DICTIONARY OF ANTHROPOLOGY

MIDCENTURY
REFERENCE LIBRARY

DAGOBERT D. RUNES, Ph.D., *General Editor*

AVAILABLE

Beethoven Encyclopedia
Dictionary of American Grammar
  and Usage
Dictionary of the American Language
Dictionary of American Literature
Dictionary of American Maxims
Dictionary of American Proverbs
Dictionary of American Synonyms
Dictionary of Ancient History
Dictionary of Anthropology
Dictionary of Arts and Crafts
Dictionary of the Arts
Dictionary of Civics and Government
Dictionary of Dietetics
Dictionary of Early English
Dictionary of Etiquette
Dictionary of European History
Dictionary of Foreign Words
  and Phrases
Dictionary of Last Words
Dictionary of Latin Literature
Dictionary of Linguistics
Dictionary of Magic
Dictionary of Mysticism
Dictionary of Mythology
Dictionary of New Words
Dictionary of Pastoral Psychology
Dictionary of Philosophy

Dictionary of Psychoanalysis
Dictionary of Russian Literature
Dictionary of Science and Technology
Dictionary of Sociology
Dictionary of Spanish Literature
Dictionary of Word Origins
Dictionary of World Literature
Encyclopedia of Aberrations
Encyclopedia of the Arts
Encyclopedia of Atomic Energy
Encyclopedia of Criminology
Encyclopedia of Literature
Encyclopedia of Psychology
Encyclopedia of Religion
Encyclopedia of Substitutes and
  Synthetics
Encyclopedia of Vocational Guidance
Illustrated Technical Dictionary
Labor Dictionary
Liberal Arts Dictionary
Military and Naval Dictionary
New Dictionary of American History
New Dictionary of Psychology
Protestant Dictionary
Slavonic Encyclopedia
Theatre Dictionary
Tobacco Dictionary
Yoga Dictionary

FORTHCOMING

Buddhist Dictionary
Dictionary of American Folklore
Dictionary of the American Indian
Dictionary of American Men and Places
Dictionary of American Names
Dictionary of American Superstitions
Dictionary of Astronomy
Dictionary of Discoveries and Inventions
Dictionary of Earth Sciences
Dictionary of Explorations
Dictionary of French Literature
Dictionary of Geography

Dictionary of German Literature
Dictionary of Hebrew Literature
Dictionary of Law
Dictionary of Mechanics
Dictionary of Poetics
Dictionary of the Renaissance
Dictionary of Science
Dictionary of Social Science
Encyclopedia of Morals
Personnel Dictionary
Teachers' Dictionary
Writers' Dictionary

PHILOSOPHICAL LIBRARY, INC.
Publishers

15 E. 40th Street   New York 16, N. Y.

Dictionary of
ANTHROPOLOGY

by CHARLES WINICK

PHILOSOPHICAL LIBRARY · NEW YORK

ISBN 978-0-8065-2919-6

Printed in the United States of America

PREFACE

It may not come amiss to say something about the nature of this book, for a dictionary of a growing science poses special problems. In common with the other social sciences, anthropology demands for itself a broad mandate—it is about "man"—but its subdivisions and special interests are more defined by what its practitioners actually *do* than by any formal definition of scope.

Although the growth of anthropology has been continuous if inevitably uneven, there has been a great surge of interest in anthropology in the last few decades. This mirrors not only a sense of urgency about contemporary social problems and the hope that anthropology can help solve those problems, but also a greater interest in the nature of man and of man's cultural and physical heritage. This growth has made anthropology certainly the most sprawling and probably the most ambitious of the social sciences. A field which includes archaeology, cultural anthropology, linguistics, and physical anthropology has boundaries and a vocabulary which are constantly expanding.

Within the scope of the whole subject exist a few domains which are neater than the rest so that it is easier to speak with assurance of the special vocabulary of a specialty like linguistics than it is to define the technical terms of cultural anthropology.

Anthropologists in the course of their research are called upon to invent special terms. Many of these terms cannot be defined with absolute precision and are used on the basis of a tacit consensus about their meanings. This agreement depends on a shared notion of the connotations of a particular term rather than on a clear verdict of the word's denotation.

Many anthropological terms carry the burden of their past history into present discourse. Kroeber and Kluckhohn have written a fascinating and sizable monograph on the many shades of meaning which cluster around so basic an anthropological concept as "culture." In other cases, the meaning of a concept is affected by the distinctive circumstances of a classic investigation or the special use to which the concept was put by a particular investigator, or it is overlaid with the remains of past polemics.

The different meanings ascribed to anthropological concepts by different scholars often reflect fundamental differences in their approach to the study of society, the relations between man and society, and social change and social causation. These differences in approach are far less important than the large core of agreement in anthropological science.

Altogether, anthropological language is rich and often very sensitive but only very little standardized. Such limitations to one side, however, most anthropologists are self-conscious social scientists who try to be as precise and explicit in their use of special terminology as they can. As time goes on, usage and custom often crystallize the range of meanings of some of these special terms, force the abandonment of some, while the process of coining new terms continues.

So fertile has been the verbal resourcefulness of anthropologists that some limits had to be set to this immense material. For the most part, the terms included are English and from the English-language vocabulary of anthropology. But in so cosmopolitan and polyglot a field there are many non-English terms which enjoy common currency. Although no attempt has been made to cover every isolated use of a term, the selection of entries has been keyed to standard source and instructional materials in anthropology.

To assist the reader into the more remote reaches of the literature, short biographical identifications of some of the leading earlier contributors to anthropology are included. Most such notices cover individuals who had made their major contribution by 1900, which for this young field is the date of its remote past and beyond which no additional identifications would appear to be necessary.

A dictionary which purports to detail the words of a growing and changing "science of man" must of necessity confine much of its effort to reporting usage, and the ordinary disposition of a special terminology as it is revealed in the established and authoritative literature of the field. And while it is proper to stress the tentative character of some special terms, anthropologists do find it necessary to speak a special vocabulary among themselves. To this special language this dictionary invites the reader.

I am grateful for the cooperation of the staff of the libraries of the American Museum of Natural History, Columbia University, New York Academy of Medicine, New York University, Queens College, Smithsonian Institution, University of London, University of Rochester, Wenner-Gren Foundation, and the staff of the New York Public Library.

Special thanks are due Drs. Gertrude Dole and Robert Carneiro. They generously made many of their definitions available for this volume.

Robert Austerlitz, Junius Bird, Gordon Ekholm, William Evan, James A. Ford, Alfred K. Guthe, Faye Mering, Benjamin N. Nelson, Alphonse Riesenfeld, Bernard Rosenberg, Joseph Rosner, S. Martin Samit, David Schendler, Gilbert Shapiro, Herbert J. Spinden, William D. Stevens, Matthew W. Stirling, Uriel Weinreich, and Jesse Winick contributed materially to the elucidation of many problems of meaning. Marilyn Kaplan provided a substantial number of entries dealing with Oceania and contributed invaluable editorial assistance. Harry Tegnaeus contributed various entries dealing with Scandinavia and Africa. The entire manuscript was critically read by Martin I. Greenfield.

I am of course responsible for all errors of omission or commission.

CHARLES WINICK

Queens College
New York City

vii

A

à dos rabattu. See BACK, BATTERED.

à froid. A term in ceramics meaning "in a cold state," or that the clay was not subjected to firing.

aba. A loose-fitting outer garment without sleeves worn in Asia for festivals and religious pilgrimages. It is characteristically made of a fairly heavy woolen fabric woven into stripes.

abacus. A device for making arithmetic computations by arranging movable counters. Some models have rods or grooves with a counter on each denoting 1, 5, 10, and 100 respectively. Among the Chinese and elsewhere, an abacus consisting of sliding counters on wires within a frame persists in use.

abacus column. See COLUMN, ABACUS.

Abakan. A form of Altaic (q.v.).

abalone. A gastropod of the genus *Haliotis*. The shell, which has a series of perforations near the edge and is highly iridescent on the inside, was used for ornamentation by the Indians of California and elsewhere.

abandonment. Deserting the sick, the aged, the young, or others who are unable to care for themselves.

abased. A heraldic term applied to an escutcheon on which a chevron has been dropped to a point lower than its normal position.

abat-jour. An architectural device used to diminish and direct the daylight entering a window. It may be a skylight or any screenlike contrivance placed so as to redirect the light.

abbatre. Any type of fabric woven so that the design gives a concave or depressed effect as opposed to an embossed or relief effect.

Abbevillian. A Paleolithic culture that lasted from the first glacial period through the second interglacial period. The type site was at Abbeville, France, and the basic tool was a large core implement serving as a crude hand ax. Core implements originate in this culture and probably were produced around 600,000 years ago in Egypt and around 450,000 years ago in France and England. An older term for Abbevillian is Chellean, derived from Chelles, France.

abbozzo. In painting and sculpture a "rough draft," or sketch, of a projected work of art.

1

abduction. 1 Carrying off or forcibly detaining a woman with the intention of marrying her. Recent research makes it unlikely that this was ever as widely practiced in ancient periods as older writers maintained. 2 The action of a muscle in drawing an organ or a limb away from the central axis of the body. The abductive muscles are largely found in the limbs and neck. See ADDUCTION.

abhiseka. The Hindu ritual of bathing in sacred waters. The term is sometimes also applied to the anointment of kings and high officials on taking office, and in the Buddhist religion, it means the 10th level of perfection.

abia. A game played with chips and disks in various parts of Africa.

abigarrado. A Mexican term used in jewelry-making or gem-cutting to describe any gem or precious stone that is variegated or not constant in color.

abiotrophy. Tissue degeneration or bodily deterioration.

Abkaz or **Abkasian.** A language of the western branch of the North Caucasian family.

ablative. In grammar, the noun, pronoun or adjective case which shows the agent, means, or source (and sometimes the time or location) of an act or occurrence.

ablaut. Regular variation in the root vowel of two or more related words so as to show changes in the meaning, e.g., run-ran. It is a type of quantitative gradation. The term apophony is sometimes used.

abong. An Ifugao house used by the poor.

aboriginal. A native of an area before the coming of European or other settlers, e.g., the American Indians were the aboriginal inhabitants of North America. The term is also rendered aborigine, although this usage has some connotations of dislike.

abortion. Delivery of a fetus before it can become a viable human being. In certain cultures abortion may be deliberately induced for economic reasons, to avoid the pains of childbirth, or to conceal illicit sexual relations. Deliberate abortion is found in almost all cultures.

abracadabra. A magic (q.v.) formula used against disease and misfortune.

abrasion. The technique of shaping rocks that do not fracture easily by using sandstone or wet sand as abrasive agents.

abraxas. A magical word in occult science which is numerically equivalent to 365, the number of days in a year. Believed to be the name of a god, a gem or stone bearing this word is credited with great potency as a charm. Abraxas also means an amulet (q.v.) engraved with a mythical figure, usually half human and half animal, and a verse or legend. Some examples have the word "abraxas" inscribed.

abri. The French term for shelter.

abris sous roche. See SHELTER, ROCK.

Abruzzese-Neapolitan. The Italian dialects spoken by the inhabitants of southern Latium, Abruzzi, Campania, Lucania, and Puglia. They are characterized by a clouding or obscuring of the final vowels

2

and umlaut distinctions in the root vowels.

absorption. In linguistics, the process of suppressing a sound or the process by which the sound is assimilated with an immediately adjacent sound.

Abuna. A patriarch of the autocephalic Coptic Christian church of Ethiopia.

abyss. The space in some early religions, without bottom or filled with water, behind or under the earth. In Babylonian thought, for example, the abyss was believed to be a primeval chaos which gave rise to the universe and to life.

acanthon. In physical anthropology, the point of the anterior nasal spine.

Acatl. The second year, in Aztec writing; also the word for cane.

accent. In linguistics, a distinguishing stress or force of voice on some syllable (q.v.) or syllables of a word.

accent, circumflex. A symbol (^) which is written over letters representing vowels to show the proper pronunciation. In French the circumflex accent also indicates that in the antecedent Latin word an *s* now omitted, followed the vowel, e.g., French *tête* from Latin *testa*.

accent, final. Emphasis or stress placed on the last syllable of a word.

accent, medial. Emphasis on a syllable other than the first or last.

accent, pitch. A comparative weighting of pitches within a single utterance.

accent, stress. See STRESS.

access, peaceful. Permission to an outsider to enter a group's territory, occasionally so that advantage of a natural resource may be taken.

accetta. A hatchet with the cutting edge parallel to the handle.

accidence. The study of the modification of words through inflection (q.v.) and root vowel changes.

accidentalism. A world view which posits the existence of actions or events that are neither caused nor predictable.

acclacuna. A female slave among the Incas.

acclimatization. The process by which organisms adapt themselves to a new climatic environment. The color of human hair and skin may be an example of the changes accompanying this process, although anthropologists are not in agreement on this.

acculturation. The process by which culture is transmitted through continuous firsthand contact of groups with different cultures, one often having a more highly developed civilization. The process may be unilateral or bilateral. It could be said, e.g., that about 1,000 years ago Japan largely received its culture from China through acculturation, acquiring such items as writing, coined money, and Buddhism, with the Chinese accepting only the folding fan from Japan. The 19th century saw a second period of acculturation for Japan, this time from the West. The German term *Kulturfall* is sometimes found.

acculturation, antagonistic. The adoption of a culture trait by a society as a means of resisting more effectively the encroachments of the society from which it is borrowed,

3

as the borrowing of the rifle by the Plains Indians.

acculturation, marginal. The process whereby the cultural interchange between two areas is largely confined to the border region.

acculturation, planitational. A mingling of two cultures over a broad area.

accumulation. The collecting of various facets of a culture, such as techniques for making implements.

acetabulum. A deep cavity on the posterior part of the pelvis which articulates with the head of the femur.

Acheulian. Referring to the lower Paleolithic age in the Old World, lasting from the early second interglacial period until the third interglacial period. The name derives from a site at Saint-Acheuil, France. The Acheulian hand axes were smaller and better than the Abbevillian (q.v.) model. Many open-air sites date from this period. There was evidence of esthetic interest in the technology, and the tools were more symmetrical, with sharper edges. Indirect percussion may have been used ca. 100,000-180,000 years ago. Acheulian culture spread from France and Spain to southern England, southwestern France, and Italy, ultimately overlapping with the eastern culture along the Rhine.

achrondoplasia. A condition in which there are defects in the cartilage at the epiphyses of the long bones. Persons suffering from achrondoplasia usually experience difficulties in locomotion and may have thick stunted limbs.

ackie. A unit of gold in West Africa equaling one-sixteenth of an ounce.

acocotl. A musical instrument named after the Mexican plant from which it is made. It is constructed from an eight- to ten-foot length of the stem. The performer produces a wheezing tone by inhaling through the tube. Another term for the instrument is clarin.

aconite. A genus of plants used in Northern Asia to provide a strong poison for tipping arrows. It is also called wolfsbane and monkshood.

acosmism. A variety of pantheism which holds that the universe exists only through the absolute.

acoustic feature. See FEATURE, ACOUSTIC.

acre. A land measure equal to 43,560 square feet. It originally involved one day's work for a plow team, and was thus variable.

acroama. Musical or dramatic productions in ancient Greece presented during meals for diversion.

acrocephaly. Condition of being high-headed. In an acrocephalic skull the height is at least 98 per cent of the breadth. In the fleshed head the height from the ear hole is at least 85 per cent of the breadth.

acrodontism. The simplest method of attaching teeth to their skeletal support. It consists of consolidation of the teeth directly with the alveolar ridge and the absence of socketed roots or fibrous connective tissue. Acrodontism is typically found in fish.

acrolith. A sculpture made of two or more materials. An acrolith

4

usually combined wood and stone, and sometimes had metal drapery. Typically the hands, feet, and head were of marble and the remainder of the body of some baser material.

acromegaly. Excessive growth of the extremities, jaw, and face resulting from overactivity of the anterior lobe of the pituitary. The affected person usually has a large chest, short legs and arms, large hands, a large head and nose, and thick lips. See GIGANTISM.

acrophony. A word sign used to stand for the first consonant of the names of an object.

acropolis. The section of a Greek city, built at its highest point, in which were the chief temples and public buildings. The word is associated with Greek cities, like Athens, Argos, and Thebes, which had citadels, but that at Athens has become known as the Acropolis.

acroteria. Ornaments made of marble or terra cotta found on top of the pediments of Greek temples.

action, frost. The process by which rocks are shoved upward when water freezes and expands.

actualization. The discernible product of the articulation of phonemic variants.

adaptation. The process by which an organism adjusts to its environment. The term is usually applied to changes in the physical organism. See ACCLIMATIZATION.

adaro. A bad soul among the Arosi of the Solomons.

adat. The native law of Indonesia.

addition. The process by which a sound is added to a word.

address, term of. The title or honorific phrase used when speaking to someone .

adduction. The action of a muscle in drawing an organ or a limb toward the central axis of the body. The adductive muscles are largely found in the limbs and neck. See ABDUCTION 2.

adessive. A declensional case of verbs in the Finno-Ugric languages which has the same meaning as the English prepositions *at* or *near*.

adhesion. The tendency for traits to be associated in diffusion, so that where one trait of a complex is present the other trait would also be present. Tylor notably espoused the concept of adhesion. The term is also used to mean an organic or functional connection between two social traits.

adiacritic. Referring to a race none of the members of which can be recognized as such by an expert.

adjective, descriptive. An adjective which follows and is modified by a limiting adjective, when the two occur in a phrase, e.g., *red* in *that red hat*.

adjective, limiting. An adjective which modifies and precedes a descriptive adjective and noun when the two types of adjective occur together, e.g., *that* in *that red hat*.

Adlet. A group of monsters believed by the Eskimo to have been produced by a cross between dogs and men.

adobe. Sun-dried unfired clay brick.

adoption. The process by which a person, family, clan, or tribe enters into a new relationship which is tantamount to a congenital relationship and may supersede the original relationship. The death of a parent, war, and economic hazards are among the reasons for adoption. Adoption of adults may occur. Adoption extends group relationships. It helps to make the social order more flexible and affords newcomers a group status which determines their relation to other members of the group.

adorno. An ornamental, usually zoomorphic, part appliquéd to a pot, and especially to the rim or shoulders of the vessel.

adret. The side of a mountain or valley which faces the sun.

Adyghe. The Cherkess and Qabardi language belonging to the Western Caucasian branch of the North Caucasian family.

adytum. A secret inner shrine of a temple, not to be entered by the public.

adze. A cutting tool with a thin arching blade at a right angle to the handle. It consists of a grip, haft, haft head, blade, and edge. It is asymmetrical around its major axis and cannot be used as an ax but is mainly for woodworking. The adze is seldom a weapon. The term celt is sometimes used.

adze, hand. See TOOL, CHOPPING.

adze, lug. See CELT, TRUNNION.

adze, shaft-hole. An adze with a hole for the shaft.

Aenolithic. Referring to the Copper Age (q.v.) or the Chalcolithic Age (q.v.)

aeotana. A tiny wind instrument consisting of seven reeds or thin strips of metal secured in a frame so as to vibrate when blown upon by the performer.

aeromancy. The art of divining knowledge of the future from weather conditions or observation of the ripples on the surface of bodies of water.

aerophone. A musical instrument in which the sound is produced by vibrating the air, e.g., the Pan pipes (q.v.).

Aetheria. A Nile oyster, the shell of which is used for fishhooks.

Affenmensch. Weinert's name for the forms of early man.

affines. Relatives through marriage. See AFFINITY, 1.

affinity. 1 The status of being related by marriage instead of blood. Mother-in-law and son-in-law, e.g., are affinal relations. 2 A likeness in the structure of languages which come from different sources. The term is also sometimes used to denote a common origin of languages.

affixation. The process of changing word meanings through adding or removing sounds, e.g., *man, manly; relatively, relative*. The elements added or removed are called *affixes*.

affricative. A compound consonantal phoneme consisting of a stop plus a spirant or another open consonant, e.g., *ts*.

African. The three families of languages in Africa. It comprises Sudanese-Guinean, Bantu, and Hottentot-Bushman.

Africanthropus njarasensis. A controversial form of man—perhaps on the Pithecanthropus-Sinanthropus level—which may have lived during the Pleistocene period

6

and appears to have had much in common with the later Neanderthal. The type is predicated on fragments of several skulls found in Tanganyika in 1935.

Afrikaans. A Dutch dialect with very simple grammatical forms, spoken in the Union of South Africa.

afrit. A malevolent spirit among the Kababish.

afterbirth. The placenta and associated structures (chorion, amnion and umbilical cord), in many cultures believed to be closely involved with the personality and future of the newly born child. See PLACENTA.

afterworld. The place to which the dead go, a conception common to almost all cultures.

agalma. A Greek term for a piece of sculpture. In modern times it has been more widely used to describe either a sculpture or a painting, especially a portrait.

agamang. Among the Ifugao, a house for unmarried women.

agamy. The absence of marriage, or a social group which does not enforce marriage relations.

agaric. A fungus used as a poison or as a spunk (q.v.). It is sometimes regarded as having mysterious properties, because of its great combustibility.

agate. A quartz, with the colors usually in bands, which was believed in various cultures to have certain beneficial properties. Jews used agate to avoid falling and Arabs to improve the blood. In medieval times it was an anti-snake medicine. North American Indians used it to make implements of various kinds. It is still a symbol of good health and long life.

agave. A slow-flowering plant genus of the amaryllis family, used as a source of fiber and to make intoxicants. It is found in Central and South America and the southwest United States.

age. A major subdivision in the history of cultural evolution. The term has been condemned as confusing, since it suggests that a given chronological period had a homogeneity of culture. Even groups living near each other at the same time may be from different "ages," as in England after 2000 B.C., when warrior herdsmen from the Bronze Age, Neolithic farmers, and Mesolithic hunters lived near each other. The early divisions into Paleolithic (Old Stone), Neolithic (New Stone), Chalcolithic (Copper), Bronze, and Iron ages are no longer seen as regular and clear-cut divisions.

age, anatomical. An individual's skeletal development compared to others of different ages. X-rays of the cartilaginous tissues in the wrist or of the closing of the fontanelle (q.v.) are often used to measure anatomical age.

Age, Bronze. Period in cultural history, beginning in the Old World in Babylonia from 2,500 to 3,500 years B.C., characterized by the deliberate production of bronze (q.v.). In the New World, in Peru, this period began ca. 500 or 1,000 A.D. Settled life and food surplus are typical in the Bronze Age. Urban life began and led to a shift of scribes, artisans, and other specialized occupational groups to the towns. Specialization of labor, leisure time, organized government, the separation of the priestly class, kingships, and organized astronomical data are found. Urbanization appeared particularly in southwest Asia and in Egypt, although its advantages were confined to certain classes. Specialists in commerce arose, as did organized thieves who preyed upon them. Trade items were sometimes buried by merchants to insure their safety. See HOARD.

The Bronze Age in Europe has been divided into periods. The first, from 2500-1900 B.C., saw flat celts, and daggers made of copper or bronze with a small percentage of tin, although stone artifacts are still found. The second period, 1900-1600 B.C., had a higher percentage of tin. Slightly raised sides are found on the celts, and the triangular daggers have a large median rib. The dagger blade lengthens and swords appear. Pottery with incised decorations is found. The third period, from 1600-1300 B.C., had early long swords with tangs—knives cast with their handles in one piece—and advanced pottery. From 1300-200 B.C., the fourth period, there were celts with wing-shaped flanges at the top, swords with a tang to go through the handle, semicircular and double razors and pottery resembling pile-dwelling ware. See AGE, EARLY BRONZE; AGE, LATE BRONZE.

Age, Chalcolithic. A transition period, ca. 4500-3000 B.C., during which copper was first used regularly. In this age the Near East flourished, and the Fertile Crescent had painted pottery of considerable beauty. Major public buildings were built, perhaps for the first time. Writing first became known ca. 3500 B.C., and the influence of temples spread. Abstract concepts like "truth" and "purity" were discussed. Fruit, cereals, and vegetables were the chief food. The period is sometimes called the Copper Age, the Copper-Stone Age, the Cyprolithic Age, or the Eneolithic Age.

Age, Copper. See AGE, CHALCOLITHIC.

Age, Copper-Stone. See AGE, CHALCOLITHIC.

Age, Early Bronze. Period in cultural history between 3000 and 2000 B.C., during which the first known organized states were formed, in Egypt and Mesopotamia. It marks the beginning of the historical period. Objects from this age include the pyramids of Egypt. Statuary and inscriptions abound. Despite the name, it is not thought that bronze was known at this time.

age, golden. A mythical period in which everyone was happy and innocent, or all was well with the world, almost always set at the beginning of history.

Age, Heroic. Period immediately preceding the time when authentic artifacts definitely establish historical facts. It is called "Heroic" because it often records a mixture of truth and of legend concerning mythical or semimythical "heroes," who are supposed to have performed superhuman acts.

Age, Ice. Name often given to the last million years. The name may be misleading since it was not the first and may not be the last period of glacial activity in the development of the earth. See GLACIATION.

Age, Iron. Period covering the 2,500 years before historic times. During it the use of iron spread only sporadically and irregularly. The Iron Age enabled the benefits of urbanization to reach more people than in the preceding Bronze Age (q.v.). Peasants could get iron tools ca. 1000 B.C., as iron was fairly cheap and a class of professional blacksmiths produced tools in abundance. Around the time of the introduction of iron, changes in the alphabet simplified writing. See IRON.

Age, Late Bronze. Period between the years 1500-1200 B.C., usually considered in conjunction with the Middle Bronze Age (2000-1500 B.C.) which immediately preceded it. There was much intellectual progress during this time. The rise and fall of the Egyptian, Babylonian, Hyksos, Hittite, and Horite empires occurred. It was then also that the Israelites finally emerged as a unified religious group.

Age, Late Stone. See AGE, NEOLITHIC.

Age, Lower Old Stone. See AGE, LOWER PALEOLITHIC.

Age, Lower Paleolithic. Period covering the time from ca. 550,000 —70,000 years before the modern era and including the pre-Chellean, Chellean, and Acheulian stages. It is also called the Lower Old Stone Age. Fire was not used during this period, nor were animals or plants domesticated. The Paleolithic men were probably hunters. The coup-de-poing (q.v.) became smaller and smaller and more regular flakes were produced during this period. Later, tools were produced by roughing out a core so that flakes could be struck from it and made into tools by retouching. Two culture areas, the Southwest-Asiatic-African-West Europe and the East-Europe (and perhaps North-Asiatic) were discernible.

Age, Middle Bronze. See AGE, LATE BRONZE.

Age, Middle Old Stone. See AGE, PALEOLITHIC.

Age, Middle Paleolithic. Period of cultural history from the third interglacial through the fourth glacial epoch. This period probably started ca. 125,000 years ago and lasted to ca. 15,000 years ago. From a cave in Le Moustier, France, it is also called the Mousterian period. This period saw the rise of Neanderthaloids (q.v.) and is sometimes called the period of the Cave Man. Finer flint implements appear. Bone tools, scraper tools, and fire were also characteristic. Man had a stable residence and buried the dead, suggesting the belief in an afterlife and religion. Along with the dead, flints, red ocher, and uneaten cooked meat were often buried. Although the dead were buried inside the caves, Neanderthal Man did not live there, but under the overhanging ledge and on the outer platforms. There may have been a curtain of animal skins used to keep out the wind. The flint

9

industry over most of habitable Europe became fairly uniform, as well as in nearby parts of Asia and Africa. This was the period of maximum Würm glaciation.

Age, Neolithic. Period from 3,500 to 7,500 years before historical times. It is also called the Late Stone Age or New Stone Age. Weaving, pottery, fine flint-working, the bow and arrow, and many metal tools were characteristic, as were the wheel, a primitive pastoralism and agriculture, and a lack of ferrous and bronze metallurgy. Lubbock, in 1865, gave this name to ground or polished implements which were found along with the bones of fairly recent animal species. The Neolithic Age ended in his view when copper and bronze were used regularly. Childe has suggested that a better criterion of Neolithic would be an economy which is self-sufficient in food production. There was a change in this age from chipped to polished stone tools. The rice, maize, barley, wheat, and other cereals then domesticated are still present today.

The Neolithic Age is so called because archaeologists saw the grinding and polishing of stone implements, instead of chipping, as the hallmark. In the Near East, man gradually changed to a producer of food from a gatherer of food. While the European climate improved, North Africa and southern Asia developed a desert and dry climate so that men did not have so much space to live in and were drawn close together, especially in oases and river valleys. These groups gradually learned to live in a more settled manner and raise their own food.

Neolithic culture came to Europe overland from the southeast by the Danube and its offshoots; from the North African coastal plains via the Straits of Gibralter, to Spain, France and England; and overland from South Russia, Poland, central Europe, and Germany. The Neolithic people colonized Greece first, probably coming from southern Anatolia ca. 3500 B.C.

The first major building of this era was found in Jericho. It was probably a temple. Religious cultism, especially phallic and fertility cults, may have been widespread. Megalithic burial structures were constructed in the Near East and Europe, although there was probably a cultural lag in the European Neolithic.

Age, New Stone. See AGE, NEOLITHIC.

Age, Old Stone. See AGE, PALEOLITHIC.

Age, Paleolithic. Period, lasting from ca. 500,000 to 1,500,000 years, during which artifacts, now found along with the bones of extinct wild animals, were produced by chipping. The Paleolithic Age, a name coined by Lubbock in 1865, is also called the Middle Old Stone Age, the Old Stone Age, or the Stone Age. It is often divided into various stages, ranging from the pre-Chellean to the Magdalenian and the Azilian, which were the transition to the Neolithic Age. In the Paleolithic Age, man slowly began dif-

10

ferentiating himself from the animal world. He lived in small groups, perhaps often in caves, where most remains are found. Europe and Asia were in the Ice Age. Man's first artifacts are usually said to have appeared during this period, along with religion.

age, physiological. The degree of development of nervous tissues, muscles, glands, and genitals relative to chronological norms.

Age, Reindeer. See MAGDALENIAN.

Age, Stone. See AGE, PALEOLITHIC.

Age, Upper Paleolithic. Period, lasting about 50,000 years, from ca. 70,000 to ca. 20,000 years before the modern era. It includes the Aurignacian, Solutrean, and Magdalenian (qq.v.) stages. Bone, ivory, and flint implements were used in this era. The Cro-Magnon men of this time probably had clothes made from animal skins and produced what is probably the first art. The bulk of the European Paleolithic culture was largely carried by Cro-Magnon man. Cultural diversity was probably greater than racial diversity. Long, fine knifelike flakes were also struck from a core. The bow and arrow and the domestication of the dog appeared. The Paleolithic period ended with the retreat of the last glacier.

Cave painting in southwest Europe began (see ART, CAVE). The arts and crafts advanced. Burials with ornaments in the grave are not uncommon. The first nude statuettes of women, in stone, bone and ivory, appear. The cave paintings and fig-

urines suggest fairly well developed magic and religious beliefs. The last stage of the Upper Paleolithic Age is called the Magdalenian (q.v.).

age, true. A person's age reckoned from the time of conception. Inasmuch as the human gestation period is around 280 days, the average infant at birth has a true age of 280 days.

age-and-area. See THEORY, AGE AND AREA.

age area. See AREA, AGE.

age grade. See GRADE, AGE.

agenitalism. A lack of ovaries or testes and of the secondary sex characteristics.

Ages of Man, Three. The three ages of the development of civilization: stone, bronze, and iron. Lucretius speculated on the existence of such ages, and in 52 A.D., a Chinese compilation gave the sequence of a Stone, Bronze, and Iron Age, although this was probably a lucky guess. In 1813, a Dane, Vedel-Simonsen, suggested that the Scandinavian area had gone through a Stone, Copper or Bronze, and Iron Age. Thomsen accepted this typology for classifying materials in his museum, and Worsaae validated the schema stratigraphically in the peat bogs of Denmark and applied it to other countries. By 1865, Lubbock suggested Grecized terms like Paleolithic and Neolithic for the Stone Age, and many further subdivisions have been made. Some scholars have suggested that so much ambiguity is attached to the Grecized terminology that it should be replaced.

The presumed cultural succession

of Stone, Bronze, and Iron Age, is likely to be truer in Greece and Denmark than elsewhere. There has not been a regular succession of metals throughout the world. Tin, for example, is scarce in many places. The early emphasis on the archaeology of the classical Mediterranean area has served to overemphasize the concept of a general succession of ages.

agglutination. In linguistics, forming words through the addition of infixes, prefixes, and suffixes to the root. In physiology, the tendency of red blood corpuscles to clump in the presence of agglutinin.

agglutinin. An antibody stimulated by an antigen (q.v.).

agglutinogen. An antigen (q.v.) which produces agglutination or clumping of the cells if mixed with blood from another group.

aggradation. The building up of deposits of material, one on top of the other. This phenomenon is used in dating archaeological finds.

Aghul. A language belonging to the Samurian branch of the Eastern group of North Caucasian languages. It is spoken in the Caucasus.

agnate. A kinsman who is related through the male line exclusively; also, more loosely, any relative on the father's side.

agnation. The system of measuring kinship only through the male members of a family. It was used in ancient Rome and is still widely found in Africa.

agnification. The literary representation of humans as sheep. It is most often found in a religious frame of reference, e.g., the pastor and his flock.

agora. A marketplace in ancient Greece or Rome. It was surrounded by colonnaded porticoes. The famous agora of Athens has been excavated since 1927 by American archaeologists, and important finds of sculpture, coins, and inscriptions have been made.

Agpo. A stage in the development of culture characterized by the practice of plant cultivation and pottery-making. The term Agpo is a synthetic word compounded from the initial syllables of "agriculture" and "pottery."

Agreement, Frankfurt. A report dealing with techniques of craniometry confirmed in 1882 by 67 anthropologists meeting at Frankfurt to standardize measurements. The 31 listed measurements were used to describe many of the specimens in German museums. In German the agreement was called the Frankfurter Verständigung.

agriculture. The process by which societies grow vegetable food. Grains and tubers are the major classes of cultivated food used by early man. The cultivation of a plant may spread from one people to another, climate permitting. The use of animal power for manpower and the use of such devices as the digging stick and plow (q.v.) are often found in early agriculture, as are food plants, the hoe, and some sort of irrigation. Many societies had guards watching over their crops, and other community participation, as in the rites surrounding the planting of seeds.

It is likely that agriculture began in South or Central Asia ca. 5,000 B.C. Brunton believes that the first grain cultivated was the emmer wheat, and Werth holds that the banana tree is probably the oldest domesticated plant in south Asia.

The area dominated by wheat includes the Near East, Europe, North Africa, and part of Asia. The area dominated by rice includes India, Japan, South China, and Southeast Asia. With agriculture are often found metal-working, the wheel, writing, larger buildings, and larger social organizations.

agriculture, maize. A system of agriculture in which the hoe was used and planting was in hillocks. Irrigation and fertilizer were only local.

agriculture, plow. A system of agriculture including the use of domesticated animals, dung fertilization, and broadcast sowing of seeds. It dates from the Neolithic Age.

agriculture, rites of. Rites concerned with preparation of the soil, sowing, and protection and harvesting of the crop. The group's magic power is used to counteract or control influences which are hostile to the crops. At sowing time, seeding may be stimulated with obscene language (India), cursing (Greece), and other techniques. The growing crops may be protected by reciting magic rituals (Japan) and carrying the deity's image around the fields. Rites are used to secure rain. First fruits are often associated with rites, and the year's last sheaf often symbolizes the corn spirit. In South America, humans were killed and their blood mixed with the cakes made of the new corn. The Chinese state religion, up to recently, emphasized the rites of agriculture.

agriculturist. A farmer who draws on animal or mechanical aids in tilling the soil. An earlier classification divided agriculturists into those who used the digging stick, hoe, and plow (qq.v.), respectively.

agwel. A bottle-shaped Moroccan hand drum.

ahimsa. The Hindu ethic of non-injury. In practice, it consists in rejecting any action which involves taking the life of another living being.

ahl. A Middle Eastern extended family (q.v.).

Ahom. A Siamese dialect which survives in part only as the sacred language of a very small group.

ahu. The Tahitian term for stone platform used as an altar in Polynesia. It is also called a heiau (Hawaii) or a tuahu (New Zealand).

Ahura Mazda. "Lord Wisdom," or Ormuzd, the supreme god in Zoroastrianism.

aid, mutual. The cooperative behavior of individuals belonging to the same species, believed by Kropotkin to be a general law of animal and human behavior.

aigrette. A heron plume used as a headdress, most commonly in dead-water stream areas of Venezuela.

aimak. A large tribal group of Mongols.

aine or ayni. A Quechua word for the loan of objects or the performance of services with the expectation of return in kind.

ainga. The name given to all relatives in Samoa.

Ainu. A Caucasoid food-gathering people who live in Sakhalin. The population is geographically stable and its language, classified as Hyperborean or Paleo-Asiatic, is linguistically unrelated 'to any other. The Ainu may be a white subrace. The physiological characteristics of the Ainu include an abundance of body hair, long earlobes, an off-white skin color, a narrow head, dark brown eyes, dark hair, a nasal index ranging from mesorrhine to platyrrhine, and a higher incidence of A-type than B-type blood. The source of the Ainu is unknown, but it is believed that they may have come from a former Siberian-European group. This group is exceptional in that it is one of the very few Caucasoid groups not confined to Europe in recent times.

air, tidal. The average amount of air, about 500 cubic centimeters, which passes through the lungs in each cycle of breathing.

airan. Soured cow's milk used among the Kazak.

akalché. A pool of water on a mud bottom in the Yucatan.

Akkadian. One of the oldest Semitic languages, widely used for diplomacy and commerce in the Near East until replaced by Aramaic. Old Akkadian, or Assyrian, was spoken from 2800-650 B.C. and New Akkadian, or Babylonian, from 650-100 B.C. The characters were cuneiform (q.v.). The literature called Akkadian consisted of emphatic, emotional compositions inscribed on clay tablets dating from the first millennium B.C. They are similar in form and content to earlier Sumerian works, which, however, are calm and restrained in mood.

Akop. A Tinguian spirit.

ak-sakal. A Kazak sib.

alabaster. A marblelike gypsum, either white or white veined with red.

alae. The lateral walls of the nostrils.

Alafin. A priest-chief of the Oyo tribe of Nigeria.

alandier. A nearly obsolete fireplace used in ceramics. It was at the base of a porcelain kiln and was fed from the outside.

alare. The wing on the most lateral point of the nose.

Albanian. An isolated member of the Indo-European language stock.

albarradon. A Mexican flood and irrigation dike.

albinism or **albinization.** A deficiency of pigmentation of the skin, eyes, and hair. This is a hereditary trait which is variable. It is often transmitted as an autosomal recessive trait which results from a gene substitution. The hair of an albino may be white, the skin white, and the eyes pink. In less extreme albinism, milder forms of these color deficiencies may be found. The complete loss of pigmentation is called albinization.

alchemy. A kind of chemical research which tried to transmute base metals into gold and to find the philosopher's stone. It developed from a secret goldsmith's science to a study of organic as well as metallic substances. Alchemy probably originated in Egypt and spread to

Greece, Rome, and Arabia. The Arabs took it to Spain, from where it went to western Europe. Paracelsus in the 16th century was the leading figure in its modern development, with his turning alchemy to the preparation of medicines.

aleatory. The fortuitous or chance element in human life.

alectryomancy or **alectoromancy.** Divination (q.v.) through the activities of a cock placed in a circle. The cock would pick grains from letters of the alphabet within the circle, transmitting an oracle in the order of picking. The term alectoromancy is sometimes used.

Alemannic. A Germanic dialect that became extinct ca. 1000 A.D. With Bavarian and Lombard, it developed into High German.

alembroth. The precipitate of mercury. It was the old thaumaturgical salt of wisdom used by the alchemists.

alette. A buttress or pilaster in classic architecture, or any small extension or wing of a building.

aleuromancy. The use of flour for divination (q.v.). A message is written on a piece of paper, which is put in flour paste and then given to persons. Fortune cookies in modern American-Chinese restaurants are a form of aleuromancy.

Aleut. Food-gathering inhabitants of the Aleutians. They speak languages similar to Eskimo.

alfa. The name given to a holy or learned man by the Arabs.

alfalfa. A widely grown leguminous forage plant. It began in the Persia-Asia Minor district, and was early domesticated. Its deep tap root

enables it to absorb water even in dry areas and to survive under unfavorable conditions.

Alfur. A physical type of eastern Indonesia characterized by a mixture of Malayan and Negroid features.

algarroba. A tree with very hard dark wood grown in cold desert regions 7,000 to 8,000 feet above sea level in Peru and Bolivia. The Peruvians used it for house posts and statues. Its nut is eaten by chinchillas.

Algerrigiowumma. An Arunta ceremony in which a boy is thrown into the air.

algoja. A musical instrument of India belonging to the flute family but played vertically. It is made of bamboo and has five finger holes. Two of these instruments are often played at one time.

Algonkian or **Algonquin.** A family of North American Indian languages consisting of six groups, which still exist: Eastern (Central and Eastern Canada), Central (the Great Lakes region), Californian or Ritwan, Blackfoot (Alberta), Cheyenne (Montana), and Arapaho (Montana, Wyoming, and Oklahoma).

alignment. A group of upright megaliths in a parallel row, e.g., the Carnac alignment in France.

allative. A declensional case found in such languages as Finnish and Eskimo, with the meaning of the English preposition *toward*.

allele. A member of a pair of genes.

allelomorph. Either one of a pair of inherited and contrasting charac-

15

teristics. The genes for allelomorphs occupy the same place in homologous chromosomes.

allelomorphism, multiple. Appearance of more than a pair of alleles in the same place.

allelotype. The genetic composition of a population.

Allen's rule. See RULE, ALLEN'S.

alley, covered. Several dolmens (q.v.) connected with each other.

allheal. Herb used in folk medicine, like mistletoe and valerian. Such herbs are also often called healall and may be used as panaceas.

alliage. See ALLOY.

allochromatic. A gem which, in a chemically pure state, would be colorless, but which shows a color or range of colors because of the presence of small quantities of 'coloring' impurities.

allometric. Referring to changes in the comparative size of parts of the body.

allometry. The study of relative growth. It is concerned with problems such as the differential rate of increase of parts of an organism. Allometry helps explain certain evolutionary phenomena.

allomorph. A positional variant of a morpheme (q.v.) which occurs in a specific environment; e.g., *are* is an allomorph of *be*, existing in the environment of *you.*

allopatric. Referring to a group which is geographically separated from other groups.

allophone. One of the variants of sound recognizable as belonging to a specific phoneme (q.v.), e.g., the two *g* sounds in gear and gore. Some occur only in specific positions, while free allophones are chance variations among the possible pronunciations of a phoneme.

allopolyploid. A fertile hybrid which has two or more haploid sets of chromosomes from each of the parents.

allosome. A chromosome (q.v.) which functions in determining sex.

alloy. A combination of two or more metals, also called an alliage. The first alloys were probably accidents, resulting from the fortuitous association of other metals with copper. Nickel and copper alloy was found in Germany, zinc and copper in India, and tin and copper in Saxony. Brass (q.v.), which is copper-zinc, and bronze (q.v.), which is copper-tin, were thus alloys which were made substantially before either zinc or tin were individually smelted. Gowland has shown how bronze could be made accidentally. In Europe and Asia, tin and copper were often found together, and even a small amount of tin could make a bronze alloy. An alloy is accomplished by fusion, and the resulting metal is stronger and more malleable than any of its component ingredients usually is.

alluvium. Sand, gravel, or soil which is deposited by running water, especially in comparatively recent eras. Such deposits are usually local and are found at the flood plains of streams, or where streams lose velocity and leave their contained sediment on the floor of a valley. In the 19th century, the term was coined by Dean Buckland to describe gravel deposits which contained the remains of recent ani-

16

mals, contemporary with man, and which flourished after a universal deluge. See DILUVIUM.

almanac. A collection of calendar and miscellaneous data, probably originating in the second century A.D. Almanacs contain calendar material and humorous sayings. They were originally linked with astrology.

almanac, clog. Primitive Danish almanac made from a piece of hardwood and notched to show the days, weeks, and months. Festivals, phases of the moon, and saint's days were inscribed on the front. The clog almanac was brought to the English mainland by the invaders from Denmark.

alomancy or **halomancy.** A technique of divination (q.v.) through throwing salt on a fire and reading the flames.

alphabet. A collection of signs which represent the sounds of a language, arranged in a customary order. Before the earliest records of writing, there were many signs which had developed a phonetic value. The early Semitic alphabets do not record vowels and represent each consonant by a separate letter. The final stage in alphabet development was writing vowels.

The Greek alphabet had a number of stages of development. The pictures were conventionalized and simplified, then acquired conventional phonetic values. The signs each stood for a single consonant, although most of them were used for word segments and words. Everything but the uniconsonantal signs was abandoned, then vowel letters were written. These steps in the development of alphabetic writing can be observed in many parts of the world.

An ideal alphabet would have only one letter for each phoneme (q.v.) or speech sound, although no alphabet has ever achieved this. Inasmuch as writing originated later than language, its development from pictures has largely been a gradual approximation to speech.

The alphabet is the most recent and most highly developed kind of writing, as well as the most adaptable. It is used everywhere by civilized people and it can be passed from one language to another. It has made writing common, and has thus facilitated education.

Diringer has pointed out two coincidences which helped the development of the alphabet. One was the combination of economic, geographic, linguistic factors which enabled the Semites to invent the alphabet. One of the linguistic factors was that Semitic-Hamitic was the only major linguistic family which is based on consonantal sounds. The other coincidence was the alphabet's being completed by passing from the Semites to the Greeks, since Greek must use vowel signs because of its euphoniousness.

alphabet, phonetic. A system of symbols to record the sounds of a language precisely and consistently. Lepsius, in 1855, developed a system, some features of which are still used. The Anthropos system remains current. The International Phonetic Association system, used

17

for over 50 years, has been revised several times. The American Anthropological Association developed a system to aid in studying American Indian languages. Modifications suggested by Edward Sapir, Bernard Bloch, and George Trager have been widely used.

alphitomancy. An ancient method of determining the guilt or innocence of a person by forcing him to eat a piece of barley loaf. The process was supposed to induce indigestion in the guilty.

alphorn. A wooden horn with a cup-shaped mouthpiece. It is found in South America, the Celebes, and the Himalaya region, and in ancient Assyria and Babylonia and medieval Europe.

Alpine. A suggested east-west central European ethnic division of Caucasoids, usually brachycephalic. This white subrace has some Ainu qualities. Dark brown hair and eyes and a mesorrhine nasal index are typical.

Altaic. A subfamily of the Ural-Altaic family of languages. Its three branches are Turkic, Mongol, and Manchu or Tungus. It is characterized by a high degree of vowel harmony (q.v.), the addition of suffixes to the root to form compact, easily analyzed speech units, and the use of inflection (q.v.) to express grammatical relationships.

altar. A raised piece of furniture used to burn or present offerings to a deity. It can also be of stone or earth. In some religions, the victim's blood was poured into the altar, where the deity presumably resided. When a fire was burning on the al-

tar, it probably was used to carry the food to the god. The altar was the home of the god, as seen in stones in which fire appeared on the altar and consumed the gift. Subsequently, there was a distinction between the altar and the sacred stone, with the altar becoming the divinity's table. The altar grew smaller as the ritual became modified for such unbloody offerings as fruit or incense.

The first altars were probably large stones or platforms of sun-baked earth, before more ornamental forms appeared. Limestone and alabaster altars were found in Assyria and basalt rock and polished granite in Egypt. Classical Greece and Rome had some altars which were small and low and used for kneeling in front of a god's image, as well as larger altars used for burnt sacrifices or offerings. The larger altars were usually in the open air. Some altars are portable, like some early Mesopotamian and Hebrew examples. "Pocket" altars are still found in India. In the ancient American civilizations, altars were tablelike, often with sculptural or other inscriptions. The altar stones were fairly low.

altar, druidic. See DOLMEN.

alternant. A different phonetic form for a morpheme (q.v.), which is used in certain conditions.

alternant, basic. The alternant which has a greater range than any other.

alternant, zero. An alternant made by a zero element (q.v.).

aludel. A pear-shaped vessel open at each end. It may be made of either pottery or metal. Sometimes two or more aludels are joined together.

alvar. A chemical preparation used to harden bones recovered from archaeological excavation, so that they can be handled without breaking.

alveolar. Pertaining to the part of the jaw at which the teeth sockets are placed; also referring to a sound made when the tip of the tongue is against the upper front alveolar ridge.

alveolo-palatal. A phonetic term used to describe any consonant (q.v.) which is pronounced with the tongue held between the ridge behind the upper teeth and the front part of the hard palate, e.g. bottom.

alveolus. A socket, especially of a tooth.

alyha. A man who lived and dressed like a woman and set up house with a "husband," after an elaborate ceremony, among the Mohave Indians. They were industrious wives, although the "husband" was teased, especially when he observed various ceremonials attendant on an imaginary pregnancy. The Mohave also had homosexual (q.v.) women.

amalaka. The bulbous shape at the top of towers on Indian temples.

amalgamation. The blending of a racial group with another through interbreeding.

amanous. Pertaining to the condition of not having hands.

amasiado. A kind of common-law relationship found in some New World Negro groups, in which the woman is the center of the family. Such matings are reasonably lasting, and probably derive from the polygynous families of parts of Africa. There is no onus attached to these unions or to the offspring.

Amazon. A generic name for a warlike woman. In Greek mythology, the Amazons were said to be female warriors who founded an empire on the Thermodon river in Asia Minor, and had excluded men from their society and conquered nearby nations.

Dahomey Amazons are women who are celibate and technically royal wives, helping with administrative and war matters. They duplicated the work of a parallel group of men. This kind of organization enabled the king to exercise more thorough control than any group in West Africa except for the Yoruba. When the Dahomey were fighting their way to the sea, these women had special functions which helped achieve victory.

ambalam. A Hindu temple where Vishnu and Siva are worshipped.

ambatch. A thorny tree of the Nile valley, with a pithlike white wood, used for making rafts.

amber. A fossil resin, which was highly prized in antiquity for its beauty as well as for the magneto-electric properties that gave it a supernatural halo. It was often used to make amulets (q.v.) The amber trade between the North and the Mediterranean may have been the means by which the southern European civilization influenced the more barbarous tribal groups of the continent's interior. Amber is found in all shades of yellow and also ranges from white to brown. Its Greek name was *elektron* from which the word *electrical* derives. Tracing amber caches is a useful method of obtaining information on early trade routes.

Ambil-anak. An adjustment of marriage custom in societies in which descent is reckoned through the male in cases in which there are no male members of the family. The adjustment involves cutting down the price ordinarily paid for the bride and reckoning descent through the woman for one generation, in addition to the newly married couple's living with the bride's family for the same generation. The term is Malay.

amelioration. The process by which a word increases its connotative stature; e.g., "knight," which originally meant "youth," "servant," or "man-at-arms," has since come to mean a person of honorific rank.

amenocal. A Tuareg chief.

America, Middle. The geographic area bounded roughly by the Rio Grande and Panama, including Mexico and Central America. It often is said to include the Antilles.

Americanist. A student of the American Indians.

Americas, theories of habitation of. Different theories have been proffered to account for the habitation of the Americas from west Asia and Africa. One theory is that early man crossed the Pacific by boat or raft. Another theory is that the crossing was made by a series of islands which are now under the

sea. The most widely held theory is that man crossed the Bering Strait from Asia to the Americas via a primitive craft over the 70-mile distance, or over a now sunken land bridge.

Most scholars believe that man crossed over from Siberia to Alaska during the last Ice Age, ca. 10,000-20,000 years ago. Inasmuch as sea water has been found frozen in an ice sheet which reached as far south as Kentucky, the sea level must have been about 300 feet below what it is now, and it was possible to make the crossing on dry land.

George Carter has reported manmade tools in California gravel terraces which are believed to be over 100,000 years old. If this is confirmed, then man may be presumed to have been in the Americas at the time of the fourth or last glacier, and must have crossed on the land bridge of the third glacier some 400,000 years ago. This compares with the age of 500,000 years which has been suggested for some European artifacts. Carter's crude rock flakes, which show controlled chipping, thus run counter to the usually accepted theory of man's having been in the Americas not more than 20,000 years. These artifacts were found on terraces of the third interglacial period, so that the putative men who made them came during a period when there was an exposed land bridge (q.v.) between Siberia and Alaska.

There are some ties, in the Eskimo, Aztec, Inca, and Maya culture, which might link Asia and the Americas. It has been suggested that there were one or more land bridges permitting travel between Asia and the Americas, and it has also been suggested that Asian culture was periodically infused into the Americas, perhaps by boat. The bulk of archaeological opinion has held that American culture developed in isolation after the initial settlers arrived. See WORLD, NEW.

Amerind. A term suggested in 1899 and used fairly widely in technical and popular writings to designate the persons resident in the New World before the Europeans arrived. It is derived from the initial syllables of American Indian.

amethyst. A violet quartz gem, which is believed to have the power of permitting a person to handle intoxicating beverages and to have curative powers.

Amharic. A language in the Ethiopic subsystem of southern west Semitic languages. It is the everyday tongue of about 3,000,000 inhabitants of Ethiopia.

amitate. The association between a nephew and his paternal aunt, in the form of the aunt either dominating or leaving property to the nephew.

Ammon's law. See LAW, AMMON'S.

amniomancy. Divination (q.v.) through the caul which sometimes covers a new-born infant's head.

amnion. A membrane which encloses the embryo and contains amniotic fluid. The amniotic membrane ruptures during the uterine contractions preceding birth.

amok. A manic and homicidal condition following a state of depression. It is often found in the Malay-speaking countries, especially among men who have left their familiar surroundings and are overwhelmed by a new environment. While it was originally noted among the Malays, from whose language the term derives, it has also been observed among Fuegians, Melanesians, and Siberians, and in India. Grief often brings on the condition, and this is followed by depression, confusion, and brooding. After working himself up into a kind of trance, the amok rushes to engage in violence. He may brood about an imaginary grievance, especially from a person who is socially superior so that there is little the amok can do about the insult. Complete postamnesia is common. The word, especially in its adverbial form, is also spelled amuck.

amole. A part of a plant which has detergent qualities and can be used as a soap.

amortizement. The architectural ornament or feature that crowns an edifice; e.g., a ridged or pointed roof, a gable, or a buttress.

ampallang. A metal rod with balls or brushes fixed to the ends. This device is worn transversely through a perforation in the end of the penis by Dyak men and is said to heighten sexual pleasure in their wives.

amphibian. A cold-blooded vertebrate class of animals. It lies between reptiles and fishes on the evolutionary scale. Gills in the young and lungs in the adult are usual. Frogs and salamanders are typical amphibians.

amphicone. The buccal cusp of the first and second upper premolar. It is a fusion of the metacone and paracone.

amphidromia. In Athens, a ceremony in which a child was carried around the hearth and thus initiated into the cult of its ancestors.

amphi-prostyle. Type of temple which has a portico at each end.

amphitheater. An oval-shaped area surrounded by rising tiers of seats, used for gladitorial displays.

amphora. A vase with two handles, chiefly found in ancient Greece. It held oil or water. Amphorae were also used by the Incas; these had two handles near the bottom that could be used to carry the amphora on the back. The amphora is one of the earliest types of vase, and is found all over the Greek world. Some were decorated by the best-known vase painters. In Oriental art, the term is used for vase forms which resemble the Greek original. Amphorae were fairly large. Of the various subclasses, the Dipylon vases were geometrically decorated, the Panathenaic were decorated with a picture of Pallas Athene, the Nolan had long, slim necks, and the Campanian had twisted handles.

amphora, Melian. Type of richly decorated Ionian vase with representations of birds and animals, both real and imaginary, painted on a cream-colored slip. There were occasional geometric backgrounds on these vases, although the oriental influence had virtually done away with this type of decoration. As in all Ionic art, the Ionic eye was present to ward off evil spirits.

Ampora. A secret society (q.v.) of Sierra Leone.

ampulla. An incense vessel used in religious ceremonies. It is often made of pewter and highly decorated. The term is loosely applied to any vessels of early times used to carry holy oils.

Amratian. An early predynastic, Aenolithic culture of Egypt characterized by finely worked implements of bone and stone.

amulet. An object, often decorative, worn to ward off various difficulties and potential dangers. This may have been the earliest type of ornament worn by prehistoric man. Some amulets were originally small parts of an ancestor's body. Representations of bodily parts, some with inscriptions, were used later as a means of ornamenting clothes and the body. In addition to protecting against danger, amulets were often also expected to provide strength, wealth, and good fortune. One type of amulet is the abraxas (q.v.).

amulet, cranial. An amulet made from the skull of a trepanned person. It was believed to have certain magical qualities.

amygdaloid. Referring to a shape like an almond. The term is often applied to Acheulian flints.

ana. A coral used as a pumice stone in Polynesia.

anabranch. A secondary channel leading to a river.

anacoluthon. In linguistics, an utterance which commences with one type of syntactical structure and without completing it shifts to another; e.g., *I like you go to the store.*

anadromous. Referring to fish, like the salmon and sturgeon, which ascend rivers in order to spawn in fresh water.

analysis, pollen. The study of past vegetation and climates through the comparative stratification of wind-carried spores in organic terrestrial sediments. Microfossils are best preserved in peatlike materials. The material is treated with a dissolving agent, like potassium hydroxide, which leaves the pollen even though it dissolves the organic matter. It is now possible to assign dates to various archaeological finds in Europe as a result of pollen-analysis studies, but the method is not as well worked out in North America. Pollen analysis is best used to give the relative, rather than the absolute, chronology of finds, or to correlate a find with other materials. The term palynology is sometimes used.

analysis, site. Analyzing the chemical and physical characteristics of an archaeological site to shed light on the habits of the occupants.

analysis, soil. A technique for the mechanical analysis of sediments, developed by Robert Lias. It can show the origin of a group of sediments and the aging of the deposition.

analysis, spectrographic. The use of a spectroscope to find the chemical elements of a given specimen. It is especially valuable in anthropology because of its accuracy and because only a small specimen is needed.

analysis, tree-ring. See DENDRO-CHRONOLOGY.

anaphora. Repeating a word or phrase at the beginning of consecutive clauses.

anaphoric. Referring to things known or spoken of; e.g., *they.*

anaptyxis. The emergence of an interpolated vowel in a word, for euphony or ease of pronunciation; e.g., *athaletic* for *athletic.*

anarak. An outer garment worn by the Eskimo as a protection against the weather while in the kayak. It is made of virtually waterproof oiled animal skins and has a hood that covers the head and extends down to the thighs.

Anasazi. A Navaho word meaning "ancient ones," used for a Basket Maker-Pueblo culture centering on the Arizona-New Mexico upland. The Anasazi sequence begins in Basket Maker II, ca. A.D. 300-500. The classic Anasazi period has been associated with Pueblo III, ca. A.D. 1050-1300, with its characteristic circular kiva (q.v.), rectangular house of masonry, and corrugated pottery. Black on white pottery was also usual.

Anatolian. A dialect belonging to the Southern Turkic group of the Ural-Altaic family of languages.

ancestor cult. See CULT, ANCESTOR.

ancilla. In ancient Greece, a warrior's shield used to beat time to music on festive occasions.

anda. In early India, a dome-shaped solid mass of brick and earth, placed over the base of a stupa (q.v.) or tomb for royalty.

Andaman. A food-gathering pygmy group on islands south of

Burma in the eastern part of the Bay of Bengal. See FIRE.

Andamanese. The language family of the Andaman Islands in the Bay of Bengal, a linguistic group lacking measurable positive relationships to other linguistic groups or families. The two variant forms are Great Andamanese, comprising Ba, Chari, Kora, Yeru, Juwoi, Kede, Kol, and Puchikvar (the northern subgroup) and Bale and Bea (southern subgroup); and Little Andamanese (Önge and Yärava). Phonologically, these languages are distinguished by the omission of *s*, by a complex system of affixes, an extensive class system, and an animate and inanimate gender.

Andi. A language spoken in the Caucasus, belonging to the North Caucasian family of languages.

androcracy. The domination of a society by male authority. An **androcentric** society is one under such domination.

androgyny. In anthropometry, the degree to which one sex has bodily forms characteristic of the other.

androsphinx. See HIERACO-SPHINX.

anemia, Cooley's or anemia, Mediterranean. A primary erythroblastic anemia characterized by splenomegaly, Mongolid facies, and bone changes. It is largely found among Mediterraneans. It is also called thalassemia.

anemia, sickle cell. A form of anemia in which the red cells assume a crescent shape in blood drawn from the veins. It seems to be more common among Negroes than other groups. The term depranocytosis is also used.

anemochore. A wind-borne disseminule, such as a seed or spore.

anepigraphic. Referring to excavated objects without writing or inscriptions. Thus, the term refers to discoveries which are purely ornamental or functional, as differentiated from inscriptions or narrative carvings.

Angakok. The priestly class among the Eskimo. The priests have the right to cohabit with women freely and derive other advantages from exploiting the fears of the ordinary person.

Angang. A kind of divination (q.v.) based on the first animal or human met on a journey.

angel. Messenger of God belonging to the family of demons. The stories of angels were especially developed in early Persian religion and were then passed on to Judaism. The heavenly demons were closely connected with functions of nature, e.g., wind and lightning. Their duties included the protection of man, mediation between man and God, divine substitution for man, and bearing revelations from God to man. A hierarchy composed of archangels originated in Judaism and became more widespread in early Christianity. After the fourth century, the angel cult became more generally accepted, and medieval Christian art abounds in representations of the Cherubim. Under Protestantism and the Enlightenment angels were relegated to the realm of fantasy.

24

angiosperm. A seed plant. The angiosperms provide much of man's sustenance. They first appeared in Mesozoic times, ca. 100,000,000 years ago, concurrent with the earliest mammals.

angle, carrying. In anthropometry, the laterally deflected angle made by the extension and supination of the forearm and the arm, e.g., in carrying. It is essentially the angle between axes of the forearm and upper arm. The human female's carrying angle is slightly greater than that of the male, although there is a great range of individual differences. The term cubital angle is sometimes used.

angle, cubital. See ANGLE, CARRYING.

angle, hafting. The angle between a blade and its tang.

Anglic. An international auxiliary language proposed by Zachrisson in the early part of the 20th century. It is based largely on phonetically spelled English.

Angra Mainyu. The evil spirit or god in Zoroastrianism.

anhistoric. Referring to antiquities that cannot be dated or elucidated by inscriptions or documentation.

animal, domestic. An animal useful to man that reproduces while captive. See DOMESTICATION.

animal, generalized. An animal that does not depart much from the generalized form of its predecessors. Man is one of the few advanced animals whose organs are largely generalized, e.g., the eye and brain. The human foot is perhaps the only specialized organ of man, having become an arched platform from a primate foot. Human hands, which remain fairly primitive, represent a good example of the adaptability and flexibility of generalized organs. The horse is an example of a specialized animal, with its strong and elongated middle toes specializing it for running.

animal, mythical. An unusual and bizarre artificial creature that may appear in folktales, e.g., the basilisk (q.v.).

animal, sacred. An animal which has a religious significance or a special meaning. Such animals may be associated with specific duties, and there may be prohibitions against eating or harming them. Some animals are associated with deities and may figure in their myths or have developed sacred qualities of their own. The horse (q.v.) used to be a sacred animal. See COW, SACRED.

animal, split. See MOTIF, SPLIT ANIMAL.

animal, white. White animals were of special supernatural value to the American Indians, e.g., the white coyote of the Yurok, who lives in the sky and is the source of all coyotes.

animal-renewing ceremony. See CEREMONY, ANIMAL-RENEWING.

animal tale. See TALE, ANIMAL.

animals, worship of. Early man, feeling himself closely akin to animals, in awe of their qualities of strength, cunning, and mystery, and dependent upon them for food, seemed to have desired to ally himself with certain animals and to protect himself from others. This may account for much of what is called animal worship. Cults perhaps arose because of man's early fear of killing and blood, coupled with the necessity for food. After grain became a staple food, various animals were associated with earth fertility. The snake was endowed with many powers, e.g., wealth and healing and fertility in field and home. As a symbol of underground waters, the snake was supposed to be the source of vegetation. It was widely believed that the souls of the dead were reincarnated in animal form. Animals were sometimes used interchangeably with nature gods because their qualities were so well adapted to symbolism. Sometimes individuals or whole tribes associated themselves with an animal species, which gave rise to many forms of totemism (q.v.).

animatism. The doctrine that many key objects in the environment are alive or have some special energy that can be communicated. These objects may be the outlets of impersonal power or may be personal. Usually, the objects do not have individual souls. The term vitalism is also used. See MANA.

animism. A belief in individual spiritual beings and in a future state. Probably originating in the Paleolithic age, such concepts as the Polynesian mana and the Indian orenda and manitou (qq.v.) represent the spiritual and nonpersonalized quality which is believed by the animist to be present in the universe. It has also been suggested that the concept first arose as a result of the difference between the dead and the living and such phenomena as sleep, trance, and dreams, so that each person might be presumed to have a physical life as well as a phantom life. Marett suggested that there was a level of preanimism in which there was no life-phantom distinction. The animist may be regarded as one who carries over to things the attitudes and procedures used to handle people.

anito. Among the Bontoc Igorot, a dead person's spirit that may cause sickness and death.

ankh. A cross with a looped top, often symbolizing the secret of life. It is found in the folklore of parts of Europe, India, and Central America. The term is Egyptian. In many representations, a god holds an ankh near the nostrils of a dead person in order to bring him back to life. The ankh is also called a crux ansata.

anklet. An ornamented or plain band or ring which is worn on the ankle.

anklung. An ancient Asian musical instrument made of bamboo pipes set in a frame. It is shaken to produce a chord.

ankteriasmus. A minor type of castration designed to keep the voices of male singers from changing.

Anlage. A predisposition, especially in the context of embryology and racial differences.

Annamese-Muong. A branch of the Austro-Asiatic family of languages spoken in the Annam district. It comprises Annamese (or Vietnamese) and Muong, each having a number of dialects.

annealing. The process of heating, firing, baking, or fusing in order to fix colors, or of heating and gradually cooling a material, e.g., glass, pottery, or metal, to toughen it or make it less brittle.

annual. A plant which completes its growth in one year, e.g., a grain or legume.

annulet. A flat band that encircles the capital of a Doric column several times. Also a flat molding which is common to parts of columns, particularly in the bases and capitals. In heraldry, an annulet is the representation of a ring on an escutcheon. It was originally meant to be the symbol of nobility, and was sometimes used to indicate the fifth son.

anointing. Rubbing oil or an unctuous substance over a person, often for purposes of consecration. It was widely used in early society. The Masai bride's wedding garments were oiled, as were the Hebrew high priest's robes. Fat and oil have been used for thousands of years in order to counteract the effect of personal demons and sickness and to give special power. Anointing is sometimes used to consecrate sacred objects and buildings.

anointing tablet. See TABLET, ANOINTING.

anomie. The condition of being only loosely integrated in a society so that the individual lacks interpersonal ties. The term was first proposed by Émile Durkheim.

anonym. A marriage class, as in Australia, for which no name is used by the natives.

ansa. In archaeology, a handle, e.g., of a vase. Ansae that are made of bronze or terra cotta are frequently ornamented or have inscriptions. The objects to which they were attached, being of less durable substance, often have disintegrated. The ansa is a more important item of study than the usual shard (q.v.). The term was developed in Mediterranean archaeology.

ansa a bastoncino. A handle made by bending a cylindrical clay stick into shape.

ansa a nastro. A handle made by bending a strip of clay of ribbon shape.

ansa a tubetto. A handle that has a small clay tube fastened against the vase wall.

ansa lunata or **ansa cornuta.** A handle that has a crescent shaped projection above. It is sometimes called an ansa cornuta (horned handle).

ant, antiquarian. An ant that digs up bright objects and deposits them on top of its ant hill. The archaeologist noting these fragments—perhaps of glass or beads—may assume that there is a site of human habitation nearby. In the study of the American Southwest, ant hills are particularly sought because of the frequency with which antiquarian ants have deposited in them turquoise beads and other shiny objects, which are exposed after rain.

ant, honey. An ant of the genus *Myrmecocystus,* a worker form of which stores in its abdomen the honey collected by other workers. In the southwestern United States,

Mexico, and Australia the honey-storing form of this ant is sought after and eaten by native peoples.

antediluvian. Term used to describe the men and objects existing before the great deluge recounted in Genesis.

anthemion. A decorative motif designed around the honeysuckle flower and leaves, used in many types of Greek and Roman architecture.

anthroarchaeologist. An archaeologist who has received training in the other branches of anthropology.

anthropic. Term referring to man as an animal among other animals, before the beginning of human culture as such.

anthropocentrism. A point of view which regards man as of central importance in the universe.

anthropogeny or **anthropogenesis.** The study dealing with the factors leading to the origin of man, such as the geological study of the physical conditions of the earth when man first appeared.

anthropogeography. The study of the interrelations between geographical environment and man.

anthropoid. An animal having the characteristics of the primate suborder, consisting of man, true monkeys, and apes. The anthropoids evolved in the Tertiary period. This suborder has true frontal eyes, well-developed brains, and stereoscopic vision. The two usual divisions are the New World monkeys (Platyrrhini, q.v.) and the Old World monkeys (Catarrhini, q.v.). Some students also single out a group of

the Catarrhini including the Hominidae, Pongidae, and Hylobatidae families (qq.v.).

anthropolatry. The devotion of an animal, e.g., a domesticated dog, to its master. Some writers have said that man's religious impulse is purely animal and is analogous to or similar to anthropolatry. Anthropolatry is also the worship or cult of a human being conceived as a god, as well as of a god conceived as a human being. Many early civilizations deified individuals. Thus the Shinto religion of Japan regarded the emperor as a visible deity and had shrines for brave warriors.

anthropology. The study of man. The word probably originated with Aristotle's description of the man with lofty ideas who is not a gossip or a talker about himself. The word anthropology is first found in English in an anoymous book on human nature, which divides the subject into psychology and anatomy. In the modern sense of the word, it is found in Hundt's *Anthropologeion* (1501), dealing with anatomy, and Capella's *L'Anthropologia* (1533), dealing with personal singularities. The contemporary science of anthropology consists of archaeology, cultural anthropology, linguistics, and physical anthropology.

anthropology, applied. The application of anthropological knowledge to meet the needs of the group for which the anthropologist is working. This may include giving advice, administration, or giving instruction.

anthropology, criminal. The study of the relationship of various traits and physical characteristics to criminality. Cesare Lombroso (1836-1909), professor of criminal anthropology at the University of Turin and founder of the science, held that criminals are persons with nervous, physical, and mental anomalies resulting from degeneration and atavism (q.v.). He regarded the criminal as somewhere between the "lunatic" and the "savage." Modern studies of crime have established the complex etiology of criminal behavior and have led to the general abandonment of theories like Lombroso's.

anthropology, cultural. The study of the behaviors of man which are learned, including among others the social, linguistic, technical, and familial. Cultural anthropology has been called the study of man and his works. It is sometimes used almost interchangeably in America for what in England is called social anthropology (q.v.), reflecting the traditional British interest in social systems and the major interest in culture of American anthropologists.

anthropology, physical or **anthropology, somatic.** The study of human biology, dealing with racial differences, the development of the human organism, changes in the body over the generations, and the relation between ecology and organism. It is also called somatology. The field of physical anthropology got great impetus from the study of anatomy. Probably the first use of anatomical knowledge in physical anthropology was Tyson's demonstration in 1669 that a pygmy (actu-

ally a chimpanzee) was a link between man and monkey. Gradually, taxonomical principles were applied to men and several different systems of classifying human beings were developed. The study of the evolution of man was another major stimulus in the development of physical anthropology. Archaeological diggings began in 1830 at Kul Oba in Scythia, and helped in the great growth of physical anthropology in the 19th century. Recent work on physical anthropology has been in the direction of incorporating ideas from genetics and the evolutionary processes.

anthropology, philosophical. The branch of philosophy concerned with the essence and distinctive character of man and the place which he occupies in the universe.

anthropology, racial. The study of the different types found within the human species and their origins and interrelationships.

anthropology, social. The study of social behavior, especially from the point of view of the systematic comparative study of social forms and institutions. The aim of social anthropology has been the application of the inductive method to society. The term was originally applied only to the study of the social organization of nonliterate peoples. Social anthropology has largely been a qualitative discipline. See ANTHROPOLOGY, CULTURAL.

anthropology, somatic. See ANTHROPOLOGY, PHYSICAL.

anthropology, synthetic. An approach which tries to integrate physical anthropology, archaeology, linguistics, theoretical anthropology, and the other cultural and historical sciences. Synthetic anthropology has been developed in the last few decades.

anthropology, theological. The study of man's nature and characteristics, from the point of view of systematic anthropology. Such subjects as man's creation and the relation between soul and body are considered. The usage is largely Continental.

anthropomancy. The use of human entrails for divination (q.v.). The humans sacrificed for this purpose were usually virgins or children.

anthropometer. An instrument used in somatometry, to measure the transverse diameters of the body and various heights. Usually it is a rigid rod about two meters long, made from hollow tubes that fit into one another. Each tube is usually graduated from zero to 2,000 millimeters.

anthropometry. The branch of physical anthropology devoted to the measurement of humans. It includes measurements that are taken on both skeletons and living persons, such as stature, bodily proportion, and the length and breadth of the head. The color of skin, hair, and eyes and similar qualitative measures are also taken. The contributions of anthropometry have been helpful in studying race crossing, the relationship between environment and physique, rates of growth, and the differences and similarities between human groups.

anthropometry, social. The study that treats social phenomena in a quantified and comparative manner.

Anthropomorpha. See HOMINID.

anthropomorphic. Having human appearance and form.

anthropomorphism. The ascription of human characteristics to objects that are not human, found in many early religious beliefs. Anthropomorphism was probably a factor in nature worship.

anthropopathism. The ascription of human emotions to objects or an environment.

anthropophagi. Mythical men of antiquity who were cannibals.

anthropophagy. See CANNIBALISM.

anthroposcopy. Visual examination and reporting of physical traits that cannot be measured exactly, e.g., eye color.

anticipation. In linguistics, the introduction into a word of a phoneme (q.v.) which belongs later in the thought; or a kind of assimilation (q.v.) in which a phoneme becomes like a subsequent phoneme or phonemes.

anticyclone. The atmospheric condition in which there are high central pressures and outward-flowing currents.

antigen. A substance in human blood that serves to differentiate one person from another. In addition to the four classical blood groups (q.v.), antigens for MN (q.v.) and Rh (q.v.) types have been discovered.

antipathy, racial. The invidious differentiation of two or more different individuals or groups because of the consciousness of presumed factors of race.

antiquarian. The usual designation for an amateur worker in archaeology. In the 18th and 19th century, the term was used for someone who collected old things.

antiquarianism. The study of ancient times and their remains, often pursued as a hobby and a precursor of archaeology, to which many antiquarians have made important contributions. W. W. Taylor has suggested that antiquarianism began in the 16th century in England. A society to preserve national antiquities was founded in London in 1572, and John Leland was appointed King's Antiquary in 1533. By the 17th century in England, many antiquaries were at work, with John Aubrey the most productive. The 18th century saw the study of antiquities invigorated by romanticism, the rediscovery of Greece, and the rise of natural history. In 1716, a London antiquarian called Conyers found some "elephant" bones and a chipped stone tool near Gray's Inn Lane in London, but was derided. In 1797, the antiquarian John Frere found the bones of some extinct animals and some hand axes in Suffolk and wrote an article suggesting that the implements and bones were from the same era, the implements being ". . . fabricated and used by a people who had not the use of metals."

antiquity, American cultural. The prehistoric development of culture in America has definitely been established only for the terminal Pleistocene. The platyrrhine tailed monkeys which branched away in the Tertiary and are localized in South America are the only non-human primates in the New World. There are practically no fossil or living anthropoid apes in America. This would appear to point to the evolution of man in the eastern hemisphere and his entering the western hemisphere rather late and fairly well developed, either neo-anthropic or Homo sapiens. The best authenticated ancient American finds probably are from the final advance or recession of the Würm-Wisconsin glaciation. This would be approximately similar to the European Upper Paleolithic, although the cultures are different. The American implements were typically large projectile points that were partly pressure chipped, while in Europe, except for Solutrean blades, hand tools were more common than spearheads in the Paleolithic. Compared with the Old World, American prehistory is shorter, its archaeology has not been worked out so far back, and its geological development is shorter.

anti-Semitism. A strong animus against Jews, expressing itself in many ways. The first record of it is in the Biblical Book of Esther (late sixth century. B.C.), when Haman in Persia said to king Ahasuerus of ". . . a certain people . . . let it be written that they may be destroyed." Renan has pointed out that ". . . anti-Semitism repeats itself everywhere and at all times." Anti-Semitism is usually rationalized on the grounds that the Jews represent a separate and unassimilable component because of their presumed differences of religion, culture, or social and political status. No one theory of anti-Semitism adequately accounts for its virulence and duration. Recent theories emphasize the irrational emotional drives of the anti-Semite.

Anubis. An Egyptian god entrusted with guarding the entombed and conducting their spirits outward. He is represented as a human with the head of a jackal and holding a staff in his left hand. Representations of Anubis were carved on the tombs containing mummies with a view to bringing him as close to the dead as possible.

anvil, hammer and. In linguistics, the action of the tongue striking the unmoving parts of the speech organs at the points of articulation.

Anyang. The site of a brilliant Bronze Age culture of the first half of the second millenium B.C. in Honan province, China.

Anyathian. Referring to a chopping-tool industry of upper Burma between the second and third glacial periods.

aorist. A past tense of no duration, e.g., *they died*.

aornarssuk. A protecting spirit among the Eskimo.

apantomancy. The art of divination (q.v.) from the first object that strikes the vision of the divine.

ape. A large anthropoid primate, such as a gorilla, gibbon, or chimpanzee. The apes evolved in the Miocene period.

Apepi. In Egyptian mythology, a tremendous serpent (the symbol of darkness) who engaged in a daily combat with the sun.

aperture, piriform. The anterior nasal opening of the human skull.

aphelion. The period in which the earth is comparatively distant from the sun, e.g., July.

apical. Referring to an articulation involving the tip of the tongue.

apiculture. Beekeeping and the collection of honey from bees. Apiculture was found at least in Upper Paleolithic times. Egyptian tomb paintings provide evidence that beekeeping was common during the dynastic period.

Apis. The bull god of the Egyptians. Most representations show him as black with white markings. When a bull god died, he was buried with elaborate ceremonies.

apnea. Elimination of carbon dioxide from the blood temporarily through forcing respiration, used for the purpose of losing the desire to breathe for short periods of time.

apobate. A Greek warrior who rode into action on a chariot, standing beside the charioteer, and leaped on and off while the chariot continued moving.

apocope. Deliberate omission or loss of the last letter, syllable, or part of a word.

Apocynum. A plant fiber used for weaving by the Anasazi.

apogee. In astronomy, the maximum distance between heavenly bodies; e.g., the moon is in apogee when at the greatest distance from the earth.

Apollonian. Referring to the cultural configuration, like that of the Zūni, marked by such qualities as introversion, orderliness, restraint, religious observances without hysteria, and sobriety. Ruth Benedict gave the term wide currency in anthropology. The concept was developed by Nietzsche and Spengler.

apophony. See ABLAUT.

aposiopesis. A speech construction in which the speaker breaks off his thought, e.g., *I expected we—*.

apotropaism. The prevention of evil through appropriate observances. Rites, blood, plants, noise, incantations, dancing, and other objects and techniques have been employed. In early society, the ceremonies often involved a group's beating, transporting, or taking the blood of a victim.

apparatus, speech. The parts of the body used in producing vocal sound, namely, lips, teeth, soft and hard palate, tongue, nose, and larynx and glottal cords.

apple, Adam's. The anterior prominence of the larynx (q.v.).

appliqué. A material consisting of one fabric sewed to another.

apposition. In linguistics, a construction in which forms joined by parataxis (q.v.) have equivalent grammatical functions, e.g., *Rover, the dog.*

apposition, close. A type of apposition (q.v.) between the components of which there is no pause pitch, e.g., *Mrs. Smith.*

apron, Hottentot. Among Hottentot and Bushmen women, an enlargement of the labia minora into a flap-like extension. There is some controversy as to whether the Hottentot apron is a genetic trait or an intentional deformation.

Apsaras. A divine water nymph in Hindu mythology. Apsarases are often represented in art dancing at a stream or waterfall. The term can also be applied in a very general sense to any representation of an angel in painting or sculpture.

apteral. Referring to a type of building colonnaded at the ends but not at the sides.

Apulian ware. See WARE, APULIAN.

aqueduct. An artificial channel for conveying water, usually by gravitation.

Aquitanian. An extinct dialect of Iberian, spoken in the Iberian peninsula during pre-Roman times. Some linguists have assumed that Aquitanian was the parent of modern Basque.

arabesque. A complex geometrical decoration of a surface, originally developed by Arabian artists.

Arabic. The language in which Mohammed spoke and which thus became the language of the Koran. It is currently spoken by some 40 million persons and is thus the most widespread Semitic language. Among its variants are Oman, Maltese, Tunisian, Hebrew, Egyptian, Syriac, Mesopotamian, and Zanzibari.

arachnodactylia. A condition in which the bones of the fingers or toes grow exceptionally thin and long, producing so-called spider fingers.

araeostyle. An architectural term used to describe an arrangement of columns in which the spacing between two successive columns is three and one-half times the diameter of a column.

Arafura. A mixed racial group of the Moluccas.

Arakan-Burmese. A branch of the Tibeto-Burmese subfamily of the Sino-Tibetan group. It consists of Arakanese, Burmese, the Kuki-Chin group, and Old Kuki.

Aralu. In Babylonian mythology, the underworld, or home of the dead. It was entered by a hole in the earth with seven doors.

Aramaic. A language originally used by the Arameans. It became an official language of the Persian Empire and was the language of Palestine in the time of Christ. It is a member of the Semito-Hamitic family. **Biblical Aramaic** is a Western Aramaic dialect in which the non-Hebrew portions of the Bible were written. **Christian Palestinian Aramaic** is a dialect of Aramaic from the Western Aramaic geographical zone. It was used in the fifth and sixth centuries A.D. for certain Biblical writings and appears in Bible translations made from the Greek.

Araucan. A family of South American Indian languages spoken near Chile. It includes Huiliche (or Kunko), Leuvuche, Mapuche, Pehuenche, Rankel, and Taluche.

Arawak. A family of languages spoken by South American Indians in South American and the Caribbean area until just before the Spanish conquest.

arblast. A kind of medieval bow consisting of a steel arc set in a shaft of wood and with a string and trigger. It was looked down upon by soldiers since it was operated by a mechanism and required no muscular strength.

arboreal theory. See THEORY, ARBOREAL.

arboriculture. The cultivation of shrubs and trees for special purposes.

arc, foraminal. The angle in degrees from the lambda to the foraminal axis.

arc, frontal. The value in degrees of the angle from the nasion to the bregma.

arc, parietal. The angle in degrees from the bregma to the lambda.

arcata. The use of the bow in playing musical instruments.

arcata in giu. The use of the musical bow with a downstroke.

arcata in su. The use of the musical bow with an upstroke.

arch. A rounded construction used in covering an open space without the use of horizontal beams. The true arch (one with a keystone and voussoirs) appeared in Mesopotamia ca. 3500 B.C. Arches are used magically and for purification.

arch, corbelled. An arch made by placing flat stones on top of one another, with each stone projecting slightly beyond the stone underneath, so that the two halves of the construction meet and are crowned by one stone. It is the most primitive type of arch, and is not capable of great width, since it does not play thrusts against one another but relies only on each component carrying the vertical thrust of the one above.

arch, dental. The arch formed by the crowns of the teeth.

arch, true. An arch made with splayed stones that press upon and obstruct one another, so that the downward thrust of gravity is translated into an outward thrust that is carried down to the supporting piers. Compared with the corbelled arch (q.v.), its outward thrust is great and is counteracted with buttresses. The true arch existed in Ur in the fourth millennium B.C., and the barrel vault (a broadened true arch) has been found in the third millennium B.C. The true arch was known by the early Egyptians but was not used for roofing. The Romans probably learned its use from the Etruscans, who used arches over gateways. The Romans used the true arch widely, e.g., in gateways, and openings in circus walls.

arch, zygomatic. A bony arch running from the upper jaw to the aperture of the ear. It provides attachment for some mastication muscles. It is large in some mammals with strong jaws and mastication muscles, while in the primates it becomes smaller as the comparative size of the jaw decreases.

Archaean. See CAMBRIAN, PRE-.

Archaeolithic. A term widely used by French anthropologists for the Mesolithic-Upper Paleolithic.

archaeology. The branch of anthropology that is concerned with the historical reconstruction of cultures no longer extant. Archaeology works with objects used by past societies, especially in daily life. As long ago as the seventh century B.C., Ashurbanipal of Assyria collected early records for his library in Nineveh. Nabonidus, in the sixth century B.C. did archaeological work and conducted restorations at Babylon. The modern study of archaeology began in the Renaissance, when Petrarch collected and tried to interpret Roman coins, and Cyriacus of Ancona collected inscriptions and drew buildings and monuments. The English journal *Archaeologia* first appeared in 1770. Winckelmann's *History of Ancient Art* (1763) was one of the earliest attempts at a systematic historical study of classical art and archaeology. One hundred French scholars went to Egypt with Napoleon in 1798 and gave great impetus to archaeology through their studies. In 1799, Championnet began the excavation of Pompeii. The 19th century saw a widening of interest in archaeology. Thomsen, in 1836, produced the first framework for interpreting inscriptionless material. By 1845, Layard began excavating at Nineveh. The mid-19th century saw an increasing study of prehistoric archaeology, with special interest in cultural styles and the degree of contiguity of different styles.

Archaeology helps reconstruct the human past in its material features, including how people lived and worshipped, how they built, their art, tombs, and travels. It provides material on man's prehistory, when no written records are available. It is concerned with all of man's material remains.

archaeology, Biblical. The recreation of the life and times narrated in the Bible. New archaeo-

35

logical discoveries have served to emphasize the general reliability of the narratives rather than the reverse. The literature of surrounding areas sheds much light on the Bible itself. Biblical borrowings from other cultures are becoming clearer, and more material is available on the strictly historical influences at work.

archaeology, classical. The archaeological study of the ancient Mediterranean area, particularly Greek and Roman civilizations.

archaeology, dirt. Archaeology actually conducted by excavation. Thomas Jefferson, in 1784, was supposed to have conducted the first such digging in America.

archaeology, field. The study of the remains of the past that are visible on the earth's surface or through examining soil discoloration and crop growth and flints, potsherds, and similar remains. It does not include excavations. The term was created by Williams-Freeman (1915). The method of study was established by Roy, who published *The Military Antiquities of the Romans in Britain* (1793).

archaeology, prehistoric. The study of those cultures which did not leave written records. It is often used to refer to the study of Neolithic and Paleolithic deposits.

archaeology, protohistoric. The study of cultures which date from the dawn of history.

Archanthropic. Referring to Paleoanthropic or Neanthropic type of man.

archetto. In ceramics, a forked or bent rod or stick with a wire stretched across, used by the potter for smoothing the clay while molding.

archiphoneme. The over-all number of pertinent characteristics shared by a pair of reciprocally neutralizable phonemes (q.v.).

architecture. The branch of art and science that deals with building construction, including execution of the original plan, actual construction, and decoration. Architecture began with the Egyptians, ca. 4,000 B.C. The development of architecture has been influenced by three discoveries: (1) two upright posts will support a horizontal cross beam; (2) an arch will support itself in addition to a superimposed weight, making arched construction possible; (3) a steel framework using the cantilever principle supports vertical walls and horizontal floors. The study of architecture is valuable to the anthropologist in helping to assess the style of life and culture of a group or area.

architecture, Aegean. The broad classification for the buildings of the Stone and Bronze Ages. Buildings of timber, stone, plaster, and adobe were constructed haphazardly and with very little skill.

architecture, ashlar. A type of architecture in which all the walls were built of stone, which was left in evidence on the outside and inside, as in Greek temples.

architecture, Egyptian. Ancient Egyptian architecture boasts many pyramids, rock-cut temples, and tombs. The style is solid, majestic, and massive. The exterior wall surfaces always sloped inward, there were many columns with no bases but many different types of capitals, and the walls and columns were decorated with a great number of sculptures in engraved outline, precisely executed and sometimes in bas-relief. The mechanical processes necessary for cutting, polishing, sculpturing, and transporting the enormous blocks of stone used in this architecture were quite remarkable in view of the inferior mechanical equipment available.

architecture, Greek. Classical architecture of ancient Greek civilization which utilized the principle of post and lintel. The different styles in order of evolution were Doric, Ionic, and Corinthian.

architecture, order of. Classification evolved by the Greeks for the different styles of columns, with bases, shafts, and entablatures. The Greeks had three "orders," i.e., Doric, Ionic, and Corinthian. The Romans used the same orders, with the addition of the Tuscan and the Composite.

architrave. A molded frame surrounding a door or window. It can also be applied in a general sense to any crosspiece resting upon two vertical columns.

archives. Records, largely official, dealing with administrative matters.

arctic costume. See COSTUME, ARCTIC.

arcuated. Type of architecture which uses the arch principle. Literally it means "curved like a bow."

ard. An agricultural implement widespread in the Mediterranean area, used to pulverize the soil so that moisture could not rise to the surface through capillary attraction. This was important because of the necessity for guarding against evaporation in the summer drought, and especially because of the comparative lack of livestock and of moisture-holding manure. The ard was usually drawn by a pair of yoked oxen. In northern Europe, ards were probably used for cross plowing. The ard probably dates from before 3,000 B.C. in Mesopotamia and Egypt. It may have been involved with the beginning of industrial food production, by enabling the growth of grain in exportable quantities. The ard probably evolved from the digging stick (q.v.).

ard, crook. An ard which derives from a forked branch. It consists of a large hoe that is dragged through the ground by the handle, with a stilt at the rear to steady it. It was used in Greece, Crete, and north Germany. The crook ard dates from the Bronze Age.

ard, spade. A Bronze Age ard used in the Mediterranean area. One end was a sole and the other the handle. A separate beam was attached near the bottom.

area. The breadth multiplied by the length of an object.

area, age. The concept that the traits of a culture area are diffused from their center at an equal growth rate and that the distance they are from the center is a clue to the comparative age of a trait. Traits at the periphery of a culture area are assumed to be early because they have spread so far, while the area's center is most typical of its culture and most long-lived.

area, culture. A region which has a relatively similar way of living common to its component socio-economic systems and cultures. The center of the culture area has uniform customs but its periphery may be less homogeneous. The concept is more relevant to material culture than to other aspects of culture. The classification by culture areas is neither historical nor natural, as it is based on the source of the material, primarily for the use of museum curators. This concept has a tendency to be used in a static way, since it is classification as of one time.

The idea of culture area was worked out first by Otis Mason for North America in 1895. A culture area in America was said to have a number of tribes which had a dozen or so clearly defined trait groups. The Arctic or Eskimo culture area was said to be characterized by Eskimo language, shamans, caribou- and seal-hunting, dog sleds, bone and ivory carving, and fur garments cut in similar patterns.

It is often difficult to distinguish a marginal area (q.v.). Another drawback of this concept is that important tribes in a culture area may not have some of the supposedly distinctive traits of the culture area, e.g., in Eskimo culture, the snow house is only prevalent in a restricted region.

area, dialect. A geographical demarcation of slight transitions in the manner of speaking a language.

area, floral and fauna. An area which has a characteristic group of species of animals or plants. As in the case of the culture area (q.v.), there is considerable diffusion, so that it is difficult to fix absolute boundaries.

area, habitation. The place where a comparatively stable human group lives.

area, lateral. In linguistics, the outside edges of an imaginary circle drawn around a center of radiation, where innovations have not disturbed the older forms.

area, marginal. The culture of communities which are at the periphery of a culture area (q.v.) and whose culture springs from the adjoining culture areas. In the Scandinavian culture area, marginal areas might be Schleswig-Holstein, Iceland, the Frisian Islands, and Finland.

area, refuge. An area into which there is immigration after pressure from other tribes. These areas are likely to be economically poor or protected by a natural barrier.

area, speech. The area within which a language or dialect is spoken.

area, wetted. The amount of moisture which is found on the body's skin surface.

area limitata. The area enclosed in the eastern half of a terramara (q.v.).

area production theory. See THEORY, AREA PRODUCTION.

area studies. See STUDIES, AREA.

areas, progressive equiformal. A series ranging from the smallest to the largest areas over which varied flora and fauna which have radiated from the same center have spread.

areca. A palm tree, *Areca catechu,* of which the nut is an ingredient of the betel nut quid.

areic. A surface which lacks streams.

aren. The equivalent of mana (q.v.) among the Ao Naga.

areography. The study of areas and of how they arise.

areola. Decorative tile, panel, or plate of earthenware, marble or stone, forming part of a pavement. Also any of the eight rectangular plates making up the circuit of the imperial crown of the Byzantine and Carolingian empires.

arête. The ridge which lies between the flaked surfaces of a flint.

arghool. An Egyptian musical instrument occasionally played by boatmen on the Nile. It is a pipe with six finger holes, fastened to a longer pipe without holes.

arghyas. The offering a Brahman makes to the sun, consisting of rice, water, sandalvil, white flowers, sesamum seed, and durra grass.

argilla. Powdered or ground granite rock, sometimes called kaolin, used as an ingredient in fine porcelains, and as a wash over clay walls in the Orient.

argillaceous. In ceramics, a term meaning claylike.

argillite. A carving first made by the western Canadian Indians ca. 1820 for sale to the Whites. Agrillites were representations of animate and inanimate forms with a high degree of sculptural design and great strength of expression.

argine. The rampart of a terramara (q.v.).

ariki. In Polynesia generally, a village or tribal chief. Also, in Polynesian legendary history, the second wave of migrants to Polynesia, who were supposed to have conquered and ruled over their predecessors, the Menehune (q.v). The term appears also in the forms aliki, ari'i, and ali'i.

Arioi, Areois, or Areoi. A troupe of professional players in Tahiti who went from village to village giving dramatic and musical performances. The women of the troupe bestowed sexual favors freely but were forced to leave the group if they bore children. The semisecret society of the Arioi was suppressed by missionary influence ca. 1820. It was pre-European and probably arose in the 16th century as a cult of the god Oro, its mythological founder, for whom the society was a missionary. The Arioi society by its dance, song, and pantomime was the major carrier of the island's mythology and tradition. Its visiting between islands helped maintain peace.

ariolist. A person who engages in divination (q.v.) by altars.

Aristotle (384-322 B.C.). The Greek philosopher who was the first zoologist. He was the first scientist before Linnaeus who classified man with the other animals, and he had some ideas concerning natural selection. He viewed man as a social animal. Aristotle bridged the gap between philosophy and science in the development of European thought.

arlequine. A precious opal. The term was originally Mexican.

armaments. Objects, largely controlled and accumulated by the state, used for warfare. In early societies, there was little distinction between armaments and devices used for everyday living. Tools and weapons were probably interchangeable originally. Armaments became more distinctive as societies developed.

armarium. An alcove or recess constructed in religious buildings as a repository for sacred vessels.

armature. A framework upon which sculpture is modeled. It is usually made of stiff wire for smaller works and wire mesh or iron pipe, for heavier works. Armature is also a rare heraldic term applied to any equipment for battle. It also designates an architectural device intended to brace a weak part.

Armenian. A language of the Indo-European family. It is spoken by some 3 to 4 million persons in Asia Minor. The present liturgical language, Grabar, is the classical form. The modern vernacular is Ashksarhik.

Armenoid. A hypothetical ethnic Caucasoid subdivision in eastern Asia Minor and the Caucasus areas. The Armenoid type has a long convex nose and is high headed.

armet. A lightweight closed headpiece in medieval armor, first introduced in the mid-15th century. It fitted the head well, allowed for reasonable movement, and had openings for sight and breathing. It was forged in many parts, which were fitted together and fastened by hooks and hinges; when closed it was firm and rigid.

armlet. A piece of personal jewelry worn by the ancient Egyptians, Persians, and Romans. It was a decorated metal band, from two to four inches wide, worn between the elbow and shoulder. Armlets were decorated in geometric style in Egypt and with engraving and precious stones in Persia. The term is also used in tailoring to denote that part of a dress at which the sleeve joins the shoulder.

armor. A kind of clothing, usually of metal, worn to protect its wearer against weapons. During the Middle Ages, it became the professional clothing of the knight.

armor, cotton. Quilted cotton soaked in brine and worn by Aztec warriors. It covered the whole body and was brocaded in several colors or embroidered with feathers.

aromorphosis. An evolutionary change which involves an increase in the energy and organization of the organism, e.g., the development of biting jaws from gill arches in the vertebrates. The term was coined by Sewertzoff.

arrangement. In linguistics, the study of the order of morphemes, words, and syntax.

Arretine ceramics. See CERAMICS, ARRETINE.

arrow. The arrow developed as a late Paleolithic weapon consisting of a shaft and a point. Although feathers help the flight of an arrow, they are not necessary and are not found in certain South Sea and South American groups. The use of the arrow is almost worldwide. It may be employed for religious purposes, magic, to improve health, and to control the weather. The culture hero is often the source of bow and arrow. Arrows may have steadying wings, a notch for a bowstring, and may be carried in a quiver.

arrow, bird. An arrow the point of which has some blunting substance, like seed, affixed so that the arrow will not injure the pelt of the animal hunted or stick in a tree and be lost. It is widely found where the bow and arrow is used, especially among the Eskimo and the Tropical Forest area.

arrowhead, transverse. An arrowhead which has its edge at right angles to the shaft.

arrowroot. An edible starch obtained from any of several tropical American plants, especially of the genera *Zamia* and *Maranta,* and used by the natives as food.

arroyo. A desert stream bed that is usually dry.

art, Assyrian. A subdivision of Mesopotamian art which flourished between 750 and 612 B.C. One of its chief characteristics was the rich wall sculpture done in bas-relief. In its early period, representations were dynamic and truthful in their interpretation of natural forms. There was a subsequent decline from which Assyrian art never rallied. In its representation of human forms, it is heavy and conventional. Great attention is paid to minute detail.

art, biomorphic. The type of designs on small stones made by men of the Paleolithic Age. The designs were based on organic forms.

art, black. This term was derived from the old practice of painting images of the devil in black. It means sorcery in general or the imaginary power of performing wonderful feats by means derived from the help of evil spirits or of the devil.

art, cave or **art, Cro-Magnon.** The art of the Upper Paleolithic Age, ca. 12,000-20,000 years ago, is found in caves in southern France and northern Spain. It consists of representations of animals, some of which are now extinct. As it is associated with Cro-Magnon skeletal remains it is also called Cro-Magnon Art. This art consists of finger tracing, bas-relief, sculpture, painting, and engraving. Its creators probably camped on the terrace of the cave or under an overhanging rock. Cave art is found where there is limestone.

Cave art is associated with blade tools in which the flake was shaped before being detached from the core, and is thus identified as Upper Paleolithic. The oldest cave art convention consists of finger tracings in the damp clay on certain cave walls. The earliest kind of engraving, consisting of simple outline drawings, is sometimes found over the finger tracings. The representations developed from rough silhouette to more precise form and in the direction of greater realism. The animals were shown with two and then with four legs. Black and red were probably the first colors used. In some engravings the animal's body is represented by long striations which suggest shading. Representations of scenes or persons together are rare. Changes in

41

style occur in several areas at once, so that it is likely that there were schools for the learning of painting technique.

The early cave engraving was probably accomplished by flint burins, which are often found associated with cave art. Natural ochers were frequently used to provide color. These ochers are iron oxides mixed with clay, earth, and other materials. Red, orange, yellow, and chocolate were used. Manganese oxide led to a blue-black and carbonacious material like burned bones provided black. Cave art did not have any green, white, or blue. The pigment was probably ground, put in shells or tubes of bone, mixed with some fatty material, and applied.

Since cave art is sometimes located far from the cave entrance, stone lamps with moss wicks burning were probably used to light the way to the paintings. Almost all Upper Paleolithic cave art is found in inaccessible and dark places, and this may be tied in with this art's supposed function in propitiating animal spirits. The frequency of artists painting pictures over earlier pictures points toward the special use of some crannies for magic and religion.

art, Cycladic. The pre-Hellenic art of the Aegean Islands.

art, decorative. The type of art that makes an artifact more attractive by adding embellishments that may not be functional.

art, Egyptian. The architecture, sculpture, and painting of ancient Egypt were among the most im-

portant in the entire history of art. The techniques employed in the various arts (including drawing, pottery, glass, carving, metalworking and gem-cutting) were far in advance of those used in later cultures. Some of the sculptures are colossal in size and many are at least 5,000 years old, dating from the 1st Dynasty, ca. 3,000 B.C. Design was highly developed and graceful.

art, geometric. An art style in which the object is distorted in representation for the purpose of achieving a better design. This style is often found, especially in the Scandinavian, Celtic, Scythian, and early Greek cultures. Greek sculpture, Celtic manuscript illumination, and Byzantine mosaics offer many examples. Geometric style emphasizes the latent rhythmic content of forms at the expense of their natural appearance.

art, Hellenistic. Greek art during the period of geographical expansion (ca. 300-100 B.C.). Hellenistic art was produced in the Aegean islands and in Asia Minor. It has been accused of lacking the vitality characteristic of older Greek art.

art, home. Art, such as sculptures and engravings, which consists of objects which actually come from the homes of early man.

art, Mayan. The art of the Mayan culture (ca. 1st century B.C.), is characterized by formalized representations of nature motifs, resulting in the most stylized decoration of stone, wood, and clay ever accomplished by any people. Mayan architecture included high truncated pyramids and the use of the corbelled arch (q.v.). The Maya also had an original complete system of writing, and there are numerous inscriptions on lofty monolithic monuments.

art, Mesopotamian. The related arts of ancient Chaldea, Babylonia, and Assyria. These arts exerted a strong influence on Greek art and therefore indirectly on all later Western art.

art, Mimbres. An unusual type of pottery made by the Indians of southern New Mexico. Most examples were black and white food bowls. They were decorated on the inside with animals, birds, insects, or fish drawn naturalistically and yet stylized sufficiently for ornamental purposes. It was the custom to break a hole in the bottom of these vessels for burial use. Research indicates that the spirit of the bowl was presumably released by this process in order to roam freely with the spirit of the dead.

art, parietal. Painting on cave walls, especially that done during the European Paleolithic period. Parietal art is distinguished from art mobilier, which comprises paintings that are movable.

art, portable. See ART MOBILIER.

art, stationary. Art objects found on the ceiling or walls of shelters or caves.

art mobilier. The decorated and carved objects found in the dwelling sites of the Upper Paleolithic Age. This work was done with ivory, bone, and stone. A group of small and round statuettes, largely of women, was found from west Europe to east central Siberia. Many

weapons and decorated tools date from this period. Valley deposits and floor accumulations have yielded a number of *art mobilier* finds. The term portable art is sometimes used.

artel. A co-operative organization, originally a group of related families in Russia, that combined forces to do work which no one family could do by itself. The term has also recently been used to designate Soviet Russian villages run on a co-operative basis.

arteriosclerosis. A circulatory disease that accompanies old age, involving hardening of the arteries.

articulation. In linguistics, the process of adjusting the shape of the passage from the larynx to the mouth to make a vocal sound.

articulation, apical. The production of a sound by touching the tip of the tongue to the top of the oral cavity, e.g., *t* or *d*.

articulation, basis of. That position of the speech organs when they are not producing sound which is characteristic of a specified speech community.

articulation, dorsal. A speech sound made by the back of the tongue touching different parts of the palate, e.g., *k* or *g*.

articulation, points of. The points which lie above the articulators, which may be approached or touched by the latter.

articulation, positions of. In linguistics, the possible combinations of the articulators.

articulation, uvular. A feature of sound produced by a vibration of the uvula, e.g., *r* in most pronunciations of French.

articulator. A vocal organ which can be freely moved, so that it can assume a number of positions. Organs such as the tongue, lips, teeth, and palate are articulators.

articulator, fixed. An articulator that cannot move, such as the soft and hard palate, upper teeth, upper lip, gum ridge, and glottis.

articulator, mobile. An articulator that can move, such as the vocal cords, the back, front, and tip of the tongue, and the lower jaw and lip.

artifact. An object of any type made by human hands. Tools, weapons, pottery, and sculptured and engraved objects are representative artifacts.

artifact, contextless. An artifact for which there is no established context, because it was found by an amateur or discovered accidentally, or because it may have been transported by various geological or other agents from its place of origin.

Arundinaria. A reed used for blowguns and panpipes in the Amazon.

arungquilta. In Central Australia, the quality which makes a medicine man efficacious.

Arunta. A tribe living in central Australia. The members have wavy hair and a receding forehead and are dolichocephalous. They are also called the Aranda.

Aryan. Tribes speaking Indo-European languages who invaded India between 1500 and 1800 B.C. War, cattle theft, and horse breeding were major activities. Pottery, the wheel, and the plow were used by the Aryans. Aryan society was patrilineal. Epic poetry was well developed. Certain writers in the 19th century developed the notion that the Aryans were the highest breed of man and that all other "races" could produce only depraved or unhealthy cultures. It has been repeatedly emphasized that the term properly belongs to a linguistic stock and that the attempt to equate "aryan" culture, race, and linguistic group must fail.

aryballoid. Referring to jars having a pointed ovoid base and a long, flaring cylindrical neck.

aryballus. A type of Greek vase. In early days, it was probably applied to a large vessel with a constricted neck used for carrying water to the bath. Today, the term is generally used to denote any bell-shaped vase with a short neck and small opening surrounded by a flat rim and used for anointing with oil.

arytenoids. Two movable hinges made of cartilage which are located on the rear of the larynx. They are attached to the vocal cords.

Asantehene. The Ashanti emperor.

ash. The solid residue from burning a combustible substance at a moderate temperature. Ashes have served as fertilizer, for religious purposes, and to bring about desired weather. Ashes from cremations have been used to bring about fertility of crops or animals and to treat different types of disease. They are symbolically used in mourning and to predict the future.

44

asheor. A 10-stringed musical instrument, now obsolete, first used by the ancient Hebrews.

asherah. A wood object, usually vertically placed, often adjacent to altars. The asherah probably was associated with the worship of trees. It probably was a sacred tree at first and then became an artificial tree symbol. It was found alongside the Jerusalem temple of Jahweh. In Phoenicia, sun and moon symbols were related to the asherah. The Hebrew asherah was sometimes in the form of a human. An asherah might also be a symbol of a deity.

ashira. A Middle-Eastern subtribe.

ashlar. A technique used in building walls in which large, carefully prepared stone blocks are used in staggered rows. Also, dressed stone as opposed to natural stone. See ARCHITECTURE, ASHLAR.

Asianic. A group of obsolete languages spoken and evolved in and around Mesopotamia and Asia Minor in distant antiquity. The term is geographical rather than linguistic since these languages have no observable relationship to one another or to any observed language. The languages are Bithynian, Cappadocian, Carian, Cilician, Cossaean, Cretan, Cypriote, Elamite, Etruscan, Gergito-Solymian, Isaurian, Khattian, Lycian, Lydian, Mariandynian, Mysian, Palwa, Pamphylian, Paphlagonian, Pisidian, Pontic, Subaraean, Sumerian, and Vannic.

asphaltum. One of the most ancient pigments in painting, also used by the ancient Egyptians in mummification. Its color is neutral brown, and it is favored as a glaz-

ing material because of its warm tone. Asphaltum has a disadvantage as an oil paint, however, since it never becomes thoroughly dry and will soften further with heat. For this reason, many paintings since the 17th century display much breaking and cracking in the dark passages. Asphaltum is also used in printing and etching. It is also called bitumen.

aspirate. The sound or letter *h;* rough breathing; a sound which is associated with *h;* an unvoiced breath.

aspiration. An expiration of unvoiced breath following the utterance of a consonant. In English the same consonant may be aspirated or unaspirated depending upon its position. Thus *p* is aspirated in *pin* and unaspirated in *spin.* Aspiration may constitute a phonemic difference (see PHONEME).

ass. An ungulate resembling the horse, but with longer ears and smaller mane, tail hair, and size. The ass is a frequent figure in folklore of the Mediterranean area. It was said to have considerable power for healing.

Assamese. An Indic language connected with Bahari and Bengali; also, a geographical designation of several languages which constitute a branch of the Tibeto-Burmese subfamily of the Sino-Tibetan family of languages.

assegai or assagai. A conically pointed slender sharp rod of ivory or bone, adapted for fitting in a wooden shaft. Assegais date from Magdalenian times. They may be forked, turn-screw shaped, and pointed or rounded at the butt. Among the Bantu, the term denotes a spear tipped with iron. The name sagaic also appears.

assemblage. The piecing together of the findings of an archaeological site, including all the types of industry (q.v.), art, bones, burials, and other remains. The term also denotes all the artifacts which have context (q.v.) together.

assibilation. A phonetic process of assimilation (q.v.) whereby a nonsibilant consonant is altered into a sibilant (q.v.).

assimilation. In *linguistics,* a type of sound change in which two adjacent or proximate phonemes (q.v.) assume shared or identical features. When the sound that remains unchanged (the assimilatory phoneme) occurs in a position prior to the assimilated phoneme, the phenomenon is called progressive assimilation. When the assimilated phoneme is succeeded by the assimilatory phoneme, the process is called regressive assimilation. Reciprocal assimilation describes the process in which two phonemes affect each other. See ASSIMILATION, INCONTIGUOUS.

In *cultural anthropology,* the process through which groups that live in a common territory but are of heterogeneous backgrounds reach a broad-based cultural solidarity that ripens into national unity. It involves a homogeneity of schemes of imagery and goes deeper than merely accepting material traits. Assimilation is found in nonliterate cultures that achieve contact with one another, in the contacts between nonliterate cultures and civilization, and in contacts between historic cultures. Assimilation may be a phase of acculturation (q.v.)

assimilation, contact. See ASSIMILATION, DISTANCE.

assimilation, distance. In linguistics, a kind of assimilation in which a phoneme (q.v.) or phonemes are crowded out by another phoneme, which is substituted for them. It is sometimes called contact assimilation.

assimilation, incontiguous. In linguistics, the process of articulation which operates in such a manner that two proximate phonemes (q.v.) separated by an intervening phonemic unit or combination of units assume shared or identical features.

assimilation, progressive. See ASSIMILATION *(linguistics).*

assimilation, regressive. See ASSIMILATION *(linguistics).*

association. In sociology, in some societies, a group of persons of common interests or of common status. Age groups often are used as definite categories within groups of this type.

In *archaeology,* objects found together in a closed find (q.v.).

association, voluntary. A group made of members that join voluntarily. In early societies, voluntary associations were fairly widespread, and Schurtz has emphasized the degree to which the like-minded persons in such an association are of the same age and sex.

assortment, independent. In genetics, the tendency of each gene to be assorted independently of its mate.

assymetry, facial. An imbalance between expression and the morphology of the left and right halves of the face.

Assyrian. See AKKADIAN.

Assyriology. The study of Mesopotamian antiquity.

asterion. A suture (q.v.) meeting point between the occipital, mastoid, and parietal bones.

asterisk. The symbol (*) used as a prefix in texts on linguistics to denote that the word or word form so distinguished is not a demonstrated linguistic unit but one the existence of which is assumed as a historical occurrence or as a hypothetical form deduced from linguistic laws and other observed data.

asterism. The starlike rays of light observed in certain gems, e.g., the star sapphire, when viewed from particular directions and exposures.

asthenic. See LEPTOSOME.

astragalomancy. Divination (q.v.) through small bones, e.g., the vertebrae. Astragalomancy may have led to such games as dice and jacks.

astragalus. The upper bone of the tarsus, which supports the tibia.

astrolabe. A circle of wood or metal, with a tube in the center for sighting. Its perimeter was marked off in degrees, either 60 or 360. The astrolabe could measure any angle. It probably was used thousands of years before the Christian era.

astrology. The doctrine that man's fate can be read in the stars. Probably beginning in Mesopotamia, astrology was adopted by the ancient Greeks and continues to the present day. Babylon, in ca. 2400 B.C., saw the first systematic astrology, which remained fairly unchanged until the Roman Empire, when the idea arose that the universe is an interrelating organism, the meaning of which could be interpreted through the stars. This viewpoint presumably made it possible to tell what would happen to anybody.

astromancy. Divination (q.v.) from the stars.

astronomy. The study of the heavenly bodies, often said to be the oldest of the physical sciences, because it is believed that early man was interested in the movements of stars, moon and sun, The moon and sun were sometimes linked with the subsistence available in a given region. Daily changes in light and darkness were related to the sun, and the phenomena of dawn, sunrise, daylight, twilight, and night were probably the first astronomical phenomena observed. The changing length of the day in temperate areas was probably noted next. The length of seasons and the measurement of dates by stars probably came later. The Pleiades cluster is generally believed to have been the first estimate of the year's length. Its rising in the evening was a sign of winter, and early husbandmen estimated reaping time by its rising and plowing time by its setting. Sirius, Arcturus, the Hyades, and Orion were also used in this way.

Asturian. Referring to a crude Spanish culture of the late Mesolithic Age. It is a specialized form

47

of Azilian (q.v.) culture. A developmental use of river pebbles as tools is found. Shellfish were a main source of food. A kind of pick made of pebble is commonly found in the northern Spanish cave deposits which characterize this culture.

astylar. Referring to a building façade with no columns or pilasters.

asyllabic. Referring to a sound unit which does not form a syllable (q.v.) by itself or serve as the nucleus of a syllable, e.g., *l* in love. The more common designation is non-syllabic (q.v.).

asylum. A place from which a fugitive cannot be taken, because of the special qualities of the place or building, usually religious or spiritual qualities possessed by the church, ruler, or other special person or institution. There the individual taking asylum is inviolate. Observance of the special qualities of a place of asylum is almost universal.

A home or a woman, because of their special powers, may represent asylum. There are many folk beliefs about the dire fate that will befall a person who violates the right of asylum. Totem centers, cities of refuge, or villages may be asylums. When some peoples were converted to Christianity, the right of asylum continued in churches, as in Spain until the 19th century.

asyndetism. The grammatical condition in which there are no connecting words between parts of a phrase or sentence.

atabal or **atabale.** A large Moorish drum, a kettle drum, or a species of tabor used by the ancient Hebrews.

Atahocan. An impersonal Algonkian deity.

Atamalqualiztli. An Aztec fasting ceremony.

atavism. The return in the offspring of a trait which was not present in the parent, although it was present in other ancestors. Atavism also denotes the belief that early ancestral characteristics will recur. This concept dates from pregenetic biology.

Atea. In Polynesian mythology, the mother of the creator god Tane. She is also called Vatea and Wakea.

Atef-crown. The symbolic headdress worn by the Egyptian gods Khnum and Osiris at all times and sometimes by other gods, including Sebek, Thoth, and Harmachis. It was occasionally used by certain kings, like the Rameses. It consisted of the tall, conical white cap of Upper Egypt, flanked with a pair of long ostrich plumes, and had the solar disk and uraeus in front. It was probably emblematic of the sovereignty of Egypt under the attributes of light, truth, and divinity.

aten. The solar disk, a religious symbol of ancient Egypt, honored as one of the important gods. With the spelling Aton, it is a parallel of Ra.

ateolotism. A well proportioned nanism (q.v.).

Aterian. An African point (q.v.) with a tang.

Athapaskan or **Athabascan.** A linguistic subdivision of the Nadené language group. This stock is perhaps related to Sinitic and includes many western North American languages. It is found in the Southwest United States, in the northwest part of Canada, and in some groups on the Pacific Coast. It includes Dene, Hupa-Matole, and Apache-Navajo.

atheism. The denial of the existence of God, or of gods. It has been said that the Tasmanians, Cimmerians, and ancient Peruvians were atheistic.

athletic. In Kretschmer's system of constitutional types (q.v.), referring to the normal or in-between type, tending toward introversion and swings in mood.

atlante. See FIGURE, ATLANTID.

Atlantic. Referring to the warm and moist climate from ca. 5000-2500 B.C., when the alder, oak, elm, and lime were typical vegetation. The Ertebole (q.v.) culture prevailed during much of this period.

Atlantis. A hypothetical land in the Atlantic Ocean where civilization is alleged to have begun. There is no evidence to support this notion.

Atlanto-Mediterranean. Referring to a hypothetical western European subdivision of the Mediterranean Caucasoids. It also denotes a Mediterranean group of substantial build, tall stature, and skin color ranging from white to ruddy.

atlas, linguistic or **atlas, dialect.** A map showing variations in the dialect of a given area, with isoglosses (q.v.) drawn in.

atlatl. An Aztec spear thrower (q.v.).

atman. The infinite essence of the soul. In Hindu religion it is described as being without magnitude, while at the same time endlessly great. It is the repository of the divine spark in the human being which exists in but separate from the body, to be returned to its source at death.

ato. A political division among the Bontoc.

Atoakwatje. Water-bringing demigods among the Arunta.

Aton. See ATEN.

atrium. An entrance courtyard surrounded on all sides by roof but open to the sky, used in Roman houses.

atrophy. The wasting away of any part of the body.

atua. In Polynesia, a supernatural being.

atypic. Referring to an unusual specimen of a species.

Audi. A primitive variety of pointed knife blade. It is small. The under surface is plain while the upper surface has several flake scars, one of which intersects with the under surface to make a sharp cutting edge. The Audi is effective when held in the curve of the first finger, as the blunted back enables pressure to be applied on the tool's sharp cutting edge. The term pointe audi is also used.

augury. Predicting what will happen in the future by observing various phenomena, usually believed to be of supernatural origin. Augury usually is associated with ceremonial observances and is very widespread. It probably stemmed from

49

predictions of the future based on birds' singing or flight.

aul. A Kazak local unit, characteristic of summer migration.

aulos. The class of reed instruments and, specifically, the most important wind instrument of the ancient Greeks. The term is derived from the Greek word for blowing. Although the aulos differed in size and shape, it was usually a double-pipe instrument, with one pipe longer than the other. The treble and bass pipes were played simultaneously by one performer. It had a double reed. The aulos came in several sizes and was often played in pairs. It was inserted in the mouth so the performer could use his mouth cavity as a wind bag and blow continually while inhaling air through his nose.

aunga. A good soul among the Arosi of the Solomons.

aunt, cross. A father's sister, so called because the relationship involves a brother and a sister rather than two sisters. A cross-aunt contrasts with mother's sister, who is called a parallel aunt.

aunt, parallel. A sister of Ego's mother, as contrasted with a cross aunt.

aureole. A glow of light around the head or body of a god or specially venerated person.

Aurignacian. Referring to the original Upper Paleolithic culture of the Old World, between the Mousterian and Solutrean levels. Bone artifacts, varied flint tools, careful burials, art objects, and ornamentation characterize this culture. The Aurignacian dates back some

85,000 years. Cro-Magnon man is associated with this period, which was marked by the Würm recession.

Implements and red ocher used by the person while alive were buried with him, along with jewelry. Flint points were used to make the bone artifacts. Some of the bone, horn, and ivory tools were treated by rubbing and sawing. The representative style of art was three dimensional. Graphic art works were executed. Bas-reliefs of persons and animals were made as mural decorations. Figurines of women were made from lumps of limestone. Aurignacian caves often have animals modeled in clay and profile engravings of game animals. Dress and adornment were used.

The Aurignacians probably began their culture in Asia and went to Europe, where their better social organization enabled them to displace Mousterian man rather abruptly. Aurignacians were tall and well muscled and had a considerable cranial capacity.

aurochs. The extinct European bison.

austerities. Behavior involving discipline or self-discipline intended to impress the deities. It is intended for mourning or magic or ceremonial purposes. Austerities may include abstention from food, flagellation, various ordeals (q.v), torture, destruction of property, and even suicide.

Australasians. The aboriginal inhabitants of Australia, New Guinea, Melanesia, and Tasmania, numbering about 1,000,000 at most and occupying about 3,500,000 square miles. The low forehead and prominent supraorbital ridges of this group are perhaps its most general characteristics. Keith has suggested that of all living forms the Australian aborigine perhaps best represents early man's generalized features.

Australia. A continent in Oceania (q.v.). It probably had the culturally least developed of living men up to the time of their discovery by the English and Dutch. They did not have pottery, agriculture, or the bow and arrow. It has been suggested that the natives of Australia constitute a fourth major race, the Australoid, distinguished by dark skin, broad nose, straight or curly hair, a narrow forehead, large mouth, fairly small brain, large teeth, considerable hirsuteness, large brow ridges, and receding chin.

Australian. A Pacific language family about which little is known. These languages, spoken by the Australian aborigines, number over 100, divided into Northern and Southern Australian groups. There is no linguistic affinity between the two groups, and the relations among the Northern Australian group are still unclear. The Southern Australian group is divided into several largely geographic groups.

Australoid. A primary geographic group or white subrace, with some survivors still in Australia. It may be the result of a mixture of Tasmanian and White types. This type is hirsute, of medium height, with large supraorbital ridges, feeble

chin, large palate, and short, broad face.

Australopithecus. A fossil manlike superape, who flourished in the Pleistocene era in South Africa. The Australopithecinae include a considerable variety of near human and human forms, ranging from pygmies to giants. The Taungs baby, a child's skull which was the first of several dozen individuals from the same area, had a thick skull and a brain which was much smaller than modern man's. The manner in which the head is set on the spine and the shape and position of the pelvic bone indicate that this creature walked erect. The teeth indicate that the jaw was hinged in a human way and that food chewing was rotary rather than up and down like an ape's.

Dart found the first examples of this type in 1925 in Bechuanaland and called it Australopithecus, or southern ape, because of its combination of simian and human qualities. Broom found a number of other specimens after 1936 around 40 miles west of Johannesburg. He sees two genera, the Paranthropus and the Plesianthropus. It is difficult to date these finds, but the animals found with them indicate that they are probably early Pleistocene or late Pliocene, so that the Australopithecinae, may be 1,000,000 years old.

The brain had a volume of around 600 cc., and the jaws were large and projecting. The nuchal crest is low and the molars large. The brain case, supraorbital ridges, and forehead have more human

51

than ape characteristics, as do the cheekbone, jaws, and the joint between lower jaw and skull base. The canine teeth are not so well developed as in apes, and the premolars have a human bicuspid shape. The front lower premolar is a simple bicuspid in man and the Australopithecinae, while fossil and extant apes have a large conical cusp in this tooth. Australopithecus' teeth are curved evenly, whereas apes have grinding teeth in straight rows, with powerful canine teeth.

Australopithecus' hip bone and femur are also human, while the ankle bone has both human and ape characteristics. In general, his limbs are sufficiently human to indicate that he stood and walked as humans do. The climate in which he lived was arid, so that he had to function on land rather than in a forest.

In general, the average height of the Australopithecinae was probably under five feet. Their limbs were human even though the brain was still small. This phenomenon of the limbs outstripping the brain is found in other kinds of mammal evolution, as in Eocene lemurs with modern limbs and primitive brains. No implements have yet been discovered with the Australopithecinae, and it is not possible to tell if they had the power of speech. There is some discussion about whether they should be classified as Hominidae or Pongidae (q.v.), depending on whether they are seen as very primitive men or apes with some human characteristics.

Austric. W. Schmidt's name for a super-family of languages that includes the Austro-Asiatic and Malayo-Polynesian families.

Austro-Asiatic. The southeast Asiatic family of languages observed in the Chota-Nagpur region of India, parts of Indo-China, the Malay Peninsula and Thailand, and in Annam and Cambodia. The component linguistic systems display a degree of affinity such that each is sometimes classified as comprising a family of languages. See AUSTRIC.

Austronesian. A Malayo-Polynesian linguistic stock, variants of which are spoken in Micronesia, Polynesia, Melanesia, Malaya, and Madagascar.

autecology. The study of the ecology of the individual and the species.

autoanalysis. The study and analysis of the society of which the investigator is himself a part.

autocephalous. Referring to a national or other major subgroup which is similar in most respects of doctrinal practice to a parent religious group but has an autonomous religious organization and its own chief, e.g., the Eastern Orthodox churches.

autogenetic. Referring to theories of evolution which say that organisms are inherently self-evolving and that the orienting qualities of evolution are within the organism.

autopolyploid. Referring to having multiple sets of chromosomes (q.v.) of the same species.

autosome. A pair of chromosomes (q.v.) of similar size. They are not

X nor Y chromosomes (qq.v), and thus do not determine sex. Of the 24 pairs of chromosomes in man, 23 are autosome. The term euchromosome is also used.

avatar. The incarnation of one kind of individual into another kind, as in a god's becoming a man.

aveia. A constellation or star used by the Polynesians as a guide.

averil. The food served at a funeral, in parts of Europe. It was usually a fairly substantial meal, since the horror of the bereaved family was linked with the quality and quantity of the food.

Avicenna of Bokhara (980-1037). An Arabian philosopher who was one of the founders of modern medicine.

avocado. A fruit, purple or green, usually pear-shaped. It is widely used in Central America as a substitute for butter and salad fruit. It was known in Mexico and Colombia before Columbus.

avoidance. The prescribed minimization of contact between relatives in certain primitive societies. The regulations governing avoidance usually apply to individuals of opposite sex. It probably stems in part from the incest (q.v.) prohibitions.

avoidance, avuncular. The custom of a man's or boy's avoiding his mother's brother.

avoidance, name. The practice of not mentioning the names of specific classes of individuals, like dead relatives or relatives through marriage.

Avongara. The noble class among the Azande.

avulsion, tooth. The removal of a tooth for reasons other than disease. Tooth avulsion is found especially among some Australian groups as part of the initiation (q.v.). In the most widespread form one tooth is removed; removal of two or three teeth is increasingly rarer.

avunculate. The relationship between a nephew and his maternal uncle, in which the nephew is subject to the authority of, and is likely to inherit the possession or position of, the uncle.

avunculocal. Referring to a couple living with the maternal uncle of the husband.

awl. A properly pointed piece of flint or stone can serve as an awl. The size of awls varies. The true awl has a carefully trimmed working end. The pseudo-awl sometimes has an untrimmed flat flake surface, with the trimming only carried around through 180°. The awl is used to pierce holes.

awl, brad. A short and nontapering awl used for punching and making holes to receive brads, screws, and similar objects. It has a cutting edge at the end.

ax. A metal or stone cutting tool which is perforated so that it can take a handle. The ax evolved from the coup-de-poing (q.v.) and changed in size and shape from that of an ostrich egg to a more oval and flat shape with straight edges. The ax is intended to strike a crushing blow. It also has a secondary function of piercing or cutting. The piercing part is usually set at an angle to the handle which is not larger than a right angle. Its eye is in the plane of the stroke. The parts of an ax are grip, haft, haft head, blade, and edge or point.

ax, anchor. An ax made of stone and shaped like the bottom part of an anchor. It is found in Ecuador and the West Indies.

ax, battle. A weapon in almost universal use before the invention of firearms. It is still used by certain uncivilized peoples. Battle axes were widely varied in size, shape, material, and decoration. Some were highly ornate, with engraving, enamelwork, and even gems. The simple battle ax had knobs or spikes for butts, and often had a well shaped and elongated butt. Scandinavia and Hungary have yielded a great variety of battle axes.

ax, double. A Minoan ax which had two blades in the same plane, with the shaft hole halfway between the two blades. The double ax was also the symbol of a widespread religious cult.

ax, fist. See COUP-DE-POING.

ax, hammer. An ax which is blunt on one side and has an ax edge on the other. It is bored for hafting and is usually employed for domestic purposes. Most hammer axes are carelessly made.

ax, hand. See COUP-DE-POING.

ax, head. An iron ax with a long, slender, crescent-shaped blade, used by the Tuinguian, Kalinga, and Igorot of Luzon. The head ax is primarily for headhunting, but also has utilitarian functions, such as cutting wood.

ax, kitchen midden. A Campignian nodule of flint chipped so as to have a straight edge and with two bevelled sides like a turnscrew. It is often found in the Danish middens.

ax, lictor's. An ax in a bundle of rods, carried by the lictor who attended the chief magistrates and caught animals in ancient Rome; hence, a symbol of government authority.

ax, monolithic. An ax made of one piece of stone, found in the Americas, especially Mesoamerica.

ax, shaft-hole. An ax of which the head fits on, rather than in, the shaft. This is accomplished by a hole in the ax head, which is parallel to the blade. This type of ax is probably attributable to the Sumerians.

ax, Shangaan battle. An implement, over two feet long, consisting of a long slender handle and a long sharp blade. It is found in East Africa and is used to make incisions in palms in order to get juice for palm wine.

ax, tranchet. An ax with a transverse cutting edge like the edge of a chisel.

ax, transverse. A shaft-hole ax in which the blade is at right angles to the shaft.

ax-adze. A double ax in which one blade is transverse to the shaft and to the other blade. Such tools have been found in the Aegean, Persia, and Hungary.

aye-aye. A lemur of Madagascar (genus *Daubentonia*) with aberrant physical characteristics. It has long curved rodentlike incisors, no canines, a "third eyelid" or nictating membrane, and a very long middle finger.

ayllu. A Peruvian social unit of the Inca period. Apparently it began as a unilineal, probably patrilineal, kinship unit and developed through conquest and population shifting into a unit primarily territorial comprising members of several unrelated kinship groups.

Aymara. A family made up of 11 South American Indian languages that are spoken in Ecuador and Bolivia by approximately 500,000 persons.

ayni. See AINE.

Azilian. A transitional culture area of the Epipaleolithic Age in France. It is named after a site at Mas d' Azil, France. The Azilian remains were found above a Magdalenian and under a Neolithic deposit. This culture is not so refined as the Magdalenian (q.v.). Round scrapers and points were typical. Fairly crude flat stag antler harpoons were found. Representational art no longer exists, and the culture seems meager.

It centered in the Pyrenees region but spread to Switzerland, Belgium, and Scotland. The climate was boreal but approached modern climate. Fauna were modern.

Where Magdalenian culture flourished, the Tardenoisian (q.v.) changed into the Azilian. Pebbles with painted dots and signs are typical. Badly made bone and stone tools, such as angle gravers and small scrapers, are characteristic of this industry.

azoic. Referring to the initial stage of the earth, during which there was no life.

Aztatlan. The legendary home of the Aztecs.

Aztec. An American Indian language, now extinct, sometimes called Nahuatl, belonging to the Nahuatlan family of languages. It was the language of the civilization of Mexico prior to Columbus' discovery of America.

B

Baalism. A type of nature religion with the chief emphasis on fertility. Baalism came out of the Near East, where it was highly developed by the Canaanites or Phoenicians. The chief deities were El, the father of the gods, Asherah, the mother-goddess, Baal, who controlled the weather, his consort Astarte, the goddess of fertility, and Mot or death. The arid climate of Syria and Palestine, with the cessation of the rains in March-April and the long dry season until October, gave rise to the symbolic legends which characterize Baalism. It was thought that the rains stopped because Baal had been killed by Mot and that in the fall, the Sun and Astarte brought Baal back to life. Finally, the earth was again fertile in the spring because of the copulation of Baal and Astarte. The ceremonies, rituals, and worship of Baalism were highly licentious, and it was this quality which gave rise to the controversy brought up by the prophet Elijah as to whether Yahweh or Baal was to be the true God of Israel.

babassú. A palm, *Orbignya sp.*, of Tropical Forest South America. The leaves are used to make baskets and as thatching and the oily nuts are eaten by the aborigines.

babiche. A French-Canadian-Indian word referring to the narrow rawhide strips found in nets, fishing lines, and similar devices.

babracot. A platform supported by three or four legs lashed together at the top in the form of a pyramid. Fish and meat are roasted on it by placing the platform over an open fire. The babracot is widely used by the Indians of tropical South America.

baby, bush. The genus Galago of the lemur family, found in East Africa, Zanzibar, and Fernando Po.

baby, water. A mythological small person living in a body of water. American Indians usually fear water babies because they may be harmful if encountered.

Babylonian. See AKKADIAN.

bacchanalia. A dance performed by the Greek priests and priestesses of Bacchus. The dancers were costumed in fawn skins and each carried an ivy-entwined spear (the thyrsus). When the dance was first taken to Rome in the 2nd century B.C., only women took part. Men later performed, and the bacchanalia was then known for such licentiousness and immorality that it was outlawed by the senate in 186 B.C. Many participants were sentenced to death or imprisonment.

Bachofen, Johann Jakob (1815-1887). A Swiss lawyer by profession, he was also a philologist who extensively studied classical life. He is best known for his book *Das Mutterrecht* (1861), in which he held that the difficulties of determining paternity in an originally promiscuous society had led to the key role of the mother and to reckoning descent through her.

back, battered. A flint blade, often triangular, which has one battered edge. This characteristic is also termed *à dos rabattu*.

back, blunted. Referring to a blade with one edge purposely blunted by secondary flaking.

backstay. On a sailboat, a kind of rigging which is near the stern and keeps the mast from falling forward.

Bacsonian. A stone industry of Indo-China in which the most characteristic implement was a chipped stone ax with a ground cutting edge. This type of ax was very similar to that of the Australian aborigines.

Badarian. Referring to a kind of pottery made in Egypt ca. 5,000 B.C. and shaped like a tulip. The Badarian people migrated from southwest Asia. They were hunters and food gatherers, who lived in settled communities and had flint tools.

badimo. A Bechuana evil spirit.

badjara. A traveling houseboat, found in deltaic areas in which waterways are widely used methods of communication. The badjara is often propelled by oars. A corrupted spelling is budgerow.

baetyl. Stone, usually a meteorite, used as an altar for worshipping some divine being.

bag, moss. A cradle of leather or skin in the form of a bag and enclosing moss on which the naked baby is placed. It may be skin-lined in the winter. It is found in northwest Canada.

bagai. A Kazak race on horseback.

bagani. Those who have killed six persons among the Mandaya of the Philippine Islands.

bagpipe, Oriental. A musical instrument consisting of a skin bag with openings at its extremities. A pipe with a single reed and a tube to blow air into the skin were inserted in the openings. The pressure of the player's arm forced air through the pipes.

Bahuma. The pastoral Negro-Hamitic higher class of East Africa.

Bahuvrihi. A syntactical distinction denoting a possessive compound of the type *red-eyed.* The term, meaning *much-riced,* derived from the grammar of Sanskrit.

baidarke. A Russian adaptation of the Kaniagmiut term for kayak (q.v.).

bairakter. A chief, e.g., in some parts of Albania.

bait, proper. Bait that consists of the food of the fish or animal which is being hunted.

bakhshish. See SYSTEM, BAKSHEESH.

baknang. A wealthy Tinguian family.

baksa. A central Asiatic shaman (q.v.).

baksheesh or bakshish. See SYS-TEM, BAKSHEESH.

Balam, Chilam. A set of books in the Maya language that were transliterated into Spanish script and that contain some of the history and mythology of the Mayas.

balance, foliot, and verge escape. An early escapement (q.v.) device in which the verge rod was turned to and fro, so that it regulated the foliot balance, thus adjusting the escape movement.

balanophagy. The eating of acorns, one of the principal items in the diet of the Indians of California.

balaua. A Tinguian spirit house.

Balbi, Adriano (1782-1848). A Venetian geographer and statistician, who compiled (1826) the first reasonably complete ethnographic atlas of the world.

balché. In the Maya area, an intoxicating drink made from honey.

baldachin. A temporary or permanent canopy which can be either stationary or portable.

baldness. A lack of hair or natural covering on the head. It is probably a dominant and sex-linked Mendelian characteristic. Women are seldom bald. Baldness is usually found associated with substantial body hair and beards. It may be useful in differentiating racial groups. There is some evidence that baldness is an inherited Caucasoid mutation that is rarely found among Mongoloids and Negroids and that the extent of baldness among Caucasoids is increasing. See HAIR.

baleen. A bony substance in a whale's mouth that serves to strain food out of the water. Baleen is widely used by the Eskimo for making implements.

balian. A Batak spirit medium.

ball, fire. A mixture of clay and coal, heated in a fire and then thrown at the enemy's dwellings. Fire balls have been found in the Swiss lakes and are believed to have destroyed many lake cities. The Norrii used this method to set fire to Caesar's camp.

ballad. A narrative folk song that deals with one incident. Ballads originated in Europe in the Middle Ages. A ballad is told in stanzas and is likely to have a refrain.

ballad, homiletic. A first-person song in which the narrator discusses his past sins as a warning to others.

ballista. A piece of ancient military equipment used to hurl large stones or spears.

balnooknook. A log drum or gong of the Australian aborigines. The name is said to derive from a dingo about whom there are many myths.

baloma. Spirits of the dead among the Trobrianders.

balsa. A cigar-shaped tied bundle of rushes used for water travel. The balsa floats by specific gravity and is either punted or propelled by paddle. It is found in Ecuador and Peru. The most seaworthy are made by the Amara Indians of Lake Titicaca. The balsa is sometimes called the pelota.

Baltic. A language group of the Indo-European family, including Lithuanian, Latvian, and Old Prussian.

Balto-Slavic. A subfamily of the Indo-European family of languages.

Balum cult. See CULT, BALUM.

bamboo. A reed plant found in southeast Asia and other warm climates. Bamboo may grow to be very high. It was widely used for artifacts because of its sharp edge. In southeast Asia it may have been used for spear heads and other artifacts for a long period until the introduction of finer stone working.

Bamiyan Buddha. An immense statue of Buddha carved into a solid breccia cliff in Afghanistan in the desert regions beyond the Khyber Pass by ancient tribes who fled persecution in India. The statue is 130 feet in height and displays excellent proportion and linear work.

banab. The temporary dwelling, made of leaves and sticks, among some Guiana groups. The word is sometimes spelled benab.

banana. A large herbaceous perennial or its fruit. The banana was brought to Brazil in the 16th century by European explorers.

banca. A Philippine dugout canoe.

band. The most primitive social group. The band is found among peoples whose techniques have not advanced much beyond hunting and gathering. An average band may have between 50 and 150 members. The internal structure is simple. Often a tribe will comprise several bands.

The band's zone of exploitation is usually the area within which a man can go in a day and return to camp at night. A hunting band claims territory which it defends against trespassers. Permanent settlement is possible for agricultural bands if an area's resources can be relied on. Each band has its own culture. Ridicule may be the most powerful weapon which the band uses against an offender. The band is likely to have a head man and to differentiate between bands in its tribe and those of another tribe. The band is held together as a result of living together rather than by kinship.

band, brow. A band around the brow and head, used as an article of adornment and to keep the hair down. In North America, brow bands are often made of beads.

band, composite. A band that has nonrelated families in it, and in which there is no exogamy (q.v.). It is believed that such bands are likely to have over 100, e.g., the Canadian Athabaskans and the Andamese.

band, head. A band worn around the head, and one of the most common elements in early headdress. Most hunting people wore head bands. The head band may consist of many materials, from leaf to iron. It keeps the hair out of the eyes and holds decorations and articles. It has evolved into the emblem of royalty.

band, hip. A ring worn around the hips. The hip band may be made of fabric, leaves, flowers, metal, or other materials. It is an early human costume. Some material may hang from the ring, and the ring may be worn with other garments. The hip band is found even in fairly advanced cultures, as in ancient Egypt.

band, patrilineal. A band that is politically autonomous and practices exogamy (q.v.) and communal land ownership, with land being handed down patrilineally. A patrilineal band consists of a lineage (q.v.) that has several households or bilateral families. It is perhaps the most common kind of band. It is found among the Bushmen and Central African Negritos, among other peoples.

band, pleated. See GUILLOCHE.

band, unilineal. A band in which all the members are kin. Most such bands are patrilocal (q.v.) and observe patrilinity (q.v.).

bandar. See BENDYR.

Bandkeramik. A type of Neolithic pottery in which the neck is decorated with bands of dots or lines, usually in spiral and meander pattern. The term band ceramics is also used.

banishment. Being ordered to depart from a society or face the death penalty, for which banishment was sometimes an alternative.

banki. A severed prepuce among the Aluridja.

banner. A large social grouping among the Mongols.

banquette. In architecture, a mass or ledge raised above the floor of a chamber. A banquette is sometimes called a bench.

Bantu. The family of African Negro languages spoken by approximately 50 million persons in South Africa. The area is south of the Sudano-Guinean area, and the two language families are thought by many to have common origins. They are similar in their class groupings of nouns and the use of an identifying prefix with all words grammatically connected with the noun. The more important of the 80 to 100 Bantu languages are Swahili, Zulu, Congo, Luba-Lulua, Luganda, and Nyanja. Some scholars believe that the ancestors of the Bantu originally came from the area around the Bahr el Ghazal, from Kordofan on the north, or the Benne and Lake Chad basins in the west. They then went to the lacustrine area which became the region from which the Bantu later spread over Africa in a series of great migrations. Other scholars believe that the origin of Bantu culture can never really be traced.

banya. A small wooden kettle drum of India. The upper portion is covered by tight parchment braced with strips of skin at the sides.

bar, currency. A flat iron bar, used as a kind of coinage in the Iron Age. Many such bars resemble partly manufactured swords. They have been found in various sizes and weights, indicating that they may have been of certain standard values.

bara. A religious ceremony in Australia, as opposed to the corroboree (q.v.), which is nonreligious, secular, and fun-making.

Baraba. A language belonging to the Eastern Turkic group of the Ural-Altaic family of languages, spoken in western Asia.

baraka. A power of holiness, believed in by many Moslems. Some natural objects have baraka. Certain persons, like children or newly married couples, also have it, as do saints, sultans, rulers, and descendants of the Prophet. It may be passed from one individual to another. See MANA.

barbarism. A Neolithic or primitive economy, or any culture that has no written language but has domesticated animals and agriculture. The term is also V. Gordon Childe's designation of the stage of animal and plant domestication that followed savagery (q.v.) and preceded civilization (q.v.). Barbarism is also a linguistic term used to describe any departure from the conventional grammatical or literary usage. Morgan gave the term wide currency in his suggested evolutionary development of society.

barbasco. The Spanish-American name for various plants, especially of the *Compostas* family, that are used to poison fish in the streams and ponds of tropical South America.

barbe. A pleated linen garment worn by mourning women in the Middle Ages. The lower estates wore it below the throat, while baronesses wore it above the chin.

barbotine. A slip (q.v.) or a clay paste used in decorating pottery in relief.

bark. The external surface of a woody perennial stem or root. Bark is easily worked and is extremely important to many peoples. It can be made into bark cloth, by soaking and pounding (see TAPA). Bark can be removed fairly easily in autumn or spring. It has been used for making roofs, flooring, shelters, the lining of fish store pits, torches, tapers, shoes, beehives, net floats, and many kinds of boxes. Its use probably stems from the Paleolithic

Age. Birch was probably the most useful bark to early man, because it so dominated the first forests which covered the open spaces at the beginning of the post-glacial period.

barley. An adaptable and ancient annual cereal, known for some 5,000 years. Barley was probably domesticated in southwest Asia, although two centers from which it may have spread are Ethiopia and Nepal and Tibet. It is used as a human food, as malt, and as an animal food. It can be grown in colder places than any other grain and is probably more widely distributed than any other cereal. It may be the oldest major cereal and was widely used even in Neolithic times.

barramundi. The large tidal perch of North Australia, widely eaten by the natives.

barrio. A Spanish term meaning neighborhood which was applied in Hispanic America to a territorial division of a populous area. Barrios often corresponded to preconquest territorial and kinship units, such as the ayllu (q.v.) of Peru and the calpulli (q.v.) of the Aztecs.

barrow. A dolmen (q.v.) that is covered by earth. Barrows were usually near settlements or villages but at a sufficient distance so that the dead would not be too close to the living. A barrow was regarded as sacred ground and was often near the temple. Another term for barrow is tumulus.

barrow, long. A type of Neolithic barrow, mostly found in England, and possibly so named because the people buried under it are presum-

61

ably long-headed, as well as the shape of the barrow.

barrow, round. A type of Bronze Age barrow found in England, and possibly so named because the people under it are presumably round-headed, as well as the shape of the barrow.

barter. The direct exchange of one kind of goods for another, with no employment of money. It is the only mode of exchange in the simplest economic systems. Four kinds of barter often distinguished are gift economy, gift barter economy, pure barter, and money barter (q.v.).

barter, dumb. The exchange of goods without the traders having any direct contact. The first group leaves its goods in a given place, then leaves. The second group puts its proferred exchange goods alongside the original commodities, and leaves. When the first group comes back, it either takes the exchange goods if satisfied, or, if not satisfied, departs with the original goods. The second group then comes to take up its goods. The term silent trade is also used.

barter, money. A transaction in which goods or merchandise are used as stand;·dized measures of value.

Bartholomae's law. See LAW, BARTHOLOMAE'S.

bas-relief. A technique of sculpturing in which the figures appear almost flat against a background.

basalt. A form of volcanic rock, dark and compact, possessing a splintery fracture and widely used by the ancient Egyptians for their sculpture. Basalt was frequently used in the construction of obelisks and tombs. The name is also applied to a pottery of basaltic appearance made by Josiah Wedgewood.

base, culture. The totality of the culture traits that obtain in a given time and place, often used for the culture which gives rise to inventions.

Bashkir. A language belonging to the Western Turkic group of the Altaic subfamily of the Ural-Altaic family of languages.

basi. Sugarcane rum among the Tinguians.

basilica. A Roman public administration hall. A great number of these halls were later converted into Christian churches, and many of the early churches were constructed on the model of the basilica.

basilisk. A two-headed mythological animal of medieval times. The basilisk was believed to be so deadly that its breath was fatal to anyone it touched. It was frequently represented in the arts, especially in heraldic emblems on shields and escutcheons.

basion. The midpoint on the anterior margin of the occipital foramen.

basket. A semirigid or stiff container, built on its own frame, or with the foundation made together with the basket. Baskets carry liquids as well as solids.

basket, boiling. A basket in which food is cooked by means of hot stones, e.g., in southern Alaska.

basket, pannier. A round flat basket with low sides, common among American Indians in California and elsewhere. Such baskets are often used in loading burdens on mules.

Basket Makers. See MAKERS, BASKET.

basketry. The art of using two connected elements, the warp and the woof, to make an object. A basket differs from an object made by felting (q.v.) in having interlaced materials.

basketry, coiled. A form of basketry in which a foundation of grass or splits is stitched together, usually with a bone awl.

basketry, plaited. A form of basketry in which there is an interlacing of warp and woof. The term hand-woven basketry is also used.

basketry, twined. A form of basketry in which a rigid warp is held together by two or more intertwining weft elements.

Basque. The language of one million inhabitants of the northeastern corner of Spain and the southwestern corner of France. The language seems to have no common origins with any other, although it is thought by some to have developed from the Aquitanian dialect of the ancient pre-Roman language, Iberian. Basque has many stops, palatals, and spirants. Many words are formed by the addition of prefixes and suffixes. The verbs do not have an active voice.

bast. The tough woody fiber which comes from the phloem, pericycle, or cortex of certain plants, especially the Tiliacea, Malvacae, and Sterculiaceae families. Bast is commonly used to make cordage and ropes.

Bastaards, Rehobeth. In South Africa, the children of Hottentot wives and Boer men, who founded the semi-independent town of Rehobeth because of their ostracism by the Dutch in South Africa.

bastard. The offspring of a union between members of different races. Among those which have been studied by anthropologists are the Reheboth Bastaards (q.v.), Dutch-Indonesian offspring on Kisar, and Jamaicans with German and African Negro parents.

Bastian, Adolf P. W. (1826-1905). A German physician who has been called the founder of ethnography. He established an ethnographic museum and spent many years in traveling extensively. Bastian opposed Darwinism and adumbrated many concepts of modern anthropology, including "elemental ideas" and "folk ideas." Bastian believed in the psychic unity of all men, and collected data on the resemblances of artifacts and of behavior. He held that the environment is largely responsible for the form which behavior and artifacts take and that migration and contact provide a mixture of ideas, some eventuating in civilizations.

bastinado. A punishment found among the Egyptians, Chinese, and Turks in which the soles of the offenders's feet are beaten. The term also may mean a cudgel.

bastion. A projection built onto the walls of a fort for purposes of defense.

batab. The hereditary civil head of a Maya city-state.

Batak. A member of the Indonesian subfamily of the Malayo-Polynesian family of languages, spoken in Samoa. The number of speakers of Batak is more than one million.

batch. In ceramics, the last mixture of ingredients in glass-making, at which point they are converted into glass by fusion.

batey. In the Greater Antilles, a large plaza, sometimes surrounded by low earth walls, used as a ball court and for ceremonial purposes.

batik. A method of making colored designs in Indonesia. Wax is placed over parts of the fabric before it is dipped into the dye. The wax is then removed by boiling. The term batik also applies to the fabrics.

baton. A stick or staff carried to denote a hierarchical position or rank.

bâton-de-commandement. An Upper Paleolithic implement, made from reindeer horns cut from the stem at an antler's root, where a hole is perforated. There is usually some engraving. Bâtons-de-commandement may have been used to straighten shafts (see STRAIGHT-ENER, ARROW). This may account for the frequency with which they are decorated with animal figures, since the arrow may have been expected to absorb some affinity with the animal intended for prey and thus hit its target more easily. It has also been suggested that these implements were used as symbols of authority, in basket manufacture, or as instruments of sorcery. The term perforated bone stave is also used.

batten. A device on a loom which is placed in the warp to beat the wefts in place.

battle-ax folk. See FOLK, BATTLE-AX.

baydar. A kind of canoe found in the Aleutian Islands. Baydars consist of a light wooden framework covered by one or more skins.

bayou. A slow moving stream or inland body of water. The lower Mississippi has many bayous.

beach, raised. A shelf of shore accumulation that is at a height above sea level not attainable by the highest modern tides. Its presence indicates that the sea once hit the level at which the raised beach exists now, so that the distance between it and the beach as it exists today has been obtained by emergence.

Beach-la-mar or **Beche-la-mer.** A trade jargon evolved in the contact between commercial colonials and native inhabitants of the Western Pacific, with a vocabulary largely English.

beak and keel. See ROSTROCARINATE.

beaker. A bellshaped vessel of pottery, found in pre-Bronze Age Europe. It characterized the culture of the so-called beakermen.

beaker, bell. A bellshaped beaker, characteristic of early Danubian culture, in which height and diameter are about the same. The bell beaker's lines are flowing and graceful. There are often varying zones of design on the beaker, e.g., a zone of chevrons and a plain zone.

beaker, zoned. A beaker, characteristic of the Rhine valley, in which the height is normally greater than the diameter. Zoned beakers are angular and coarse, and their lines are not graceful. The term also refers to a beaker which has horizontal band ornaments as zones.

beam, carrying. A board or similar strong pole from which a suspended load can be carried by two or more men.

beam, yarn. A device found on advanced looms, which is used instead of a bobbin to wind and unwind the threads of the warp as necessary.

bean, broad. A widely distributed flat brown bean, growing on gray-green plants. It has been grown from Paleolithic days, with centers of variation in Afghanistan and Ethiopia.

Bear, Kicking. A Teton Dakota shaman who became a leader of the Ghost Dance (q.v.) cult in 1890.

beating up. The weaving technique by which each warp thread is pushed into its appointed position.

beauty, illuminating. A theme of many folk tales dealing with a woman so beautiful that she shines even in darkness.

bec-de-flute. See GRAVER.

bec-de-perroquet. A flint graver with a curved point.

bêche-de-mer. A sea slug, which may be up to 18 inches long, in the Pacific area. It is gathered from the sea bed, boiled, dried, and smoked. It is eaten and also used as a soup stock by Australians and Chinese in Southeast Asia.

Beche-la-mer. See BEACH-LA-MER.

bedacryl. A wetting agent used to strengthen archaeological finds so that they can be removed.

Beddoe, John (1826-1911). An English physician, who conducted a major anthropological survey of the residents of Great Britain and studied the relation between vocation and physical structure. He is the author of a major anthropological survey of Europe (1891) and is probably the first person who made detailed measurements of living peoples. As early as 1861, he did a study of eye and hair color of the Irish.

bedrock. The solid rock that underlies superficial formations.

beehive. One of the very oldest types of house, round and dome-shaped. It consists of two windbreaks (q.v.) in semicircular form, woven together. It is found in Australia, Africa, and North America.

beena. See MARRIAGE-BEENA.

beer. A stimulating drink, the first recipe for which dates from 2,800 B.C. in Babylonia. It is made from the germinated seeds of barley or malt. The malt is mashed and a sugary solution—wort—is extracted, to which yeast is added, after which some of the sugar is converted to alcohol. The resulting dilute alcoholic solution is flavored by hops and similar ingredients.

beer, banana. A beer made from bananas, drunk in Central America. It was probably made in areas that were under the influence of pirates, who raided cities where they believed silver and other valuables were. In Nicaragua, a common form of banana beer is called mishla.

beer, honey. A honey-based beverage drunk in East Africa.

begging. Soliciting aid from strangers, which developed with the rise of private property.

Beigaben. Companion offerings left in a grave to provide assistance for the dead in the world to come.

beijú. A round, flat cake made by baking manioc flour on a griddle. It is a staple dish among most of the Indians of Tropical South America.

Beil. See COUP-DE-POING.

Bela. A nomadic slave class among the Tuareg.

bell. A hollow sounding device, often metal, which has a clapper. The bell has been used for religious purposes in the Occident since the classical civilizations. Its use has often been linked with that of the gong (q.v.). One of the bell's major purposes is to generate emotion through plangent or stirring sound. The bell is made of bell metal, a tin-copper alloy. A hammer or clapper may be suspended inside or outside the bell or kept separate from it.

bell, clapper. A musical instrument consisting of a hollow bell which has a striker suspended inside. The striker usually swings or strikes the sides if the bell is swung. The bell has an opening at the bottom.

bell, pellet. A hollow, globular object containing loose pellets that rattle if shaken. Pellet bells are usually made of metal and with a thin opening in the casing.

bellows. A device, used in metallurgy, consisting of an orifice that takes in air and expels it forcibly through a tube. The first bellows probably consisted of a compression and influx of air in a bag of animal hide. This kind of bellows is shown on an 18th dynasty Egyptian tomb, ca. 15th century B.C. The Bible mentions bellows, in association with the smelting of lead, and the smith in Hebrew is *nappahu,* or bellows user. There is philological evidence that the words for bellows date from the first Accadian stratum, or around the beginning of the second millenium B.C.

bellows, bag. See BELLOWS, SKIN.

bellows, concertina. A bellows between the piston and the dish bellows (q.v.), which developed in Eastern Asia. The concertina bellows is like a dish bellows, but it is larger, with a skin containing a number of rings that are separated by pistons and fall with the bellows' raising and lowering.

bellows, dish or **bellows, drum.** A bellows consisting of a loose diaphragm that fits over a solid chamber, with air inhaled through a diaphragm slit or by a chamber flue. It is intermediate between the bag and piston bellows. It was developed in Central Asia and India and is widely used in Central and South Africa. Sticks, as in Africa, or strings, as in Malaya, may be used to move the bellows.

bellows, house. A leather bellows that has an accordion shape and is inflated and deflated between two wooden boards. The first mention of this form is in the fourth century A.D. by Ausonius.

bellows, piston or **bellows, pump.** A device to fan a fire, found in

southeast Asia. It consists of a pipe
or box from which air is pumped
by a piston into the furnace or
hearth pit. It probably developed in
South or East Asia. The pipe or box
in which the piston moves is of
bamboo or wood. A horizontal piston was used in the Far East and
became the Japanese or Chinese
tatara or box bellows. A vertical
piston was used in India, Indonesia,
Madagascar, and Burma. Two cylinders are generally used simultaneously in order to keep up a continuous stream of air.

bellows, skin. A bellows made by
sewing animal skins together, leaving a slit with two rims, probably
wooden. It developed in Central
Asia and the Near East. It was probably the first bellows and went from
the Near East to Africa and Europe. Two pairs of bellows were
generally used together. The term
bag bellows is sometimes used.

beloid. Referring to a skull which
when viewed from above is narrow
in front and broad at the back.

belomancy. The use of arrows
for divination (q.v.).

belt, chastity. A metal girdle with
a lock which women in Medieval
and Renaissance Europe were sometimes forced to wear in order to
prevent them from having sexual
relations with any man but their
husband or lord.

Belzoni, Giovanni B. (1778-
1823). An Italian circus strong man
and salesman of irrigation equipment, who was among the most
successful robbers of Egyptian tombs
and materials. He has been praised

for his recovery of many Egyptian
art treasures.

benab. See BANAB.

bench. In the archaeology of the
American Southwest, a mass of material elevated above the floor of a
chamber or level, as in a kiva
(q.v.). The bench is from one to
three and a half feet above the floor
and is usually at least a foot wide.

bendyr. A hand drum popular in
the Algerian region of Africa. It
has a barrellike frame covered at
one or both ends with stretched
animal skin. The name is sometimes
spelled bandar.

Bene Diambe. A hemp-smoking
society in the Congo.

Bengali. The Indic language of
some 75 million inhabitants of Bengal.

benge. A strychnine-like poison,
used among the Azande to predict
the future. It is given to chickens,
and whether they live or die determines what action the person
will take.

Benninghof's lines. See LINES,
BENNINGHOF'S.

bennu. An Egyptian sacred bird,
which was an emblem of the resurrection. It is heronlike, with two
long feathers flowing from the back
of its head.

Berber. A language group belonging to the Semito-Hamitic family.
With the extinct Libyan it constitutes the Libyco-Berber branch of
the Hamitic subfamily. The languages are Tuareg, Shluh, Kabyl,
Zenaga, Zenete, and Gaunche (extinct).

berdache. One who behaves and
dresses like a member of the oppo-

site sex. Some of the berdaches were hermaphroditic. Early French explorers in North America first used the term to describe passive homosexuals. Angelino and Shedd have proposed that the term be used to designate persons of one sex who assume the role and status of the opposite sex, and who are so regarded by the community. Some berdaches cut themselves to simulate a menstrual flow and stuff their clothes to simulate a pregnancy. See HOMOSEXUAL; ALHYA; SHAMAN.

Bergmann's rule. See RULE, BERGMANN'S.

Bering. Referring to the earliest period in Eskimo art from which artifacts have been discovered. Objects include kayaks, bone, ivory, and stone. This period centered ca. 500 A.D. Bering designs were abstract and often drawn around the eye of a fish or mammal.

berm. A short flat strip of ground, usually separating a vertical defensive rampart from a ditch.

berserker. In Norse tradition, a warrior overtaken by frenzy and rage in battle. The berserkers foamed at the mouth and howled and were presumed to be invulnerable.

Bertillon method. See METHOD, BERTILLON.

Beschlagwerk. Patterns originating in the technique of weaving and subsequently made into geometric arrangements which are then applied as decoration to other types of handcrafts, e.g., pottery or metalwork.

bestiary. A book with written descriptions or pictures of real and mythical animals.

betel. A part of the areca nut, which is chewed as a stimulant. Betel originated in India. It has a bitter taste and it darkens the teeth and gums. In Indonesia, it is chewed with lime. Betel is also consumed in East Africa.

betel box. See BOX, BETEL.

betrothal. An engagement between a man and a woman that they will marry in the future.

Beweddung. Among Teutonic peoples, the contract committing the suitor and the father, providing for the exchange of the bride for certain valuable objects. The Beweddung subsequently became a contract between the suitor and the girl, with provisions made for her support in the event of the husband's death.

bezel. A sloping edge; also, the part of a ring which holds the stone.

bezoar. A very hard object which occurs in the digestive tract of some animals. It is used for medicine or magic.

Bhudas. An inbreeding community in Hyderabad, India, in which there is hereditary toothlessness among males. This trait is recessive and sex-linked and is accompanied by baldness and extreme sensitivity to heat.

bias, sex. The degree to which feminine or masculine potentials are developed at a given time.

bicentric. Referring to a species or a genus with two centers of evolutionary development.

Bicol. A member of the Indonesian

subfamily of the Malayo-Polynesian family of languages, spoken in the Philippine Islands by about 700,000 persons.

bicuspids. The teeth which are behind the canine teeth. On each tooth, the crown has two small cusps, one each on the outer and inner side.

biddazze. A stone hut found near a nuraghe (q.v.).

bier. A stretcher-type device used to carry an uncoffined body or a coffin to a grave.

biface. A large pear-shaped piece of stone trimmed flat on both sides.

bifacial. Referring to an object the opposite surfaces of which are similar.

bifid. A cleft stem, looking like an open jaw, found on the fore end of the Alaskan kayak.

bifurcation. The difference between relatives of the same type when one is reckoned through the males and another through the females, e.g., a maternal and a paternal aunt. Bifurcation is the termonological reflection of the differences between the mother's and father's side of the family.

Big Head. See HEAD, BIG.

Bihari. The Indic language of some 37 million inhabitants of northeastern India. There are three dialects, Maithili, Magahi, and Bhojpuri.

bilabial. In linguistics, referring to the production of consonants by the coordinated convergence or contact of both lips, e.g., *b.*

bilabiodental. In linguistics, referring to the articulation of a sound produced by contact of the upper lip and upper teeth with the lower lip.

bilateral. Referring to the transmission of property rights or descent through both the female and the male, in a manner which is either equal or does not emphasize either line.

bilharziasis. A disease resembling hookworm which has been found in Egypt since early times. It is probably spread by refuse containing the Bilharzia blood fluke and contaminating the water and food supply.

bilinear. Referring to kinship groups that include both paternal and maternal relatives.

bilingual. A person who speaks two languages with a fair degree of facility and accuracy.

bilithon. A large horizontal stone slab supported by a vertical slab.

bill, brown. A bill-hooked weapon used from medieval times until the invention of firearms. The brown bill is so called because it was blood-stained, the warriors not being accustomed to keeping their weapons bright.

billabong. An Australian term for a lagoon, derived from a New South Wales aboriginal dialect in which *billa* is a river and *bong* is dead.

billikin. A carved ivory figurine made by the Eskimos of the Diomede Islands.

bilocal. Referring to a married couple living near or with either spouse's parents. The comparative affluence or importance of the spouses' families or personal preferance may be responsible for their matrilocal or patrilocal residence.

bilophodont. Referring to cross crested molars, usually associated with specialized teeth. The summits of the opposite cusps are linked by prominent cross crests on the slope of the four main cusps. The trait is found in tapirs and other ungulates and in Old World monkeys.

Bimana. See QUADRUMANOUS.

bimanual. Referring to movement or posture in which the hands are used to swing or hang on branches.

biogenesis. The doctrine that only living organisms can produce living organisms. Schwann enunciated this in 1837. Theologians were once strongly opposed to biogenesis, since it seemed to deny the possibility of a "special creation" by God.

biogenetic law. See LAW, BIO-GENETIC.

biolinguistics. The scientific examination of language with particular emphasis on the neurophysiological and genetic factors.

biology, human. The study of human beings from a zoological point of view.

biometry. The statistical analysis of biological studies, especially as applied to such areas as disease, birth, growth, and death.

biomorph. The representation of a living organism.

bion. The physiological person, marked by independence and definiteness of function.

bionomics. The study of the relation between organism and environment.

biosphere. The air in which there are living organisms, including the

atmosphere, lithosphere, and hydro-sphere.

biota. The plant and animal life of an area.

biotope. The minimum area which has a unique environment.

bipedal. Referring to an upright posture and movement using the hind legs.

bipenne. A double ax.

bipolar. See TECHNIQUE, BIPOLAR.

bird, fire. A bird which presumably brought fire to earth for man's use. There are animal tales (q.v.) which attribute this to both the raven and the robin.

birth, virgin. Unusual, miraculous, or supernatural conceptions are widespread in the writings of ancient religions. In the less complicated cultures, conception sometimes occurred through contact with an amulet (q.v.), fetish (q.v.), or image. Many of the early rulers of the Mediterranean area were given prestige by stories of divine parentage. Legends of these unusual happenings are frequent in the Egyptian, Greek, Roman, Zoroastrian, Hindu, and Buddhist religions. The Christian chronicle of the virgin birth of Jesus as it appears in the gospel according to St. Luke closely parallels the pattern of supernatural conception as set forth in earlier writings in the Old Testament. The later account in the gospel according to St. Matthew places more emphasis on the virginity of Mary. By the middle of the second century, the doctrine of the virgin birth through the impregnation of Mary by the Holy Ghost had attained universal acceptance since it was only by insistence upon it that the divine and human essences could be held to have united in Jesus to make him a sacrifice acceptable to God.

birthright. The right to inherit property or to have a particular social status as a result of one's birth. The child's legitimacy, birth order within the family, sex, and rank are relevant.

biru. A Babylonian linear measure which gives the distance between districts.

biscuit. Pottery which is unglazed.

bisque. Clay after the first firing. More generally, bisque denotes the hardened state of clay products before the glaze is applied.

bissixt. The intercalation (q.v.) day in the Julian calendar, added in February every fourth year. It came after the sixth day before the calends of March, and was thus considered a second sixth day.

bit. A jointed or solid metal rod which goes between the jaws of a horse to restrain and control the animal.

bite, edge-to-edge. A form of chewing in which the incisal edges of the anterior teeth meet when in centric relations. It is found in some primates but in very few humans, notably the Eskimo. In them the edge-to-edge bite is attributed to the wearing down of teeth from chewing hides to soften them.

Bithynian. An ancient extinct language, examples of which are to be found in writings and glosses set down by classical authors. Most linguistic authorities consider it a language of unknown origin in the Asianic class.

bitumen. See ASPHALTUM.

bivallate. Referring to a ditch with a bank on both sides.

black, bone. Carbon black pigment used in prehistoric times, made by burning animal bones in a closed container.

black drink. See DRINK, BLACK.

blackfellow. The name popularly given to the dark brown Australians, although they are not Negroes.

blackjack. A large drinking vessel, originally made of waxed leather and later of thin metal.

blacksmith. See SMITH.

blade. A parallel-sided narrow, long flint (q.v.) flake, fairly flat and thin, and often fairly large. The blade is also the front of the upper surface of the tongue.

blade, backed. A knife made from a flint blade, with one blunt edge, probably to protect the user's fingers. The blunt back enables the user to place his finger alongside it and control the pressure and movements.

blade, notched. A blade with a notch in it, probably used to prepare a shaft or to point an arrow. It is also called a strangulated blade.

blade, strangled. A flint (q.v.) blade which has a lateral notch at the same level on each of its margins.

blade, strangulated. See BLADE, NOTCHED.

blank. A piece of stone that bears marks of having been worked with the intent of making an artifact but which is not finished.

blastogenic. Referring to characteristics that are hereditarily transmitted.

bleeding. The working-up of pigments from the undercoat of a painting into the succeeding coats, imparting to them a certain amount of the color of the underpainting or imprimatura.

Blemmyes. Legendary headless people. The mouth and eyes were situated in the upper part of the breast. Ancient Roman writers described them as an Ethiopian tribe inhabiting Nubia and Upper Egypt.

blend. See CONTAMINATION.

blessed, islands of the. The area to which the gods go when they die, in many religions. These islands are usually in the west, to symbolize the setting of the sun. The island of Atlantis is an extension of this idea, as is the Arthurian Isle of Avalon.

blessing. A helpful word which probably was believed to be effective because the utterer was in touch with a divinity. Priests, magicians, and those near death had special powers for blessing. A prayer may be used if a divinity is active in the blessing's efficacy. The effectiveness of the blessing varied with the status of the person who uttered it. Blessing was usually a private matter but it was used as a public ritual in higher religions.

blockhouse. A fort which blocks or covers the access to a bridge, landing, or other military target. It is also a heavy log defense structure with holes for weapons to fire through or a house made of squared logs.

block-on-block. See TECHNIQUE, BLOCK-ON-BLOCK.

blondism. Partial loss of pigmentation.

blood. The blood is a combination of red corpuscles, white corpuscles, and plasma. It constitutes about 8 per cent of the body's weight. It circulates in the vascular system and carries oxygen and nutriment to all parts of the body, while it brings away waste products to be excreted. Blood coagulates when it is removed from the body through the formation of threads of insoluble fibrin.

In nonliterate societies, blood is often equated with life. Some societies prohibit drinking blood, while others may require it as the symbolical absorbtion of another person's qualities or of qualities attributed to certain animals. Blood may be linked with vengeance or used to confirm a bond. Blood is the symbol of relationships. It is often regarded as having great potency. It may give strength to the old, enable a victor to have a dead enemy's courage, give the power to prophesy, sustain the dead, fructify marriages, alleviate disease and evil, and purify. Blood from menstruation and childbirth is often regarded as dangerous. Some peoples drained blood into a trench from a sacrificed animal or strangled the animal to avoid spilling its blood. Blood was widely used for purposes of purification. The blood baptism of various mysteries is an example of blood as purification. Outsiders were often admitted to a clan or other groups by exchanging blood with one of its members.

blood, blue. A hypothetical kind of blood possessed by certain elite and aristocratic groups. The expression came from some Spanish families of Castile, who were inter-marrying. They were fair skinned, so that their veins were more no-ticeably blue than those of the pre-vailing dark-complexioned popula-tion. Veins, of course, are white and blood is dark red. The blue appear-ance is caused by the refractive qualities of the tissues through which veins are seen. "Blue blood" is a direct translation of the Span-ish *sangre azul*.

blood, good. A hypothetical type of blood possessed by persons of good family background. This er-roneous belief assumes that a per-son's destiny is predetermined by his blood type.

blood, half. A person born to parents each of whom is of a dif-ferent race. In general, such children have the status of the socially in-ferior partner to the mating. This term is colloquial, as the concept of mixtures of blood has long been in-validated. The term half-breed is also used.

bloodedness, warm. The organ-ism's ability to keep a constant body temperature, e.g., birds and mam-mals.

bloom. Iron in a spongy condition, resulting from charcoal absorbing oxygen from iron ore when the ore is fired with a bellows. The term loupe is also used.

blower, cloud. A straight tubular pipe used by the Pueblo Indians. It was from a few inches to a foot long.

blowgun. In tropical areas, a long tube from which darts are blown. It is used in hunting and warfare. The blowgun is found in Indo-nesia, the Malay Peninsula, and in parts of South America. Curare (q.v.) in South America and Ipoh sap in Asia are poisons used to tip blowgun darts. Inasmuch as blow-guns are not found elsewhere in the world, it may be supposed that they were invented independently in Asia and in South America.

blowing, glass. The technique by which a mass of viscid glass mix-ture is placed at the end of a blow-ing tube and inflated by blowing through the tube. The earliest known descriptions of glass-blow-ing techniques were found portrayed on the bas-reliefs of Beni Hassan about 2,000 B.C., but the process is still used today in the production of the finest glass articles. The develop-ment of glass blowing, which was accelerated around the first century B.C., permitted the making of larger and more types of glass objects.

blue, Alexandria. The famous bright blue pigment used on wall paintings by the ancient Egyptians. It is composed of silicates of copper and lime.

blue, Egyptian. A stable pigment, made primarily of copper, found in ancient Egyptian wall paintings. Its hue is bright and rather pale and closely resembles the blue Egyptian pottery glaze. Some examples of paintings made with this color are over 3,000 years old and show virtu-ally no deterioration. It was used from the Fourth Dynasty through 600 A.D., after which the method of manufacture seems to have been lost.

Blumenbach, Johann Friedrich (1752-1840). A German naturalist, one of the founders of physical anthropology. He established craniology and divided men into five races: Caucasian, Mongolian, Ethiopian, American, and Malay, each in a different part of the globe. His criteria were hair, body structure, and skull form, with the last especially important. Blumenbach believed that races arise by degeneration and differentiate themselves by a *vis formativa.* His collection of craniological materials was world famous. He exposed the non-authenticity of Wild Peter, an alleged feral child found in 1724, and thus shook the prevalent belief in the existence of feral men.

blunderbuss. An early firearm having a large bore and a funnel-shaped muzzle. It was capable of holding a number of balls or slugs and was intended for use at close range.

board, memorial. See BOARD, MUMMY.

board, mould. The curved plate in a plow that turns over the earth. Plows with this equipment were first used ca. 100 B.C. in northwest Europe.

board, mummy. A large piece of wood exactly the same size and shape as the Egyptian mummy and used to conceal the mummy bandages and beautify the mummy. It was decorated with an image of the deceased and various gods were usually carved on it in relief. The reverse side of the board, which rested on the mummy, was painted violet.

board, osteometric. A wooden block, about two feet long and a foot wide, with a wooden upright

and marked off in metric scales. It is used to measure bones.

board, scraper. A tool for designing pottery. The whole pot is painted and then is scraped in order to display the color underneath. Some examples of this method, in Greece, are about 5,000 years old.

board, throwing. See THROWER, SPEAR.

boat, bark. A craft made of several pieces of bark sewed together. The bark boat is almost as old as the dugout (q.v.).

boat, basket. A light craft made of narrow strips of split bamboo which are woven into stiff matting in an elongated oval form. Both ends are spoon-shaped. The basket boat is found in Indochina.

boat, bull. A simply constructed skin boat, formerly used by various North American Indians, notably on the Plains. The bull boat usually resembled a circular bowl, with vertical sides and a flat bottom. Its framework was usually of willow rods at right angles to each other and bound together by thongs. A buffalo hide was stretched over this framework. The bull boat was propelled by a short-handled, broad-bladed paddle. It was used by the Hidatsa and other tribes to cross the Missouri and was used by the Plains Indians to transport goods by water. These boats make no distinction between stern or bow.

boat, tub. A short tub used in China and Japan for water transport.

bob, plumb. See PLUMMET.

bobbin. A reel on which the free end of a thread is coiled in continuous weaving. The weight of the bobbin helps keep the thread extended.

Bochica. A Chibcha anthropomorphic white god.

bodkin. An implement with a sharp point used to make holes in fabric; also a blunted needle with a large eye.

body, preservation of the. The methods by which the body of the deceased can be preserved indefinitely include cold storage, injecting a germicidal and antispetic fluid into the blood vessels, and desiccating the body and keeping it dry. The last was used by Egyptians in mummification (q.v.).

bogadi. An African term for bride price.

Bogenkultur. A Kulturkreis (q.v.) found in New Guinea. Bogenkultur has the bow and a maternal organization with no exogamy. It is sometimes called bow culture.

bohío. A type of house with a rectangular floor plan and a gabled roof, built by the Taino of the Greater Antilles. See CANEY (1).

boiling, stone. Heating or boiling liquid by placing the liquid in a container and dropping in heated stones. Tylor first noted this mode of cooking and gave it a specific place in the history of cooking. The technique is also called hot-rock cooking.

boiler, pot. A piece of flint which has been crackled and whitened by fire and was presumably used to keep water heated.

boiler, rice. A double cooking vessel with the lower vessel containing hot water so that the food does not scorch.

bokung-elong. A secret society (q.v.) of the Pangwe, in the Southern Cameroons.

bolas or **bola.** A weapon consisting of stone balls tied by sinews in groups of two or three. The bolas is hurled at animals' legs in order to entangle them. This hunting method is used by some South American Indians and some Eskimos even today. The term is sometimes spelled bolo.

Bole-Maru. A phase of the ghost dance (q.v.) cult, characterized by some features of clothing and the dances.

bolo. See BOLAS; KNIFE, BOLO.

boloi. The antisocial acts of a Bechuana witch doctor.

bolson. A land basin.

boma. A thornbush fence or palisade built around villages in central Africa to ward off predatory animals.

Bomai and Malu cult. See CULT, BOMAI AND MALU.

bombylius. A moderately sized Greek vase used as a container for perfumes and for pouring water. It varied between the aryballus (q.v.) and the lecythus (q.v.) in general structure.

Bon. The religion of nomads e.g., the Kazak of North Central Asia.

bonder. A stone built into a wall to strengthen it. The bonder is long enough to go through the entire thickness of the wall.

Bondu. A female secret society (q.v.) in West Africa.

bone. In *anatomy*, the hard tissue that composes the adult skeleton of most vertebrates. Bone is a dense connective tissue, rigid and hard because of its inorganic material. It is covered with periosteum and it is porous internally, with different sized cavities. About 70 per cent of bone consists of mineral salts, with about 60 per cent of this calcium phosphate. Organic matter represents about 30 per cent of the bone (nerves, bone marrow, blood-forming elements, white blood-cell-forming organs, platelet-forming organs, lymph vessels). The only animal whose bones break longitudinally, in artificial splitting, is man.

In *ethnology*, among the Riffs, a group of families related through the male line and descended from a single ancestor. The Riffian bone is analogous to a clan.

bone, ice. An ice skate made of bone, mentioned in the Edda. The ice bone gave rise to iron-bladed wooden skates in Holland in the 13th century.

bone, Inca. See BONE, WORMIAN.

bone, parietal. One of the two bones which meet at the sagittal suture and form a substantial part of the top and sides of the cranium. This pair of bones forms various sutures with the frontal, temporal, occipital, sphenoid and other bones.

bone, sphenoid. One of the most complicated bones in the human skull. It is made up of greater wings, lesser wings, lateral and medial pterygoid plates, and the body. It contains the sphenoidal sinus. The sphenoid bone forms the floor of the middle cranial cavity and part of the nasal fossa. The sella turcica (Turkish saddle), which supports the pituitary gland, is largely composed of the two sphenoid bones.

bone, Wormian. A supernumerary bone that occasionally forms between cranial sutures, especially in the back of the skull between the occipital and the two parietal bones. As the occurrence of this bone is especially common in the skulls found in ancient Peruvian sites, it is also sometimes called the Inca bone.

bones. Four pieces of the ribs of horses or oxen used as a musical instrument. The bones are held in the hand and struck together for the purpose of marking time in accompaniment to a voice or to another instrument.

Bones, Black. An aristocratic class among some Asiatic nomadic herding peoples, e.g., the Kirghiz and Kazak.

bones, oracle. A technique of divination (q.v.) using the bones of some animals.

bones, utilized. Bones from the toes of bison or horses that were cut and used as anvils in Middle Paleolithic times.

Bones, White. A dependent class among some Asiatic nomadic herding peoples, e.g., the Kirghiz and Kazak.

Boni. The festival of the ancestral soul return in Japan.

Bontok. A member of the Indonesian subfamily of the Malayo-Polynesian family of languages, spoken in the Philippine Islands.

bonze. In Buddhism, a priest or religious functionary.

book, dream. A formalized statement about the meaning of dreams, used for thousands of years. One of the earliest such books was an Egyptian papyrus of the 12th Dynasty, ca. 2000-1790 B.C.

Book of the Dead. Any one of a group of ancient Egyptian inscriptions describing the magic, ritual, and myth of the period. The original texts have been found inscribed on tombs, monuments, and papyrus. Some of the earliest examples are on walls of the chambers of the pyramids of Unas, Pepi, Teta, and Merenra (ca. 3000-2200 B.C.). The original Book of the Dead was a collection of 200 chapters on customs for the beautification of the dead among the Egyptians. The deceased was to recite the various chapters so he could gain power and privileges in his new life.

Book of the World. The tremendous literary project started during the Ming Dynasty under the direction of Yung-lo, the third emperor. It was an encyclopedia of all knowledge which contained 22,877 full volumes and required two years and an enormous staff to complete it.

bookbinding. The design and production of covers for books. As early as 800 B.C., the Babylonians made two layered clay tablets, the inner layer of which was inscribed with cuneiforms, the outer with the title. It was necessary to break off the "title" before the cuneiform characters could be read. Egyptian papyrus books were surrounded by wooden cases. Later in the fifth century, parchment and vellum manuscript sheets were stitched together. Some bindings were made

of intricately tooled leather and sometimes studded with precious gems or decorated with gold and silver.

boom. One of a number of poles used to attach the outrigger to a canoe. It is also any pole used to extend the foot of a sail.

boomerang. A wooden weapon, with a curved upper and flat lower surface, some models of which return to the thrower. The thrower gives the weapon as much rotation as possible, so that after some 50 yards of flight, it will turn over on its flat side, curve to the left, and rise. Each end of the boomerang is on a different plane, and it can use the physical principle of the screw. Boomerangs are flattish seen in section and curved seen in outline. In those boomerangs that return, the surfaces are likely to have a small spiral twist. Another term for boomerang is comeback club.

boot, Patagonian. A high riding boot found amond the Tehuelche Indians of the Patagonian pampas.

Bopal. An artificial language or modification of Volapuk, originated by St. de Max in 1887.

bord-droit. A kind of straight-bordered bronze ax.

boreal. Referring to the forests of the north, which cover 9 per cent of the earth's surface. Most of the inhabitants were hunters. The term also refers to the northern and mountainous area north of the equator, including much of North and Central America.

boreal, pre-. Referring to a cold climate, becoming warmer, especially from ca. 7900-7000 B.C., when birch, pine, and willow were typical vegetation. During preboreal times the Ahrensburgian culture flourished.

boreal, sub-. Referring to a cool and dry climate. The term subboreal has particular reference to the beginning of the Neolithic period.

borer. A variety of coup-de-poing (q.v.) which is smaller than the normal and has its point drawn out in a narrow spike shape. Generically, a borer is cylindrical, has a sharp edge, and is used to make holes in materials. The term perçoir is also used.

borer, fire. A round stick which is rapidly turned in depressions in another stick. This turning continues until there is smoke in the sawdust, which is then gently blown on and breaks into flame.

borer, tap. A large and fairly coarse kind of awl, found in the Middle Aurignacian period.

Borreby. A hypothetical Cro-Magnon or northwest European Caucasoid element found in the present population of Germany.

borrowing. A taking-over by one culture of a feature of another culture, often through the influence of important persons.

borrowing, cultural. Linguistic borrowing which involves taking features from another language.

borrowing, dialect. Linguistic borrowing between dialects of the same language.

borrowing, intimate. Borrowing of speech forms which takes place when two languages are spoken in one community. There is a dominant or upper language spoken by the senior or more powerful group, as well as a lower language spoken by the less powerful group in the society, e.g., the immigrants in the United States. The lower language primarily borrows from the upper language.

borrowing, linguistic. Adopting language features which are not the same as those of the main tradition.

Bos primigenius. A wild ox. It may have given rise to the cattle of today.

bosing. A percussion method in which a hammer, lead-filled tin, or the central socketed part of a pick, held vertically, strikes the ground. It is an archaeological method for testing what is below the ground's surface. It was first used by Pitt-Rivers. Undisturbed material beneath shallow topsoil gives a thud, while a filled-in area will give a different kind of sound.

botanomancy. Divination (q.v.) or fortune-telling by leaves. Messages were sometimes written on the leaves and they were left for the wind to blow. The answer was derived from the leaves that were left. Another method was to note the way the leaves crackled when scattered on a fire or crushed in the hand.

botoque. In tropical South America, a type of circular, disklike lip plug, usually of wood, which is inserted into an incision in the lower lip. In Africa, this type of lip plug is inserted into the upper lip as well and reaches six to eight inches in diameter. See TEMBETÁ.

78

bottiglia. A vase shaped like an Italian wine flask.

boucher. See BOUCHER DE PERTHES.

Boucher de Perthes (1783-1868). A French customs official who studied Paleolithic implements and their geological associations in both cave and river deposits. He claimed that man was contemporary with extinct animals. In 1838, he suggested the hypothesis that humans have developed over hundreds of thousands of years. He is considered the father of human paleontology and modern prehistoric archaeology. The term boucher, derived from his name, is sometimes used for a coup-de-poing or a flint.

boundary. The limit of a land holding, often very strictly observed by early peoples. Sometimes the boundaries had religious meanings and the boundary had marginal properties. Such early gods as Min and Hermes are concerned with protecting roads and boundaries.

boundary, language. A hypothetical line drawn around a particular speech community, usually enclosing a number of small circles indicating various speech islands.

boustrophedon. Writing which goes from left to right and right to left, with the alternate lines often inverted, so that it is necessary to turn the tablet around after each line.

bout, drinking. A ceremony in which alcoholic beverages are drunk usually until the participants collapse. It is especially common in the West Indies and among the Caribs of Central America. Among the Garif, after a drinking bout the participants fall drunk alongside a grave and return with reports of conversation which they presumably heard in the underworld.

bow. A weapon used to propel an arrow by placing the arrow notch in the bowstring and pulling the bowstring toward the operator, then letting the arrow go forward. A single bow consists of one stave with no additions to make it more elastic. The bow may have been invented in the Old World and was not found in the New World till fairly recently. In the Pacific area, it was used mainly for sport and the hunt.

bow, composite. A bow with a resilient shaft made of at least two different elements, e.g., wood joined to horn, sinew, whalebone, or another type of wood. A sinew backing may be corded or it may be found in layers.

bow, compound. A bow made by fastening several pieces of wood together, e.g., hickory and yew. It is more powerful than the simple bow. The compound bow was known before 2,000 B.C.

bow, compound musical. Two or more musical bows joined in order to play polychordal music. A compound musical bow may have a common resonator, with the plane of the line of strings parallel to the resonator surface.

bow, cotton-cleaning. A bow around the string of which tufts of raw unspun cotton are wrapped. When the string is twanged the dust is shaken off and the cotton is thus cleaned.

bow, knuckle. A finger guard or protector which is attached to a sword.

bow, musical. A bow used for playing music. A shooting bow may be used, with the string divided into two unequal parts by making a string loop around bow string and bow. The string may be plucked, struck, or friction-vibrated. The musician's teeth usually hold part of the bow, magnifying the sound, if he plays for himself. If he plays for others, the sound may be magnified by resting the bow against an outsider resonator like a pot or gourd. The musical bow may consist of a bent stick with both ends connected by a fiber or string.

bow, pellet. A bow used to shoot pellets or bullets rather than arrows.

bow, self. A bow made of a single piece of wood.

bow, sinew-backed. A bow made of horn, driftwood, or some other fairly brittle material, with wrappings of sinew, found in northwest America. It is likely that this bow is a development of the Asian bow made of wood, horn, and sinew, with a thumb ring to release the bowstring.

bow, sinew-lined. An American Indian one-piece bow the back of which is strengthened by sinew glued on. The sinew-lined bow is found among the Navaho and others.

bow, trussed. A type of bow made of one or more pieces of inferior wood reinforced by adding longitudinal withes or sinews and wrapping many times with sinew or fiber to give added strength.

bowl, effigy. A bowl, usually of pottery, modeled in the form of an animal or plant or other object. Effigy bowls were a highly developed art form among certain South American Indians.

bowlegs. See LEGS, BOW.

bowlegs, postural. The appearance of bowlegs stemming from standing with the knees in hyperextension and internal rotation, although the leg bones are not truly bowed.

bow-wow. Referring to Herder's theory that language arose by primitive man imitating animals, e.g., *bleat* sounds like a sheep's bleat. It is also called the onamatopoeic theory.

bowsprit. On a sailboat, a spar attached to and projecting from the hull at the ship's bows.

bowstring. The string used to hold the two ends of the bow together. The bowstring is usually made of animal material, like tendons or sinews, or vegetable material, like twined bast.

box, betel. A box which contains a slice of the areca nut, usually powdered with coral rag or lime and wrapped in a betel pepper leaf.

box, sounding. An apparatus found in the kiva (q.v.). The sounding box looks like a subfloor vault. It is thought that it was used as a type of drum when the top was covered.

boxadi. The lobolo (q.v.) among the Bakatti.

boy, salt water. A coastal native of Manus Island.

brace. The distance between the tips of the middle fingers of each hand with the arms outstretched. It is almost six feet.

bracer. An archer's rectangular wrist guard, drilled for attachment at each end. The bracer was usually made of stone or bone.

braces, additional. Smaller tribes added to the Iroquois League.

brachiation. Movement by a combined use of hind and fore limbs. It was developed by arboreal apes and is helpful for tree life.

brachycephalic. Referring to a person with a comparatively broad head, characterized by a cephalic index (q.v.) of higher than 81 on the dry skull and higher than 82 on the living head. Primary brachycephaly is a sign of incomplete differentiation and is associated with evolutionary development and is positively correlated with increasing stature.

brachycephalization. The process of a population becoming more brachycephalic. Brachycephalization may result from an increase in brain size without stature increasing. The major factor in the brachycephalization of historic Europe probably was the continual appearance of Asiatic roundheads and their mixture with early European dolichocephals, with brachycephals resulting. Early man was long-headed and his mutations were in the direction of brachycephaly. These mutations were probably independent and repeated. Weidenreich has pointed out that the shorter jaw and wider braincase attendant on brachycephalization help achieve head balance in a bipedal organism like Homo sapiens. Vision improves as the eyes are farther apart, and the jaw functions more easily. Brachycephalization is also called globularization.

brachychouranic. Referring to a maxillo-alveolar index (q.v.) of more than 115.

brachycranial. Referring to an individual with a comparatively broad skull, characterized by a cranial index (q.v.) of between 80 and 84.9.

brachycolic. Referring to having a short colon, of up to 160 cm.

brachydont. Referring to a tooth with short roots and a broad crown used in crushing by carnivores.

brachylogy. A phrase or style of speaking which is grammatically incomplete or abbreviated in some manner.

brachyskelic. Referring to a stem-leg length index between 75 and 79.9.

brachystaphyline. Referring to a palatal index (q.v.) of more than 85.

brachyuranic. Referring to a skull with an alveolar arch the external breadth of which is at least 115 per cent of its length, so that the maxillo-alveolar index (q.v.) is more than 115.

bracteate. A pendant made of thin plaques of gold resembling coins. Bracteates were found in the Scandinavian countries. They were at first copies of Roman medallions and ca. fifth century A.D., animal motifs were found.

bradyesthesia. Blunted sensation.

Brahman. The most desired goal of the Upanishads and the Vedas. Brahman is the state in which the human and divine exist together in an absolute impersonal union. The Brahmans are also the highest caste among the Hindus, i.e., the priests. See ATMAN.

Brahmanas. Priestly writings of the Hindus, attached to the Vedas and probably dating from 800-600 B.C. They show a stage between Vedic religion and philosophical Hinduism. In repetitious detail, they give the ritual's significance and directions for sacrifices.

braiding. Entwining several strands by passing each strand of material over the others so that each strand makes a sinuous path in the texture.

brain, full. Referring to primates which have a brain that is approximately the same size as modern man's.

brain, half. Referring to primates that are extinct and had a brain of a size on a level below the hominine (q.v.) and who had a putative culture.

branch, green. A green branch has wide usage as a peace symbol, especially in Australia and Oceania. It is a specific sign of peace, especially in East Australia.

branding. Burning a symbol deep enough into the flesh to make a scar. Branding was used to mark slaves or criminals.

Brandwirtschaft. An early European type of fertilizing in which fire was used to clear patches of forest. The ashes from the fire provided a potash dressing for the soil, which was sown and cropped for a season or two, after which the farmer went to another tract. This technique probably survived longest among the Finno-Ugrian peoples and is still in use in part of Carelia.

brash. Small pieces of ice mixed in with the ice resulting from pressure between ice bodies.

brass. An alloy made of copper and zinc in different proportions. Brass was not made as a deliberate product in very early times, and references to it in Biblical translations are probably inaccurate. It occurred by accident in different places, but since brass is the deliberate mixing of copper and zinc, it could not have been made intentionally until metal zinc was localized toward the end of the medieval era. Brass of the contemporary period has 67 per cent copper and 33 per cent zinc. Probably the first brass objects are some bracelets in Kameiros, a Rhodes city which was wiped out in the sixth century B.C. In the fourth century B.C., a kind of brass was evidently made by the Mossynoeci, who lived on the south shore of the Black Sea.

brazier. A basin-shaped portable vessel used to burn charcoal with no draft. It develops heat to warm the extremities. Braziers are usually of metal but may be pottery. Braziers are widely distributed but are most often used in the southern temperate and tropical zone. The brazier contains a portable fire and may thus be among the first takings of fire from its base level on the hearth.

brazing. Joining two pieces of metal by heating their edges almost to the point of melting and then hammering the edges together.

bread, persimmon. A bread made by Indians in the eastern United States, especially Virginia, of sun-dried persimmons.

bread, Piki. A dry thin bread made from corn and used by the Hopi. It keeps well and resembles an extra-thin Mexican tortilla.

breadth, bi-acromial. With the subject standing normally, the distance between those margins of the acromion processes of the scapula which are most lateral.

breadth, bi-cristal. The iliocristale distance.

breadth, bi-orbital. The distance from the center of one lateral orbital border to the other.

breadth, bigonial. The distance between the gonia, the two points which are the most laterally located on the angle of the lower jaw.

breadth, bizygomatic. The distance between the most lateral points on the zygomatic arches.

breadth, chest. The average of measurements of the transverse distance between the most lateral points on the chest, made at inspiration and expiration during normal breathing.

breadth, head. The distance, measured by a spreading caliper, between the points on the side of the head above ear level that project laterally the farthest .

breadth, hip. The distance between trochanterion and trochanterion.

breadth, interorbital. The distance between the left and right dacryon points.

breadth, maxillo-alveolar. The greatest distance between the external lateral alveolar borders.

breadth, maximum bizygomatic. The maximum breadth separating the two zygomatic arches.

breadth, maximum cranial. The distance between euryon and euryon.

breadth, maximum facial. The distance between zygion and zygion. It is the most widely used measure of facial breadth.

breadth, maximum head. The maximum transverse diameter on the head. It is usually measured over each parietal bone.

breadth, maximum physiognomic nasal. The greatest transverse distance between the most lateral points on the wings of the nose.

breadth, minimum frontal. The minimal distance between the origins of the zygomatic processes of the frontal bones.

breadth, minimum frontal cranial. The minimal breadth between the temporal crests of the frontal bone.

breadth, nasal. The greatest distance between the lateral margins of the pyriform aperture.

breadth, orbital. The distance between the ectoconchion and maxillofrontale, or between the dacryon and ectoconchion.

breadth, physiognomic. The distance between the subaurale and the superaurale.

breadth, physiognomic ear. The distance between postaurale and preaurale.

breadth, shoulder. The distance separating the acromial points when the subject is standing normally.

breadth, thoracic. The breadth of the chest multiplied by 100 and divided by the anterior trunk length.

breathing, rough. Aspiration at the beginning of a word.

breccia. A rock composed of angular pebbles or fragments embedded in a matrix which may have the same origin. Breccia has long been used for ornamentation. Egyptian breccia vases are collector's items.

breccia, osseous. Heaps of rock and fossil bones cemented together by calcareous or ferruginous mud.

breechclout. A garment consisting of a string around the waist to which is attached a cloth between the legs.

breed, half-. The child of parents who are of different racial groups, e.g., of a Caucasoid and an American Indian parent. See BLOOD, HALF. A silver and copper nugget, as found in Alaska, may also be called a half-breed.

breeding, selective. See SELECTION, ARTIFICIAL.

breeding out. A method of maintaining the standard of a given species by bringing in other specimens to breed. When some forms of Arabian horse, e.g., the barb, began to degenerate, out-breeder horses were used. The Japanese maintained the family of the Mikado by bringing in semiroyal out

breeders. Some authorities have maintained that if there is no defect in the specimens, in-breeding is not harmful.

bregma. The point on the summit of a skull at which the two parietal bones meet the frontal bone.

breve. A curved symbol (˘) placed over the character for a vowel to indicate the correct sound. The breve frequently indicates that the vowel is short, e.g., *fĭnăl*.

bridge, land. A land connection, usually in the glacial period, between two areas now separated by water. Land bridges resulted because ice sheets absorbed such vast amounts of water that the ocean level dropped almost 200 yards. The Bering Strait, e.g., was a land bridge between Siberia and North America. The hypothesis of land bridges helps explain relationships between fauna and flora in the disconnected areas, as well as similarities in culture, e.g., between northeast Asia and the New World. See HYPOTHESIS, CONTINENTAL BRIDGE, and HYPOTHESIS, CONTINENTAL DRIFT.

bridge, liana. Interwoven bridge shaped like a basket and made of liana, a climbing plant. There are anchoring posts at the shore or in the water and a rail.

bridge, tow. A bridge spanning an abyss, fastened at both ends. The traveler may be in a seat or attached to a stick.

Brinton, Daniel G. (1837-1899). The leading American anthropologist of his generation, who did important work in religion and mythology. To Brinton, anthropology

84

meant physical anthropology, ethnology was the social study of man, and ethnography collecting facts on peoples. His *Races and Peoples* (1890) contains a discussion of physical and psychological components of ethnography, races, and the effects of insular and littoral living.

Broca, Pierre (1824-1900). A French surgeon who was the founder of the formal study of physical anthropology. He started the first anthropological scientific society in 1859, the first anthropological journal in 1872, and the first school of anthropology in 1876. He studied the physical makeup of the French people. He discovered Broca's area on the brain, which is linked with speech and its pathology. This area is usually on the right side of the brain of left-handed persons and vice versa. Many of Broca's methods in craniometry and osteometry are still in use.

broch. A kind of small circular stone house in Scotland, probably developing from an aisled round house, and adapted for defense. The broch dates from the Iron Age, and some 500 are extant. The walls are about 20 feet high and 15 feet thick. There is often a circular court and a guard cell.

bronze. An alloy of tin and copper. Bronze probably occurred from noticing that copper ore with certain impurities was more useful than pure copper, and then isolating those impurities. About 10 per cent tin and 90 per cent copper is the optimum ratio, but early bronze may have from 2 to 16 per cent. Lead was sometimes added in early

times. Bronze is superior to copper because the addition of tin increases hardness and strength, lowers the melting point, and increases liquidity, thus making casting operations easier. Copper is not a good metal for casting because it contracts on cooling and absorbs gases, thus becoming porous; the presence of tin helps check this absorption.

Although bronze is an alloy of tin and copper, some archaeologists have confused copper and bronze, and some have used bronze to refer to copper mixed with metals other than tin.

Ancient societies used bronze most successfully for making works of art, which is one reason that it plays an important part in the classical metal cultures.

Both the Old World and the New World show considerable variation in the tin-copper relation, indicating that the early metallurgist did not use tin precisely. There is no bronze period as such in North America, because the tin ores in this area are not bound with copper.

Bronze was first developed in Asia, with the earliest appearance at Ur, ca. 3,500 B.C. Bronze artifacts in Egypt are found in the 18th dynasty, ca. 1580-1350 B.C., although the use of bronze became established only ca. 663-609 B.C. The Danubian region saw the use of bronze ca. 2300 B.C., with European bronze use beginning ca. 2000 B.C.

bronze, Corinthian. A highly prized alloy made at Corinth. It was noted for its superb quality and the works of art which were made from it were of the highest order technically and artistically.

Bronze Age. See AGE. BRONZE.

brotherhood. A close association of affection and service that stems from kinship or membership in a common society. The members have the same standing and have equal shares in the group's obligations and benefits. They may be organized for many different reasons. Various ritualistic observances may characterize initiation into a brotherhood, e.g., sucking one another's blood, eating a ceremonial meal together.

brotherhood, blood. A symbolic exchange of blood between two men who are not brothers and who thus create strong kinship ties. Those entering such a covenant become loyal brothers. It is thus a close bond between two people who have mingled their blood, and it developed from the early view of kinship as a blood association.

brothers, war. Men who count war honors together among the Plains Indians of the United States.

Brünn. Referring to a hypothetical Aurignacian central European subdivision of the Caucasoids.

Brythonic. A Celtic language group which includes Breton, Welsh, and Cornish.

buccal. Referring to the interior wall of the mouth and the portion of the tooth and the bone supporting it that are adjacent to the cheek.

bucchero. Black polished pottery found in several parts of Italy in the so-called Etruscan period.

buccina. An ancient Roman horn used by the infantry, as distinguished from the kituus, which was used by the cavalry. The buccina had a cylindrical bore that expanded into a bell, and the tube was curved to nearly a circle, with the bell resting on the player's shoulder. It was pitched at the second G above middle C.

buchu. An aromatic South African plant used for medicinal and cosmetic purposes.

Buckland, Dean (1784-1856). An English geologist, who used catastrophes as a method of reconciling the evidence of fossils and geology with the Biblical account of the creation.

buckler. A shield, especially one that is small and round.

bucranium. A decoration in Roman architecture, an ox skull. It is most frequently seen on altars and temple friezes.

budding, generation by. A process by which new groups are formed. A part of a group may leave in order to obtain more subsistence, although it still recalls the relatives and ancestor of the original group. Descent continues in both areas and ultimately the ancestor is not recalled, so that the lineage (q.v.) has been superceded by the clan (q.v.).

budgerew. See BADJARA.

Buffon, George Louis (1707-1788). A French naturalist who emphasized that human beings constitute a species that became broken down into several subgroups.

Buhl. A minor glacial advance following the fourth, or Würm (q.v.), glacial period, and occurring ca. 18,500 B.C.

86

builders, mound. Prehistoric peoples who were widely scattered over the eastern half of the United States. They are named for their practice of building burial mounds.

building ceremony. See CEREMONY, BUILDING.

Bukvitsa. A modified version of the Cyrillic (q.v.) alphabet, which displays influences of the Glagolitic (q.v.) alphabet. It was formerly used by Catholic Slavs in Bosnia and Dalmatia.

bula. A small vodun (q.v.) ceremonial drum, about 8 inches wide and 18 inches high.

bull, winged. A symbolic animal of ancient Assyria used as a representation of force and domination. It had a bull's body, wings, and a human head. The winged bull appears frequently in sculptured form and is placed so as to guard the doors of a palace.

bulla. A locket or pendant worn around the neck by Roman children as an amulet (q.v.). Protection was believed to be effected by the precious material from which the bulla was made or by some substance enclosed within it.

bullock. A castrated bull; a young bull.

bumpkin. On a sailboat, a spar which attaches to and projects from the stern.

bun. A Congo term for soul.

bundle, ceremonial. A bundle containing paraphernalia supposed to have supernatural properties. Among certain of the American Indians, these bundles were considered to be links between the in-

dividual and the source of his spiritual power.

bundle, diplomatic. See STICK, DIPLOMATS'.

bundle, medicine. A package of objects, used by some North American Indian tribes and believed to have special magical or ritualistic properties. Medicine bundles were the property of either an individual or a group and were usually enclosed in a skin cover. The source of these bundles stems from supernatural persons. They may be kept in special places. Sometimes they were sold.

bundling. An early country practice in parts of Western Europe and New England. Bundling consisted of engaged couples, or others, lying dressed in the same bed in order to save fuel when on visits.

buni. Harplike Egyptian musical instrument made from a hollow sound box covered with parchment. The strings are stretched on a rod that goes through the center. Twisted cords with tassels on them increase the tension of the strings for tuning.

bunodont. Referring to a tooth with a rounded cusp, used mainly for grinding.

bunt. An arrowhead with a round or square rather than a flat end.

burdock. A plant widely used to cure fever, colic, and ringworm.

burén. A circular pottery griddle used by the Indians of the Caribbean area to bake manioc cakes.

burial. The ceremonial interment of a corpse, probably first occurring in Mousterian times.

burial, bundle. A bundle of defleshed and disarticulated bones tied or wrapped together for burial.

burial, chariot. Burying a warrior along with his chariot. It is found in the late Hallstatt (q.v.) epoch, north of the Alps. The chariots were mostly four-wheeled, light, and luxurious. The harness gear was not usually buried.

burial, collective. A burial in which two or more bodies were put in the same grave or tomb.

burial, contracted. See POSITION, CONTRACTED.

burial, crossroads. The practice of burying suicides or criminals at crossroads. Some early European groups offered human sacrifices at crossroads altars.

burial, extended. Burial in which the body rests on its back in an extended position.

burial, flexed. A form of burial in which the arms or legs or both are bent, making the corpse more compact and easier to inter.

burial, niche. A form of burial in which the body is placed in a niche lateral to the grave shaft. It is found in many parts of the world.

burial, olla. A method of interment wherein the body is placed in a large urn and set in a subterranean chamber, practiced by the Zapotec Indians. Excavations at the Tres Zapotes site in the early 1940s unearthed five complete ollas.

burial, platform. A method of disposing of the dead in which the body is placed on a platform above the ground and left to be defleshed by scavengers.

burial, secondary. A final burying of a person's bones, after the first temporary burial during which the flesh has decomposed. Secondary burial has been found in many parts of the world. The bones are usually concentrated in packages or in a skin.

burial, tree. The practice of putting a corpse inside the hollow trunk of a tree or on a platform constructed among the branches. Tree burial was common among certain North American Indian tribes. The body was done away with by carnivorous birds and natural decay.

burial, urn. Placing corpses or their ashes in vessels. The urn was either sealed by a slab or stone or by an urn placed over it, mouth to mouth.

burial, water. A method of body disposal in which the deceased is either cast into an ocean or set adrift in a boat.

burin. A flake tool for sculpturing or engraving. Basically it consists of a blade with the sides sliced obliquely at one end so that they form a narrow chisel edge when they meet. There were over 20 major kinds of burin. They were especially associated with the Upper Paleolithic cultures. The burin is pointed by a facet being removed along an edge in such a manner that it can be repointed again merely by removing another facet. See TECHNIQUE, BURIN.

burin busqué. A nosed flint graver (q.v.) found in Aurignacian times.

burin-ciseau. See CHISEL, ENGRAVER.

burin, ordinary or **burin en-bec-de-flûte.** A small, straight-edged chisel.

burití. Any of a number of palms of the genus *Mauritia* with fan-shaped leaves widely used by natives of the tropical forest of South America, especially for making cordage and for thatching roofs. These palms are also called miriti or iti.

burumbi. A circular dwelling of the East Congo made of banana leaves.

Burushaski. A language sometimes considered to be related to the Dravidian or Munda languages, but more currently held to be unrelated to any other language. It is spoken in northwestern India.

busby. A large bushy wig; or a high fur hat worn by English hussars, with a bag with the regimental facings hanging from the right.

Bushmen. Geographically, members of the Bushman-Hottentot pygmy population, speaking Bushman languages of the Khoisan stock. These are food-gathering groups in South Africa. Their physical traits include yellowish skin, steatopygy (q.v.), thin lips, short stature, slight prognathism (q.v.), broad nose, narrow head, slight body hair, and tufted hair. It has been suggested that the Bushmen and Asiatic pygmies may have left a hypothetical native country, with the Bushmen migrating south and the pgymies going east. Bushmen culture has received many foreign influences. In moving to South Africa, the Bushmen may have met with an earlier Caucasoid group, the Strandloopers. The Bushmen have been regarded as degenerate Negroids or as relics of a Eurafrican-steppe hunting culture. See PYGMY.

busk. A Creek celebration in which there is a pardon for previous injuries and crimes. It is an annual harvest observance in which there are rites for the purposes of new fire and purification (qq.v.). The busk is also called the green-corn dance.

busked. Referring to a shape like the nose of an animal (e.g., a horse) in profile; a kind of Upper Paleolithic graver.

buso. An evil spirit among the Bagobo.

Busycon. A large conch shell found in Florida and the area of the Gulf of Mexico and used by Indians to make trumpets, ladles, dishes, gorgets, and other implements.

butt, faceted. A flake the striking platform (q.v.) of which has been part of the steep end of a tortoise core (q.v.) and is crossed by portions of the preparatory flake scars.

butter. A food made by skimming and churning cream.

buttress. Outside support built against a wall designed to counteract the pressure exerted by an inside arch or vault.

buxea tibia. An ancient flutelike musical instrument made of boxwood and with three finger holes.

Buzu. The sedentary slave class among the Tuareg.

buzzer. A toy consisting of a disk with two perforations through which two cords are passed. When the cords are twisted and untwisted rapidly, a buzzing sound is produced. The buzzer was used by the Indians throughout the Americas aboriginally and occurs also among the Australian natives. See ROARER, BULL.

byssus. In ancient Egypt, winding sheets in which dead bodies were wrapped in the last stages of mummification; also mummy cloth (q.v.).

C

Caaba. The most sacred Moslem shrine. On this site, Adam is believed to have first prayed after he was told to leave the garden of Eden. It is the central chamber of the magnificent mosque of Mecca and houses the well-known sacred black rock. The name is also spelled Kaaba.

caballito. A Peruvian paddled float consisting of several bundles of reeds lashed together. The caballito is made by forming a bundle of reeds into a tapering cone shape, which is then built to full size.

cabane. A supporting framework, often of skin, in some kinds of ships.

cabochon. A precious stone, the surface of which is rounded and smooth instead of faceted.

Caboclo. A Brazilian cult group that worships Indian and African gods. It is an aspect of Negro non-Christian American religion that points toward the early settlers of the area where the group is found. A Caboclo is a rural Brazilian, usually of mixed ancestry, having descended from Whites and Indians or Negroes or all three.

cacholong. A white surface that flint assumes when it is long exposed to air.

cache, fire. A method of keeping a fire or flame going by placing three balsa logs together in such a way that they hold fire like a punk. The logs form a kind of triangular shape. The fire cache is found among the Paya, Mesquito, and some forest tribes of Central America.

cacique. An Arawak term for the paramount village or tribal chief. It has come to be employed widely throughout Latin America with the same meaning.

cacogenics. The study of the effects of bad heredity.

cacography. The misuse or poor choice of words, or incorrect or inappropriate use of language in writing.

cacuminal. Referring to an articulation made by the tongue against a point quite high up on the palate. The term domal is sometimes used.

cadastral. Referring to land ownership.

cadence. The rise and fall of the voice in speaking, produced by the alternation of louder and softer syllables. Cadence is applied in particular to the change of the voice at the end of a sentence or at a pause.

cadi. A judge in a Moslem community.

cadro. A main street in ancient Rome.

caenogenesis. Youthful characteristics which do not have an effect on the adult.

caesaropapism. A government where the same person is in charge of political and religious matters.

caid. A secular healer who is equivalent to a sheik among the Arabs.

cairn. Ancient Gaelic memorial. A cairn was usually a heap of stones placed to serve as a grave marker, a landmark, or as an indicator of the place where some valuable was stored.

cake, bride. A cake baked in connection with a wedding ceremony. Such cakes are common in many parts of the world.

cake, ice. A piece of ice which is not so large as an ice floe (q.v.).

cake, obley. A cake that has symbolic value at a religious ceremony. Obley cakes are found in many religions. They may have special shapes or be specially arranged.

calabash. A gourd, or the bottle gourd used for pipes; also, an implement made of the dried shell of the gourd.

calabaza. A gourd-shaped clay vessel used by the Peruvians from the tenth to the eighth centuries B.C. It was filled with food, placed alongside the body of a priest, and then wrapped with the body between the undergarment and the outer strips of the mummy wrapping.

calamus tibialis. A primitive Roman reed pipe with three or four finger holes. The calamus tibialis was usually played by shepherds.

calcaneum. The heel bone.

calenda. The mock battle dance of some New World Negro groups. Verses were often sung to accompany the dance.

calendar. The technique employed to reckon the sequence of days and special observances. The calendar relates the number of days and appearances of the moon in a year.

calendar, Constantinian. A calendar decreed by Constantine the Great in 321 A.D. It used the seven-day week as part of the calendar. It had 52 such weeks and thus had to borrow one day from another week in order to complete the year, so that the calendar must change every year.

calendar, Egyptian. A calendar with 12 months of 30 days each, with 5 additional days at the year's end. The Egyptians had three seasons of four months each, representing inundation, sowing, and harvesting.

calendar, Gregorian. The calendar adopted in 1582 by Pope Gregory XIII. It is a correction of the Julian calendar. Each year has 365.2422 days, or 365 days, 5 hours, 48 minutes, and 46 seconds. The calendar must borrow a day from another week to fill out the year, so that it must change every year. There are actually 14 different kinds of calendar years. The calendar is adjusted to the seasons so that it will be 4905 A.D. before a one-day correction is necessary, and this can be made by regarding a leap year as an ordinary year. The Gregorian calendar was not adopted immediately by non-Catholic countries and not until 1912 by China and 1918 by Russia.

calendar, Julian. The calendar adopted by Julius Caesar. It was originally corrected in 238 B.C. by Ptolemy III. The Julian year has 365.250000 days. Some eastern Orthodox groups still use this calendar.

calendar, Mayan. The calendar of the Mayans, whose year had 365.-242129 days. This calendar was extremely modern and accurate.

calendar, permutating. A calendar made by permutating two unequal series of time units against each other. The Aztec had a 260-day cycle (tonalpohualli), as did the Maya (tzolkin). They meshed the 260-day cycle with the 365-day year, the length of which they had measured, and had a cycle of 365 multiplied by 260 and divided by the common denominator 5, leading to a 52-year cycle.

The Chinese have a permutation calendar in which the 12 zodiac animals are permutated against the ten celestial systems. Multiplied by each other, this is 120 divided by their common denominator 2, or a cycle of 60 years. Bali has a complicated permutating calendar which leads to a 35-day cycle.

The concept of the week is the result of permutation of names of the planets against the day's 24

hours, with each day named by its first hour.

Calendar, Round. A period of 52 365 day years, in Mayan computation. This period of 18,980 days was actually a very accurate calendar, and it was copied by the Aztecs, Mixtecs, and Zapotecs.

calendar, 13-month. A hypothetical calendar suggested by some. It would have a new month, Sol, between June and July. Each month would have 28 days. June 29 would be Leap Day, and December 29 would be Year Day.

calendar, world. A proposed calendar sponsored by many groups. It would be the same for every year, with four quarters of 91 days each and month dates falling on the same days of the week. World Holidays would account for the extra days.

caliche. The crust on top of arid soils. The chemical formula is $CaCO_3$.

caliper, spreading. An instrument used to measure various diameters of the head.

Call'arco. Bowing a stringed instrument, as opposed to plucking (pizzicato).

callaïs. A precious stone, the source of which is not known. It resembles turquoise chemically and is a translucent green. Beads and pendants made of callaïs have been found in various parts of Europe.

calli. An Aztec word for house or for a four-year period.

callosity, ischial. The horniness of certain areas of the buttocks of primates. Ischial callosities are not present in man because of gluteal muscle padding.

calmecac. A type of advanced school among the Aztecs in which priestly functions were taught. The training was difficult and complex, and included fasting and self-torture.

calorimetry, partitional. The analysis of the heat interchanges between environment and body to establish the simultaneous influence of evaporation, convection, and radiation in their relation to heat change and metabolism.

calotte. The upper part of the human cranium.

calpullec. Among the Aztecs, the head of a calpulli (q.v.), whose principal duty it was to supervise economic affairs.

calpulli. A territorial and administrative unit of the Aztec capital of Tenochtitlan (Mexico City), which seems to have originated as a localized clan.

calthrop. A weapon with points and spikes arranged so that at least one is always facing up if thrown at the ground. It is also called a cheval trap.

calumet. A lavishly decorated wood shaft or pipe on which there are symbolic paintings and objects. It was used extensively among some Plains tribes. The ritual smoking of the calumet, or pipe of peace, held an important place among many American Indian groups.

calva. The top of the skull.

calvaria. The skull exclusive of the facial bones.

calypso. A witty Trinidad folk song concerned with topicalities and sung in English.

camas. A plant of the genus *Camassia*, resembling the hyacinth, whose bulb served as an important source of food for the Indians of the Columbia River basin.

cambium. The part of a tree lying between the bark and the old wood and which forms the tree's annual growth ring.

Cambrian. Referring to a life period of the Paleozoic or primary era, characterized by invertebrate life only. The Cambrian lasted from perhaps 520 to 420 million years ago.

Cambrian, pre-. The period in geological time in which the earth was formed, perhaps from 3,000,-000,000 to 520,000,000 years ago. The term Archaean is sometimes used.

camel. A ruminant animal of deserts. It can store water in the stomach and thus go long distances without drinking. Camels were found in Babylonia ca. 1,000 B.C.

cameo. A gem of which the design stands out boldly in relief.

camomile. A strong-smelling bitter herb, used for medicinal purposes. The Egyptians consecrated the herb to their gods. It is still used in Europe today as a medicinal tea.

camote. The sweet potato staple of the Ifugao.

campanilismo. A point of view about in-group (q.v.) belongingness which excludes from the in-group anyone outside a narrow range.

94

campanology. Bell ringing or bell manufacture.

Campignian. Referring to a late Mesolithic culture in northern France. It is characterized by pottery, hewn axes, and oval huts with a fireplace in the center. The huts were made of sticks and clay. The pottery had embedded grains. The Campignian tranchet ax, a cross-cut ax, was the chief flint industry product. There were no microliths or blades. The Campignian was a crude coastal culture.

canal. An artificial inland waterway.

canalatura. A furrowed ornament produced on pottery through incising with a blunt stick.

canarium. An almond eaten in the Solomons.

candle. An accumulation of wax, fat, or resin around a central wick. These substances are used because they melt and create a fluid supply for the wick, which uses capillarity to attract the fluid to the flame. The candle is essentially a torch (q.v.) with a wick. It probably developed for use in confined areas and appeared fairly late, probably in the Iron Age. It typically uses a rigid material for combustion, and is unlike a torch in that it has a central capillary wick. One type of candle is the taper, a flexible wax-covered cord or wick that can be coiled.

candlenut. The oily seed of the candleberry tree (*Aleurites moluccana*) of Indonesia and Polynesia. When dry, candlenuts are used by the natives as candles, whence their name.

candomblé. A society originally from Africa, found in parts of Brazil. It is primarily for religious purposes, and the major activities are conducted by women.

canec. The provincial head of Itsa cities in the Peten.

canephora. A sculpture of a woman with a basket on her head.

canette. Any container used as a dry or liquid measure.

caney. 1 A type of house with a circular floor plan and a conical thatched roof built by the Taino Indians of the Greater Antilles. See BOHÍO. 2 A kind of funeral mound of alternating layers of snail shells, earth, and ashes made by the Ciboney Indians of the Greater Antilles.

cannibalism. Using human flesh as either a symbolic or regular food. Cannibalism has been found for reasons of hunger, vengeance, religion, filial piety, and justice. It may be found even in cultures on a fairly high level and is often linked with ceremonials. Cannibals often also eat dogs. The term anthropophagy is also used.

cannibalism, burial. Eating the flesh of a dead person, often to get part of his spirit, as among the Liverpool River people of eastern Arnhem Land in Australia.

cannibalism, endo-. Cannibalism in which the victim is a member of the tribe that eats him.

cannibalism, famine. Eating human flesh solely as a means of surviving in times of starvation, rather than as a customary or ceremonial practice. Famine cannibalism occurs notably among the Eskimo.

cannibalism, gastronomic. Eating human flesh as a dietary supplement or because of an acquired taste, rather than as a ceremonial practice in which the objective is to incorporate into oneself the desirable traits of the deceased.

cannibalism, revenge. Eating human flesh for revenge, as is the case with the Ngarigo of Australia, who eat the flesh of dead enemies and speak contemptuously of them.

cannibalism, ritual. Eating all or part of the body of tribal members who have died. The eaters are either close relatives or a special group.

canning. Placing food in an airtight container.

canoe. An early small boat, which is fairly narrow and long. It has sharp ends, is paddle propelled, and is without a sail or rudder. Oceania has the most complex, and Africa the simplest, canoes.

canoe, double. Two canoe hulls joined by beams that carry a deck platform with a mast.

canoe, five-piece. A canoe made by heightening each side of two dugouts by a plank on edge and connecting them at stem and stern with an end piece.

canoe, magic. A canoe found in American Indian stories. It propels itself at certain signals from its owner.

canon, Greek. A division of the human body into mathematical proportions, so that the total body height is equal to that of eight heads. Polyclitus of Argos (450-420 B.C.) made the first exact Greek canon, which Vitruvius re-constructed with the palm of the hand as the basic unit.

canon, Morgan's. The axiom postulated by the British psychologist C. Lloyd Morgan (1852-1936) that the best theory is the simplest one which accounts for all the facts. It is a restatement of the principle associated with William of Occam, known as Occam's razor (ca. 1325).

canon, Ptolemy's. A listing of the dates during which the Babylonian kings of the period 747-323 B.C. reigned.

Canonchet. A chief of the Narragansett tribe who was associated with the Indian King Philip's war against the English. He is also called Nanuntenoo.

canthus. The angle caused by the meeting of the eyelids.

cantico. A dance or social gathering among some American Indian groups.

capacity, cranial. The total capacity of the cranial cavity. It is often measured by the amount of small shot or mustard seed in cubic centimeters that the cranial cavity will hold.

capacity, measure of. The measure used to express the capacity of a unit, such as the hollow of a hand, an armful, a gourd load, a man's load, or a basket load.

capacity, population. That part of the world population which can be kept alive and productive by the available world resources.

capacity, vital. A measure of the lung capacity, consisting of the air expelled from the lungs after full inspiration. Vital capacity is measured with a spirometer. About 4,000 cubic centimeters can be inhaled and then exhaled.

capillus. The long, thick, and coarse hairs found on the eyebrows, scalp, and beard. A capillus may also be called a terminal hair.

Cappadocian. An ancient Near Eastern language, now extinct, examples of which may be found in inscriptions from the end of the third millenium B.C. See ASIANIC.

Capsian. Referring to the Aurignacian culture in North Africa. This Upper Paleolithic culture is a blade culture. The flakes are fairly narrow and somewhat prismatic. The blades became smaller and turned into microliths, and there was an increase in bone tools. Land snail shells were often found. As the Capsian developed, new culture elements were added, mostly by diffusion from Egypt.

capstan. A vertically cleated cylinder that revolves on an upright spindle and is surmounted by a drumhead. It has pawls at the foot of the drum and is used to raise or move heavy weights or to exert power on a rope that passes through the drum. The capstan may be operated by hand, steam, or electricity.

capstone. The coping or topmost stone.

capture, marriage by. A rare form of marriage in which one mate captures the other. Mock capture is more common. In China, the bride's brothers drive her suitors away. In groom capture, her brothers bring him to the bride.

capture, mock. The practice of the groom's seizing his bride at the wedding feast and withstanding a beating by the bride's relatives. The groom is successful in the marriage if he withstands the beating and keeps holding onto his wife. Mock capture is common among the Bushmen.

carabao. An East Indian water buffalo.

caraguata. A Chaco plant with usable fiber and fruit.

carbet. A Carib community house.

carboniferous. Referring to a life period in the Paleozoic Age in which the first true amphibians, first insects, and early reptiles appeared. The carboniferous lasted from perhaps 275 to 220 million years ago.

carbuncle. A red unfaceted garnet; a deep red gem, like a garnet or ruby. The carbuncle has been extensively used as an amulet (q.v.). It is mentioned as having special qualities in the Koran, Christian tradition, Arab and Indian folklore, and elsewhere.

cardial. Referring to pottery which is decorated by lines made with the edge of a shell.

cardinal point concept. See CONCEPT, CARDINAL POINT.

cargo cult. See CULT, CARGO.

Carian. A language spoken in antiquity on the west coast of Asia Minor, now extinct. It is preserved in about 80 short inscriptions and glosses recorded by classical authors.

Carib. A language family of South America. See ARAWAK.

caricature. An art form involving the deliberate distortion of a person's features for the purpose of mockery. It is said to have been introduced by the brothers Carracci

97

in Italy at the end of the 16th century.

caries. Tooth decay. The degree of decay of teeth of fossil men is often an important clue to the kind of food they ate, their general health, and related factors, and thus helps date them and their culture. Caries is a disease characterized by inorganic breakdown followed by organic disintegration of the tooth. In modern civilized cultures, the high incidence of caries is considered to be in direct proportion to the high degree of refined carbohydrates in the diet, although some research suggests that the caries are linked with the change from hard to soft foods, so that this would be an example of the effects of disuse on organs with mechanical functions. Australian aborigines and Maoris who had excellent teeth two generations ago now generally have the same high decay rate as the English, underlining the importance of change in diet in causing caries.

caritive. Referring to a syntactical classification used to designate verb forms in certain languages that have the same denotation as the English preposition *without.*

Carmel, Mount. The fossils found in the Mount Carmel caves date from the third interglacial period, probably before the early Upper Paleolithic era. The culture was probably Levallois-Mousterian. The skeleton is heavy, the neck short, the forearm bones straight and long. The head is more like that of an early Homo sapiens than Mousterian. It is possible that Homo sapiens and Neanderthal man cross-bred to produce hybrids like the Mount Carmel people.

carnelian. A red chalcedony (q.v.), widely used for seals. It is supposed to cure disease, embolden in battle, and protect against injury. Mohammed had a carnelian ring.

carnival. A community celebration which has been observed from the Middle Ages to the present, in Europe and the New World. Parades, floats, and noise making are often found. Carnivals used to begin at the start of spring and may be a relic of early ceremonies for celebrating the disappearance of winter and its harm to the crops.

carnivore. A meat eater.

carol. A song in English, usually tied in with Christmas celebrations. The carol may have originally been an accompaniment to a dance.

cartilage. A translucent elastic tissue that composes a good deal of the skeleton and embryo of vertebrates. It is converted to bone in the higher vertebrates. Cartilage in mammals lines the surfaces of joints and provides a resilient surface between moving bones. Cartilage is also called gristle.

cartomancy. Divination (q.v.) through the use of cards or playing cards. Gypsies traditionally use this technique.

cartonnage case. See CASE, CARTONNAGE.

cartouche. A scroll design; an ornament shaped like a scroll; a tablet with its edges rolled up. In Egyptian finds, the cartouche is an oblong device which carries the sovereign's name.

carucate. In Denmark and Norman measure, what could be filled by a caruca; plowland. It was 80 acres in two-field and 120 acres in three-field culture, excluding fallow land.

carvel. A ship built with the boards meeting flush at the seams. It originated in the Mediterranean area and was the only kind of boat built in the Greek and Roman era.

carving, Maori. A highly developed South Sea island art. Symbolic representations were carved in the fine-grained totara wood with a cutting tool made of the sharp nephrite greenstone. Most specimens were of objects in nature. Some large panels have fine examples of a complicated circular carving.

caryatid or **karyatid.** A tiptoeing dancer in early Greek times who performed at the feast for Artemis Karyatis and was the model for a kind of pillar. In the ancient feasts at Karyai she carried flower baskets on her head. The female figure used as an architectural column is also called a caryatid.

caschrom. See CASHCROM.

case, absolute. A grammatical designation for the noun which is the subject of a sentence but is grammatically isolated from the other sentence elements.

case, cartonnage. In ancient Egypt, a mummy case intended to cover the mummy wrappings. It was made of many layers of linen solidified with plaster. The cartonnage case was decorated like a coffin, with the head end bearing a likeness of the face. It was placed inside one or more other coffins.

case, brain. See CRANIUM.

case, common. The form of a word without inflection which is used in uninflected languages, either with or without prepositions, where inflectional languages would use various case forms.

cashcrom or **caschrom.** An angular digging stick with a footrest used for tilling the soil in Scotland and Ireland, where it has survived in much the same form from pre-Roman times. It has a very sharp point and is very thin.

cashirí. A native beer made in the Caribbean area and in the Tropical Forest of South America from masticated and boiled manioc. It is also called caxirí and cachirim.

cassareep. A sauce or paste made by boiling down juice extracted from manioc roots. It is used as a condiment in the pepper pot (q.v.) and is also an excellent meat preservative.

cassava. A plant of the genus Manihot, which has fleshy roots yielding a nutritious starch. The cassava juice has hydrocyanic acid, which cooking removes. Intoxicating drinks like cashirí can be prepared from it. It is widely distributed in the tropics, and it is also known as yuca or yucca, tapioca, and manihot. It probably originated in South America, long before Columbus.

casseta. A coffin made by placing stone slabs together in the ground.

casse-tête. A mace or a club.

cassiope. A white heather resinous plant which is perhaps the best arctic fuel. It is dry in winter and burns easily.

cassowary. A bone, used to make daggers in New Guinea.

cast, brain. A cast of the skull's interior. It gives an impression of the brain's size and shape. Brain casts of fossil skulls are made of plaster. Some fossils may have natural brain casts through the induration of the contents of the skull cavity.

cast, endocranial. A plaster cast of the interior of a skull.

castanets. Two similar wooden hollow clappers which a dancer snaps together between thumb and forefinger. Castanets help provide rhythm. They may be of Phoenician origin.

caste. An hierarchical system of social control in India, with each subgroup assigned a ranked status, depending on its origin and religious strictness. In Europe, a minority group with its own culture, such as the Gypsies. In the United States, a hereditary class status, the members of which are limited in residence, job, marriage, and economic possibilities.

In India, theoretically there are four castes: Brahmans, warriors, farmers and business men, and workers. When seven years old, members of the three top castes have a spiritual rebirth. In actuality, there are more than four castes, and Brahmans are not all priests. Pollution by leather and contact with the lowest group is a common religious idea, as is the idea that only persons of the same caste can eat together. Some foods are forbidden. Endogamy is the rule. Hereditary occupations for caste members are common.

caste, half. An individual born of parents each of whom came from a different racial group. See BLOOD, HALF.

castellation. A battlement or castle. The term is often used to describe a steplike design on the border of pottery.

Castle, Pink or **Castle, Montezuma's.** A high cliff dwelling in the Verde Valley of Arizona, called "pink" because it was burrowed out of red sandstone. The people that lived in this dwelling for 300 years were a tribe of farming Indians. The mummy of a baby excavated at the site in 1923 was wrapped in perfectly preserved cotton cloth, showing that cotton was cultivated and woven. The Indians also made pottery and mosaics.

casting. Shaping metal by pouring it while molten into forms. The early castings were probably in open sand molds and consisted of flat thick sheets. An ingot cavity carved in rock was the next likely development, and this led to the hollow mold. Lugs were used to help carry the molds. The original cast was open, with one side hammer-flattened. This led to the double mold and then the solid mold. Casts are also made of objects that cannot be moved away from their original location or that have perished but have left impressions in the earth where they lay. Molten bronze and plaster of Paris are widely used to fill molds in casting conducted in connection with archaeological research.

casting of the skin. See SKIN, CASTING OF THE.

Casuarina. A tree genus with no leaves and with drooping reed-like branches. Riesenfeld has attributed importance to these trees in connection with some megalithic (q.v.) rituals.

catacomb. A subterranean burial chamber. Many catacombs are near Rome. The greatest number were built by Christians during the second, third, and fourth centuries. Each consists of a maze of passages from three to four feet wide and six or more feet high. The walls were excavated to accommodate tiers of bodies which were sealed in with tiles or cemented slabs. There were sometimes as many as seven levels of passages, the estimated length of which came to several hundred miles. The Christian belief in the resurrection of the body made the current Roman practice of cremation untenable, and therefore the catacombs were publically recognized Christian cemeteries.

catadromous. Referring to fresh water fish, like the eel, which go down to the sea to spawn.

catafalque. A temporary construction used to exhibit the remains of prominent persons at funerals. It used to be a temporary construction over a tomb.

catamaran. A float or raft made of two pieces of wood tied together. The catamaran is propelled by sails or paddles. It is used in South America and in the West Indies and the East Indies. The term also applies to a vessel which has twin parallel hulls.

catapult. A device that hurls a missile by placing it in front of a bowstring which connects two bundles of stretched sinews. The catapult could send arrows and one-pound weights almost 1,000 feet. The first artillery is found in Roman catapults. Later catapults threw spears and flaming torches.

Catarrhini. Nostrils that are narrowly spaced and directed downward. The term also means the Old World monkeys, who have the same number of teeth as men and are diurnal and arboreal.

catastrophism. The belief that the earth's history consists of a series of great catastrophes. Cuvier publicized this doctrine, and Dean Buckland, in the early 19th century, used it to reconcile fossil deposits and the Bible. By assuming a number of special creations of life, it was possible to concede the comparative recency of man and yet avoid the heresy of deriving him from lower forms. See DILUVIUM.

catching, soul. The attempt to return a soul to the body of a living person, usually done by specialists.

catenary. Referring to a curve like that of a hung chain.

catlinite. A red pipestone of the upper Missouri region used by the Indians there for tobacco pipes, whence its name Indian pipestone.

catoptromancy. Divination (q.v.) practiced by the ancient Greeks in which images reflected in a mirror suspended in a fountain were observed.

catre. A platform bed used among Andean Indians and in areas influenced by Andean culture.

cat's-eye. A stone which has a touch of light across its dome when the cut is not faceted but convex. The cat's-eye was used to cure eye troubles and to protect the wearer against his enemies, witches, and the evil eye. It is found mainly in the Far East.

Caucasian. The language spoken in the Caucasian mountain area. Georgian is one of the few to be the vehicle for an early literature, in the fourth century A.D. There are some 300 Caucasian languages. This is a geographical rather than a linguistic rubric. The divisions are the North and South Caucasian families. About one million persons speak North Caucasian. South Caucasian, spoken by about 2 million, includes Georgian, Laz, Mingrelian, and Svanian.

Caucasiocentrism. See CENTRISM, CAUCASIO-.

Caucasoid. A racial group, also called Europoid, centering around the Mediterranean Sea. Some typical characteristics are light skin, medium to tall height, narrow to medium broad face, straight or wavy hair of fine to medium texture, considerable body hair, and eyes ranging from light blue to dark brown, with a nose likely to have a high bridge. This group includes the Dinaric, Nordic, Alpine, and Mediterranean subgroups. There is usually no facial protrusion and the blood group is usually higher in A than in B.

A generalized white race was probably the earliest Homo sapiens. This early form is likely to have had light brown skin and dark hair and dark eyes, with repeated mutations giving rise to depigmentation.

Caucasoid-Mongoloid. In Boas' classification, a basic human division.

caul. Part of the amnion, which may remain attached to a child at birth. It is sometimes considered good luck to be born with a caul.

causality, circular. A relationship between two factors such that they are mutually interacting, e.g., personality influences culture and culture influences personality.

cavate. An excavated cliff dwelling actually hewn out of a natural cliff, as differentiated from the masonry cliff houses which were built by the Pueblo Indians.

Cave, Fell's. A site in southern Chile, discovered by Bird, which contains artifacts and nonhuman bones that have been indirectly dated by the radiocarbon method as $8,639 \pm 450$ years old. The dating is derived from the radiocarbon dating of Pallaike Cave (q.v.), which is from the same cultural horizon and has the same kind of extinct fauna.

cave, Gypsum. An early American culture characterized by spearheads consisting of a short-stemmed long triangle. Fragments of shafts, butts, and tips of light spears are also found.

Cave, Pallaike. A site in southern Chile, discovered by Bird, which is the only New World site yielding extinct animal remains, artifacts, and associated human skeletal remains, all in stratigraphic association. It has been dated by the radiocarbon method as being $8,639 \pm 450$ years old.

cavesson. A metal noseband used to break horses and train them.

cavities, glenoid. The cavities in the base of the cranium into which the articular extremities of the lower jaw fit.

Cebidae. A family of the Platyrrhini (q.v.). Among the Cebidae are the only primates with grasping and prehensile tails. Species with such a tail include squirrel and capuchin monkeys. The members of this family have 54 chromosomes.

cedilla. A sign placed under a letter to indicate the proper sound to be used in pronunciation, e.g., *garçon.* The mark is also used to indicate nasalization of a vowel.

cell, germ. The reproductive cell that maintains its continuity regardless of the somatic cells. DeVries in 1900 advanced the theory that germ cells can mutate and create new species. See PLASMA, CONTINUITY OF THE GERM.

cell, sickle. See SICKLEMIA.

cella. The main interior space of a temple. It is usually surrounded on three sides by walls and occupies the entire width of the building.

celt. An ungrooved ax head made of a hard metal. This term is also used for an adze. The celt was mounted on a staff or shaft of wood or was attached by a thong to a handle.

celt, constricted. A tool that combines the features of a winged celt and a palstave (q.v.). It is characteristic of the Middle Bronze Age in Bohemia and Moravia, hence it is sometimes called a Bohemian palstave.

celt, flanged. A celt with ridges on the sides of either face. These ridges give greater longitudinal rigidity to the tool.

celt, flat. A metal celt which is almost flat on both faces and the sides of which are almost parallel. Flat celts were used in predynastic Egypt and in Crete, Spain, parts of Russia and elsewhere.

celt, petaloid. A type of highly polished celt made of very fine grained stone by the Taino Indians of the Greater Antilles.

celt, shoe-last. A polished adze or hoe arched on one face and flat on the other. The shoe-last celt is universally found in the early phases of Danubian culture.

celt, socketed. A celt which has a surface to engage the end of the shaft, largely eliminating side slip, and which does not require splitting the shaft end. The socketed celt was the predominant type in the Late Bronze Age.

celt, trunnion. A celt in which the shoulders have been turned into definite lugs which project on each side. The implement is sometimes called a lug adze.

celt, winged. A celt with flanges on each face widened in order to make wings that might be hammered around the shaft prongs on either face. The winged celt was found in parts of Italy and Germany.

Celtic. See KELTIC.

cementation. The binding of deposits by lime and similar materials.

cementum. On a tooth, material which surrounds the root and is very similar to bone.

cenotaph. An empty tomb for a person who is buried in another location.

cenotes. Sink holes or limestone wells in the Yucatan.

Cenozoic. Referring to the tertiary (q.v.) period in the geological development of the world, beginning some 58,000,000 years ago and including the Eocene, Oligocene, Miocene, and Pliocene periods. The term Kainozoic is sometimes used.

census. An official enumeration of the people of a governmental unit, together with the collection of appropriate statistics on the people. Egypt had a vital statistics system by 1250 B.C., and Roman citizens were required to report the birth of children within thirty days, by the sixth century B.C. The classical civilizations often required such records for revenue or military purposes, with the first civil registration systems found among the Incas of Peru, who kept thorough records by quipus (q.v.) because of their lack of a written alphabet.

Recording vital statistics was originally the concern of the clergy, who recorded baptisms, weddings, and burials, rather than births, marriages, and deaths. The recording of the clergy's payment for these ceremonies did not provide a thorough register. Japan had a system of registration of births, deaths, and marriages in 720 A.D. Europe's first systematic registration system was in Spain in the fifteenth century, when Cardinal Ximines introduced regular parish registers. Thomas Cromwell in 1538 in England required the clergy to keep records, with France establishing a similar system in 1539. In North America, Massachusetts had the first record of actual births and deaths and first (1639) made this a civil function.

centaur. A mythological creature, partly horse and partly man. Centaurs were noted for their warlike and amatory exploits, which are depicted in artistic representations through the centuries. In the 8th century B.C., the centaur is shown as a human being in front with the body and hind legs of a horse. As time progressed, he became a man to the waist only.

center, Broca's. The third frontal convolution in the brain's left hemisphere, presumably a center for controlling speech. In 1861, Broca demonstrated that damage to this area was related to aphasia.

center, culture. The place where a specific culture trait or culture complex is to be found in its most representative form.

centimeter. Ten millimeters.

centrism, Caucasio-. The doctrine of the white race's being the best equipped and most deserving of all racial groupings.

centrography. The statistical method employed to analyze geographical distributions.

centromere. The structure within the chromosome which attaches it to the spindle.

centrosome. The structure in animal cells which forms the head of the spermatozoa. It appears in animal cells at the spindle poles during cell division.

cephalic. Referring to the head.

cephalometry. That branch of somatometry (q.v.) which involves measuring the face and head.

cephalotaphy. Preserving or burying the head without the body.

ceramics. The art and science of making baked clay objects or the objects themselves. Since its invention, this art shows more comprehensively than any other, man's cultural development, as ceramics are fairly indestructible. See POTTERY.

ceramics, Arretine. Roman pottery made of fine red clay, decorated with bas-relief stamped on the outside and covered with a red glaze. The bowls were gracefully shaped and the designs were well spaced.

ceramics, band. See BANDKERAMIK.

ceramics, comparative. A technique of determining the chronology of ancient peoples by studying their ceramics.

ceramics, string. See SCHNURKERAMIK.

cerauniae. The name given to carved flints by the early Greeks and Romans. The name means lightning stones.

Cercopithecidae. A family of the Simians consisting of the two subfamilies of Cercopithecinae and Colobinae (qq.v.).

Cercopithecinae. A Simian (q.v.) subfamily that has cheek pouches, large buttock callosities, developed thumbs, and no stomach pouches. In this subfamily are black apes, talapoin monkeys, and macaques.

cereal. A grass the grain of which is consumed by humans. The major cereals are rye, barley, wheat, oats, rice, and maize. The cereals contain food which is fairly concentrated and dry, so that it can be stored, ground, and baked. They provide much of the human food supply.

cerebral. Referring to a form of coronal (q.v.) articulation in which the tip of the tongue articulates against the highest point of the palate.

cerebretonia. In Sheldon's typology, the sensitive and introverted personality. The cerebrotonic type is distinguished by restraint, inhibition, thoughtfulness, and quiet behavior. His is the temperament associated with ectomorphy (q.v.). See TYPES, CONSTITUTIONAL.

ceremony. A fixed or sanctioned pattern of behavior which surrounds various phases of life, often serving religious or aesthetic ends and confirming the group's celebration of a particular situation.

ceremony, animal-renewing. An increase rite which has as its objective the proliferation of a type of animal.

ceremony, building. An appropriate ceremonial at the construction of a new building.

ceremony, Morning Star. A Pawnee ceremony involving the sacrifice of a young maiden to the Morning Star, an important Pawnee deity.

ceremony, new fire. The Aztec ceremony of extinguishing the old altar fire which had burned for 52 years and kindling a fresh fire in recognition of new life. Runners lit torches from the new fire and rekindled the altars in the temples of many towns, and the residents in turn took fire to their hearths. Before lighting the new fire, the residents of the towns destroyed their clothing, implements, furniture, and ritual objects to symbolize the destruction of the old and the taking over of the new. Related ceremonies are found in other parts of the world.

ceremony, seasonal. A ceremony performed during a specific part of the year.

ceremony, turtle. A ceremony found in Mexico and the American Southwest, consisting of a fertility dance for warriors. The turtle is a symbol of fertility and the patron of childbirth. As part of this respect for the turtle, the umbilicus of a child was often carried about in a small ornament in the shape of a turtle.

cerography. Wax painting. The wax is used as a binder with the pigment and is heated with hot irons to make the colors flow and to fix them. The ancient Romans inscribed wax tablets with a stylus by this technique.

ceromancy. The art of divination (q.v.) by observing melted wax dropped on the floor. The shapes and sizes of the drops had a special significance.

cestrum. An ancient painter's tool. Pliny describes it as a pointed instrument which is used with wax.

cervix. The constriction of a tooth where the crown meets the root.

cestus. See KNUCKLEDUSTER.

chabbabeh. A flutelike musical instrument of ancient Persia. It has a mouthpiece, is about 12 inches long, and has 6 or more finger holes at the sides.

Chac. The Maya rain god.

chacmool. A sculptured semirecumbent human figure in the form of a bench, probably of ceremonial significance, found in Maya centers in Yucatan.

chacra. A plot of farm land in Peru.

Chagatai. An Oriental language of the Central Turkic group of the Altaic subfamily of the Ural-Altaic family of languages.

chain tale. See TALE, CHAIN.

chair, sedan. A closed litter (q.v.) used to transport and hide the face of noblemen in Babylon, and parts of the classical world.

Chaka. The last Zulu king to revolt against White dominion.

chalcedony. A translucent quartz gem, usually blue. Chalcedony has been used in seals and amulets and for good luck in Greece, Egypt, Palestine, and Western Europe. Chalcedony is a mineral which is deposited by siliceous solutions in hollow flint and the steam cavities of lava. It is called jasper when yellow and carnelian when red. The term also denotes a waxy, whitish flint.

Chalcolithic Age. See AGE, CHALCOLITHIC.

Chaldean. A designation which is often erroneously used for Biblical Aramaic (q.v.).

chamaeconch. An orbital index (q.v.) of less than 75.9.

chamaecranic. Referring to a cranial length-height index (q.v.) of less than 69.9.

chamaedont. Referring to teeth with fairly low crowns.

chamaeprosopic. Referring to a person with a short and broad face. The face, measured from the nose root to the bottom of the chin, as a percentage of the greatest facial breadth across the zygomatic arches, is not high. A living person with a facial index of less than 88 and a skull with a facial index of 90 is chamaeprospic.

chamaerrhine. Referring to a broad-nosed person; also, a nasal index (q.v.) between 51 and 57.9.

champlevé. Referring to ground which has been lowered or cut out. The term is used in reference to enameling.

Chancelade. A site near Periguex, France, where in 1888 some cultural remains of the Magdalenian period were found, along with a skeleton with Eskimolike characteristics that may be pre-Mongoloid.

change, ameliorative. A change in the denotation of a word that leads to an elevation in meaning.

change, analogic. The creation of a new word form which has the same relation to an existing form as prevails between an analogous form and its previously existing form. The change is usually made by analogy. Thus, the plural of *brother* used to be *brethren*, but by analogy with *sister* and its plural *sisters*, it changed to *brothers*.

change, culture. Changes in a culture may include acculturation, assimilation, and diffusion (qq.v.). The field of cultural dynamics usually involves the study of the time dimension of culture. The early 19th century studies of culture change emphasized the evolutionary approach. By the turn of the 20th century, the diffusionist approach was predominant. By the 1920's, the functional emphasis became predominant, and the 1930's saw the use of the configuration and psychodynamic emphases in culture change.

change, evolutionary. A definite and continuous process of adaptation, with an increase in differentiation to accompany changes in function.

change, linguistic. A change in language which may be the result of internal or external processes. The internal changes may result from sound change, analogy, semantic change, and creation. Sound change is usually a regular process, although certain conditions will result in irregularity. Analogy is the process by which a given pattern is extended to similar cases so that the older forms are replaced by newer and more regular forms. Analogy is a continuing process in language and is usually retarded by written language. Semantic change is a change in meaning. Creation involves making new forms or new morphemes (q.v.). Creation usually conforms to the pre-existing phoneme (q.v.) patterns. It may give rise to a new combination not previously found. External change often takes place through borrowing, which arises from culture contact with other peoples. New forms appear on the basis of what already exists in the language.

change, name. Procedures and regulations for changing personal

107

names vary from society to society. Among the Tikopia, for example, both partners to a marriage take a new name. An individual's name may indicate his standing in the society. Some societies do not regard it as important to have a name indicate a person's sex. There are nonliterate groups where the name memoralizes important events.

change, pejorative. A change in the meaning of a word, so that an originally exalted meaning gives way to a more contemptible connotation.

change, phonetic. A change in the representation or articulation of a word as the result of a change in speech habits, usually independent of its semantic content. Carefully expressed statements of phonetic change seem to be very regular.

change, semantic. A change in the meaning of a word through its being analogized to respond to a new situation.

change, sound. Any change in a particular speech sound, whether it is inherent in its character or caused by its surrounding elements.

change, substratum sound. See SOUND CHANGE, SUBSTRATUM THEORY OF.

change, symbolic. See GRADATION, VOWEL.

changeling. A child who is in some way defective, born of gnomes, witches, or fairies, who substitute him for a normal child stolen before baptism or other ceremonies. This reflects the ancient belief that infants are vulnerable until certain rites take place. A changeling can be disposed of by making it laugh.

channelled ware. See WARE, CHANNELLED.

chant. A monophonic type of singing or reciting in free rhythm. Many cultures use chants for sacred rituals or other important occasions.

chaomancy. The art of divination (q.v.) by the observation of atmospheric changes.

chapap. A pit in the floor of an American Indian ceremonial chamber.

chaparral. Vegetation largely consisting of shrubs with broad, small, evergreen leaves, usually found in Mediterranean areas.

chape. A bronze device in which rapier and sword sheaths terminated. Some chapes were looped, some were winged, and some were diamond-shaped. The chape protects the point of a sword sheath.

chaplet. A wreath worn on the head. It is usually of flowers and is usually worn on ceremonial or special occasions.

character, acquired. A modification in an organism caused by environmental factors and not inheritable. In 1809, Lamarck suggested that adaptive behavior led to inheritable alterations. Darwin (1859) and Weisman (1892) disputed this view. See PLASMA, CONTINUITY OF THE GERM.

characterization, area of. An area in which a particular societal group develops its identifying attributes. The term area of characterization is often used to indicate the area in which a race develops as a result of adaptational processes. It is also used to describe a culture area (q.v.).

chariot. Perhaps the earliest known vehicle, usually with a round wood front and a small platform behind and drawn by two or four horses. The chariots used by the Romans and Persians had two spoked wheels which rested without springs upon an axle.

charisma. The authority or power to change custom, law, etc., by virtue of position and attributes, as of a king or messiah; the qualities of leadership which inspire unquestioning adherence in the leader's followers.

charivari. A French medieval wedding celebration, which became a kind of public expression of disapproval at an unpopular wedding through noise making and violence. Charivaris were finally prohibited by the Church.

charm. Behavior or a verbal formula which can bring about harm or good. A charm is often seen as a small object which can be carried on the person. It also includes spells and incantations (qq.v.). A charm which carries good fortune is a talisman (q.v.), while a charm which has a protective function is an amulet (q.v.). Charms have been made of all kinds of objects, for a variety of reasons. Color, rarity, shape, and other associations may lead to the selection of a charm. Artificial charms are often made by a professional magician in early society. Charms are almost universal.

charpoy. A cot or bedstead in India.

charqui. A Quechua word for thin strips of meat, especially beef, that have been dried in the sun or over a fire. "Jerked" beef is a corruption of this word.

chasing. Metal embossing. This technique can only be used on a hard alloy, since the engraving tool will cut too deeply into a softer metal and leave ridges on the sides of the grooves which cannot be removed without scratching the adjacent surfaces. Chasing was invented by the ancient Greeks and was used in the ornamentation of armor.

chasqui. Professional messengers in Inca Peru who were sheltered in special hut stations at intervals along the roads. By running in relays, they could cover up to 150 miles in a day.

chastity. Sexual purity in a woman for biological, religious, economic, or proprietary reasons. See TEST, CHASTITY.

Châtelperron. See POINT, CHÂTELPERRON.

chattas. Ceremonial umbrellas of ancient India which were attached to the central post of a memorial tomb.

chattel. An object of personal ownership.

chatty. A Hindu household pot used for holding liquids.

chatzozerah. The biblical silver trumpet used by the Hebrews in battle and ceremony. Moses was instructed to make these trumpets from a single piece of silver. Josephus described them as being under one cubit long, with an oblong blowing end and a bell at the far end.

Chavín. An Andean culture with stone masonry platforms, symbolic

109

art, and a strong religious cult. It dates from approximately the first century A.D.

checkerwork. A form of plaited basketry in which each element of the woof set alternately crosses under and over each element of the warp.

cheese-making. In cheese-making, curds (q.v.) are treated with rennet and other substances, exposed to certain temperatures, and ripened to make a more edible food.

cheilion. The most lateral point on the corner of the lips.

cheironomy. The association of parts of the hand with specific musical notes, so that a melody could be carried or conveyed merely by indicating a particular part of the hand.

Chellean. See ABBEVILLIAN.

Ch'eng-tzu-yai. See POTTERY, BLACK.

Cheremiss. The language of about 375,000 persons in Asiatic Russia. It is a Finno-Ugric language considered by some linguists to be a member of a Lapponic group, including Lapp, Cheremiss, and Mordvin.

cherkesska. A male saber dance, found in the northern Caucasus.

chernozem. A type of soil in which the lower layers have living elements. It is fertile and particularly suited for the growth of grains. The spelling tchernozem is also found.

chert. An impure kind of flint (q.v.). Chert is siliceous, but is coarse and not texturally as homogenous as the pure flint. It is usually brown or gray-black and is found in carboniferous limestone.

Chert is often used as a flint substitute.

Cheruma. The rice-cultivation slave caste of Cochin.

chess. A game in which the players move pieces alternately on a board until the king of one player cannot escape. Chess has been attributed to some 14 different ethnic groups, although most scholars think India was its birthplace. It probably passed through Persia to Europe. Its name is from Old French, from the Hindu *chaturanga,* which refers to the components of an army: horses, elephants, chariots, and infantry. Its relation to warfare is seen in the Buddhist story that Buddhists invented it instead of war, which they abhor. There is no element of chance in a game of chess and skill is the determinant of victory. Chess is played all over the world.

chest, sepulchral. A case for holding the canopic jars in the Egyptian mummification process. The canopic jars contained the organs removed from the corpse before the embalming process. The chest had four wooden dividers and reposed in the tomb with the mummy.

chester. A town surrounded by a wall.

chesting. Placing a body in a coffin, in early English speech.

cheval trap. See CALTHROP.

Chibcha. A group of languages in central America and a culture in Colombia.

chicha. A native American beer made from maize, usually by chewing the kernels and spitting them into a container with water, the saliva serving to promote fermentation. Chicha is made from Mexico to Bolivia.

chief. A leader in a social organization on a low technological level. Sometimes the chief's position is inherited. A chief may have eloquence, skill as a warrior, religious qualities, and other desirable traits.

chief, dual. A chief who has an associate of equal status. Often this involves a peace chief who handles civil concerns and a war chief who is more temporary and in charge only during war time, as among some North American Indians. Thus, the Cherokee peace chief is a hereditary office, while the war chief is elective. In East Africa, dual chieftainships are also widely found, and they occur also in Alaska, the Torres Straits, and New Guinea. The peace chief usually stands for the group's continuity in most of these societies.

chief, investiture of the. A chief's formal induction into office, often involving appropriate rites. Special objects, such as regalia or insignia, may be necessary before a chief can reign.

chief, peace. A chief who primarily concerns himself with directing civil affairs. See CHIEF, DUAL.

chief, talking. A representative of the chief who publicly addresses the people in those societies in which the chief does not himself speak publicly. In Polynesia, the talking chief is a tribal official who knows the genealogy of everyone in his village and the history of the tribe and relates this information during ceremonies and to visitors. The talking chief handles much of the religious activity of the tribe because the priest-king is so often surrounded by taboos that force him into inactivity. In consequence of this substitutive role, the talking chief is sometimes called a spokesman.

chief, war. A village, tribal, or confederacy leader, skilled in military exploits, who takes command in time of war but is subordinate to the regular or peace chief (q.v.) in civil matters.

child, fatal. A child whose fate was seen at birth to hurt or kill his parents or an official. Like Oedipus, these youngsters were usually exposed to die but survived and consummated the childhood prophecy.

childbed, men's. See COUVADE.

ch'i-lin. One of the most frequently represented mythical creatures in Chinese art. It has a scaly antelope body, a bushy tail, and a head like that of a dragon. The ch'i-lin has long been regarded as a very wise creature which portends well for the future.

chilkat. A goat's hair and cedar bark blanket made by the western Canadian Indians. Chilkats are highly decorative and of the highest artistic quality. They were first made on the Queen Charlotte Islands and developed by the Chilkat mainland tribe.

chilwa. A musical instrument which is intermediate between the ugubu and the goura (qq.v.). The chilwa consists of a bent stick and a split cane chord. It is found among the Tchivokué.

chimerat. The Swedish folklorist von Sydow proposed this term to designate the kind of tale usually called fairy tale or märchen.

chimpanzee. An anthropoid which is perhaps the ape closest to man. The chimpanzees spend much time on the ground, but they also practice brachiation (q.v.). The average weight is about 110 pounds and the average height less than five feet. A chimpanzee is built like an undersized human being.

chin. Among the Chinese, signs of the extraordinary in natural objects.

ch'in. Symbolic ancient Chinese musical instrument. There are five strings representing the five known elements of the time, the round upper section representing the heavens and the flat bottom the earth. The strings are stretched over a bridge and fastened to pegs at one end. Since performance on the ch'in requires considerable skill and rigorous training, it is sometimes known as the scholar's lute.

China, Great Wall of. The tremendous structure for the defense of China, designed as a deterrent to invading northern tribes. Construction was begun by Emperor Tsin Chi-Hwang-Ti in 214 B.C. and was substantially completed in 204 B.C. A great deal of work on the Wall was done as recently as the fourteenth century. It averaged 22 feet high and 20 feet thick. Running between China and Mongolia, the Great Wall was approximately 1500 miles long and has been called the world's largest defensive work.

chinampa. One of the artificial islands built by the Aztecs in Lake Texcoco to provide additional agricultural land. It was made by scooping up mud from the bottom of the shallow lake and throwing it into areas enclosed by wattle work. The present "floating" gardens of Xochimilco are examples of chinampas still in use.

chindi. A Navajo evil spirit inhabiting the bodies of the dead.

Chinese. The subfamily of the Sino-Tibetan family of languages which is made up of Wen-li, the classical literary language of China, Kuo-yü, the new "National Tongue," and a great number of Chinese dialects and vernaculars. It is spoken by nearly 600,000,000 persons. Chief among the Chinese vernaculars are North Mandarin (Peiping region), which provides the foundation of Kuo-yü; Wu, appearing around the Yangtze Delta as the language of approximately 40,000,000; Cantonese, or Yueh, spoken by about 30,000,000; and Min, spoken in the province of Fukien by about 30,000,000.

Ch'ing. The Ch'ing dynasty in China (A.D. 1644-1912) was one in which blue and white porcelain and monochrome glazed porcelain were perfected (K'ang Hsi reign, (1662-1722). The Yung Cheng reign (1723-1735) was famous for its egg-shell porcelain. The Ch'ien Lung reign (1736-1795) saw the development of fine monochromes and transmutation glazes, and the Chia Ch'ing, and Tao Kuang reigns (1796-1850) saw graviata ware and some fine monochromes.

Chinoi. Flower spirits among the Semang.

Chinook Jargon. A vernacular, used by the natives of Oregon, which is a mixture of French, English, and Indian dialects.

chip, buffalo. A piece of dried dung of the American bison, used as fuel by Indians.

chipping, stone. Shaping stones by chipping them. In the anvil method, the stone is struck on a fixed stone and held in the hand. In the hammer method, the stone is held by the feet or hands, or by wood or fiber strips, or buried in the ground; it splits differently according to the manner in which the stroke is cushioned. The bipolar technique consists of holding the stone on another stone, thus combining the hammer and anvil methods and giving rise to bulbs of percussion (q.v.).

chiripa. A loin cloth in South America.

chisel. A celtlike tool with a narrow blade. Also a Mousterian flint tool in which a small section of the flake's edge is separated from the rest by small semicircular chips on each side. The cutting part is made in a thin edge, so that its cutting line lies parallel to the flake's plane. The term ciseau is sometimes used for chisel.

chisel, engraver. A chisel in which the cutting section is in a thick edge of the flake, so that the section's cutting line is at right angles or is oblique to the plane of the flake. The engraver chisel is sometimes called the burin-ciseau.

chita. A Mexican carrying net.

chitemene. A method of agriculture, found in Northern Rhodesia, which involves cutting down trees in an area which is larger than the area to be cultivated. The branches are cut and burned, destroying weeds and leaving ashes which absorb the seed. Kaffir corn and finger millet are the major crops. The land is worked for a few years and then abandoned.

chiton. A woolen, cotton, or linen garment worn by all Greek men and women. It was a simply designed oblong piece of fabric which was wrapped around the body, fastened at the shoulder, and belted. Variations were achieved with different colored fabrics, rich brooches and pins, and contrasting belts and borders.

Chokata. The guardian of the calendar in old Japanese culture.

Cholula. An archaeological site north of Puebla, Mexico, which was an important religious center. The Teotihuacan-Toltec defeated the original inhabitants and converted the many temples into a single platform to honor Quetzalcoatl.

chopper. A circular flint disk which is trimmed like a coup-de-poing (q.v.), of which it is probably a variation, dating from Acheulean times. The chopper is made from modules of flint or other appropriate material, part of the circumference of which is flaked into a sharp working edge. See AX, KITCHEN MIDDEN. The term chopper is often used generically to describe a class of tool, like an ax, which has a cutting edge but is heavier than a knife. These tools are used by hitting a chopper against the object to be cut.

Chordata. See VERTEBRATES, PHYLUM.

chordophone. A musical instrument in which the sound is produced by stretched string, e.g., the musical bow.

chorion. A fetal membrane which is outside the amnion (q.v.). It comes out along with the afterbirth.

chorography. The study of fairly large regions.

chorten. A Tibetan monument in memory of a lama or saint. It may contain sacred relics, like the ashes of dead lamas. Important persons have their own chorten, while an ordinary person's remains are thrown into an old chorten. A chorten's five parts stand for the elements: fire, water, earth, air, and ether. They are usually made of dried mud. Devout Tibetans pass chortens on the left.

chorus, cyclic. A group of 50 dancers who sang and danced in a circle around the altar of the god Dionysus in ancient Greece. They performed mythological tableaus.

Choshiu. A slender Japanese.

chott. The bed of a former lake in a desert.

Chou. Referring to archaic unglazed pottery of the Chou dynasty in China, ca. 1122-249 B.C. This period had triggered crossbows, coins, iron, and perhaps steel swords.

chreia. An old gnomic writing, originally a cryptic saying created by one writer and borrowed by another. It is now used for an apposite remark used for literary embroidery.

Christian, Rice. A Chinese who pretended to be converted to Christianity in order to be fed.

Christy, Henry (1810-1865). An English archaeologist and banker, who financed Lartet (q.v.). He collaborated with Lartet in 1864 on a famous paper on Paleolithic art.

chromatid. A split chromosome.

chromatin. The material in a chromosome which is in an area stained by certain dyes.

chromomere. The smallest part that can be morphologically distinguished in a chromosome.

chromosome. The 24 tiny filaments in the human egg and sperm which carry and transmit hereditary potentialities, so that the fertilized egg has 48 chromosomes. Each chromosome consists of genes (q.v.). The chromosome is string-shaped.

chronology, absolute. Dating an object in terms of years, through the study of gravel or other deposits in which it is found, especially by the study of radioactive minerals in igneous rocks.

chronology, relative. Dating archaeological finds relatively to each other, even though the age in terms of years is not known.

chrotta. See CRWTH.

chryselephantine. Referring to ivory and gold used in the construction of the magnificent cult statues of the early Greek. Some statuettes using the technique have been found in Egypt and Mesopotamia, pointing to the Oriental origin of the technique. The best known examples of the tremendous Greek statues were the Athena and Zeus by Phidias, the Asklepios by Calamis, and the Dionysus by Alcamenes. The term is sometimes used for statues made of a framework of metal and wood, with ivory and gold incrustations.

Chthonion. Referring to the underworld, especially to the gods of the underworld. The Chthonic deities were worshipped in Greek religion. These deities may have been ancestral spirits, who stand for ghosts of the deceased. The symbol of the snake is found in both Chthonic deities and ancestral spirits. A number of the gods of Olympus had a Chthonic counterpart, who was often greatly feared.

Chukchee. A language and culture among the Paleoasiatics of the Chukchee Peninsula in eastern Siberia.

chultun. An artificial cistern of Yucatan.

chumbo. An Arab fanatic who will devour a live sheep.

chunkey. A form of the hoop-and-pole game (q.v.) played by the Indians of the southeastern United States with a stone disk and a stick with a crook at one end. Also the stone disks when found archeologically.

chuño. A flour made by dehydrating frozen potatoes. This was a staple food in the highlands of pre-Columbian Peru.

churinga. Sacred flat pieces of stone or wood at central Australian totem centers. One is prepared for each person on birth, so that each native has one for his soul. The churinga is believed to have some of the person's soul, and thus they are kept by the survivors even after death to be used in ceremonies. They are often taboo to women and children. The name derives from

the Arunta word for sacred. The pieces of wood or stone used were usually elliptical, with incised symbols. The spelling tjurunga is also found.

churn dasher. See DASHER, CHURN.

chymotrichous. Referring to the possession of wavy hair.

cibobe. See SIPAPU.

cicada. An arrow or spear point shaped like a cicada.

cicatrix. The tissue that develops at a wound and helps to complete healing by contracting and forming a scar. **Cicatrization** is the deliberate scarring of the body in order to make it more beautiful. Sometimes battle scars are regarded highly; a holdover from this belief is found in the prized duelling scars of students at German universities.

cicisbeism. Permitting a married woman to have a lover.

Cihuacoatl. An Aztec goddess of fertility and death, also called the Snake Woman.

Cilician. A language of the Near East, now extinct, which has no traceable linguistic origins.

cincel. A South American Indian stone chisel. The cincel was used for carving and making inscriptions.

cingulum. A swelling on the incisor teeth at the upper portion near the fusion of the crown and root.

Cippi of Horns. Small Egyptian tablets with magic formulae.

circ. A prehistoric stone circle.

Circassian. A language, originally from the Caucasus, which has moved with the people who spoke it to Asia Minor and Syria. It belongs to the Adyghe group of the North Caucasian family.

circle. A circle or a series of concentric circles of standing stones. There may be an avenue of approach and a central stone.

circle, camp. A tribal circle formed by the components of an Indian tribe, often used while hunting buffalo. When there were concentric circles, each circle stood for a separate political or kin group. A subgroup might have a given place in the circle. The camp circle is associated with the Plains Indians.

circle, culture. In the usage of the Kulterkreis (q.v.) school, a culture complex (q.v.) which comprises the major categories of human activity, including social, aesthetic, ethical, economic, political, and religious.

circle, fairy. An increase in the intensity of the green color of a circular area of a field or grass caused by a fungus growth. These circles are not to be disturbed since fairies are supposed to dance in them.

circle, home. The kin group.

circle, hut. A ring of large stones mixed with smaller stones. The hut circle may be covered by a bank of earth or be overgrown by grass. There is an entrance gap in the ring. The ring represents what is left of a low wall on which there was a roof.

circle, magic. A circle drawn around a person as a kind of supernatural defense. The magic circle probably stems from the early practice of using a circle of fire as a defense against the dark. Thus rings and bracelets and similar circular objects have at various times had a special value. Pebbles, thorns, fire, and water are among the materials that have been used to mark the circle. A black magician, when calling up spirits, usually stands inside a circle of this type for safety.

circular tale. See TALE, ENDLESS.

circumambulation. Ceremonially walking around an object, often while the right hand points to it. This is done for such magical or religious reasons as to obtain good luck, cure disease, give protection, consecrate a site, and identify with a sacred person or object. The object is often circumambulated three times, and the walk may be made in the direction of the sun to connote respect and loyalty. When done in the opposite direction, disrespect is indicated. Circumambulation was found with special frequency among the Celts, Hindus, and Greco-Romans, but it is almost universal.

circumcision. Removal of the foreskin in the male, or the clitoris or labia minora in the female. Circumcision probably originated in Chaldea. It is known to have existed in Egypt in the fourth millennium B.C. The early followers of Christ insisted on circumcision as a prerequisite for conversion but this was resisted by some potential converts, and Paul and Barnabas began accepting converts who were not circumcised, so that after approximately 50 A.D. pagans could be converted without being circumcised.

The removal may be partial

116

or complete. As a kind of initiation, circumcision is widely distributed throughout the world. It usually takes place before or during puberty, or at any time from a few days after birth to shortly before marriage. Special persons may perform the task. Among the theories which have been advanced to explain circumcision are that it is a sacrifice, a measure of pain tolerance, a marriage preparation, a consecration of the genitalia, a symbolic recognition of the dangers of sexual intercourse, a hygienic measure, a symbolic castration, and a sacrifice redeeming the male from the god who gave him life. No one of these theories is generally accepted. The Hebrews, Egyptians, Mohammedans, and various American Indian groups were among those practicing circumcision. Many early societies kept it confined to specific class or status groups. It has been estimated that about one-seventh of all males are circumcised.

circumflex accent. See ACCENT, CIRCUMFLEX.

circus. An ancient Roman arena for public entertainment. Events in the circus included chariot races, athletic games, battles between gladiators, mass executions, aquatic spectacles and wild beast hunts.

cire perdue. See TECHNIQUE, LOST WAX.

cirque. A kind of amphitheater along the mountain crest at the head of a valley. A cirque is caused by glaciation.

ciseau. See CHISEL.

cist. A kind of Neolithic burial; a burial chest or early coffin; a tomb made of upright stone slabs with a cover stone or stones. The terms coffre en pierre, kist, and kistvaen are sometimes used.

cist, stone. A dolmen (q.v.) of grave size.

cithara. See KITHARA.

city. A large urban community. The first city was probably Uruk, a Sumerian settlement founded ca. 3,500 B.C. in Mesopotamia. Cities maintain themselves by exchanging goods and services for raw material and foodstuffs. They require good transportation for ingress and egress. Chinese cities originated ca. 2,000 B.C. and European cities ca. 850 B.C.

city, petrified. The Upper Egyptian city of Ishmonie, so called because of the legend that the numerous sculptures there were once living beings who were transformed into stone by a miracle.

city-state. An autonomous state, consisting of a city and its outskirts. Usually there is a well-defined distinction between a peasant and a bourgeois class, as in Phoenecia or Greece.

civilization. A degree of fairly advanced culture, in which the arts and sciences, as well as political life, are well developed. V. Gordon Childe sees the essential characteristics of civilization as internal social hierarchies, specialization, cities and large populations, and the growth of mathematics and writing.

civilization, coldward march of. The doctrine that civilization and technique flourish in colder cli-

117

mates, which presumably incite a higher energy level and have more storable foods than warmer climates.

Clactonian. Referring to Lower Paleolithic technological areas in northwest Europe. Clactonian industries are found in the same deposits as the coup-de-poing (q.v.). They are probably contemporary with Chellean and Lower Acheulian times. Flake tools, rough scrapers, and disks are found.

clamp. A device to bind things together or to wedge adjacent parts against other elements of a unit.

clan. A matrilineal sib (q.v.); or a unilateral kin-group, often exogamous. Membership in a clan hinges on kinship through one parent. A clan should provide mutual security, legal help, government, marriage regulation through exogamy and economic institutions, religion, and ceremonies, property regulation, social control, and role allotment.

Murdock has suggested that the essential similarity between clan and gens (q.v.) should lead to clan being used only for a kin group which hinges on both a rule of descent and of residence—this he calls a compromise kin group. His criteria for a clan are its basis in unilinear descent, residential unity, and genuine social integration.

In most contexts, a clan is a unilineal group of relatives often living in one locality though sometimes multilocal and with common property. The members of the clan trace stipulated descent from their original ancestor, who may exist only in the mythological past and is perhaps neither animal nor human but a spirit or a landscape feature. It differs from a lineage (q.v.), which traces descent by demonstration from a human ancestor, and it often tends to be an overgrown lineage.

clan, complex. A clan stratified internally on the basis of the person's degree of closeness to the original ancestor, which establishes the access to clan benefits. The term geneological clan is sometimes used for complex clan.

clan, equalitarian. A clan in which all the members can have an equal opportunity to enjoy its benefits. In the equalitarian clan, the individual adopts the clan's name and takes part in all its activities.

clan, geneological. See CLAN, COMPLEX.

clappers. A musical instrument consisting of two like objects that are struck against each other. A pair of clappers is rattled or struck rhythmically, usually when held between the performer's fingers. The term cliquette is sometimes used.

clappers, spring. Clappers that have two parts connected at one end, so that the free ends strike each other.

clarin. See ACOCOTL.

class. A group within a society distinguished by its social and economic level from other groups. Such characteristics as age, occupation, and nativity have been used to differentiate classes. In the contemporary sense of the word, classes are not common in early communities, and the classes which do exist are very static; rich persons in early society, e.g., are rich usually because their hereditary status brings riches with it. Usually, a man in early society lives and dies in the same class. Most early societies use age as a stratification criterion rather than wealth.

class, age. See SET, AGE.

class, form. The totality of the language forms that can functionally perform a position.

class, marriage. One of a number of social divisions operated to regulate marriage found in many native tribes of Australia. Members of one marriage class may marry those of only one other class. Membership in such a class is determined by double descent (q.v.). Marriage classes are called sections when there are four and subsections when there are eight.

class, word. A syntactical form class, e.g., a substantive.

classicism. The qualities of restraint, simplicity, dignity, serenity, repose, and perfection of form, particularly in art. Classicism is thus the totality of traits supposedly characterising the art of Greek and Roman antiquity at their apogee.

classificatory. See SYSTEM, CLASSIFICATORY; TERM, CLASSIFICATORY.

classifier. See DETERMINANT.

clavicle. The collar bone.

claviform. Referring to having a clublike shape. The word claviform is also used of the upright bars with a small side projection found in early art.

clay. A plastic colloidal secondary material deriving from decomposition of certain primary rocks. The major ingredient of clay is hydrated aluminum silicate, along with a number of natural impurities, like alkalies, iron compounds, calcium carbonate, humus, quartz sand, and water. The water is either mechanically mixed or chemically combined.

clay, bolus. See KAOLIN.

clay, boulder. A compact and hard soil which resembles dried and tightly compressed mud. Boulder clay comes from the surface of the mountains and rocks over which glaciers passed. The material was reduced to mud and left along the glaciers' paths. Boulder clay consists of unstratified tough clays, with angular lumps of flint and other fragments.

clay, china. Kaolin (q.v.), or decomposed granite rock, an ingredient of fine porcelains.

clay, potter's. Clay used in pottery. Potter's clay is made up of aluminum oxide and silica.

clazomene. A seventh-century type of Ionian vase decorated with pictures of the riotous revels of many satyrs. The borders and backgrounds are animals, birds, and much foliate ornamentation. The Ionian eye appears—as it does on all Ionian pottery—to ward off the ever-present evil spirits.

cleaver. A coup-de-poing (q.v.) ending in a broad cutting edge formed by the intersection of two flake scars that incline to each other at a small angle.

clepsydra. An ancient forerunner of the clock, used by the Greeks and Romans to measure time. The clepsydra measured the controlled flow

119

of mercury, water, or other liquids through a narrow opening.

cleromancy. The art of divination (q.v.), through observing pebble shapes when thrown on a flat surface.

click. A sound made by sucking in or interfering with outgoing breath, common in the Khoisan and Bantu languages.

click, labial. A sound made by the larynx being lowered when the glottis is closed. The labial click is found in the Khoisan and Bantu languages.

cliff dwelling. See DWELLING, CLIFF.

cliffhouse. A cliff dwelling made of masonry. Cliffhouses are found among extant and extinct Pueblo tribes.

climate, continental. A climate which has large extremes. Continental climates are found in extensive land areas.

climate, glacial. A climate in which the average temperature is below freezing every month.

climate, social. Folkways, mores, and other patterns of living that may be difficult to measure objectively but that constitute the social background of living in a culture.

climax, culture. The point of maximum intensity of a culture, e.g., the Northwest coast of North America.

clincker or clinker. A craft used for fishing, dating from Viking times. The clincker is made by having the upper edge of each plank in the sides overlapped by the lower edge of the plank above.

cliquette. See CLAPPERS.

clitoridectomy. The operation in which the clitoris is removed, practiced particularly by Nilotic Negroes.

clock. The most common of all machines, a device for telling time. In 1370, one of the first perfected clocks was produced, by De Vick in Paris. Earlier, in 1345, the sexagesimal system had been introduced. Derek Price has reported Chinese documents which describe a 30-foot clock tower built in 1088, which had gongs sounding every quarter hour as well as an escapement-like mechanism for regulating the water wheel which powered it. Price has suggested that the medieval "planetary computer" and the Chinese clock tower may be traced through Islam to Greece, on the basis of a 2,000 year old "clock-machine" which was found between Greece and Crete at the turn of the century. The major parts of a clock are concerned with creating and transmitting power and regulating the clock's speed. The study of clock development is a valuable clue to the level of technology of a culture.

clock, shadow. An early type of clock that tells time by shadows. The shadow clock is T-shaped. It is put in an east-west direction at sunrise, with the higher and vertical crosspiece eastward to the sun, so that the crosspiece throws a shortening morning shadow along the base, which is graduated into "hours." The clock was turned around at noon, with the lengthening shadow of the afternoon then falling along the long part of the T.

The Egyptians used the shadow clock.

clock, water. A clock consisting of a vessel with water that escapes drop by drop from a small hole near the bottom. The inside of the vessel is graduated into divisions roughly like hours, and hence the water level is the indicator. A conical shape was often used to insure a steady flow. Later water clocks became fairly complicated, with wheels and pinions.

cloisonné. A type of ceramic decoration which involves incising the surface and filling the incised portions with paint or other kinds of inlay.

clone. A group of organisms that stem from a common ancestor through mitotic divisions without rearrangements of the chromosomes (q.v.).

closure. In linguistics, the process by which a stream of air is blocked by one or more organs of speech. The sound that results from closure is an occlusive or stop (q.v.) sound.

cloth, bark. Cloth made from the spongy bark of some trees through felting (q.v.). Bark cloth is made by removing the bark, scraping it, and then pounding it thin. The bark is often soaked in water. See TAPA.

cloth, Kasai. Plaited raffia fiber cloth of the southwest Congo.

cloth, mummy. Winding strips of linen from 3 to 5 inches wide and 3 to 13 feet long. For the most part, the Egyptian mummy cloths were not decorated, but in the later Greek (Ptolemaic) period, ornamentation and colors were used.

The terms mak, nu, and mennui are sometimes used.

clothing, anatomic. A type of garment that is fairly close fitting. Anatomic clothing often consists of an upper garment and trousers or skirt. It is roughly equivalent to tailored clothing.

clothing, gravitational. A type of garment that is loose and flowing and derives its shape from the fabric's natural fall. It may consist of a loose jacket and flowing trousers or skirt or a single garment, such as a sari or a toga.

clout, breech. A garment made of skin or cloth. The breech clout is connected to a belt before and behind and goes between the legs.

clown. A person who engages in ridicule and aggressive behavior or simple-minded language. Clowns may be identified with natural forces, the dead, or supernatural elements. Clown analogues are found in many parts of the world. The clown may have magical qualities and enjoy great liberty in ridiculing superiors. Their behavior is often contrary; e.g., they will talk if ordered to be silent. They often wear special masks or costumes, which may represent the forces with which they are presumed to be connected. Clowns are found in many North American Indian ceremonies and were often organized into societies.

club. A pointed or knobbed stick, often used as a weapon.

club, ball-headed. A round-headed war club used by the Iroquois and some other Indian groups.

club, bat. A type of long slender weapon resembling a bat, used in parts of Oceania and South America.

club, comeback. See BOOMERANG.

club, morning-star. A starshaped club found in some Pacific areas.

club, sword. A club in the form of a sword, as among the Fijians.

club, throwing. A club with a large head and a small straight shaft. The throwing club generally goes to its target end over end.

clubfoot. A foot deformity in which the foot is twisted out of shape or out of position, or both. Some Egyptian mummies show clubfoot.

cluricaune. A wrinkled old elf of Irish folklore. The cluricaune is a shoemaker to the fairies by trade and has a tendency to play tricks, but he knows the whereabouts of buried treasures. He has become the leprechaun of modern literature.

coa. A digging stick found in Mesoamerica (qq.v.).

coaction. The interaction of plants and animals or of organisms generally.

coaming. A raised frame around an opening on a house or ship. The coaming prevents water from running into the opening.

coarticulation. The simultaneous action of two or more articulators.

coca. A shrub that has cocaine in its leaves, which are chewed by some South American Indians as a stimulant.

coccyx. Man's hidden tail, consisting of the four last caudal vertebrae at the bottom of the spinal column.

cochineal. An insect, *Coccus cacti*, the female of which, after being dried, yields a brilliant red dye. The dye stuff was extracted by the Indians of Mexico in pre-Columbian times, and the dye was widely used in native paints and textile dyes.

Cochise. Referring to a southwest American culture, dating from ca. 9,000 B.C. The Cochise people were food gatherers, who used grinding stones and had few hunting tools.

cocksnook. A denigratory gesture made by thumbing the nose. It is also called a snook.

cocoa. The chocolate tree, grown in Central America and elsewhere. It has small yellow flowers. Dried cocoa seeds are widely used to make a drink or food. The plant probably originated in the New World long before Columbus.

coconut. The coconut palm fruit, which has an outer fibrous husk and a hollow nut of thick edible meat. It may be the world's most important cultivated plant, since it supplies so many people with timber, drink, food, oil, condiments, and fiber. It was probably first domesticated in southeast Asia.

codex. A book with leaves placed flat on each other rather than being rolled together as a scroll. The codex was introduced some time around the second century A.D., and it is associated with the early Christians. It was introduced because the papyrus roll was inconvenient to use, in that rolling and unrolling it were troublesome and it was difficult to refer to a specific passage. Codices were bound in quires, which gave rise to the development of modern books, when paper replaced papyrus.

Codex, Dresden. A Mayan book dealing with astronomy and mathematics. Mayan astronomy, as given in this document, was prob bly superior to European astronomy, and Mayan mathematics was probably as good as European mathematics at the time of the Spanish conquest.

codpiece. A pouch covering the male genitals, introduced ca. 1450 A.D. in Europe, where it was very popular for several hundred years. The clinging hose of the middle Ages and the shortness of the doublet were both so revealing that the Church ordered wearing of the codpiece .

Codrington, Robert Henry (1830-1922). An English anthropologist who based several important books on the language and customs of Melanesia on his 30 years of missionary service there. His discussion of the Melanesian belief in mana (q.v.) became famous.

coefficient, creatinine. The ratio of the body's excretion of creatinine in a 24-hour period, measured in milligrams, to the weight of the body in kilograms. The creatinine coefficient is used to measure obesity, although it has not been completely validated.

coelanaglyphic. Referring to hollow relief in sculpture.

coemptio. A symbolic sale of a bride to her husband, used as a priestless marriage ritual in ancient Rome.

coffee. A small tree or shrub in which the interior ovary of the flower becomes the berry. There are some 40 species of coffee in Africa and India. They have been used to minimize fatigue for thousands of years, most frequently by making a tea from the leaves, although it is more usual in the West to make a beverage of the pulverized berries. Coffee was probably domesticated in the Middle Ages and introduced commercially by Red Sea Arabs. A third of the world currently uses coffee.

coffin, inner. The case immediately surrounding a mummy (q.v.). The inner coffin was made of fine materials, was richly ornamented, and was tailored to the exact proportions of the corpse, with an allowance for the bandages or mummy cloth (q.v.). The construction was usually of two-inch thick sycamore planks, fastened together with dowels, and the cover was sealed with liquid plaster.

coffre en pierre. See CIST.

cofradía. In Latin America, an institution that combines Christianity, social life, and some native and political functions.

cognate. A person related to another through birth, especially on the mother's side.

cogwheel. A wheel with teeth or cogs. It was probably developed in Egypt.

Cohuna skull. See SKULL, COHUNA.

coif. A cap that largely covers and conceals the hair. The coif is a close-fitting headdress. It was worn by sergeants-of-law in England and by medieval women, and it was originally used to cover clerical tonsures. The term is also used for a closely fitting cap of mail.

123

coil, bee-skip. A kind of simple oversewn coil in which the stitches are wide apart and connect the coil at intervals. Each stitch passes just behind and looks as if it is emerging from the stitch of the coil below.

coil, furcate. A kind of simple oversewn coil in which a new stitch splits the preceding coil's stitch. This leads to a forked effect.

coil, simple oversewn. A kind of coiling in which a stitch goes over the new part of the foundation coil and through a part of the coil below.

coil, spiral. See COILING (basketry).

coil without foundation. A technique for making coiled basketry (q.v.) with interlocking loops.

coiling. In *pottery,* a hand-manufacturing process in which one sausage of clay is added to another, in a spiral formation, or in which one coil of clay is built up to the wanted height. The pot is created from the bottom up until the appropriate height is reached, after which the outer and inner surfaces are smoothed.

In *basketry,* a technique in which a spirally coiled foundation is bound in place by pliable material, whence the designation spiral coil. It is sporadically distributed around the world. In this technique, the warp is inactive, as the weft goes around it before going on to the next stitch. A pointed implement makes a hole through which a weft goes. A spiral foundation of materials such as leaf strips or grass is sewn together in ascending or flat coil.

coin. A standard metal form of money, probably beginning in 700 B.C. in Lydia, when the kings stamped lumps of silver or fixed weight with the royal symbol.

coin, sounding. See MONEY, MOON.

coin, tooth. A medium of exchange generally employing unusual animal teeth.

coir. The fiber extracted from the husk of the coconut, or the cordage made from it, especially in Oceania.

collateral. Referring to consanguine relatives not directly connected by descent to the next generation. Thus, of two such relatives neither need be directly related to the other as ancestor or descendant, although there is a line of descent to a common ancestor. Collateral relatives may be of the same or another generation.

collection culture. See CULTURE, COLLECTION.

Colobinae. A Simian (q.v.) subfamily with ischial callosities and small or no thumbs. Included in this subfamily are langurs, proboscis monkeys, and guenons.

colonate. A form of servile land tenure which was prevalent throughout the later Roman Empire.

colonization, language of. The language adopted by a subject or dependent nation from the conquering or culturally superior nation or imposed by it. It is customarily used as the official language, in business transactions, and as a cultural medium, equal to or replacing the native language. A example of a language of colonization is French in England following the Norman conquest.

colono. A farm laborer in Latin America who is partly paid for his work by the temporary use of land belonging to his employer. The colono complex probably originated in ancient Rome and has remained almost entirely unchanged throughout its development. The institution of colonato is found most widely in countries with a plantation economy and with a substantial proportion of indigenous persons or of mestizos (q.v.). The colono has no exact analogue in the tenure arrangements of parts of the world which are relatively advanced. He constitutes a well-defined class in the various Latin American countries, although complete census data are unavailable.

colors, hot. A group of colors encompassing all hues of red and those near red, e.g., yellow and orange. Any colors associated with heat or showing the tones of fire belong in this classification.

colors, primitive or colors, primary. Red, yellow, and blue, so named because of the old fallacious belief that all colors could be obtained by mixing these three.

coltello-ascia. A celt (q.v.) with a nearly semicircular cutting edge.

coltello-sega. A flint knife with sawlike edges.

colugo. The "flying lemur," not really a primate.

columbarium. An underground burial chamber used by the Romans for mass burials, slaves, freedmen, and burial clubs. Columbaria were built with rows of niches in which the ash-filled urns were deposited.

column, abacus. The uppermost portion of the head of a column, used to support the superstructure. The abacus column is variously ornamented in the different classical architectural styles. In the Greek Doric, e.g., it is completely simple and square without decoration; while in the Ionic, it is more delicate and has side moldings. In the Corinthian style, in complete contrast to the Ionic, it is quite ornate. with concave sides and truncated corners.

comal. A pottery griddle used by the Aztecs to cook tortillas.

comb. A pronged device used to "beat up" a pick of the weft.

comb, composite. A type of comb in which the teeth consist of separate pieces bound or woven together with fiber. It is the common form of comb among the Indians of Tropical Forest South America.

comb, dental. An arrangement of the lower incisors and canine teeth found in lemurs. These teeth are in a row at the front of the jaw and have the shape of a comb.

combat, regulated. Prearranged or sham battles. Regulated combat between the two clans is sometimes a feature of exogamous marriages.

combat, transformation. A battle between two persons in which each transforms himself into various forms in trying to beat the other. The transformation combat is a widely found folktale motif.

commensal. Referring to persons who usually eat together.

communication, density of. The comparative incidence of language communication in a speech community (q.v.).

communion, phatic. The maintenance of emotional rapport in a social group, in Malinowski's terminology.

communism, primitive. A socioeconomic arrangement whereby all the productive resources belong to the community, within which there is an equal distribution of the output. Primitive communism was the ideal of early Christian monasticism.

communism, sexual. A hypothetical early state of extreme sexual permissiveness. Very few societies have been proven to practice sexual communism.

community. Mutually dependent families living and working together in a given area and usually in face-to-face association.

community, campsite. A social group on the band (q.v.) level.

community, endogamous. A social organization in which endogamy (q.v.) prevails. The endogamous community is sometimes called the local group.

community, speech. A group of persons interacting through the use of speech. The size of such communities varies, and they may sometimes merge with each other.

community, village. A group, comprising more than a single family, living in fairly close contiguity, and dividing the meadow area among its members. Such communities have been found over a good part of the world. Sanderson has classified them into the migratory agricultural village, which is seminomadic and lasts for a few months; semipermanent villages, which last for a number of years, and permanent settlements. There has been considerable discussion on the beginnings of village communities, with different countries being named as the source. Thus, their beginnings have been attributed variously to Germany, Russia, India, Greece, and China. Village communities seem to have existed from the beginnings of agriculture and were kindred-centered, except for England. They were likely to be patrilineal. Common open fields were generally a feature.

compadrazgo. The relationship which develops through taking godparents, in Central America. The compadrazgo is Spanish in origin, but its great importance suggests that it replaced a formal friendship organization that existed before the Conquest. The relations are those between godparents and godchildren and between the godparents and their godchildren's own parents.

comparison, base of. The study, analysis, and classification of phonemic relationships having an affinity with respect to some characteristics.

compass. A device for getting directions on the earth's surface through a magnetic needle that swings freely to indicate magnetic north. The compass was invented by the Chinese and introduced to Europe ca. 1,000 A.D.

compass, sliding. An instrument for measuring lesser diameters, e.g., of the nose.

complement, phonetic. An added phonetic element that indicates the proper pronunciation or significance of a symbol in systems of writing employing the use of pictograms and symbols that stand for one or more words. Phonetic complements are used in Japanese, e.g., to indicate the pronunciation of the characters, which have been taken from Chinese.

complex, culture. An organically related group of culture traits in a culture area, e.g., the cattle complex of East African cultures. In diffusion (q.v.), the traits of a culture complex will probably remain associated. These traits are usually logically associated with each other.

complex, Folsom. A group of tools consisting of some projectile points, a fluted knife and a knife made from long thin flakes chipped off the fluted knives. They are associated with the culture of early man in Folsom, northeast New Mexico, from 10,000 to 12,000 years ago.

complex, megalithic. A culture in which large stone monuments play an important part.

complex, Oedipus. An emotional conflict, hypothesized by Freud, which involves repressed hate for the parent of the same sex and repressed love for the parent of the opposite sex. Freud suggested that the successful resolution of this situation is prerequisite to a healthy personality. Anthropological data have been used in attempting to determine the universality of the Oedipus complex. Malinowski challenged the universality of this complex by showing that the Trobriand Islanders, who have a matrilineal (q.v.) society, do not display the kind of emotional link with the parent postulated by Freud but show Oedipus-type reactions toward the mother's brother, who directs a good deal of the child's life. This was held to demonstrate that the Oedipus complex, in Freud's formulation, was culture-bound. Kardiner has pointed out that the Oedipus complex is present only in cultures that interfere with the sexual goal in childhood, which in his view, is why it is not found in Marquesan and Trobriand culture.

complex, trait. A functional combination of culture traits, constituting the smallest functioning unit of culture.

component, gynandromorphic. Sheldon's name for the extent to which the male body resembles the female and the female the male. The gynandromorphic component is rated on a seven-point scale. A male high in this component would have, e.g., large hips and breasts.

compound. A word made by putting together elements with which the average speaker of the language is familiar. Compounding is a widely used method for coining new words.

compound, fused. A compound in which the elements are not easily distinguishable as separate words, e.g., *likelihood.*

compound, phrasal. A compound the components of which are easily recognizable, e.g., *nevertheless.*

compound, synthetic. A compound word that has special kinds of word formation.

compressor. A bone anvil or chopping block usually associated with the Middle Paleolithic Age.

compurgation. The process by which a person cleared himself by taking an oath, along with a number of others who took their oaths that the principal's oath was credible. The other persons who took the oath along with the accused were chosen by him. The practice of compurgation persisted into medieval times.

concept, cardinal point. The ascription of special significance to the cardinal directions and also to the top, bottom, or middle, especially as found in Indian groups of the American Southwest and Mexico.

conch. A marine shell, univalve or bivalve, of the type used for a horn, e.g., among the Aztecs.

concha. A Mexican musical instrument that resembles a lute. It has five double strings.

conchology. The study of the shells of mollusks. Conchology is used to help date archaeological deposits by giving clues to ecological factors.

concretion. A collection of concentric mineral matter, often surrounding an organic nucleus.

concubinage. A marriage or sustained sexual relationship that has no juridic consequences, such as devolution of property.

concubinage, group. A number of men who have concubines in common.

concubine. A lawful cohabitant of a man who is instead of, or in addition to, a wife or wives. The children of such an arrangement usually are legitimate, but in some cases they may not be allowed to take the father's name. The man is usually obliged to support the concubine.

concubitancy. A social framework in which individuals are born into a situation of mutual marriageability; or a condition in which a person has a status with another equivalent to marriage without actually having to be married to that person.

condyle. A bony prominence in the ramus of the lower jaw which articulates the temporo-mandibular joint. It rotates, slides forward, and moves laterally in mastication. The occipital condyle is a bony prominence which articulates with the first cervical vertebra (atlas). See OCCIPITAL.

cone. A small polished stone object, usually round and made of hematite, formerly used by the American Indian. Its function is not established.

cone, funerary. A rough cone of terra cotta, about 3 inches across and 10 inches high, found in Egyptian graves. An inscription on the funerary cone gave the name of the deceased. The cones were probably models of cakes placed in the tomb.

cone, talus. See TALUS CONE.

confarreatio. A patrician marriage ceremony in ancient Rome. After the parties to the marriage gave their consent in the home of the bride, she was carried to her husband's home by torchlight. After her husband carried her over the threshold, the bride and groom ate a sacred meal made of *far*, an ancient grain. This made it possible for the bride to become familiar with the worship of her new husband's household gods.

confederation. A league of two or more Indian tribes for mutual defense and offense, e.g., the Iroquois confederation, which comprised five tribes.

confession. The discharge of guilt by admitting wrongs or errors, and thus cleansing the soul or the community of guilt. Confession is found among the Eskimo and other nonliterate cultures, as well as in its better known Christian forms.

configuration, cultural. The basic integrative theme of a culture. In the concept of Ruth Benedict, the cultural configuration might be viewed as the polarizing element that gave a distinctive flavor to each element of a culture. Those whose personalities were in consonance with the cultural configuration would function successfully.

congeners. Organisms that belong to the same generic stock.

congeries. Facets of a culture that are not organically related.

congruence. Agreement between the various classes and forms of an expression.

conjugation. The system by which the mood, tense, voice, person, or number of a verb is changed. Conjugation is accomplished by the use of infection, prefixation (qq.v.), and auxiliaries, among other means.

conjugation, chromosome. The intimate association of homologous chromosomes.

conjunction. A grammatical term used to describe any word that connects words or sentences and indicates the relationship of the connected elements. This category is broken down into coordinating and subordinating; connective and disjunctive; affirmative, adversative, copulative, and continuative; causal, concessive, hypothetical, correlative, negative, and temporal.

connotation. The suggestive meanings and overtones of a word apart from its denotation, or explicit meaning.

connubium. A lawful marriage, or the right to enter into such a marriage.

consanguine group. See GROUP, CONSANGUINE.

consanguinity. Relation either by blood or from a common ancestor. The term is generally used for blood relations that have been socially ratified. Marriages within prohibitively close degrees of consanguinity are incestuous. One related by consanguinity is a *consanguine*.

consciousness, race. The knowledge that one is a member of a racial group, usually with feelings of race interest and race superiority.

consecration. The dedication or setting aside of specific times, objects, animals, or persons as sacred. Consecration may be effected by sacrifice, charms, amulets, teaching, singing, and other methods.

consonant. A sound characterized by a closure (q.v.), either complete or partial, in the vocal tract, e.g., *k, b, l, n,* in contrast to a vowel (q.v.), which is not closed.

consonant, ejective. A plosive (q.v.) which is pronounced simultaneously with a glottal stop (q.v.). It occurs in Caucasian languages.

consonant, geminated. A combination in which the same consonant appears twice in succession, e.g., the *tt* in *flattop.* The two occurrences are separated by a glottal stop.

consonant, kinetic. A consonant that cannot be extended without change in quality, e.g., *t.* See CONSONANT, STATIC.

consonant, labialized. A consonant in the expression of which the lips are rounded, e.g., the *s* in *soup.*

consonant, labiovelarized. A consonant that is both velarized and labialized, e.g., the *kl* in *pickle.*

consonant, static. A consonant that can be extended without change in quality, e.g., *f.* See CONSONANT, KINETIC.

consonant, velarized. A consonant produced while the back of the tongue is raised toward the velum. Velarized consonants are common in certain Caucasian languages.

consonant, vocalic. See MATRES LECTIONIS.

consonantism. The systematic investigation, either descriptive or historical, of the system of consonants of a language or dialect.

consonantization. The process by which a vowel becomes a consonant. It is rare.

constant, radiation. The heat flux per degree of temperature differ-ence between the mean body surface temperature and the temperature of the air. The radiation constant is stated in terms of calories per person or per square meter an hour.

constituent. That part of two or more complex forms (q.v.) which is contained in common.

constituent, immediate (abbreviated IC). One of the parts into which a form (sentence, phrase, word, syllable, etc.) is analyzed first. Usually there are two ICs. The sentence *the girls giggled* has the ICs *the girls* and *giggled. The girls* has the ICs *the* and *girls. Girls* has the ICs *girl* and *s.* IC analysis shows the hierarchy of the levels of construction of utterances.

constituent, ultimate. A part of a construction that is arrived at when IC (q.v.) analysis is carried to its final point. In the sentence *girls giggled,* the ultimate constituents would be *girl, s, giggle* and *d.*

constituent, unique. A morpheme (q.v.) occurring only in one construction, e.g., *cran* in cranberry.

construction, absolute. A syntactical construction that is not linked grammatically to any other part of the sentence, e.g., the absolute ablative.

construction, endocentric. See ENDOCENTRIC.

construction, exocentric. See EXOCENTRIC.

construction, syntactic. A meaningful and significant set of taxemes (q.v.).

consummation, deferred. The postponement of the marital consummation, usually for religious reasons.

contagion, law of. Frazer's name for the magical process that operates because things that used to be in contact are still regarded as being in contact.

container. A device used to carry, store, cook, and preserve. Some containers, like shells, are used as they occur in nature, while others are fashioned from hide, wood, fiber, and other materials.

contamination. The change in meaning of a word on the basis of analogy with an unrelated but similar-sounding word. Thus, *dastard,* originally meaning "coward," by analogy with *bastard* acquired a more pejorative meaning.

context. In archaeology, the surroundings of an artifact in the place where it was found. The context is significant because it is often assumed that the object was made near where it was found. The stratigraphy and horizontal position of a find are part of the context.

continence, ritual. A couple's refraining from sexual intercourse for religious or similar reasons.

continental bridge hypothesis. See HYPOTHESIS, CONTINENTAL BRIDGE.

continental drift hypothesis. See HYPOTHESIS, CONTINENTAL DRIFT.

continuant. A consonant (q.v.) made by partial obstruction to the outgoing air, e.g., *m, v,* so that the sound can be prolonged.

continuum, folk-urban. The distinction between a relatively small, homogeneous, isolated, technologically backward society and a modern civilization. The folk society as contrasted with the urban civilization is said to have more feeling of belongingness, solidarity of members, family emphasis in all aspects of social life, and sacred elements in all institutions. The family and religion permeate all institutions rather than being relegated themselves to specific institutions. The urban community has opposing characteristics. This concept of folk-urban continuum has been developed by Robert Redfield.

contour, intonational. The shape of the intonation over a syntactic unit, e.g., rising or falling.

contours découpés. Silhouette carvings in which the details are completely worked out on both sides. Contours découpés date from Paleolithic times.

contradance. A dance in which the participants are a number of couples face to face. This type of dance was highly developed in Europe.

contrafforte. The wooden or stone buttress that supports the rampart of a terramara (q.v.).

conuco. In the Caribbean area, an agricultural plot, especially a manioc field cultivated by the slash-and-burn (q.v.) method.

conventionalization. The use of religion to obtain approval for something that might not be tolerated in a nonreligious context.

convergence. The process by which distinctive culture traits from different areas become similar or merge. Convergence is a possible alternative to choosing between invention and diffusion (qq.v.) in explaining similarities between cultures, although it gives only a partial answer to the problem.

convergence, flexion. The ability of the primates to splay the five digits out and bend them together in a converging manner so that they can grasp small objects.

Conze, Alexander (1831-1914). An Austrian archaeologist whose account of his excavation during 1873-75 at Samothrace has been called the first modern excavation report. Photographs and architectural drawings were copiously used as illustrations.

Cook, Captain James (1728-1779). An English explorer of the Pacific islands and pioneer in the collection of native objects. Cook made three substantial trips, one of which, on the *Endeavor* (1769-1771), was the first known long sea trip without deaths from scurvy. His seamanship was daring and intelligent. He traveled around the world and wrote excellent accounts of the ethnography and artifacts of Polynesia. The first European to land on Hawaii (1779), he was taken for a deity and killed by the natives.

cooking. The preparation of food for eating by the use of heat. Roasting was probably the first phase, followed by baking and boiling.

cooking, hot-rock. See BOILING, STONE.

coolamon. An Australian aboriginal dish of wood or bark used for holding water and food.

Cooley's anemia. See ANEMIA, COOLEY'S.

coonti. A plant used for flour and bread by Florida Indians. The Seminole still eat it to this day.

copal. A resinous substance burned as incense in Mexico.

Copan. A major Maya site in western Honduras, noted for its sculpture and fine stelae. Dating from ca. 300-900 A.D., it is one of the largest Maya sites of the classic period.

Cope's law. See LAW, COPE'S.

Copilcoc. A burial site near Mexico City belonging to the Formative (Archaic or Middle) culture period of Mexican prehistory. It was completely covered by the Pedregal lava flow.

copper. Early man was probably attracted by the bright appearance of copper and probably discovered that it could be hammered into various shapes. The earliest artifacts of metal are Egyptian pins and beads made of beaten copper. In time it was realized that copper can be cast into any shape when it is molten and can be given a good edge. The earliest fused implements of copper are from ca. 4000 B.C. in Egypt and Babylonia. Implements of copper are not common in Europe because the metal is scarce there and existing objects were melted down when bronze was introduced. The discovery of copper smelting helped contribute to human progress since it released man from dependence on rare native copper and permitted him to make more tools by using the relatively plentiful copper ores. It is likely that two millenia intervened between the initial use of hammered copper and copper smelting and casting.

The use of native copper marks the commencement of each of the metal cultures, since silver and gold, though malleable, are not industrially useful to early man. Once it was discovered that the soft copper could be hammer-hardened, its use began to spread. When it was observed that too much hammering made the copper brittle, heat was probably used to take care of this defect.

In their elemental condition, lumps of copper are purplish-green or greenish-black, although they turn yellow-red by scratching and rubbing against other pebbles in the stream. Native copper was a link between stone and metal.

There is a general scarcity of copper relics in graves, perhaps because burial customs are conservative and early man would hesitate to place copper tools in a grave for fear of causing trouble in the next world.

Copper was probably first found in the Sinai peninsula and was used in Egypt more than 1,000 years sooner than in central and western Europe.

copper, drift or **copper, float.** Copper which has been carried by natural forces from its original site, like the nodules of copper south of the Great Lakes area. They were torn by glaciers from their beds in Lake Superior. The Indians used this drift copper.

copra. The dried meat of the coconut, an important source of food on many Oceanic islands.

coprolite. Fossil excrement, which can give information on the habits and food of now extinct groups. It also means vertebrate remains in the form of phosphatised casts.

Coptic. The modern survival of the ancient Egyptian language. The characters are modifications of Greek letters.

copula. In grammar, a word used merely to express the relation between predicate and subject, e.g., Jim *is* sick.

coraca. The lower hereditary nobility among the Incas, from whose ranks came the municipal chiefs and certain other administrative officials.

coracle. A craft shaped like a shallow basket, made of latticed framework. It is waterproofed with tar and pitch. Coracles have been covered by tarpaulin and hide, as well as flannel. They are especially used for fishing in shallow rivers with many rocks and are still found in parts of England.

coracora. A large war canoe of Tahiti.

corbel. A projecting block of wood or masonry built into a wall in order to support a beam or other feature. Corbels are sometimes carved or molded.

corbelling. Covering the area between two walls by making successive rows of bricks project a little more inward than the row below, until the two walls join in a false arch.

cord, throwing. See THROWER, FLEXIBLE SPEAR.

cord, umbilical. A cord, terminating in the naval, which connects the placenta with the mammalian fetus. The umbilical cord permits blood to circulate between placenta and fetus and is about 20 inches long and almost one-half inch wide. Many nonliterate groups regard it as being involved with the child's future and make special arrangements for its disposal.

cordiform. An early Mousterian coup-de-poing that is flat and small and equilaterally triangular. Its edges are sharp and straight and trimmed with small flake scars.

cordophone. A musical bow with one string, the ancestor of all string instruments.

cords, vocal. Two parallel bands of muscle going from the front to the back of the larynx. The glottis is the space between them. The vocal cords can be very delicately adjusted.

core. A piece of flint, obsidian, or stone from which flakes were struck to make implements.

core, blade. A core of flint with a striking platform (q.v.) which yields blades when struck with a hammer.

core, polyhedral. A prepared core with a roughly conical shape.

core, tortoise. A flint nodule so shaped that it is possible to detach a flake which could be used as an implement without further working. It looks like an inverted tortoise shell. Striking one end of a tortoise removes an oval flake consisting of part of the more gently domed side and resembling a flat hand ax when viewed on its outer face. Such a flake has sharp, thin margins and can easily be used as a skinning knife. The tortoise-core technique developed near the end of the second interglacial period in Europe during the Levalloisian period, whence the term Levalloisian technique.

core, turtleback. A flint core which is roughly prepared and has a large flake bed. It is characteristic of the Acheulian-Levalloisian period.

corita. A float (q.v.) which is a woven basket cemented with pitch. The corita was used as a ferry along the Lower Colorado.

corium. The part of the skin which is chemically treated in the process of tanning.

corn, Kaffir. A grasslike seed plant used as a fodder grass in Latin America. It was developed in South Africa.

corn, pod. A corn with a pod covering over each kernel.

corn, pop. A type of corn that was probably an ancestor of maize and the earliest kind of corn to develop in the Americas.

cornu. A large coiled trumpet with a narrow bore. The cornu was used in the Roman Empire to signal large bodies of troops.

coromandel. A catamaran (q.v.) which consists of several carefully shaped logs lashed together in a definite order. A rowing rail and stern parts are usually added. The coromandel is used by Tamil fishermen.

coronach. A Scottish lament, often chanted at funerals.

coronal. Referring to an articulation involving the blade of the tongue.

coroplast. In the ancient world, a maker of clay figurines.

corposant. See FIRE, ST. ELMO'S; LIGHT, CORPSE.

corrasion. The process of producing river channels through the operation of mechanical force.

correlation, spurious. A relation between two variables which results from factors other than those to which the relation is mistakenly attributed.

correspondence, phonetic. A greater than chance similarity in meaning between two or more languages. The concept of phonetic correspondence is useful in historical linguistics to help reconstruct languages, as in the deduction of the proto-Germanic mother language of the languages of West Europe.

corroboree. An Australian feast that lasts six weeks. There are witty, partly improvised dances and dance operas, which begin a half hour before sunset and extend into the night. The participants rest during the day. Corroborees are performed to assure peace, after a successful hunt, before battle, and on similar occasions. The term is now used by nonnatives to describe any native ceremonial activity.

corrosion. The process by which exposed surfaces of the earth wear away.

corrugated ware. See WARE, CORRUGATED.

corvée. Labor drafted for the performance of public works or nonmilitary work for the government. This was practiced by the Incas of Peru.

cosmogony. A group's beliefs about the beginning and composition of the world or universe. There are different stories of the creation. A god is usually the creator. He may use a magic word to start the world (Hebrews), make the world by sacrifice (India), or be a master artificer (Egypt), a potter (Egypt), or a weaver (Babylonia). The sexual union of Earth and Heaven is widely found in early cosmogonies, as is the idea of a cosmic egg (Polynesia). In early cosmogonies, it was generally believed that before creation, there was a vast collection of waters in darkness, rather than a creation from nothing.

Cossack. A lightly armed horseman, a Russian term. Cossacks were organized in small groups and engaged in military operations on their own authority.

Cossaean. An Asianic language which was spoken in the Zagros Mountains area, east of Mesopotamia. Its written records date back to the 17th century B.C.

costume, arctic. Garments worn in arctic areas usually cover the whole body and fit it fairly closely. Trousers may have originated in the Arctic, since some sort of bifurcated garment is needed to cover the limbs closely and minimize heat loss. It is possible that some Mongol groups pioneered in arctic clothing, because they could not migrate southward due to the barrier of the Himalayas and thus had to learn to adapt to the cold. Since the decline of the Graeco-Roman civilization, this type of clothing has been pre-

135

dominant in European male dress. See CLOTHING, ANATOMIC.

costume, tropical. Garments worn by persons in a tropical climate are usually loose fitting. They probably began with a skirt-type garment suspended from the hip band (q.v.). Tropical costume is usually made of vegetable material. This type of clothing may have given rise to European women's clothing. See CLOTHING, GRAVITATIONAL.

cosy, tea. See SCRAPER, CORE.

Cottian. A language formerly spoken on the Agul in eastern Siberia. It is related to Yenisei-Ostyak.

cotton. A downy, soft-textured, white, fibrous substance found attached to the seeds of certain plants of the malvaceous genus. Cloth from cotton was first made as early as 3000 B.C. in India. Its use and manufacture spread until the Spanish Moors and Sicilian Arabs began to produce it in 912 A.D. in Europe. Its first known appearance in England was in the 12th century. The development of cotton in the western hemisphere was roughly parallel. Recent researches show its existence in Peru as early as 200 B.C., in pre-Inca times. The filmiest cotton fabric is Dacca muslin, made in the Indus valley. This is famous for its lightness, with 73 yards to the pound, while the next lightest fabric, made in Switzerland, weighs 16½ yards to the pound.

coulter. A piece of metal held vertically in front of a plowshare. Plows with coulters were first used ca. 100 B.C. in northwest Europe.

council. A group of adults who advise the chief of a group. The nature and influence of the council vary from society to society.

count, stone. The study of moraines through the study of erratic (q.v.) stones.

count, winter. Among the Plains Indians, a picture history painted on buffalo skins.

coup. Among the French Canadians, a prestige-making tap given to the enemy's body with the hand or by an object in the hand. The first person near the body delivered the first coup. Among the Plains Indians, a coup was a brave or victorious act. A coup was granted for scalping or killing an enemy, or for being the first person to strike him. The implement used to strike the blows was called a coup stick.

coup, counting. The system among certain Plains Indians whereby status and prestige were conferred for performing certain feats. Coup counting is also the practice of announcing coups publicly. A distinguishing eagle feather indicated the warrior's rank in the system. Touching an enemy, or an object belonging to him, was often the lauded feat.

coup-de-poing. A superficially flaked core-tool probably used as the first formal implement. These heavy triangular artifacts were probably general utility weapons. Coups-de-poing became extinct in Europe around the Mousterian Age. Their lower and upper faces are trimmed and there is a sharp edge between the faces. The two major types of coup-de-poing are pointed and pear shaped, and flat and oval. The flat, oval type was probably mainly used for scraping and cutting, and the pointed kind for stabbing and piercing hides before skinning.

The first recorded discovery of a coup-de-poing was made in 1690, by some workmen digging at Gray's Inn, London. It was believed to be of Roman origin. About 100 years later, similar implements were found by John Frere in Suffolk. In 1825, John MacEnery began digging in Torquay, and in 1828 Townsend found implements with some Quaternary fauna in France. In 1837, Boucher de Perthes (q.v.) published his famous account of the discovery of chipped flints in the Somme alluvial deposits. The coup-de-poing is also called the hand ax or fist ax, the Beil, or the Faust Keil.

coupoir. See TRANCHET.

coursing. The architectural arrangement of stones or bricks in continuous horizontal or inclined rows. This technique is characteristic of advanced architecture only.

court, royal. A ruler's court in which the culture and power of a regime are concentrated, as in the Old Kingdom of Egypt.

cousin, cross. The child of a parent's sibling of the opposite sex. The relationship of cross cousins involves a crossing from female to male in the connecting relatives, e.g., the child of the sister of the father.

cousin, parallel or **ortho-cousin.** The child of a parent's sibling of the same sex, e.g., of an individual's father's brother or mother's sister. Parallel cousins are often regarded as siblings and often are not permitted to intermarry.

couvade. The imitation by the father of many of the concomitants of childbirth, around the time of his wife's parturition; it is also called men's childbed. The father may retire to bed, go into seclusion, and observe some taboos and restrictions in order to help the child. Among the theories that have been suggested to account for the couvade is that during this period, the father has to take care of himself to avoid an injury that could be transmitted to the child by sympathetic magic. Another is that the father asserts his paternity through appearing to share in the delivery. A third explanation is that the father simulates the wife's activities in order to get evil spirits to focus on him rather than on her.

covenant. An agreement based on a moral obligation. Marett has said that the conscious use of covenant began with exogamy (q.v.) and dual organization (q.v.). It is often linked with blood, gifts, peace-making, and marriage. Among early men, the covenant implied a union of being, often through a rite. A sharing of blood, representing life, between two persons, or of animal blood, indicate a sharing of life. Salt stands for blood, and the covenant of salt is another example of the blood covenant. The family's first altar was often the dwelling's threshold, and this led to a threshold covenant, in which the blood of a slaughtered animal is shed on the threshold in order to make a covenant union with a newcomer.

covenant, blood. An agreement between two persons confirmed by each having drunk or smeared himself with the other's blood or by the two having mingled their bloods.

covolo. A fairly small rock shelter.

cow, sacred. India is the major culture area which has adopted a special set of codes, institutions, and folkways in connection with cattle, indicating reverence for them. The pious Hindu has an attitude of ahimsa (q.v.) toward the cow. Early Vedic teachings contain numerous references to killing cattle, and the beginning of the prohibition seems to date from the Jain religion, ca. sixth century B.C. Although Buddhism led to a diminution in the killing of cows, the cow was not inviolable in Buddhist India, ca. 300 B.C. to 1000 A.D. In the period A.D. 800-1200 the cow became inviolable as a Hindu countermeasure against Moslem invaders and liberal Buddhism.

The present Indian constitution specifically preserves the inviolability of the cow. Of the approximately 85 per cent of the Indian population which is Hindu, probably the higher caste persons observe the cow's special status, while lower castes and outcastes probably are less observant. Of the non-Hindus, only the Jains observe the cow's inviolability. Moslems still oppose the sacredness of the cow, perhaps because the dogma of the cow was one means by which the Moslem invaders were originally opposed. It has been suggested that approximately 125,000,000 persons in India do not observe the cow's inviolability.

A recent census indicated that India has about 5,500,000 cattle which are being protected in accordance with the ahimsa principle, although 6,600,000 cattle were slaughtered in the same year. There are over 3,000 organizations established to care for cattle.

cowrie. A thick-edged shell of a kind of snail. The cowrie shell is used as money and as a medium and store of value. The snails are obtained by putting coco leaves in the water and then picking them up after the snails have settled on the leaves. The use of cowrie shells is believed to have originated on the island of Mafia off East Africa and on the Maldive Islands southwest of India. The shells are used in Africa, especially in inland regions.

coyness, ceremonial. An assumed reluctance by a participant in a ritual, especially the feigned resistance of a bride during some phase of the marriage ceremony.

crack, ice. A narrow split in ice over which persons can walk or sledges can pass.

crack-lacing hole. See HOLE, CRACK-LACING.

crackle. In making pottery, the deliberate fracturing of the glaze on vessels during firing. Crackle can be finely controlled by mixing certain clays so that bands of different kinds of crackle may appear on the same vessel. See CRAZING.

crackle, Chinese. A method of decorating pottery by giving it a crackle finish. It was originally done by placing the hot pottery in cold water. The marks which resulted could be emphasized by adding color. The piece might be retouched so that the pattern above and below could be seen.

cradle, cat's. A game in which string figures are made by the hands, or sometimes by the toes and teeth.

cramp. In building, a device used to fasten together stones of the same course. Cramps were of wrought iron and bronze and were usually hidden and lead-sealed.

craniology. The study of crania and skulls, including their measurement (craniometry), photographic or pictorial representation (craniography), and description (cranioscopy).

craniometry. The measurement of the facial skeleton and the braincase.

craniophor. An instrument used to hold a skull in any desired position in order to take measurements or photographs.

cranium. The skull exclusive of the lower jaw and the facial bones. The cranium, also called the brain case, fits around the brain closely enough to provide a sign of the individual's cerebral development. As the cranium increases proportionately, the facial part of the skull seems to withdraw below it. As the front part of man's brain developed, the forehead became vertical. Since the human brain case is globular and large in surface, the muscles of mastication and the neck muscles can be attached without any special flanges or crests such as are found in lower animals.

crannog. An artificial island, generally used as a fortress, made of transversely laid logs covered with stones, brushwood and earth. A crannog may be surrounded by a stockade or a timber platform on which huts and hearthstones were erected. The crannog was usually circular or oval, with an average diameter of some 60 or 70 feet, but ranging from 20 feet in Neolithic times to as much as 120 feet in the Bronze Age. A gangway usually connected with the shore. Scotland and Ireland had a good many crannogs, but they are also found in Wales, England, Switzerland, and Austria. The huts built on the crannog were probably thatched and timbered. Zigzag stepping stones have been found on some crannogs, and it has been suggested that their purpose was to cause intruders to stray into the mud. Crannogs were first systematically explored in 1839, by W. R. Wilde.

crasis. The production of a new sound from two distinct sounds, resulting from the combination of the last sound of one word with the first of the following word. Thus in Greek a word that ends in a *t* sound and is followed by a hard breathing becomes a *th* (or theta), as seen in the English word *method,* which is a combination of the Greek *meta* and *hodos.*

crater. A Greek bowl used for mixing wine and water. The crater had two handles, one on either side, a large body and a wide mouth. Craters were made of gold, silver, and pottery. They date back as far as the fifth century B.C., with the famous black glazed François vase placed ca. 560 B.C. The Athenian calyx craters of the fifth century B.C. and the simply designed volute-craters of the fourth century are excellent examples of this creative craft.

crazing. In making pottery, the accidental fracturing of the glaze. Although it is not intentional, Oriental potters often regard this as an enhancement of the vessel's beauty, as they do many other accidental effects of firing.

creation, analogic. Creating new word forms by analogy with pre-existing forms. Thus, given *dove* as the past of *dive,* since we have a form *drive,* its past tense by analogy should be *drove.*

creation, special. The theory that each kind of organism was individually created and thus is not related through descent to any other kind of organism.

creeper. A primitive skate carved from a walrus tusk. The Eskimo hunter, nearing his prey on the ice, places creepers on his boots to facilitate his movements.

creeper, ice. An attachment to the underside of shoes to help in walking on ice.

cremation. Destroying a corpse by burning is favored by many groups because it prevents the possible return of the dead, dispels the pollution of death, protects the body from wild beasts and evil spirits, secures warmth and comfort in the future world, and eliminates the possibility of transformation (q.v.). Cremation was widely practiced in many cultures before Christianity.

crembala. A castanetlike musical instrument used by female dancers and singers of antiquity to accompany themselves.

crenelation. Indentation, notching, or channeling of an object.

Creole. A person who springs from the hybridization of a higher invading culture with a native culture and who retains many features of the latter. The term also means of foreign origin but bred or growing in a colonial or remote country; thus it applies to a person born in the West Indies or Spanish America but of European descent. The Louisiana French language is termed a Creole.

creolization. The process by which a language degenerates into a trade language.

Crescent, Fertile. Lower Mesopotamia and Egypt, the site of the most advanced human development to ca. 1000 B.C.

crest. A painted or carved design which is often used on the northwest coast of North America to explain the mythical origin of a family. A crest may represent an animal and be connected with a sib (q.v.). It occurs often as a decorative design.

crest, nuchal. A ridge of bone that goes up to the back of the skull and attaches to some neck muscles. The nuchal crest is well developed in modern apes and is found on a lower level on some fossil human skulls.

crest, sagittal. A high bone wall running the length of the skull, found in male gorillas. It supports the antagonistic muscles of the jaw.

140

crest, temporal. A ridge on the temporal bone.

Cretaceous. Referring to a life period of Mesozoic times. It is characterized by mammals becoming divided into placentals, marsupials, and monotremes, and by the development of specialized reptiles. The Cretaceous lasted from ca. 70 to 140 million years ago. The end of this period saw the extinction of the great reptile dynasties.

Cretan. The language of ancient Crete. Very little is known about it. There are three inscriptions, which have never been deciphered, and four short texts written with Greek characters.

cretinism. Cretins have short extremities, dry skin, sallow complexion, and large faces and abdomens. They are usually short. See HYPOTHYROIDISM.

crevasse. A crack in land ice caused by the unequal flowing motion of the ice.

cribble. The process of decorating wood or metal by making small punctures or dots on the surface.

crime. Conduct for which there is some punishment provided by the whole community's sanction, rather than by the hurt person alone. In this sense crime does not exist in a society that provides only vendettas or other private means of redress.

crimping iron. See IRON, CRIMPING.

criosphinx. See HIERACOSPHINX.

criteria, sorting. The morphological or metric features used to select the members of a race or subrace.

crithomancy. The art of divination (q.v.) from the pattern formed by grain or particles of flour. Crithomancy is usually practiced with sacrificial rituals.

crochet. To make a fabric with a hooked needle by alternately drawing a thread into a loop and attaching the thread to other loops in the fabric.

Cro-Magnon. The western European population, probably Caucasoid, associated with the Aurignacian and later cultures. Remains were first found in 1868, in the rock shelter of Cro-Magnon in the village of Les Eyzies, Dordogne, France (Cro-Magnon is French patois for great hole). Five skeletons were found there, although similar findings have been made in Western Europe. It is believed that the Cro-Magnons were absorbed into later populations. This type was fairly tall and had a larger cranial capacity than modern man, with a high forehead and prominent chin.

Cro-Magnon is probably the prehistoric Homo sapiens of whom we know the most. His culture went through the Aurignacian, Solutrean, and Magdalenian stages. There were many stone instruments, and flint chipping reached its highest development. Reindeer horn, bone, and ivory were also used to make various implements. Cro-Magnon dwellings were in rock shelters and caves, where the dead were buried. Red ocher was found in many graves, although the exact significance of this is not known. Ornaments such as necklaces were in the graves of the period, and the fine arts, including painting, drawing, and sculpture, probably first appeared in the Aurignacian period.

Cromerian. Referring to a flake industry (q.v.) found in the early Pleistocene, in the Cromer Forest area.

cromhorn. An obsolete European reed instrument.

cromlech. A megalith (q.v.) made of menhirs (q.v.) placed in a circle.

crook, furrow. A heavy wooden hack (q.v.) which was pulled by hand to make small furrows for sowing.

crook, plow. An agricultural implement consisting of a share and pole.

crop mark. See MARK, CROP.

crops. The foods grown by a culture. The major crops of western civilization are millet, barley, and wheat. Rice is the staple in large parts of Asia. Breadfruit, maize, taro, yams, and coconuts are other staple crops. Almost all the agricultural crops of today were known to nonliterate peoples.

cross. Two or more lines intersecting transversely. The cross was used as a religious symbol by the Chinese, American Indians, Buddhists and Egyptians. It may have symbolized the four winds, the active or passive component of the phallic in nature, or a hammer. The cross was used as a symbol of punishment and suffering before the time of Jesus.

cross, St. Andrew's. A design consisting of two lines intersecting one other in the shape of an X.

cross, Tau. A design in the shape of a T.

crossbow. A bow which is mounted on a stock. The stock has a groove or barrel to direct the arrow or bolt. The stave can be composite, compound, or single. Crossbows in late medieval times were drawn by cranks and released by triggers. The propulsive force might be sufficient to penetrate armor.

crosser. A go-between in legal matters among the Yurok.

crossing over. In the process of reduction division, the exchange of genes (q.v.) between the two chromosomes of a pair.

cross-reference. An agreement in language, in which a subclass includes some mention of the form with which it is joined.

crowd. See CRWTH.

crown. The portion of a tooth which is usually visible in the mouth. The crown is covered by enamel and extends from the occlusal surface to the cervical line.

crown method. See METHOD, CROWN.

crural. Referring to the thigh or leg.

crux ansata. See ANKH.

crwth. A stringed musical instrument shaped like the lyre. The crwth is the earliest known instrument in Europe that is played with a bow. It has five or six strings and round soundholes. It was known before 400 B.C. and is an ancestor of the violin. The term chrotta or crowd is sometimes used.

cryanesthesia. Inability to perceive sensations of cold.

crypt. A small secret room usually built underneath a religious structure and often used as a repository for sacred relics or a tomb. The term is derived from the Greek word *kryptos,* meaning hidden.

cryptogam. A low seedless plant type.

cubit. A length measure, originally the forearm from the end of the middle finger to the elbow. It was variously 17.58 inches (Hebrews), 18.22 inches (Greeks), 17.5 inches (Romans), 20.7 inches (Egyptians), and 18 inches (English).

cucumber. A monoeicius trailing vine with a rough stem. The cucumber needs good soil and much water. Its use as a garden vegetable is very widespread. It has been grown in India for thousands of years, and probably originated in northern India.

Cucurbit. The plant genus that includes squashes and pumpkins. There are about a dozen species. They are creeping annuals found in the warm parts of the world.

cuesta. A gently sloping ridge.

Cuicuilco. A circular terraced burial mound of the Formative (Archaic or Middle) culture period of Mexican prehistory. The mound is situated south of Mexico City and was partially covered by the Pedregal (q.v.) lava flow.

cuirass. A piece of armor that covers the body from neck to groin; by extension any stiffened garment.

cult. The ritual observances involved in the worship of, or communication with, particular supernatural persons or objects or their symbolic representations. A cult includes the collection of ideas, activities, and practices associated with a given divinity or social group, e.g., the cult of Dionysius. Thus, the Greek gods each had their own cults, which were different although they had some fairly distinctive characteristics in common, e.g., their human qualities. Durkheim has stressed the periodic reappearance of a cult's ceremonies. The cult is a symbolic presentation, as well as an aid to, the growth of both men and gods. It is not merely ritual activities but also the beliefs and myths centering around the rites. The objects of the cult are often associated with the daily life of the celebrants, so that the Malay have a rice cult and the Ainu a bear cult. The cult often changed under the effect of migration and conquests. Jane Harrison has pointed up the cult's importance in the growth of religion.

Sacred persons may have their own cults. The cult may be tied to a given place, cover a wide area or be confined to an individual or object. There may be officials entrusted with the rites or anyone who belongs may be able to engage in them.

cult, ancestor. Those activities involved in the worship of, or communication with, the souls of a group's ancestors.

cult, Balum. Boys' initiation rites in parts of Melanesia.

cult, Bomai and Malu. A secret society (q.v.) of the Torres Straits.

Cult, Buzzard. See CULT, SOUTHERN DEATH.

143

cult, cargo. A New Guinea cult in which ancestors return by ship, bringing quantities of European and other goods with them and helping to drive the colonizers out.

cult, hero. The ritual observances involved in the worship of dead heroes or their spirits.

cult, individual. A cult in which a person has his own spirit helper or guardian spirit (q.v.). In some North American groups, each adult is expected to acquire spiritual experience by a dream or vision, perhaps induced by a vigil of fasting or the like. The guardian spirit revealed is frequently an animal.

cult, Kolaskin. A prophetic religious movement of the Indians in the Plateau area of the United States.

cult, Kuksu. A north central California cult in which there is an initiation of young men who learn to disguise themselves as Kuksu, ghosts, or other gods.

cult, Lumawig. A Bontoc ancestor worship (q.v.) cult.

cult, mystery. Any secret cult into which proposed devotees are not admitted until they have undergone secret rites, the meaning of which must not be told to those outside the cult. In ancient times, some cult officials acted out symbolic plays based on the lives of the gods and goddesses and interpreted their secret meanings to the initiates. See RELIGION, MYSTERY.

cult, priest-temple-idol. A ceremonial complex characteristic of the higher aboriginal cultures of America, in which a class of specialists attended deity images in ceremonial structures.

cult, Southern Death. An exaggerated emphasis on death by the leaders of the Natchez Indians and some other groups of the American Southeast. It probably spread from Mexico. The Southern Death cult bears some resemblance to the Egyptian Pharaoh's great concern with death and the afterworld. The term Buzzard Cult is also found.

cultigen. A plant which is dependent on man for its survival.

cultivation, dry. Crop cultivation in which rain provides the necessary moisture. Using this technique, most plots can produce only a few croppings before becoming exhausted.

cultivation, shifting. Cultivating a plot for a few croppings until it becomes exhausted, then moving a settlement to a new plot to start again.

cultivation, wet. Crop cultivation in which springs, rivers, or torrents provide all or part of the necessary moisture.

culture. All that which is nonbiological and socially transmitted in a society, including artistic, social, ideological, and religious patterns of behavior, and the techniques for mastering the environment. The term culture is often used to indicate a social grouping that is smaller than a civilization but larger than an industry.

Gustav Klemm offered in the mid-19th century an extremely modern definition of culture as "customs, information, and skills, domestic and public life in peace and war, religion, science and art. . . . it is manifest in the transmission of past experience to the new generation." Tylor, in 1871, helped establish the importance of the concept by his definition of culture as ". . . capabilities and habits acquired by man as a member of society."

Herskovits has characterized culture as being learned, structured, divisible into aspects, dynamic and variable, and stemming from every component of human existence. Moreover, its regularities permit it to be analyzed and it is the means by which a person adjusts to his environment and expresses himself.

Culture is not organic. It can only exist where there is human life, as the lower animals do not have the ability to perpetuate their learning. The residue of social knowledge passed on through social transmission is the basic mechanism in culture which differs from the processes of biology. Culture is nongenetic. It is not learned by individual experience but socially. Culture is tradition which is handed down. Language is the most important means of social transmission.

Ants, bees, wasps, and termites are examples of animal societies that have some sort of communication system. These societies are tightly knit and the members are subsumed more completely in their social roles than in human society. They do not have ethics or religion. As their "experience" is probably transmitted through the genes, rather than through the kind of social learning by which human culture is transmitted, their type of social life cannot be termed culture.

Culture is an historical process, with any culture composite and hybrid and showing variations within groups.

Kroeber and Kluckhohn have classified definitions of culture as descriptive (broad statements), historical (social tradition), normative (the rule, ideals), psychological (adjustment, learning, habit, psychological, patterning), and genetic (artifact, idea, symbol).

culture, bow. See BOGENKULTUR.

culture, collection. The beginning of human culture, in which there are no artifacts nor any provision for the future. The state of collection culture is purely hypothetical, since it is not found in any extant or known society and since prehistorical societies are evidenced only by their artifacts.

culture, core. A culture characterized by the use of the coup-de-poing (q.v.).

culture, cross. Having references to more than one culture or to comparative studies among several cultures.

culture, flake. A culture characterized by the use of edged flake flint tools.

culture, folk. A culture characteristic of a small, tightly knit society, in which kinship is all-important.

culture, hoe. The earliest kind of agriculture. It is supposed to have been developed mainly by women, who used a hoe or pointed spadelike tool as their major implement. This culture is still widespread today. Usually, one type of plant provides the basic means of subsistence in a hoe culture. Roots often cultivated with the hoe are potatoes, yams, and taro. Grains often cultivated are rice and maize. The hoe was usually associated with a seminomadic life, except in those cases where it was found in a river valley that had fertile soil because of irrigation or fruit-tree cultivation.

culture, holistic. The culture of mankind, considered as a unit.

culture, nonliterate. A term used to describe what is often called preliterate or primitive culture. Many modern writers prefer the term nonliterate because it does not assume (preliterate) an inevitable advance to writing or (primitive) an early type of culture that will later mature.

culture, nonmaterial. Those elements of a culture that are intangible.

culture, partitive. The specific culture of a given society.

culture, plow. A culture characterized by the use of the plow (q.v.), a complicated system of irrigation, and regular fertilizing of the soil.

culture, preliterate. A culture which has never used writing. See CULTURE, NONLITERATE.

culture, two-class. A culture with a mixture of totemism (q.v.) and mother right (q.v.).

culture, universal pattern of. The common elements in all known culture.

culture area. See AREA, CULTURE.

culture epoch. See THEORY, CULTURE EPOCH. The theory that the individual recapitulates human cultural development, in his own cul-

tural development. It is associated with G. Stanley Hall .

culture historical. Referring to a school of anthropological thought, largely German-Austrian, which represents a modified diffusionist (q.v.) point of view. The culture historical school emphasizes worldwide diffusion and hypothesizes contacts among cultures, which are used to reconstruct man's history. General history and the productions of a culture are woven together, with some reliance on psychological factors. This school was founded by Fritz Graebner, although its most prominent recent leader has been Father Wilhelm Schmidt, who added some mystical elements.

culture subarea. See SUBAREA, CULTURE.

culturology. The science dealing with culture as a distinct class of phenomena and which seeks to explain elements of culture in terms of other cultural factors rather than by reference to biological or psychological phenomena. The term *Kulturologie* was first used by Wilhelm Ostwald, the German chemist and philosopher, before 1915. More recently, Leslie A. White has proposed the term culturology as the proper designation for the science of culture, which he points out is not coextensive with sociology or social psychology.

cumin. A carrot that was widely used as a medicine and a condiment.

cuneiform. Referring to a writing method of antiquity, characterized by wedge-shaped signs. It was developed by the Sumerians in Meso-

146

potamia as early as the fourth and third millennia B.C. Cuneiforms appear in Babylonian, Persian, and Assyrian stone inscriptions and were the chief means of written communication for many languages of antiquity as late as the second and first millennia, until the development of the Egyptian pen, ink, and papyrus just prior to the Christian era. Cuneiform writing, however, continued till the Christian period. Business and private writing dropped it first, while officials were more conservative. By the beginning of the fifth century B.C., it fell into disuse as Babylonian declined. In the third to first century B.C., it reappeared briefly because of the favor of the Seleucid dynasty. The last known cuneiform writing dates from 6 B.C. Cuneiform was not deciphered until the 19th century. Early Persian script, the most recent, was understood first, and the earliest Sumerian cuneiform script last.

cup, incense. A small urn-shaped vessel often found in early cremations. Incense cups are usually found upside down. They may have been used to light the funeral pyre. Usually they were perforated at least once.

cup, paint. A natural geological formation in the shape of a cup with ocher placed inside. The paint cup was used for painting by the Virginia Indians and others.

cup and the pin. A game of the western hemisphere in which a skull, or an object with holes, is swung by a cord toward a pointed stick. The holes, or the parts of the skull, are assigned a numerical value, and the player swings the "cup" toward himself and aims the stick at the hole with the highest value.

cupola. Rounded roof or ceiling. Cupola also may mean a small projection built onto a roof or building.

cupping. Using small glasses or cups for bloodletting by holding them over the skin and creating a vacuum.

cupreous. Referring to copper.

cupule. A concavity or pit shaped like a cup.

curar con blanquillos. See CURING, EGG.

curare. A dried extract of the woody vine *Strychnos toxifera,* used as an arrow poison.

curdling. The process by which bacilli separate the curds from the whey in milk.

curds. The comparatively solid protein component of milk, which becomes separated by the lactic acid bacilli in the milk. Some nomadic groups dry the curds and use them as staple foods.

curers, animal. Animals that were presumed to have the ability to cure disease.

curing. The process of making skins impervious to water as well as reasonably pliable. Animal fats may be used for curing. The most lasting technique is tanning (q.v.).

curing, egg. In Central America, rubbing a patient's body with an uncooked egg to diagnose or cure. For diagnosis, the egg is broken so that an examination will reveal the disease. For treatment, the egg is usually placed in a stream of water, in order to get rid of the heat from the patient's body. The process of egg curing is also known by its Spanish name of *curar con blanquillos*.

curragh. A skin-covered craft resembling a coracle (q.v.). The body is made of paired wands in a bowl shape. There is a wooden seat in the center. The gunwale is constructed first, with the sides and bottom put in position later. The curragh is found in Ireland.

currying. Removing the hair from a skin by soaking it in water after rubbing in wood ashes.

curse. The words used to invoke forces outside man to cause trouble. Curses are almost universal. They call on a power against which there is little defense and they may be effective in the future. A curse is injurious because it puts the speaker in a special relation with a deity or demon or is effective through its own inherent power. Priests, magicians, and those on the verge of death had special powers for cursing. Cursing was usually private, but it was used as a public ritual in higher religions. An oath (q.v.) was often worded as a curse which would take effect if the speaker did not fulfill certain conditions. A qualified person could destroy a curse's effect by a blessing (q.v.) or a countercurse.

curse, conditional. An invocation that difficulties or bad luck will strike the object of a curse if certain conditions are realized or if the alleged facts are not true.

cursive. Referring to writing which has joined strokes and often has rounded angles. Cursive writing has been found on Pompeiian wax tablets from 55 A.D. Roman cursive writing gave rise to European national scripts and to italic printing.

curtailment. A tendency for a diphthong (q.v.) to become a simple vowel in rapid speech.

Curtius, Ernst (1814-96). A German archaeologist and writer who, in 1875 at Olympia, organized the first modern systematic and cooperative archaeological research.

curve, Praxiteles. Inverted S-curve developed by the Greek sculptor Praxiteles in arranging the human form. He obtained sensuous representation of the body in repose by erecting the figure in a relaxed vertical position, the weight on the right foot which was forward, the left foot swung back, the left arm outstretched to the side, the right hip curved out, and the head turned to the right.

Cushite. A language branch of the Semitic-Hemitic group, spoken in the south of Egypt. It includes Galla and Somali.

cushma. An untailored garment in the form of a long shirt. It is made by sewing together the edges of one or two rectangular pieces of cloth to form side seams, while leaving apertures to serve as sleeves and as a slit for the head. It is found in the Montaña area of South America and in adjoining parts of the Tropical Forest.

cusp. A high point on the crown of a tooth, part of the mastication surface.

custom. A group behavior pattern that may be established by tradition, by contemporary social habits, or religious precepts, as differentiated from a legally enforced institution (q.v.). Customs are enforced by social disapproval of their violation. They lack the coercive backing of the state (q.v.) and the sanctions of the mores (q.v.). Fashion and convention are less important than custom.

Custom, Yam. The Ashanti yam harvest ceremony.

customs, birth. The observances before and after the birth of a child, usually established to protect both the mother and the child.

customs, death. Ritual observances of a death, usually based on the fear of death by nonliterate people.

Customs, Grand. A ceremony performed at a Dahomey king's death.

cut, strata. An excavation, usually small (perhaps two by four meters), made to determine the stratigraphy of an area. Strata cuts are generally made at arbitrary levels.

cutting, clear. Removing all trees from a wooded area.

Cuvier, Georges (1769-1832). A French scholar, the founder of comparative anatomy and of paleontology. He hypothesized that each epoch was successively destroyed and then recreated as a result of a series of catastrophes. Cuvier was tremendously influential in his day and flatly denied that there were any fossil human bones. He created the concept of homology. He suggested a trifurcate classification of humans, into Caucasian, Mongolian,

and Ethiopian, which is still the most popular classification of races.

cycle. A large time span or period, usually featured by a dramatic beginning, a steady development, and a catastrophic finale that eradicates all preceding occurrences. The basis for this belief is the general concept of ages of the world, e.g., the Golden Age, Silver, Bronze Age, and the concept of the calendar round, or calendar series, at the conclusion of which the series recommences. Cycles are often based on the movements of the heavenly bodies. The Babylonians and the Mayans both estimated a cycle of about 33,000 years, although they arrived at this conclusion independently. The Hindus estimated the cycle of a "Day of Brahm" to be 4,320,000 years long.

cycle, life. The lifetime of a person or group, with particular reference to the nodal points of the cycle, which is often seen as repeating itself in the future.

cycle, Sothic. The period in early Egyptian reckoning when the calendar date and the actual date coincided. Because there was no allowance for leap years, the Sothic cycle took 1,460 years.

cycle, type life. The period between the introduction and the final disappearance of an artifact type, with special reference to its period of growth and decline.

cyclometer. A device to measure the distance covered by a wagon or cart.

cyclothymia. In Kretschmer's system of constitutional types (q.v.),

149

the personality found associated with pyknic (q.v.) persons.

cylix. Greek ceramic drinking cup with a wide bowl, extensively used from Mycenean times through the best years of Athenian vase painting. The shape varied from the squat early Corinthian cylix of the sixth century B.C. to the tall and graceful Athenian cyclix with its simple black-figured decorative band. Most later cylixes bore representations of dancing and drinking scenes.

cymotrichous. Having curly hair.

Cynocephalus. The dog-headed ape, associated with the Egyptian god Thoth.

Cypriote. The ancient language of Cyprus, now extinct and virtually unknown, which is preserved in twelve inscriptions which are sup-

posed to date back to the fourth century B.C.

Cyprolithic. See AGE, CHALCO-LITHIC.

Cyriac de Pizzicolli (b. 1391). An Italian merchant who is often called the first archaeologist. He went to Greece and conducted excavations there.

Cyrillic. An alphabet invented around 900 A.D. by the followers of Cyril. It is based on ancient Greek capital letters and is less complete than the Glagoljica, also originated by Cyril. Present-day Russians, Bulgarians, and Serbs use it in their script.

cytogenetics. The study of the area common to both cytology and genetics.

cytoplasm. The contents of a cell other than its nucleus.

D

D pestle. A rocker-shaped stone used for grinding. It is found among the Totenac of Mexico and several other groups.

dacryon. The point of intersection of the maxillary, frontal, and lacrimal bones at the medial point of the orbit.

dactylomegaly. Possessing unusually large fingers.

dagger. A hilted, fairly short weapon with a blade. The earliest daggers had a triangular blade that was flat on each face and was usually less than six inches long. They were used for stabbing.

dagger, Cypriote. An early dagger characterized by a shank that extends through the handle and is held in place by bending the end of the shank back into the handle.

dagger, ogival. A dagger in which the blade's edges are parallel for some distance before tapering to a point.

dahlia. A tuberous-rooted thistle herb. It has been cultivated in Mexico for a very long time.

Dahl's law. See LAW. DAHL'S.

dahut. A hunting practical joke in which a novice hunter is left waiting indefinitely for the game while his associates leave him. The dahut is found in North Africa and France.

daimon. A special kind of supernatural entity that is distinct from the soul (q.v.) of an individual person. The term is also spelled daemon.

daimonism or **daimonology.** The body of knowledge dealing with spirits, their involvement in the activities of human beings, and the procedures for handling them.

dakhama. A deep pit circled by a tower, with a grating on top, on which bodies were placed to be eaten by carnivorous birds until the flesh-cleaned bones dropped through the grate into the pit. It is found among the Parsees of India. See SILENCE, TOWER OF.

dalca. A canoe built of planks and used by the Indians of the region of Chiloe Island in Chile.

daluka. A Sudanese drum, one end of which is covered with parchment.

damam. An Indian ritual drum made from two human skulls fastened together at the crowns. After the lower parts of the skulls are cut away, human skin is stretched over the cavities. The damam is used in certain temple ceremonies.

damascening. A decoration on metal widely found in India and Persia. A triangular groove is cut into the metal and silver and gold wire are hammered in. The term damascening is also used for designs with a watered appearance that are obtained by hammering previously soldered iron rods into a homogeneous mass.

damper. A bread of the Australian Bushmen, made of a mixture of flour, water, and baking powder and cooked in smoldering ashes.

dance. In its broadest sense, dance is moving the body and/or the feet in time to rhythm and is mainly a co-operative group art. It has been generally accepted that dance is an almost universal expression of man in all ages and nations. The dance is probably the most ancient art expression and has sometimes been called the major recreation of early man. Since birds and animals have been observed dancing and since the rhythm can be provided by clapping, etc., dance must have been an almost universal form of precultural play (see DANCE, PLAY). It may have been an overflow of joy, a need for self-dissolution, or a link with magic and religion. The dance may be engaged in either for its effect on the dancer or on an onlooker. It may both stimulate excitement and be an outlet for excitement. Dancing has been used to induce delirium and autointoxication by religious functionaries. Some groups, like the Bororos of South America, have made the ability to attain this kind of ecstacy the criterion of priesthood.

Dance has many functions in nonliterate societies, serving social, occupational, and religious ends. In labor based on unity of action, a dance leader often set the pace. Dance was also used to integrate a group engaged in warfare and to give training in preparation for combat. Groups which engage in battle, like the Maori, have war dances. Funeral dances are widespread and often mimetic, so that the dead could be influenced by sympathetic magic (q.v.).

dance, abdominal. A dance based on certain stylized movements of the pelvic region. The abdominal dance is usually performed by women and is believed to have originated as a fertility dance. The belly dance or *danse du ventre,* is considered a late variant.

dance, astronomic. The most ancient Egyptian dance, in which the dancers' movements symbolized the movements of the heavenly bodies. The astronomic dance was accompanied by the music of the flute and lyre. The dancers circled around the altar of the sun god Ra in groups representing the signs of the zodiac. This dance was also performed by the ancient Greeks around the burning altar of Zeus. The term is also used for a dance in which the stars, moon, or sun are worshipped. The expression celestial dance is sometimes found instead of astronomic dance.

dance, belly. See DANCE, ABDOMINAL.

dance, big-head. See KUKSU.

dance, bird. A symbolic dance of Madagascar, usually performed by women, in which the dancer leans forward with arms outstretched and beats the ground with her feet as the starting movement. She then draws her arms back, lets them fall, and extends them overhead. The dance then begins to accelerate as the music rises to a crescendo and the audience starts a handclapping accompaniment. The dancer's arms beat more and more frenziedly and she runs in a circle, twisting her fingers and arms convulsively, and finally falls to the ground exhausted.

dance, bison. A ceremonial dance of the Mandan, an Indian tribe of the upper Missouri. Eight male performers, dressed in buffalo hides, their bodies painted with bands of red, black, and white, imitate the movements of the buffalo.

dance, blackmailing. A dance in which the performers visit the dwelling of a person from whom they hope to obtain money. They sing and dance, shouting threats, until the victim agrees to pay.

dance, bread. An American Indian dance symbolizing sustenance, like the Shawnee dance for good hunting addressed to the female deity Kohkomhoena.

dance, calumet. An Indian ceremony centering around a smoke offering to the Great Spirit. The Indians of the Great Plains were particularly devoted to the calumet dance. It was used for rejoicing, to confirm peace pacts, and to welcome visitors.

dance, candle. A dance in which lighted candles are carried by the participants.

dance, celestial. See DANCE, ASTRONOMIC.

dance, chain. A dance in which the performers are arranged in a a long weaving line, as differentiated from dances in which the performers are paired or arranged in a circle.

dance, character. An interpretive dance in which the performer represents an animal or a person other than himself. In the character dance, the interpreter becomes the portrayer of another's experience and thereby loses his individual identity.

dance, corn. A dance, widely found in the New World. It is directed to the powers responsible for the growth of maize and asks them for rain and a bountiful harvest.

dance, couple. A dance symbolizing a man's courtship of a woman. The bolero in Spain is a well-known current example. Originally the couple dance was probably a fertility dance.

dance, courtship. A widely practiced form of dance used in courtship. Among Australasians, men dance while women watch. The dancer may show his skill in handling weapons, with the woman selecting the man she likes the most. Courtship dances excite sexual impulses as well as express them.

dance, death. A dance for the deceased or for representatives of Death. Death dances may be intended to commune with or propitiate the dead or to exorcise a dangerous spirit.

dance, demon. A ceremonial masked miming of extranatural forces. The demon dance is intended to get the help of these forces or to exorcise them.

dance, duck. A North American Indian dance that represents the duck. The object of the duck dance is to increase the supply of wild fowl.

dance, eagle. An American Indian dance that mimes the eagle's flight and thus tries to reach the powers in charge of rain and thunder, in whose realm the eagle presumably lives.

dance, Egyptian. A dance that combines writhing and bending motions with sharp, angular posturings, as represented in ancient Egyptian drawings and engravings.

dance, eland bull. A ceremonial dance among the Bushmen.

dance, fish. A North American Indian dance in which a fish's motions are suggested.

dance, folk. A form of dance that is supposed to spring spontaneously from the desire of the common people of a nation for communal expression. Folk dances are handed down within the community or nation. They are performed for the sheer joy of the activity, in distinction to the art dance, which attempts to communicate specific ideas.

dance, ghost. A ceremonial that acted out the symbolic return of the Indians and the departure of the whites from the North American continent. The ghost dance was developed ca. 1870, by the Nevada Paiutes, and it became popular 20 years later among the Plains Indians. The dance reflected the unhappiness of the Indians at the disappearance of their way of life under the onslaught of white civilization. With the evident failure of warfare, hope developed that there would be a millenial restoration of the past.

dance, goat. A dance in which the male goat is impersonated. Goat dances are often associated with licentious and mischievous behavior. Greek tragedy is believed by some authorities to have arisen from the goat song associated with these dances.

dance, green-corn. See BUSK.

dance, horse. A symbolic ride on a horse or a hobbyhorse. The purpose of the horse dance may be to express martial vigor or the horse's importance. Many American Indian tribes had such a dance.

dance, hot. A dance in which the participants put their arms in very hot water and remove immersed dog meat or splash each other while assuring themselves that the water was cold. The hot dance was found among the Plains Indians.

dance, John Canoe. A West Indies drinking bout in which the participants consume canoe loads of beer.

dance, jumping. A ceremonial dance of the Hupa and Yurok Indians. There are many dancers and a display of wealth. The jumping dance is intended to dispel sickness and procure food. The steps are chiefly leaps, and a "dancing basket" is used.

dance, leap. A dance with leaping. The leap dance often involves sympathetic magic (q.v.), since the leap is believed to be a sign of the vital impulse, with a high leap betokening a tall crop. Such dances may be used for therapy, inducing martial fervor, or as a display of strength. See DANCE, PHALLIC.

dance, lift. A dance in which a girl is raised from the ground by her male partner. Lift dances were probably associated with fertility magic, since a defiance of the law of gravity is presumed by many peoples to effect reproduction, on the analogy, perhaps, of penile erection.

dance, limping. A Plains Indian dance in which a limp is suggested by dragging one foot or lifting it off the ground.

dance, line. A dance in which the participants form in one or more straight lines.

dance, longways. A dance in which the participants are aligned in two facing parallel lines.

dance, owl. An American Indian dance in which the movements and activities of an owl are suggested.

dance, phallic. A dance with the theme of fertility. Upward leaps and kicks often symbolize fertility. The sexual elements of the phallic dance may be overt or symbolized. Stamping of the leg is common, with the leg identified with the penis and the earth being entered symbolically. See DANCE, LEAP.

dance, play. A dance which serves the function of play. Such dances are found among birds, insects, and fish, as well as humans. They help to release a surplus of energy. The conclusion of play dances is often orgiastic.

dance, puberty. A dance to celebrate a young person's attaining puberty. Often the participants are the older members of the society. Such dances are often in circular formation.

dance, rabbit. A dance that centers around the rabbit and imitates rabbit movements and activities. It is found among many North American Indians.

dance, scalp. A dance performed by American Indians after collecting scalps. The performers usually dance in circles around the scalps after mounting them on poles. The dance often involves a symbolization of battle activities.

dance, snake. A dance in which a snake is either handled or its activities or movements are imitated. The snake is often regarded as a fertility symbol, and such dances may represent fertility rites. Among the Hopi Indians, the snake dance is traditionally performed every two years around August 20. Snake priests may carry live rattlesnakes in their mouth in the ceremony. Nine days of elaborate ritual precede the dance. In groups of three the snake priests proceed by a kind of hopping step to a hut in which the snakes are kept. The priest carrying the snake is given a snake and holds it at the middle in his mouth. The other two priests wave feathers at the snake to distract it as they walk the other priest around the plaza. A new snake is taken after the third trip around, until all the snakes have been carried. Rain is one of the goals of this ceremony.

dance, snake-antelope. A Hopi dance of priests who carry several kinds of snakes and then release them to the cardinal directions, in order to get rain. The snake-antelope dance was performed every other year up to 1912.

dance, solstice. A dance which is designed to help the sun change its course. It is very widely distributed and is especially common at the winter solstice as a celebration of the sun's return. Traces of the solstice dance may be found among the Pueblo Indians today.

dance, stick. A dance in which a stick is handled. The stick is often used as a phallic symbol.

dance, sun. A fertility dance directed at the sun as a symbol of life, widely found in early America. The best known of the sun dances is that of the Great Plains Indians, which lasted for several days and was centered around a special tall pole. It often included self-inflicted torture or deliberately induced exhaustion designed to obtain visions. There is often a symbolic bird in the ceremonies. See SWINGING, HOOK.

dance, sword. A dance for men in which the participants handle and manipulate a sword either alone or with others. A sword dance may be used in various ceremonial settings, such as weddings or solstice observances. It is possible that the sword is a phallic symbol.

dance, torch. A religious or feast dance in which lighted torches are carried aloft by the performers.

dance, turkey. A North American Indian dance that imitates the turkey.

dance, turtle. A dance of some American Indian groups involving a symbolic contact with the turtle's fertility.

dance, war. A dance in which combat is mimed or which represents a prebattle emotional reinforcement, with a possible sham battle. The war dance has had fertility overtones. Women had roles in some North American war dances.

dandy. A North India palanquin.

danse du ventre. See DANCE, ABDOMINAL.

dao. A straight-edged blade which is about a foot long and fits into a bamboo handle. The dao is very widely used among the Lhota and neighboring groups.

dapay. A Bontoc men's house.

daphneomancy. The art of divination (q.v.) from the crackling sound made by a dried laurel branch when thrown into a fire.

Darmesteter's law. See LAW, DARMESTETER'S.

dart. A small missile weapon consisting of a shaft with a pointed head. The shaft may also be pointed. A butt of soft material is often found. Darts may be hurled at their target by a blowgun.

dasher, churn. The piston that goes up and down in a churn.

dating, cross. The process of establishing the relative age of cultural phenomena that are not directly connected to each other, i.e., objects found archaeologically in different hemispheres.

dating, direct. Dating a particular object in years by the study of the object itself.

dating, fluorine. Using the comparative amount of fluorine in bones and teeth to determine their comparative age, since these remains absorb fluorine in the ground. The method was adumbrated in 1806, when two French chemists discovered that ivory absorbs fluorine when in the soil. In 1892, Adolphe Carnot showed how the technique could be used to date bones comparatively.

dating, guess. An estimate of the chronological sequence or approximate date of an archaeological site or culture made on the basis of evidence that is not completely confirmable.

dating, indirect. Dating an object by its connection with another object the age of which can be estimated.

dating, lexico-statistical. Obtaining a time index of the linguistic changes in a dispersed speech community, based on the fairly constant rate of replacement of the noncultural daily vocabulary. Two test vocabularies from different areas are obtained. The comparative percentage of cognate words found in the test vocabularies provides an index to the time since which they began diverging and hence an indication of when the speech community was still unified.

dating, radioactive. Determining the age of rocks and other materials by the analysis of the constant rate of breakdown of radioactive materials into a number of decay products. Thus, uranium 238 will decay into a lead isotope over several billion years, and the age of the rock can be determined by comparing the ratio of the uranium to the end product. New techniques permit very small quantities of ores to be used in dating and also permit many different substances to be analyzed from the same sample, each checking on the other, so that one rock sample may be analyzed through its thorium, uranium, lead, rubidium, strontium, and potassium. Small amounts of isotopes can be separated through the ion-exchange resin columns, and they can be measured by the isotope-dilution technique and the mass spectrometer.

This new method permits many different kinds of rocks to be dated, because it is not confined to highly concentrated ores, and it permits more samples of a single rock structure to be used. Radioactive materials found in granite show fewer discrepancies in age than materials from other areas. Although most of the previous work has been done with uranium and lead end-products, the rubidium-strontium system is increasingly employed because it permits the use of more varied granite materials than do other radioactive combinations. Radioactive dating by the isotype-dilution method of measuring has lead to the discovery of some of the oldest rocks in the world. Granite from Manitoba, Canada, has been found to be 3,500,000,000 years old, while the Bikita Quarry in Southern Rhodesia has yielded rocks 3,300,000,000 years old, and Jakkalswater, South Africa, rocks 2,400,000,000 years old.

dating, radiocarbon. The analysis of radioactive carbon (C 14) in archaeological samples to help date the remains. The method is especially useful in dating materials originating within the last 20,000 to 30,000 years. It is important that unaltered organic materials be used.

In 1950, W. F. Libby and his associates developed a method of carbon-dating archaeological specimens by measuring the activity of carbon-bearing samples with a screen-wall type of Geiger counter. This was the first accurate technique for dating archaeological remains that bore no inscriptions or were not the subject of contemporaneous literary references.

Late in 1953, scientists from the University of Manitoba announced a method of dating all matter which has radioactive carbon—like vegetation, fossils, and bones—from as long as some 40,000 years ago, with a probable error of 10 years. The new process employs a scintillator counter. The material to be dated is immersed into the liquid scintillator and produces light flashes that are registered by an electronic eye. In an average human body, 100,000 carbon atoms disintegrate each minute. If part of a body were preserved 5,000 years, the number of disintegrations would be reduced by 50 per cent.

All of the methods of carbon-dating developed so far require the destruction of the sample being dated. The age of the sample and the degree of accuracy of the desired dating are positively correlated with the size of the piece that has to be dissolved or burned. The Libby method uses a piece that weighs an ounce or more.

dating, sequence. A method of finding the relative chronology of objects in an archaeological find, developed by Sir Flinders Petrie in Diospolis Parva, Egypt. He discovered pots with a wavy handle, which became less wavy on pots of similar shape found in later graves, with the original handle a scratched decoration on the most recent pots. Petrie put the objects found along with the pots in chronological order. Not knowing the pots' absolute date, Petrie divided the period of their use into 70 parts, dating each type from S.D. (sequence date) 30 to S.D. 100, permitting room for earlier finds. S.D. 79 was later discovered to be around the beginning of the dynastic period, 3200 B.C., and Petrie estimated that S.D. 30, or the beginning of the series, was ca. 4800 B.C. Recent carbon 14 tests have somewhat reduced the dates of these periods.

datu. A Bagobo chief.

Daun. Following the fourth glacial period in Europe, the third, and last, minor glacial advance, from 7500 to 6500 B.C.

David, star of. A star with six points, made of two superimposed triangles. The triangles presumably represent male and female. The star of David was believed to quell demons. The term Solomon's seal is also used.

days, epagomenal. The 5 days added to the ancient Egyptian year of 12 months, each having 30 days, in order to bring the calendar up to the true year's length.

days, halcyon. The good weather which presumably occurs in the seven days before and after the winter solstice. Halcyon days are so called because the halcyon (king-fisher) is supposed to be able to float undisturbed in the absolutely calm water that prevails in that period.

dawak. Spirit possession of Tinguian mediums.

dead, abode of the. The place where the dead are believed to live. The abode of the dead may be in the sea, sky, or under the surface of the ground. The dead may have a ruler. It may be possible to visit the residence of the dead while still alive, as did Odysseus, Aeneas, and Orpheus.

Dead, Book of the. See BOOK OF THE DEAD.

dead, cult of the. Ceremonial activities to get the help of the dead or make them comfortable. The cult of the dead is found in Polynesia and elsewhere.

dead, disposal of the. Many different techniques have been used to dispose of the dead. At first, it is likely that bodies were simply left where they fell. Burial was the next step, followed by a period of partial cremation. Gradually, cremation became obsolete, and burial began to be the most widely used technique. Egypt embalmed its dead, although incineration was the practice in most of the ancient world.

Christianity has generally been opposed to cremation on the grounds that the substance to be resurrected at the Last Judgment must be kept intact. The body may be disposed of by placing it in or on the ground, leaving it on a platform, burning it, or placing it in an urn.

dead, door of the. A portal built in a house for the express purpose of removing a dead body from the dwelling in order that the ghost will not be able to find its way back to haunt the survivors. This door is ordinarily sealed up again after the corpse has been taken out.

dead, fate of the. The problem of what happens to the dead after death is variously answered. They may die several times, stop existing, continue as they did when alive, be reborn or reincarnated, or possess the living.

dead, feasts for the. A feast held in association with a death, shortly after a death, or even continuing for several years after it has taken place. A feast for the dead may be eaten at the funeral, at the grave itself, or at some distance from the grave. The major motives in these feasts are probably the desire to feed the deceased, to help him obtain rest and happiness, to take a meal with him and therefore create a closer union, or to propitiate his spirit. The desire to obtain descendants may also figure.

dead, prayer for the. A prayer to help the deceased, beginning with leaving food at the grave. This developed into communication with the deity on behalf of the deceased and of oneself. Those religions that have the concept of an intermediate state often use prayer as a means of getting the deceased to the next higher state.

deadfall. A trap that drops a weight or lever on its victim once a trigger has been released.

deanthropomorphism. The movement originated by the cynic Xenophanes and continually developed by rationalists, away from the practice of endowing idealized images with human characteristics.

death. Most cultures have a concept of a life after death. Confucianism is one of the few religions in which a "good death" is accepted as the proper end of a good life.

In early societies, the concept of death may have been difficult to accept. Disobedience, women, curiosity, etc., were held attributable for death. A person's death was perhaps not often accepted as natural but as the result of some malevolent person or influence.

There are many ways of handling the dying and the dead. Many early societies regard the corpse as dangerous. Weeping is not a universal phenomenon. A funeral may be held. Some precautions may be taken against the soul's return, e.g., turning the body around while en route, crossing water. Burial may be in crouching, sitting, or extended position. The facial orientation is usually prescribed, with east the favored direction. Some objects may go into the grave along with the corpse for the afterlife. A feast may be linked to the death observances (see DEAD, FEASTS FOR THE). Those who were in touch with the corpse may have to be purified. See DEAD, DISPOSAL OF THE.

death, letter of. A letter which calls for the death of the bearer.

deception, auricular. A tale dealing with an element or a natural force that speaks, usually by an echo.

decimal. Referring to a counting system based on 10. The decimal system probably springs from the use of both hands as a major unit.

decimeter. Ten centimeters.

declension. The scheme by which differences in case, gender, and number of a noun, pronoun, adjective, or number are shown. The modifications are accomplished by inflection (q.v.).

decoction. Boiling something in water to extract its essence.

décolleté. A woman's garment that exposes the neck and part of the upper bosom. Décolleté was introduced at the end of the Middle Ages.

decumanus. A road in a town in ancient Rome.

decury. A company or group of 10; a group or class of any number; an Inca tribal unit.

deff. An African percussion instrument from Algeria. It is constructed of a wooden frame with parchment covering both sides and is beaten with the hands to produce the sound.

defilement. The state of being unclean, resulting from contact with death, giving birth, disease, sacrilege, bloodletting, or similar associations. Defilement is a concept that is midway between spiritual and physical uncleanliness.

deflector. See SCREEN, FIRE.

defloration. Taking away a woman's virginity, usually during and in connection with the observances surrounding her marriage. A man other than her husband or mechanical techniques may be employed.

deformation. Changing or disfiguring part of the body. The waist, lips, ears, nose, head, and feet have been the parts most usually deformed. The nose is often flattened or bored, and the ears and lips can be made longer through weights. The head shape is changed by pressure applied to the skull and the waist by constriction. Deformation has been practiced more by women than by men. Darwin pointed out that there seems to be a tendency to exaggerate characteristics already present, so that people with large lips make their lips still larger.

deformation, cranial. The deformation of the head for cosmetic or other reasons. The largely membranous head of the infant is easily changed in shape by flattening the forehead or occiput or by cylindrically or conically lengthening the crown or occiput. Boards, bandaging, and similar devices are widely used to change the shape of the head in infancy.

deformation, nasal. Deforming the nose by piercing the septum, the alae, or the tip, or by making it smaller or larger.

degeneration. Continual hereditary deterioration in the development of a species.

degradation. The theory that man was originally civilized but that some men, the nonliterates, had fallen from grace and had had themselves and their cultures degraded. The theory of degradation was based on theological reasoning.

dehiscence. A gap, resulting from total ossification, in the tympanic plate of the temporal bone.

deicide. Literally god-killing, usually referring to the symbolic or actual murder of a totem animal or of a priest-king in early religion.

deictic. Referring to uninflected particles that are added to nouns to indicate their position, e.g., *here.*

deification. The process of making objects, natural phenomena, ideas, and persons into deities. Deification was probably an expression of man's desire to be godlike, especially after death. The deification of fertility was especially common. The Egyptians, Indians, Greeks, and Romans were particularly prone to worship gods who were deified men or forces.

deiseal. In Ireland, a circumambulation (q.v.) around certain sacred objects. Good luck presumably comes from this imitation of the sun's circuit.

delabialization. The change in a sound produced by the unrounding of the lips, e.g., from Anglo-Saxon *cyng* to English *king.*

delative. Referring to a declensional case having the denotation of a descending motion. The delative appears in certain non-Indo-European languages.

delftware. A brown pottery is covered with a white opaque glaze, on which decoration is painted. Delftware takes its name from Delft, Holland.

delta. An alluvial deposit near a river's mouth, often forming a large tract of land. It may be in the triangle shape of the Greek letter delta, because of the river's division into separate branches. Deltas may be formed on the open coast, on lakes or bays, or where two rivers join.

deluge. The great flood that appears in the religious traditions of virtually all peoples and that destroyed all but a few inhabitants of the earth. Scientific study gives little credence to the belief that there was a universal flood. However, it is probable that there were many disastrous local floods, and therefore the legends were magnified by time and molded by theology. It is probable also that mutual influence and borrowing had an effect on their spread. The story which appears in the Bible is closely akin to the Babylonian legend and tells of how Yahweh willed the flood and gave advance notice to Noah. The Persian high god told Yima to build a walled compound to save the good people. These two examples show how the legend was used to demonstrate moral concepts. In India, however, the flood was one of a series of cosmic calamities which periodically destroyed the world. The Chinese flood was a local affair.

demography. The statistical analysis and description of populations. Demography considers distribution, vital statistics, age, sex, birth rate, death rate, and mobility over a period or at one time.

demon. A lower type of superhuman person, thought to be an enemy of mankind, found in a number of religions. Demons are believed to be responsible for misfortune and trouble. The demons are usually believed to be in the lower parts of the earth, although they could make themselves felt throughout the universe. They had the power of invisibility and could sometimes effect possession of the personality of humans. Much attention was given to ridding the possessed of these demons, often by exorcism (q.v.). Some demons, however, were believed to be benevolent toward men. **Demonology** is the study of demons.

De Mortillet. See MORTILLET, GABRIEL DE.

demotic. The cursive modification of hieratic (q.v.) writing used for the vulgar dialect. Demotic was used from 900 B.C. to the fourth century A.D. The term, meaning popular vulgar characters, comes from Herodotus. Hieratic writing deteriorated, and demotic, having become a proper system of writing in Lower Egypt, became the popular writing of Egypt. At first used for letters, it was gradually adopted for long compositions. Demotic was written from right to left. It is difficult to read. The term enchorial is sometimes used.

demulcent. A substance, like gum arabic, which can sooth or protect an inflamed member.

dendrochronology. The analysis of tree rings to date artifacts. A layer is added to the tree's circumference each year; it is thin in a dry year and wider in a wet year. Each layer's end is indicated by a dark ring from the most recent growth. The layers can be counted and the tree's age determined as of the time it is cut. Since the climatic sequence has been worked out for certain areas, it may be possible to determine the date a tree was cut from the configuration of the rings. Even burned wood can be dated. The physicist A. E. Douglass worked the method out to date climate. He first applied it to archaeological remains in 1914, when he began dating some beams from Pueblo Bonito. He published his results in 1935. The Southwest was the first area studied by dendochronology, and the method has been applied to other areas in the United States and Europe.

dendromorphic. Referring to beings, especially gods, who resemble trees.

Deniker, Joseph (1852-1918). A Russian-French anthropologist whose book, *The Races of Man* (1900), was widely influential. He emphasized that the criteria for race should be physical rather than linguistic. Deniker classified humans into six races and 29 racial groups on the basis of a wide variety of characteristics.

denotative term. See TERM, DE-NOTATIVE.

dental. Referring to a sound made by the tongue used in conjunction with the teeth, e.g., *t*.

dental formula. See FORMULA, DENTAL.

dentalium. A genus of gasteropodous mollusks with a tubular arcuate coned shell open at both ends. It was widely used for money, beads and belts by the American Indians.

dentine. On the tooth, the material found between the enamel (q.v.) and the pulp chamber and between the cementum (q.v.) and the pulp chamber. Dentine is softer than enamel.

depas amphikypellon. A double cup. It has two handles or one divided by a partition. Homer refers to a depas amphikypellon which, it is generally agreed, was a two-handled vessel that flared upward from a nearly pointed vase.

Depéret's law. See LAW, DE-PÉRET'S.

depigmentation. The loss or diminution of an organism's pigmentation.

deposit. The remains left by the living habits of early human groups. Examples are kitchen middens and graves.

deposition, travertine. The rate at which stalactites (q.v.) and stalagmites (q.v.) grow. Travertine deposition is used to date archaeological sites.

depranocytosis. See ANEMIA, SICKLE CELL.

depth, bi-iliac. See DEPTH, PELVIC.

depth, chest. The transverse distance of the most lateral points of the chest, averaging the expiration and inspiration of a normally breathing subject.

depth, pelvic. The distance between the iliocristales. The pelvic depth is also called the bi-iliac depth.

derbouka. An earthenware drum found in Arabia. The derbouka is a long hollow tube with a parchment or skin head stretched over one end. It is played with the fingers of both hands.

derivation. The process of making a new word out of a pre-existent word by adding a prefix or suffix, or by some other method. The term derivation also means giving the source and development of the elements in a word.

derivative term. See TERM, DE-RIVATIVE.

dermatoglyphics. The analysis of the ridge patternings of the skin of the fingers, palms, soles, and toes. In 1823, the Breslau physiologist Purkenje used fingerprints for identification and classification. In 1858, Sir William J. Herschel used native hand prints as a seal on documents and in 1877 began using them for official purposes. Sir Francis Galton (q.v.) made the study of fingerprints scientific.

dervish. An Islamic ascetic, chiefly remarkable for the mode of prayer. Frequently chanted, the devotions are accompanied by prescribed bodily movements that increase in intensity and speed until a kind of ecstasy is achieved.

descent. The several kinds of degree of closeness of association with others through kinship. Matrilineal and patrilineal descent refer to the mother's or father's sib (or other group), respectively. Bilateral descent (q.v.) has reference to either indifferently or both equally. Double descent (q.v.) is restricted to a maternal group of one type and a paternal group of another type. The family in the United States observes bilateral descent.

descent, agnatic. See PATRI-LINEAL.

descent, asymmetric. Descent which is decided differently by each sex.

descent, bilateral. A method of reckoning descent in which the individual has equal affiliation with his four grandparents and no unilinear emphasis. The kindred (q.v.) is the most widely found kind of bilateral descent group. A comparatively small percentage of societies, including that of the West, follows bilateral descent.

descent, cross-sex. A system of reckoning descent in which females are related to the mother of their father and males to the father of their mother. Cross-sex descent is a type of mixed descent.

descent, double or **descent, double unilineal.** An individual's simultaneous association with one social group from his father and another from his mother, so that he may belong to his father's patrilineal sib and his mother's matrilineal sib.

descent, indirect. A system of descent whereby a child belongs to the totemic clan of its father's father rather than to that of its mother or father. Indirect descent is found in Australia and Papua.

descent, mixed. See DESCENT, SEX-LINKED; DESCENT, CROSS-SEX.

descent, sex-linked. A system of reckoning kinship in which females are related to the females in the mother's line and males are related to males in the father's line, e.g., among the Sula of Indonesia. Sex-linked descent is a form of mixed descent.

descent, uterine. See MATRI-LINEAL.

descriptive. The name given by Lewis H. Morgan (q.v.) to methods of expressing kinship by using specific technical terms for specific individual relationships, e.g., in western civilization. See SYSTEM, CLASSIFICATORY; TERM, DESCRIPTIVE.

desert. A comparatively waterless area in which the annual rainfall seldom exceeds 15 inches. There is little vegetation or animal life and few water sources. Some gardening is possible near oases.

desert, hamada and erg. A desert consisting of rocky plateaus with only slight relief, sometimes with some sand-filled basins.

desert, mountain and bolson. A desert in which there are either scattered ranges or mountains separated by fairly substantial basins.

detection, louse. The study of the relations among given animal species through tracing the kinds of lice carried by them.

determinant. An additional character added to a word symbol to indicate which of more than one meaning is relevant. A determinant is also sometimes called a classifier.

determination, cultural. The molding of a culture by ecological, biological, or other factors.

determination, phosphate. A method for discovering the most densely inhabited part of a site without excavating the whole area. Settlement rubbish leaves a high content of phosphate in the soil, and soil samples from different parts of the site can be studied to determine the area with the greatest amount of phosphate.

determinism, economic. The theory that economic factors and the distribution of economic power in a culture determine cultural life. Karl Marx is prominently associated with the doctrine of economic determinism.

determinism, environmental. The position that the physical environment and such factors as natural resources and climate largely determine the development of a group.

detritus. The loose material resulting from the disintegration of rocks. It is often called debris.

Deutero-Malay. See MALAY, DEUTERO-.

Devanagari. The form of script in which ancient Sanskrit and modern Hindi are written.

devoicing. The process by which a voiced consonant becomes unvoiced. Devoicing, or unvoicing, occurs when the vocal bands cease vibrating during production of the sound.

devolution. Retrogression from a more advanced and differentiated condition to one which is less advanced and differentiated. Devolution is the reverse of evolution.

Devonian. Referring to a life period in the Paleozoic Age in which lung fishes and bony fishes first appeared. The Devonian lasted from perhaps 320 to 275 million years ago.

dewclaw. A rudimentary function-less mammalian hoof or claw. A dewclaw is also a small bone or nail behind the foot of an ungulate or the small uppermost claw in a dog that does not touch the ground.

dextrality. Using and favoring the right hand over the left.

dextrality, index of. See HANDED-NESS.

dextrosinistral. A naturally left-handed person who has been taught to use his right hand in drawing, carving, writing, and working.

dhola. An Indian percussion in-strument that combines some of the qualities of the drum and the tam-bourine. The dhola is made by bor-ing a hollow shell from a solid wood block and stretching parchment over both ends and fastening it with leather strips and hemp hooks. The dhola sometimes has metal rings fastened to the sides that are struck with sticks. It is played mostly at feasts and weddings.

dhoti. An Indian one-piece gar-ment. The dhoti is a T-shaped long piece of cloth worn around the waist and hanging down between the legs so that it forms an extem-porized kind of trousers.

diabolism. Believing in the exis-tence of a personified agency for evil, usually the Devil.

diachronic. Referring to the his-torical or developmental approach to the study of culture. See SYN-CHRONIC.

diacritical. A sign attached to a letter in order to distinguish it from others of similar form or to indicate that the letter represents a particu-lar sound, e.g., ō and ö. Diacritical also means an act the function of which is to separate an individual from one group and reinforce his identity with another, in the study of society. The term in that sense has been taken from linguistics.

diaeresis. The written symbol placed over one vowel that is next to another to indicate that the vowel is not pronounced as a diphthong with the other vowel but is to be assigned its customary independent phonetic value in pronunciation. The most common diaeresis is (¨).

diagraph. See DIGRAPH.

dialect. A provincial or local lan-guage form. A dialect usually differs from the standard form of the lan-guage in morphology, vocabulary, pronunciation and idioms. Although a distinct entity, it is not different enough from other dialects to be a separate language but can be under-stood by speakers of the remaining dialects. In strict linguistic usage, the standard form is itself but one among the dialects of the language. See AREA, DIALECT. The term *dia-lectal* denotes phonetic units that have the characteristics of, or belong to, a dialect, e.g., the gerundial ter-mination *in* instead of *ing* in Eng-lish. *Dialectology* is the systematic investigation of dialects.

diam. A chant of Tinguian medi-ums.

diameter, biacromial. The meas-urement of the greatest breadth of the bony shoulder girdle.

diameter, bigonial. The lower jaw's outside breadth, measured at the hinder angles.

diameter, bizygomatic. The diameter of the face in front of the ears.

diameter, extracanthic. The distance from the junction of the lateral point of the lower and upper eyelids of one side to the other.

diameter, intercanthic. The distance from the midpoint of the juncture of the lower and upper eyelids of one side to the other.

Diamond Scripture. See SCRIPTURE, DIAMOND.

diaper. A repeat pattern of geometric or floral designs used to decorate a whole surface.

diaphoretic. Referring to a substance that can increase perspiration.

diaphysis. The shaft of a long bone.

diaspora. From the Greek word dispersion, a term usually applied to those countries to which the Jews were exiled or to the exiles themselves. The diaspora is sometimes used to denote converts from Judaism to Christianity who were not inhabitants of Palestine.

diastema. A natural space between the teeth. It is usually found in the upper anterior region of the mouth.

diastrophism. The changes in the form of the earth's surfaces which result in its major physiographic features.

diathesis. A grammatical term used to describe the relationship of the subject to the verb, according as the subject is the instigator or the recipient of the action. Diathesis also means a predisposition to a disease.

dibble. A Neolithic tool, sharp- or chisel-pointed, which evolved from a root digger, and which probably led to the plow (q.v.) and the hoe (q.v.). The dibble was probably the first agricultural implement and was originally a stick for making holes in the ground. It was a refinement of the root digger and was probably used from 10,000 to 4,000 B.C.

dice. Small ivory or bone cubes, generally used in pairs in games of chance. The faces of a die are marked with one, two, three, four, five and six spots, respectively. Dice have been known for thousands of years, long before there was any writing. Even loaded dice and other forms of cheating were fairly common in antiquity. Dice were very common in Greece and Rome, and the latter periodically had antidicing laws. Dice probably stem from divination (q.v.) through animal knucklebones or vertebrae by reading meaning into the cast.

dichorial. Referring to the notion that twins have two chorions (q.v.).

didjerido or didjeridoo. A hollow wooden trumpet of north Australia.

differences, race. Those individual differences which are presumably typical of the race to which a person's ancestors belonged. Race differences are regarded as due to heredity rather than environment.

diffusion. The method by which a part of a culture spreads to other areas. Diffusion is a means by which an institution, invention, culture trait, or complex may spread to other areas. It occurs in space, by migration or borrowing, from one

167

culture to the other. Although it is found in every example of acculturation (q.v.), it can take place without the contact necessary in that process. See ASSIMILATION; CHANGE, CULTURE.

diffusion, stimulus. Diffusion in which the general idea of a cultural element is taken over.

diffusionism. A theory that emphasizes the role of diffusion in the study of the genesis and transmission of culture, to the neglect of other factors. The heliolithic (q.v.) and culture-historical (q.v.) schools of thought represent the extremes of this point of view, which was vigorously fought by such functionalists as Bronislaw Malinowski. Although every culture borrows a good deal, this extreme position is no longer held by most anthropologists. G. Elliott Smith and other English diffusionists concentrated on the importance of Egypt, while Schmidt and other German-Austrian diffusionists emphasized the role of the large culture unit—the Kulturkreis (q.v.)—which spread to large parts of the early world from a number of centers of diffusion.

digastric. One of a pair of muscles attached to the chin and that depresses the jaw.

Diggers. The Shoshone, so called because they dig for roots and eat them. See GATHERING, FOOD.

digit. A finger's breadth, used in ancient measures, e.g., among the Hebrews and Greeks. A digit is also a number under 10 or one of the parts in which the limbs of vertebrates terminate. The digits are numbered, with the great toe and thumb the first.

digit, toilet. Among lemurs, a lengthened claw on the second toe used to scratch.

digitigrade. Referring to walking on the digits. Most mammals (excluding man) are digitigrade; e.g., cattle and horses walk on the tips of one or two digits on each foot. See PLANTIGRADE.

digraph. Any two letters which represent one phonetic unit, e.g., *ou* in pour. The term is sometimes diagraph.

digraph, consonantal. A grouping of two consonant letters which represent one consonant sound, e.g., *th* in English.

dilly-bag. A container with a drawstring. The dilly-bag is used to transport nonliquid materials.

diluvalism, catastrophic. See CATASTROPHISM.

diluvium. A drift (q.v.), originally presumed to be the product of a deluge. These gravel deposits were believed to contain the remains of animals which existed before man. The name was coined by Dean Buckland and the diluvium hypothesis was defended by Cuvier. See CATASTROPHISM.

dimorphism, sex. The extent to which females and males of the same species differ in form. Dimorphism in social mammals has largely been attributed to the sexual selection presumably resulting from the males' struggle for the females. This selection usually leads to males who are bigger and more aggressive than their females.

Dinaric. Referring to a hypothetical European Caucasoid racial group in the Dinaric Alps region of Yugoslavia, often characterized by a large convex nose and a long face. Medium to light pigmentation and acrocephalic round heads are typical.

ding-dong. Max Müller's theory that language arose through a harmony between sense and sound, e.g., *thud, clang.*

dinghi. A small skiff with sharply pointed graceful bows and a stern usually higher than the bow. The dinghi is used for fishing and carrying passengers and cargo. It is particularly common on the Ganges.

dingo. A feral dog, which is believed to have been introduced by man. The dingo destroys sheep and has a wolflike face. It is kept by some Australian tribes.

Dionysian. A cultural configuration, such as that of the Kwakiutl, characterized by extravagant behavior, use of drugs, extroversion, emphasis on the individual personality, and similar patterns. Ruth Benedict is largely responsible for the use of this concept in anthropology.

diorite. An igneous crystalline and granular rock, used to make implements in Australia and other parts of the world. Diorite is hard and has a speckled black and white surface. The Sumerians and Egyptians particularly valued it.

diota. Any Greek vase with two handles, but most commonly the amphora (q.v.).

diphthong. A compound phoneme consisting of two vowels, e.g., those in *boy, out.*

diphthong, falling. A diphthong in which the syllabic part precedes the nonsyllabic part. This type of diphthong occurs in German and English, e.g., the *i* in *bite.*

diphthong, rising. A diphthong in which the nonsyllabic part precedes the syllabic, e.g., the *ye* in *yes.*

diphthongization. The process by which a diphthong is produced from a simple sound.

dipinti. Painted characters, often classified as inscriptions by archaeologists even though they are not carved. It is the opposite of graffito (q.v.).

diploë. A spongy middle layer of tissue between outer and inner cranial bones.

diploid. Referring to cells carrying the full number of chromosomes (q.v.). The fertilized ovum and the body cells growing from it are diploid.

diplomacy. The method by which a large social group conducts its external affairs. The earliest diplomatic communication probably consisted of sending messengers from one group to another. North American Indians used both messengers (q.v.) and envoys. Numelin has pointed out that although diplomacy is customarily dated from the Oriental historical peoples, it can be shown that certain basic diplomatic usages have developed among early human communities, and that it was necessary for the leaders of early societies to maintain mutual relations, originally by messengers and later by envoys and other representatives.

diptote. Referring to a noun that has incomplete declensions consisting of only two cases.

dirt, child. Dirt which is washed off a Hottentot girl at puberty.

dirt archaeology. See ARCHAEOLOGY, DIRT.

disc. See DISK.

discoid. Referring to having a flat and circular shape; a stone artifact which is disk-shaped (e.g., in the southeast United States), often with a central perforation.

discovery. Perceiving the existence of something which had been in existence before but had not previously been observed. Dixon has drawn a distinction between discovery and invention by the absence of purpose in a discovery as opposed to its presence in invention (q.v.). He has, however, recognized the close relation between them. The conditions said by Dixon to be necessary for pure discovery are opportunity, observing, and a combination of the ability to appreciate and imagination. Curiosity and need, he feels, are also usually necessary, while need is a factor in both discovery and invention.

disease, bronze. Light green spots on early bronze caused by salts which have gone through the metal's surface.

disjunction. Longitudinal chromosome (q.v.) splitting during cell division.

disk or **disc.** A flint implement which is either oval, round, or fairly square, with irregular edges. The intersections of the trimming of the lower and upper faces form the sharp edge.

disk, Phaistos. Found in July, 1908, and dating from about 1700 B.C., it consists of a terra-cotta tablet which is almost circular, some six to seven inches in diameter. The characters of the Phaistos disk are stamped on the two sides along spiral lines that divide the face into five coils. The characters are pictorial but have no association with Cretan pictographs. Diringer has called the disk the most remarkable inscription in Crete. Pernier, who found it, reported 45 different symbols. There is no trace outside Crete of a similar script, and its origin is obscure.

disk, sun. A small gold disk, with concentric circle decorations, about 2¾ inches in diameter. It was found in Ireland and is probably linked with sun worship.

dissimilation. A type of sound change in which one of two identical phonemes occurring relatively close to each other is replaced by another, e.g., the Latin *peregrinus* being replaced in Romance languages by *pelegrinus,* leading to the English *pilgrim.*

distaff. A staff or stick which supports fiber that is being spun.

distal or **disto-.** 1 Away from the center of the body. 2 The surface of a tooth furthest from the center of the dental arch.

distance, measure of. The means usually used to express distance, such as the length or breadth of nail or finger, the span from thumb to the tip of the forefinger or little finger, a pace, a spear length, bowcast, bowshot, the distance covered in a day, a cubit, fathom, etc.

distance, social. The relative accessibility in a society of two statuses to one another.

distichiasis. Having double eyelashes.

disto-. See DISTAL.

distribution, complementary. The principle that no two sounds that are phonetically similar ever function in such a way as to lead to distinctions of meaning between two utterances. The *t* in *till* and in *still,* e.g., are phonetically different, one being aspirated and the other unaspirated, although English has no situations in which this contrast effects word meanings, so that they can both be assigned to the same phoneme. The *t* sounds, thus, are allophones (q.v.) of one phoneme (q.v.).

dithyramb. A poetic song performed by the Dionysian choruses. Although it was a most popular early Greek lyric form, there are no authentic examples in existence today.

diver, earth. In American Indian mythology, the animal that goes down into the primeval waters and comes up with some dirt, which then expands to become the world. Usually one animal succeeds only after a number of others have failed.

divination. The process of reaching a judgment of the unknown or future through the study of incomplete evidence as found in various signs. Divination is found all over the world, and various techniques have been used. It is usually fairly standardized in each culture. Omens (q.v.) may be used. Divination can be regarded as one kind of magic (q.v.) and it is closely linked with religion (q.v.). See AEROMANCY; ALECTRYOMANCY; ALEUROMANCY; ALOMANCY; ALPHITOMANCY; AMNIOMANCY; ANGANG; ANTHROPOMANCY; APANTOMANCY; ARIOLIST; ASTRAGOLOMANCY; ASTROMANCY; BELOMANCY; BENGE; BONES, ORACLE; BOTANOMANCY; CARTOMANCY; CATOPTROMANCY; CEROMANCY; CHAOMANCY; CLEROMANCY; CRITHOMANCY; DAPHNEOMANCY; HARUSPICATION; HEPATOSCOPY; HIPPOMANCY; ICHTHYOMANCY; LAMPADOMANCY; LECANOMANCY; MARGARITOMANCY; MYOMANCY; NECROMANCY; NEPHELOMANCY; ONEIROMANCY; ORNITHOMANCY; PYROMANCY; SCAPULOMANCY; SCIENCE, MANTIC; SCRYING; SORTITION; THEOMANCY; XYLOMANCY.

diving motif. See MOTIF, DIVING.

divinity, tutelary. A deity or guardian spirit (q.v.) which is protective.

division, dual. See MOIETY.

division, reduction. The process by which each parent's pairs of chromosomes (q.v.) are reduced by half (from 48 to 24 in the human), so that each parent contributes 24 chromosomes. When each pair of chromosomes splits, each gamete has only one instead of two chromosomes of each type.

divorce. Legal dissolution of a marriage, along with regulations for the status of the spouses and their children. Divorce is common in some early societies. Sterility of the female is a major cause and involves the return of the bride price (q.v.). The bride's lack of status may also lead to a dissolution of the marriage.

Almost every society has recognized divorce although the conditions under which it has been granted have been varied. The Code of Hammurabi has the oldest recorded divorce regulation, providing that a man could get a divorce from his wife without giving a reason. Some preliterate groups, like the Veddas of Ceylon, do not permit divorce, while there are societies, like the Zuni, in which the wife who wishes to leave her husband merely places his personal property at the entrance to their house as a sign to him to return to his parents.

divorce on the drum. See DRUM, DIVORCE ON THE.

Djisakid. An Ojibway juggler.

djoged. A flirtation dance of Bali, in which a professional girl dancer is courted by a man, who tries to approach her to smell her perfume. Other men cut in on the original man and continue the flirtation.

djundagalla. A pole erected in North Australia after a novice has been subincised.

dobo. A tree house, as in New Guinea.

doctor, snake. A person who has become immune to snake venom by swallowing increasing quantities and can presumably make others immune by rubbing his sweat into their skin.

doctor, talking. A Northwest Coast Indian shaman (q.v.) in Oregon. The talking doctors recited a creation myth as a means of curing the sick. These doctors also officiated at various ceremonies.

doctor, witch. A shaman (q.v.), especially in Melanesia and Africa.

dodecahedron. A 12-sided figure.

dog. The earliest domesticated animal, probably first domesticated in the Baltic area in Mesolithic times. The dog is probably a descendant of the Asiatic wolf. The Andamanese and Tasmanians are among the few peoples who did not have dogs.

dohol. An ancient Persian drum, much varied in shape and size, made of a metal or wood shell covered with parchment at both ends. The dohol was beaten with the hands.

dolcimello. See DULCIMER.

dolicho-. A prefix used in physical anthropology to mean long; e.g., *dolichocephalic.*

dolichocephalic. Referring to an individual who has a comparatively narrow or long head, and a cephalic index (q.v.) of under 75 on a dry skull and under 77 on a living head. The great majority of ancient men are dolichocephalic, indicating that this is an earlier form than the mesocephalic (q.v.) or the brachycephalic (q.v.).

dolichocolic. Referring to having a long colon, over 175 cm.

dolichocranic. Referring to a cranial index (q.v.) between 70 and 74.9.

dolichohieric. Referring to a length-breadth sacral index (q.v.) of less than 99.9.

dolichuranic. Referring to a maxillo-alveolar index (q.v.) of less than 109.9.

doline. A hollow due to the collapse of a cave.

dolion. A rough jar with two levels, found in the Late Bronze Age Villanova culture in Italy. The dolion often contained the ossuary (q.v.).

doll, medicine. A small carved representation of a woman, of ivory or jade, in full figure. Since only the husband was permitted to touch his wife, the wife would indicate to the doctor the place of her ailment by pointing to the appropriate spot on the doll. The doctor would not examine the patient, but would prescribe on the basis of the doll. The medicine doll is primarily associated with the Ch'ing Dynasty (A.D. 1644-1912) in China.

Dollo's law. See LAW, DOLLO'S.

dolmen. A megalith (q.v.) consisting of a room-shaped series of slabs, including one for a roof. Dolmens were used for burial purposes. These structures date from the Neolithic and Bronze Age. Many dolmens were covered by a barrow. There are usually at least three slabs of stone in a dolmen. Dolmens are sometimes called druidic altars or stone tables.

domal. See CACUMINAL.

dombeg. An ancient Persian hand drum, made from a goblet-shaped wood shell. One end was parchment-covered.

dome, snow. The dome capping the series of spirally tapered blocks of snow that support each other in an Eskimo snow house. The dome covers the opening at the top.

domestication. The supervised control of groups of animals by human beings. The breeding of such animals is controlled, and they are protected against other animals and weather, in addition to being fed regularly and having their mobility restricted. Features which are desirable for human purposes are developed by progressive breeding under artificial conditions. Some of the characteristics which often result from domestication include excess fat on the rump, short jaw, drooping ears, and depigmentation or melanism. Domesticating animals is an artificial process which is probably linked with the growth of agriculture. Taking care of animals properly is time consuming, and early food gathering (q.v.) communities could not spare persons for domestication, assuming that its techniques were known. Domestication also refers to the regular growing of plants.

dominant. Referring to a gene that blocks the influence of a weaker, or less overtly influent, gene, called recessive (q.v.). The dominant gene is abbreviated A.

doon. See TOWER, PICTS.

door. A place through which entrance to or exit from a building is made. The door often had a special significance for early man, probably because of its having separated the outside world and its troubles from the world inside and its comforts. Some doors were believed to be inhabited by guardian spirits and others bear amulets or charms. Death may be seen as a door.

door of the dead. See DEAD, DOOR OF THE.

dorsal. Referring to sound made by the back of the tongue, e.g., *k* or *g*. The term also refers to the back of the body.

Dorset. An early coastal Eskimo culture in the central and eastern areas of Arctic North America,

173

thought by some to have flourished until ca. 1000 A.D.

dorsum. The back part of the tongue.

doshi. A Congo term for a ghost-like second self.

doublets. Two or more words appearing in the same language which came from the same basic word but are used as having different meanings. An example is *cherry* and *cerise,* the first meaning the fruit and the second the color. Cherry came into English from the Old Norman French *cherise,* while *cerise* was adopted in recent times directly from the modern French word for cherry.

dovekie. A small auk, eaten by some Eskimo groups.

dowel. A device used to hold stone of different courses together. Dowels have different shapes for various needs. They were often of wrought iron packed with molten lead.

dower. The part of the estate of a husband that goes to his widow (dowager) by operation of law, regardless of testamentary dispositions, when he dies.

dowry. Valuables that the relatives of either party to a marriage contribute to the marriage. The dowry is usually found in societies with established family and property institutions. It has been suggested that this term be reserved for the valuables or gifts that the bride's father or group pays to the bride or bridegroom.

dragon. A crocodilelike mythical creature with some characteristics of an eagle, hawk, or lion, often with wings. Its physical features varied, but it often made frightening noises, breathed smoke or fire, and lived near water. The populace subject to the dragon often must offer it a living sacrifice. Many folktales give the story of the hero who kills the dragon and saves the life of the potential sacrifice, usually a beautiful virgin. The dragon is often linked with a culture's deities. As a myth the dragon may be of Babylonian origin and subsequently have spread to the East. The dragon was the Taoist vitality symbol. It was regarded as the major source of evil in the world in early Hebrew tradition.

drama, ritual. A symbolic representation of struggle between opposing forces, which is enacted and then resolved. Ritual drama has given rise to some of the world's masterpieces of the theater, as in Greece. It may symbolize a natural or religious conflict toward some practicable goal. The conflict may be concerned, e.g., with a conflict between deities and humans, seasons of the year, moral principles. Humor is sometimes found in the ritual drama.

Dravidian. A linguistic family of the south of India, perhaps the leading family before Iranian and Indo-European appeared. It is spoken also in central India, on the east coast of India, in northern Ceylon, and in the eastern Beluchistan mountains. The total using these languages numbers over 100,000,000. The chief branches are Tamil-Kurukh, Kui-Gondi, Telugu, and Brahui.

drawknife. A knife with a handle at both ends. It is used for cutting in a drawing motion and for shaving.

dray, dog. See TRAVOIS.

dream, sought or **dream, traditional.** A dream which is induced, as among the North American Indians. It usually contains much cultural symbolism and usually has a relation to the group's culture patterns.

dream, unsought. A spontaneous dream which occurs in sleep.

dream book. See BOOK, DREAM.

dream interpretation. See INTERPRETATION, DREAM.

Dreaming. The aboriginal name for a person's totem (q.v.), among the Australian aborigines. It is believed to be part of the person before birth and to be transmittable to his children.

Dreaming, Eternal. The Australian aboriginal term for the conception of life as a continuum, a whole with the past, present, and future essentially one.

dreams, primitive. Dreams of persons in nonliterate societies. It has been said that primitive dreams often played a major function in medicine, magic, career selection, art, ceremonies, war, naming, myths, and other activities. Géza Roheim has commented that these dreams have fairly clear-cut symbolism because of the closeness of unconscious and suppressed material to the surface among non-literates. Lincoln has reported primitive dreams which have symbols not unlike Freud's, such as father, mother, phallus, womb, birth, death, night-

mares, and sexual fantasies. Such dreams can be divided into sought dreams (q.v.) and unsought dreams (q.v.) as in Polynesia, Melanesia, Australia, Africa, and North America. The manifest elements in a dream are related to its culture, while dreams which follow the culture patterns may almost be stereotyped. The culture-pattern dream may disappear as the result of acculturation. The dreams of early men are related to animism and religion. See INTERPRETATION, DREAM.

dreikanter. A quartzite boulder which is faceted by sand blowing against it, usually from the direction of the prevailing wind.

Dresden Codex. See CODEX, DRESDEN.

dress. A means of decoration and protection against the elements consisting of a covering for parts of the body. Dress is supposed to have originated in Upper Paleolithic times. It may be used as a means of warmth, self-display, conspicuous consumption, etc.

drift. Material carried along by glaciers.

drift, continental. A horizontal movement of large parts of the earth's crust, e.g., continents. South America, for example, is believed by many scholars to have drifted away from Africa.

drift, genetic. A chance rise or decrease in mutant gene frequencies, primarily found in small isolated groups. The phenomenon is also called the Sewall Wright effect.

drift, linguistic. A long-range movement in time of a language,

175

which helps to explain how a linguistic prototype slowly changes. Edward Sapir developed this concept.

drift, river. A deposit along a river course, which includes silt, sand, and loess (q.v.).

drill, bow. A fire drill in which the stick is twirled by twisting the string of a bow around the stick and moving the bow. Some scholars maintain that the bow as a device for propelling missiles developed from the drill bow.

drill, fire. A most common device for making fire, consisting of a stick which is twirled in a pit in a piece of wood until a spark is drawn. There is a record of the fire drill in the Bible, in Ezekiel. The Egyptians, Babylonians, and Homeric peoples used the drill. In Africa, the fire drill is still used. The vertically worked drill is widespread in Asia and in the western hemisphere. It is believed that the fire drill, in one form, or other, antedates writing, and is very ancient. It has been suggested that the fire drill developed from a slender rod manually twirled on a lower stick, into a rod held in a socket and turned by a cord in a slot in the lower piece of wood and finally into a pump drill (q.v.).

drill, pump. An American Indian method of making fire that uses spindles and strings to make drilling easy. It is a kind of fire drill. In some parts of the world, e.g., Madagascar, the pump drill may also be used to drill holes.

drill, shaft. A drill the shaft of which is alternately turned in different directions manually, e.g., as used by the pre-Columbian Indians.

drill, strap. A drill used both for perforating and as a fire drill. A wood headpiece, held in the teeth, maintains the shaft in position. The shaft is alternately turned from right to left by a thong wound around the shaft and turned manually. The strap drill is found in Greece, Egypt, India, Greenland, and America.

drill, tubular. A drill, often made of a reed, with the drill shaft turned by the palms while sand and water were at the drill's bottom. A tubular drill makes a cylindrical hole and is used in manufacturing stone bowls and axes.

drink, black. A beverage made by the Indians of the southeastern United States by boiling the leaves of the plant *Ilex cassine*. The effect of the drink was purgative and vomitive; it was also thought to invigorate the body and to instill spiritual power in the drinker.

drinking bout. See BOUT, DRINKING.

droit de seigneur. See JUS PRIMAE NOCTIS.

dromedary. A camel which is especially trained for riding, or the one-humped camel, as distinguished from the two-humped variety, the Bactrian.

Druid. A Celtic priest, diviner, or magician with great wisdom and a rank just below the king's. The druid's decision was final. His learning was not written down. He officiated at rituals involving naming, sacrifice, and burial. The druid was a physician and astronomer, among his other skills. He could cause people to become ill, fall asleep, or die. Druids are often associated with the use of mistletoe (q.v.) in magic.

drum. A percussion musical instrument. The drum in its many forms is perhaps the musical instrument most widely used.

drum, basket. An inverted basket that is beaten with a drum stick in the rituals of some American Indian tribes.

drum, canoe. A tapered hollow tree trunk with closed ends and an orifice on the upper surface. The canoe drum is both a canoe (q.v.) and an incision drum. It is found in Assam, Java, and the Fiji Islands.

drum, dervish. A type of Egyptian drum made of ceramic ware or metal. The head is parchment and it is usually played by beating it with a leather strap. It is used by dervishes (q.v.) in their devotions.

drum, divorce on the. A divorce ceremony among the Cheyenne.

drum, double-membrane. A drum consisting of membranes drawn across both ends of a hollow body. Sometimes both membranes are used to make sound. There are also drums with only one membrane vibrating, with the other a means of attaching bracing cords that strain the membrane which is played.

drum, fetich. An African percussion instrument that supposedly has a close connection with the deity. The owner of the fetich drum is reputed to have special influence with the deity.

drum, fontomfrom. An Ashanti drum used to transmit proverbs. The fontomfrom drums are divided into female and male and are dressed accordingly.

drum, friction. A drum with a string or stick attached to the center of the membrane. The fingers are rosined or moistened and drawn along the string or stick and the resulting vibrations are transmitted to the membrane. Friction drums are often used ceremonially.

drum, hourglass. A drum that narrows between its two openings. Hourglass drums are usually quite small.

drum, incision. A musical instrument consisting of a hollow cylinder, which may be a few inches to 15 feet long. The incision drum is made from a hollow tree or bamboo internode, with its ends closed by the trunk sections or nodes. There is a narrow longitudinal slit, almost as long as the cavity, on one of the drum's sides. The drumsticks are applied to the lips of the slit. The incision drum is often regarded as female. The manner of playing suggests sexual intercourse, and the use of the drum may be related to fertility rites or the associated moon worship. The term slit drum is sometimes also found.

drum, jar. A vessel of pottery that is sometimes filled with grain and water and used as a drum by placing a skin across its mouth. The jar drum is sometimes called the pot drum.

drum, kettle. A metal vessel which has a membrane as a head.

drum, magic. An Eskimo or Lapp drum made of wood covered with reindeer skin. The magic drum is used by magicians in rituals designed to establish communication with the spirit world and for divination (q.v.).

drum, membrane. A wooden cylinder with a tightly stretched hide membrane over one or both heads. The membrane drum is beaten by a stick, the hand, or the fingers.

drum, pot. See DRUM, JAR.

drum, sacred. An instrument found in the home of every early Lapplander for use with magical incantations. The sacred drum was made out of birch or pine and the top was stretched animal skin. It was beaten with the antler of a deer.

drum, sand. A tunnel made of sand, used to produce a resonant sound by slapping the palm against it. The sand drum is often associated with fertility rites.

drum, slit. See DRUM, INCISION.

drum, single-membrane. A drum consisting of one tensely drawn membrane of hide or similar material drawn across a hoop, cylinder, or vessel orifice. Fingers or beaters are used to play the single-membrane drum.

drum, stamping. A fairly long hollow cylinder one end of which is open and the other closed. The stamping drum is usually struck by a handle while on the ground.

drum, talking. A drum rhythm which is, or which is a clue to, the lyric or text of a song. See DRUM, FONTOMFROM.

drum, water. A container which holds water and is beaten like a drum, often in connection with rain-making activities.

drumlin. An oval or elongated hill of glacial drift.

Drums, Stone. Ten inscribed chiselled boulders in the Peking Confucian Temple. They are from 1½ to 3 inches high and about 7 inches in circumference. They probably date from the reign of King Hsiian (827-782 B.C.).

drumstick. The object used to beat a drum. It is usually made of wood and slightly larger at one end, and it is sometimes padded to dull the tone. The drumstick can be used to play other percussion instruments, e.g., triangle, cymbals, gong.

drunkenness, ceremonial. Intoxication resulting from the consumption of alcoholic beverages during festive or ritual occasions, such as a drinking bout (q.v.).

dryas. A rosaceous plant of the arctic and alpine areas of the northern hemisphere. The dryas has simple leaves and yellow or white flowers.

drying. A technique of preserving food staples, often by exposing them to the heat of the sun.

Dryopithecus. Miocene ground-dwelling and erect apes, one group of which probably evolved into man. Their arms and legs were approximately equal in length.

dualism. The doctrine that there are two different major principles in the world, each opposed to the other. The two principles are usually those of good and evil, as found in Zoroastrianism.

178

dualism, ethical. Having one ethical code for members of the in-group and another for members of the out-group (q.v.).

dubu. The men's house in eastern Melanesia.

duck tablet. See TABLET, DUCK.

duel. A battle in conformity with specific regulations, between two persons fighting to obtain satisfaction for particular grievances. The weapons used may be purely verbal, as in the Greenland Eskimo nith song, where the weapons are disparaging witty songs.

dugout. A boat made from a single log, using an adze (q.v.) and fire. The dugout is perhaps the most widespread of all early boats. It was probably developed from the floating tree trunks originally used for water transport. The term monoxylon is sometimes used.

dujo. Among the Indians of the Caribbean area, a type of one-piece carved wooden stool, often with a backrest, used by persons of the higher classes and by shamans in curing ceremonies.

duk-duk. A secret society (q.v.) found in the Bismarck Archipelago.

dulcimer. A forerunner of the piano, appearing in nearly all ancient European countries and originating in the Near East. The dulcimer has strings stretched over two bridges from pegs on the side of the sounding board. The sound is produced by striking the strings with small hammers. The dulcimer is approximately three feet wide at the broadest point and has from two to five strings with a range of from two to three octaves. It is now found

only among certain itinerant Hungarian Gypsies. The term dolcimello is sometimes found.

dún. A fortification in which ancient Irish nobles and kings lived.

duration. See QUANTITY.

durian. A genus of trees found in the Malay archipelago. Its fruit, which ripens in the early summer, is very large and is a favorite of the natives.

dvergar. In the mythology of northern Europe, a dwarf who was very intelligent and could become invisible. Dvergars appeared at night and had their homes and workshops underground.

dwarf. An underground person of small stature who figures in the folklore of Europe, North American Indians, and Eskimos. Dwarfs are long-bearded, have wrinkled skins, and enjoy revels. They can predict the future. Although they are very generous, they also steal.

dwellers, cliff. Peoples who lived or live in homes in the cliffs, e.g., the Pueblo and some contemporary Spanish groups.

dwelling, cliff. A tribal house of the American Southwest. Descendents of the ancient cliff dwellers are the Pueblo Indians. Cliff dwellings were made of masonry (cliffhouse proper) or evacuated or hewn from the natural cliffs (cavate).

dwelling, lake *or* **dwelling, pile.** A dwelling or population center built on piles, usually over water. The Swiss lake dwellings represented a Neolithic culture which showed signs of farming, earthenware, domesticated animals, and ground stone axes. The German term Phahlbauten is sometimes used.

dwelling, pit. A bowllike cavity in the earth, probably roofed over with boughs, brush, mud, plaster, and similar protection from the elements and used as a dwelling by some prehistoric peoples. The roofs of pit dwellings were usually oval or circular. The Basket Makers (q.v.) had such homes.

dyadic group. See GROUP, DYADIC.

dye, purple shell. A purple dye made from a shellfish found in the Mediterranean and in pre-Conquest Middle America.

dyeing, ikat. A form of tie dyeing (q.v.) in which hanks of threads are bound and dyed before weaving. The bound areas do not absorb dye and are arranged in such a way that, after weaving, the colored threads form a design. Ikat dyeing was practiced in Indonesia and in pre-Columbian Peru.

dyeing, negative. See DYEING, TIE.

dyeing, resist. Dyeing only parts of a fabric, often by soaking part in wax or clay so that the dye will not take there. Resist dyeing is found in the Punjab and in Indonesia. See BATIK.

dyeing, tie. A technique for dyeing only a part of a fabric or hank of threads. Knots are tied in the fabric or hank before dipping so that the part within the knot is not exposed to the dye. It is also called negative dyeing. See DYEING, IKAT.

dynamism. A term sometimes used to describe belief in mana (q.v.).

Dyoro. A secret society (q.v.) on the Ivory Coast.

dyphyodontism. A type of denti-

tion in which the temporary, or milk, teeth of infancy are replaced by permanent teeth. Dyphyodontism is a typical mammalian trait.

dyschiria. Awkwardness in performing manual tasks.

dysharmony. A relation between face and skull which is unusual. A long narrow face is usually associated with a dolichocephalic (q.v.) skull, and a round short face with a brachycephalic (q.v.) skull. Heads in which this positive correlation is not found, as in the case of the long-headed and broad-faced Eskimos, are called dysharmonic.

dysostosis. Weakened or inadequate ossification, especially in fetal cartilage.

dysplastic. In Kretschmer's system of constitutional types (q.v.), the deformed disproportioned type that tends toward introversion.

dyss. A small chamber used for individual or collective burial. It consists of four uprights that support one large capstone. From one to six skeletons have been found in them. The dyss was especially common in Denmark. One end stone is usually larger than the other uprights, so that there is an aperture which permits later burials after the tomb is completed.

dysteleology. The study of organs that do not seem to have any function and have become vestigial.

dziggetai. An organism intermediate between the ass and horse, used around 3,000 B.C. by the Sumerians to draw chariots.

dzo. The concept of mana (q.v.) among some West African tribes.

Dzhudezmo. The spoken form of "Judeo-Spanish" (q.v.).

E

eagle-beak. See ROSTROCARINATE.

earth, brick. The altered superficial zone of loess (q.v.) that was recently deposited.

earthenware. A major division of pottery. It is clay baked to a temperature sufficient to harden it while still leaving it porous, so that glaze must be added to make it impervious to liquids. See STONEWARE.

earthquake. A movement of the earth's crust caused by forces acting from beneath. Many early societies thought that the earth is supported by animals and that earthquakes result from the animal's shaking or movements. The Algonkian Indians believed the tortoise supported the earth, and in the Celebes, the hog was believed to provide this support. In the Moluccas a serpent, in Persia a crab, and in Mongolia a frog were believed to be under the earth. Other early groups attributed earthquakes to the earth's being carried by strong persons, who shook at times.

earthworks, classification of. In classifying earthworks, *A* is a promontory fortress (q.v.), *B1* a hilltop fortress, and *B2* a fortress on high ground which is less dependent for protection on natural slopes.

eater, sin. A person who was paid to take on himself the moral trespasses of the deceased and their consequences in the afterlife. Sin eaters were common in England until about the early 19th century. The sin eater might partake of food placed on the corpse or accept food or money passed over it.

eburnation. The abnormal hardening or ossification of a cartilage or bone so that it resembles the texture and hardness of ivory.

ecad. A noninheritable change in an organism.

ecesis. The germination and establishment of plants.

echeia. A metal or pottery bell included in the architecture of ancient theaters in order to amplify the voices of the actors and chorus by vibration. An echeia is also a gong or drum.

échelle des êtres. The scale of living organisms, referring to a scale of organisms, arranged in terms of increasing complexity, used by early French naturalists to exemplify organismic gradation. The term may be literally translated ladder of beings.

éclat. A chip, splinter, or flake of flint.

ecliptic. An imaginary circle in the sky along which the lunar and solar eclipses occurred. The concept was used in early astronomy.

ecology. The study of the relationships between humans and their environment or between organism and habitat.

economy, collecting. An order of human existence predicated on gathering wild plant foods.

economy, handicraft. A society the major economic support of which derived from manual labor applied to handicrafts.

ecotype. A species subdivision the distinguishing features of which are determined by its living in a specific ecological environment.

ecstasy. The state of emotional rapture, exhilaration, and mental exaltation in which the subject goes into a sort of trance. While in this state one is highly insensible to ordinary external stimuli. Ecstasy is characterized by a oneness of consciousness, exclusion of the world of sense, passivity, intensity of joyous emotion, visions, and the claim of an immediate divine experience that has intellectual value and yet cannot be communicated. Early peoples induced ecstasy by the use of drugs, fasting, flagellation, and dancing and interpreted it as spirit possession. Later groups accomplished it by mystic practices, including the rigid discipline of the body, lengthy contemplation, and constant auto-suggestion. The results of the experience are varied and different types of satisfactions are attained, such as sensuous, intellectual, aesthetic, and religious. Most observers agree that certain individuals have a higher susceptibility to the experience than others.

ecthlipsis. The process of deleting or suppressing a consonant, either written or spoken.

ectocanthion. The outer corner of the eye.

ectoderm. The outer germ layer in the embryo. The ectoderm forms the skin, hair, nails, mouth tissue, anal tissue, and part of the brain.

ectomolare. The point on the outer surface of the alveolar margins which is most lateral.

ectomorphy. In Sheldon's system of constitutional types (q.v.), the condition of being distinguished by fragility and linearity. The ectomorph has fragile long bones and a highly developed nervous system that is comparatively unprotected by other tissues. This body build, according to Sheldon, is characterized by cerebrotonic temperament, i.e., is restrained in behavior, solitary, timid, ambitious, and intent.

Eden. A type of longitudinally grooved stone projective point of considerable antiquity in western North America. It is long and narrow, with grooves made by the removal of large conchoidal spalls about half its length and with fine transverse flaking.

edge, feather. The edge of a flint flake which has a smooth flake scar, with no ridges to impede a finger passing over the scar.

eduk. A noble among the Haida.

effect, Massenerhebung. The effect which the size of a mountain mass has on the altitudinal limits of climatic formations.

effect, Sewall Wright. See DRIFT, GENETIC.

effigy. A representation of a person. An effigy is often made of a dead person, both as a memorial and a home for his spirit.

Egbo. A secret West African fraternity centering around the leopard. The Egbo has some educational functions. The name is also written Ngbe.

egg, cosmic. The early idea of the world or mankind arising from an egg, e.g., in Egypt, where Khnum forms it. The cosmic egg is also called the world egg.

egg, Nuremberg. A large watch made ca. 1500 A.D. by Henlein of Nuremberg. It is said to have been the first spring-driven watch.

egg, world. See EGG, COSMIC.

egg curing. See CURING, EGG.

Ego. A person who is the basic point of reference in determining and tracing kinship and organizational relationships. The customary usage is to present Ego at the apex of a chart in which the relationships are indicated graphically. Although usually a male, Ego may sometimes be female.

Egyptian. Formerly one of the Semitic-Hamitic (q.v.) languages. It was replaced in the 17th century by Arabic. See COPTIC.

Egyptian fabric. See FABRIC, EGYPTIAN.

Ehringsdorf. A cranium reported in 1928 from Ehringsdorf near Weimar, Germany. It was found near Mousterian (q.v.) implements and tropical flora and fauna. It probably dates from the second half of the last interglacial, ca. 120,000 years ago. It is slightly more like the modern human skull than the Steinheim (q.v.) skull, with a brain capacity of around 1,450 cc., a substantial forehead, rounded occipital area, and fairly high vault, while the lower jaw and eyebrow ridges have some primitive qualities.

Eibib, Heitsi. A Hottentot culture hero (q.v.).

eidolism. The belief in disembodied souls or ghosts, i.e., an eidolon.

eidolon. See EIDOLISM.

eidos. The explicit content of a culture, or its outward appearance, as opposed to its essential or non-manifest significance.

eight-class system. See SYSTEM, EIGHT-CLASS.

einkorn. An ancient form of wheat, still grown in parts of central Europe.

eisteddfod. An assembly of Welsh bards to examine candidates and hold contests.

ejido. In Latin America, the publicly owned land around a town reserved for pasture or for the future expansion of the community.

ekera. Galla souls of the dead.

Elamite. An ancient language of Iran. It existed from at least 2500 B.C. until the first century A.D.

electrum. A light yellow natural alloy of gold and silver. It is so called because its color is like that of amber, the early Greek word for which was *electron*.

element, culture. See TRAIT, CULTURE.

element, floating. In syntax, any word which serves no purpose in a sentence.

element, zero. A single phonetic form which is used to convey different meanings, e.g., the singular and plural of *deer,* in which nothing —zero—is added. See MARKER.

Elementargedänken. According to Bastian (q.v.) the basic fundamental ideas presumably universally held by man.

elementary term. See TERM, ELEMENTARY.

eleusine. A milletlike Congo food plant.

Eleusinian. Referring to Eleusis in Attica, Greece, the main place of worship to the goddesses Demeter and Persephone. It was at Eleusis that the initiation into the Eleusinian mysteries took place.

elfstone. A stone on which offerings were made to the elves.

ell. A measure for cloth which is seldom used today. The present American value is 39.37 inches, the Danish 24.7 inches, the Dutch 27 inches, and the Scottish 37 inches.

ellipsoid. Referring to a skull that looks elliptical when viewed from above.

elliptocytosis. A red corpuscle condition in which the cells are biconvex. It is probably an inherited simple Mendelian dominant.

eluviation. The process by which coarse soil concentrates at the surface and finer particles of soil are removed through the action of rain water percolating downward.

Elysian fields. See FIELDS, ELYSIAN.

emaciation. The condition in which the body has a disproportionately small fat content. Emaciation is sometimes associated with some degree of muscle atrophy.

embalming. Treating a dead body with certain preparations to prevent it from decaying.

embouchure. The mouth hole of a musical instrument.

embrasure. The space between teeth.

embroidery. The patterns made on a finished fabric by stitching.

emerald. A green beryl which has been treasured for its value and appearance for thousands of years. It was mentioned in the Bible as a foundation stone of the New Jerusalem, and emerald composed the first Mohammedan heaven. Looking at an emerald was thought to relieve eyestrain, and they were worn, orally ingested in the form of powder, and in other ways used for their healing properties. Dysentery, epilepsy, and snake bite were among the ailments which they could presumably help cure. Emeralds were used to predict the future, for good luck, and to increase forensic and other qualities.

eminence, chin. A localized thickening of the bone on the front part of the jaw, on both sides of the region of the symphysis, often used to distinguish Homo sapiens.

emir. An Arabian ruler.

emissary, war. A messenger (q.v.) whose role largely consists of bringing a declaration of war, or warning other groups of the trouble to come, and calling people to arms. This custom was found in many different places, such as the Marquesas, New Caledonia, New South Wales, Northern Rhodesia, and parts of North and South America.

emmer. A wheat grown in Russia, Germany, and parts of North America as a stock feed. It was cultivated by the Neolithic lake dwellers in Switzerland. This 28-chromosome wheat was grown wild in Syria and Trans-Jordan, and is in some early Mesopotamian village finds, as well as Badarian sites.

empaistic. Any inlaid, embossed, or stamped article made of parchment, leather, or wood.

empire. A foreign area brought under a sovereign's dominion. Empires were common in the Old World and may have begun with Near Eastern city rivalries. Tribute is often exacted by the ruler of the subject peoples.

empire, Lunda. A large native empire of the South Congo.

en biseau. Chisel-ended.

enamel. In *ceramics,* a glass-like substance fused on to a metal surface. An enamel is a glass which has had coloring agents like metallic oxides added. It may be opaque or translucent. Pigments used to decorate pottery are also termed enamels.

In *anatomy,* an ectodermal derivative that forms the crown of a tooth. It is the hardest structure in the body. The ectodermal derivative produces enamel on the various teeth in the human mouth at different times in relation to the eruption of the tooth, e.g., the enamel for the third molar which erupts

between the ages of 16 and 20 is laid down around age 12.

encaustic. A method of painting using pigments mixed with a wax base. It is necessary to heat the medium in order to apply the paint. Encaustic was used throughout the classical period but went out of existence during the ninth century. It is thought that the well-known Fayum mummy portraits were executed in this technique.

enceinte. The wall or rampart surrounding a place.

enchorial. See DEMOTIC.

enclisis. The process of pronouncing a word as one with the word immediately preceding it without a stress on the word itself. An enclitic word is sometimes written as part of the preceding word, e.g., *que* in Latin.

encomienda. The practice of giving land to Spanish settlers in America, provided that they convert and rule the natives of the area, who are forced to work for them.

enculturation. The process by which a human being adapts to his culture and learns to fulfill the function of his status and role (qq.v.).

endama. An extended and socially sanctioned kind of extralegal mating, found among the Black Caribs of Honduras.

endless tale. See TALE, ENDLESS.

endo-cannibalism. See CANNIBALISM, ENDO-.

endocanthion. The inner corner of the eye.

endocentric. Referring to a combination of free forms in a phrase in which the phrase form class is the same as that of one or more of the free forms that compose it. The whole phrase together cannot be used functionally like any of its components, e.g., *with Robert* cannot be used after another preposition or before another noun.

endocranial. The inner surface of the cranium.

endoderm. The innermost of the three embryonic germ layers and the various tissues which stem from it. The endoderm forms the digestive tract and parts of the liver, pancreas, and other organs.

endogamous status group. See GROUP, ENDOGAMOUS STATUS.

endogamy. The compulsory restriction of marriage to members of the same segment of the population or class. An instance is found among the Masai blacksmiths. Marriage within a group because of convenience is not endogamy.

endogamy, royal. The practice of siblings in royal families marrying each other. Royal endogamy was found in Egypt. See INCEST, DYNASTIC.

endomolare. The point which is most lateral on the inner surface of the lingual margins of the alveolar processes.

endomorphy. In Sheldon's system of constitutional types (q.v.), the extreme of soft roundness and of importance of the digestive viscera and the abdominal region. This body-build type has flabby muscles. Sheldon said that it is associated with the viscerotonic temperament, which is distinguished by sloth, interest in good living, good fellowship, and depending on other peo-

ple. The theory suggests that this build is related to the development of the endoderm (q.v.).

endophasia. A method of communication of language, which may be subconscious or conscious, in which no sounds are produced and none are heard.

endoskeleton. The internal or supporting bone framework of an animal, which makes up most of the skeleton of vertebrates. The endoskeleton contrasts with the exoskeleton of such phyla as the arthropods and mollusks.

endozoochore. A seed or sport disseminated by being carried inside an animal's body.

endscraper. An implement of flint which has a blunt end for planing and scraping. It may also be called a grattoir.

Eneolithic. See AGE, CHALCOLITHIC.

engadji. A Masai cow dung hut.

En-Gai. The Masai supreme being.

English, Basic. A simplified form of the English language in which there are only 850 words. It was invented by C. K. Ogden and enthusiastically backed by such prominent persons as G. B. Shaw and Winston Churchill.

English, Broken. A creole English that incorporates certain African linguistic features, such as a contact vernacular (q.v.) in Liberia and Sierra Leone.

English, Bush-Negro. A creole English spoken in Dutch Guiana by the Bush Negroes. It is also called Jew-Tongo.

English, Pidgin. An English dialect used for communication between Chinese and white persons. It is characterized by the use of concrete for abstract.

engobe. Using colored slips (q.v.) in pottery. The engobe technique is found as far back as in Chinese pottery of 3000 B.C., which had a red body and colored clays painted on over the body.

engraver. An Upper Paleolithic flake knife in which the chipping gives a small edge, usually at right angles to the plane of the blade. It was used to make horn, bone, and ivory implements.

engraver, angle. See ENGRAVER, LATERAL.

engraver, curved. An engraver in which the engraving edge is bordered by a convex surface and another surface which is either straight or slightly convex. The convex face has the caniculate flakings reminiscent of the carinate scraper (q.v.), from which the curved engraver is believed to have evolved. It dates from the Middle Aurignacian period.

engraver, hafted. A beaver incisor artifact that is hafted, transversely in an antler tine. Hafted engravers are found in the Intrusive Mound Ohio culture and the Point Peninsula New York culture.

engraver, lateral. A flake implement the working edge of which is formed in the upper angle of the left hand edge. The angle point may be beaked. It began appearing in the Lower Aurignacian period. The lateral engraver is also called the angle engraver.

ennead. A cycle of nine deities in Egypt.

enseigne. During the Middle Ages, a small lead badge given to pilgrims at the shrine of a saint. The badges were made in the lead foundry associated with the shrine. There was a hole to permit attachment to the hat. Many enseignes have been found in river beds.

ensellure. The lumbo-sacral curve.

ensi. A Babylonian civil governor.

entablature. In the architecture of the ancient world, the wall which rests on the column capitals and supports either the roof plate or the pediment, depending on the entablature's position in the building's flank or front. The entablature is divided into the cornice (upper and projecting moldings), frieze (central area), and architrave (just above the column).

entoconid. The disto-lingual cusp of the first and second lower molar and second premolar and the lingual cusp of the first molar.

entrochite. A fossil joint in a crinoid stem.

environment. The totality of the external conditions and influences that affect man. Environment is important in influencing human society through such natural factors as rainfall, climate, and vegetation and through the actual location of a society in relation to other societies, which becomes increasingly important with advanced cultures that have centers of growth and advancement. Environment has a tendency to remain stable and yet there may be different cultures in the same environment. Environment modifies culture and is also influenced by culture.

environment, ethnic. See AREA, CULTURE. The term ethnic environment was first used by Otis Mason in 1895.

environmentalism. The doctrine that environment is the most important single factor to consider in studying culture. Buckle explained differences in civilization by environment. The anthropogeography movement started by Ratzel and fostered in this country by Semple emphasized the influence of environment on cultures. Most anthropologists regard environmentalism as an oversimplification and share Boas' view that environment is only one factor in explaining culture.

envoûtement. A form of sympathetic magic (q.v.) in which the apparent object of the magic is a representation of its real ultimate object. Thus, after an image of the target person is made, e.g., of wax, some part of the victim's body (like hair) may be incorporated in the image, which is then treated in the same way in which the magician wants to influence the target person. This procedure is extremely widespread even today.

eo-. A prefix used to mean a very early form or period; e.g., *Eo-anthropus dawsoni.*

Eoanthropus dawsoni (Piltdown man). A presumed fossil predecessor of modern man. Charles Dawson found some cranial fragments, along with an anthropoid lower jaw, in Sussex, England, between 1911 and 1915. There had been some disagreement over the extent to which the cranial fragments are of the same provenience. Some eoliths were also found nearby.

Recent research has shown that the major Piltdown finds are bogus, having been deliberately faked for reasons which are not clear. These finds consist of the stained jawbone of a modern ape with teeth filed to show human wear, an ape canine tooth which probably had ancient gravel put into the pulp cavity to simulate age, and at least one eolith with a reddish brown stain made with a chromate solution in order to simulate great age. A special bulletin of the British Museum in November, 1953, confirmed the hoax. Dr. Franz Weidenreich, in 1932, had written that the Piltdown jaw belonged to an ape and that the skullcap was that of a modern man. Weidenreich criticized the find because the inverse relationship between the form and size of brain case and jaws—the larger the brain case, the smaller the jaws—which is true in all anthropoids and hominids, is violated only by Piltdown Man.

In the summer of 1954, a further announcement was made on the results of the study of the fraud. The jaw was revealed to be that of a recent immature orangutan. The black coating on the eye tooth was oil paint. The presumed turbinal bone was probably an animal limb. The flint implements were artificially iron-stained. A steel knife was used to shape the bone implement. The associated fauna were probably "planted." Some of the bones were replaced by gypsum to some extent, as a result of being treated with iron sulphate. None of the Piltdown finds actually stems from Piltdown.

Eocene. The earliest major subdivision of the Tertiary era, usually used for the period before the Oligocene but sometimes referring to the whole Cenozoic period before the Miocene. It saw the development of tarsioids and lemuroids and of mammalian orders. It lasted from perhaps 70 to 45 million years ago.

eolian. Referring to wind-borne.

eolith. A type of chipped flint found and named in 1883 by De Mortillet. Often called "dawn stones," there is some controversy over the extent to which these objects were man-made, or were created by the elements and merely look man-made. Some eoliths date from the Tertiary and Quaternary era.

eonism. The practice of persons of one sex wearing, or wanting to wear, the clothes of the opposite sex. The term was used by Havelock Ellis for the Chevalier d'Eon de Beaumont, an 18th-century figure who was painted in female clothing by Sir Joshua Reynolds. Hercules and Achilles, among other mythical heroes, spent time wearing women's clothes.

Eotechnic. Referring to the phase of technical development in western civilization in which wood, wind, and water were predominent. The experimental method in science developed at that time, and the guild system prevailed in manufacturing.

Eozoic. Referring to the period in which life began on the earth, prob-ably in the form of simple plants and radiolaria. The climate at this time was probably warm.

epanalepsis. The practice of repeating a word to emphasize it or obtain a particular effect. In a more specific sense, epanalepsis is using a personal pronoun in place of a word that has been mentioned before.

epenthesis. The addition of a sound or letter to a word without etymological justification. The added sound is anaptyctic (see ANAPTYXIS) or excrescent. This anaptyctic sound or letter is frequently used to make a difficult transition between two other letters less difficult. An example is *athaletic* instead of *athletic*.

ephod. An official garment of the Hebrew High Priest. It had two front shoulder pieces and was heavily embroidered.

epicanthic fold. See FOLD, EPICANTHIC.

epicanthus. See FOLD, EPICANTHIC.

epicanthus, inner. The point at which the lower and upper eyelids meet, near the nose.

epicanthus, outer. The point at which the lower and upper eyelids meet, farthest from the nose.

epicene. A noun that indicates ambisexual gender.

epigonal. A Peruvian cultural period during which a highly conventionalized and formalized art prevailed. The term was coined by Max Uhle.

epigonium. A harplike musical instrument of ancient Greece. Although existent descriptions are

189

vague, it seems to have had 40 strings, which were played by plucking with the fingers.

epigraphic. In archaeology, referring to any matter that is written or inscribed, as opposed to purely decorative and uninscribed matter found in excavations.

epigraphy. The science of deciphering and explaining inscriptions. It is a subdivision of history, philology, and archaeology. Inscriptions carved on hard material, like stone or baked clay, constitute the subject matter of epigraphy proper, while crude engravings on walls are graffiti and painted characters are dipinti.

epilepsy. An ailment that causes unexpected and sometimes paroxysmic loss of conciousness. It was believed to be an indication of the possession of the epilept by an extranatural force, so that oracular qualities were sometimes assumed to be associated with the condition, which was thus sometimes welcomed as a means of linkage with supernatural forces. Various remedies were proposed for epilepsy, from rhinoceros horn shavings in the 14th century, to three drops of sow's milk in parts of modern Ireland. Contemporary medical opinion is not agreed on either the cause or treatment of epilepsy. Some psychoanalytic thinkers suggest it is psychogenic and should be treated by psychotherapy, and other authorities regard it as a physiological or structural ailment that requires diet or physiological therapies. Electroencephalograms have been found very useful in diagnosing epilepsy.

Epimesolithic. Referring to a culture which exhibits such Neolithic traits as polished axes and pottery in Neolithic times but still retains features of Mesolithic economy, e.g., hunting, fishing, and food gathering.

Epipaleolithic. Referring to the transitional development level between the Old World Upper Paleolithic and Neolithic era.

epiphany. The appearance of a deity in a certain locality.

epiphysis. A subordinate part of a bone formed by a separate ossification center and remaining distinct from its main portion. An epiphysis is also the end of a long bone, as distinguished from its shaft.

episememe. The meaning of a tagmeme (q.v.).

epistasis. A factor of one gene pair that masks the expression of the factors of another pair, or the process by which one gene inhibits the action of another (nonallelic) gene.

epoch, culture. See THEORY, CULTURE EPOCH.

eponym. The individual whose name is taken over by a tribe or larger social group. He may be a mythical or real person. Greek mythology contains numerous eponymous myths.

equator, caloric. The latitude at which there is a minimal radiation fluctuation.

equinox. The time at which the center of the sun crosses the equator and night and day are everywhere equally long, about September 23 (autumnal equinox) and

March 21 (vernal equinox). See SOLSTICE.

equivalence. The doctrine that all men have similar capacities and that these similarities account for the similarities among institutions. In effect, it is the doctrine that the ends of the various human cultures are, in essence, similar.

equivalence, brother. The classification of brothers in a single kinship status.

equivalence, generation. Classifying relatives of the same generation level in a single kinship status, even though they have different genetic relations.

éraillure. A bulbar scar on the bulb of percussion (q.v.) of a flint.

erawng mōt k'rak. A forked stick representing a buffalo, among the Wild Wa of Burma. These sticks, 7 to 10 feet high, are placed in front of houses to represent sacrifices of buffalo by the house owner. Buffalo horns and head may be stacked up at one end of the house, as confirmation of the sacrifices. The sticks may be painted, usually red and black.

erbeb. An Arabian rebec (q.v.) that was a forerunner of the violin. It is a stringed musical instrument played with a bow.

eré. A childlike aspect of the personality which temporarily dominates a participant in initiation ceremonies. It is a state of mind midway between possession (q.v.) and ordinary behavior. This word is used in some candomblé (q.v.) cults and by the Trinidad Shango sect.

erg. A sand basin in the desert.

ergeron. Recent loess (q.v.).

ergology. The study of artifacts that were made for use rather than trade. It is also the study of the effects of work on the human organism from a physiological and psychological point of view.

erh. A Chinese word for the combined forces of yang (the active male principle) and yin (the female or passive principle) (qq.v.), which come from the Tao and are the origin of all things.

erosion. The process by which natural agencies wear away rocks on the surface of the earth.

erratic. Referring to material that has been carried from its original site by natural forces, especially ice. Rock and gravel are often so carried.

Ertebole. Referring to a culture in Denmark, probably from 5000-3000 B.C. Kitchen middens, pottery, and the bow are identified with this era, which was probably humid.

erythrocyte. A red blood corpuscle.

escapement. The part of a watch or clock through which the energy of the mainspring or weight is transmitted to the balance or pendulum by means of impulses that keep the balance or pendulum vibrating. It is in control of the motion of the train of wheel work. There are several hundred different kinds of escapements.

escargoteries or **escargotières.** Extensive mounds (up to 12 by 500 feet) characteristic of Upper Paleolithic sites of inland North Africa. The mounds consist for the most part of ashes and snail shells, indicating an important source of food of the occupants.

191

escarpment. The ground surrounding a fortification, which is cut away almost vertically in order to hold the enemy off. An escarpment is also a deep cliff, often caused by faulting.

escort, grave. Persons, usually of low status, who are sacrificed at a funeral in order to provide the dead person with escorts to go with him and serve him in the other world.

eskänye. An Iroquois Indian shuffle dance for women. It was a bread dance (q.v.) intended for the food spirits. The songs associated with the dance deal with the crop cycle and the growth of the plants and are accompanied by a rattle and drum.

Eskimo. Inhabitants primarily of arctic areas who speak a branch of the Eskimo-Aleut linguistic stock. They number some 35,000. They are Mongoloid (q.v.) and have a broad face and long head. The Eskimo language and culture are fairly conservative. The Eskimo travel widely among themselves. Perhaps with the exception of some northeast Siberians, they are the most warmly dressed of any early culture group. They live in a snow house most of the year and a skin tent in the mild weather. The kayak (q.v.) and umiak (q.v.) provide transportation in water. Dogs, not reindeer, pull their sleighs. Food is often a problem. The harpoon (q.v.) and the bow and arrow are major weapons.

The Eskimo economy is closely linked to seasonal variations. Animals provide most of the food which the Eskimo need. For re-ligious reasons, animals from sea and from land are kept separate. The Eskimo have a wide variety of implements, and their technology is noted for its suitability to a trying environment. Their artistic activity is largely utilitarian. Their primary social organization consists of a local group with a few families and little political structure. The religion is free of a great deal of ritual. Shamanism is fairly widespread, with the shaman (q.v.) functioning mainly to cure disease. There is evidence of Eskimo culture for about 2,000 years.

Eskimo-Aleut. A family of languages with a high degree of incorporation, or polysynthetism, which is spoken in the northern and western parts of Alaska and along the shores of Labrador, Greenland, Hudson Bay, and the northern coast of North America. It appears in the far regions of northeastern Asia and in the Aleutian Islands.

esparto. An Algerian or Spanish grass used for making simple rafts, cordage, and shoes.

Esperanto. An artificial universal language invented in 1884 by Ludwig Lazarus Zamenhof.

espringale. A round dance for couples, associated with the Minnesingers in the 14th century. The dance was a carole dealing with verdure and nature. The German term Springtanz is also used sometimes.

estampie. A stamping dance which flourished from the 12th to the 15th century. Every third beat was accented.

Esthonian. A Finno-Ugrian language.

estufa. An underground chamber used by certain southwest Indian tribes as sweat houses. See KIVA.

Eta. Outcasts who were traders in early Tokogawa Japan.

ethnic. Referring to a group distinguished by common cultural characteristics, e.g., a linguistic group like the Bantu or Malayo-Polynesian.

ethnobiology. The study of ethnology in its relation to physical anthropology.

ethnocentrism. The feeling that one's group has a mode of living, values, and patterns of adaptation that are superior to all others. It is coupled with a generalized contempt for members of other groups. Sumner defined ethnocentrism as ". . . the view of things in which one's own group is the center of everything, and all others are scaled and rated with reference to it . . . each group thinks its own folkways the only right ones, and if it observes that other groups have other folkways, these excite its scorn." Ethnocentrism may manifest itself in behavior such as warfare or in attitudes of superiority or sometimes hostility. Violence, discrimination, proselytizing, and verbal aggressiveness are other means whereby ethnocentrism may express itself.

Anthropology has been called the least ethnocentric of the social sciences.

ethnogenic. Relating to the beginning of ethnic groups.

ethnography. The study of individual cultures. It is primarily a descriptive and noninterpretive study.

ethnohistory. The use of the records of literate groups to help write their history.

ethnolinguistics. The systematic investigation of the relationship between languages and ethnology.

ethnology. The study of culture on a comparative basis and the theory of culture; it is often called cultural anthropology. Ethnology is distinguished from ethnography (q.v.) as being more inclined toward theory and the comparative study of institutions. It was widely used as a synonym for anthropology, being selected in 1839 by W. F. M. Edwards for the name of the Société Ethnologique de Paris, an anthropological group. The term is also found in some European usages as meaning ethnography.

ethnomusicology. The comparative study of musicology.

ethnos. A group of people, linked by both nationality and race. These bonds are usually unconsciously accepted by the members of the group, but outsiders observe the homogeneity.

ethnosociology. Sociology applied to early man.

ethos. The totality of the distinctive ways of living that separate one group from another, especially its values. Ethos also denotes the emotional quality possessed by socially patterned behavior. Ruth Benedict, adopting Oswald Spengler's terminology, has suggested that an ethos may be characterized as either Apollonian or Dionysian.

etiological tale. See TALE, ANIMAL.

etiquette. A part of a group's folklore that sets up stylized accepted kinds of behavior between individuals or between an individual and a group. Etiquette is often a feature of a hierarchical society.

Etruscan. An Asianic language spoken in pre-Roman and Roman Italy, now extinct, with no demonstrable linguistic affinities. The oldest records date back to the eighth century B.C.

etumo. Money paid to compound murder among the Wakamba.

etymology. The study of the history and derivation of words.

etymology, false. An accidental resemblance between words that makes them appear related, e.g., *religious* and *sacrilegious*. False etymologies may lead to gross distortions, e.g., the *Route Le Roi* in London became *Rotten Row,* and the medieval commercial courts of *Pied poudré* (French "dusty foot") were transformed into *Pie Powder.*

etymology, folk. An etymology of a fairly complex word which changes it into a more easily graspable form. Folk etymologies are usually made by nonprofessional linguists and are usually incorrect, e.g., *angnail* becoming *hangnail.*

etymon. The basic part of any word that serves to indicate its etymology.

euchromosome. See AUTOSOME.

eugenesis. The theory that the hominidae (q.v.) were always fertile with one another. The term was invented by Broca.

eugenics. The analysis of the mechanisms of inheritance and development of human traits, with a view toward improving the quality of the human race. Eugenics emphasizes the improvement of the human stock by applying the principles of heredity. Galton (q.v.) became interested in these problems (1869) and started a laboratory (1904) for eugenics research.

Eugubine Tablets. See TABLETS, EUGUBINE.

euhemerism. The belief that deities are merely deified men and women of prominence and that myth is a distorted version of history. It is attributed to Euhemerus the Messenian (330-260 B.C.), who first advanced it in his *Sacred History,* although others of his period had also suggested it. Christian theologians pointed to his theories to prove that the classical deities were not real gods.

eumelanin. Black pigmentation.

eunuch. A human male who has been castrated. This custom probably began in Mesopotamia. Many Near Eastern priests are eunuchs. They have been widely used as guards, often of women's dwellings. Some eunuchs, like Potiphar, have been prominent persons. Eunuchs are the very lowest of classes in India. Some societies castrate males for certain offenses. A eunuchoid build may result from gonad underdevelopment. It is characterized by infantile appearance, feminine hips, scanty pubic hair, and hypogenitalism.

euphemism. A reference to a deity, the devil, spirits, animals, or specially powerful persons, using a name or designation other than the usual one. The object of euphemism is to placate or deceive. If the Devil is referred to by name, he may come, so in England, e.g., he is Old Nick. The Sioux Indians call a beaver a water person, and in the United States people "pass away" rather than die. Yahweh, the Hebrew's deity, could not be mentioned by name. The term euphemism has come to mean a roundabout or pleasant way of stating something unpleasant or difficult.

Euphorbia. A Congo fish poison.

Europoid. See CAUCASOID.

eurycnemic. Referring to a platycnemic index (q.v.) of more than 70.

euryene. Referring to an upper facial index (q.v.) of 45 to 49.9.

eurymeric. Referring to a platymeric index (q.v.) between 85 and 99.9.

eurymetopic. Referring to transverse fronto-parietal index (q.v.) of more than 69.

euryon. The point on the side of the head that is most lateral.

euryprosopic. Referring to a broad-faced person or to a total facial index (q.v.) between 80 and 84.9.

eurysome. A short broad person.

eustasy, glacial. The process by which the water level rises and declines as glaciers melt and are formed.

eustatic. Referring to a land area which does not undergo either depression or elevation.

euthanasia. See KILLING, MERCY.

Evans, Sir Arthur (1851-1941). A British archaeologist who discovered a new civilization at Crete, which preceded the Mycenaean civilization and probably gave rise to it. He also uncovered a Neolithic culture under the earlier Bronze Age civilization. Evans' discovery has been recognized as one of the great archaeological triumphs.

evaporation. The amount of heat loss that results from evaporation from the oral and skin surfaces of the body within a given time period. It is usually stated in terms of calories per person or per square meter of the surface of the body.

eversion, lip. The extent to which the lips are turned outward.

evolution. A continuous development distinguished by each stage's growing out of the one before. It is implied that there is an unfolding of forces that were always potentially present. The concept of evolution is used in physical anthropology in tracing the development of Homo sapiens. Some cultural anthropologists also apply it to the development of human institutions from simple to more complex, although many scholars believe that the viewpoint has uniformistic and deterministic assumptions that are not justified.

evolution, biological. The development of organisms from simple and homogeneous to complex and heterogeneous forms. The fact of biological evolution is deduced from the study of living forms as well as the remains of past forms. It is a never-ending process. Another term sometimes used is organic evolution.

evolution, cultural. The continuous growth of a culture from simple to complex forms and from homogeneous to heterogeneous qualities. The fact of cultural evolution is deduced from studying contemporary societies as well as the remains of past societies. It is presumed to be an ongoing process, still occurring.

evolution, cumulative. The growth of related phases of a society, such that the several processes of growth combine to give a general effect.

evolution, divergent. Evolutionary development that leads to several progressive modifications of an original common form.

evolution, emergent. The appearance, through mutation, of developments that are quite new because of unique combinations of pre-existing elements.

evolution, explosive. Evolution in which certain groups change very rapidly.

evolution, lineal. The theory that each society's cultural development will be parallel with that of all other societies.

evolution, monotypical. Evolution in which the process happened only once in a given species. Applied to man, this theory would hold that the different human races developed only after the human condition had been reached at one certain time. See EVOLUTION, POLYTYPICAL.

evolution, organic. See EVOLUTION, BIOLOGICAL.

evolution, orthogenic. The concept of evolution as a straight-line process.

evolution, parallel. The type of evolution in which the same fea-

ture evolves independently in two or more groups.

evolution, personal. The development of personality, confirming a pattern present in childhood.

evolution, polytypical. Evolution in which several parallel groups evolved. Applied to man, this theory would hold that different primate groups evolved so that each of these early subhuman primate groups developed into a race. See EVOLUTION, MONOTYPICAL.

evolution, supraorganic. The doctrine that societies grow in a manner similar to the growth of organisms. Herbert Spencer, in his *Social Statics,* first called attention to this presumed relationship. Thus, early societies, in this view, are merely arrested in growth, and are examples of the early stages of society's growth. E. B. Tylor is the best known of the English evolutionary anthropologists.

evolution, unilinear. A general progress in a cultural area, without the benefit of diffusion (q.v.). Each stage in a culture presupposes a lower stage, according to this theory. It is often associated with Spencer.

evolution, universal. The trend toward development and unfolding in all aspects of life.

evolutionary unity of species. See SPECIES, EVOLUTIONARY UNITY OF.

evolutionism. The theory that all of life and the universe have developed by growth and change. It includes the concept that individual species grew out of one another by modification and adaptation. The origin of this concept is buried in antiquity, some of the earliest statements having come from the ancient Greeks, including Anaximander, Anaximenes, Empedocles, and Aristotle. In modern times, however, the work of Charles Darwin offers the most comprehensive and meaningful exposition of this theory.

ewi-ngbe. A secret society (q.v.) among the Ekoi of the Northwest Cameroons.

Ex Oriente Lux. The concept, expounded by Montelius and a group of German archaeologists near the end of the 19th century, that all of European cultural development is based on what was taken from the ancient East. The term literally means "light from the East." This concept was disparagingly called "Le Mirage Oriental" by some.

exchange, affinal. The practice of the two kin groups making exchanges so as to engage in an enduring contract as a result of marriage. The relationship between the two groups may outlast the marriage which it validated.

exchange, gift. Reciprocal exchange of gifts.

exchange, marriage by. Marriage resulting from two men exchanging sisters or daughters as wives for themselves or their brothers or sons. It usually helps unify both groups, and is associated with Australia, Melanesia, and Arabia.

excision. Removal of the clitoris, an operation practiced especially on prepubescent girls among some Sudanic tribes.

exclude. To refuse entry to a member of an out-group (q.v.) on the part of an in-group (q.v.).

exclusion, policy of. The policy of keeping out of a group those individuals whose presence may be a threat to its integrity. The policy of exclusion governs many phases of immigration law in the United States.

excommunication. Expelling a person from a religion or a religious community.

excrement, talking. A man's feces that give him advice. This notion is often found in the western part of North America and in some Ojibwa and Pequot-Mohegan folk myths.

excrescent. See EPENTHESIS.

exemplum. A medieval illustrative story used to enliven sermons.

exocentric. Referring to a combination of free forms in a phrase in which the phrase form class differs from that of any of the free forms composing it. There are not many such constructions in a language. An example is the noun phrase *letdown*, in which one element is a verb and the other an adverb.

exogamy. The practice of a person seeking a mate outside his group, usually found in clans and moieties (qq.v.). The term was coined by McLennan (q.v.).

exogamy, local. Exogamy in a local group.

exolinguistics. The study of the relation between a language and the rest of the culture of which it is a part.

exophasia. Language that is spoken and heard.

exorcism. The ritualistic expulsion from the body of those spirits which are presumed to be responsible for some undesired condition or behavior. Verbal formulae, flagellation, sacrifice, and many other methods are used. The work of exorcism is usually accomplished by the religious leader of a community.

exostosis. An unnatural protuberance of a bone.

expansion. The process by which a word that represents an individual becomes used for a class. See NARROWING.

expansion, chest. The difference in the measurement of the chest between inspiration and expiration.

Expedition, Torres Straits. An expedition to the Torres Straits in 1898 led by A. C. Haddon and including C. S. Myers, C. G. Seligman, W. H. R. Rivers, and A. Wilken. It was the first anthropological field trip in which the interdisciplinary team approach was used. Rivers' paper, *A Genealogical Method of Collecting Social and Vital Statistics* and Myers' work on the psychology of sense organs resulted from the expedition, which also set high standards for future field work and publication.

expiation. The belief that the person committing a crime must be killed or punished so that the gods who had been angry at his group would be appeased. The idea of expiation is that a wrong can be cancelled by some equal activity or behavior.

explosion. A phonetic term used to describe the process of suddenly opening a closure of the oral air passage, causing exhalation of air.

exposure. Killing infants by leaving them in unfrequented areas, or abandoning corpses in similar areas so that they could be destroyed either by weather or animals.

expressivity. The extent to which the effects of a gene vary from one individual to another.

extension, analogical. Extending the use of an affix through analogy with already existing words built up in a similar way.

exuviae. The parts of the body which have been eliminated, such as excreta or nails.

eye, apotropaic. The representation of a human eye appearing frequently in Greek art. The apotropaic eye is used to ward off evil, and is most often seen on vases and the prows of ships.

eye, coffee-bean. A type of appliqued eye on early Mexican clay figurines characterized by a longitudinal depression resembling a coffee bean.

eye, dog. A Chinese designation for the typical Caucasoid eye, which does not have the epicanthic fold (q.v.).

eye, evil. The belief that an eye can cause injury or trouble by looking at a person. Certain people are believed to have evil eyes, and folklore often suggests means of warding off their effect. This superstition probably originated among the Egyptians. Sometimes a gesture rather than a glance may transmit the harm.

eye, substitute. A folk hero exchanges his eyes with those of an animal, usually a jackrabbit's, among the North American Indians. These substitute eyes enable the protagonist to be alert continually.

eyedness. Preferring the use of one eye or the other, in activities like sighting.

eyefold. The relationship between the skin and the upper eyelids and canthi.

eyeglass. See SPECTACLE.

eyes, god. A god's eyes, as presented in art. The eyes may exist apart from the god.

F

fable. A short story in which the protagonists are talking animals, with both human and animal traits. These stories point a moral, which is often explicitly stated at the end. Since fables represent an oblique commentary on human beings, they stem from fairly sophisticated cultures. They probably began with the Semites, but Aesop's fables, ca. 600 B.C., is the first extant collection. Aesop is supposed to have been an Ionian slave, whose fables were probably transmitted orally. Their transformations are found in the Middle Ages, Renaissance, and down to modern times. LaFontaine's fables are still studied to this day, as brilliant statements of human nature. The fable is a highly developed literary form in certain cultures of Negro Africa and has left its traces in Negro folklore in the New World.

fable, cante. A narrative partly transmitted in song, in which the song is the most important part. The prose narrative usually provides background for the song.

fabliau. A short verse story of the 12th to 14th century, especially in France. The themes and treatment of the fabliaux were satirical or burlesque. Many ridicule women, the clergy, or cuckoldry.

fabric, Egyptian. The earliest known textile with nap. It was a pile structure material, produced by pulling up loops of weft. These loops were irregular in length and frequency of appearance.

fabricator. A flint implement used in pressure flaking.

façade, flying. A façade that juts out in front of a building so as to give an impression of greater than actual size. It was a common feature in Mayan architecture.

face, disharmonic. A face that is short, with the head width smaller than the space across the cheekbones.

facet, graver. A flake scar that results from holding the flake or blade vertically and striking a vertical blow at the point.

faceted. Referring to a striking platform (q.v.) that is artificially prepared.

facies. An aspect of a species or its subdivision; a geological layer differing by its character or fossil content from another layer of the same age; a collection of closely related parts or components.

factor, leptosome-pachysome. A factor of body morphology isolated by Sir Cyril Burt through factor analysis of physique. The leptosome-pachysome factor is a bipolar factor positively associated with girth and negatively with height and limb length. It may be related to Sheldon's factor of ectomorphy (q.v.).

factors, multiple. Genes that are nonallelic and affect the same visible character.

factory. A workshop area, indicated by a considerable number of implements and flakes of flint in one place.

fado. An urban Portugese song, accompanied by two guitars. The fado is very popular. Typical subjects are love, despair, and prominent persons. The style of singing is free and emotional.

faet fiada. A power that can be used to make the Irish druids and the Irish Christian saints invisible.

faïence. A decorative earthenware that is made of coarse fabric which is enameled and decorated. It probably dates from the second Predynastic period in Egypt.

faire quelques sondages. A technique of attacking the problem of developing an archaeological site by trial pits in various spots. A disadvantage of this method is that it may injure an important object and it does not show the meaning or plan of any objects found. The term may be translated as *to make several diggings.*

fairy. A small supernatural person, often living underground and wearing green, who has the ability to make himself invisible. Fairies usually are helpful to humans, but they may be mischievous pranksters or deliberately evil. They may live by themselves or be associated with a vocation, home, or place. In fairyland, fairies live forever, and quite lavishly, in their own communities. Fairies sometimes marry humans. A fairy may kidnap a human child and leave a changeling, a fairy baby, in its place. Human beings, like True Thomas in the ballad, who stumble into fairyland are sometimes held there for a term of seven years before their release.

fakir. An ascetic, usually found in the Orient, who concentrates on religious contemplation, lives on donations, and may perform miracles.

falconry. Hunting in which trained hawks are used.

familial. Having to do with family life.

familiar. A spirit, bird, or animal that is closely associated with and works with a wizard or religious functionary. It may be a double of its master and is also usually his servant and attendant. The concept of the familiar is found all over the world.

familiarity. Certain freedoms which can be taken with specific relatives. A typical example is the joking relationship between nephew and paternal aunt in many nonliterate cultures.

familism. A social organization in which the continuity and functioning of the family group are paramount. Familism is particularly associated with China.

family. The key institution in society, consisting of one or more women living with one or more men and their children. A socially approved sex relationship, and various rights and obligations, characterize the family. In the order of their comparative incidence, the major kinds of marriage-family relationship are monogamy, polygyny, polyandry, and group marriage. Common residence and economic co-operation are usually associated with the family. Death or marriage of children may radically change the family. The family is the first institution into which the individual is born.

The origin of the family is not clear. Every record of early man shows evidence of family life. Every known society has the institution of the family. Most of the writings on the early development of the family are purely speculative.

The reproductive functions of the family are often secondary to the larger economic and social functions of the authentic institutional family. An oft-debated but recently reestablished example of a society where reproductive functions are secondary to the needs of the social system is the Nayar of India, who have a husbandless family where there is no recognition of the role of the biological father, and there is no place in the family for fathers or husbands and hypergamy prevails.

Murdock reports that of 192 societies on which there are data, 92 are extended families, 53 are polygamous, and 47 are nuclear families.

Attempts to define the various forms of the family in primitive society often may represent fundamental differences in points of view about the nature of the society and there is still some disagreement about how best to classify the forms of the family.

family, bilateral. A family in which there is bilateral kinship, with relatives counted equally on both sides, as in America today.

family, biological. See FAMILY, CONJUGAL.

family, composite. At least two related nuclear families in one household. The composite family may also be several related individual families, such as a man and his son's families, living in a household, or a man living with several wives.

family, conjugal. A family in which the husband-wife-children relationship is functionally primary, while other individuals are subordinate. The conjugal family is sometimes called the small family or the biological family. The personality of the partners is formed outside the unit, and their new roles are created at marriage. It is small, with extension difficult. Private property generally prevails. It is a nucleus of spouses surrounded by a fringe of relatives.

family, consanguineal. An extended family where the husband-wife-children relationship is functionally subordinate to the father-son or mother-daughter relationship. The clan has some functions of this kind. There is a nucleus of blood relatives surrounded by a fringe of spouses. The members grow up with the family. Division of labor is established. It is fairly large, with economic security and protection of aged and young. There is little private property.

family, domestic. The family which usually occupies one homestead.

family, elementary. One husband, one wife, and their children, including adopted children.

family, extended. A family consisting of a series of close relatives along either the male or female line, usually not along both. A woman, her husband, their children and her married daughters with their husbands, or a man, wife, his children, his sons and sons' wives would each be extended families. The extended family is the most commonly found kind of family in primitive societies for which data are available.

family, joint. Several related families in one household, usually referring to a parent and his or her children of the same sex and their families. Common residence is important in maintaining the joint family functionally. Labor is pooled. All are responsible to the same authority. It differs from the extended family in comprising two or more nuclear families, while the extended may have one nuclear family and assorted nuclear kin without full families.

family, linguistic. Two or more languages that have the same source but are not related to other lan-

guages in the same degree, e.g., the Germanic and Indo-European language families.

family, maternal. A family in which relationships are counted through the woman. It consists of a woman and her male and female descendants. The maternal family almost never extends beyond six generations.

family, nuclear. A married couple with their children.

family, paternal. A family in which relationships are counted through the father.

family, patriarchal. A family in which the father or the eldest male (patriarch) rules. The development of private property is regarded as contributing to this kind of family. The patriarchal family in ancient Rome was a self-contained social, economic, legal, and religious entity. At an early date the paterfamilias (head) even had the authority to kill any member of the family.

family, small. See FAMILY, CONJUGAL.

family, stem. A nuclear family plus one or more related individuals who do not comprise a second nuclear family.

family, unilateral. A family in which the relationship is channeled through either the male or female side, e.g., the susu (q.v.). The term "unilateral" is more frequently used to describe a kinship (q.v.) system than a kind of family. The extended family is unilateral.

family tree. See THEORY, FAMILY TREE.

famine. Extreme hunger resulting from failure of the food supply, which was not uncommon in early society.

fan, fire. An Indian device used to rekindle fire when it threatens to go out. It consists of a handle with a fan-shaped body.

fan, winnowing. A fan used to separate grain from chaff.

fandango. A sensuous courtship dance of Spain, danced to a guitar.

farandoule. A Provençal round dance, performed by peasants, which may be an extension of early vegetation dances.

farming. The process of tillage of the land, developing from the gathering of wild roots and the use of the dibble and hoe.

farming, dry. Producing crops under conditions in which the crop yield is usually limited by low rainfall.

fashion. Beginning in the 15th century among the urban and court population, the prevailing custom or mode of dress, usually set by the social arbiter of the community. Changes in fashion are usually short-lived.

fasting. Deliberately not partaking of drink or food, often for religious reasons or to communicate with extranatural forces through the hallucinations engendered by privation. Fasting is a purifying activity. A whole society may fast simultaneously, or groups within a society may fast on special occasions. A kind of incomplete fasting, in which small amounts of food and water were taken, was widely found, e.g., during menstruation or while mourning.

Inasmuch as prolonged hunger gives rise to visions, early man's mental and physical experiences during periods of lack of food may have led to the religious use of fasting. The American Indian used the fast to acquire a private totem, shamans (q.v.) fasted to make contact with spirits, and those consulting the Greek oracles fasted. The suffering occasioned by fasting made it a good method for obtaining penance. It had wide use as a preparation for ceremonies like initiation and first fruits (q.v.).

fatalism. The doctrine that forces exterior to man are at work in the world, minimizing the human contribution to a situation, so that things happen in accordance with a pre-established pattern.

fatherhood. Social acknowledgment of existence as a male parent, including the broader definitions of the character of such a parent and his role in society. Most known early societies and most civilized groups place the father in a dominant position in family life. Fatherhood is thus treated with much respect and even in some instances with religious awe.

fatherhood, sociological. The practice of having the husband of a child's mother function as the child's father no matter what the biological relation is.

fathom. A unit of measure, consisting of an arm span, often applied to measuring hides. It is measured from finger tip to finger tip with the arms outstretched.

faucal. A general name for sounds produced in the throat, including pharyngeal, glottal, and laryngeal.

faulting. Breaking of the crust of the earth.

fauna, mixed. Fauna the remains of which are found together even though they may come from different temperature types. Thus, even though some warmth-loving fauna might be found, cold-loving varieties might have begun to appear.

Faust Keil. See COUP-DE-POING.

fautasi. A Samoan canoe.

fawi. A Bontoc men's house (q.v.) annex.

feast. A communal or official meal, usually undertaken in connection with a joyous occasion. The hearth and the shared meal are usual signs of hospitality. Feasts are found in almost every kind of society. Feasting is often associated with religion, probably because of religious ideas about food and from a desire to propitiate the gods. Often an abundance of food provides its own occasion for feasting, or important events like birth, adoption, victory, elections, and rites de passage may be linked with the feast. Religious feasting may be preceded by fasting as a kind of purification. One of the oldest feasts in Europe is the final harvesting feast in the autumn, or harvest home. The feasting of the dead at the time of harvest—All Souls' Day—is widely found.

feast, communal. A community meal with a symbolic meaning and often a special sacramental nature. A communal feast accompanies important points in the life of the social group or person, e.g., a birth, marriage, the beginning of the hunting season, the solstice.

feast, totem. The practice of the members of a clan eating the totem (q.v.) object, usually once a year in a totemic communion. At the totem feast, the impersonal power which the individual shares as a clan member and which is in the animal is renewed.

feature, acoustic. A characteristic of the sound of a particular utterance as it exists or may be recorded experimentally. When these features influence semantic interpretation and are therefore an essential part of communication by speech, they are called distinctive acoustic features, and when they do not have a bearing on meaning, they are called nondistinctive. In the *k* sound of *cool,* the aspiration is nondistinctive but the dorsal and voiceless features are distinctive.

feature, suprasegmental. A significant feature of speech sound, such as stress or pitch, which is superimposed, as it were, on a sequence of several regular ("segmental") phonemes.

febrifuge. A medicine that can alleviate or end fever.

federation. A political grouping made up of independent groups cooperating voluntarily. It was a common form in the Americas, e.g., the League of the Iroquois. The federation was not common in Europe and Asia. It is usually based on an alliance.

feeling, race. A feeling, either positive or negative, associated with the distinctive traits of any race.

fei. Coins made of white stone called argonite, used by the Yap. The fei are flat, large, round, and have a hole in the middle.

feldspar. A group of minerals that become rock. They are found in North America, Scandinavia, Italy, and the U.S.S.R. They are used in the manufacture of glazes for ceramics. The Chinese added feldspar to clay in order to make it suitable for use by a potter. Weathering causes feldspar to decompose into china clay, which is very important in making porcelain. Pure feldspar has no color but is often tinted by mineral impurities.

fell. A bleak Norwegian plateau.

fellah. A peasant or agricultural laborer in the Middle East. The fellahin usually are persons who stem from race mixture (q.v.). Turks call Egyptians fellahin.

Fell's Cave. See CAVE, FELL'S.

felting. Rolling, beating, and compressing such objects as animal fibers, as originally developed by some Neolithic Asian peoples. Fabrics made this way are good for hats, shoes, and tent covers but not for clothing, because of their inflexibility. In Tibet today yak hair is felted.

felucca. A vessel that used to see much service in the Mediterranean. It has oars and lateen sails, and its helm may be applied to stern or head as the situation requires.

femur. The thigh bone in vertebrate animals, or the first bone of the leg. It articulates with the acetabulum and the knee joint.

fender, rat. A disk around piles used on Ifugao houses. Its purpose is to prevent rats from climbing up the piles into the houses.

fennel. A parsley herb widely used for reducing weight, improving vision, and improving mothers' ability to nurse their children.

Fenno-Scandia. The name sometimes given to the area covered by Norway, Denmark, Sweden, and Finland.

fermentation. Using bacteria to transform the sugar in some foods into alcohol.

fern. A spore-reproducing plant with no flowers, widely used to cure toothache and skin complaints.

Ferninterpretation. In Fritz Graebner's usage, one culture's borrowing from another in spite of the distance between them. According to this idea, two culture elements that are similar on the basis of the criteria of form and quantity, even if they are in different places, come from the same source.

Ferrell's law. See LAW, FERRELL'S.

festival. Collective rituals, often centering around magical operations. A festival may also be a period which is specifically for public religious observances. Festivals probably spring from the early communal feast and its attendant sacrifice. They are social in nature and symbolize the feeling of a whole community. Usually they are very durable and are marked by their holiday character. As society developed, festivals became more elaborate, numerous, and stylized. There may be festivals to mark the emergence of a season or the end of one. Thus, April Fool's Day is probably

a holdover of vernal equinox ceremonies. Anniversaries of important
community events also generate festivals. Festivals become secularized
as the society develops, e.g., the
Jews tied the Passover tabernacle
and Pentecost agricultural festivals
in with their early history.

festival, harvest. A festival held
after the crop has been gathered
successfully. Some groups regard a
corn spirit as dwelling in the grain,
especially its last sheaf. Thus the
gathering of the last sheaf may involve the corn spirit's being killed,
departing. or entering its collector.
If the spirit is killed or leaves, there
is rejoicing at the festival, because
the imitated corn spirit has done no
harm; and if the spirit enters the
collector or is captured. there is also
occasion for rejoicing because it is
then held to the next harvest. A
period of license may ensue and the
corn spirit may be so confused that
it is not able to identify the people
who have taken over some of its
rights. Early festivals did not exhibit much gratitude for collecting
a satisfying harvest, although the
festival later became one of gratitude.

fetalization or **foetalization.** The
process whereby the organism's development is arrested at a fetal
stage. Louis Bolk gave this name to
fetal characteristics that pass into
adult life. Man's hairless body, for
example, is found in a fetal stage of
the anthropoid body and in man is
conveyed from fetal stage to adult.
Keith has pointed out that man's
small face and the large size of the
brain-containing part of the head

represent a prolongation of infan-
tilism into adult life.

fetish or **fetich.** An object which
has supernatural potency, often because of its association with a spiritual being. The name probably derives from magical objects owned
by West Coast African Negroes. In
a number of cults, and especially in
West Africa, carved objects such as
images are believed to be the temporary home of spirits. These objects get special attention if the
spirits are immanent, but not otherwise. The word fetish comes from
the Portuguese *feitigo,* meaning a
good-luck charm. The simplest type
of fetish might be a stone over
which a native tripped and then
felt awe at its power.

fetishism. The doctrine that objects or persons may be possessed by
spirits that are not their own souls,
or a religion emphasizing the use
of fetishes. From 1760, when De
Brosses maintained it was the earliest type of cult, to its replacement
by Tylor's animism, it was regarded
as a key category of comparative religion.

fetishism, nail. The use of wooden
fetishes into which the suppliants
drive nails so that the fetish is sure
that they are praying to it. Nail
fetishism is found in the Congo
region of Africa.

feud. Mutual hostility among intimate groups, where violence may be
expected.

feud, blood. The practice of the
family of a victim taking over the
responsibility for avenging his murder or mistreatment by taking vengeance in kind on the offender or

his family. After social ties became more established, the king often took over the responsibility for extracting the blood revenge.

fiber. The basic unit in making textiles.

fiber, bast. See FIBER, SOFT.

fiber, leaf or fiber, hard. A fairly stiff and long strand, usually from a leaf, e.g., Manila hemp. Leaf fiber is found in heavy rope materials rather than in spinning.

fiber, soft or fiber, bast. A fairly pliable and long strand on the inside of a plant, e.g., jute. Soft fiber is made into longer lengths manually, through thigh rolling or a spindle.

fibrolite. A white or gray mineral that has a fibrous to columnar structure.

fibula. In archaeology, a clasp, buckle, or brooch that looks like a safety pin. Fibulas were probably introduced by the Dorians ca. 1350 B.C.

In anatomy, the smaller of the lower leg's two bones. It articulates with the femur and the ankle bone.

fibula, boat. A fibula with an arch resembling a canoe, found in ancient Greece.

fibula, bow. A fibula with an arch. The bow fibula is often formed like a series of beads or is adorned with rings in ancient Greece.

fibula ad arco di violino. A fibula shaped like a violin bow.

fibula ad arco semplice. A fibula shaped like an arched bow.

fibula gomito. A fibula with a bow shaped like a bent arm.

fibula serpeggiante. A fibula with one or more cusps in its bow.

ficron. French workmen's slang for a kind of coup-de-poing (q.v.) with a heavy butt and a long tapering point.

fictile. Referring to the quality in any ceramic substance that makes molding it possible. The term is usually applied to the process of molding by manual rather than mechanical means and it is also used to refer to pottery or clay artifacts.

fief. During the feudal system, the land of a vassal who had pledged his military and other support to an overlord.

field, ice. A segment of pack ice (q.v.) some miles in dimension.

fields, Elysian. The heaven of Greek mythology and the home of the dead who had lived a good life. The Elysian fields are described as having eternal spring, flowers, and an abundance of happiness. They are located by early Greek writers in the western ocean or at the western edge of the world.

fig. A small, self-pollinating tree with broad leaves. The fruit is oblong or almost globose. There are many varieties of fig. It was probably domesticated in Southern Arabia.

figure, atlantid. A figure in sculpture or architecture that acts as a support, e.g., a caryatid (q.v.). If the figure is male, it is called an atlante.

figure, string. A form made of string wound around the fingers. String figures are very widely distributed and may have religious meanings. Rivers and Haddon have developed a descriptive terminology for figures: radial refers to a string on the side of a finger near the thumb and ulnar on the little-finger side; proximal means near and distal away from the palm; a loop goes around a digit; palmar refers to a string on the front of the hand, dorsal on the back.

figure, Venus. A limestone figurine of a woman, dating from the Aurignacian period. Usually the hands, feet, and head are sketched in and the features of the face are not defined, while the middle portion of the body is represented more clearly. The form of the Venus figures suggests mammary overdevelopment and steatopygia.

figure eight. A kind of simple oversewn coil (q.v.) in which a stitch encloses two coils in a figure that looks like the number "8." The stitch goes behind, up and over, and in front of the new coil, as well as behind, and down and out under the preceding coil.

figure eight, crossed. A kind of simple oversewn coil in which the stitch goes in front of the new coil, as well as behind and down under the previous coil. The thread comes between the two coils, coming to the right of and crossing the last long stitch. The crossed figure eight gives the appearance of a row of knots between the coils.

figurine. A small carved or moded representation of a human being, animal, or bird.

filament. A very long fiber, e.g., silk.

file, Indian. A single file of men.

fillet. A narrow band worn as an ornament on the head; especially a

band of feathers sewed together or affixed to a band of fabric.

filetting. Making a brow band (q.v.).

filling. Yarn that runs the width of a fabric or woof as opposed to the warp of a woven cloth. Also, the yarn or material that is to be used for this purpose.

filling motif. See MOTIF, FILLING.

final accent. See ACCENT, FINAL.

find, associated. A method of dating objects by considering the objects that are in deposits with various industries (q.v.). The associated find method is usually employed as a check on stratigraphy or typology (qq.v.). It is important to determine whether the association is real and original. If, for example, an industry is sealed in a rock shelter layer and is associated with some remains of extinct fauna, the association must be regarded as authentic and the industry must be accepted as being from the same period as the extinct fauna.

find, closed. An archaeological discovery in which all the remains were placed there at the same time and thus belong together contemporaneously. The term association is sometimes used for the assemblage of objects.

find, depot. See HOARD, FOUNDER'S.

find, open. An archaeological discovery in which the remains do not belong together and are not contemporaneous but were thrown together through the site being reused or through animals' burrowing or materials' slipping from higher layers.

209

find, Trinil. A lower jaw, a skull, and three other finds made in Java. The lower jaw was first found in 1936. The leg bone shows a height of 5 feet 6 inches or more. The skull was very thick and heavy. The forehead is very low and the profile is apelike. The Trinil man's teeth are large and his dental arch narrow. The jaw is heavy and chinless. This is the only fossil accepted as a man to have a diastema (q.v.).

findspot. The place in which an artifact or human remain has been found.

finestra. Any aperture, especially in a rock tomb.

fingers, sun. See OBELISK.

Finnish-Lapponic. Part of the Finno-Ugric subfamily of the Ural-Altaic family of languages. Within it are the Finnish group and Lapp. Some linguists include Cheremiss and Mordvin with Lapp in a Lapponic group, while others maintain that they are two distinct branches of Finno-Ugric.

Finno-Ugric. A subfamily comprising the Finnish-Lapponic, Ugric, Permian, and Samoyedic branches and belonging to the Ural-Altaic family of languages. It is characterized by agglutination and vowel harmony.

Fiorelli, Giusseppe (1823-1896). An Italian archaeologist who was in charge of the excavation of Pompeii from 1860 on. He developed new scientific methods for complete excavations of houses without damaging them, so that they could be studied *in situ*. He taught his principles of stratigraphic analysis at a school that he founded in Pompeii.

fire. Fire produced by deliberate combustion probably dates from the pre-Mousterian era. The strike-a-light (q.v.) and friction techniques are the two major methods of fire-making. Almost every known tribe has known how to light or use a fire, while no animal species has this knowledge. The Andaman Islanders are the only known group which seems not to have known how to make fire, although they are reported to have known how to carry fire. The East African site at Olorgesailie is an example of a group of human beings who left no ash or charcoal and thus may not have had fire. The control of fire and the development of language and of agriculture are three of the most important steps in human development. Fire is used for agriculture, cooking, light, warmth, signals, cremation, religious rites, and many other purposes. Among the first signs of fire discovered with human remains are the bits of charcoal with the Ehringsdorf jaw and the Choukoutien caves where Sinanthropus was found.

Volcanoes, fire in coal seams, earthquakes causing trees to ignite through friction, lightning, and tree branches ignited by wind-caused friction may have provided the fire that was used by early man. Wood-friction heat is probably the first means of making fire artificially, and it probably stemmed from working with wood and vegetable fibers. The difficulty of effecting artificial fire is emphasized by the fact that few woods are suitable for the fire drill or fire saw (qq.v.), **the** lack of tinder, the difficult concept of the wood channel, and the time required to raise a spark to a blaze.

Fire has influenced architecture, with a beehive-shaped house with a fireplace in the center very widely distributed throughout the world. The central fire minimizes the danger of burning down the house and maximizes heating of the floor space, while the exit for smoke and fire—the conical roof—coincide.

The earliest controlled fire was probably built near a camp, in front of a cave, in front of a rock shelter, and the like. The possession of fire by early man betokens responsibility for its control. Economy in the use of fire seems to characterize early man. Cultures with a simple technology usually prefer to keep a fire going rather than make it anew, with groups like the Tierra del Fuego Indians carrying fire with them by water craft to avoid having to make new fire at their destination.

fire, Chinese. A substance containing saltpeter and charcoal, mixed with pitch and animal fats, used in the Far East as an kind of gunpowder long before the Christian era.

fire, Greek. An incendiary mixture used in earthenware pots that were catapulted into besieged cities. Greek fire included materials like sulphur resin, naphtha, and petroleum oils, which caused the fire to spread and also emitted noxious fumes.

fire, marriage. A fire which plays a part in the marriage ceremony. The Romans led the bride to her bridegroom's home by torchlight, and the Ainu and Hindus used fire in their marriage ceremonies.

fire, need. A new fire that is started and then used to bring good luck to the group or else to minimize the possibility of disease or of injury to crops or domesticated animals. The new fire was used to relight the household fires. Traces of this custom persisted up to fairly recently. The need fire was sometimes placed in the main entrance to a city.

fire, new. A newly lit fire, often the occasion for ceremonial observances. The fire may be lit in a religious center or in a home. Fires are often lit and extinguished to mark special observances.

fire, perpetual. A fire that is kept burning indefinitely. The continuity of the fire is here linked with the continuity of life, because warmth and life are associated. The perpetual fire may also be a survival from a period when the art of fire making was not so well known as today and it was necessary to preserve a fire. Perpetual fires are maintained in synagogues and were a prime responsibility of the Vestal Virgins in Rome.

fire, pure. A kind of fire that is especially pure in compliance with regulations about fire. For example, Persian fire worshippers (Parsees) believed that lightning provides the purest fire.

fire, St. Elmo's. A glow of light seen at the tips of parts of a ship. It is so called after the Mediterranean sailors' patron saint. It may mean bad luck, good luck, a lost soul, or good weather. The term corposant is sometimes applied to St. Elmo's fire.

fire, wild *or* fire, strange. Fire that is not in accordance with regulations dealing with the purity of fire. Fire which has been stolen from a family hearth is wild fire, since it may become a means of malevolent witchcraft.

fire, world. A North American Indian belief that the world was once almost or completely destroyed by fire.

fire ceremony. See CEREMONY, NEW FIRE.

firearm. A weapon that emits a shot through the action of an explosive, e.g., gunpowder. The Chinese used gunpowder in the 6th century A.D. and projectiles in the 12th century A.D. Firearms in war date from the 14th century.

fired ware. See WARE, FIRED.

firedrake. A fire-emitting dragon that protects a treasure in a cave.

firestone. See FLINT.

firstling. The first born child or offspring of humans or of domestic animals, often used to refer to the first born used as a sacrifice (q.v.).

fischietto. A terramara (q.v.) vase that might have been used as a strainer.

fish, lung. A fish that can live on dry land as well as in the water, since it has both lungs and gills. The original air-breathing vertebrates may have their evolutionary ancestors in the lung fish.

fishing, bottom. Fishing in which bait is near or on the bottom.

fishing, kite. A method of fishing in which a large kite with baited lines is sent out over the water. The kite can go out much farther than the fisherman can, so that he has access to deeper waters where fish are likely to be. Kite fishing may have originated in China, from which it spread to Melanesia.

fishing, mid-water. Fishing in which bait and line are suspended in the water. There is likely to be a float (q.v.).

fishing, surface. Fishing in which no sinker is used. The bait is usually cast on the water or it hangs from a kite (q.v.). Sometimes chopped fish, called chum, is spread on the water with occasional hooks scattered about.

Fison, Lorimer (1832-1907). An Australian anthropologist, who specialized in social organization.

fitching. Twining that uses two wefts.

fittest, survival of the. Darwin's doctrine that the organisms that adapt most easily survive through the operations of natural selection (q.v.).

five-color ware. See WARE, FIVE-COLOR.

fjord. A narrow sea inlet lying between high rocks or banks, e.g., on the Norwegian coast.

flag, prayer. A pennant that is strung across the entrance gates to the larger Tibetan cities. The Tibetan believe that these fluttering flags carry prayers through the skies to Buddha.

flagellation. A whipping or beating that takes place in conjunction with a ceremony. Flagellation may be part of an ordeal (q.v.), it may exorcise evil spirits, or it may satisfy sado-masochistic needs. It may be used in religious observances, as among the Pueblo Indians and Christian anchorites.

flageolet. A small wind instrument that is played by a mouthpiece inserted in a bulb.

flail. An implement used in threshing. It consists of two heavy unequal sticks, connected end to end by a flexible leather joint. The handle is the larger piece, while the shorter piece is brought down on the grain so that it strikes flat on the floor.

flake. An implement made by removing flakes of flint from a large piece and using the flakes as tools. A flake results from directing a blow obliquely near the edge of a piece of material which breaks conchoidally.

flake, channel. A flake taken off the center of a fluted point.

flake, Clactonian. A flake with a non-faceted striking platform at an angle of 120° to the main surface.

flake, Levallois. A flake form that replaced the coup-de-poing (q.v.). The Levallois flake was made by trimming a nodule, as if making a core tool, with a square or stubby base. Striking the base produced an oval flake that had a presharpened edge, so that the underside was flat while the upper side had small flaking.

flake, notched. A knifelike flake with secondary chipping over the top and along both edges. There is a shallow concavity in one or both edges. The notched flake began to appear in Lower Aurignacian times.

flake, plunging. A flake that did not come away level with the core when it was struck off.

flaker, arrow. A piece of reindeer horn dovetailed into a handle of wood or fossil ivory and kept in place by thongs or plaited tendons, which shrink as they dry and thus make the fastening more secure. The Eskimos use the arrow flaker to make weapons.

flaking. Removing flakes from a lump of flint.

flaking, controlled. Flint flaking made by the use of wooden mallets rather than hammer stones. The softer wood produces a kind of pressure action instead of the sharp percussion of the stone hammer.

flaking, fish-scale. Pressure flaking that gives rise to a characteristic scaly appearance. It is often found on early metal age flint tools.

flaking, free. Flaking in which the implement that strikes the blow goes right through the flint and into the air again before losing its force. This gives rise to a clean flake and a feather edge (q.v.).

flaking, pressure. A method of removing tiny flakes from flint by applying pressure on a flint edge through a stone or bone implement at a given point. It was widely used in the Solutrean period and was also used in Upper Paleolithic times for secondary working. Pressure flaking is suitable for fine workmanship, because the craftsman can bring appropriate pressure at just the point he desires.

flaking, primary. Forming the upper surface of a flint tool by trimming its surface and removing any

213

unnecessary lumps. Primary flaking is also the flaking needed to produce and shape a tool.

flaking, prismatic. A fairly advanced method for making flint implements, introduced in the Aurignacian period. A conical core is first made from a flint nodule; then a pointed tool is held along the edge of the striking platform (q.v.) and hit with a hammer stone, resulting in some narrow long flakes.

flaking, resolved. See FLAKING, STEP.

flaking, ripple. A very delicate parallel and rhythmic flaking found on the most highly finished implements.

flaking, secondary. Trimming a tool so that surface irregularities are reduced and its cutting edge is refined or modified. The term retouche is also used.

flaking, step. Flaking in which the force of the blow into the flint is spent before it gets through to the other side, so that there is a flake scar shaped like a step. This type of flaking was widely used in the middle Paleolithic era for secondary working. The term resolved flaking is also used.

flap. A sound consisting of a single tap, produced by a very short vibration of one of the supraglottal organs; e.g., the *tt* in *matter*.

flat, strand. A marine terrace the landward border of which consists of a sea cliff. Seaward it ends in a series of skerries (q.v.).

flat, alkali. A marshy area in an arid region that is rich in salts.

Flatheads. A group of American Indian tribes which artificially flat-ten their children's heads, including the Catawba and Chinook. The Salish, often regarded as the generic Flatheads, did not flatten their children's heads.

flaw, ice. The point at which the shore ice (q.v.) is in contact with the ice pack.

flax. A cultivated textile plant that played an important part in early Europe and the Near East. It probably spread from the Mediterranean area to temperate Europe. Linen is woven from spun flax.

fleece. The wool covering a sheep or similar animal. Some religions attribute magical properties to fleece, e.g., magically transferring the properties of the animal to its wearer or protection against disease. Fleece was often used in ceremonies, especially the fleece from a sacrificed animal.

flesher. A blunt tool of bone, flint, stone, or metal used in fleshing (q.v.).

flesher, hide. A bone or metal gougelike implement, usually with serrated edge, used to remove flesh from the inner side of an animal skin. The term hide scraper is sometimes used.

fleshing. Scraping off the flesh on the inner side of a skin.

flexion. See INFLECTION.

flight, magic. A world-wide mythological theme centering around the ability to fly, as on a magic carpet.

flint. A brittle and homogeneous hydrated silica, often found in sedimentary limestone or as bands of nodules in deposits of chalk. Flint is comparatively easy to work and is associated with early man. It has a variable amount of water, which is loosely held. It is harder than steel. The natural color ranges from gray to black. When flint is sharply struck, it breaks with a conchoidal fracture and a very smooth surface. Before metal, it was the chief material for cutting tools, and many early societies are identified by the flint implements associated with them. On the basis of flint tools which he found, Boucher de Perthes (q.v.), a French customs official, suggested in 1838 that humans have developed over a period of hundreds of thousands of years. He was at first ridiculed, but ultimately his work was accepted.

Flint was an early item of commerce. It was used for ceremonial purposes in many communities even after iron was introduced. In various parts of the world, flint implements are believed to have fallen from the sky and are called thunderstones. In parts of the British Isles, they were believed to have been shot by fairies at a human. Many American Indians regarded flint with veneration. Flint is also called firestone from the facility with which sparks can be struck from it.

flint, eccentric. A flint implement made by elaborate pressure flaking. Eccentric flints are found among the Maya of Mexico and in the Southeast United States. They may suggest a human figure in profile.

flint, pygmy. Tiny flint splinters, in a variety of shapes. Some have a small tang. Their distribution is widespread. It has been suggested that they were used for harpoon teeth, tattooing, arrowheads, and fish hooks. Pygmy flints were probably also hafted into wooden frames and used as different kinds of knives and saws.

flint, tabular. Flint found in layers at least a few inches thick.

flint and pyrites method. See METHOD, FLINT AND PYRITES.

float. A craft that keeps afloat because its material has a specific gravity of less than one. In the upper Nile area, floats are made of papyrus or ambash shafts tied together. A float cannot easily be used against the current or for a long trip. Another name for a float is a raft. A float is also a device used to keep fish bait at a specific depth in water, as well as a means by which to signal a fisherman that his bait has been taken.

float, swimming. An accessory device used to assist the body in supporting itself while swimming, e.g., among the Tamil.

float, tree trunk. A tree trunk stripped of its branches, which is straddled by the rider in transporting himself on water.

floats. Loosely fastened warp or weft threads that appear either on the surface or back of a fabric.

floe, ice. An ice mass smaller than an ice field (q.v.).

floor. An archaeological level below the present surface on which there are undisturbed traces of early man.

floral and fauna area. See AREA, FLORAL AND FAUNA.

flounce, Nilotic. A flounced effect that occurs when some African tribes do not have enough grass or other thatching material, so that layers of thatching are omitted at regular intervals.

flume. An inclined channel for transporting water from a distance.

fluorapatite. A mineral that results from ground-water free fluorine ions combining with the hydroxyapatite in the teeth and bones. Fluorapatite changes gradually with time and so is helpful in determining the comparative age of associated bone finds. It is not useful where there is too much fluorine or in the tropics.

fluorine dating. See DATING, FLUORINE.

flute. A musical instrument consisting of a tube, played by the musician's blowing across the edge of a hole in the tube. Flutes were extensively used for ceremonial purposes and appeared as early as the Paleolithic Age. The Neolithic Age saw the introduction of finger holes so that different tones could be made. Flutes differ in shape, mouth hole location, and manner of playing. They may be played with one hand while the other plays another instrument. The flute's shape gives it a phallic, and thus a fertility, power. Flutes are often made of bone and thus may have the bone's phallic overtones as well. The flute is often found in ancient burials as a charm to revive the dead. Shepherds often play the flute. The term flue pipe is sometimes found.

flute, Aeolian. A musical instrument consisting of a hollow object with perforations. The wind blows across the perforations of the Aeolian flute to produce sounds.

flute, crooked. An ancient Egyptian musical instrument that looked like a bull's horn, very much like the Hebrew shofar (q.v.).

flute, duct. A flute in which there is a duct used to direct the air against the tip of the sound hole.

flute, end. A flute consisting of a tube open at both ends. The performer blows into the upper edges and manipulates the several stops at the bottom of the tube. The end flute is held vertically while being played.

flute, nose. A flute played by blowing through the nostrils rather than through the mouth.

flute, notched. A flute with a notch in the upper opening. It is held vertically while being played. The notched flute usually has stops.

flute, transverse. A flute that is closed at one end, near which is a sound hole. The performer directs air against the edge of the sound hole. The transverse flute is usually held horizontally while being played.

flute, wailing. One of the earliest musical instruments known to man. It is Egyptian in origin and examples of it have been found in mummy cases. The wailing flute consists of a group of slender pipes that are bound together, although there is no clear evidence of the kind of mouthpiece used. It is also called the gingroi.

fluting. The flaking characteristic of Upper Paleolithic times, in which long, narrow, shallow, parallel-sided flakes were removed.

fluvialism. The doctrine that geological strata can only be interpreted by assuming that they were formed by agencies which operate in a uniform way and rate comparable with the action of contemporary agencies. Lyell was the best known fluvialist writer. The term uniformitarianism is also used.

fluviatile. Referring to rivers.

foehn. An Alpine down-mountain wind.

foetalization. See FETALIZATION.

fogous. See SOUTERRAIN.

fold, complete Mongoloid. An eyefold (q.v.) in which the skin over the upper eyelid is loose and hangs over the eyelid's free margin.

fold, epicanthic or **fold, Mongoloid.** On the upper eyelid, the fold of skin from the nose to the eyebrow. The epicanthic fold is most pronounced among the Neo-Asiatic Mongoloids and is usually found associated with a smooth forehead, conspicuous cheekbones, and a flat nose. From 20 to 50 per cent of Chinese display the epicanthic fold and about 2 per cent of Europeans.

fold, external epicanthic. An eyefold (q.v.) in which the skin hangs over the external canthus.

fold, internal epicanthic. An eyefold (q.v.) in which the skin hangs over the inner canthus.

fold, median. An eyefold (q.v.) in which the skin hangs over the middle of the upper eyelid's margin, leaving both canthi exposed.

fold, Mongoloid. See FOLD, EPICANTHIC.

fold, Nordic. An extra fold of the upper eyelid that masks the outer epicanthus. The Nordic fold is found on some Europeans and is not common among Chinese.

fold, pseudo-Mongoloid. A simulated complete Mongoloid fold often found in the first years of life or in older persons.

foliate. Referring to a laurel-leaf or willow-leaf point, typical of the Solutrean cultures.

folk. A group of associated peoples; a primitive kind of post-tribal social organization; the lower classes or common people of an area.

folk, battle-ax. Certain Scandinavian Neolithic groups, whose typical implement was the battle ax.

folklore. The common orally transmitted traditions, myths, festivals, songs, superstitions, and stories of all peoples. The term was first used by William J. Thoms (Ambrose Merton) in 1846. The three major folklore areas of the world are Africa, Europe, and Asia; South and North America; and the South Sea region. Each of these areas has considerable folklore unity. Thus, e.g., the trickster story is common in the Africa, Europe, and Asia area, the explanatory tale in South and North America, and elaborate creation myths in the South Sea area.

Most folklore consists of survivals (q.v.), which continue to have functional value. Sir Lawrence Gomme (1853-1916) tried to make the study of folklore scientific and emphasized the historical, ethnological, and sociological components.

Folklore has come to mean all kinds of oral artistic expression. It may be found in societies that have no writing and it may be unwritten in a literate society. Originally folklore was the study of the curiosities of culture, but gradually it became

217

specialized as the study of popular literary activities.

folklore, historic-geographic method of or **folklore, Finnish method of.** The method of studying folklore that assumes that every tale had its own history and therefore must be independently examined before larger generalizations can be made. The historic-geographic method of folklore emphasizes the study of the time and place, origin, original form, and variations of folktales. Julius and Kaarle Krohn of Finland developed this method in the late 19th century.

folktale. A traditional narrative, passed along from one person to another. Folktales are found in nearly all cultures.

folktales, mythological theory of. Jakob Grimm's theory of the beginning and significance of folktales, in which folktales are represented as the residue of Indo-European myth. This theory would point to the necessity of examining the relation of myth to folktale. Andrew Lang's work largely discredited the mythological theory of folktales.

folkways. The totality of those widely observed traditions in a society the breach of which is punished informally. Punishment is likely to be by such means as avoidance, ostracism, and exclusion. Taking off one's hat to a lady in the United States is an example of a folkway.

follicle, hair. The sheath from which the hair grows.

Folsom. Referring to an early American hunter culture of which there are no skeletal remains. It was spread over the Great Plains area, and there are similar finds in other sites. The relation of the Folsom to the Anasazi (q.v.) culture is obscure. See POINT, FOLSOM.

fonds de cabane. The remains of a prehistoric habitation or hearth which was built in the open. The term may be translated as *foundation of a hut.*

fono. In Samoa, a district parliament composed of the chiefs of several villages.

fontanelle. An interval, covered by a membrane, formed between the angles of an infant's cranial bones. One of the fontanelles is between the posterior medial junction of the parietal bones and the occipital bone. The other two are behind the ears between the temporal and occipital bone. The fontanelle is sometimes used to measure anatomical age.

food, associations with. Associations with food were responsible for many of the religious activities of prehistoric man. These ceremonies blended the practical and the religious or emotional qualities. There were many rules about the use of food and about specific foods that might not be eaten. Women or children might be forbidden to eat some foods. The totem animal might not be eaten. Some societies observed a closed season, to protect food sources which were growing scarce. First fruits (q.v.) observances helped the crop to maturity. There was sometimes a prohibition against eating some foods lest their characteristics be acquired. Food was often given to the gods and to the deceased.

food, inexhaustible. A recurrent folktale theme dealing with the self-revival of food as it is being eaten or when it is in a container. The Greek horn of plenty, in the story of Philemon and Baucis, and the North American Indian legends dealing with a nut that never can be finished are typical stories of this type.

food, phallic. The sex organs symbolized in foods. Fish and cake are common phallic foods. Such foods are eaten for religious or ritual reasons. The ancient world had many such foods, and they are still eaten today.

fools, leafy. A ritualistic Swiss dance performed by masked men who are costumed in leaf-type clothes and carry bells and twigs. The rhythm of the leafy fools' dance is provided by drummers. The entire company goes from inn to inn all day long without stopping.

foot, ice. Ice attached to the shore.

foot, web. A condition in which there is skin webbing between the toes. It afflicts males only and so is a sex-linked character carried by a dominant Y gene.

foramen. An opening, usually in a bone, for carrying nerves or vessels.

foramen magnum. A large opening that contains the connection of the spinal cord with the brain and along which are the occipital condyles that articulate the skull with the neck region of the backbone. Man's foramen magnum faces down and is on the underside of the skull, since his backbone is vertical with the skull at its upper end. Most primates have the foramen magnum displaced from the back of the skull to its undersurface, with the extent of the displacement greater as the evolutionary scale is ascended. The position of the foramen magnum on a fossil skull thus gives valuable clues to the manner in which the individual carried his head and his general posture.

foramina, lacerate. Jagged openings to admit nerves and arteries at the base of the skull. The comparative size of the middle lacerate foramina is correlated with skull development, as these openings reach their greatest size in human groups with large brains.

foramina, parietal. Small apertures in the parietal bones near the middle line. If present, they transmit blood vessels. Their presence and size seem positively correlated with more highly developed human groups.

foreshaft. The connection between the head and shaft of implements like a spear.

forest, boreal. A northern forest, with very long winters and short summers. In a boreal forest there are many fur-bearing animals and hunters predominate.

forest, Mediterranean scrub. An area near sea and desert in the temperate zones but closed off by mountains from the desert. Summer is hot and dry, while winter is rainy and mild.

forest, semideciduous rain. A tropical rain forest (q.v.) in which rains fall only seasonally and trees annually lose their foliage, so that undergrowth can develop.

forest, temperate. A well watered forest in which summer and winter seasons are clearly defined and in which game is common. There are both evergreen and deciduous trees in a temperate forest. Much clearing must be done before large groups of people can be supported.

forest, tropical rain. An equatorial forest with heavy vegetation, much rain, and very high temperatures.

forest, true rain. A tropical rain forest in which there is rain every day.

forestay. On a sailboat, a kind of rigging that is near the bow. The forestay keeps the mast from falling backwards.

forge. An area used for metalworking, usually heating and hammering.

fork. A pronged implement for carrying food to the mouth, which first became known in Italy in the 14th century.

forking. The terminological difference used to distinguish male from analogous female relatives.

form. In linguistics, the meaningful part of an utterance.

form, absolute. In linguistics, the form assumed by a phrase or word when spoken by itself. See SANDHI.

form, attested. A spoken or written word or a variant word form actually observed as having occurred in a linguistic system, in contradistinction to hypothetical forms.

form, bound. A linguistic form that is not spoken by itself nor used as a sentence, e.g., *ed* in *laughed*. A

bound form may also be called a bound morpheme.

form, cognate. In linguistics, a word that resembles another in phonetic form and meaning.

form, complex. A linguistic form that resembles another phonetically and/or semantically.

form, criterion of. A similarity in the form of two cultural objects that does not stem from their nature or function. Ratzel suggested that this criterion indicated the likelihood that the form of one of the objects was borrowed from the other. He developed this concept while studying the development of the bow in Africa.

form, familiar. Any form of a word, usually a verb or pronoun, which shows affection, kinship or familiarity, and sometimes lack of respect, on the part of the speaker toward the individuals addressed.

form, finite. Any form of a verb that shows the relationship of the action to a particular subject, as opposed to the infinite forms. This distinction is particularly relevant in the Indo-European languages and somewhat in the Semitic and Finno-Ugric languages, but it has no importance in most other language groups.

form, free. In linguistics, an element of a language that can be spoken by itself in normal speech, e.g., a word. See FORM, BOUND. A free form may also be called a free morpheme.

form, hesitation. A parenthetic statement when a speaker hesitates, e.g., *Mrs. -er- Jones.*

form, nonsense. A statement that has no denotative meaning, e.g., *urtch.*

form, nursery. A speech form that has an infantile connotation, e.g., *mamma.*

form, relic. A speech form that is a holdover from a previous speech feature. It is especially used in dialect geography.

form, starred. A word form that has an asterisk (*) in front of it to show that it is a hypothetical form or one reconstructed on the basis of known data and linguistic laws, e.g., Latin *auricula* for ear.

form, tactic. In linguistics, a taxeme (q.v.) that appears as a grammatical arrangement.

form, underlying. In linguistics, the free morpheme appearing in a complex form; e.g., *boy* in *boyishness.*

formula. A verbal technique for handling problem situations or disease, among several American Indian tribes, e.g., the Cherokee.

formula, dental. A formula for expressing man's dentition, usually written $\frac{2.1.2.3}{2.1.2.3} \times 2 = 32$ indicating that a normal mouth has 32 teeth, consisting of two incisors, one canine, two premolars, and three molars on each side of the upper and lower jaws.

formula, story. A formula used to begin and end a folktale, among the North American Indians.

formula tale. See TALE, FORMULA.

fortis. Any consonant that is produced tensely and strongly, e.g., *p* as against *b.*

fortress, hilltop or fortress, contour. Earthworks that consist of artificial defenses that follow a hill's natural lines.

fortress, promontory. Earthworks that defend a piece of high ground that is not accessible because of water or precipices on the one side and artificial works on the other.

fossa. 1 The moat of a terramara (q.v.). 2 A concavity in teeth or bones, e.g., the temporal fossa on the temporal bone and the distal fossa on the first molar.

fossa canina. A depression in the outer surface of the upper jaw bone serving as an attachment for the muscle that lifts the corners of the upper lip and exposes the canine teeth. It is a distinguishing characteristic of Homo sapiens.

fossa, glenoid. The depression in the temporal bones of the skull into which the condyle of the lower jaw fits.

fossil. An object that has been preserved in rocks or earth.

fossilized. Referring to bones in which organic material is replaced by deposits of minerals. Narrowly speaking, fossilization means merely that the animal fats and gelatine in a bone have been lost, but not necessarily that they have been replaced by anything. See MINERALIZED.

fossorial. Referring to a digging habitat or organism.

fostering. Giving a child to others than its parents to be taken care of.

fovea. An area in the retina that makes sharpness of vision possible.

fracture, conchoidal. A shell-shaped fracture on flint, produced by pressure flaking (q.v.).

fracture, hinge. A method of removing a flake from a core so that part of the flake's edge is rounded or curled over, in contrast to the normal flake's sharp cutting edge.

fracture, starch. A kind of fracture of flint resulting from thermal changes, in which the results are bars of flint of long parallel facets, looking rather columnar. This kind of fracture probably results from breaking due to shrinkage of the flint.

fracture, vowel. See DIPHTHONGIZATION.

Frankfurter Verständigung. See AGREEMENT, FRANKFURT.

fraternity. Siblings; a society of men.

fraternity, tribal. A fraternity that includes all of a society's men.

freemartin. A nonfertile female calf which is twin to a bull calf. When dissected, the freemartin usually is found to have imperfect organs of both sexes.

free-standing. Any carved figure or column that is not attached to another structure.

frequency, gene. See METHOD, GENE FREQUENCY.

fret. An ornament made by a combination of fillets or bands, originally used in the prehistoric era and later by the Greeks. The French word *grecque* is sometimes applied to the fret.

friable. Referring to the physical quality of a substance that makes it easy to crumble.

fricative. Referring to a type of articulation in which the air passes through a narrow groove, e.g., *th* in *timothy*.

friction, wood. The most widely used technique for making fire among nonliterate peoples. One piece of wood is horizontal on the ground and the other piece is twirled rapidly into it; or else one piece is rubbed along the grain of another or sawed across its grain. Usually the two pieces are different kinds of wood, of different degrees of hardness. Both pieces should be very dry.

frit. A compound used to glaze, or to give density to, soft porcelain. It was used on Greek pottery.

frit, blue. A blue color found in ancient Egyptian and Mesopotamian wall paintings, possessed of great lasting qualities. See BLUE, EGYPTIAN.

Fritsch, Gustav (1838-1927). A German anatomist who wrote a widely influential book on anti-Semitism and emphasized the relation of human types and geographic factors.

frontality, law of. The doctrine that the human body, when represented in a work of art, should not be shown twisting or turning. It is characteristic of much early statuary. Early artists usually present the figures in a work of art in their most familiar expression. In sculpture, this is usually a frontal representation. The law of frontality is that a vertical nose-navel line could equally divide the statue, apart from arms and legs. Early Greek sculpture, in the sixth century, B.C., showed this law, as did much Egyptian sculpture.

222

frontotemporale. The deepest point on the incurving of the temple above the orbit.

frost action. See ACTION, FROST.

fructivore. A fruit eater.

frugivorous. Referring to eating fruits rather than grain.

fruit, forbidden. The belief that there was once a tree, the fruit of which was not to be eaten except under special circumstances. Adam's expulsion from the Garden of Eden resulted because he partook of the Tree of Knowledge of Good and Evil contrary to God's command.

fruits, first. The initial catch of fish or animals, or the initial offspring of domesticated animals; also, the ceremonies surrounding their consumption. The object of first-fruit ceremonies is to placate the gods and reassure them that they will get their share, thus minimizing the danger that lurks in everything new. The ceremonies may involve sacrificial offerings, or elaborate feasting. The earliest agriculture products that became ripe were often presented to a god in order to celebrate. These ceremonies probably originated as a method for protecting the food supply until it could reach maturity and be used. Ancestors who were given credit for control over the food supply got the first fruits. Sometimes the practice was extended to cover the first infant born. The priests of Israel and the shrines of Greece made their revenues from first fruits.

frutescent. Referring to the form of a shrub or bush.

fucoid. Referring to an alga fossil.

fuller. A groove that runs all or most of the length of a sword.

fulling. A process of making cloth stronger and smoother and cleaning it. It was originally done by beating the cloth in water, so that it shrank and the pattern of the weave was less visible. Oil might also be removed from the cloth. The early Middle Ages saw fulling by hand, while the later Middle Ages developed fulling by the feet. More recently, the fabric is kept for several days in a container of alkaline solution, while this solution is mixed with a stick or similar device, thus softening the fibers and giving the fabric a more uniform surface.

functional theory. See THEORY, FUNCTIONAL AND STRUCTURAL.

fundament. That part of the earth's land surface which has not been altered by men; the earth's face before man appeared.

funeral. The ceremony attendant on disposing of a dead body. Such ceremonies vary among cultures, and there is not much agreement on the time lag between death and burial. Narrowly speaking, the funeral is a torchlight procession, with the name itself derived from the Latin for *torch*, because burials used to take place by torchlight at night.

The funeral ceremonies usually show a blend of affection and fear. Attempts may be made to confuse the ghost so that it cannot return to its home on earth. Great grief is likely to characterize the funeral. The fires at or en route to the funeral are probably to warn and light the spirit, as well as to put off the ghost. The mourners may purify themselves after the funeral through bathing or other devices. Funeral feasts may be conducted in which the deceased is presumed to partake. Funeral games are probably intended to keep the ghost away, and some are intended to wake the procreative urge to counteract death.

Second funerals may be held to effect final cutting off of the spirit from the living, as well as the spirit's formal acceptance in the other world. Such funerals are often found where the spirit presumably stays around the body until the flesh decays.

funeral, mock. A funeral involving temporary mourning for a nonhuman object, like a locust. The ceremony is believed to have magical effect, as in driving away locusts.

furnace. A device used for metallurgical processes effected by heat from fuel combustion. The fuel burns in a fire box and the metal is in the hearth, although the two parts may be combined. In a shaft furnace, Osmund furnace, hearth furnace, or kiln, the fuel and metal are in contact. In a crucible furnace, the heating chamber can be moved.

Roasting furnaces were used in antiquity to remove undesirable substances, like water from iron ore or sulphur or arsenic from galena and pyrites. Perhaps the earliest smelting furnace was an open fire, although the bowl furnace, a hole lined with clay, is the earliest kind found. The pot furnace, a later development, was more efficient than the bowl furnace. See HEARTH.

Furtwängler, Adolf (1853-1907). A German archaeologist who conducted excavations in Greece and with Löschcke published a list of all the Mycenaean pottery in the Aegean islands, probably the first corpus of finds in archaeological history. Furtwängler made important contributions to the study of the chronology of pottery.

futhark. The first six letters of the runic alphabet which are used as its name.

fuzzy-wuzzy. The name given by American soldiers in World War II to the frizzly-haired Oceanic Negroes. Rudyard Kipling had given the term currency by referring to the Sudan Fuzzy-Wuzzy tribe in his *Ballad of the Sudan Expeditionary Force.*

fylfot. See SWASTIKA.

G

gad. A pointed bar of wood tipped with metal, or a metal bar resembling a crowbar. The gad is shorter than a crowbar.

gaff. On a sailboat, a spar attached to the head of a sail. The jaws keep it on the after side of the mast. A gaff is also a fish hook the shank of which is attached to the handle.

gaff, double. A fish hook consisting of a handle in the shape of a Y and with a barb on each arm's inner face.

Galen, Claudius (130-200). A Greek physician who lived in Rome. He explicated many facts about the human anatomy. His writings were almost the only textbooks on medicine and anatomy for approximately 1,500 years.

galena. A lead ore widely used in the central United States by various American Indian groups, especially the Mound Builders of the Mississippi Valley. It was used to make numerous objects.

gallop, flying. A method for graphically representing a quadruped, such as a horse, in the act of running rapidly. The hind legs are extended to the rear, and the front legs extended forward together. The flying gallop is stylized and artificial, as such a position is not assumed by quadrupeds in flight. It is found in art practically all over the world.

Galton, Sir Francis (1822-1911). English founder of eugenics, who developed the correlation table and studied hereditary genius. He emphasized the study of individual differences and is probably one of the founders of the mental test. Galton demonstrated that physical and other characteristics are distributed in a society in accordance with the normal probability curve. He is largely responsible for developing the field of eugenics.

gamal. The men's house (q.v.) in New Hebrides.

Gamblian. The second of the two great pluvial periods recognized from the geological strata of Kenya. It is sometimes considered to be two separate pluvial periods.

gambling. Risking something valuable on a chance of gain. Gambling is worldwide and flourished in ancient times.

game. Play-acting in which there are participants who compete with each other in accordance with rules.

game, ball. One of the most popular men's games of the American Indians, especially in the East. Netted rackets were used to bat a stuffed deerskin or wooden ball to the opposite goal, with the hands not permitted to touch the ball. The ball game is the ancestor of modern lacrosse.

game, charming. Attracting game by special persons reciting formulae. Charming game was rather common among some American Indian groups, e.g., the Paiute.

game, deer's-foot. An American Indian game in which perforated bones from a deer's foot are strung on a cord with a needle at one end. The bones are thrown so that one will light on the needle.

game, dice. A game widely played in Canada and America among Indian groups. Two or four lots—each of which has a different value—are thrown into the air, and a score is kept of the value. It is the ancestor of the modern game of craps.

game, four-stick. An American Indian game in which four marked sticks are hidden under a flat basket, with the participants guessing the location of each stick.

game, hand. An American Indian game in which two bones or objects, one marked and the other unmarked, are held behind a player's back or hidden and it is necessary to guess where the unmarked object is. This game is an early variant of our "button, button, who's got the button?" The hand game was enormously popular.

game, hidden-ball. Game played in the Southwest. An American Indian game in which a ball or stick was hidden under one of four cups or tubes, with the player required to guess under which one it actually is.

game, hoop-and-pole. A North American Indian fertility game in which a hoop is set rolling along the ground and is shot at by arrows and other weapons. The game is scored by the relation of the fallen arrows and other weapons to the hoop.

game, kickball. A game found in northwest Mexico in which the participants run fairly long distances while kicking a ball along.

game, masters of the. In South America, gods or god-like persons or entities who are special protectors of game or of a particular kind of animal.

game, mocassin. A game played by the Indians of the southern Great Lakes area. It consists of hiding an object in one of a number of moccasins and then having the participants guess which moccasin it is in.

game, ring-and-pin. A game in which a hoop or similar object attached by a cord to a small stick is flipped and caught on the stick.

game, slow. Slow-moving animals like the tortoise that are easily collectable, often by women and children.

game, snow-snake. A game played by throwing a long pointed stick along smoothed snow, e.g., among the Iroquois.

game, stick. A game widely distributed among Indian groups of

Canada and America. It involves shuffling bundles of sticks and then guessing in which bundle a given stick is.

game, wheel-and-stick. A widely distributed American Indian game in which one player rolled a stone wheel forward while the other slid a curved stick after it, so that the wheel would rest in the curve of the stick. It was also used in divination (q.v.) and to help cure the sick and is probably related to sun myths.

gamete. The male (sperm) or female (ovum) sex cells.

gametophyte. The part of an organism's life cycle which results in gametes being produced.

gamilan. The Indonesian orchestra, which makes varied tones and depends largely on percussion. The leader plays a *rabab*, or kind of viol, and there is often a *suling*, or bamboo flute, and a *selompret*, an oboe-like instrument. The other instruments are gongs and bullet-shaped drums. There may also be a big drum and bamboo rattles.

gap, wind. See VALLEY, WIND.

gardener. A farmer who uses man power exclusively in working the soil.

gargoylism. A condition of substantial abnormality, with unusual bony structure, opaque corneas, and enlarged liver and spleen.

gash. Reed pen used by ancient Egyptian scribes. It was approximately 10 inches long and was made with either a split point or a bruised end, which gave a feathery effect.

gastromancy. The art of divination (q.v.) by looking steadily into

a water-filled container or by listening to the sounds made by a ventriloquist.

gastrula. An embryonic stage in which the embryo encloses a cavity, is opened at one end, and is essentially an outer layer of cells.

gathering, food. Obtaining subsistence by collecting fruits, berries, roots, moss, fungi, insects, fowl, and fish, as well as some forms of mud and earth, and hunting some animals. Among the food-gathering peoples are the Ainu, Veddas, Bushmen, Andamanese, and most North and South American Indians. It is the simplest form of economy.

Most food-gathering communities were fairly small, on the order of about 50 persons. Women usually foraged for plants and fruits and men engaged in fowling, hunting, and fishing. There was little in the way of individual ownership, and migrations were common in following wild herds for food. Apart from the dog, which was probably domesticated early, other animals were not domesticated by food gatherers, since they lacked time for specialized activities. The search for food took up most of their time, and they were often near starvation. There was little trading or internal commerce, as well as little in the way of individual wealth or class differences. Food gathering was common up to fairly recent times, and it has been estimated that man has had agriculture for only about 1 per cent of his existence.

Gedänken. Objects or things that serve as reminders of previously existing persons, groups, or periods.

They are usually fortuitously found rather than specifically recovered.

gee-string. A garment made by wrapping a cloth around the waist, with one layer between the legs and under the belt part, so that the front hangs down like an apron.

Ge'ez. The ecclesiastic and literary language of Ethiopia, dead for some time as a spoken language but long used in Ethiopian literature and by the Ethiopian Church.

geloscopy. The art of divination (q.v.) by observation of a person's way of laughing.

gematria. The study of cryptographs in Hebrew literature, or the explanation of the Hebrew Scriptures by studying the words' cryptographic meanings.

Gemeinschaft. The concept of a community, or of traditional or sacred society. In Tönnies' formulation, the Gemeinschaft is a group based on "natural will," i.e., a major purpose of the members in forming the group is to associate with each other. The later literature on this subject emphasizes what Tönnies saw as a consequence of this "natural will," a feeling of belongingness and solidarity among the members. Maine's concept of status, MacIver's concept of community and Cooley's concept of primary group are analogous. See GESELLSCHAFT.

geminate. Referring to the lengthening of an articulation, e.g., in *cat-tail* the *tt* sound, produced by interposing a glottal stop between the two occurrences of the consonant.

gemination. The practice of doubling consonants in particular and any sound or written symbol in general.

gender. A syntactical classification of words most often evident in the Indo-European and Semitic languages. Nearly all of these languages show the difference between a masculine and a feminine gender, some have a neuter gender as well, and some have an animate and an inanimate gender.

gene. The minute globules within the chromosome (q.v.) which seem to be the ultimate carriers of specific hereditary potentialities. The genes are ordinarily passed unchanged from one generation to the next. Man has been estimated to have from 10,000 to 80,000 genes, with several authorities estimating about 20,000-40,000. There is no reliable estimate of the number of separate gene loci in any organism, although approximations are available for some forms like *Drosophila*. The estimates of the number of gene loci in man are analogized from *Drosophila*.

Genes can reproduce and mutate. They are arranged linearly in the chromosomes. It has been estimated that all humans have some 90 per cent of the genes attributed to humans, while only 10 per cent of the genes account for sex and racial differences. See MENDELIAN.

gene, complementary. A gene that produces a character through working together with another gene. The character does not appear unless the complementary genes are found together in an organism.

gene, lethal. A gene that may cause the death of the person carrying it.

gene, linked. A gene which does not segregate from other genes in meiosis because it is linked with them in the same chromosome. The characters determined by the linked genes appear in one organism.

gene frequency method. See METHOD, GENE FREQUENCY.

genealogical method. See METHOD, GENEALOGICAL.

generalization. In evolution, an organism remaining fairly close to the form of its predecessors. Man is an organism that is highly developed and yet is generalized. See ANIMAL, GENERALIZED.

genetic group. See GROUP, GENETIC.

genetics. The study of the process of inheritance.

genna. Among the Naga, something prohibited under supernatural penalties. It is similar to the Lushia *thianglo,* the Lakher *ana,* and the Garo *marang.*

genophagy. The supposed complete replacement of recessive by dominant genes in an entire population. This does not take place in actuality; rather, an equilibrium of dominant and recessive genes is reached and maintained.

genosome. The protoplasmic material of a chromosome in which the genes are located.

genotype. The genetic framework of the individual. The genotype is also an organism in which the genes determining a trait are either recessive or dominant, so that the organism's somatic appearance is in accordance with its gene arrangement.

gens. A kin group, unilinear and exogamous, usually a patrilineal clan.

genuflection. The act of kneeling on one or both knees in a religious observance.

geochronology. The development of time scales for the earth, so that those periods to which the calendar is not applicable can be dated in terms of years.

geognosy. A branch of geology that deals with the elements making up the earth.

geography, dialect. The analysis of localized differentiations within a speech area.

geography, linguistic. The study of the geographic distribution and characteristics of the dialects of a language.

geomancy. Divination (q.v.) by observation of lines or figures. It was originally done by the study of topography or by throwing down a handful of sand. In China, geomancy is used to locate dwellings or tombs. The Arabs study the pattern of points in the sand.

geomorphic. Referring to the shape, content, appearance, and physiography of various feature of the earth's surface.

geophagy. The practice of eating various types of earth and clay. Geophagy is found in Africa, China, Indonesia, and South America. In the 17th century, some Spanish noblewomen ate so much earth that penalties were imposed by the religious authorities and the government. Geophagy has been

229

attributed by some authorities to dietary deficiencies, especially of salt, but this explanation has been disputed.

geosyncline. An area with substantial marine deposits and where the sea bottom tends to sink.

geotype. A species subdivision, the major distinguishing features of which are defined by geographic localization.

ger. The Mongol name for yurt (q.v.).

Germanic, Primitive. A lost language spoken between the first century B.C. and the first century A.D. Its descendants are included in the Germanic family of languages, one of which is English.

Germanic sound shifts. See SHIFTS, GERMANIC SOUND.

Geronimo. An Apache prophet and medicine man who opposed the American authorities in the late 19th century and spread terror. He fled to exile in Mexico several times.

geronticide. See SENILICIDE.

gerontocracy. An early form of government in which the old men of the community were the rulers because of their special powers, wisdom, and prestige.

gerontomorphic. Referring to morphological traits most commonly found in an older representative of a species.

Gesamtkunstwerk. The theory that all areas of the arts should be included in one interrelated subject.

Gesellschaft. The concept of society, association, or secular society. In Tönnies' formulation, a group based on "rational will," i.e., a

major purpose of the members in forming the group is to achieve some common objective. It is not unlike MacIver's concept of association, Maine's concept of contract, Weber's concept of *Zweckrational* action, and Cooley's secondary group. See GEMEINSCHAFT.

gesta. A rectangular slab used by ancient Egyptian scribes as a pallette to hold inks. The gesta was made of wood, ivory, or stone and contained two or more "wells" for inks, a half cylindrical groove for the pens or reeds, and usually a cover of stone or wood. They were about 12 by 3 inches. They have been found in tombs dating to the Fourth Dynasty. Many gestas had the name of the reigning king inscribed upon them.

gesture. A communication by moving parts of the body, especially the upper parts. It is often used by persons who are of different language backgrounds and is a technique for the expression of emotion and artistic feelings and ideas. There is some evidence to show that the gesticulatory part of early religion is more important than the role of words. See THEORY, GESTURAL.

gethaka. See KITHAKA.

gharnao. See RAFT, CHATTY.

ghat. In India, a large stairway leading to a river. A ghat usually goes from a temple to the river.

ghi or **ghee.** Boiled butter, which will keep solid at high temperatures. Ghi is found in parts of East Africa, India, and Central Asia. In India, it usually comes from goat and sheep milk and in Africa from camel milk.

ghost. 1 In folklore, the soul of the deceased when it is believed to be perceptible to humans. 2 In archaeology, the deduction of the nature of a destroyed object from circumstantial evidence. Thus, the existence of the harp of Shub-ad at Ur was deduced through the study of the traces in the ground left by the strings, and Garrod reconstructed a wooden spear by a hole it left in the pelvis of a Paleolithic hunter in Palestine.

ghost, ash. A clown among the Inland Pomo.

ghost, rousing the. Taking liberties with a corpse before burial, or playing practical jokes on the relatives of the dead. Rousing the ghost has been common at various times and places and was forbidden in 1367 at the Council of York.

ghoul. A monster that eats humans, both living and dead. Ghouls are common in lonely places.

ghutru. A goblet-shaped percussion instrument from India consisting of a hollow shell and a parchment drum head.

giantism. The condition of being exceptionally strong and large. The term comes from the mythological characters who were larger and more powerful than men but less than gods.

giants. Very large humans, birds, or animals. They are often mentioned in North American folklore. Giants are often male and often cannibals. Belief in giants is practically universal. Giants are often

heroes of tremendous strength and may have mythological qualities.

gibber-gunyah. An Australian term for a stone shelter.

gibbon. The smallest of the apes, less than three feet tall. It has very long arms, which enable it to brachiate with great skill.

gieres. A Lapp boatlike sled.

gift. A present given to someone, which may be a major distribution technique in early society. Giving presents has an important economic function in all the North American tribes and Polynesia. It is closely linked with a strong sense of personal dignity and self-appreciation. Gift-giving peoples often have institutionalized boasting and indulge in intentional and conspicuous waste. A gift as a voluntary offering to please or propitiate is often found on ceremonial occasions.

gift, fatal. A gift given to an enemy, who unwittingly takes and uses it as if it came from a friend. Fatal gifts may bring the recipient death or misfortunes.

gift, Indian. A gift for which it is understood that another gift is to be given in return. The term arose from the common American Indian custom of asking a gift for a gift.

gift, morning. A gift given by the husband to his wife on the morning after the wedding takes place.

gifta. The process of handing over a potential bride to her suitor, symbolizing the move from her father to her potential husband. The gifta followed the Beweddung (q.v.).

gig. A fish hook lowered on a shoal to catch a fish.

Gigantopithecus blacki. A type of fossil hominoid, known also as the Chinese Giant Ape. The original evidence found by G. H. R. von Königswald consisted of three large molar teeth that were obtained in Hong Kong apothecary shops in 1935. Von Königswald has maintained that the teeth are from a non-human form while Weidenreich has said they are human.

gigantism. Acromegaly (q.v.) that occurs before the limb bones are ossified, so that there is a great increase in stature. The effect results from pituitary hyperfunction.

gin. An Australian squaw or woman.

gingival. Referring to a speech articulation in which the tongue is against the ridge above the upper teeth, e.g., *t* in English.

gingroi. See FLUTE, WAILING.

girth, axillary chest. The girth of the chest, measured across the axillary fossae and averaging readings during expiration and inspiration.

girth, mesosternale chest. The chest girth, averaged during inspiration and expiration and measured across the mesosternale.

giving, gift. The exchange of gifts among primitives. When there is no trade or barter, gift giving helps equalize the distribution of goods. Gifts may be presented on a special occasion, such as a visit.

glabella. A point halfway between the supraorbital ridges over the nose. It usually forms a slight prominence.

glabrousness. A lack of hair on the body. It is an important trait in differentiating racial groups from one another. Negroids and Mongoloids are relatively glabrous. See HAIR.

glaciation. The covering of large parts of the earth by a thick layer of snow and ice. Glaciation makes it difficult for most flora and for some fauna to grow. Early Europe has been covered by four ice ages— Günz, Mindel, Riss, and Würm— named after four Swiss streams. Glaciers still exist in parts of the north and the Alps. It is believed that Homo sapiens appeared in the intermediary period between the Günz and Mindel eras. The term glacier was coined by McLennan. The poet-naturalist Schimper first wrote on a Great Ice Age, and the naturalist Agassiz confirmed his findings by studying the Swiss glaciers and their effects.

North America also had four major glaciations: Nebraskan, Kansan, Illinoisan, and Wisconsin. These periods were probably almost contemporary with the European ice ages. The interglacial periods were longer than the glaciations, and the Second, or Middle, Interglacial was especially long.

The four extremes of the Glacial Age named by Penck and Brückner in their study of Alpine glaciation have been correlated with three or more glacial extremes in England, northern Germany, and Russia. There is some doubt about the number and contemporaneity of the successive glacial stages and their relation to climatic changes. The second and third glaciations were probably the most severe and were probably separated by an intermediate warm phase which may have exceeded all the others in extent. The onset of the first glaciation was preceded by a long period in which the temperature gradually fell; and the final glaciation was divided into a number of small oscillations of lessening intensity.

It has been suggested that the Glacial Age can be regarded as a series of temperature undulations that increased to a maximum and then diminished. Some authorities have even suggested that the period called post-glacial is perhaps merely an intermission between the last glaciation and the one yet to come.

Some traces of an Asian glacial cycle have been observed in the Himalayas, in the area north and east of Tibet, in northern Formosa, northeastern Korea, and central Japan. It has been suggested that the Asian cycle was parallel to that of Europe and that the north European ice sheet extended over northern Siberia. The glaciations of the north were in all probability contemporaneously duplicated in the southern hemisphere.

Zeuner has estimated that the four glaciations began, respectively, 600,000, 500,000 250,000, and 120,000 years ago, with the last reaching its terminal period ca. 20,000 years ago. Some areas that had no glaciation, like Central Africa, have had alternating rainy (pluvial) and dry (interpluvial) periods, which may be correlated with glacial periods.

glacier. An ice stream that flows from higher to lower levels.

glacis. A long slope running from a ditch to the top of a defensive rampart.

gladiolito. A lanceolate ground stone artifact of unknown function found archaeologically in Ciboney burials in Cuba.

Glagolitic. An alphabet with symmetrical geometric forms with appendages. It resembles Ethiopic and probably had some connection with the Cyrillic alphabet. It was used by some Slavic speaking peoples.

glass. A brittle, hard, transparent substance made by fusion, often by fusing silica particles in sand. Glass was first used in Egypt ca. 4000 B.C. Most glass consists of silicates, soda, and lime, and often contains potash and lead oxide. Under the Romans glass became very popular and common.

glass, eye. See SPECTACLE.

glass, homogeneous. Glass that is uniform in composition throughout its structure as differentiated from glass made up of layers of different structure.

glaze. A layer of molten glass that is fused to the clay surface of a ceramic object through firing. This layer seals the porous surface of the clay so that it is shiny, hard, and smooth. The origin of glazes is not definitely established. Probably the oldest glaze that survives is one with the name of King Mena, ca. 3000 B.C.

Alkaline glaze, made of silicic acid with alkali, potash, or soda, was found among the early Egyptian, Persian, and Syrian pottery makers and was used for several millenia. It did not spread because it does not stick to potter's clay and must be used with a clay made of silicious sand.

Lead glaze is the most widely used type. It sticks to practically all clay bodies. When tin oxide is added, it forms an opaque glaze found in Assyrian, Babylonian and Egyptian pottery.

glazing. A technique of giving pottery a high sheen through the application of salts in solution, silica, lead oxide, or a slip (q.v.), under high temperatures. Not many primitives could use this technique.

Gletschermilch. An opaque glacial melt water with sand and clay in suspension.

glide. In linguistics, the transition from one sound to another or from vocal organ inactivity to the production of a sound.

glide, off or **glide, final.** The last phase of the articulation of a phoneme when the vocal organs go back to their usual position or take a position before forming another sound.

glide, on or **glide, initial.** The first part of the pronunciation of a phoneme, in which the organs of speech are in the position to produce the sound.

globularization. See BRACHYCEPHALIZATION.

Glockenbecher. A bellshaped cup.

Gloger's rule. See RULE, GLOGER'S.

glory, hand of. A good luck charm made from a dead man's dried hand. The hands of criminals that were hanged are especially prized. The hand of glory may make the possessor invisible or motionless.

glosseme. The smallest meaningful linguistic unit. It is used differently by Bloomfield and by Hjelmslev and there is controversy over its exact meaning.

glossematics. A school of language theory developed by Danish linguists since the 1930's. It emphasizes the relation between language units of expression as well as of content.

glossolalia. An unintelligible jargon spoken while in a state of religious excitement. In Christian terminology it is sometimes called "speaking in tongues."

glossopetra. Aldrovarde's name for flint arrowheads, because of their presumed resemblance to a human tongue. Pliny thought they fell from heaven during the moon's eclipses. The Japanese call them axes of the fox, since the fox is their symbol of evil.

glottal. Referring to a sound produced by the larynx (hence also called laryngeal) by a closing or restriction of the vocal chords, e.g., *h*.

glottalization. The modification of a speech sound by producing a compression of air by means of a rising glottis rather than by the lungs, as in the Caucasian languages.

glottis. The V-shaped area between the vocal cords (q.v.). It is about 1.8 centimeters in males and 1.2 centimeters in females.

glottochronology. The chronological comparison of languages by comparing their basic vocabulary sampled at different times. Since the basic vocabulary of a language is fairly constant, its changes can help show changes in related languages.

glottology. See LINGUISTICS.

glutton motif. See MOTIF, GLUTTON.

glyph. A character or carved figure that is in relief or incised; a pictograph (q.v.) that is carved.

glyptography. The study of engraving on precious gems.

gnathic. Having reference to jaws.

gnathion. The midpoint of the lower end of the symphysis of the jaw.

gnome. A dwarf, usually hunchbacked, who either lives in or swims through the earth. Jewish cabalism locates gnomes in the earth's center.

gnomon. A stick or vertical rod that is stuck in the ground so that the shadow shows the position of the sun. In Borneo, it is used to tell the seasons of the year.

goatta. A tent used by the only arctic tribe in Europe, the Lapps.

go-between. An intermediary, often used to describe a person who helps arrange a marriage.

Gobineau, Count Arthur de (1816-1894). A French writer on the development of society. His essay, *The Inequality of Human Races* (1853) was probably the first and most influential of the selectionist writings on society. He said that there were inferior and superior races, and that most races were not capable of civilization.

goblin. A mischievous but helpful house spirit. A goblin does peculiar things, like unexpectedly moving furniture around.

god. A particular god was believed to be in charge of various parts of the world or of specific activities or qualities. Communication with them is necessary to insure that they are on our side. They may be any powers that are superior to men yet helpful to them. Gods usually are the nucleus of attention of their social group. Among the factors that have been suggested as giving rise to gods are the focusing of attention on the problems of food and sex, a feeling of mystical projection of human emotions, the effect of exalting group ceremonies, the idea of a just cause, the idealized image of a priest, and the mixture of hero-soul and spirit.

Gods have been classified as nature powers (Dawn, Moon), fertility gods (Great Mother), functional gods (war gods, healing arts), mediating gods (avatar of Vishnu), high gods (Chinese T'ien, Hindu Brahman), supreme universal ruler (Allah or Ormazd).

A god's history is clearly linked with its believer's life and development. Conquest, moral growth, and economic and other changes may radically change the nature of gods.

god, air. A supernatural being associated with meteorological and atmospheric phenomena: storms, rain, winds, lightning, and thunder. Wind gods were found in America, India, and China. There are several storm gods, e.g., Woden and Thor. In the Shinto religion, lightning is personified in the Dragon-Sword. The early Yahweh, as well as the Babylonian Enlil, were tied in with wind, cloud, and storm.

235

god, finite. A god who has power limited by factors beyond his control. Almost all primitive gods were finite, since they limited each other and were also limited by the original chaos of the world. The Olympian deities of the Greeks were themselves subject to Fate.

god, high. A supreme deity, especially in connection with the religion of primitive peoples. Some Catholic anthropologists, notably Father Schmidt, have attempted to demonstrate that peoples of lowest cultures have a concept of a high god in order to prove that belief in a supreme deity characterized the earliest religion and is an inherent item of human belief. Andrew Lang questioned that such gods result from extensive evolutionary development by showing that they existed among some fairly undeveloped Australians. While Tylor said that the high god was a general culminating development, Lang maintained that it was entirely separate from other cultural items.

god, momentary. An object which is presumed to be possessed by a god when it is worshipped. A momentary god is also a god who has a limited existence for a specific purpose and place only.

god, mountain. A god believed to be (or to live in) a mountain, because of its size, its meteorological concomitant, or the mythology created around it. The Greek Mt. Olympus is a well-known example of a mountain associated with gods.

god, tribal. A deity worshipped by a particular tribe, found usually among transient or nomadic peoples. Some of the early nomadic Hebrews originally worshipped tribal gods. They are believed to take care of a particular tribe and look after its welfare.

goddess, mother. A mother-figure deity. Most early nature cults included the mother goddess, or Great Mother, as a central figure, since the maintenance of fertility is of prime interest in the religion. The traditional mother goddesses of the eastern Mediterranean area were Isis in Egypt, Astarte in Phoenicia, Cybele in Phrygia, and Demeter in Greece. This goddess functioned as the patroness of agricultural productivity and the giver of blessed immortality for the dead whose life-giving power was transferred to the souls of men. Each mystery religion had a mother goddess, with the exception of Mithraism, which was for men only. The goddess Cybele was the only one to be given the official sanction of the state.

goggles, snow. Goggles made of wood or ivory with narrow slits, used by the Eskimo to prevent snow blindness.

Goidelic. See CELTIC.

gold. A precious yellow metal, probably the most precious substance used as an ordinary commercial medium. Gold is widely distributed, mostly in the metallic state. It is seldom found pure but usually has some 8-10 per cent of silver and occasional traces of copper or iron. It is found in veins in quartz rock or in alluvial sands deriving from the debris of gold-bearing rocks washed into watercourses.

Gold is very ductile and malleable and is little altered by climate or corrosion because of its resistance to oxidation and its insolubility. It is too soft for ordinary use and is hardened by alloy with copper or silver. Gold has always been highly valued and has been used for various religious functions, for representations of the gods, and to give to the gods. Some peoples, like the Chinese, used it widely in early medicine.

Gold nuggets and ornaments were found in Paleolithic deposits. Inasmuch as early man had discovered that copper was useful in making tools, it is possible that gold, which looks like untarnished copper and is malleable and untarnishable, was used for adornment. Gold has been mined wherever the rock surface is not overlaid with jungle, moss, or drifting sand. Pieces of shiny gold could be picked up by early man, after which he probably sifted the sand and used water to wash the gold out of gravel. Since gold is easy to concentrate, gold washing was one of the first forms of mining. The first systematic attempt to get gold in quantity was probably a placer, or deposit of sand or gravel along a stream.

Golden Horde. See HORDE, GOLDEN.

golem. An incomplete object or person, from the Hebrew word meaning embryo. A Czech golem of the 16th century has been made famous in literature and film. Rabbi Löw, the owner of the golem, forgot to uncharm it one Friday afternoon, and it went about wreaking havoc. It disappeared forever when he found it near the synagogue and uncharmed it. The activating force of this and other golems consisted of a charm with one of the names of the deity written on it. This charm was put in the mouth of the golem, which would do as instructed until the charm was removed.

gonad. An organ containing germ plasma. In the mammals, the gonads differentiate into ovaries and testicles, which influence the rest of the body by sex hormones.

Gondwanaland. A presumed sunken continent, of which only Java, Sumatra, and Borneo remain today. Africa, Australia, and Brazil were the suggested components of Gondwanaland, which was said to have persisted through the Mesozoic era, during which these southern lands were believed to be separated from northern lands by the Sea of Tethys.

gong. A curved resonant plate which is struck by a stick, usually in its center. The gong is a major instrument in parts of Asia, where it is used in religious ceremonies and in curing the sick, as well as in signaling. Gongs date from at least the sixth century A.D. They developed from drums and are especially associated with the dance. They are often used to remove bad influences, get the god's attention, and please the gods, notably in the Mongolian Orient, Mexico, and Central America.

gong, slit. An elongated gong with a slit usually in its middle. It is widely distributed.

237

goniocraniometry. Measuring the head's angles.

goniometer. A device used to measure angles.

gonion. The most lateral outer connection point between the ascending and horizontal rami of the lower jaw.

goods, grave. Adornments, weapons, food, and similar materials buried along with a corpse. They are of great value to the archaeologist in reconstructing the culture of which the grave was typical. Grave goods often denoted status and were often placed in the burial place to assist the corpse in the afterlife.

goongooroo. Indian ankle bells. They are attached to a card worn around the ankle of a dancer or news carrier. The bells sound sonorously when the wearer is walking or dancing.

gorge. A small lanceolate device attached to a cord and used to catch fish and small mammals. The gorge usually is covered with meat or solid fat and becomes imbedded transversely in the throat when the bait is swallowed.

gorget. A bone, shell, or stone artifact which is perforated so that it can be suspended. A gorget is also a piece of throat armor, a collar, or a woman's neck ornament.

gorilla. An African anthropoid (q.v.) which is the heaviest extant primate. Its weight may average 400-500 pounds. It usually moves on all fours.

gouge, shell. A kind of adze (q.v.) made of shell, especially found in Micronesia.

goura. A stringed-wind musical instrument found among the Hottentots and Bushmen. It consists of a flexible bamboo rod with a flat quill and peg inserted. A string goes from the quill to the other end of the rod, where it is attached. The performer plays by blowing while the quill is between the lips, which are closed lightly. It is also called the ugwala.

gourd. A fruit with trailing tendril-bearing herbs. Gourds were cultivated in the New World before Columbus and in the Old World. Floats, dishes, and water bottles have been made from the dried and cleaned shell of the gourd, which is the most widely found elementary container.

gracile. Referring to a tendency to be light-boned and thin.

gradation, quantitative. The range of possible vowel gradations, including vanishing, reduced, normal, and lengthened gradation.

gradation, vowel. The alteration of vowels within a word to show differences in meaning. e.g., the different tenses in a verb like *come* and *came*. Vowel gradation is also called symbolic change.

grade, age. A level of social status, or of segregation, which is distinguished by age. Age grade usually involves males only but may involve females also. Ceremonies generally mark the transition from one group to another. With younger persons, these may take the form of an ordeal (q.v.), as in Melanesia, Eastern Africa, and among the Plains Indians. The age grades may consist of the natural physiological periods of life, such as puberty and menopause. Age sets in men usually comprise graduated steps, each of a specific number of years. Youths who are of the same age may remain close for many years and call each other "brother." The age-grade dimension may cut through the vertical dimensions of clan or lineage to develop horizontal ties, thus strengthening the social fabric. Members of an age grade sometimes wear distinctive garments and have special responsibilities.

gradient, growth. An increment in the rapidity of growth, measured by the position of a tissue with relation to a fixed point.

grading, age. An extension of the relationship between old and young siblings to groups of persons of approximately similar age.

graffito. Any wall marking or scratching that could be considered an inscription, e.g., ancient letters, characters, or hieroglyphics. Graffiti frequently give valuable clues to the colloquial tongue, as opposed to the standard language that would typically be found in an inscription. Generically, a graffito is a scratched inscription, as opposed to painted or fired inscriptions. See DIPINTI.

grammar. The branch of linguistics dealing with the meaningful arrangement of a language's form, and with word classes and their relation with each other and their functional relations in larger units. A grammar includes general statements, paradigms, rules, and exceptions.

grammar, comparative. The branch of grammar that investigates comparatively the grammatical features and phenomena of a number of languages for the purpose of discovering the nature and degree of their relationship.

grammar, diachronic. The study of grammar from a historical point of view.

grammar, synchronic. The study of the grammar of a particular period or stage of a language.

grammar, universal. The investigation of languages in general and of the broad principles basic to the syntax of all languages.

Grand Soleil. See SUN, GREAT.

grape. A juicy smooth-skinned berry, which is the edible fruit of the vines of the Vitis and Muscadinia genera. Both color and size vary. The use of the grape for raisins and wine is widespread. It was widely consumed in early Neolithic times and probably originated in the Transcaucasus-Turkestan area.

graph, chronological. A graph showing the type frequencies of related artifact types over a given time span. It is a representation of the type life cycle (q.v.).

graph, Red. A technique for analyzing wrist X rays that permits the investigator to evaluate carpal bones of varying maturation rates and enables maturation to be studied from the viewpoint of a zone rather than of a single point.

graphemics or **graphonomy.** The systematic investigation of methods of writing and the relationship of writing systems to systems of language.

grass, kunai. A sharp, high, long grass found in dry areas.

239

grassland. Land used only as meadow or pasture or kept in grass.

Grassman's law. See LAW, GRASSMAN'S.

grater, fire. A Polynesian method of making fire in which a pointed piece of hardwood is rubbed in a softer log until the sawdust bursts into flame.

grattoir. A flake planing tool or endscraper (q.v.).

grattoir à bec. See SCRAPER, BEAKED.

grattoir caréné. A fairly oblong Aurignacian keeled endscraper (q.v.).

grave. The place in which the dead are buried. Many groups made the grave as comfortable as possible, leaving objects which the deceased could use in the next world. Coffins of varying kinds were often used. The body might be left in a specific direction or position, and the grave's shape and depth varied widely. The ground used generally became sacred. Graves might be scattered or grouped together.

grave escort. See ESCORT, GRAVE.

grave, ocher. A grave in which the corpse has been thickly covered with red ocher (q.v.). Ocher graves are found with considerable frequency in Russia north of the Caucasus.

grave, passage. A long funerary corridor made of upright slabs and covered with capstones.

graver. A flint tool used for shaving or cutting, probably the first type of chisel. It has a transverse cutting edge and may have been used to make slots for shafts or handles. A graver has at least one graver facet (q.v.). The ordinary type of graver may also be called the bec-de-flute.

graver, angle. A graver with trimming from the graver facet (q.v.) to the other side of the working edge. If the trimmed edge is at right angles to the flake's longer axis, the angle graver is called transverse. If the trimmed edge is at an angle to the flake's longer axis, it is called oblique.

graver, beaked. A graver the point of which is shaped like a nose. The beaked graver is made by a large graver facet (q.v.) intersecting with several small facets, which curve away to the flake's opposite edge.

graver, flat. A graver in which at least one graver facet (q.v.) is parallel to the main flake surface.

graver, gouge-angle. A graver with a gouge as a working edge. The gouge-angle graver is made by several graver facets (q.v.) at angles to each other so that the edge is curved. The other side of the edge is trimmed.

graver, gouge-single-blow. A graver made by several graver facets (q.v.). It has a curved working edge and is made on a small core (q.v.).

graver, polyhedric. A graver made by several graver facets (q.v.) struck at angles to each other so as to make a convex curve. The opposite side to the facets usually has a hollow made by a large negative bulb of percussion (q.v.) at the top of the polyhedric graver facet on the inner side of the working edge.

graver, screwdriver-core. A graver made on a small core. It has a screwdriver type point.

graver, single-blow. A graver in which the graver facet (q.v.) is produced by a single blow to the end of a blade or the pointed end of a flake.

graves, Grimm's. In the Upper Paleolithic period, mines in England that show evidence of having been used for mining flint for sale or export. Limestone posts held up the mine roofs. Antlers used as picks and stones dislodged the flint.

gravette. A fairly advanced kind of slender, small, and pointed knife blade. The blunted back of the gravette is practically parallel with its sharp working edge. It is likely to have a squared or pointed tip. Two or more gravette knife blades, hafted in a longitudinal groove in a stick, formed a kind of knife and might have been the first tool made of more than one component part.

Gravettian. Referring to Upper Paleolithic times.

gravity, specific. The extent to which something is lighter or heavier than an equal volume of water or other standard substance.

Great Spirit. See SPIRIT, GREAT.

Great Wall of China. See CHINA, GREAT WALL OF.

greathouse. A very large single house in which the whole community may dwell, as in Borneo today and in the Ukraine in prehistoric times. A greathouse may be more than 100 yards long.

grecque. See FRET.

grid, mummy. A lift for a mummy made of slats of white and yellow wood and resting at the bottom of the coffin.

gridiron. A structure of wood or iron consisting of rods on crosspieces supported by forked sticks. The gridiron preserves food through semicooking, drying, and smoke. It is very widely used.

griffin. A fantastic animal with the body, legs, and tail of a lion, the head of an eagle, two wings, and long sharp claws. The griffin is often seen in medieval escutcheons and in illustrations of myths. Its function was guarding hidden treasures. It is sometimes found in Greek architectural design as a gargoyle (q.v.).

Grimaldi. Fossils from the late Pleistocene believed by some to have Negroid features. The remains of a woman and boy were found in 1901 in the Grotte des Enfants, near Monaco. They have an upright and bulbous forehead and a strongly projecting tooth-bearing bony gum.

Grimm, Jacob Ludwig Karl (1785-1863), and **Wilhelm** (1786-1859). Two German philologists who made great contributions to folklore, comparative mythology, and language. The Grimms were brothers. See LAW, GRIMM'S.

Grimm's graves. See GRAVES, GRIMM'S.

grinding, tool. Making a tool through abrasion of the material by a harder sand or stone. Tool grinding developed in late Paleolithic times.

Griqua. South African halfbreeds.

gristle. See CARTILAGE.

grit. A siliceous sandstone that is coarse-grained, sharp-grained, or has grains of unequal size.

groove, stick and. See PLOW, FIRE.

Grotefend, George F. (1775-1853). A German philologist who, in 1802, discovered the meaning of characters in cuneiform (q.v.).

ground, happy hunting. A popular designation of the afterworld of the American Indians. The term is not used by Indians, who do not envisage hunting as a major activity in the afterworld. In the daytime, the Indian afterworld is quiet, while there is much social activity at night.

group, blood. One of the four kinds of human blood, distinguished by the absence or presence of two chemical elements. Each major human racial grouping is different with respect to the comparative incidence of each blood type, namely, O, B, A, and AB. The ABO group is usually the one meant when "blood group" is used. Groups A and AB are divisible into A_1 and A_2, and A_1B and A_2B_1, so that there are really six categories in this system. Some human groups are largely O, or O and A. Blood group frequency differences probably are related to the mixing of stocks. In a small area, blood group similarity is a good clue to ancestral similarity. For example, in North Wales, persons with Welsh names differ in blood group frequency from persons with English names. There are two other established systems of blood grouping. See RH; MN. Landsteiner discovered in 1900 that some blood would cause other person's red corpuscles to clump, and in 1901 he identified three blood groups. In 1907, Jansky divided blood groups into O, B, A, and AB. Boyd has suggested that blood groups probably represent the one characteristic of man that is genetically based on a limited number of genes and is nonadaptive, not unduly subject to mutation, and objective. He proposed that blood groups be more widely used by anthropologists in classifying races and subraces.

group, consanguine. A blood-related social group in which the relationship may be hypothetical or fictitious. In a fictitious relationship, nonblood relatives may be included in, and blood relatives excluded from, the group.

group, dyadic. A pair of human beings in a social relationship.

group, endogamous status. A bilateral kinship group within which the individual must marry, e.g., a caste in India.

group, genetic. A group of persons who are all related by some degree of common descent. Thus, in the genetic group there are no outsiders who are brought in by marriage, adoption, or otherwise.

group, horizontal. A social subgroup from a homogeneous social stratum.

group, in-. See IN-GROUP.

group, kinship. A social organization based on blood relationships. The residential kinship group has a common residence and may exclude some consanguineal relatives while including some affinal relatives. Husband and wife are, although sister and brother are not, included in a residential kinship group. The rule of residence shapes the nature of the group. The consanguineal kinship group is not characterized by common residence. It includes only consanguineal relatives. Only one spouse is usually a member of the consanguineal group, while all siblings belong. The rule of descent is the major influence in shaping the consanguineal kinship group.

group, lineage. A social group composed of living members of a lineage (q.v.). A large group, which is several generations removed from its original ancestors, may be broken down into several sublineages.

group, linkage. The genes in the same chromosome. They are jointly transmitted, except for crossing over.

group, local. See COMMUNITY, ENDOGAMOUS.

group, out-. See OUT-GROUP.

group, status. See STATUS GROUP, ENDOGAMOUS.

grouping, archaeological. The several successive levels of archaeological material, e.g., site, industry, culture, civilization.

growth, accretionary. A multiplication of tissue components in an organ without qualitative functional change.

Gschnitz. Following the fourth, or Würm, glacial period in Europe, the second minor glacial advance, from ca. 13 500 B.C.-8500 B.C.

guaca. An ancient Peruvian grave. The word *quaquero* from which it

is derived means one who looks for the graves either to study them or to steal from them.

guacal. A decorated calabash of the modern Maya.

Guanche. A language belonging to the Semitic-Hamitic family, within the Berber group of the Hamitic sub-family. It was spoken in the Canary Islands until the end of the 17th century.

guanín. An alloy of gold and copper used in the Antilles to make jewelry. The alloy was probably imported from South America. Guanín is also a pendant made from the alloy worn by Arawak Island chiefs as a symbol of their office.

guano. Bird droppings containing phosphate that makes them excellent fertilizer. The Chincha Islands, off Peru, provided millions of dollars worth of guano in the 19th century.

guard, counter. A part of a sword connecting the guard and pommel.

guardian, tutelary. See SPIRIT, FAMILIAR.

gubo. An African stringed instrument made of a narrow wooden strip over which a fiber string is stretched. A resonator made from a gourd shell is attached to one end. The performer produces the sound by holding the instrument against his body and plucking the string with a plectrum or his fingers. It is very infrequent for the string to be bowed. The gubo is found among the Zulu and Kafir tribes.

gueesting. The Dutch name for bundling (q.v.).

243

guenon. A genus of African monkeys with many different species.

guest. A visitor to a group who is accorded hospitality. The guest may have to prove his friendly intentions, but once accepted, he may be treated with cordiality, be given food and shelter, and sometimes be allowed even sexual access to the host's wife. The guest is often expected to leave after a fixed period, when he may get gifts and an escort to the frontier. See HOSPITALITY; STRANGER.

guffa. An Arab coracle (q.v.) used on the Tigris-Euphrates.

guilloche. An ornament made of two bands twisted over each other so as to leave round openings that are filled with circular ornaments. The guilloche is sometimes called a pleated band.

Guinea-Sudan. An African linguistic stock, found in the area from the Atlantic to the Sudan.

guitar. A flat stringed instrument that is plucked by finger. It accompanies much folk music. The guitar is sometimes associated with evil forces.

gum, black-boy. A tree resin used by Australian aborigines for hafting stone tools.

gummanda. Horizontal body marks in Australia.

gunbad. A square, domed burial chamber of India. This tomb or monument is often inscribed with word or picture stories telling of events in the life of the person buried.

gunwale. The part of a vessel where deck and topside meet.

gunyah. In New South Wales, an aboriginal bough shelter or hut.

Günz. The first glacial period in Europe, from ca. 1,000,000-600,000 years ago. See GLACIATION.

guttural. See VELAR.

guttus. An ancient ceramic vessel with a narrow neck. The only knowledge of this vase is derived from the writings of Juvenal and Pliny, since no examples have been found.

gynaecocracy. See GYNECOCRACY.

gynandromorphic component. See COMPONENT, GYNANDROMORPHIC.

gynecocracy or **gynaecocracy.** A hypothetical society in which women were the rulers, suggested by Bachofen (q.v.) in 1861. He believed that gynecocracy developed after a hypothetical primeval promiscuity against which the women rebelled. Robert Briffault has been a recent exponent of this idea. There are few known societies in which women had both domestic and political power.

gypsophily. The characteristic of a species being confined to, or flourishing unusually well on, soils that have much gypsum.

Gypsy. A traditionally wandering minority group, mainly found in Europe and stemming in part from the zone of the foothills and plains parallel to the Himalayas, from which they moved north and west. There are approximately 2,000,000 gypsies. By and large they try to keep their customs, language, and costume unchanged.

gypsies, sea. Sea-faring groups in the Sumatra area noted as traders.

Gypsum cave. See CAVE, GYPSUM.

gyromancy. A method of divination (q.v.) in which a person walks continually around a chalked circle until he collapses from exhaustion and the diviner notes the position of his body in relation to the circle.

gyttja. A sediment that largely consists of organic remains.

H

habitability. The suitability of an area for settlement.

habitat. A geographical area in which a person or group can take care of the key activities of living. The term is also used to refer to such features of a region as altitude and climate.

habitus. Body build, generally used in connection with a system of constitutional types (q.v.).

hache. A flint implement with a square head; the successor to the tranchet (q.v.). The hache has been found in parts of Germany and Scandinavia.

hack. An early agricultural implement resembling a pick. It consisted of a heavy stick with part of a branch remaining to be used as a spike.

hackamore. A loop of rope placed around the neck and through the mouth of a horse, generally used to break the animal. A hackamore is also a halter with a loop that can be tightened around the horse's nose.

Haddon, Alfred Cort (1855-1940). A physical and cultural anthropologist, who had the first chair of anthropology at Cambridge. He was particularly interested in the technology and art of different cultures. His *Study of Man* (1898) emphasized that anthropology dealt with more than man as a biological creature. He used "ethnography" to denote the study of an individual group and "ethnology" for the comparative analysis of groups, a usage still found today. Haddon divided ethnology into subfields, like religion, sociology, linguistics, and technology. He was the leader of the famous Torres Straits Expedition.

Haeckel, Ernst (1834-1919). A German biologist who popularized the law of ontogeny (q.v.). In 1866, he wrote that the theory of evolution cast important light on anthropology. His *History of Creation* (1868) postulates the existence of 36 races.

haft. The handle of a tool or weapon used for cutting.

hagiology. The study of the lives and activities of the saints.

Haida. Indians of the Pacific Northwest, flourishing in the Queen Charlotte Islands off southern Alaska; a linguistic group probably stemming from Athapaskan.

hair. A pigmented cornified derivative of the ectoderm (q.v.).

Both head and body hair are important in classifying racial groups. Texture is one of the most important classification criteria, as it is closely linked to hereditary factors that are little affected by external influences; it is measured microscopically and by degree of straightness. In general, Caucasoids have wavy to intermediate hair, Negroids wooly hair, and Mongoloids straight hair. The body hair is differentiated by kind of beard and the extent of down. In this regard, Caucasoids are generally hairy, while Negroids and Mongoloids are fairly smooth-skinned. Individuals with much body hair and substantial beards often are bald.

hair, peppercorn. Frizzly hair which grows in little tufts leaving small spaces between the tufts, as found on the Bushmen of South Africa.

hair, terminal. See CAPILLUS.

hairiness. The degree to which a person has a beard and hair covering the body. Hairiness is used to differentiate racial groups.

haka. Among the Maori, a mourning, war, or diverting dance. Also, the stem and stern strake (q.v.) on Solomon Island canoes.

hakari. A ceremonial distribution of wealth like the potlatch (q.v.).

hako. An elaborate form of calumet dance (q.v.) originated by the Pawnee. It was a prayer for longevity, crops, and children.

halak. A Semang shaman (q.v.).

halam. A stringed musical instrument found in West Africa. The halam is constructed from an oblong piece of wood hollowed from a solid block. One side is scooped out like a trough and covered by a parchment with a sound hole. A long rod through the body of the instrument protrudes to form the neck, from which gut strings are stretched over a bridge just above the sound hole.

halberd. An Early Bronze Age triangular dagger that was hafted at right angles to a staff. The blade is not always symmetrical. The halberd probably originated in Portugal or Spain.

half-breed. See BREED, HALF.

hallcist. A megalithic tomb which is a degenerate form of the passage grave (q.v.). In it there is no chamber and the passage end is used for a burial place.

halliard. See HALYARD.

Hallstatt. The early phase of the Iron Age (q.v.) in Central Europe, dating ca. 1500-500 B.C. and named after an Austrian site. Hallstatt culture can be traced over a large territory from Hungary to Spain and Portugal. Although incineration of corpses was the rule at the beginning of the epoch, inhumation developed widely toward the end. The Hallstatt is sometimes called the epoch of the barrow (q.v.); there were two types, those in which the central sepulture was on the ground level, and those in which the sepulture was an underground pit. The swords of the period were fairly uniform, compared with the variety used in the Bronze Age. The homes were largely made of perishable materials. Pottery was well developed and there was considerable artistic activity, including some signs of Roman influence. Domesticated animals were widely found.

The Hallstatt excavations demonstrate the gradual change from bronze to iron. The iron is used successively as an ornament, an edge, to copy bronze objects, and finally for objects to which it is best suited.

halomancy. See ALOMANCY.

halyard or **halliard.** A kind of rigging used to hoist a sail. The halyard is identified by linking it with the name of the sail to which it is connected.

Hamacha. An Arab fanatic who cudgels himself.

hamada. A rocky plateau ,in a desert.

hamadryad. A mythological tree or forest being that can be friendly or opposed to human beings. Hamadryads derive from the power of trees and plants. If they join with the souls of the dead, they become tutelary spirits.

Hamatsa. The highest grade of the Seal Society of the Kwakiutl.

Hamitic. A linguistic family consisting of some north and east African languages including Berber, Galla, and Somali. The name comes from that of Noah's second son, Ham. These languages are related to Semitic languages and are very old. Their grammar is simple, and they have not developed a notable literature. The first Hamitic inscriptions are in Ancient Egyptian, ca. 5000 B.C. Some writers speak of an Old Hamitic culture, which was common to Hamites, half-Hamites, and Nilotes. Other sources recognize a North Hamitic culture, which has Near Eastern and Old Mediterranean elements. An East Hamitic culture, linked with East African cattle breeding, has been identified.

Hamito-Semitic. A hypothetical linguistic ancestor of the Semitic and Hamitic languages.

hammers, Purgatory. The name given to a flint arrowhead in some parts of Europe. The term derived from the belief that the arrowheads were the hammers used by the dead to knock at the gates of Purgatory.

hammering, cold. Forming metal by beating it while cold. Cold hammering was the first method of working metal. It was used by groups near meteoric iron or free copper.

hammerstone. A round stone which is used to hammer, possibly the most ancient implement.

Hammurabi, Code of. A compilation of laws made by Hammurabi, ruler of Babylon. It is based to a great extent on earlier Sumerian laws. The code has almost 300 paragraphs on social, domestic, moral, and business matters, and it has a good deal in common with the Hebrews' laws. De Morgan found a copy of the code in Susa in 51 columns of cuneiform text on a round-topped stele of black diorite about six feet high. It dates from 1940 B.C.

hamstring. To incapacitate by cutting the large tendons in the rear of the knee on either side. Hamstringing is a common method of controlling domestic animals in technologically backwood cultures.

248

Han. Referring to bronzed pottery with a deep green glaze, of the Han dynasty in China, ca. 206 B.C.-220 A.D.

hana. A soft-skinned yam of the Solomon Islands.

hand, third. A prehensile tail found in certain monkeys and used to grasp objects or in brachiation.

hand, Buddha's. An Oriental citron fruit resembling a hand. The Buddha's hand is often incorporated in Oriental art.

hand and thigh method. See METHOD, HAND AND THIGH.

hand-breadth. A linear measure based on the breadth of a hand. It may have a value ranging from 2.5 to 4 inches.

handedness. The comparative ease and facility with which one hand is used as against the other. The index of dextrality is a measure of preference for one hand over the other in a number of activities.

handfasting. The ceremonies attendant on a betrothal, which may be a kind of trial marriage. The heart of the ceremony is the two participants' clasping hands. A pregnancy or childbirth renders handfasting a marriage, while otherwise the relationship can be dissolved. It is a folk custom of Europe.

handja. An African musical instrument made from a number of progressively larger hollow gourds. The gourds are attached to a frame of reeds about three feet long and one and a half feet wide. Thin wooden strips fastened across the tops are struck with wooden rods. The modern counterpart of the handja is the xylophone.

hands, laying on of. The practice of placing the hands on a part of a person's body, usually the head, in order that one in authority may transmit blessing or grace to him. Thus, new members of the Sanhedrin among the Hebrews received the authority for their offices from the Prince of the Sanhedrin in this manner. Egyptian and Babylonian kings and priests were endowed with the authority for their offices by contact with the hands of divine images. A departure from the usual meaning of laying on of hands appears in the ancient Hebrew ceremony in which the priest transfers the sins of the people to the scapegoat (q.v.) every year. The basic concept motivating all these rituals is that of a mysterious power transferrable by contagion.

handstone. See MANO.

haplodont. A tooth with a single cone, like the incisors.

haplography. See HAPLOLOGY.

haploid. Having the chromosome number characteristic of the gametes of the species, i.e., half the number in the somatic cells.

haplology. A form of anticipation (q.v.) in which one of two similar phonemes (q.v.) is dropped, along with whatever phonemes are otherwise normally between them, e.g., *prob-bly* for *probably*. The omission of letters in writing is termed haplography.

happu. A Chinese drum made from a wood shell filled with rice powder and with both ends covered with parchment. The sound produced was a "clack." The happu was almost always ornamented with carvings representing a phoenix rising from the flames.

hara-kiri. A ritualized Japanese suicide by disembowelment. It is also called seppuku.

Harappa. An archaeological site in the Punjab. It gives its name to urban culture represented there in the third millenium B.C.

harlotry, sacred. The practice of having women serve as religious prostitutes. Sacred harlotry was often associated with temple rites. The sexual acts might constitute part of the worship, while the fees were an offering.

harmattan. A hot, dry wind blowing from the Sahara Desert to the west coast of Africa from December to February. It makes the atmosphere hazy and withers the crops.

harmika. A structure resembling a balcony, found in monumental tombs in India.

harmonica, stone. A percussion instrument, now obsolete, made of a series of graduated rock slabs. The sound was produced by striking with a hammer.

harmony, vowel. A term in phonetics used to describe the regular practice in the Finno-Ugric, Turkish, and Manchu languages of limiting the use of certain vowels within a particular word. For example, a back vowel and a front vowel may not occur in the same word, while any number of like vowels may occur. Vowel harmony determines the proper suffixes or case endings.

harp. A musical instrument consisting of many chords. It usually has a resonator and a neck; the chords are stretched between them, at right angles to the surface of the resonator. The fingers pluck the strings. Since the framework is not rigid, the strings cannot be tuned accurately.

harp, Aeolian. One of the most ancient of musical instruments, constructed with one or two sets of strings, a frame, sound board, and bridges. It was usually placed near an open window, so that the sound was produced and the harmonies varied by the wind.

harp, jew's. A musical instrument made of a frame with a tongue attached by one end. The jew's harp is held in the mouth, and the tongue is usually finger-plucked. In early types, frame and tongue are in one piece and the tongue is straight and is vibrated by plucking the end of the frame or by pulling on an attached string. Later models, of metal, show a bent tongue with a free end that is plucked. Different notes are sounded on the jew's harp by the vibrations of the tongue being communicated to air in the hollow of the mouth. The instrument is found over much of the world. The name is probably a corruption of jaw's harp.

harp, Western. A harp with a prop between the neck and resonator. The prop makes the framework rigid, so that it is possible to tighten the strings of the Western harp and thus tune them accurately.

harpoon. A barbed assegai (q.v.) used in hunting. It consists of a head with its blade, shank, and tang or socket, a foreshaft, shaft, butt, and wings, and a line attached to the harpooner. The head of the shaft remains in the animal after impact, and the shaft itself usually floats away. The earliest harpoons have a stem with a suggestion of barbs on both sides. The next stage showed well-made barbs on one side of the stem. Double-barbed harpoons followed, with the barbs well separated and alternate or opposite. The barbs became angular in Upper and Middle Magdalenian times. Reindeer or stag's antler often was used in making harpoons. Retrieving javelins and arrows with a cord at the shaft are also classified as harpoons.

haruspication. See HARUSPICES.

haruspices. Roman diviners who foretold the future by studying the entrails of slaughtered animals. They also used portents and the flight of birds to make predictions. Pig livers are used for haruspication in Borneo today.

harvest festival. See FESTIVAL, HARVEST.

hashish. A narcotic made from the sprouts and tops of Indian hemp. It exaggerates and upsets the sense of the passage of time and may cause delirium. It is also called bhang (India), dakha (South Africa), and fasukh (Morocco). The Assassins of the Crusades era got their name from the practice of consuming hashish.

hasina. The equivalent of mana (q.v.) among the Malagasy.

hat, basket. A woven hat typical of the Northwest Coast and the Far West of the United States, made of locally available materials, like willow bark. The Northwest Coast had broad hats, while more southern areas like Oregon had smaller cap-like versions.

hat, cloud. A conical hat worn by boys when they come of age in some Indian tribes in Alaska. A hat of similar shape is called a *diba* in parts of New Guinea. Some non-literate societies require their men to glue such a hat to their head and not remove it, even in sleep. In the Middle Ages, this conical hat became the headgear of witches and evil spirits. The victims of the Spanish Inquisition and European Jews during the 11th century were compelled to wear conical hats.

hat, yellow. A lamaist sect of Buddhism in Mongolia.

hau. A bush which is used to make twine in Hawaii.

Haustafel. A German word meaning house-tablet, usually applied loosely to the unwritten domestic and private moral code. Haustafel, thus, is differentiated from an ancient, possibly written, code of public morality. It is concerned with an individual's duties to his gods, country, parents, children, spouse, friends, and, depending on his status, master or slaves.

Hawaiki. The mythical western homeland of the Polynesians, also called Havai'i.

Head, Big. A phase of the ghost dance (q.v.) cult, centering around a special kind of headdress.

headman. A leader of a tribe or similar group who does not have precisely specified authority. A headman is also a leader below a chief in status, or the leading person of a social group whose authority is based largely on personal influence.

headrest. A device to support the head when sleeping, the ancestor of the pillow. It may have practically any shape, from a log to a handsomely carved bench.

healall. See ALLHEAL.

heald. See HEDDLE.

heart. In ancient cultures, the heart was considered to be the place where all emotion originated or the center of life or the residence of the soul. In a culture that conceived the personality as being composed of more than one soul, the heart-soul was always among them. In some early and several later cultures, the heart was the center of courage and strength; thus, the heart of a brave man or of a wild beast might sometimes be eaten to gain those qualities. In ancient Mexico, the heart was the portion of the victim offered as a sacrifice to the gods.

hearth. The pavement used for a fire, especially a furnace in which ore or metal can be exposed to a flame. The first hearth was probably a campfire. This led to a hole to collect molten metal. Clay was next used to line the hole, because it is fire-resistant and keeps the metal clean. Stones were used later to line the hole in the hearth floor, and the furnace (q.v.) developed. Early metallurgists discovered that carbonized wood was a good fuel. They kept their twigs under an earth cover to carbonize easily without complete combustion and become brittle so as to be breakable into small pieces for furnace use.

hearth, back. The floor of the inside of a fireplace on which the fire is built, or the portion supporting the grate.

heath. A waste land area, often, as in Britain, with characteristic undershrub vegetation of the genus Erica.

heaven. The place in the sky where the souls of the blessed live after death. Divine persons also usually live in heaven. There may be different heavens for various vocations or degrees of blessedness.

heb-sed. An early Egyptian ceremony in which the Pharaoh (q.v.) magically renewed his power and gave it over to the earth. It may have been a successor to a earlier ceremony in which the sick pharaoh was killed.

hecatomb. A sacrifice of a substantial number of victims. It is from the Greek term for sacrificially slaughtering 100 oxen simultaneously.

hectare. An area measure equivalent to 10,000 square meters or 2.471 acres.

heddle or **heald.** In weaving, a set of parallel doubled cords in a mounting. The heddle constitutes the harness to guide the warp threads to the lathe or batten in the loom. It permits the shuttle to go rapidly through several warp threads at once by means of an opening called a shed. A loom forms a shed when the heddle is raised; then the weft goes through the shed and the weft is "beaten up" by a sword (q.v.), comb (q.v.), or reed (q.v.).

heddle, bar or **heald, bar.** A heddle made of several loops connected with a rod. Each loop surrounds a warp thread. The rod in

252

rising causes the warp threads to form a shed, or opening.

heddle, frame or **heald, frame.** A heddle with two bars linked by loops. Each loop has an eye to permit the passage of warp threads. Narrow bars may be used instead of the loops. The warp threads that are to be raised or lowered go through the eyes and those remaining stationary go through the spaces between the loops or bars.

heddles, reciprocating. Heddles built so that one goes up while the other is down, giving rise to a larger shed that provides less strain for the warp.

heem. A flutelike musical instrument from Siam. Several pipes are mounted in a hollow box or gourd that forms a common mouthpiece.

heiau. See AHU.

Heidelberg Man. See HOMO HEIDELBERGENSIS.

height, auricular head. The projected vertex-tragion distance, measured by subtracting the height of the tragion above the floor from the subject's stature.

height, basion-bregma. The distance from the bregma to basion.

height, cranial. The distance between the ear opening and the top point on the skull. Inasmuch as it is not easy to take this measurement on living persons, there is little information on the head height of contemporaries; however the cranial height is important in classifying skeletal remains.

height, morphological facial. The distance between gnathion and nasion.

height, nasal. On a living subject, the distance, measured by a small sliding caliper, between the nasion and the subnasal point, where the upper lip meets the lower end of the nasal septum. On a skeleton the nasal height is the distance between the nasion and the nasospinale.

height, right acromiale. The distance from the floor to the furthermost lateral projection of the outer border of the acromion of the scapula.

height, right dactylon. The distance from the floor to the tip of the middle finger. It is measured with the subject standing and the finger pointing directly toward the floor.

height, right iliocristale. The distance from the floor to the point on the crest of the right ilium which projects most laterally. It is measured with the subject standing erect.

height, right iliospinale. The distance from the floor to the right anterior-superior iliac spine, measured with the subject standing.

height, right radiale. The distance from the floor to the high point of the head of the radius.

height, right sphyrion. The distance from the floor to the inner surface of the medial malleolus.

height, right stylion. The distance from the floor to the distolateral end of the styloid process of the radius.

height, right tibiale. The distance from the floor to the upper surface of the medial condyle of the tibia.

height, right trochanter. The distance from the floor to the upper surface of the greater trochanter of the femur.

height, sitting vertex. The distance from the highest point of the head to the surface on which the subject is sitting.

height, standing. The distance between the floor and the highest point of the head with the subject standing erect.

height, suprasternal. The distance from the floor to the center of the anterior-superior border of the manubrium sterni.

height, symphysion. The distance from the floor to the symphysion, when the subject is in the standard erect position.

height, total cranial facial. The distance between the nasion and gnathion.

height, total jaw. The distance between the gnathion and subnasale measured with the jaws closed normally.

height, total morphological face. The gnathion-nasion distance in the median sagittal plane.

height, trunk. The straight distance between the suprasternal notch and the upper edge of the pubic symphysis.

height, upper cranial facial or **height, upper face.** The distance between the nasion and prosthion.

height, upper morphological facial. The nasion-prosthion distance in the median sagittal plane.

height, vertical auricular. The porion-apex vertical distance, or the apex-bi-porionic axis distance.

heitiki. In New Zealand, a small contorted human figure carved of jade or whalebone and representing an ancestor. It was worn around the neck as a charm and at death was passed on to a descendant.

heke. A great migration from Rarotonga to New Zealand, ca. 1350 A.D.

hekistotherm. A polar plant that grows beyond the forest limits.

heliacal. See RISINGS, HELIACAL; SETTINGS, HELIACAL.

Helicon. An ancient Greek musical instrument supposedly invented by Ptolemy to aid him in the study of musical intervals. It had nine strings stretched across a square sounding board.

heliolithic. Referring to the school of diffusionism (q.v.) in anthropological thought, usually associated with several English scholars. G. Elliott Smith was its moving spirit. According to the heliolithic theorists, borrowing was almost the only method by which culture change (q.v.) took place, with invention (q.v.) practically never occurring. One heliolithic school favors a pan-Egyptian theory.

heliotropism. A phototropism in which the light of the sun is the orienting factor, e.g., the sunflower's head turns to and the roots away from the sun. Copernicus first developed this hypothesis in 1543, although it had been earlier adumbrated by Pythagoras (6th century B.C.), Aristarchus, (third century B.C.), Martianus Capella (fifth century A.D.), and Cardinal Nicholas de Cusa (15th century A.D.).

helix. A spiral object; the incurved rim of the external ear; a spiral ornament in architecture, i.e., a volute on an Ionic capital.

hell. The world after death, where the souls of the dead live, especially those being punished because of their behavior on earth. There are often demons and a god. Hell is usually regarded as being underground.

Hellenic. An Indo-European language family, which includes Attic and some modern Greek dialects.

helper, spirit. An individual protective spirit, or a malicious spirit controlled by magic.

helve. The handle on a weapon or tool.

hematite. A powder made of iron ore and grease, used by various peoples to protect the body from cold. The use of hematite was responsible for the designation "Redskins," erroneously applied to the American Indians. Hematite may range in color from light red to chocolate.

hemophilia. A condition in which the blood cannot form clots when exposed to the air. It usually appears in men and results from one recessive gene which is X-carried. The prevalence of hemophilia in some royal families of Europe has been attributed to inbreeding.

hemp. A fiber plant very similar to flax. It usually grows five to eight feet high and has female and male plants. It is perhaps the oldest important fiber crop, and it probably originated in the Orient, where the Chinese cultivated it almost 5,000 years ago. Hemp is used for drugs, oil, and fiber. See HASHISH.

henge. A sacred stone circle, like those at Avebury and Stonehenge in England.

hennin. An extremely elongated headdress held on by a chin band and usually worn by women. The hennin first appeared in the 15th century in Europe.

henotheism. The practice of making different gods in a pantheon successively supreme. It was found, said Max Müller, in the Vedic religion. It is supposedly intermediate between monotheism and polytheism. The term henotheism has been used for the stage of the Jewish belief in God from the time of Moses to the Exile.

Hepalidae. A family of Platyrrhini, usually called marmosets. They have bushy tails, furry covering, clawlike nails, and a nonopposable thumb.

hepatoscopy. Predicting the future by studying the livers of slaughtered animals. It was also used to determine the god's will and to get advice on life. Hepatoscopy spread from the early Assyrian and Babylonian state religions to the Mediterranean area. It was based on an ancient notion that the seat of life was the liver.

herald. An agent who relays a chief's orders in Plains and Plateau society.

heraldry. An art that began during the Third Crusade (12th century), perhaps because it was necessary to identify knights by symbols, since their faces were completely covered by helmets. An individual mark or sign was painted on each shield. Heraldry includes the designing and execution of coats of arms, their authentication, their histories and connections with family genealogies, and the devising of new emblems (e.g., as military insignia).

herb. An aromatic plant used in seasoning and medicine, as well as for magical purposes. Herb lore was the major weapon of early medicine. There is not much agreement among various peoples on the properties of specific herbs. Color is important in magical properties, e.g., yellow herbs cure jaundice. Some societies follow specific rituals in growing herbs and gather them on special days only. They may be used externally, or merely being near them may effect a cure.

herbivore. An animal that is exclusively a vegetable eater.

herd. A group of persons with uncontrolled common desires. Some theorists hypothesized the herd as an early social grouping of man.

heredity. The totality of biological traits transmitted by the parents and determining the individual's capacity for growth and development.

herm or **herma.** A bust of Hermes, the protector of travelers, mounted on a square base. The herm, which may be derived from a phallic column, was used as a marker on the roads of ancient Greece. Other types of markers in use elsewhere included the cairn (q.v.) and stones.

hermaphrodite. An individual that simultaneously or successively displays the characteristics of the two sexes. Hermaphroditism is alternating in the oyster, which has successive male and female stages, and simultaneous in certain worms. A hermaphrodite may also be an individual of a species normally made up of males and females which combines the characteristics of both sexes. While partial hermaphroditism appears occasionally in human beings, it has been asserted that there is no authentic case of a human who was capable of producing both male and female gametes.

hermeneutics. Scripture interpretation; the art and science of the interpretation of any authoritative document.

hero, culture. A mythical personage, perhaps a god, who was regarded as being a group's protector. The culture hero is believed to be responsible for the group's present position, as well as for many of its arts. He regulates crops, game, and the elements, and he is often presumed to be waiting in the west before his return. The culture hero, often as trickster (q.v.), is common in almost all North American Indian folklore, in which he usually has a colleague. In some instances the culture hero is a bird or animal.

hero cult. See CULT, HERO.

Heroic Age. See AGE, HEROIC.

Herodotus (490-409 B.C.). A Greek historian and geographer. In his systematic analysis of the peoples of his time, he was perhaps the first anthropologist. Half of his writing on the Persian Wars was devoted to the peoples of Persia. He was a fabulist who reported as truths a good many myths and superstitions, e.g., that the Ethiopians have black semen. His candor was exceptional, as in his saying that things never happen quite as they should, or very often they never happen at all, so that the

256

conscientious writer will learn to remedy these deficiencies. Herodotus' materials were used by some anthropologists, e.g., Bachofen.

Herrschaft. A type of political structure characterized by strong individual leadership.

hetaerism. The institution of prostitution in ancient Greece, which drew on both free women and slaves. Some hetaerae were famous for erudition. Hetaerism is also a hypothetical early sexual communism (q.v.).

heterochromosome. A differentiated chromosome involved in sex determination. See X.

heteroclite. In syntax, referring to a word the declension or conjugation of which is an exception to the rule established for words of the same class.

heterodont. Referring to the possession of teeth differentiated for specialized functions like gripping and cutting. Homo sapiens is heterodont.

heteronym. Any word written the same as another word of the same language but sounding different and with a different meaning. A heteronym is also a literal translation of a word from another language.

heterophenogamy. Mating between persons who do not somatically resemble each other to a greater degree than would be expected under random mating.

heterosis. See VIGOR, HYBRID.

heterosome. A chromosome that is either X (q.v) or Y (q.v.). See AUTOSOME.

heterozygosity. A condition in which genes are not similar, or the combination of two unlike germ cells or factors.

hetman. The elected head of a Cossack group.

hetzmek. A Central American ceremony conducted when an infant is first carried on the hip, at about three to four months of age. The hetzmek is designed to arouse the qualities that are hoped for in the child. A grandparent holds the child on the hip and puts a tiny machete, hoe, and axe in a boy's hands and in a tiny needle, scissors, and mano in a girl's hands.

hex. A witch, or witchcraft. The term is found in the Teutonic languages. There are professional "hex doctors," who are supposed to counteract spells, control nature, and cure difficulties by using formulas. Many hex doctors practice even today.

hexadactylism. The possession of six toes or fingers. It is a Mendelian trait.

hiatus. The cessation of sound between two successive vowels. An internal hiatus occurs when the vowels are within the same word. An external hiatus occurs between two words when the first ends and the second begins with a vowel.

hide. An English unit of land, estimated to be from 48 to 125 acres, equivalent to the amount that could be plowed in a year by an eight-oxen plow and could support a free peasant family in England in the Middle Ages.

hieracosphinx. A type of Egyptian sphinx with a hawk's head. The criosphinx and androsphinx had a goat head and a human head respectively. See SPHINX.

hierarchy of science. See SCIENCE, HIERARCHY OF.

hieratic. Referring to an ancient Egyptian cursive hieroglyph writing at first used generally and then only for religious material. The term originally denoted the sacral or priestly. Clement of Alexandria first used "hieratic" for this priest writing, as opposed to the "demotic" (q.v.) or popular. Hieratic developed out of the hieroglyphic (q.v.) system, in which the signs increasingly becoming bolder and more cursive because of the technique of writing with the brush pen on papyrus. The hieratic signs are really cursive transcriptions of hieroglyphic symbols. Hieratic writing was present in the first Egyptian dynasty. By the seventh century B.C., it was largely taken over by the priests for transcribing traditional texts and was used fairly extensively up to the third century A.D. It was first written vertically, then horizontally from right to left.

hierodule. A temple slave, often one who serves as a sacred prostitute. See HARLOTRY, SACRED.

hieroglyphic. Referring to the stylized picture writing of ancient Egypt that later became script. The invention of script itself was attributed to the god Thoth. After 300 A.D., the meaning of the hieroglyphic characters was lost, until the discovery of the Rosetta Stone (q.v.) in 1799 permitted their deciphering. Some signs stand for sounds (phonetic) and some for ideas (ideographic). The phonetic characters are of two kinds, alphabetic and syllabic. There are some 500 characters. Hieroglyphic was one of the most important writing systems of the ancient world. Its early history is fairly parallel to that of cuneiform (q.v.) writing. It is generally believed that the system was successively a kind of pictograph (q.v.), ideograph (q.v.), and rebus (q.v.) writing. Hieroglyphic was used for word signs, phonograms, and determinatives. The writing usually ran from right to left, with the signs facing the line's beginning, although occasional inscriptions ran from left to right, or in both directions. The Egyptian scripts had their whole development in Egypt. See DEMOTIC; HIERATIC.

High. When used before the name of a language, High describes the form used in the highland parts of the country. It may also mean the form of the language that is the best usage. E.g., in Middle High German, it means both the best usage and the highland (southern).

Hina. The first woman, according to Polynesian mythology.

Hinayna. A conservative Buddhist sect.

Hindu. A Caucasoid racial stock characterized by narrow head, brown skin, tall stature, considerable body hair, wavy hair, and some prognathism.

Hindustani. A Western Hindi dialect, the lingua franca of India.

hinterland. The tributary areas of a seaport.

hippocampus. A mythological monster with a horse's head and forequarters and a dolphin's tail.

hippolectryon. A theme in art representing a cross between horse and cock, found in Persia and elsewhere. It was probably a solar symbol.

hippomancy. A method of divination (q.v.) based on the gaits of horses.

hiri. A trading expedition involving lakatois (q.v.).

hiss. See SIBILANT.

historiated. Referring to an object decorated with significant figures, e.g., flowers or animals, rather than with a geometric or repetitive design. During the Middle Ages, manuscripts were illuminated with historiated animal letters.

Hittite. An extinct Indo-European language.

hlonipa. A prohibition against mentioning a dead person by name.

hoard. A collection of artifacts, vessels, or ornaments buried together. Hoards first became widespread in the Bronze Age and reflect the considerable trade of that time.

hoard, domestic. A hoard that belonged to one person or household and thus indicates contemporaneity of the constituent articles. A domestic hoard usually had one specimen of each artifact, all generally showing signs of use.

hoard, founder's. A hoard, consisting of old and broken tools, scrap metal, and implements for metallurgy. The objects in these hoards may be from different dates and probably belonged to groups of Late Bronze Age itinerant tinkers, who collected metals and made repairs, or to a smith who buried his stock and tools.

hoard, trader's. A hoard that belonged to a trader. It usually contained several examples of each kind of artifact, either new or half finished. A trader's hoard was probably created when an itinerant merchant buried his stock, biding the time that some danger would have passed and allowed him to recover it.

hoard, votive. A hoard found, e.g., in a swamp, a spring, or at the foot of a tree, and thought to be offerings presented to a deity inhabiting the spot. The objects in the hoard may not have been in simultaneous contemporary use.

hodji. In some parts of central Europe, a sage or philosopher who enjoys great prestige.

hoe. A Neolithic tilling device with a flat blade at right angles to the handle. It was the most important tool of early agriculture.

hoe, cylindrical. A Neolithic hatchet with a sharp blade, round back, and circular transverse section. The culture based on this implement, according to Menghin and Heine-Geldern, is the first productive agricultural economy and appeared in south or central Asia or perhaps China. The cylindrical-hoe culture spread rapidly. It was often combined with raising pigs.

hogan. A Navaho dwelling shaped like a cone or a beehive and made of earth, sticks, or stones chinked with mud.

hogback. A steeply sloping ridge.

hogshead. A large barrel or cask, usually containing from 63 to 140 gallons.

Hohokam. A culture of southern Arizona, ca. 450-1450 A.D., roughly parallel to the Anasazi (q.v.) development. Hohokam means *the ancients* in Pima-Papago. There was no masonry building. Cremation was practiced. An oxidized red or buff pottery was common. Bow and arrow were probably used. A ritual ball game was played. Four major periods in Hohokam development are usually distinguished. Maize was grown almost from the beginning of this culture, with cotton grown from the second period on. Copper bells date from the third period. The fourth period has contiguous houses with packed earth walls and multicolored pottery. The Hohokam Indians built pit and surface houses grouped into small villages and had a fairly well developed agricultural economy because of their irrigation systems, from which they are sometimes called the Canal Builders. Their chief crafts were pottery and jewelry-making. Examples exist of a ware on which figures of animals, men, and birds are freely sketched. Their jewelry, made for personal ornament or burial purposes, was carved of shell and included necklaces, rings, bracelets, and pendants in the shape of frogs, sheep, birds, or humans.

Hokan. A part of the Hokan-Sionan linguistic stock, the existence of which is hypothesized by some linguists.

holandric. Referring to genes in the male (Y) chromosome.

Holarctica. The land mass consisting of Asia, North America, Europe, and North Africa.

hole, crack-lacing. A hole on either side of a crack in a piece of pottery. String is placed connecting the holes, so that the crack will be reduced and confined sufficiently for the vessel to be used.

hole, cup. A hole cut in the stone of tombs with symbolic intent.

hole, ghost. A hole at the base of the cinerary urn presumably made to permit the soul of the deceased whose ashes it held to escape.

hole, kettle. An undrained hollow, often formed by the thawing of a piece of dead ice.

hole, pry. An incision half to three quarters of an inch deep and two to three inches long cut into the upper surface of a stone to give purchase to a crowbar used to pry another stone into place. A pry hole is at right angles to the motion to be given the upper stone.

holes, shift. Holes cut into the upper surface and under surface of a stone. They were used to move stones.

hole, smoke. An opening in a tipi or other dwelling made to permit smoke to go out of the dwelling. It is often in the top center of the structure.

holiday. A day of rest, originally a holy day of a feast, during which no work was to be done, in order to express reverence for a deity.

holly. An evergreen used for religious ceremonies. The Cross was supposed to be made of holly wood, which thereupon developed thorny leaves and red berries (blood).

Holly is especially displayed around Christmas time. It is used to cure a variety of diseases.

hollyhock. An herb used as a skin lotion and for stomach ailments and gout.

holocaust. A burnt offering, usually when consumed by fire; a substantial sacrifice.

Holocene. The most recent life period, ca. 25,000 years ago, characterized by the rise of Homo sapiens. The climate was temperate.

holocoenotic. Referring to environmental forces acting mutually among themselves and in concert against organisms.

hologenesis. The theory, enunciated by Rosa and Montandon, that different parts of the organism respond at different speeds to the process of evolution. According to hologenesis, those parts that develop most rapidly cease developing early, while the slowly changing parts eventually become more adjusted.

holophrase. A phrase entirely contained within one word, as in the incorporating languages (q.v.).

home, harvest. One of the oldest European feasts, held at the time of the last autumn harvesting.

homeostasis. The term proposed in 1932 by Walter B. Cannon (1871-1945) for the constant self-adjusting states maintained by physiological processes. Homeostasis has also been used by some anthropologists to describe the individual's and society's methods of internal self-regulation.

homestead. A habitation of which the occupants represent a household. It may be one or several dwellings.

homiletic ballad. See BALLAD, HOMILETIC.

hominid. Referring to the human being, from Pleistocene times on; also, the family of the Hominidae, which currently includes only the species Homo sapiens. The hominids originated in either Africa or Asia. It is possible that the Hominidae originated in the early Pliocene.

hominine. Referring to all the members of genus Homo, regardless of whether they belong to the species sapiens.

hominoid. A fossil type which is human-like.

hominy. An American Indian food. It is coarse, hulled maize, broken and boiled.

homme moyen. Quetelet's conception of an individual who is an average of a larger group, with respect to various characteristics, especially racial.

Homo. The genus to which the living forms of man belong. Surviving forms all belong to the sapiens species. This genus of the Hominidae (q.v.) has a mean cranial capacity of over 1,100 cc. Homo probably originated in the last interglacial period, ca. 50,000 years ago. If the specimen found at Swanscombe (q.v.) is regarded as a member of the genus Homo, then it goes back to the second interglacial period, ca. 100,000 years ago. If the mandible of Homo heidelbergensis (q.v.) is included, the genus began ca. 200,000 years, in the first interglacial.

Homo faber. Man the smith, the name applied to Neanderthal man.

Actually, Neanderthal man was not able to forge anything, although he could chip stones.

Homo heidelbergensis. A type of fossil man known from a large mandible found in 1907 in a sand quarry from the second interglacial period. This fragment (from Mauer, near Heidelberg), was near horse and rhinoceros remains. Some scholars regard Homo heidelbergensis as an ancestor of Neanderthal man and probably earlier than sinanthropus pekinensis (q.v.). The jaw is huge, with a very broad upright blade and no simian shelf (q.v.). The teeth have human characteristics. The great width of the vertical ramus indicates a probably powerful masseter muscle in the jaw. It is likely that the upper jaw and face were massive, with stout zygomatic arches.

Homo modjokertensis. A Lower Pleistocene (q.v.) fossil, related to Pithecanthropus. The sole find is the remains of the cranium of a two-year-old child made in 1936 at Modjokerto, Java.

Homo mousteriensis. This name is sometimes given to Neanderthal man because of the frequency with which Mousterian implements are associated with Neanderthal skeletal remains.

Homo neanderthalensis. This form of man has many variations, often divided into four subgroups, the Rhodesian (see HOMO RHODESIENSIS) the Mousterian, or Spy, the Ehringsdorf, and the subgroup closest to modern man, including the Skhul Mount Carmel and the Galilee remains. Homo neander-

thalensis was first found in Gibralter in 1848 and was intensively studied in 1936. It was named in 1864 by William King. Elements of over 100 Neanderthal remains have been found. It flourished during the third and fourth glacial periods.

Classic Neanderthals are probably from the fourth glacial advance. Their dead were buried, along with their tools. The presence of speech may be inferred. Mousterian culture predominated. Primarily because they buried their dead and because they lived fairly recently, ca. 100,000 to 50,000 years ago, a good deal is known about Neanderthal man. The brain of Neanderthal was probably slightly larger than the contemporary brain and the skull longer and wider than any contemporary type. The skull is broad behind the ears, and the back of the head protrudes. The head is not balanced and does not have a large forehead. The nose was probably large. There was little prognathism and not much of a chin. The mouth was large and the face was puffed around the nose. Neanderthal man stood an average height of 5 feet 3 inches; the posture was stooping, with the knees semiflexed. Neanderthal's teeth were robust. His bones were heavy and thick and his joints large. Although the feet were generally human, the big toe was not separated from the other toes.

In many ways, Neanderthal had a number of apelike characteristics. Thus, while Neanderthal has simian limb features, fairly modern limb bones were found as long ago as

262

Pithecanthropus, in Pleistocene times. It is now believed that Neanderthal is not an intermedite step in Homo sapiens' evolution but an evolutionary sideline in which some features were exaggerated. Some of these features, like the brow ridges and taurodontism (q.v.), are unique. A number of the earlier Mousterian specimens, when chronologically studied, have fewer Neanderthal characteristics than later Neanderthals, so that these early forms are nearer Homo sapiens than the later ones. There are no post-Mousterian remains that show a transition to modern man, suggesting that the extreme Neanderthal may have become extinct ca. 70,000 years ago. Neanderthal's brain being larger than modern man's, it is difficult to see how it fits in with the general development of the brain.

Clark has suggested that the development of Pithecanthropus' brain led to a generalized Neanderthal, with two kinds of development around Acheulian times. One had a large brain and large brow ridges, jaws, and palate, with specialized skull and teeth, and limb changes, which gave rise to the extreme Neanderthal. The other development saw the brain being enlarged while the brow ridges and jaws receded, the teeth became smaller, and a vertical forehead, and rounded cranium, appeared, as well as the limb characteristics of earlier Pithecanthropus. Clark has suggested that this line of development led from Acheulian man to Homo sapiens.

Homo primigenius. Primeval man, the name used up to fairly recently for Homo neanderthalensis (q.v.) when it was thought that Neanderthal was a step in the development from ape to Homo sapiens.

Homo rhodesiensis. A possible type of Homo neanderthalensis, found in 1921 in Northern Rhodesia. The specimen was an almost complete skull and some leg bones. It had a large face and teeth with caries. The specimen is also called Rhodesian Man and Broken Hill Man. It was not buried and was found in a cave shaft. The skull was thick, long and low. Rhodesian man had a brain capacity of 1,300-1,500 cc. The brows and palate are very large. The mouth is human, but the cranium is low and the brow ridges are more massive than any other human skulls. The jaw, palate, and brain case are Neanderthaloid, while the foramen magnum and some of the nose and ear features differ somewhat from Neanderthal. The antiquity of Rhodesian man is not clear. The artifacts are late Levallois (q.v.), while the freshness of the skull and the associated animal bones seem to indicate considerable modernity, as do the caries. Rhodesian man probably became extinct because he was too specialized.

Homo sapiens. The species to which all extant humans belong. First found in the Upper Paleolithic, the skull is thin-walled and the face light-boned. The forehead is high and the head dome-shaped. The hair is thrown into high relief because the face is pulled in under the forehead. There are cheek hollows not found in Neanderthal man and a chin. Homo sapiens appeared with Aurignacian (q.v.) culture, in which flint blades were the most important tools. In the middle of the Upper Paleolithic, Homo sapiens entered the Solutrean (q.v.) period, characterized by excellent flint working. The Magdalenian (q.v.) period, which followed, saw the slight deterioration of stonework and the rise of bone for tools.

In Europe, Homo sapiens with his Aurignacian culture probably drove the Mousterian Neanderthals away. It is possible that there were Negroid and Mongoloid elements present, in addition to some Australian elements. The races of today were probably present by the last glaciation, although they probably had rugged and large crania. See MAN; MAN, EVOLUTION OF.

Homo soloensis. A type of fossil man, represented by 11 skulls without facial skeleton found in 1931 by W. F. F. Oppenoorth, near the Solo River in Java. These skulls are regarded as an enlarged Pithecanthropus type and they also have much in common with Sinanthropus. Homo soloensis is probably from an era comparable to the third European interglacial period. The brow ridges are like those of Homo rhodesiensis, although not so large. The posture was also like Rhodesian man's. The foramen magnum is like that of Homo sapiens, and the brain volume was around 1,150-1,300 cc. The one shin bone found is quite modern. The Solo man probably became extinct because he was too specialized.

Homo wadjakensis. A type of fossil man, represented by two skulls found in 1889 by E. Dubois but first reported only in 1930. The remains are regarded by some as very similar to modern aboriginal Australian, but this connection is controversial because of the delay in reporting the find and because it was so damaged. The skulls were large. Both the Australian skull and the Wadjak man have heavy brows, a receding forehead, and are chinless and prognathous (q.v.). The Wadjak skulls have the brain size (1,650 cc. in males) and construction which is that of Ice Age Homo sapiens (q.v.) in Europe, so that it has been said that the Upper Paleolithic European has the same relation to the contemporary European as the Wadjak man has to the contemporary Australian aborigines.

homodont. Referring to the possession of teeth that are almost all alike.

homogametic. Referring to the female, because a woman has XX sex chromosomes. See X.

homograph. Any word which is the same in written form as another word of the same language, but different in sound and meaning.

homologies. The basic structural and developmental resemblances on which zoological relationships are based.

homomorphy. The identity between inflections of a word, so that different meanings have the same form, e.g., deer, put.

homonymy. The identity in sound of two words, e.g., *sew* and *sow*. It is seldom that the meaning of homonyms is confused, as the context usually shows which meaning is intended. Homonymy causes less confusion in a highly inflected language.

homophone. A word that has the same sound as the word represented by a pair of symbols taken together. Homophones are often found in Chinese. Perhaps the term's major use is as an equivalent for homonym.

homophony. The characteristic of being like in sound but different in meaning.

homosexual. An individual who engages in sexual relations with a person of the same sex. Ford and Beach report that some kind of homosexual activity was acceptable in 49 out of 76 societies on which information was available.

Primitive societies exhibit a wide range of attitudes toward homosexuality. Some societies, like the Siwans of North Africa, expect all young men and boys to practice homosexual sodomy. The Big Nambas of New Hebrides had institutionalized homosexuality, as did the Zūni. The Manus of New Guinea are typical of a group indifferent to homosexuality. Some groups permit homosexual practices but ban sodomy, and others prohibit all homosexual practices. In communities where homosexuality is believed to be rare, there are pressures which are directed against its open manifestation. Some societies have a recognized class of men who enjoy an intermediate man-woman status, and may dress like women, marry men, and do female work, like the alyhas, berdaches, or shamans (qq.v.).

Sir Richard Burton, in the "Terminal Essay" to his translation of the *Arabian Nights,* uses the comparative method to report on the extent to which homosexual practices have been endemic in many parts of the world, especially the Mediterranean and Far East areas. Students of primate behavior have observed homosexual alliances between primates even where a member of the opposite sex might be available.

Homosimius precursor. A hypothetical creature that immediately preceded man in the genealogical scale. This name is often used as a quasi-algebraic symbol, to refer to the putative but yet undiscovered organism which came directly before man.

homozygosity. A condition of similarity of genes, so that the group will breed true, with traits preserved.

hook, fish. In Magdalenian times, a thin piece of pierced bone pointed at both ends. If a fish swallowed it, a strong pull would cause the hook to stick in the gullet. Other kinds are V-shaped.

hook, fisherman's. A device used to penetrate the fish's gullet or mouth. It acts as a support for the line or bait. The fisherman's hook consists of a shank, point, and head. There are solid and composite hooks.

hook, pruning. A smaller sickle (q.v.).

hookah. A pipe with a long flexible stem that enables the smoke to be cooled.

hookswinging. An annual initiation rite among the Mandan Indians in which the candidate had skewers with heavy weights attached stuck into his flesh. The candidate is raised by ropes attached to the skewers and revolved until he faints.

hoopoe. A long billed bird that has figured in folklore throughout the world. It has been regarded as a war bird, a messenger, a wise bird, as well as an evil portent and an unclean bird.

hopper. A trough or funnel in which some substance is put in order to be fed into a mill.

hopper, mortar. An object, frequently funnel-shaped, used in a mortar to keep the substance being ground from falling out. Indians in California and Nevada often make the mortar hopper of basketry and use it in grinding acorns.

hops. A climbing herb used to cure insomnia, for skin disease, and for tooth and ear troubles, as well as for making beer.

hora. A Rumanian and Palestinian folk dance.

horde. A social group that is not tightly organized. Some 19th-century anthropologists believed society developed from a tribal horde, as did Freud. A horde is also a collection of nomads that claims exclusive rights for hunting and grazing in the area within which it usually wanders. See ORDA.

Horde, Golden. The Tartar tribes that invaded northern Europe and Russia over the steppes, in contrast to the Tartars led by Tamerlane and others who invaded the Middle East. See ORDA.

horehound. A bitter perennial herb, widely used to treat chest diseases from the ninth century to the present. It has also been used for stomach disorders, to improve vision, and as a snuff.

Horizontal, Frankfurt. See LINE, FRANKFURT.

horn. A wind instrument, made of animal horns or metal. They are used to signal, to expel evil spirits, or for other ceremonial or magical purposes. They figured in bull worship in Mesopotamia, and are used by Jews for some religious observances (see SHOFAR). The horn is a symbol of the great power of the bull. Many Middle Eastern deities, along with kings and priests, wore horns as signs of their power. Since the bull is associated with fertility, the horn often symbolizes prosperity, as shown in the cornucopia.

horn, ram's. See SHOFAR.

horse. A large solid-hoofed herbivorous mammal, with long mane, tail, and hair, a small head, short ears, and a callosity on the inside of the hind legs. It was first used as a draft animal in Babylonia ca. 2300 B.C. The domesticated horse probably spread to Europe and the Near East in the Indo-European invasions of the second millenium B.C.

The horse has been called the reason for the collapse of the Western Roman empire. Cavalry had not been important in the Roman army, which had one horseman for each 15 or 20 men on foot; and the mounted barbarians drove the Roman troops from the field. Mohammed is believed to have gone from Mecca to Jerusalem on the wonderhorse Alborak. Horses helped in the Arabs' military successes, as later with Genghis Khan. The horse figured in the Middle Ages as a result of the knights' power. With a horse and armor, they could exact a grant of land from a lord.

The horse has also been important in the development of the New World. Although the oldest Equidae fossils date from Eocene strata in northwest America, the native equine species were completely extinct centuries before Columbus' arrival. It is the European horse that was diffused among the Indians of the Great Plains. Wissler (1927) suggested that the Plains Indians' horses came from horses left by the De Soto and Coronado expeditions in 1541. Haines (1938) believed that Spanish settlements of the Santa Fe area in the early part of the 17th century were responsible for the Indians' adopting the horse. The diffusion was north and east to the Indians on the fringe of the Spanish Southwest settlements. The 18th and 19th century saw a steady diffusion of horses to the northern Plains tribes, with ca. 1800-1880 the period of maximum development of the Plains horse culture complex. The elements in the complex were diffused with considerable uniformity over a fairly wide area and played an integral part in transforming the economy from a food-gathering to a buffalo-hunting basis. Some traits in the horse complex are European in origin, although most were Indian inventions or modifications. Until the buffalo's extermination, ca. 1880, the Plains Indians regularly used to hunt buffalo. The horse was also used in war and as transportation.

Wissler believed (1914) that the Plains Indians' adoption of the horse probably did not change their culture to any great extent, while Kroeber later (1939) questioned this kind of "essentially static conception." Ewers (1955) has surveyed the available evidence and concluded that the horse caused both qualitative and quantitative changes in the previous pedestrian hunting and gathering economy. He also emphasized the change to a class from a classless society on the Plains, based primarily on the ownership of horses.

horse, crazy. Among the American Indians, a person who goes against his group's ways of living.

horseshoe. A metal device, usually iron, covering and protecting a horse's hoof. Its widespread magical use may be due to its being made of iron, which is traditionally opposed to harmful spirits. The nature of the horseshoe's position is important in effecting its potency. It has been used as a fertility symbol in Mexico and by the Aztecs.

horticulture. Hand tillage of the soil, using such implements as the hoe (q.v.), which can be operated by human power. The digging stick (q.v.) is probably the most frequently used tool. Women engage in a large part of horticulture. Shallow cultivation is generally the rule.

267

Dogs are often found in horticultural populations and pottery is not uncommon.

horticulturist. See GARDENER.

hoshio. A Mongol petty state unit.

hospitality. Receiving a guest (q.v.) or a stranger (q.v.) cordially. It has been found to be almost an institution among many nonliterate peoples and is linked with religion. The visitor may bear news and be expected to carry powerful blessings. Even hunting peoples, such as the Damas of southwest Africa, exhibit considerable hospitality. The Oriental and classic countries and the Old Testament and Mohammedanism emphasize hospitality. The original European visitors to nonliterate groups were generally received with hospitality. Group hospitality may show itself in one group's visiting others. Hospitality includes the procedures by which a stranger is made welcome to a social unit, often in accordance with definite rules of kin and tribe. Eating together, shaking hands, and wife lending (q.v.) are common techniques.

hospitality, wife. See LENDING, WIFE.

hotel. An establishment offering commercialized hospitality, originally arising along trade routes or near religious centers.

hothouse. An artificially heated building made of glass for the cultivation of plants. It was first used in France in 1385.

Hottentot apron. See APRON, HOTTENTOT.

Hottentot-Bushman. A language family (sometimes called Khoin or Khoisan) used by approximately 300,000 inhabitants of southwest Africa, mostly pygmy tribes. It is made up of Hottentot or Nama, which has four dialects, and Bushman, which has two. The chief phonetic characteristic of this family is the clicking sound produced by the inspiration of air. The Hottentots themselves are sometimes regarded as the result of a mixture of Bushmen and Hamitic or Semitic people, which may have occurred in the Limpopo-Zambezi area. Hottentots have also been called a blend of East Hamitic and Eurafrican elements.

hourglass. A transparent vessel made up of two upright sections connected by a very narrow neck. It is filled with the amount of sand or other substance that will take exactly one hour to run from the upper section through the neck into the lower section.

house, bachelor's. A community house used by warriors in totemic societies.

house, bone. An ossuary (q.v.), among the Indians in the southeastern United States. Bones were cleaned and put in a cane hamper before going to the bone house.

house, communal. A large and well built house, often found in matriarchal societies in which 15 to 20 persons lived.

house, grass. A warm-climate dwelling with grass over a pole framework, often beehive shaped and with a fireplace which was sacred. It is found among the Caddoan Indians and others.

house, long. A long rectangular building, the traditional dwelling of the Iroquois.

house, men's. A separate dwelling often found in early societies, in which married and/or unmarried men live. Erhard Schlesier has pointed out that in Micronesia, the term men's house is used to refer to six different kinds of house: the bachelor's house, club house, men's workshop, dance and feast house, cult house, and council house.

house, pit. A house built by embedding the floor in the ground over the site of a pit before erecting the superstructure. The pit house can be made roomy with fairly short side walls and can be heated fairly easily. The earliest house sites, dating from approximately 12,000 B.C., seem to have been pit houses.

house, quadrangular. One of the oldest types of house. It was made by placing a roof on the area between two parallel vertical windbreaks (q.v.).

house, snow. A spiral Eskimo winter dwelling made of blocks of snow that melt in the spring.

house, sweat. A lodge used for sweat baths, especially among Indians. These baths figured as war preparation, religious rites, or part of the puberty rite. The sweat house consisted of an airtight building in which very hot water was dropped on stones, giving rise to steam. The Navaho and Iroquois used them often. See LODGE, SWEAT.

houses, Jews'. Artifacts found in Cornwall, the ruins of dwellings that date back many centuries before Christ. Similarities in the construction place them in a period when trade had been established between Britain and the eastern Mediterranean region.

houses, Picts'. Primitive subterranean structures found in the western region of Aberdeenshire and the Orkneys and dating from the early Metal Age.

Howitt, Alfred William (1830-1908). An Australian anthropologist who studied kinship and backed Morgan (q.v.) in the controversies of the period.

huaca. A Quechua word meaning "sacred." By extension it was used for burials and hills, since both were venerated in pre-Conquest times in Peru.

Hubbard, Mother. A long, full, shapeless type of cotton dress adopted by natives, especially in Oceania, under the influence of Christian missionaries.

huehuitl. An Aztec drum made from a hollow log about one foot in diameter and three feet long. The dried skin or leather head could be easily adjusted to produce a difference in pitch. The huehuitl was mounted on a tripod and beaten with the fingers and wrists.

huipilli. A Mexican woman's sleeveless shirt.

hula. A Hawaiian dance, simultaneously an art, a recreation, and a religious activity. It was taught by priests in a sacred hall.

hull, reed-bundle. A hull consisting of three cigar-shaped bundles of reeds tied together.

human. Referring to man. The emotional connotations of the term make it difficult to use in a taxonomically correct manner.

Humboldt, Baron Alexander von (1769-1859). A German naturalist who travelled extensively and made many contributions to geography, including the concept of the isothermal line, which permits the comparison of the climate of different countries. His comparisons of the cultures of Polynesia, Asia, and America, strongly influenced Tylor and the Kulturkreis school.

humerus. A bone of the upper arm that articulates with the glenoid fossa and the forearm bones.

Humka. A friendship ceremony among the Dakota.

hummer. See ROARER, BULL.

hummock. A fairly short pile of pressure ice (q.v.).

humpy. In Queensland, an Australian aboriginal bough shelter or hut.

humus. Black or brown organic soil material formed from decomposing animal or vegetable matter.

Hunt, James (1833-1869). An English anthropologist who identified himself with the cause of the South in the American Civil War and buttressed his belief in slavery with anthropological data. He also used anthropology in discussions of other controversies of the period, e.g., the status of women, the Celts, and the Irish. He started the Anthropological Society in 1863. Hunt emphasized that anthropology is concerned with the whole problem of the development of human beings.

hunting, fire. Hunting animals by burning sections of prairie or forest. The animals would be fascinated by the fire and would succumb to the smoke. Fire hunting was a considerable aid in technologically backward cultures.

hunting, head. Raiding hostile tribes to obtain heads of the enemy, either for religious use or as trophies. Head hunting seems to be linked with ritual cannibalism (q.v.) and human sacrifice, as in parts of Indonesia, South America, and West Africa. The complex of practices may reflect a fertility cult that sees life as an almost tangible and finite substance especially found in the head and transferable through taking the head. Thus, a misfortune that is believed linked with an absence of life stuff may be a signal for a head hunt. Heads removed for prestige and religious reasons may be preserved.

hunting, higher. The economy of those tribes that use advanced hunting devices for the chase.

hurdy-gurdy. A large medieval musical instrument that is mechanically run by a wheel turned by a crank. It was used to accompany singing.

hush. See SIBILANT, ABNORMAL.

husk, verb. Any form of a verb which no longer functions grammatically as a verb.

Hutukhtu. See KUTUKHTU.

Huxley, Thomas Henry (1825-1895). An outstanding English student of comparative anatomy and evolution. He followed Darwin's ideas in studying human development. In 1865, he used hair to classify mankind. In 1870, on the basis of hair and skin color, he suggested classifying man into the Australoid, Negroid, Xanthocroid, and Melanochroid races.

hüyük. In Turkish achaeology, an artificial mound resulting from human occupation over an extended period. See TELL.

hyalography. The art of engraving on glass. This may be accomplished with the use of a substance harder than glass, e.g., emery, diamond, or in some cases with acid.

hybrid. The offspring resulting from the mating of two persons from different geographical areas or with different gene structure. It has been held by some that hybridization is beneficial, as in the case of the amalgamation of several groups in Greece which led to a great cultural effervescence. Those who deplore hybridization have maintained that disharmonies arise when stocks are crossed, although the evidence for this has been severely challenged. The hybrid is usually rejected by one of the parental groups. See MESTIZO.

hybridization. The process by which hybrids are developed.

hydramnios. A surplus of water in the fetal membrane.

hydraulis. A musical instrument consisting of a water organ, used in the Roman circus and army. Air was pumped into a hemispherical container in a cylinder half full of water and was held in constant pressure by the water. A tube led to flue pipes and keys.

hydria, Caeretan. A type of Ionian vase made in the seventh century B.C. The Caeretan hydria is identified by mythological picture stories painted in white, black, and dark red. Somewhere in the abstract or animal decorated background, the Ionian eye is always present to ward off evil spirits. These vases were highly utilitarian and generally were used to carry the household water.

hydrocephaly. A kind of mental deficiency resulting from an excess of cerebrospinal fluid in the brain ventricles. The head is generally large and the individual's physical condition is poor.

hydrochore. An organism with water-disseminated seeds.

hydrophyte. An organism, often aquatic, that flourishes under conditions of high moisture in the environment.

hydrosphere. The earth's aqueous envelope, which includes vapor, underground water, and all bodies of water.

Hylobatidae. The small anthropoid family that includes siamangs and gibbons. They have fine soft hair, with a small oval head, and large orbits and ears.

hylotheism. The doctrine that matter and deity are one and the same.

hylozoism. The theory that life and matter are inseparable and identical, that each particle of matter contains the spark of life in addition to the original motivation for motion and change. This theory arose in early Greece from the Milesian school.

hyperbole. Changing word meaning by deliberate exaggeration.

Hyperborean. 1 A Greek mythological people believed to live in a country of perpetual sunshine, beyond the north wind, so that the term is used for extreme northerly areas. The Hyperboreans sent an annual offering to Apollo's temple at Delos. The term Paleo-Asiatic is also found. 2 A group of languages to which the Chukchee-Kamchadal, Gilyak, and Ainu families belong. It is spoken by approximately 50,000 people, who live in the far northeastern corner of Asia. The term indicates a geographical distinction, since none of the families belonging to the group display any relationship.

hyperbrachycephaly. Exceptional round-headedness, with a cephalic index (q.v.) of more than 85.9.

hyperbrachycranic. Referring to a cranial index (q.v.) between 85 and 89.9.

hyperbrachyskelic. Referring to a stem-leg length index (q.v.) of less than 74.9.

hyperchamaerrhine. Referring to a nasal index (q.v.) of more than 58.

hyperdolichocranic. Referring to a cranial index (q.v.) between 65 and 69.9.

hypereuryene. Referring to an upper facial index (q.v.) of less than 44.9.

hypereuryprosopic. Referring to a total facial index (q.v.) of less than 79.9.

hypergamy. In the caste (q.v.) system, encouraging a girl to marry within her own caste or into a higher echelon, although she cannot marry into a caste beneath her.

hyperleptene. Referring to an upper facial index (q.v.) of more than 60.

hyperleptoprosopic. Referring to a total facial index (q.v.) of more than 95.

hypermacroskelic. Referring to a stem-leg length index (q.v.) of more than 100.

hypermorph. The highest form of man, in some classifications, e.g., the Mediterranean.

hyperpituitarism. See ACROMEGALY.

hyperplatycnemic. Referring to a platycnemic index (q.v.) of less than 54.9.

hyperplatymeric. Referring to a platymeric index (q.v.) of less than 74.9.

hypertrichosis. Excessive hairiness in humans. It is possible in such cases that the lanugo (q.v.) was not shed.

hypertrophy, law of atrophy and. See LAW, WOLFF'S.

hypocaust. A furnace that heats air and transmits it through flues under the floors and in room walls. It was known to the Romans and Greeks.

hypochoristic. Referring to a pet name or a familiar name.

hypocone. The disto-lingual cusp of the upper first and second molars.

hypoconid. The disto-buccal cusp of the lower second molar and the central buccal cusp of the lower first molar.

hypoconulid. The disto-buccal cusp of the first lower molar.

hypogeum. In ancient architecture, the parts of a structure or building that lie underground. The catacombs or lower levels of castles are examples of hypogea.

hypogonadal. Referring to subnormal development of the secondary sexual characteristics as a result of a deficiency in the testes' or ovaries' functioning.

hypomorph. A lesser developed form of man, in some classifications, e.g., the Negrito (q.v.).

hypostasis. The process by which a gene may be inhibited by another (nonallelic) gene.

hypostyle. See TEMPLE, PYLON.

hypotaxis. A sequence of predications in which at least one subordinate predication uses special attributive forms, e.g., I hope *that* you will arrive home. See PARATAXIS.

hypothesis, catastrophal. See CATASTROPHISM.

hypothesis, continental bridge. The hypothesis that continents used to span the areas where oceans are today, thus forming bridges between what are now separate land masses. See BRIDGE, LAND.

hypothesis, continental drift. The hypothesis that continents may not always have had the position they have today and that they probably split away from a larger land mass and drifted to their present position. Wegner has suggested that continents which formed a uniform mass separated from each other and drifted apart, on the analogy of

icebergs. Thus, the contours of the west coast of Africa and the east coast of South America roughly fit each other, and have some fossil types which are similar.

hypothesis, modesty. The hypothesis that modesty at least partly accounts for the origin of clothing. Sergi has suggested, to the contrary, that modesty is a result of wearing clothing.

hypothesis, protection. The hypothesis that clothing originated as a means of protecting the body from the elements and from animals.

hypothesis, solar radiation. The hypothesis, usually linked with the name of Milankovitch, that the Ice Age resulted from slight variations in the solar radiation which the earth's surface received.

hypothesis, wave. The hypothesis that language changes spread in a wavelike manner over a particular speech area and that a change may happen in one section that is different from the section covered by an antecedent change. Johannes Schmidt (1843-1901) promulgated this hypothesis in 1872 to explain similarities between geographically contiguous branches of the Indo-European languages.

hypothyroidism. Inadequate thyroid functioning. It is called cretinism (q.v.) if it exists from birth and myxedema (q.v.) if it occurs later.

hypsicephaly. Exceptional high-headedness; a skull, the basion-bregma height of which is at least 75 per cent of the maximum length of the skull.

hypsiconch. Referring to an orbital index (q.v.) of more than 85.

hypsicranic. Referring to a cranial length-height index (q.v.) of more than 75.

hypsiloid. Referring to an arch or curve in U-shape, after the Greek letter upsilon.

hypsodont. Referring to teeth with long crowns.

hypsodonty. The relation between the vertical and horizontal on teeth.

hysteria, arctic. A mental disturbance, culturally related to the technologically backward Siberian societies where it is found.

I

I fraction. The ratio between the time in which air is inhaled (I) and the duration of the entire respiratory circle (D). It is from .04 to .45 in ordinary breathing and about .16 in speech.

ibâda. In Islam, during the Middle Ages, the view that man's task and goal was the service of God.

Ibn Khaldun (1322-1406). A Mohammedan scholar whose writings on North Africa and Arabia are valuable ethnographical sources.

IC. See CONSTITUENT, IMMEDIATE.

ice, drift. A floating ice pack.

ice, landfast. See ICE, SHORE.

ice, needle. Ice formed from fresh water that freezes and breaks up in the spring into crystals as long as the original ice was thick. The ends of the crystals are very sharp.

ice, old. Ice dating from the preceding year or years. It has angular hummocks and pressure ridges.

ice, paleocrystic. Ice that is a number of years old. Thaws and rains will have rounded its fracture angles.

ice, pressure. Ice broken by the pressure of currents or of wind. It may be in hummocks or ridges.

ice, shore or **ice, landfast.** Ice one end of which touches the beach, while the other meets the ice pack.

ice, young. Ice that has been formed recently and is too weak to support a man walking on it. It usually refers to ice made of salt water.

ich-kanava. The long migration myths of the Mohave Indians.

ichthyomancy. The art of divination (q.v.) from indications in the entrails of fishes.

ichthyosis. Having a scaly skin. It is a sex-linked condition, chiefly in males.

iconoclasm. A hostility to images, found, e.g., in Ikhnaton's substituting the sun for other gods ca. 1375 B.C. and in the Old Testament prophets' attacks on image worship.

iconogenetic. Referring to eyes that form images, so that they gather information about light as well as about the objects from which the light is reflected. Iconogenetic eyes are found in complex animals.

iconology. The branch of art history that attempts to analyze the subject matter portrayed by artists without taking into account the personalities of the creators.

ideas, elementary. Bastian's concept of inherent unconscious psychic processes that are common to all mankind.

identic. Referring to a declensional case that shows likeness, sameness, or identity. It is found in certain non-Indo-European languages.

ideograph. A written symbol for a word that conveys the idea intended rather than the sound. Thus the Chinese character meaning "well" or "happy" combines elements representing a woman and a son, since, according to the traditional etymology, the mother-son relationship is the happiest state conceivable.

ideophone. A vocable in the languages of the Bantu group the purpose of which is to modify a term of the utterance.

idiographic. Referring to a study the purpose of which is to establish particular, specific, or factual propositions or statements. See NOMOTHETIC.

idiokinesis. A process of change in a person's hereditary characteristics.

idiolect. The variety of a language that is peculiar to the individual.

idiom. Any distinctive utterance peculiar to a language that communicates a particular meaning, which is sometimes opposed to, and not necessarily explained by, the syntactical rules and is not equivalent to the additive meaning of the component parts, e.g., *to wear a*

chip on one's shoulder. An idiom is also the general character of a language.

idiophone. A musical instrument with which the player creates the vibration in the instrument itself, e.g., xylophone or gong.

idol. A three-dimensional representation of a man or an animal which is believed to be the seat or receptacle of a supernatural entity and before which appropriate acts of worship are performed. Early man, attributing special power to some specific objects, often expressed his anthropomorphism by cutting human features in a stone or tree, thus making it sacred. In Egypt, composite human-animal figures, like the sphinx, are also found. Having spirits within them, idols were often believed to show signs of being alive, e.g., by winking or turning the head. It has been suggested that the word idol should not be used because of derogatory associations.

idol, dolmen. A type of stone standing on one end and found from Morocco to Troy. A dolmen idol is shaped to resemble a human figure.

idolatry. The worship of idols. The practice may have had its origin in Aurignacian times, and have expanded into the eastern Mediterranean area.

igloo. An Eskimo snowhouse (q.v.), often dome-shaped. In Eskimo terminology an igloo is any shelter for humans or animals, and thus to the Eskimo a cathedral could be an igloo. Some travelers designate by igloo the type of Eskimo house they know best. Accordingly, Stefansson suggests that the word has almost lost its meaning and that more specific words be used wherever possible.

igname. The sweet potato in New Caledonia.

ignis fatuus. The pale flame seen over marshy grounds. It is often explained on the basis of disintegrating organic matter which causes spontaneous ignition of marsh gases.

ikat. A silk chiné fabric of southeast Asia. See DYEING, IKAT.

ilium. The upper portion of the hip bone.

illa. Amulets and similar devices among the Incas and their descendants.

image. A representation of another object, often invested with special properties by early man. See MAGIC, SYMPATHETIC; IDOL.

image, divining. A carving, usually of wood, used in Africa and Central America for magic.

imagery, apotropaic. Any symbolic representation the purpose of which is to ward off demons or evil influences. Quite frequently it takes the form of staring eyes (related to hypnotism). Apotropaic imagery exists in most primitive cultures and is based on the assumption that any likeness has the power of what it represents.

Imam. The head of a mosque.

imbrication. Overlapping the edges, as in laying tiles; or any elaboration of structure.

immortality. Living indefinitely, or living after death in some place other than on earth. It is possible to infer that very early man believed in immortality, on the basis of burial customs, which preserve the body so that there may be a place for the soul.

impaction. A tooth's being embedded in the alveolus so that eruption is prevented.

impaling. An ancient form of capital punishment. Either a stake was driven into the body below the breast bone, or the victim was thrown onto stakes or spears set in the ground.

impastation. Making a paste from the ingredients of a ceramic mixture.

impasto. The prepared clay used to make pottery.

implement. An object with which work can be accomplished.

implements, Yuma. Projectile points that are longer and narrower than the Folsom point (q.v.). Yuma implements are unfluted.

implosion. A temporary articulation of the speech organs in such a way that there is no exit for breath and the closure is effected. See STOP.

impossibilities. In folklore, tasks that are impossible or silly.

impregnation, magical. Conception through processes not usually associated with conception, like Danae's being impregnated by Zeus in the form of a shower of gold.

impulse, decorative. A hypothetical drive for self-ornamentation, which, according to some theorists, is responsible for the origins of clothing.

in norma verticali. Viewing a skull from above, in order to classify it. The Italian anthropologist

277

Sergi, particularly, has used this as a race criterion, instead of the cephalic index (q.v.).

inao. Among the Ainu, a whittled stick used for ceremonies.

inbreeding. The marriage and reproduction of close relatives. It is popularly believed to deteriorate a strain, but it may also effect an improvement. Recent studies have shown that inbred stocks, like the Hawaiian royal family, may be physically superior.

Inca. One of three archaeological periods in Andean cultural development, dated ca. 1400 A.D. The civilization was based on intensive agriculture, with foods preserved and stored. There were basketry, weaving, ceramics, metallurgy, stoneworking, building, water transportation, and good roads. The class division was rigid, with the Inca class on top. Its members were of the royal lineage and were considered descendants of the sun. Religion was in state hands, and the sun temple was the center of political and social controls. War was conducted for political conquest and the vanquished peoples were forced to pay tribute. The conquest empire reached from mid-Ecuador to mid-Chile. The Inca Empire was an example of a planned economy and welfare state. Defeated enemies who could not be absorbed into Inca society were exterminated. The Empire was destroyed by Francisco Pizarro and his comrades. See ROADS, CLASSIFICATION OF.

incantation. Saying or singing special phrases in order to get a special power to take effect, e.g., bewitching someone or exorcising a demon. The words in an incantation are believed to have a magical effect when recited.

incarnation. The process by which a deity takes over or inhabits temporarily, or for the full span of its life, a human or animal body. The authority for this exchange is received by direct contact with the gods in a number of different forms, e.g., vision, possession by the Holy Spirit, lineal descent from the deity, or endowment with divine illumination. The idea of incarnation is present in all religions. In ancient Persia, the kings were crowned with the "royal glory" or the "divine light" of the Moslem Imams. Egyption Pharaohs were divine because the sun god Re inhabited their bodies in order to impregnate the queen. Greek religion and myth abound in stories of temporary incarnations of the gods, such as the frequent appearance of Zeus, Poseidon, and Apollo in other forms.

In Hinduism, the beneficent god Vishnu is the most frequent hero of incarnation stories. His coming commonly accompanies the sinking of the world into decay, the rise of iniquity, and desperate need. He functions in those perilous times as a teacher and savior. An incarnation of Vishnu is spoken of as being his avatar.

In early Buddhist theology, the emphasis was upon salvation without the help of the gods, but later the Bodhisattva was defined as a human being who had acquired superhuman powers by his rigorous disciplines on the road toward

Buddhahood. Whenever the world is covered with darkness, truth is obscured, and mankind is going downhill, one of these Bodhisattvas appears.

Jesus, the Christian savior, was recognized as a god in the early second century. Since one of the primary concepts of Christianity is monotheism, Christ was maintained to be an incarnation of the divine being. To preserve the monotheistic framework, he was defined as one of the three "persons" comprising the unitary God.

The purpose of these stories of divine incarnation seems to have been manifold—to elevate great men, to unify religions of diverse origins, to give the value of a god to a savior, or to bring the protection and assistance of the divine being closer to mankind by presenting it in human form.

incense. An aromatic substance given off by certain trees and used in worship. It was believed that the incense was desired by the god, and it has been suggested that its fragrance showed it had a supernatural quality that made it the god's property. Its ability to dispel odors might have been regarded as a means of driving away demons.

incense cup. See CUP, INCENSE.

incest. Sexual or marital relations between two persons so related that their marrying is prohibited. Incest prohibitions exist in all human societies. In more than 200 studied by Murdock, not one allowed marriage between father and daughter, brother and sister, and mother and son. A few societies permitted a purely sexual relationship, as opposed to a marriage, outside the primary relationship.

The Inca, and Hawaiian nobility probably had brother-sister incest. Sometimes marriage is permitted between partly collateral relations: Marquesan society allowed men to marry their mothers-in-law; in parts of Sumatra a man can marry a half sister by the same father; in Haida society a man could marry his brother's daughter.

Society decides on the delimitation of incest, which always extends beyond the nuclear family although the taboo is intensest there. There is a high positive correlation between incest taboos and kinship groupings. The incest taboos are emotional and intense and their sanctions are usually religious. They are often violated, especially in fairly modern times, but are enforced with some vigor in many early societies because of the power of affinal ties and because of the great role of kinship in societies with a weak political framework. The horror with which incest has long been regarded is seen in the extent to which duplicity is deemed necessary to entice another person into incest, in the Old Testament. Absalom raped his sister Tamar but only by pretending to be sick, so that she nursed him, and Lot's two daughters cohabited with Lot only by getting him drunk first, after their husbands had been killed.

Although a great many theories to explain incest have been put forth, no one theory is universally accepted. Freud, writing of a hypothetical primitive society in which the father forced the sons to leave the home, suggested that the sons' desire for the mother had to be suppressed so that the strength of their revulsion would make them seek outside women. Westermarck maintained that it is biologically bad to interbreed and that to this factor was added the condition of revulsion provoked by familiarity and contiguity, as in avoidance (q.v.).

Briffault's theory is based on his concept of an early matriarchate (q.v.) in which the mother keeps her sons from women except those at home, with the sons breaking away from the jealous mother and marrying women from outside the home.

Economic determinists explain incest prohibitions as due to simple desire for gain, with early marriage serving the social purpose of realigning property concentrations. A sexual alliance within a family reduced the possibility of increasing the wealth of the family through profitable exogamy (q.v.) Proponents of this view cite the politically inspired marriages of European royalty as modern extensions of this ancient principle.

The Tylor-White theory of incest has it that one must "marry out or be killed off." Marrying out of the group permits its extension to include outside groups so that enemies are eliminated and persons who marry out of their group last longer. Marriage occurs between groups rather than individuals in this theory.

The Wilson Wallis theory em-phasizes that the consanguineal kin unit is the basic co-operative unit, and that there is no evidence dealing with the relationship between affinal groups. A numerical disparity led to looking outside the group for mates, and the simple unavailability of partners caused persons to marry outside the family in order to get a spouse. The Malinowski-Seligman theory is that an institutionalized incest taboo arises because of the necessity for eliminating intra-family sexual rivalry, as there are males and females who are mutually attractive and must be separated, lest spouses spend too much time watching one another. Brenda Seligman's theory is that every member in a family has a vested interest in his own sexual prerogatives and excludes the children of his own sex from sexual access to the other spouse and to the siblings of opposite sex.

In general, the punishment for incest is related to the social disequilibrium caused rather than to the resultant intra-family difficulties. Except in advanced societies, the punishment is usually not penal but social in its nature.

incest, dynastic. In some royal families, the arrangement of marriages between close relatives whose marriage would otherwise be forbidden by the general incest prohibition. Dynastic incest existed among the Ptolemies, who inherited the empire of Alexander the Great from Ptolemy I, a general in Alexander's army. The Ptolemies, who were Macedonians, frequently married their own full sisters.

In the ancient East and especially in Egypt, kings sometimes married their half-sisters. This was done because the surviving female member of a royal family, often the daughter of a main royal wife, might have a more legitimate claim to the throne than the surviving heir-apparent or king who might be the son of a second wife. In order to strengthen his claim to the throne, he thus married his half-sister for dynastic reasons. Cleopatra thus married her oldest brother, and after his death married her younger brother, with both brothers reigning by right of the marriage, just as Julius Caesar may have married the queen to be acknowledged as ruler.

incision. A mutilation (q.v.) performed on males. It consists of making a longitudinal slit in the dorsal part of the prepuce. It is often associated with initiation activities. See SUBINCISION.

incisors. One of two teeth with a cutting edge and a spatulate form in the front of the jaws on each side. They are used to bite off food, which is then moved to the back for the grinding teeth.

incisor, shovel-shape. An incisor that has a shovel shape because of a thickened rim around the lateral and lower borders on the inside. Hrdlicka suggested that only enamel participates in the formation of the ridge but more recent work has shown that the dentine also participates. The shovel-shape incisor is widely found among Mongoloids. It is also found in Sinanthropus pekinensis (q.v.), which is one reason

why Sinanthropus is believed to be a Mongoloid precursor.

incorporation. Using noun-derived primary affixes to express the object of a verb, as in Nahuatl.

indemnity. An object of value which one individual or group gives to another so as to cancel out or eliminate rights of the recipient that have been infringed. Indemnities are obligatory in specific circumstances.

index. The relationship, mathematically expressed, between two anatomical measurements.

index, acrocranic. A cranial breadth-height index (q.v.) that is more than 98.

index, acromio-cristal. The bicristal breadth multiplied by 100 and divided by the bi-acromial breadth.

index, bodily fullness. The relation between height and weight. It is the result of the division of the weight by the stature's cube and then multiplying the result by 100. Age and sex are linked with this index.

index, brachial. The length of the forearm multiplied by 100 and divided by the length of the upper arm.

index, cephalic. The relation between the maximum breadth and maximum length of the head, measured from the glabella (q.v.) to the farthest occipital (q.v.) and computed by multiplying the breadth by 100 and dividing by the length. If the cephalic index is 90, then the breadth of the skull is 90 per cent of its length. The index is two points higher on the living than the dry skull, because of the tissues on the side of the head. The cephalic index is inherited, but its genetics are not clear. The index is established around the time of birth and shows no consistent postnatal change, but it is subject to modification with certain limits. Thus, the increase in the height of the children of Europeans in the United States tends to lower the index because the length of the head is more positively correlated than is head breadth with stature. The index is also modifiable by artificial deformation of the head.

In central and east Europe, and perhaps Polynesia, round-headedness may be associated with some constitutional or other qualities that have survival value. See DOLICHO-CEPHALIC; BRACHYCEPHALIC; MESOCEPHALIC.

index, cranial. The relation between the maximum breadth and maximum length of the skull, from the glabella (q.v.) to the most distant occipital (q.v.) point computed by multiplying the breadth by 100 and dividing by the length.

index, cranial breadth-height. The height from bregma (q.v.) to basion (q.v.) multiplied by 100 and divided by its maximum breadth.

index, cranial length-height. The height from bregma (q.v.) to basion (q.v.) multiplied by 100 and divided by its maximum length.

index, crural. The length of the shin multiplied by 100 and divided by the length of the thigh.

index, facial. The total height of the face multiplied by 100 and divided by its breadth, measured from

nasion (q.v.) to gnathion (q.v.) and from zygion (q.v.) to zygion. The facial index is not so useful as the cranial index (q.v.) because it is more susceptible to change due to age, function, and sex. In general, prehistoric man probably had a longer and narrower face than more recent groups.

index, femero-humeral. The length of the upper arm multiplied by 100 and divided by the length of the thigh.

index, forearm-hand. The hand length multiplied by 100 and divided by the length of the forearm.

index, gnathic. The endobasion-prosthion distance divided by the endobasion-nasion distance and multiplied by 100.

index, hand. The hand breadth multiplied by 100 and divided by the length of the hand.

index, intermembral. The length of the entire arm multiplied by 100 and divided by the length of the whole leg.

index, ischium-pubis. The pubis length multiplied by 100 and divided by the length of the ischium.

index, length-breadth sacral. The anterior sacral breadth multiplied by 100 and divided by the anterior sacral length.

index, lower leg-foot. The length of the foot multiplied by 100 and divided by the length of the lower leg.

index, Manouvrier's skelic. See INDEX, STEM-LEG LENGTH.

index, maxillo-alveolar. The biectomolare breadth multiplied by 100 and divided by the maxillo-alveolar length.

index, morphological. Naccarati's index of the relation of height to weight.

index, nasal. The relation between the length and width of the nose. This is determined by multiplying the greatest nasal breadth of the nasal aperture by 100 and dividing by the nasospinale-nasion height. The nasal index is based on so many factors that it is not widely used in genetic analysis. The nose form is affected by the temperature of the air which a person breathes habitually. The nasal index is related to sex as well as age. A woman's nose is likely to be shorter and broader than a man's. The nasal index grows smaller as the person grows older.

index, orbital. The greatest orbital breadth multiplied by 100 and divided by the greatest orbital length.

index, palatal. The greatest palatal breadth multiplied by 100 and divided by the maximum palatal length.

index, pelvic breadth-height. The greatest pelvic height multiplied by 100 and divided by the greatest pelvic breadth.

index, pelvic inlet. The sagittal diameter of the pelvic inlet multiplied by 100 and divided by the transverse diameter of the pelvic inlet.

index, pilastric. A cross-sectional index of the femur (q.v.) established at the middle of the shaft.

index, platycnemic. A cross-sectional index of the tibia (q.v.), established at the middle of the shaft.

index, platymeric. The anterior-posterior platymer diameter multi-plied by 100 and divided by the medio-lateral diameter.

index, sicklemia. A measure of the extent of sicklemia (q.v.) in the blood, determined by using vaseline to seal a drop of blood between the cover slip and slide. If sodium hydrosulfite is used the process takes only about 15 minutes instead of several hours as with vaseline.

index, stem-leg length. The leg length multiplied by 100 and divided by the length of the stem, i.e., the sitting height or the height from the top of the head to the pubic symphysis. The stem-leg length index is also known as Manouvrier's skelic index.

index, thoracic. The depth of the chest multiplied by 100 and divided by the breadth.

index, tibio-femoral. The length of the lower leg multiplied by 100 and divided by the length of the thigh.

index, tibio-radial. The length of the forearm multiplied by 100 and divided by the length of the lower leg.

index, total facial. The height from gnathion (q.v.) to nasion (q.v.) multiplied by 100 and divided by the bizygomatic breadth (q.v.).

index, trunk. The bi-acromial breadth (q.v.) multiplied by 100 and divided by the sitting suprasternal height (q.v.).

index, transverse fronto-parietal. The frontotemporale-frontotemporale distance, divided by the euryon-euryon distance and multiplied by 100.

index, upper facial. The height from prosthion (q.v.) to nasion (q.v.) and divided by the bizygomatic breadth (q.v.).

index, vertical lumbar. The sum of the dorsal vertical diameters of the centra, multiplied by 100 and divided by the sum of the ventral vertical diameters.

index, vital. The number of births in a population multiplied by 100 and divided by the number of deaths. If this ratio is over 100, then the population is growing and is biologically healthy. If this ratio is under 100, the population does not show natural biological growth.

Indian, American. 1 A Mongoloid racial stock of composite race, characterized by brown skin, broad face, straight hair, slight body hair, and some prognathism (q.v.). Eye color ranges from dark brown to black. The blood group (q.v.) is almost completely 0, with occasional high A and some B. Man probably arrived in the New World ca. 20,000 to 15,000 years ago. The name comes from a letter of Columbus in February, 1493, where he spoke of "Indios." **2** The languages of the Western Hemisphere, many of which are now extinct. They are spoken by about 16 million persons, of whom approximately 250,000 live in the United States and Canada. They are structured differently, although many of them are synthesized from many sources so that the common origin is dubious. It is difficult to classify them precisely since little is known about many.

Indians, Blanket. Those American Indians who do not wish to wear modern clothes and prefer their ancestral costume.

Indians, canoe. A name applied to the Yahgan and the Alakaluf of Tierra del Fuego because of their reliance on canoes for fishing and travel.

Indians, Digger. A designation, derogatory in intent, which was applied by white settlers to tribes of the Basin area of the western United States, such as the Paiute, who subsisted largely by digging roots out of the ground.

Indians, White. A hypothetical group of white-skinned Indians in the interior of the United States.

Indic. A branch of the Indo-European family of languages which belongs to the Indo-Iranian group. It is spoken in India and Ceylon. The modern languages are Hindi, Urdu, Bengali, Bihari, Marathi, Punjabi, Rajasthani, Gujarati, Oriya, Sindhi, Pahari, Bhili, Khandesi, Assamese, Sinhalese, Kashmiri, Nepali, and Gypsy (Romani). They have all developed from Indic. Classical Sanskrit and the medieval Prakrits are members of this group also.

Indio. A descendant of a pre-conquest group in Latin America who preserves pre-Conquest language and customs, e.g., a Tarascan of central Mexico.

individual cult. See CULT, INDIVIDUAL.

Indo-Chinese. A language family, which includes the languages of China, Burma, Tibet, and Siam.

Indo-European. A language family which includes the Germanic,

Italic, Celtic, Baltic, Slavic, Albanian, Greek, and Indo-Iranian subfamilies. The comparative method was developed largely in the study of this family, and to this day comparative linguistics is often identified with Indo-European comparative studies. Indo-European includes the classical or inflected languages, in which ample use is made of affixes and in which roots are often subject to alteration depending on the affix. The source of the Indo-European languages has been variously identified as the Baltic coastline, Southern Russia, and elsewhere.

Indonesia. An island group of Oceania (q.v.), consisting of Sumatra, Java, the Celebes, the Philippines, and Indonesia. The degree to which its flora and fauna are coterminous with the Asiatic mainland probably indicates that some of the islands were only fairly recently separated from the mainland. The Indonesians are mostly Mongoloid, although there are some Negritos on the Philippines and the Andaman Islands.

Indonesian. 1 In physical anthropology, an attenuated Mongoloid type of man, showing some Caucasoid elements, followed by Malays, who are truer Mongoloids. The Indonesians are often called proto- or deutero-Malays. 2 In linguistics, the subfamily of the Malayo-Polynesian family of languages, which includes at least 200 languages and dialects, chief among which are Malay, Javanese, Balinese, Batak, Bicol, Bisaya, Bontok, Buginese, Dayak, Formosan, Ilocano, Macassar, Ma-

duran, Malagasy, Sundanese, and Tagalog.

induration. The process of hardening.

industry. A collection of artifacts of the same age found at a given site constitute the site's industry. If a site was inhabited successively, so that there are artifacts belonging to different ages, the one site represents different industries.

inessive. In linguistics, referring to a case in languages such as Finno-Ugric that means the same as the English preposition *in* or *within.*

infanticide. The practice of killing infants at birth or soon after. It is still found in some societies and used to be fairly common, i.e., the Polynesians killed two thirds of their children for economic reasons. The West African Jagas formerly killed all children who might otherwise hinder their marches. Some peoples have practiced infanticide for motives of religion, cannibalism, or economy, including the destruction of infants with physical defects that would hinder their usefulness. Suffocation, choking, drowning, and exposure are the usual methods.

infantilization. The arrest of the development of the organism at an infantile stage.

infection. In linguistics, a vowel change due to the influence of a near-by vowel.

infibulation. Attaching a device to the female genitals to prevent sexual intercourse, or an operation on the female genitals, often in order to make sexual intercourse more difficult. Sometimes infibulation is

285

accomplished by partially sewing the edges of the labia majora together.

infinite, idea of the. The view that the major phenomena of nature cause an idea of the infinite to arise in early man. According to Max Müller, such phenomena as sun, sky, and wind gave rise to this idea, which led to the beginning of religion. Müller's views were based on his erroneous assumption that the Vedas were the productions of primitive men, so that he imputed to very early men powers of abstraction which they probably did not have.

infixation. The process of affixation within a word. An infix is a morpheme (q.v.) which is inserted within a root. Infixes are common in Semitic languages.

inflection. The syntactical term denoting the practice of adding particular endings to the root of a word in order to show grammatical relationships. This process is found primarily in the synthetic languages and almost never appears in the analytic languages. Inflection is a type of accidence.

inflection, base of. The prime or fundamental form of a word which is augmented with flectional terminae. It is either the root base or the stem base.

informant. A person who assists the anthropologist studying a group by answering questions, providing background information, and engaging in discussions. There is usually more than one informant in each group, in order to give the field worker the benefit of varied points of view. In linguistics, an informant is a native speaker of the language under study who demonstrates the sounds, indicates words, typical utterances, etc. He does not explain the grammar or structure of the language, but provides the linguist with the material necessary for a scientific description.

ingada. An Arunta chief.

Ingiet. A secret society of New Britain.

in-group. A group of persons as seen from the viewpoint of a member of the group, in contrast with other groups and persons who are not members of the group.

inheritance. The procedures that apply to the transmission of property, such as matrilineal or patrilineal, depending on whether the male or female line is followed. Although inheritance refers only to the succession of the living to the property of the dead, transfering property during life will affect it. The rules of inheritance show a person's obligation to his relatives and his desire to indicate choice in disposing of his property. Rules of inheritance usually emphasize an obligation to one's relatives. Most early societies do not have inheritance by will.

inheritance, avuncular. The transmission of property and privileges to a man from his mother's brother upon the death of the latter.

inheritance, collateral. The practice of having siblings inherit property from each other rather than having the children of the sibling inherit it.

inheritance, Darwinian. Inheritance of physical characteristics in accordance with Darwin's theory of natural selection. In Darwin's view, the variations which arise by chance in a species' form or function persist only if suited to the environment, so that the variations which best fit the organism to survive are perpetuated.

inheritance, lateral. The transmission of property to a collateral relative of the deceased, especially a person of the same generation, as from a man to his brother. See INHERITANCE, LINEAL.

inheritance, lineal. The transmission of property to a lineal descendent of the deceased, as from a man to his son. See INHERITANCE, LATERAL.

inhumation. Burial of the dead.

inhumist. Referring to a group or society that buries its dead.

ini. See SNOWHOUSE.

inion. The base of the occipital external protuberance of the skull, on the back of the skull. It is the point at which two ridges made by neck-muscle attachments meet.

initiation. The transition and attendant ceremonies, such as ordeals and rites, involved in passing from one state or status to another. An example is obtaining membership in a secret society (q.v.). The ordeal (q.v.) measures the initiate's worthiness to enter his new status. Initiation may mean the cessation of contact with noninitiates. Many early societies had grade initiations. Their purpose was both to induct the young person into the full status of an adult and into the group's re-

ligion. The elders usually arrange and handle the ceremonies. They are usually mandatory and not going through the rites may mean disgrace. Aliens are usually excluded, while almost all of a tribe attends. The ceremony of initiation is among the leading social institutions of early man. Seclusion, mutilation, symbolic representation of death and resurrection, the display of some sacred objects, special instruction, and restrictions on the young person are frequent characteristics of initiation ceremonies. See RITES DE PASSAGE.

innominate. An irregular large bone formed by the fusion of three of the pelvic bones.

inscription, house. A legend written on a dwelling or other building, often near its entrance, and often containing sacred inscriptions.

insectivores. A small mammalian insect-eating order. It has been suggested that primates (q.v.) may have arisen from such insectivores as the tree shrew.

inselberg. An isolated desert rocky hill.

insolation. The energy that the earth receives from the sun.

instinct. A key inherited drive in higher animals, the existence of which among humans is debatable. Several thousand presumed instincts have been listed, but the current tendency is to use the concept of a physiological drive rather than instinct in explaining apparently automatic and unlearned behavior.

institution. A fairly permanent cluster of social usages. It is a reasonably enduring, complex, integrated pattern of behavior by which social control is exerted and through which basic social desires or needs can be met.

instrument, percussion. A musical instrument, including objects of any shape or size, from which sound is elicited by striking either with the hand, a stick, or other beating device. Simpler examples of the percussion instrument, such as the drum, gong, and triangle, usually provide accompaniment for other instruments. However, the piano, which is the most complex of percussion instruments, is a solo instrument in its own right.

instrument, stringed. A musical instrument that has a resonator to amplify the sound made by plucking or picking with a bow. A calabash, or even the player's chest, may serve this purpose. The musical bow, which consists of a string that is plucked while the other hand produces pitch changes by varying the length of the part allowed to vibrate, is the most elementary stringed instrument. Stringed instruments are less widely used by early man than wind and percussion instruments. String instruments are usually classified by the technique used to set the strings in vibration, i.e., plucked strings (plucked or strummed by fingers or plectrum, or hammer-struck), bowed strings, and struck strings (finger plays on a keyboard).

instrument, valve. A musical instrument played by a valve mechanism used to establish vibrations in the air column produced inside the instrument by blowing.

instrument, wind. An instrument in which the player blows into a device. Wind instruments are particularly useful to musicologists because they show the scales and intervals of the music of extinct peoples. Some wind instruments, like the trumpet, may be used for signalling.

intaglio. A gem with the design cut in, so that an impression made from the stone duplicates the design in relief. Intaglios were frequently used for seals.

intensification, rites of. Ceremonial activities that hinge on community-wide situations, e.g., preparing for the harvest.

intercalation. Adding additional days to the calendar in order to make it coincide with the solar year. An example is the day added to February every fourth year in the Julian calendar.

interdental. An articulation made by the tongue placed between the lower and the upper teeth, e.g., θ.

interdigitation. Interlocking, as two hands the fingers of which are joined.

interglacial. The period between major glaciations.

intergrade. A mixture of races that shows characteristics of two or more. Intergrades often arise from an admixture of contiguous populations. The existence of intergrades has emphasized the difficulty of race classification.

interjection. A word or phrase that mainly occurs as a minor sentence (q.v.) and is mainly used by parataxis (q.v.), e.g., *aha.*

interjectional. Referring to the theory that language originally arose as a response to emotional stress that elicited interjections that in turn gave rise to words. The term pooh-pooh is sometimes applied to this theory.

Interlingua. An international artificial language, based on modified Latin. Giuseppi Peano invented it in 1903.

interpretation, dream. Lincoln has suggested that nonliterates either interpret the explicit manifest content of a dream without looking for latent meanings, like the Huron, or go beyond the explicit manifest content and look for latent symbolic meaning, like the Ashanti. The concept that different groups have of dreams varies, but dreams do appear to be important in many cultures. Tylor (q.v.) first emphasized how early cultures often gave the dream a reality like that of the external world. See DREAMS, PRIMITIVE.

intersexuality. A blending of feminity and masculinity resulting from an incomplete distinction of secondary and primary sexual characters.

interstadial. The period between glacial phases, within a major glaciation. The three last glacial phases, which are phases of one glaciation, were separated by cool-temperate interstadials.

intervocalic. Referring to a consonant or group of consonants written or spoken between two vowels, e.g., in *abacus* the *b*.

intichiuma. A Central Australian ceremony the purpose of which is to supply food and other necessities through certain magical activities apportioned to the various totem groups. The ceremonies usually were directed at supplying more of the edible totem animals. The intichiuma is also called the talu.

intonation. In a sentence or thought unit, the melody or pitch accent used to modify meanings. In English, intonation makes the distinction between statement and question, e.g., *He has gone* is a statement if the final pitch falls, a question if it rises. In the so-called tonal languages, notably Chinese, the intonation (or tone) is an integral part of each word along with the other phonemes (q.v.).

introvert. A type of person, described by C. G. Jung, who is more concerned about his relationship to himself than with the outside world.

Inuit. The Eskimo name for themselves, literally meaning "men."

inuksuk. An Eskimo likeness of a man, made by piling up several rocks a few feet high. It is set up to serve as a convenient guidepost for hunting, especially ambushing caribou. These guideposts are 50 to 150 yards apart. Real persons stand in line with the inusksiut (plural) approximately every half mile. When the caribou appear, the real persons begin moving, and evidently the caribou then thinks the inuksiut are humans.

invalidicide. The killing of invalids.

invention. A change or adjustment in objects or practices so that a new kind emerges. Every change in human activity which is deliberate and designed is an invention. The change, according to Dixon, is always new and basically better. Invention may apply to nonmaterial as well as to material culture. See DISCOVERY. Some theorists believe that the presence of similar or identical traits in different cultures may be explained by independent invention instead of by convergence (q.v.) or diffusion (q.v.).

invention, basic. The original and seminal invention of its kind.

invention, improving. An invention designed to add to or modify a basic invention.

invisibility. In folklore, the state of not being seen through the operation of some magical object, such as a cap, cloak, or ring.

invisibility, cap of. An object that permits its wearer to see while remaining invisible. Such objects are found in folklore from different parts of the world, e.g., Hades' cap, or the northern European Tarnhut.

Io. A god of the Maori who is known only to the upper classes and includes everything in himself.

Ipiutak. An early northwest Eskimo culture from which many stone and carved bone artifacts of Neolithic type have been found near Point Hope, Alaska. This culture appears to have arisen from the earliest Eskimo culture and to have flourished during the first half of the first millennium A.D.

I.Q. See QUOTIENT, INTELLIGENCE.

Iranian. An Indo-European language family related to Sanskrit. Many of the Zoroastrian hymns were written in Iranian.

Iranian Plateau. A white Mediterranean subrace including peoples living in Mesopotamia, Iran, and northwest India. Important traits are prominent cheek bones, a high hooked nose, large skull, long narrow heads and faces, brown eyes, brown or black wavy hair, and considerable hirsuteness.

iron. Iron is harder than bronze, making it desirable for weapons and tools. It is probable that the first iron used was meteoric iron (q.v.), as iron in the native state is otherwise scarce. Its smelting probably began ca. 2000 B.C. south of the Black Sea. It was used industrially in Egypt ca. 13th century B.C. and began replacing bronze in the Aegean ca. 1200-1100 B.C. African Negroes used iron widely, often passing directly from stone to iron. Iron was first fused in Europe in the 15th century A.D. It has been widely used because it can be hammered, cast, or molded in different forms and because of its hardness, strength, and magnetic properties.

Iron is widely used as a charm and its use is often prohibited in religious ceremonies, e.g., the Hebrews did not use it in building altars. Some people regard iron as having come from heaven, e.g., the Egyptians and Babylonians.

It is not known how iron was first discovered. Suggestions are that a piece of ironstone may have been reduced in a campfire, copper rich in iron was smelted, or a metal believed to be tin or lead was smelted inadvertently.

iron, crimping. An iron bar embedded in two parts of a stone wall to hold them together.

iron, meteoric. Iron coming from meteors. This nickeliferous iron was widely used by early man, as most of it is very malleable. Moreover, the dark stones look like copper and might have been used because of this resemblance. Some of these meteor fragments were small and lent themselves to tool-making, e.g., the meteor of Canyon Diablo, Arizona, which is in thousands of small fragments. Attila and the Caliphs also had their "swords from heaven." The words for iron in ancient languages show that most had a celestial source. In Babylonia, iron is indicated by two characters for "heaven" and "fire." In Egyptian, iron is represented by "marvel from heaven."

Iron, Teutonic. The time, ca. 500 B.C., of the merging of the Hallstatt and La Tène periods, primarily in northern Europe and Germany.

iron, wrought. Bloom (q.v.) which has had its slag removed and which has been reheated and beaten into solid pieces.

Iron Age. See AGE, IRON.

Iroquoian. A North American language family. It is found from the Gulf of St. Lawrence to Lake Erie, and among some groups in North and South Carolina.

irregular. Referring to grammatical forms that are exceptions to a general statement and that must be presented in a separate list.

irreversibility, law of. The doctrine, based on orthogenesis (q.v.), that a biological group which has

become extinct cannot return, that an organ which has lost its physiological usefulness cannot again become useful, and that a species which degenerates into inferior forms cannot become powerful again.

irrigation. Supplying water by artificial means for areas where there is insufficient rainfall.

irrigation, basic. Irrigation resulting from dependence on a river's natural rise, as in Egypt's Nile Valley before 1902, when the Aswan dam was built to regulate the river's rising.

irrigation, perennial. Irrigation that can continue at all seasons because water can be conducted to the fields in irrigation canals and ditches.

ischium. The lower portion of the hip bone. The body weight rests on the ischium when seated.

Islam. The religion of the Moslems, the youngest of the great religions of the world. It arose in Arabia in the seventh century and is largely derived from heretical gnostic Christianity and Judaism. The major dogma of Islam is the absolute unity of Allah.

island, mythical. In folklore, an island where life is ideal and everything is delightful. The Islands of the Blessed, of Greek and Celtic folklore, are typical.

island, speech. A small circumscribed speech community within which all the people speak a different language from the inhabitants of the much larger surrounding area, e.g., the Pennsylvania Germans or the Dutch in New Holland, Michigan.

isobase. An imaginary or map line connecting points which had the same elevation in a given time period, e.g., since the last glacial era.

isocephaly. The systematic distortion of the natural proportions of the subjects of a visual composition so that they will all be of the same height for the purposes of design, e.g., in the classical Greek artistic style.

isogenous. Referring to stemming from the same origin.

isogloss. A line on a dialect map that separates areas with different dialects. Although linguistic differences have their own boundaries, these dialect boundaries are not usually very sharp.

isoglosses, bundle of. A group of isoglosses which runs in the same direction and is fairly contiguous geographically.

isograph. A line drawn on a linguistic map that denotes a likeness in the use of sounds, vocabulary, grammer, or inflection.

isohet. A line connecting all points in an area with the same annual rainfall.

isolation. The separation of one group from similar groups; an individual in a group being apart from, and not organically participating in, the group of which he is nominally a member.

isophenogamy. Mating between persons who resemble each other somatically to a greater degree than

would be expected under random mating, e.g., short persons marrying one another.

isopoll. A line that connects points with equal pollen percentages during equal periods of time. The term is applied to fossil pollen.

isostasy. The process by which the earth's crust gradually rises as glaciation melts.

isotropic. Referring to an object that has the same properties in all directions.

Israel, Lost 10 Tribes of. The unconfirmed belief that King Sargon of Assyria in 721 B.C. sent 10 of the 12 tribes of Israel to captivity. These tribes have been reported in different parts of the world and have been identified with the American Indians, Anglo-Saxons, and other groups.

ithyphallic. Referring to those objects of worship in phallic religions that contain exaggerated sexual organs; more specifically, the phallus carried during the festival of Dionysius. It also refers to a graphic representation of males with erect penes. Thus, Greek vases of the fifth century B.C. often show satyrs with erections in hot pursuit of reluctant nymphs.

Itzcouatl. The first ruler of the Aztec tribes.

ivy. A plant that has been widely used for medicine as well as symbolically. It was sacred in Egypt, crowned victorious athletes in Greece, represents the soul's immortality in some religions, and also represents the female or fertility.

J

jacales. Square Pashetuake huts.

jackass, laughing. See KOOKA-BURRA.

jackstone. A small stone, or a game played with several such stones.

jade. A name given to nephrite and jadeite, both of which take a high polish and were highly prized in Neolithic times. They were used for implements, to effect cures, to rejuvenate the dead, in prayer gongs, in sacrificial knives, and as charms. Jade is exceedingly varied in color, with white, green, coral, and black being among the most highly prized varieties.

jandi. An early type of water transport consisting of a large tanned skin with holes around the edges. Dry grass is placed on the skin and hide ropes are passed through the holes and over the grass. Both goods and persons were carried on this device. It is still in use in Gojam province in Ethiopia.

jangada. A fishing raft of Brazil.

Japhetic. A term originated by G. W. von Leibnitz (1646-1716) to designate a language group which corresponds approximately to the Indo-European family of languages. It also is a theoretical language family, supposed to include North Caucasian, South Caucasian, Sumerian, Elamite, Asianic, Basque, Etruscan, and other extinct European languages, advanced by N. Marr, and now generally repudiated.

jar, canopic. See JARS, CANOPIC.

jar, whistling. A pottery vessel, usually double, having a system of passages which admit air as liquid is poured out, making a whistling sound. The whistling jar is especially characteristic of pre-Columbian Andean and Middle American ceramics.

jargon. A spontaneously developed language, with limited vocabulary and grammar, often found in a situation in which there are several languages in contact with each other. It is also a simplified and conventionalized version of a dominant language (q.v.); or the specialized terminology of a science, trade, or profession.

jargon, Chinook. A lingua franca of the Pacific Northwest region of America, which is a combination of Chinook, Nootka, English and French words.

Jarmo. A mound in northern Iraq, discovered by Robert Braidwood, which has been carbon-14 dated at 4758 B.C. + 320. It is one of the sites which has been discussed as perhaps the first beginning of agriculture, since it shows traces of cereal cultivation and of domestication. Jarmo was a prepottery culture.

jars, canopic. The set of four jars used by the Egyptians to encase the organs removed from the dead body during mummification. The jars accompanied the body in the tomb chamber so that the whole body would be present for the journey to the next world.

jasper. An opaque quartz used for statues, vases, and gems. It was sometimes a medicine, a magical stone, a protection against lightning, or a charm to lead to success in war.

jasper ware. See WARE, JASPER.

Java Ape Man. See PITHECANTHROPUS ERECTUS.

javelin. A spear for throwing, as opposed to thrusting.

jerkin. A fairly short coat.

jestbook. A collection of short stories directed against a disliked class, often incorporating apparently innocent jokes. The period from 1500 to 1700 saw the full flourishing of the jestbook. Mottley's 18th-century collection, attributed to Joe Miller, has become well known.

jet. A fossilized coniferous wood that was probably washed to sea, and, after impregnation with salt water, was embedded in mud that hardened into a sort of shale. It has many of the properties of amber (q.v.), and was used for ornaments in the Neolithic and Bronze Ages.

jettatura. The spell cast by a person with the evil eye (q.v.).

jettatore. Someone who is believed to have the evil eye (q.v.).

Jew. A Jew must be regarded simply as a person with the religious or cultural background called "Jewish." Jews are neither a race nor a racial subdivision, nor is any group of Jews anatomically dissimilar from the larger culture of which it forms a part. Although certain elements of religion are common to all Jews, many new subcultures were developed by Jews in the diaspora (q.v.), through integrating and adapting parts of neighboring cultures with the more traditional elements of Judaism.

The Jews have formed a number of languages of their own, such as Yiddish (q.v.) and Dzhudezmo ("Judeo-Spanish"), while retaining Hebrew for religious purposes and reviving it as the national language of Israel.

The Jews emerged as a group ca. 1200 B.C., when they arrived in Palestine, probably from southern Mesopotamia. They had largely Mediterranean physical features. Palestine at the time was populated by Philistines and Amorites, who were Mediterranean, and by some Iranian Plateau (q.v.) groups. After 586 B.C., when the Temple was first destroyed, many Jews dispersed in neighboring countries and developed new traits and racial mixtures. By 70 A.D., when the Temple was again destroyed, the racial makeup of the Jews was fairly diverse.

The Jews of today are often divided into Sephardic Jews, centering around Asia Minor, North Africa, and eastern Europe, who are largely Mediterranean in type, and Ashkenazic Jews, who are found in Europe and America and have no clear-cut physical characteristics, except perhaps for some Mediterranean and Iranian Plateau features.

Seltzer has pointed out that the high and frequently convex nose of the Iranian Plateau and the thick wavy hair, lips, and large lidded eyes of the Mediterranean may be found often enough in Jews of today to help in distinguishing them as such, although none of these characteristics is exclusively Jewish. Many Jews in Israel (founded as a Jewish state in 1948) are blond, blue-eyed, and light in complexion, while 45 per cent of the Polish Jews had light eyes and 29 per cent of Lithuanian Jews were blond.

Non-Caucasoids have adopted the Jewish religion, including some Chinese, the Falasha in Ethiopia, and some American Negroes.

Jews' houses. See HOUSES, JEWS'.

Jew-Tongo. See ENGLISH, BUSH NEGRO.

jhuming. A form of agriculture in which trees in virgin forests are cut down and burned, and seeds are sown in the charcoal. When the land was exhausted, the group moved further into the forest. This kind of agriculture was found in the New Stone Age, although the term comes from the hill tribes of Burma, who practiced it up to recently.

jihad. A holy war, fought to convert nonbelievers to the Moslem doctrine.

jimsonweed. A plant with a toxic white bell-shaped flower, the center of a cult in southern California and Arizona. It is chewed and drunk as an intoxicant in Colombia and Ecuador. From it the drug toloache is extracted. It is also used as an aphrodisiac, an anaphrodisiac, or a poultice.

jingler. An early type of rattle (q.v.) found among some nomadic groups. Jinglers are often made of animal hoofs.

jinn. In Moslem lore, a long-lived being who is invisible and can assume any shape. Jinns may cause diseases, especially if they are annoyed. They quickly punish even inadvertent violators of their many rules.

jinrikisha. See RICKSHA.

John Canoe dance. See DANCE, JOHN CANOE.

joiking. Lapp singing.

joss stick. See STICK, JOSS.

jötunn. In Teutonic mythology, a giant representing hostile natural forces.

"Judeo-Spanish." A language of Sephardic Jews which in its spoken form is often called Dzhudezmo and in the stylized form used for the Bible and semi-sacred texts is called Ladino.

juju. In West Africa, a fetish or its power.

jujube. A large brush or small spiny tree which has a small dark-brown fleshy drupe. Its fruit is olive-sized. The jujube has been grown in China for thousands of years.

Junggrammatiker. The neogrammarians (as Leskien, Osthoff, and Brugmann were called), who espoused the principle that sound changes follow laws without exceptions. This position has been attacked by those who maintain that phonetic laws do not have the validity of physical laws.

junk. In shipping, a vessel with neither a sternpost nor a keel. It has both a transom head and a transom stern. The rudder is rectangular and is suspended in a well in the center of the stern projection hanging over the upper works of the keel.

In music, an ancient Arabian stringed instrument made of a 26-inch wood case fitted with a sound box in the shape of a triangle and containing one sound hole. The six strings are attached to a polished wood neck at one end.

juoigen. A specially sacred prayer of the Lapps used to communicate with ancestors.

Jurassic. A life period of the Mesozoic era characterized by the earliest birds, modern fishes, and the peak of reptile development. In this period, the seas swept over large areas of Asia, Europe, and North America. It lasted from perhaps 170 to 140 million years ago.

jus primae noctis. A custom found in various early cultures and perhaps in medieval Europe. It gave the head of the tribe or other group the right to sleep with a woman on the first night after her marriage. There is considerable scholarly controversy over whether or not the jus primae noctis actually obtained in Europe. The term literally means the "law of the first night." Another term is the droit de seigneur (French "lord's right"). In parts of Polynesia, the chief publicly performed a defloration ceremony on a woman just before her marriage.

K

ka. In ancient Egyptian belief, a special phase of the personality that is born simultaneously with the person. The ka helped the person during life and after death. It was one of the seven parts of man.

Kaaba. See CAABA.

kabaka. The Baganda king.

kabalai. A leather water bucket in southern India.

kachina or katcina. A mask, statuette, or other object, used in rituals by the Arizona Hopi and other Pueblo Indians. Men wearing or carrying the kachinas represent supernatural persons, who are often identified with the dead. These supernatural persons are mythical ancestors of human beings who are believed to visit the earth during the winter and to spend the other half of the year in the spirit world. Their appearance and departure is an occasion for dramatic ceremonies. When kachinas are killed, they are believed to turn into deer. The kachinas used to bring corn, rain, and melons; they gave their masks to men so that they could accomplish benevolent acts through impersonation. The masks are not realistic and vary greatly in design.

The term kachina was also used to describe the niches in the ceremonial chambers in which the objects were placed when not in use. The form kokko is sometimes found.

Kadaklan. The supreme being among the Tinguian.

kadangian. A rich family head among the Bontoc.

Kafir-Sotho. A southeast African group of Bantu languages in which there are clicks made by inspiring air to create a smacking sound like a kiss.

kaftan. A wool or cotton padded coat often worn by the Kazak but also used throughout the Middle East.

Kageen. The Bushman name for the Mantis (q.v.).

kahunga. See TOHUNGA.

Kainozoic. See CENOZOIC.

kakina. A method of staining the skin by drawing a needle and a soot-impregnated thread under and through the skin.

kakko. A small Japanese drum. It originated in Tibet or Turkestan. The kakko has a parchment head stretched over hoops that are of greater diameter than the shell. The edges of the head project and are laced togethed with cords of skin.

kakoshi. An African stringed instrument played with a bow. It is made from a hollow body and may or may not have a sounding board. Halfway down its length is a crossbar from which the strings are stretched to pegs that are roughly inserted in the long neck. The crossbar is fastened into position with long strips of skin.

kaldebekel. In the Marianne and Caroline Islands, clubs organized by young men so that they may associate with unmarried girls in a special resort called a Bai.

Kalevala. The national hero epic of Finland.

kaloa. A log raft of northern Australia.

kalu. Among the Fijians, anything marvelous or relating to the deity.

Kamasian. The first of the great pluvial periods recognized from the geological strata of Kenya.

kami. In Japan, deities resident in shrines. They are ancestral spirits or gods in the Shinto religion.

kamitok. The killing of the aged among the Chukchee.

kampong. A Malayan term for a house.

kamui. Among the Ainu, specially exalted objects.

Kanaka. A usually derogative term for native tribes in the Pacific, especially common among French colonials in New Caledonia.

Kanarese. A language belonging to the Dravidian family of languages, spoken by approximately 15 million persons in southern India, Mysore, and Hyderabad.

Kane. See TANE.

k'ang. A Chinese heating device consisting of a horizontal subterranean flue that forms a platform in a room. Fuel is burned with as little draft as possible. The k'ang is a permanent installation in a building.

kanoon. An ancient Turkish musical instrument with 75 gut strings stretched over a wooden body in sets of three. The strings are fastened to pegs at one end, stretched over a bridge, and anchored to the interior. The upper face is formed of wood and the lower of parchment.

Kant, Immanuel (1724-1804). A great German philosopher who wrote a book on "anthropology" and made basic contributions to the study of race. In 1775, he gave and published lectures on the "various races of man," probably the first formal lectures on anthropology. Kant emphasized theories rather than the external traits of race.

kantele. The national musical instrument of Finland. It is a trapeze-shaped psaltery. Finnish legend tells that Wainomoinen, the heavenly musician, originally constructed its frame from the bones and its tuning pegs from the teeth of a pike.

kanuna. An ancient Indian stringed instrument made of a three-sided wooden body. Each of its 26 strings is attached to a separate peg and stretched over a single bridge to the opposite end. The strings are struck with hammers.

kaolin. The white China clay used to make porcelain (q.v.). It is a decayed feldspar rock. Kaolin requires a fusing agent because it is nonfusible itself. The term comes from the Chinese for "high ridge," where it was first found. Kaolin is sometimes called bolus clay or china clay.

kaolinite. An ingredient of certain types of clay. It is a soft, white, earthy mineral.

kap kap. An ornament from Oceania made from carved tortoise shell mounted on polished sea shell.

karma. Among the Hindus, the relations between cause and effect, or the law governing those relations in the case of individual conduct. Karma concerns the relation of a person's ethical behavior to what will happen to him in future incarnations. In effect, the individual's condition in any of his incarnations is the merited result of his behavior in past existences; thus the individual and his karma may be said to be one.

karnal. An old Persian metal trumpet about two feet long. It has a cup mouthpiece and the other end is in the form of a bell.

kaross. A robe made of sewn skins held together over the shoulders by a thong.

karst. An area with sinks, abrupt ridges, protuberant irregular rocks, underground streams, and caverns.

karyatid. See CARYATID.

karyotype. The morphology of the chromosomes of a type, usually showing length, breadth, number, and similar information.

kasso. An African stringed instrument, most often found on the West Coast. It is made from a large gourd section sealed with a parchment membrane. The parchment is pierced with a long straight wooden stick. Underneath the membrane are four more sticks that protrude from the edge of the gourd, two parallel to the strings and two at right angles. The strings are fastened with loops.

katakana. One of the systems of syllable writing used in Japan. It derives from the standard Chinese ideograms and is chiefly used in scientific literature and official documents.

katcina. See KACHINA.

kathenotheism. The term used to describe the Hindu practice by which each god is supreme in his turn. The word was invented by Max Müller. Its literal meaning is "one-at-a-time theism."

katikoro. The Baganda prime minister.

katta. A digging stick (q.v.) in Australia.

katun. A Maya time period of 20 years of 360 days each.

kauri. A tall timber tree of New Zealand, *Agathis australis,* from which the Maori made their large dugout war canoes.

kauwa. Hawaiian slaves.

kava. A drink made from pepper plant roots in Melanesia and Polynesia. It is nonalcoholic.

kayak. A canoe made of skins, as found among some Eskimo and Indian peoples. It has an enclosed cockpit in the center and a deck of skin and is sharp at each end. The kayak is built upside down, and its cover is often the skin of the bearded seal with the hair removed. Only a racing shell can approach its speed. The kayak can be used in rough waters and breakers. The traveler gets into the cockpit and has his legs stretched out at an almost 90-degree angle. In Greenland and elsewhere, a waterproof coat covers the kayak cockpit and the neck and wrists of the traveler, so that the kayak and the clothing are contiguous and waterproof. Learning to get out of a kayak takes considerable skill.

kazoo. A musical instrument consisting of a tube with a vibrating membrane that changes the quality of the voice.

Keet Seel. A cliff village of the Anasazi Indians that was constructed in the tremendous Laguna Canyon in northern Arizona. There are more than 150 rooms and underground kivas (q.v.) in the village. The name in Navaho literally means "broken pottery."

Keilor. A South Australian skull found in 1940, probably some 100,000 years old, of the third interglacial level or post-Pleistocene era. It is very similar to Homo wadjakensis (q.v.). The skull capacity is ca. 1,590 c.c., while recent Australoid skulls average 1,290 c.c.

kelek. A raft buoyed up by 50 to 1,000 inflated sheep- and goatskins. It is found in Iraq and Armenia. The kelek existed thousands of years ago and is still in use today, primarily to carry cargo.

kelim. A technique of weaving in which slits are left between contiguous warp threads in the finished cloth. This technique was used in ancient Peru in the making of ponchos.

keloid. A raised scar. A keloid results from initiating a scar or introducing foreign matter into the skin or from a tumor.

kelp. A large seaweed used by the Northwest Coast Indians. The floating bulbous end piece serves for bottles, and the long hollow stalk is a speaking tube in various ceremonies, including some of a slapstick nature.

kelpie. An Australian sheep dog developed ca. 1870 from a smooth-haired collie and a bitch that was part collie and part dingo (q.v.). The kelpies are smooth-haired and prick-eared.

Keltic or **Celtic.** 1 A Caucasoid subrace with light eyes, dark or red hair, and long heads. It is concentrated in Ireland. 2 A group of the Indo-European family of languages. It is divided into the Goidelic branch (Irish or Irish Gaelic, Scots Gaelic, and Manx) and the Brythonic branch (Breton, Welsh, Cornish). Gaulish, the oldest member, has been long extinct.

Keokuk. A Sauk Indian, who became chief of that tribe because of his outstanding ability, despite the fact that he was not of the chiefly clan. He advocated peace and remained neutral during the Black Hawk war.

Keo-phay. Referring to hewn axes of a type found in Tonkin.

kere-kere. A system of reciprocity among the Fijians.

kernel. Among words related by affixation (q.v.), the root phonetic element common to all the words.

300

kero. A beaker or cup made of pottery or wood during the Inca period in Peru.

kerres. An open Lapp sleigh consisting of thin canoe-shaped planks about five feet long.

ketosis. A condition in which acetoacetic acid and acetone are in the blood.

key. In many religions, a key represented a technique of reaching heaven, and many deities were supposed to carry keys. Keys also have magical and medicinal qualities.

khamsin. A warm dry wind which blows over Egypt for some 50 days in the spring.

Khan. A Mongol sovereign.

khasm beyt. A subsection of the Kababish tribe.

khetem. An ancient Egyptian roller seal about one to four inches long. It was inscribed in intaglio or relief and dipped into pigment or dye before being rolled to make an imprint. Some good examples of the khetem are made of ivory, wood, porcelain, and copper. The type dates back to the Sixth dynasty and developed into the signet ring worn on the finger.

khipu. See QUIPU.

Khoin or **Khoisan.** See HOTTEN-TOT-BUSHMAN.

kia. A Pima carrying bag.

kiama. The second age grade (q.v.) of the Kikuyu.

kiaotsu. A Chinese palanquin.

kibitka. A permanent yurt (q.v.) built on a platform and drawn by oxen.

Kieselguhr. A clay of very fine quality used not only for ceramics but also for painting.

killer, slave. A clublike implement used to kill slaves on the Northwest Coast. The slaves were killed to show their owner's disregard for property during potlatches.

killick. A small anchor; or an anchor made by a stone enclosed by pieces of wood.

killing, mercy. Killing a person for humane reasons, in a minimally painful manner. Mercy killing is also called euthanasia.

killing, second. A method used to keep the body from escaping from the grave. Nails are driven through the skull or the body to boards in the grave.

kiln. A large stove used for hardening, burning, or drying pottery and similar objects. The kiln is sometimes called the pot oven.

kilolo. The parliament among the Lunda of the Congo.

kimbugwe. The keeper of the royal umbilical cord among the Baganda.

kin. Blood relations. The recognition of the relationship may be culturally conditioned.

kin, mother-. Tracing relationships and transmitting names through women.

kinandi. The "devil's harp" of Africa, a stringed musical instrument similar to the Greek lyre and thought to have been brought to Africa by the Phoenicians. Sometimes very crude kinandis are made from ordinary tin pans with stretched camel skin across the top. It is believed by many tribes that the kinandi has magical power.

kindred. The grouping of relatives by bilateral descent (q.v.). The kindred is the most frequently found kind of bilateral kin group. Murdock uses the term to mean a group of individuals with a relative in common, while *Notes and Queries* uses it for a group of individuals with an ancestor in common.

kinesics. The systematic investigation of nonvocal movements of the body that are relevant to communication.

king. A male sovereign ruler, often with spiritual as well as temporal powers. Special religious activities may be attached to the kingship if the king is associated with certain deities.

kinnikinnick. A mixture of red willow bark, the inner leaves of a kind of dogwood, other leaves, and tobacco. It was smoked by hunters and Indians in the western part of the United States.

kinnor or **kynnor.** A musical instrument that looks like a small harp. Among the ancient Hebrews, it was played along with percussion instruments by street musicians.

kinship. The social recognition and expression of genealogical relationships, both consanguineal and affinal. Kinship systems may include socially recognized relationships based on supposed as well as actual genealogical ties. The study of kinship systems is one of the oldest, and is still considered by many to be one of the most important, elements in the study of social organization. Kinship terms (q.v.) can be studied linguistically, ethnographically, sociologically, and psychologically. It has been suggested by Radcliffe-Brown that there is a high

correlation between social organization and kin terminology. Rivers has noted that particular terminological features reflect particular features of social organization, and Kroeber has emphasized the role of language in systems of terminology.

kinship, agnatic. See KINSHIP, PATRILINEAL.

kinship, classificatory. Placing relatives of different genetic relationship in the same kinship status.

kinship, matrilineal or **kinship, uterine.** Kinship that is traced only through females.

kinship, patrilineal or **kinship, agnatic.** Kinship that is traced only through males.

kinship, totemic. A blood relationship between the members of a sib (q.v.) who have a common totem (q.v.).

kinship, uterine. See KINSHIP, MATRILINEAL.

kinship group. See GROUP, KINSHIP.

kirn. The last sheaves of the harvest, or a harvest festival.

kissar. An ancient African musical instrument, like a lyre. It is usually made of a gourd but sometimes of a tortoise shell or even a human skull. Attached to this body are two vertical rods with a crossbar. The strings are attached to the crossbar and stretched over a bridge to the lower edge of the body.

kist or **kistvaen.** See CIST.

kite. A kind of float (q.v.) used by the fisherman to keep the bait moving along the water's surface.

kithaka. Land holdings of the Kikuyu.

kithara. A musical instrument consisting of a heavy wooden body with a crossbar to which strings are attached. There was a handle used to change the instrument's pitch or slacken the string's pitch. There were up to 11 strings. The kithara was used for instrumental solos and played by virtuosi. The spelling cithara is sometimes found. It is associated with the ancient Greeks, and Apollo as leader of the Muses was sometimes called a kitharedus.

kithito. A charm used in oaths among the Wakamba.

kiva. An underground chamber built by the Hopi Indians of the southwest United States for ceremonial uses. The earliest forms were circular and it is thought that they doubled as dwellings. Later kivas were rectangular and were entirely for religious rites and for relaxation and meetings, mainly by men. These chambers always contained benches (q.v.). The entrance to the kiva is on its roof. Kivas existed in the pueblos of New Mexico and Arizona and in the early pueblos of Utah and Colorado.

kiva corner, exterior. Triangular spaces that resulted when a circular kiva was built within a rectangular room.

Klallam. See SOCIETY, KLALLAM.

Klemm, Gustav (1802-1867). A German, who from early childhood was a passionate collector of specimens and facts. He anticipated Tylor's classical definition of culture and was familiar with the notion of evolution (q.v.) before Darwin. He postulated three stages of cultural development.

Klintidie. A society for old men with prestige among the Kiowa Apache.

klong khek. A Siamese drum. It is a hollow cylinder, both ends of which are covered with tightly stretched parchment fastened with laced hoops of tree bark or animal skin.

knapping. Shaping artifacts of stone, usually flint.

knife. A cutting implement with a longitudinally edged blade. Knives have been made of different materials, with the earliest probably of stone. Knives from the first two epochs of the Bronze Age are rare but are more frequent in deposits of the third and fourth epochs. Three kinds of knife appear in that age: knives attached to the handle by a tongue, knives with a socket for hafting, and knives with handles and blades cast in one piece. Knives are often classified into knives proper, used to cut; knife-daggers, used in a cutting-thrust; and stilettos, used only to thrust. The knife may be a folklore symbol of bad luck, or on the other hand, an iron knife may symbolize good luck.

knife, bolo. A knife used in the Philippines as a utensil and weapon. There are various shapes and sizes of bolo knife.

knife, leaf. A knife that was used to strip leaves from trees as winter feed for cattle. It is a sickle-blade which is in line with the handle.

knitting. Netting which has meshes drawn so tightly that it forms coherent fabric. Knitting is done with movable needles or pins that are fixed and then withdrawn. The garment or fabric is made from one yarn by using two needles which alternately hold the material and make a new row of interlacing loops.

knobkerrie. A knobbed throwing club found in South Africa.

knock-knee. The condition in which the feet remain apart while the knees come together.

knot, magic. Knots in magic and religion symbolize a holding together or a keeping apart. In Brahman marirage, e.g., knots on the sacred girdle stand for marriage's binding character. The Jew's phylacteries represent the Torah's (Law's) binding qualities. In Saxony and India, during parturition, knots were untied so as not to impede the child's birth. Knots have served as magical contraceptives. Many early peoples untie knots in order to avoid disease, a taboo, or a spell.

knot, starting. The beginning of a piece of basketry, usually made by crossing the first warp sticks in pairs and then binding them together, so that the weft can be manipulated.

knuckleduster. A device used in boxing to protect the knuckles and add force to a punch. An example is the Roman cestus.

ko. A New Caledonian spirit leaving the body during sleep.

kobong. A totem (q.v.) social group in Australia.

kohau. Pictographic tablets carved by the early inhabitants of Easter Island.

kohl. A black and green cosmetic used by the Egyptians to paint the eyebrows and eyelids and make the eyes look larger. It consisted of lead sulphate, lead sulphide, and green carbonate of copper.

koilorachic. Referring to a vertical lumbar index (q.v.) of more than 102.

koine. A language customarily used by a group in a self-contained region within a broader linguistic area. Ordinarily it results from a compromise among several dialects of a language. Koine is also a standard system for writing based on the Attic characters and adopted by the Macedonian kings in the fourth century B.C.

kokko. See KACHINA.

köksskal. A conical kitchen hut, found in Sweden. It is made of round poles bound together in a cone shape. The lowest third of the hut is covered with spruce rind.

kola. The bitter nut of two tree species found in tropical America. It is about the size of a chestnut. Kola contains caffeine and theobromine and is chewed as a stimulant and condiment and its extract used as a tonic.

Kolaskin cult. See CULT, KOLASKIN.

kole-kole. In the Banks Islands, a feast in honor of something achieved or built. The kole-kole permanently sets the honored object aside from similar objects.

koli. A Hindu farm labor group of farmers and tenants, in India.

Kolotl. A dog-faced Aztec god.

komag. A Lapp winter boot.

Kona. The Japanese area of Hawaii.

kona. Hawaiian coffee.

kondo. The main chamber or hall of worship in a Buddhist temple. The literal meaning is "golden hall."

kookaburra. A big-headed Australian kingfisher. Its call resembles human laughter more than that of any other wild bird.

Koran. The most sacred Mohammedan book. It includes all the moral laws of the religion, a chronicle of the life of the prophet Mohammed, and a graphic description of heaven, hell, and the day of judgment.

kore. See PO.

koro. A neurotic condition found in Chinese residents of Indonesia and South China. The affected person feels that his penis is retracting to the abdomen. Pathologies like hernia or edema of the abdomen may provoke koro.

koshung. A political group of the Mongols equal to a banner (q.v.).

kosi. The Trobriand Islanders' soul substance.

Koterey. A mutual-aid society among the Songhoi.

Kouali. An archaeological site on the Algerian seacoast, excavated in 1949. In the several layers of artifacts that were uncovered there were flint tools, stone implements, and stone chips, indicating that implements were fashioned at the site. Blade tools like those of the Aterian culture of the Paleolithic Age were also found. Underneath these layers were mingled late Neolithic and early Roman pottery, establishing that elements of the latest prehistoric cultures were still in existence in Roman times.

kouitara. A pear-shaped African musical instrument, chiefly Moroccan, with four pairs of strings. Usually it is highly decorated.

koundyeh. An African stringed instrument from the Sierra Leone region. It is constructed from half a coconut shell covered by a parchment with a central sound hole. One string is stretched on a long wooden neck. The term ngiemah is also used.

kowtow. A Chinese ceremonial of respect involving touching one's head to the ground several times while kneeling on both knees.

kra. In the Gold Coast area, a ghost-like second self.

kraal. An enclosure which holds sheep, cattle, or elephants, or a small native village in South Africa and its way of life, often used by Kaffirs or Hottentots.

kratzer. See SCRAPER, END.

kris or **kriss.** A Malay dagger.

kstau. A turf, stone, or wood winter hut of the Kazak.

Kuksu cult. See CULT, KUKSU.

Kukulcan. A Maya deity whose name means "plumed serpent." It is equivalent to the Quetzalcoatl of the Aztec.

kula. A circular system of exchanging goods, found in New Guinea. See RING, KULA.

Kulturfall. See ACCULTURATION.

Kulturgeschichtliche Methode. See KULTURKREIS.

Kulturkreis. The area that is characterized by, and radiates outward, a specific culture circle. The theory, usually associated with Wilhelm Schmidt, postulates a diffusion (q.v.) of successive culture aggregates.

It holds that it is possible to trace the paths along which culture complexes have diffused by plotting the geographical points at which the constituent traits are found. The application of this technique is called the Kulturgeschichtliche Methode. See METHOD, CULTURE HISTORICAL.

Kulturkreistheorie. The school of anthropological thought, associated with Foy, Graebner, and Schmidt, which deals with the influence of the Kulturkreis (q.v.). See METHOD, CULTURE HISTORICAL.

kumara. The Polynesian name for the sweet potato. It is thought to have reached Polynesia in pre-Columbian times from Peru, where it was known as *kumar*.

kumiss or **kumyss.** A brandy made from camel and donkey milk, fermented with butter. It probably originated in the Far East.

Kunai grass. See GRASS, KUNAI.

Kupe. A mythical explorer from Tahiti, who is credited with the discovery of New Zealand in the middle of the 10th century.

kurdaitja. A sorcerer, and often executioner, in Australia, especially among the Arunta.

kurgan. In South Russia, a burial mound dating from Neolithic and Bronze Age days.

kurtar. A musical instrument found in India. It is made of two clappers with curved handles. Small metal disks are inserted into the clappers and small bells jingle at the sides.

kurtorachic. Referring to a vertical lumbar index (q.v.) ranging up to 97.9.

kurtosis. A relatively flat frequency curve, as compared with a normal frequency curve.

kussir. A Turkish musical instrument, stringed and percussion. The body of the kussir is similar to a kettle drum, with its top covered with skin across which the five strings are stretched.

kutturu. A stick used for fighting in central Australia.

Kutukhtu or **Hutukhtu.** The Lamaist high priest living at Urga.

kwanga. The African name for a manioc cake.

Kwat. A secret society (q.v.) of the Banks Islands.

kwatje-purra. A rain-making stick among the Arunta.

Kwi-Iru. A secret society (q.v.) of the Kru of West Africa.

Kylver. A fifth-century Scandinavian memorial stone honoring the dead. It was ornamented with elementary linear designs and inscribed with runes (q.v.). It dates from the period just before the Viking culture of the sixth to the eighth century. The Kylver was used very successfully to decipher the old runic alphabet.

kymograph. A device utilizing a pen attached to one of the speech organs to study its movements.

kynnor. See KINNOR.

L

La Tène. The second part of the Iron Age, dating ca. 400 B.C.-100 A.D. It is primarily centered in France.

la'a. A fish net of the Solomon Islands.

label, mummy or **label, wooden.** The identification tag for a mummy or a thin slab of wood on which the name of the mummy is inscribed. It was usually about two by five inches. It had a hole in one end through which a papyrus string was run so that the label could be tied around the mummy. Archaeologists call it the wooden label, and the term mummy ticket is also used.

labial. A sound made by using the lips, e.g., *f*.

labio-dental. A phonetic term used to describe any consonant produced with the lower lip touching the upper front teeth, e.g., the *f* in *forward*.

labio-velar. A term used in phonetics to describe any consonant produced with rounded lips and the back portion of the tongue arched toward the soft palate, e.g., the *w* in *water*.

labrale inferius. The midpoint of the upper margin of the lower membranous lip.

labrale superius. The midpoint of the upper margin of the upper membranous lip.

labret. An elongated wooden plug, worn in the lower lip, e.g., among the Aleut and Eskimo.

labrys. A double-bitted ax. It was a religious object in Crete.

lacustrine. Referring to or inhabiting a lake.

ladang. A dry land rice field.

ladder, Indian. A ladder made from a small trimmed tree, with the branches used as steps.

Ladino. 1 In Central America, persons who are urban-born, Spanish-speaking, and non-Indian. 2 The language used by Sephardic Jews for the translation of the Bible and other sacred and semi-sacred texts.

Ladinoization. The process in Central America of persons moving from the Indian culture to the Ladino culture.

ladle, socketed. A ladle with a perforated projection as a handle.

Ladogan. A hypothetical Upper Paleolithic element in parts of the

307

present-day European population; a hypothetical Caucasoid racial subdivision of the East Baltic area.

lag. A kind of assimilation (q.v.) in which a phoneme becomes like a preceding phoneme. Lag with substitution is the commonest kind.

lag, cultural. The retardation in the rate of change of one part of an interrelated culture complex as against another part, often used for a delay in translating a change in material culture to the nonmaterial techniques for controlling it.

lakalaka. A Fijian dance derived from the Tonga.

lakatoi. Large rafts on the south coast of New Guinea used for trading expeditions between Port Moresby and the Papuan Gulf.

lakay. A Tinguian headman (q.v.).

lake, subglacial. A water channel which forms below glacial ice and becomes a lake when the glacier disappears.

lake dwelling. See DWELLING, LAKE.

lakkek. Among the Lapp, a covered sleigh for carrying foods and provisions. It is made of thin planks with a covered oval or square opening.

lama. A priest in Tibet or Mongolia.

Lamarck, Jean Baptiste (1744-1829). A French zoologist who first made the distinction between vertebrates and invertebrates. He was the exponent of the idea of the inheritance of acquired characteristics and was perhaps first to develop a thorough theory of evolution.

lambda. The point where the sagittal and lambdoid sutures meet.

lambdaism. The use of another phoneme (most often r) in place of the phoneme l.

lambdoid. Referring to a shape like the Greek letter lambda, e.g., the lambdoid suture.

lame à encoche. See SCRAPER, NOTCHED.

lamellar. Referring to a long thin blade taken off a polyhedral core in a blow, or referring to layers.

lamia. In Greek mythology, a mythical woman who ate children.

lamp, float. A lamp consisting of a bowl filled with water and oil and a floating wick. It gives only a feeble light, although it is economical in using oil and was fairly safe because of the water. Float lamps are often correlated with cults.

lampadomancy. A method of divination (q.v.) in which omens are seen in the flame of a lamp.

lance. A weapon made of a fairly long handle and a sharp head.

lanceolate. Referring to being narrow and tapering to a point at the peak.

landmark. A specific point on the body from which anthropometric measurements are taken. Landmarks are intended to insure that these measurements are standardized.

lane, ice. A crack in the ice which is not narrow enough to be stepped over but can be crossed by emergency methods.

Lang, Andrew (1844-1912). An English folklorist and anthropologist, who was originally an ardent defender of Tylor's views on religion against the attacks of Max Müller. His *The Making of Religion* (1898) conflicted with his

own earlier defense of a chronological development of religion from
low to high gods. He demonstrated
that gods need not become more
ethical in higher cultures, and that
a high god could be found in simple
groups like the Baiamai of southwest Australia. Lang believed that
the high god was a separate development away from the major evolutionary line. He emphasized the
extent to which the high god was an
exaggerated man rather than a spiritual being.

langsuir. Among the Malay, the
spirit of a woman who died in giving birth.

language. A system of arbitrary
vocal symbols, used to express com-
municable thoughts and feelings,
and enabling the members of a social group or speech community to
interact and cooperate. Language is
essentially a convention in a speech
community, whereby certain sounds
are associated with certain ideas. At
the present time, there are at least
2,000 languages.

Language is as old as human society. From its possible origin in
Mesopotamia, Egypt, and China,
language may have spread over the
rest of the world within the limits
of history. Many students, however, consider it impossible to determine the origin of language.
Many languages are spoken by il-
literates and it is possible that a
great many more languages have
not been written down by their
speakers. Every language has dialects. There is a close relationship
between language and culture (q.v.).
Language is part of culture and is

socially transmitted. It is basic for
culture, as social cooperation without language is difficult. There is
evidence of a continuing cultural
tradition in the early Pleistocene,
and it may be assumed that language was present at this time.

Ethnology uses verbal behavior
as a valuable guidepost. The relation between semantic elements and
the people who speak the language
is important. Morphemes (q.v.)
seem to be correlated with environment, e.g., the Arabs have more
than 1,000 words for camel.

language, agglutinative. A language with many dependent morphemes (q.v.) or elements that appear in an established sequence
within words, e.g., Turkish. The
many summatory elements in such
a language have definite meanings
and are used in different words
where a similar meaning is necessary. The elements of agglutinative
languages are sometimes regarded as
"stuck on" to each other, hence the
name.

language, amalgamating. An inflected linguistic system in which
the affixes lose their independent
identity through a close linkage
with the roots of the words.

language, analytic. A language
wherein words that have no complete meaning in themselves except
in conjunction with other words
bearing an independent meaning
are the main or only method of
formulating syntactical relationships. An analytical language, thus,
becomes completely or partially uninflected. English and Chinese are
regarded as analytical languages in-

sofar as they depend on prepositions and conjunctions, rather than on word order, to express syntax.

language, animal. The language employed by animals to communicate with each other. Animal sounds are fairly uniform, within a species and in an individual. Animals do not seem to imitate each other, and it is not clear whether they imitate sounds. Animal cries are simple and there is some evidence that they are used to express recognition, and thus to express simple emotions.

language, auditory. Verbalization, as opposed to written, gesture, or other language.

language, centum. An Indo-European language characterized by the use of *k* to represent the proto-Indo-European guttural *k* sound, i.e., Greek, Italic, Celtic, Germanic, Hittite, and Tokharian.

language, classificatory. A language belonging to the Bantu family in which particular prefixes serve to indicate the class of a word.

language, creolized. A morphologically simplified version of a language of colonization (q.v.) which has become the only method of ordinary communication within a socially or politically subject group.

language, dead. Any language that has ceased to be used as a general medium of spoken communication, although its use among scholars and in writing and ritual may persist, e.g., Latin, Old Church Slavonic.

language, dominant. See BORROWING, INTIMATE.

language, flectional. A language in which syntactical relationships of words and/or shades and modifications of their meanings are accomplished by adding prefixes or suffixes to the roots. Agglutinative and amalgamating languages (q.v.) are flectional.

language, formless. A term used to describe the nonflectional languages, with particular reference to the languages in this category in which the words are unaltered by prefixes or suffixes and the meaning of which is conveyed purely by position in the sentence and the associated linguistic elements.

language, fully synthetic. See LANGUAGE, INFLECTIVE.

language, genderless. Any language in which no differentiation of words as to grammatical gender is found.

language, hybrid. A language made up in large part of borrowed words.

language, incapsulating. See LANGUAGE, POLYSYNTHETIC.

language, incorporating. See LANGUAGE, POLYSYNTHETIC.

language, inflective. A language in which there is a close relationship between the stem of a word and its prefix or suffix, and in which the relation between linguistic component and idea is less mechanical than in the agglutinative languages (q.v.). The Indo-European is the most important family of this type. The bound forms (q.v.) of inflective languages represent a merger of distinct features. The meaning of a word in these languages is changed by making changes to a stem or root, as in declining nouns in Latin. The term fully synthetic language is sometimes used.

language, isolating. A language in which there are no bound forms (q.v.) and the single word does not change form, e.g., Chinese. Each word represents a number of ideas, and it can be treated like any part of speech, depending on its position in the utterance.

language, juxtaposing. A language that shows syntactical relationships by putting classifiers in front of words representing the chief concepts, e.g., the Bantu languages.

language, living. A language which is the chief means of communication used by the larger number of the inhabitants within a particular area, geographical or national.

language, lower. See BORROWING, INTIMATE.

language, morphology of. The study of the construction and interrelations of words and their parts. There is great variation in the morphology of languages.

language, polysynthetic. A language that uses bound forms (q.v.) to designate objects, instruments, and other details of an action that in other languages are represented by separate words. Eskimo and many American Indian languages are polysynthetic. The term incapsulating language or incorporating language is sometimes used.

language, primary. The spoken language, as opposed to the written language, which is called secondary.

language, pure. A language with no foreign elements and no borrowed words, and which does not combine its own forms with others to produce new words. The notion of a pure language is essentially an invention of nationalistic theorists, since on careful study any language appears as an amalgam of diverse elements.

language, ritual. The language employed in ritual activities. Often it is not the same as the community's usual language. It may have many archaic elements.

language, sign. Communication by stylized movements of the hands, or using smoke or other signal devices. The Plains Indians used hand movements for intercommunication, and some Hindu groups communicate by stylized gestures. Sign language is often used by groups speaking different languages, or by persons who cannot speak. Words are portrayed by pantomime that closely follows natural ideas. It may include movements of the arms, head, and body, as well as the hands. These movements usually represent the most obvious and conventionalized features of an object or action.

language, standard. A language used in official communications and in writing and schools. It is usually associated with, and comes after, political independence.

language, subordinating. A language in which the modifying elements occupy a subordinate position to the elements expressing the central idea.

language, synthetic. A highly complex formalized language, allowing classificatory ideas to be con-

311

veyed within the single word, mainly through the frequency of bound forms (q.v.), e.g., Latin.

language, theories of. See BOW-WOW; DING-DONG; INTERJECTION-AL; THEORY, FAMILY TREE; THEORY, GESTURAL; THEORY, NATIVISTIC; THEORY, SING-SONG; YO-DE-HO.

language, tone. A language in which words made up of identical sound elements may have different meanings if they are spoken in different tones (inflections), e.g., the Indo-Chinese languages.

language, weakly synthetic. A language with a moderately formal elaboration of a word, e.g., Italian.

languages, classification of. The basic method of classifying language is historical, grouping together, if possible, languages with a common origin and some link to an actual historical fact. Genetic classification is based on relationship of form and meaning. Typological classification is based on such special relations as class, morphological methods, meanings, etc. Isolating (e.g., Chinese), agglutinating (e.g., Turkish), and inflecting (e.g., Sanskrit) languages are often typologically classified. The genetic classification permits the historical reconstruction of language and culture, and can be used to reconstruct culture and history, while the typological classification is not historical.

langur. A fairly large Asiatic monkey. The langurs eat vegetarian food and have large stomachs.

lantaka. A Moro bronze cannon.

lantern, horn. A lantern made of a cow's horn.

lanugo. The fine hairy down with which the human fetus is covered during its sixth to eighth month. It is usually shed before birth.

lapidarian. Referring to stones or gems.

lapidaries. Discussions of the special properties of precious stones. They may deal with magic (q.v.), medicine, or related matters. Such discussions are first found in Babylonian astrological writings.

lapis lazuli. A sapphire-like stone with some golden highlights from pyrites. It was sometimes used to represent gods, to cure fevers or other ailments, or as a sign of virginity.

Lapp. In northern Scandinavia, a racial subdivision of the Caucasoids, which has some Mongoloid elements. Some scholars believe the Lapps to be neither true Caucasoids nor true Mongoloids but a step in the development of the Mongoloids and Upper Paleolithic Europeans. They are brachycephalic, with an average breadth-length index of about 84. The upper part of the face is usually broad, with protruding cheekbones. The chin is often narrow, making the face pear-shaped. Lapps are usually short and small-bodied. The hair is mostly brown, with some black, and it is often straight. The nose is usually straight. Some 1,000 years ago, the Lapps in Fennoscandia were divided into three groups, the Eastern, Central or Western, and Southern. This distribution is reflected in Lapp dialects: Russian Lapps speak Eastern

Lappish as do the Fisher Lapps in Finland, and Central Lappish is spoken by Finland's Mountain Lapps and by the Norwegian and Swedish Lapps. The Fisher Lapps and the Forest Lapps of the South are seminomads. Some scholars have suggested that there is a Northern Lapp group (Kola-Lapps, Skolt-Lapps, Fisher Lapps, and the Sea-Lapps along the Arctic coast), which differs from the Southern Lapp group (all other Lapps) in relative height of the skull and in blood group characteristics.

lapse. A linguistic change that is unintentional and is observed by its auditors with disapproval or amusement. Noticed lapses are usually ignored by polite society. Subphonemic lapses may be involved in the changes that a phoneme undergoes.

lares. The spirits of the Roman family and of the Roman political organizations. They were beneficent spirits who became identified with the dead. The lares having to do with the family founder's spirit were most important and were worshipped within the home.

Lartet, Edward (1801-1871). A French paleontologist who made some major finds of Upper Paleolithic man. He found fossils of *Pliopithecus* in 1836 and *Dryopithecus* in 1850. He discovered perhaps the first examples reported of French art of the Upper Paleolithic period. In his subdivision of the Paleolithic period, Lartet for the first time used nonarchaeological data to classify archaeological materials.

laryngeal. See GLOTTAL.

laryngoscope. A mirror device for examining the vocal cords.

larynx. A cartilage box which is at the head of the windpipe. It is the first place at which air coming from the lungs can be checked. From the outside, it is seen as the Adam's apple (q.v.).

lasso. A noose thrown to encircle a running target. It may be attached to a pole.

latah or **lattah.** A state, usually occuring among women, involving extreme suggestibility, compulsive imitating, and sexual delusions. Almost any incident can precipitate it. It often occurs in women who have failed to meet the demands an unfamiliar environment makes on them. Complete post-amnesia is common. Latah often occurs in equatorial areas including Indonesia, and the Philippines, but it has also been found in and among the Ainu. The chronic form is sometimes called young-dah-hte.

lateral. Referring to a type of dental articulation in which an air passage goes around either or both sides of the middle line of the month, e.g., *l* as in *let*.

lateral, palatal. A lateral in which the breath can pass along either or both sides of the tongue and in which the back of the tongue touches the palate's highest point, e.g., *gl* in Italian.

lateral area. See AREA, LATERAL.

laterite. A kind of tropical soil.

lathe, turning. A machine in which two blocks turn the material being worked on two bronze pegs.

313

latifundia. The great estates, especially in ancient Rome, which were owned and exploited by absentee landlords.

lattah. See LATAH.

latte. Stone columns in the Marianas.

Latvian. An isolated member of the Indo-European language family.

lava. A stone mixture of several minerals erupted by a volcano. It flows like a liquid before hardening.

lava-lava. A garment consisting of a straight piece of cloth, usually cotton or bark, wrapped tightly around the hips and sometimes around the torso as well. It is common attire in much of southeast Asia and Oceania.

lavo. A disk and board game of Fiji.

law. A social norm sanctioned by the possibility of the application of force by appointed authorized persons. Thurnwald has emphasized that law is separated from usage and custom because organized force stands behind it. Law is distinguished by the communal approval extended to the action taken as a result of the violation of a norm. Kinship plays an important part in primitive law. Law may turn to religion if its technique is inadequate to develop enough evidence.

Hoebel has described four major functions of law: defining relationships, allocating the power of coercion, handling cases of trouble, and adapting social relations to changing conditions of life. Almost every society has a procedure for halting feuds.

law, Ammon's. The generalization that the taller a person is, the larger his skull, or that the correlation between the cephalic index (q.v.) and stature is negative. The correlation is usually not very high. This generalization is applicable only to males in a homogeneous group.

law, Bartholomae's. A systematic formulation of the factors associated with sound shifts in the Indo-Iranian languages, which states that under some conditions an aspirated voiced consonant followed by a voiceless consonant becomes unaspirated and the voiceless consonant becomes voiced and aspirated.

law, biogenetic. Haeckel's formulation that the individual's development, or ontogeny, is a shortened recapitulation of phylogeny, or the race's evolution. The biogenetic law is sometimes called the recapitulation of phylogeny in ontogeny.

law, Cope's. The law of biology that the degree of survival of a species is directly related to the extent to which the species remains unspecialized and in the main line of evolutionary development, and, correlatively, the extent to which it does not enter into a specialized branch of development.

law, Dahl's. The general rule operating in the Bantu languages to the effect that when a vowel or diphthong occupies the position between two unvoiced consonants, the first consonant becomes voiced.

law, Darmesteter's. The rule that in the change from Latin to French, the syllable immediately preceding the accented syllable disappears or becomes silent, unless it includes the vowel *a*.

law, Depéret's. The supposed law of biology that the measure of the success of an organism's adaptation is its increase in size throughout its evolution.

law, Dollo's. A general statement of the irreversibility of evolution, namely, that an organism cannot go back to its ancestors' conditions.

law, Ferrell's. The law that when a body moves on the earth's surface, there is a force from the earth's motion which deflects it to the right in the northern hemisphere and to the left in the southern hemisphere.

law, frontal or **frontality, law of.** A procedure followed by many early sculptors in which the top of the head and the nose, spine, and navel lie along an imaginary straight line. The legs also follow this straight median plane. Up to ca. 500 B.C. there are few exceptions to this rule. Julius Lange of Copenhagen first named it.

law, Grassman's. A linguistic law that when two syllables next to one another in Greek language begin with aspirates, one of these aspirates (ordinarily the first) loses the aspiration.

law, Grimm's. A linguistic law that a series of sound changes occurred in the development of Primitive Germanic out of Primitive Indo-European. Voiced stops *b, d,* and *g* became the voiceless stops *p, t,* and *k*; voiceless stops *p, t,* and *k* became the voiceless continuants *f,* hard *th,* and *x;* and *bʰ, dʰ,* and *gʰ* became *b, d,* and *g*.

law, Meinhof's. A rule of phonetics relative to the interchanging or displacement of nasalized consonants in languages classified in the Bantu group.

law, palatal. A law of phonetics promulgated in 1875 by V. Thomsen. It holds that in Sanskrit, a Proto-Indo-European velar or guttural *k* or *g* which precedes the vowel *a* becomes the palatalized Sanskrit *c* and *j* when the Sanskrit *a* corresponds to Latin or Greek *e,* but the *k* and *g* which precede *a* are unchanged when the Sanskrit *a* corresponds to Greek or Latin *a* or *o*.

law, Peschel's. A law postulating an inverse relationship between the amount of clothing worn and the amount of skin pigmentation. There seem to be many exceptions to this rule.

law, phonetic. A schematized statement of a change in the place or manner of a specific articulation, or a systematic formulation of the principles governing a phonetic change, e.g., Grimm's law (q.v.).

law, private. The law governing private wrongs (q.v.).

law, sumptuary. A law which regulates expenses or luxurious displays either for the society as a whole or for the lower classes, which are required to observe a sober demeanor. Ancient Rome and feudal Japan enforced sumptuary laws by restricting the types of clothing that might be worn.

law, von Schwann's. The statement of a relation between contraction and length of muscle fibers such that when muscle fibers shorten, there is a diminution of the tension of contraction.

law, water. The laws for regulating water, found even in early civilizations. Herodotus and the Code of Hammurabi both had discussions on the regulation of water. Mediterranean concepts of water law, generalized into Roman law, which sees running water and the sea as common property, still influence our thinking today.

law, Williston's. The observation by Williston, an American paleontologist, that the parts of an organism tend to reduce in number, with a specialization in function on the part of the fewer parts; e.g., in the evolutionary scale from fish to humans, the dermal bones in the skull roof diminish in number while their individuality increases.

law, Wolff's. The theory that an organ is enlarged when its functions increase and becomes smaller when its functions decrease. It is also known as the law of atrophy and hypertrophy.

Lawrence, Sir William (1783-1867). An English anatomist who was a precursor of modern ideas on race and of the relation between environment and organism.

Layard, Sir Austen Henry (1817-1894). A British archaeologist who made major excavations at Nineveh. His *Nineveh and Its Remains* (1848-1849) was perhaps the first archaeological book that was a bestseller.

leaching. The process by which soluble minerals in the soil are dissolved by rain water and carried off through streams to the sea. Leaching ultimately results in soil made up of insoluble residue only.

lead. A heavy, pliable, inelastic metal. It is bright blue but oxidizes to a dull gray. It is obtained from the ore easily but is so soft that it cannot readily be used for implements. Lead was probably discovered not long after man found silver, because of the frequency with which they occur together in nature, but it was probably not widely used at first. Lead does not occur often in its native state, although its sulphide (galena) has a brilliant luster that makes it highly visible. The lead lumps in the lowest Hissarlik layer suggest that it was in use ca. 3000-2500 B.C. It was used as money in early times, e.g., in India, and as votive offerings. Bronze and other coins were often made with some lead in order to debase them. In the classical period water pipes were frequently leaden, as in Pompeii and Herculaneum.

lead, ice. A crack in ice that is too wide to be crossed by foot or by vehicle. An ice lead may be miles wide.

lead, shore. Open water resulting from the ice pack moving apart from the shore ice.

leaf, blank. A layer of stalagmite or some other material laid down when humans did not inhabit a particular area, so that it separates two industries (q.v.).

leangle. An early curved implement.

lean-to. A primitive shelter consisting of a few tilted branches

316

covered with leaves. It is used by some Australian groups and others.

leasing, wife. Permitting a man to have the use of another's wife. It especially applies, as among the Eskimo, when the benefited man's wife is ill or unavailable. See LEND-ING, WIFE.

leather. An animal skin that has been tanned or dressed. Leather is either bark-tanned, tanned with alum or similar substances, or oil-dressed. Dipping the skins in lime-water in order to loosen the hair and prepare the skin for the dress-ings is frequent. Hall nuts, sumac leaves, and various barks and berries have been used as tannins. In addi-tion to its use for shelter and cloth-ing, leather was often a writing material, e.g., among the Hebrews, whose law was written on cattle hides.

leben. A nonalcoholic drink made of sour camel's milk found in the Middle East.

lecanomancy. A method of divi-nation (q.v.) by throwing an object into a full basin of water and inter-preting the image or the sound of its fall.

lecythus. A flask used by the early Greeks for oil in the bath, the gym-nasium, and funeral rites. The finest examples of this type of vase were gracefully shaped cylinders taper-ing to a base, with a thin handle fastened to a long neck and a flat shoulder. Funeral vases were deco-rated with brown paintings over a yellowish-white slip in which the home life of the departed one was depicted. The spellings lekythus and lekythos are also found.

ledger. A fishing tackle with a sinker attached to the line above the bait. Thus, some of the line and bait are on the bottom.

leek, house. A pink-flowered plant found on roofs and walls. It is often regarded as a good luck sign, and it is also used as a medicine for skin disorders.

Legba. A Dahomey god who is a messenger to other gods, propitiat-ing them on behalf of men and carrying messages to the diviners who predict the future.

legend, local. A legend closely tied in with a particular place or locality. A local legend often gives an origin for the place name or its meaning.

legend, migratory. A short prose narrative existing in a number of variants, especially in the places where the events are situated. The Anglo-Saxon Beowulf epic is based on an old migratory legend in which the hero defends a homestead against a demon, whose arm he wrenches out and whom he follows to a body of water, where the demon is killed.

legs, bow. A leg alignment in which there is an outward bowing of the bones.

leguminosae. Plants, like peas and clover, that fix atmospheric nitro-gen in the soil because of the nodule bacteria which live in symbiosis on the roots.

lei wen. A basic motif in Chinese art, representing the generalized primitive concept of the forces of nature. See T'AO T'IEH.

leiotrichous. Referring to the pos-session of straight hair.

leister. A fish-spear of a type first made of bronze and then of iron with three or more prongs; also, a fish hook with four arms and at least four barbs.

lekythus or lekythos. See LECY-THUS.

lemur. A Paleocene and Eocene primate suborder, which survives in Africa and Madagascar. It is small, foxlike, and furry, with a project-ing snout and many nonhuman fea-tures, such as having only two pairs of incisors. The lemur is arboreal and mainly nocturnal. It is the most primitive extant primate.

lending, wife. The practice of a host's permitting a guest sexual access to his wife, as an expression of brotherhood. The practice is also called wife hospitality or hospitality prostitution.

length, anterior trunk. The su-prasternal height minus the sym-physion height above the floor.

length, arm. The distance between the longest finger tip and the acromial point with the arm stretched out.

length, face. The distance be-tween the low point of the center line of the upper jaw and the na-sion.

length, feet. The pternion-acro-podion distance parallel to the long axis of the foot when the weight is supported by both feet equally.

length, forearm. The stylion height subtracted from the radiale height.

length, head. The distance, meas-ured by a spreading caliper, from the glabella to the opisthocranion.

length, leg. The distance between the tibiale and the lowest point of the medial malleolus on the ankle.

length, lower arm. The distance from the stylion to the radiale, measured with the palm facing the body, the arm hanging down nat-urally, and the subject standing.

length, lower leg. The sphyrion height subtracted from the tibiale height.

length, maxillo-alveolar. The prosthion-alveolon distance.

length, maximum cranial. The distance from opisthocranion to the glabella.

length, maximum foot. The dis-tance between the most posterior point of the heel and the most an-terior tip of the toe, measured when the subject is standing.

length, maximum head. The dis-tance between the glabella and the farthest point on the back of the head.

length, mid-facial. The prosthion-endobasion distance, in the median sagittal plane.

length, nasal. The distance from subnasale to nasion.

length, palatal. The staphylion-orale distance.

length, physiognomic facial. The distance from the gnathion to the trichion.

length, total arm. The distance from the stylion to the acromiale measured with the palm facing the body, the arm hanging down nat-urally, and the subject standing.

length, total leg. The distance from the surface on which the sub-ject is standing to the upper edge of the great trochanter.

318

length, total upper extremity.
The distance from the dactylion to
the acromiale, measured with the
subject standing.
length, upper arm. The distance
from the radiale to the acromiale,
measured with the palm facing the
body, the arm hanging down naturally, and the subject standing.
length, upper facial. The nasion-
endobasion distance, in the median
sagittal plane.
lengthening. The change of a
short sound to a long sound, e.g.,
the change from Medieval German
Sägen to modern German *Sägen*.
lengthening, compensatory.
Lengthening that takes place when
a consonant near a vowel is suppressed.
lenis. A sound pronounced with
comparatively weak force and little
muscular tension.
lenition. In Celtic languages, the
change that consonants undergo
when they are placed between
vowels, as well as the change of the
initial consonant of a word under
the influence of the last sound of
the word immediately preceding.
See MUTATION, INITIAL.
lentil. A small annual legume, the
seeds of which are often used for
porridge or as a meat substitute. It
is widely grown in many parts of
the world. Lentils probably originated in western Asia in the Neolithic period.
leopard society. See SOCIETY,
LEOPARD.
leprechaun. See CLURICAUNE.
leprosy. A disease, essentially of
the peripheral nerves, which di-
minishes tactile sensation and causes

skin lesions. Leprosy is highly in-
fectious and is usually a slowly
developing and, until recently, in-
curable chronic complaint. Among
ancient peoples and in Medieval
times lepers were banished or were
required to carry bells and wear
distinctive clothing as a warning of
their approach. Some authorities
have maintained that certain pur-
ported descriptions of leprosy in
ancient documents really indicate a
venereal disease, possibly syphilis.
Lepsius, Karl R. (1810-1884). A
German Egyptologist who was a
pioneer teacher, museum director,
and archaeologist.
leptene. An upper facial index
between 55 and 59.9.
lepto-. A prefix used in physical
anthropology to mean narrow, e.g.,
leptosome.
leptocytosis. Possessing abnormally thin erythrocytes in the blood,
as in Cooley's anemia (q.v.).
leptokurtic. Referring to a frequency curve with an unusually
high peak at its center, as compared
with a normal frequency curve.
leptoprosopic. A comparatively
narrow face, or a total facial index
(q.v.) between 90 and 99.4 on a
skull, or above 80 on a living person.
leptorrhine. Referring to a nasal
index (q.v.) of less than 47 on the
skull, or less than 70 on the living
head; also, a narrow nose.
leptosome. One of Kretchmer's
constitutional types (q.v.), with a
tall and slender physique. Associated with it are schizothymic traits
of idealism, introversion, and for-

malism. A leptosome individual is said to have an asthenic physique.

leptosome-pachysome factor. See FACTOR, LEPTOSOME-PACHYSOME.

leptostaphyline. Referring to a palatal index (q.v.) of less than 79.9.

letter. A conventional symbol standing for an elementary or compound speech sound.

Letter, Black. A cursive German script of the Middle Ages.

letter, vowel. See MATRES LECTIONIS.

leucoderm. A light colored skin; also, Von Eickstedt's name for Caucasoid.

Levallois. A flake industry found in West Europe associated with Middle and Upper Acheulian materials, as well as with Mousterian tools. The industry consists mainly of flakes.

level, base. In a river bed, the limit below which erosion cannot be carried.

leverage, axis of. The path followed by the central axis of weight stresses as they are passed through the forward part of the foot in forceful leverage.

levigation. The rubbing of ceramic ware with abrasive agents to purify them without water.

levirate. The practice of requiring or permitting a man to marry the widow of his brother, or of another close relative. As practiced among the ancient Hebrews, the children who were the offspring of a levirate marriage were considered to be descendants of the deceased brother.

levirate, anticipatory. The practice of a husband's permitting his younger brother limited sexual privileges with his wife, with the view that the younger brother might inherit the wife eventually. The term attenuated polyandry is also used.

levirate, junior. A levirate in which a younger brother inherits the widow of his older brother. It was encouraged among the Biblical Hebrews.

level, dumpy. A revolving telescope with an attached spirit level. It is set on a tripod and made horizontal by screws. The dumpy level is used to determine the height of various points in archaeological research.

lewis. An iron device in sections, which can be fitted into a mortise. It is used in lifting large stones.

lex talionis. See RETALIATION.

lexicology. The systematic investigation of a linguistic stock from the point of view of semantics or morphology.

lexicography. The study of the words in a language as entities by themselves. Lexicography contains language material not included in grammar (q.v.). It involves listing every meaningful element in the language and stating the meaning. Thus, lexicography includes words, morphemes (q.v.) which may not be words, and grammatical elements and their form classes.

lexicon. The total collection of morphemes (q.v.) in a language.

ley. A pasture that is worked in rotation.

liana. A climbing and twining plant found in tropical areas, used in many cultures as a kind of string.

libation. Pouring a liquid on the ground, or on a symbolic representation of a deity, e.g., the Romans to their lares and penates. By extension, a libation is a liquid given or drunk as an offering.

libation table. See TABLE, LIBATION.

license, ceremonial. Sexual activity that is socially approved because of religious or other celebrations.

lichgate. A roofed timber building found at the entrance of many churchyards. The corpse was placed here during the first part of the burial services, because the church would have been profaned by such use. Lichgates are found in modern burial grounds, although there is no longer any need for them. The term derives from the German *leiche*, "corpse," and the Anglo-Saxon *lic*, "body."

lid, pot. A flake split from a lump of flint through the action of frost. A pot lid is usually rounded.

life, after. The life after death. Most cultures have some concept of an existence after death. Persons may have to master esoteric knowledge to prepare themselves, or their after life may depend on the funeral, mourning, or burial rites. The belief in an after life is not necessarily linked with personal immortality or moral beliefs. It is tied in with acts or, more usually, omissions of the relatives which may lead the dead to cause trouble. The dead, however, may be responsible for benefits also. They may return in dreams or materialize in their own or an animal guise. The tie between dead and living is often effected through a cult of spirits of the dead.

life, development of. The universe is believed to be about three or four billion years old, with the dawn of life around two billion years ago when carbon and soft-bodied sea organisms presumably existed. Fish and early marine animals appeared about a half billion years ago with amphibians appearing 300 million, reptiles 200 million, and mammals 150 million years ago. Man is believed to be about one million years old. Although a descendant of early primates, he does not seem to be directly related to living monkeys or apes. Although some suggest that humans appeared in different places simultaneously, others feel that southwest Asia is the cradle of humanity. Robert Broom reported fossil man-ape remains in South African cave deposits believed to be one million years old. See AUSTRALOPITHECUS. There are no Western Hemisphere animals which might have been a human ancestor, and the one species of ape in this hemisphere did not flourish. Living monkeys and apes may have had a common ancestor over one million years ago, with one branch becoming man and the other primate.

life, tree of. A marvelous perennially blooming tree, the quintessential tree, which guarantees immortality to eaters of its fruit. Different national groups had different trees of life. This tree is usually guarded by some sort of animal.

life, type. See CYCLE, TYPE LIFE.

321

lifter, mustache. Among the Ainu, a device to keep the mustache out of the soup.

ligature. A single compound letter which combines the major features of each component in the compound letter, e.g., successive occurrences of *f* are printed as the ligature *ff*.

light, champion's. The light believed to radiate over the heads or faces of warriors in a battle.

light, corpse. A phosphorescent glow observed over marshes or lakes. It means death in the folklore of many peoples.

light, jack. A light carried on the forehead and used by various Eastern Indians of the United States in night hunting of deer and other animals.

light, ultraviolet. Light lying beyond the spectrum's violet end and invisible to the naked eye. It is used to uncover restorations which cannot be determined through ordinary techniques, and even though an object may not evidence any restoration, ultraviolet light will probably show the changes in different colors.

light and darkness. The phenomena of light and darkness were profound realities to early man, who was probably afraid of darkness and saw it as associated with evil forces. Irregular occurrences of darkness, like eclipses, were especially terrifying. Compared to animals, early man was in an unfavorable condition in darkness. Religion helped overcome the fear. In early symbolism, light and darkness are symbols for good and evil. Most early religions suggest that darkness

prevailed before the world began. Later religious thought dichotomizes ethical thinking in terms of light and dark. Thus, in Zoroastrianism, light conquers darkness; Buddhism equates light with the Buddha; and the gospel in the New Testament is called the "light" and the peoples without it are "in darkness."

lightning. Atmospheric electricity discharged from cloud to earth, or between clouds, with its attendant light flash. Most cultures fearfully regard lightning as a god or a sign of the god. In some cultures it is believed involved with the weather.

lignite. A brown coal used for bracelets and other ornaments in Neolithic times.

likeness, coefficient of racial. Karl Pearson's formula for the extent to which the groups of men or crania are like or unlike. Some anthropologists have objected that it is too delicate a tool for the data on which it depends.

lily. A plant of the genus Lilium, cultivated for many years. Lilies represent fertility, war, and purity. They are used as a medicine for skin troubles.

limande. An oval, generally flat, coup-de-poing (q.v.) with pointed ends and the maximum thickness at the middle. Limandes date from the early Acheulian period. In French, the word means "flounder."

limbo. In Trinidad, an acrobatic dance for males. The dancer goes under a horizontal stick.

lime, bird. A sticky substance used to trap birds. The hunter places the substance where birds are likely to

322

alight and then catches them by hand or shoots them.

limonite. An ocher ranging in color from yellow to orange.

line, basion-prosthion. The distance from the prosthion to the basion.

line, Frankfurt or **plane, Frankfurt.** A line along which either the lower border of two orbits and one porion, or two porions and the lower border of one orbit, are oriented. The Frankfurt line is used to help adjust a skull to a position approximating that of the living, inasmuch as most skulls are asymmetrical.

line, frontal convergence. The meeting place of the crown stream (q.v.) and the glabellar stream (q.v.) of hair. The frontal convergence line varies in position in different individuals.

line, international date. The line, mostly on the 180th meridian, at which the date changes. A ship or plane crossing this line westward loses a day, and one eastbound adds a day.

line, isolexic. A line drawn on a linguistic map that shows the approximate limits of areas of speech in which a sameness in the vocabulary (lexicon) and grammar is found. See ISOGLOSS.

line, isophonic. A line drawn on a linguistic map that shows the approximate limits of areas of speech in which like phonetic features are observed in the pronunciation of the language.

line, isosyntagmic. A line drawn on a linguistic map that shows the approximate limits of areas of

speech wherein a likeness in syntax is found.

line, oil and butter. An imaginary line that crosses Europe and divides it into a northern area where fixed fats are found and a southern area where oils are found. Matthieu Williams, an English chemist, popularized this concept. The oil and butter line is important in developing the influence of temperature on the evolution of the tallow candle. The concept is useless in accounting for the wax candle, which is less affected by the temperature and is used in warm climates.

line, set. A fishing line attached to a stake on the beach, with the other end weighted. A set line has attached hooks.

line, snow. The geographical line above which snow fields remain throughout the year.

line, Wallace's. A narrow but deep sea line which divides Borneo and Bali from Celebes and Lombok. On the two sides of the line the indigenous animals are quite divergent.

lineage. A consanguineal kin group resulting from unilinear (q.v.) descent and either patrilineal (q.v.) or matrilineal (q.v.). It consists of members with a common relation in the prevalent line of descent as the result of a specific group of genealogical ties, and in which descent must be demonstrated, thus differing from a clan (q.v.). Lineage may be unilocal or multilocal, and it extends through a number of generations, some of which may be dead. It is usually exogamous, although the Arabs are an important exception, and generally observes special rituals and property rights. Particular offices or skills may be found in the lineage.

lineal. Referring to consanguine relatives connected by a line of descent. Two such relatives are never from the same generation.

lines, Benninghof's. Lines of tension and small splits that radiate from a hole made by piercing the skull with an awl. These lines demonstrate where there are large forces of pressure, traction, and stress and indicate that the skeleton of the face is mainly responsive to chewing stresses, although the cranium seems to be sufficiently thick to resist them.

lines, shatter. Lines radiating from the point of impact on a flint. They show lines of weakness on the flint and indicate that the original blow was too strenuous.

lingam or **linga.** The stone phallus representing the god Siva, the most common Hindu object of worship. It was sometimes used to deflorate girls before marriage to effect a union with the source of fertility. The lingam is often associated with the yoni (q.v.), the Hindu symbol for female reproductive energy; when the two are represented together, the lingam arises out of the yoni. The lingam is found as early as the third millenium B.C. in the Indus Valley. In its earlier forms it followed the penile anatomy rather closely, but in time it more typically assumed a symmetrical columnar shape.

lingua franca. A language common to, and widely understood in, an area where it is in general use among persons of different native speech. Thus, Hindustani is the lingua franca of the many parts of India. A langua franca may be spontaneously originated or artificially formed. The term was first used of the contact vernacular (q.v.) spoken in Mediterranean ports, which is a blend of Italian, Arabic, Greek, and other languages.

lingua geral brazilica. In Brazil, a contact vernacular (q.v.) for communication among Whites, Negroes, and Indians, as well as among Indians who speak different tribal languages. It is based on the Tupi language.

linguistic change. See CHANGE, LINGUISTIC.

linguistics. The comparative study of the structure, nature, interrelationships, history, and development of languages, also called glottology. Language is of interest to the anthropologist as a prime distinction between the hominidae and other anthropoids, as a reflection of social contact or ethnic association, and as a sample of a group's psychology or of an attained culture level. Albert Gallatin (1761-1840) classified American groups on the basis of language, and J. W. Powell (1834-1902) and D. G. Brinton (1837-1890) studied the language of American Indians. Wilhelm von Humboldt (1767-1835) had used classification by language, and by the mid-19th century, the connection between ethnology and linguistics was well established, with philological ideas used to help solve European ethnological problems, although Max Müller emphasized in 1891 that ethnology and linguistics must not be confused.

Descriptive linguistics studies the structure of individual languages and dialects. Historical linguistics deals with the development of languages. The comparison of related languages for the purpose of reconstructing their common ancestor is comparative linguistics. General linguistics is the study of the range of variation of linguistic structure, e.g., the maximum and minimum number of phonemes found in any language.

linguistics, comparative. The systematic investigations of the likenesses and differences between related languages.

linguistics, descriptive. The branch of linguistics concerned with a particular form of speech at a particular time. It is the basis of historical linguistics and of comparative grammar. At any given time, a language is not only a definite collection of word forms but is constantly changing.

linguistics, dynamic. The study of languages in the light of their development and history.

linguistics, historical. The study of the history of a language, or of language generally. It is concerned with changes in systems of language and with the family relationships of languages.

linguistics, related. The study of languages that resemble each other and are thus related.

linguistics, synchronic. The study of the elements of a language during a particular period in its development.

link, missing. A hypothetical organism which, when found, would complete the picture of man's evolution. In the 19th century, there was much speculation on the nature of the links between the apes and man. Current anthropological thinking no longer finds it necessary to speculate on the nature of such links, since the evolution of man and primate interrelationships can be traced fairly clearly in an almost logical sequence. Perhaps the major gap in the evolutionary record is in the step from Miocene apes to the Australopithecinae.

linkage. The tendency for genes to be transmitted together without recombining, e.g., a gene for a particular kind of hair and a gene for a particular kind of eye color. Such genes are usually on the same chromosome.

linkage group. See GROUP, LINKAGE.

linkage, sex. Gene association in the sex chromosomes. Some hereditary characters only oppear in one sex, and are said to be sex-linked.

Linnaeus, Carolus (Carl von Linné) (1707-1778). A Swedish naturalist who devised the system of nomenclature for organisms that is still used. Linnaeus was responsible for the division of organisms into phyla, orders, classes, genera, and species. In his system, an organism is known by its generic and specific name in that sequence. When the later practice of appending the discoverer's name to a species developed, the species named by Linnaeus were indicated by an L. Linnaeus classified men as a member of the class Quadrupedia, order Anthropomorpha, in the 1735 edition of *Systema Naturae*. In later editions, the Primate order included bats, lemurs, apes, and man. The species of man (genus Homo) listed by Linnaeus included sapiens, ferus, americanus, europaeus, asiaticus, afer, and monstrosus.

lintel. A piece of lumber or stone set over a doorway or spanning the horizontal space between two uprights.

lionila. A wooden battle ax found in South Australia.

lip, Negroid. A lip the membranous part of which is fairly large, heavy, and everted. Inasmuch as the ape's lips are neither everted, large, nor red, the Negroid lip would appear to be an advanced kind of lip and not in the least apelike or primitive, contrary to a popular belief.

Lippert, Julius (1839-1909). A German sociologist and anthropologist who made contributions to the study of the evolution of culture.

liquids. Vocalic consonants that are smooth, flowing, and vowel-like, e.g., *l* and *r*.

lira. An African reed musical instrument made of a short bamboo tube with a split end. When the performer blows a current of air on the lira, the split section vibrates in controlled tone.

Lissapol. A wetting agent used to strengthen archaeological finds so that they can be removed.

lissoir. A spatulate and slender bone implement that was probably used for burnishing.

liter. A volume measure equal to 1.81 pints.

literature, oral. Art forms, such as mythology, epics, songs, and legends, which were not written down.

litham. A veil worn by men in the Sudan.

lithosphere. The solid part of the earth.

litter. A device for transporting a person. Two or more bearers carry one passenger. A litter may be a hammock or a chair attached to two poles. It was developed from the carrying beam (q.v.). In Africa and China, the litter is still widely used.

littoral. The shore or the adjacent area, or a habitat along a shore or in estuaries. A littoral is also the ancient geographical boundaries of a culture, either the shore, beach, or cliffs at the edge of an ocean, sea, or large lake.

lituus. A small straight conical Roman horn with an upturned bell.

livres de beurre. Flint cores called "pounds of butter" by the French peasants who find them.

liwan. In Moslem Persian architecture, an open hall or chamber which led to an enclosed court. The liwan was generally a large barrel-vaulted room. The deep interior afforded shade and the open end ventilation in the hot Persian climate.

lizard. A tailed reptile, with four legs, a scaly skin, and usually fairly small but with a long body. Men may identify with the lizard and regard it as a god, an ancestor, or a messenger bearing portents of the future. The dead lizard is used in magic.

lo. A large platter-shaped Chinese gong which is suspended by a string and struck with a mallet. It is used by servants to tell of the arrival of guests, with the number of strokes indicating the rank of the individual; by the army as a signal for retreat; and by mourners to frighten evil spirits away from funeral processions. It sometimes announces the departure of ships.

loam. Impure pottery clay containing iron ocher or mica.

lobelia. An herbaceous plant used by some North American Indian groups to prevent storms, to calm disputes, and as an aphrodisiac.

lobolo. A bridegroom's paying the bride's father a number of cattle or goats for his bride. This custom is widely found among South African tribes. It serves the function of stabilizing marriage, protecting women against bad treatment, and establishing the legal position of children.

local group. See COMMUNITY, ENDOGAMOUS.

localism. Any word or group of words limited in use to a particular physical area or community.

loculus. A tomb or chamber designed for the burial of a body. The bones of St. Peter were supposedly discovered in 1950 in the loculus of the hypogeum (q.v.) at St. Peter's Basilica in the Vatican City.

locus. The place in a chromosome occupied by a gene or its allelomorphs.

lodestone. An oxide of iron which points toward the north. It was used in alchemy, medicine, and magic. Its property of attracting iron has made it a subject of intensive study.

lodge, conjuring. A primitive séance cabinet used by North American Indians.

lodge, earth. A ghost dance (q.v.) cult, centering around the construction of special subterranean houses for protection from catastrophe. An earth lodge was also a Pawnee Indian dwelling, circular and partly underground, made of thatch covered by sod cut like shingles.

lodge, juggler's. A lodge used by the shaman (q.v.) of a number of Indian groups north and south of the Great Lakes area, including the Winnebago, Chippewa, and Menominee. The spirit under the control of the shaman made the lodge shiver.

lodge, sweat. In North America, a small airtight hut in which steam for bathing was made by sprinkling water over heated stones. The steam baths were usually taken by groups of people, often linked with a vow to the sun. The baths were generally entered four times. Once inside, the men usually told stereotyped repetitive dreams. See HOUSE, SWEAT.

loess. A yellowish and nonstratified sandlike material carried by the wind and deposited at a distance. Loess deposition is a continuing process that occurs in the dry and cold steppe flanking the glacial maxima. Loess is exceedingly fertile soil, but because of its extreme compressibility and powderiness, agriculture is difficult. Especially thick loess deposits exist in regions of China bordering the Manchurian and Mongolian plains.

log, swimming. A log used as a float, as in Hawaii.

log, tapa. A log used to make tapa (q.v.) cloth.

loggia. A roofed gallery with one or both sides open.

logogram. A sign indicating a quality of a group, e.g., *wet;* a direction for action, e.g., *stop!;* a symbol representing an object not adequately limned by a picture.

loincloth. An early garment consisting of a cloth around the loins. It is usually fairly short, although the Dyak dandies have loincloths which may contain as much as 14 yards of material.

Lombroso, Cesare (1836-1909). An Italian criminologist, professor of criminal anthropology at the University of Turin. His theory that the criminal is midway between the savage and the lunatic and is the result of physical, nervous, and mental anomalies has since been disproved. Lombroso believed that the criminal could be detected by physical stigmata and atavisms.

look, fatal. A glance so potent that it can cause instant death. In the beliefs of some peoples, death is sometimes caused by looking at, or being looked at by, one endowed with the fatal look.

loom. A device used in weaving to hold the warp taut and lift several warps simultaneously, thus permitting the weft to go through the warps.

loom, Arawak. A type of weaving frame consisting of two upright posts set into the earth and around which a continuous warp is wound. A fabric woven on this type of frame is endless, e.g., the cylindrical tipoy (q.v.). The frame is so named because Arawak-speaking peoples are supposed by some anthropologists to have introduced this "loom" into the tropical forest of South America.

loom, high-warp. A loom in which the warp threads are attached to an upright frame vertically. It is probably the most primitive loom.

loom, low-warp. A loom with a horizontally placed warp. It is necessary to bend over the loom when operating it.

loom, one-bar. The simplest type of loom, consisting of a bar between two poles. The warp threads hang down, while the weft is passed through the warps thread by thread.

loom, Oriental. A two-pole weaving device which supports two horizontal rollers. The warp thread is wound around the upper roller and fastened to the lower roller in order that the rug may be rolled up as it is being woven.

loom, two-bar. A loom in which two wooden bars stretch the warp threads.

loom, two-beam. A loom in which the threads of the warp are attached to revolving cylinders.

loop. A principal pattern in dermatoglyphics (q.v.) in which the ridges of the fingerprints go around one head and toward the margin of the fingerprints. An ulnar loop opens toward the inside of the hands, a radial loop toward the outside.

lordosis. An exaggerated forward curving of the spine, typically in the lumbar region.

loris. A lemur family with four genera, found in India, Southeast Asia, and Africa.

loss. In linguistics, the process by which a sound is dropped from a word.

loss, soul. The soul's leaving the body, often believed to be the cause of disease or death. Soul loss may occur through sleeping or sneezing, by malevolence on the part of a natural object's spirit, or by witchcraft. Covering the mouth in yawning and blessing one who sneezes is probably a holdover of an ancient practice designed to keep the soul in.

lost wax. See TECHNIQUE, LOST WAX.

lotus. An ancient flowering water plant. It is associated with the East and is first recorded in the third millenium B.C., in the Indus Valley. Among its meanings have been health, luck, beauty, fertility, divinity, resurrection, and purity.

loupe. See BLOOM.

loup-garou. A shapeless animal with neither head nor limbs, which French Canadians believe they will become if they do not take the sacrament for seven years.

louse detection. See DETECTION, LOUSE.

loy. An angular digging stick (q.v.).

lozenge. A design consisting of a four-sided figure other than a square; also, a small thin leaf-shaped arrowhead.

Lubbock, Sir John (1834-1913). An English anthropologist who used an extreme evolutionary approach and upheld the concept of a state of communal marriage. He suggested that communal changed to individual marriage after marriage by capture began. Lubbock invented the terms Paleolithic and Neolithic.

lubra. A generalized term for an aboriginal woman in Australia, from the extinct Tasmanian term.

Lucretius (98-55 B.C.). A Roman philosopher whose poem, *De Rerum Natura* ("The Nature of Things"), summarized the naturalistic view of the world that the ancients held. He presented civilized society as the product of a long process of development. He adumbrated the later finding that the culture of men developed from stones to copper and iron.

ludus naturae. A stone with a general resemblance to an object touched up to increase the resemblance. Thus, a stone might resemble the head of a wolf and features would be added to enhance the likeness. The term literally means "nature's joke." Some scholars maintain that the ludi naturae represent the first form of human art.

lug. A protuberance, as on some forms of early pottery, to assist in taking hold.

lugger. A vessel with a lugsail, a four-sided sail that hangs obliquely on a mast, slung at a third or a quarter of its length from the forward end, and lowered and hoisted with the halyard.

Lumawig cult. See CULT, LUMA-WIG.

lunate. Having the shape of a crescent.

lunation. The time between two consecutive new moons. It averages 29 days 12 hours 44 minutes 2.8 seconds.

Lunda empire. See EMPIRE, LUNDA.

Lung-shan. See POTTERY, BLACK.

lunulae. Early Bronze Age crescent-shaped neck ornaments, made of thin gold plate. They have been found in parts of Western Europe.

lur. A Scandinavian brass musical instrument dating from prehistoric times. It was a cone-shaped tube that rested on the performer's left shoulder and curved forward over his head.

lure. An artificial object that looks like the usual food of the fish or animal being hunted. In music, a lure is a wooden trumpet resembling the alphorn (q.v.); it is found in Norway.

Luschan, Felix von (1854-1924). A German anthropologist who early showed that the concept of a Jewish race was erroneous.

lustration. A ceremonial cleansing or purification; in antiquity, a ceremony for purifying areas or groups of people from defilement.

lustrum. A 20-year period, as among the Mayas.

lusus naturae. A freak of nature.

lute. A stringed musical instrument with a neck and body. It is used as a background for dances and songs, besides being a solo instrument. The lute's strings are plucked with the right-hand fingers, while the left-hand fingers stop the strings on the frets. The lute was particularly popular in ancient Egypt, and appears on much Egyptian sculpture. In Arabia it was called *el ond* and in Spain *laud*. The mandolin is related to the lute.

lute, scholar's. See CH'IN.

lycanthropy. In folklore, the idea of a human becoming a wolf. It has been speculatively suggested that man originally subsisted on gathered fruit and then became a lupine carnivorous hunter, and that the superstitions about werewolves reflect this change. Such rites as those of the Moroccan Isawiyya brotherhood, in which the participants work themselves into a frenzy and tear living animals to pieces with their bare hands, have been cited as atavistic examples of lycanthropic behavior. In these rites, the men disguise themselves as animals by wearing pelts or painted garments.

Lycian. An Asianic language preserved in about 150 inscriptions and some coins, formerly spoken in the southwestern part of Asia Minor. It dates back to the fourth and fifth centuries B.C. and has no demonstrable linguistic affinity with any other language.

lykwake. The practice of watching a corpse for payment. Among the reasons for lykwake were that the relatives were loath to leave the person for whom they had been caring and the possibility that life might return to the body.

lynchet. A low ridge resulting from soil being washed down from the upper edge of a field to an uncultivated strip at its bottom. The study of lynchets helps in dating Late Bronze Age cultivations.

lynchet, negative. A hollow in the ground often resulting from early plowing which has worked the soil down from the top of a field, where the lynchet is formed.

lynchet, positive. A ridge in the ground often resulting from early plowing which has worked the soil down from the top of a field, where the lynchet is formed.

lyra. A lyre-shaped Greek string instrument with a tortoise shell body and an ox-hide tympanum. A yoke of antelope horns or wood was attached to the shell. The strings were held to the yoke's cross piece by fatty hide. The instrument was tuned by twisting the hide. There were gut strings, never more than seven. The left hand plucked the strings accompanying the song,

while the right hand, with a plectrum, bridged the pauses in the song. The lyra was used by dilettantes and novices.

lyre. A harplike musical instrument, played manually or by bow. It has been known for some 5,000 years, although it achieved special attention in Greece, where it was used for solos and for accompanying recitation and song. The lyre has a hollow and resonant body with two rods to which a transverse bar is connected and an open rigid framework. The strings, which are plucked by the fingers or a plectrum, run between the resonator and the transverse bar. The lyre was believed by the Greeks to have magical qualities.

lyre, Mercurian. One of the most ancient stringed instruments. It was made of a tortoise shell which had seven vibrating strings.

M

ma. A sour paste made from breadfruit in Polynesia, especially in the Marquesas.

maal. A Dinka name for a gift of cattle.

macana. In Mexico, a wooden sword or club.

macaque. A commonly found member of the Cercopithecidae (q.v.), with some 50 species. The macaques are hardy and stout.

macaroni. Fairly parallel wavy lines that were probably originally made on clay walls by fingers, and were subsequently made on harder surfaces with pronged implements. They constitute the earliest kind of engraving.

mace. A metal club often used offensively, originally to break armor in the Middle Ages; by extension, a staff which is a symbol of authority. Mace also denotes an aromatic and fragment spice made from dried nutmeg and a Malay money unit worth one-tenth of a tael.

mace, star-headed. A mace found on the Atlantic coast of Honduras and in Peru. There is a hole in the middle for the handle and the head bears a number of points.

maceualli. The Aztec common class.

McGee, William John (1853-1912). An American anthropologist who anticipated the study of human ecology.

machrocheilia. Unusually large lips, which are usually everted.

machwa. A sail-carrying harbor boat of the Malabar Coast.

McLennan, John F. (1827-1881). A Scottish lawyer who coined the terms exogamy and endogamy. He emphasized the importance of matrilineal descent, and he believed that all the civilized nations of antiquity passed through a totemic stage. He had many of the same ideas as Bachofen (q.v.), but developed them independently.

macquaitl. An Aztec obsidian-edged sword.

macrocephaly. An abnormally large head, usually found associated with mental deficiency. The skull does not bulge laterally or at the forehead, as in hydrocephaly (q.v.). The brain may weigh as much as 2,800 grams.

macrodiacritic. The condition in which 80 per cent or more of the members of a race, or stock are recognizable as such.

macroevolution. One-step speciation; substantial mutations; pedomorphosis (q.v.).

macron. The symbol placed over a vowel to show that it should be pronounced long, e.g., the *ā* in lāme.

macroskelic. A stem-leg length index (q.v.) between 95 and 99.9.

macrospecies. A large species.

macrosplanchnic or **megalosplanchnic.** In Viola's system of body types, referring to the fat extreme.

macuahuitl. An Aztec swordlike weapon consisting of a flat wooden club into the edges of which were inserted sharp flakes of obsidian.

macuba. A drink imbibed in some ceremonies of the Nañigo in Cuba. The initiate bites off the head of a rooster, lets its blood drip into the rum, and then drinks the mixture.

madder. A red dye or pigment used in painting since classical times. Pliny mentions it as *rubia* and examples have been found in Egyptian and Greco-Roman paintings. It is made from the root of the plant *Rubia tinctorium*. It is no longer used since synthetic dyes, such as alizarin, have replaced it.

madinada. A Baganda xylophone.

madness, Vailala. A New Guinea cult of nativism (q.v.).

maeroglossia. A large tongue, which may interfere with clear speech.

magadis. An Egyptian musical instrument like a harp. It consisted of a small sounding board over which the strings were stretched to attach to a crosspiece.

magani. Among the Bagobo, one who is the killer of two persons.

Magdalenian. The last level of the Upper Paleolithic Age in its European development. It was characterized by the increase in antler and bone working, such as the bone harpoon head; and from the prevalence of reindeer it is sometimes called the Reindeer Age. It lasted for some 6,000 years and ended ca. 7500 B.C. Many thin long blades date from this period. Ivory was used for carving. The art work of this period was representational. The climate was fairly arctic and was damper than in Solutrean times and steppe conditions were not so rigorous. Many large animals died off after the Ice Age ended and man lived on lake shores or grassy land.

Magdalenian culture is largely a French development, although it ranged from Bavaria to parts of Spain. In Magdalenian home art, single geometric patterns were used, but animal engravings were also common. The fifth Magdalenian period had the best engravings, with degeneration appearing in the sixth period. Conventionalization occurred with increasing frequency toward the end of Magdalenian times. The graphic arts also included polychrome paintings. Composite implements, like the harpoon (q.v.) and atlatl (q.v.), were common. There was more use of organic materials, shaped in a variety of ways.

Aurignacian (q.v.) culture developed where the Solutrean did not penetrate and gave rise to Magdalenian culture, which has been divided into six parts. The first three have different types of bone lance points and no harpoon. In the fourth a primitive harpoon appears and in the fifth a harpoon with a single barb row, and in the sixth a harpoon with a double row of barbs. Red ocher and shell necklaces were often included in the graves.

The few Magdalenian human remains that have been found are not unlike the contemporary Eskimo and suggest the Cro-Magnon type. One skull at Chancelade, in the French Dordogne area, has some Eskimo characteristics in its brain case, narrow nasal aperture, broad cheek, and lower jaw. Some scholars have suggested that such evidence, and the similarity of artifacts, make it likely that Eskimos lived in West Europe in the Magdalenian era, and that the reindeer and Eskimo both went north when the ice retreated in the final phase of the last glaciation.

maghoula. A mound, especially a mound of debris in Thessaly.

magic. The techniques of coercion, based on what we would consider false premises, by which persons, usually nonliterates, try to obtain desired practical ends. Regarded by many as the first use of the concept of causation, and as closely allied with the beginnings of religion, magic may be the property of a special group of magicians, or it may be the property of everyone. Many current superstitions represent holdovers of magic. Frazer described sympathetic magic as that based on something which had once been in contact with an object maintaining a permanent association even after contact ends, and mimetic magic as that which gets results by imitation, e.g., a sterile woman's handling a child's picture to assist her in becoming pregnant. Leuba divided magic functioning into the principles of repetition, sympathetic magic, and will-effort. Magic that is expected to produce evil is called black magic, while magic expected to bring about good is white magic. Malinowski has emphasized the importance of the verbal component of magic. In some groups, like the Dobuans, the effects of the magic may be spoiled by changing the recital.

Tylor gave four reasons for the nonliterate's belief in magic: some magic results do take place; the magician may use trickery or deception; believers in magic are more impressed with positive than negative cases; and it may be assumed that counter-magic is responsible whenever the rite is not effective.

Magic gives a kind of sanctity to the activity with which it is connected, as Malinowski has pointed out. He has also stressed that it makes for confidence in its users.

magic, aversive. Popular magic (q.v.) geared toward avoiding trouble, as in the scapegoat (q.v.) ritual.

magic, black. Magic used to effect evil. A typical technique is reversing the practices of the Christian religion, so as to work the contrary of its beneficent effects. Thus, the mass is said backward, and the sign of the cross is made on the floor with the left foot instead of in the air with the right hand.

magic, contagious. The doctrine that once some objects or persons have been connected, they will still influence each other and be connected in the future.

magic, defensive. Any practice of magic incantations of rituals for the sole purpose of protection from, or destruction of, evil influences.

magic, destructive. Magic used to cause bad weather, trouble, sickness, unhappiness, or death. Sorcery and witchcraft (q.v.) are often described as examples of destructive magic.

magic, effigy. Magic performed by using an effigy as if it were the actual object of the magic, e.g., piercing the eye of a wax image of a person in order to blind the person represented.

magic, exuvial. A type of black magic in which the magician performs rites and incantations with nail parings, strands of hair, skin scrapings, or other of the bodily products (exuviae) of an intended victim.

magic, homeopathic. Magic that works on the assumption that like will have an effect on like.

magic, hunting. The practice of placating supernatural spirits that control game animals before embarking on a hunt, so as to ensure success.

magic, imitative. The belief that magic can be wrought by working on symbols of a thing or person, so that action taken against the symbol will have a similar effect on the real object of the magic.

magic, love. A charm that causes a person to fall in love. It may be a drug (philter). In some types of love magic, the would-be beloved mixes some part of the bodily exuvia, e.g., the hair, in the food or hides it in the clothing, of the passional object.

magic, mortuary. Any magic rituals the purpose of which is to insure the continued good fortune of a deceased person in the next world. This type of magic was developed into an art and science in ancient Egypt.

magic, popular. The practice of a group's trying jointly to reach spirit powers either to prevent trouble or achieve a desired end.

magic, productive. Popular magic (q.v.) directed toward achieving fertility in agriculture, animals, or humans, e.g., fertility rites.

magic, public. Magic performed ritually on behalf of a community or tribe. The performer is important in his community and is often the tribal chief.

magic, sympathetic. Magic based on the principle that an object can influence other objects similar to it.

magic, white. A type of magic using supernatural abilities for the benefit of others.

magic and religion, distinctions between. The criteria usually given for distinguishing magic and religion are several. The religious act has a socially approved purpose, while black magic, at least, is socially abhorred and feared. Religion involves reverently praying for something, while in magic results are expected to follow automatically.

Religion is a social activity, while magic typically is individual. The goals of religion are diffuse and general, while those of magic are specific and limited. These distinctions, however, are at best tenuous. Thus, popular magic (q.v.) and productive magic (q.v.) are social activities, while the intensest form of religious life — mysticism — is quintessentially solitary. Moreover, especially in its more popular expressions, religion may seek individual, mundane results instead of expressing a general reverence of deity.

magician. A professional worker in the field of public magic (q.v.).

Maglawa. The Tinguian afterworld.

Maglemosian. An Epipaleolithic culture area in north central Europe. It was a bog or lake culture, with a ground-stone industry, bone-working, wood-working, canoes, and some flint-working. It probably saw the domestication of the dog and the people probably lived on birds, fish, and grass. Some engravings consisting of conventionalized dots were found. A single-barbed harpoon (q.v.) was the typical tool. The climate was cool and dry, with pines and hazels common. The type site is in Denmark, although the Maglemosian culture was distributed from northern England to Finland and Poland and was largely associated with the Baltic.

magma. A crude mixture, especially of inorganic matter.

magnetism, remanent. The magnetism created in an object heated above a critical temperature called the Curie point. Such magnetism (also called paleomagnetism), in a substance which contains magnetite—many rocks, the majority of soils, potter's clay—provides a method of dating archaeological finds. The object becomes magnetized in line with the environment's magnetic field, and retains its specific magnetism for an indefinite period after cooling. (Potter's ovens usually reach the Curie point, as do most large fires.) In most cases, the environment's general magnetic field is the same as the earth's, or magnetic north. However, since magnetic north varies about 10° in 100 years, measuring the remanent magnetism of a hearth theoretically should permit dating the last time the oven was heated, $\pm$ 10 years. A major defect of the method is that there are no records on the magnetism of the earth during the periods of prehistory. Another is the possibility that the earth's magnetic changes are repeated in about 500-year periods, so that a find should be located within a given 500 years in order to use this method.

magot. In art, any small grotesque figure. It is usually found in Oriental art in the form of knobs on covers of large vases and other decorative vessels. The word comes from French and means "ape."

In northern Mexico, magot is a plant that provides a poison for arrows.

Magyar. A Finno-Ugrian language; Hungarian.

Mahabharata. An Indian epic poem, the world's longest, of 220,000 lines. It was begun before the beginning of the Christian era and finished by 400 A.D.

mahambi. See MARIMBA.

Mahayana. A branch of Buddhism with elaborate ritual and images.

mahol. Derived from the Hebrew *hul*, "to twist or turn," a word used to describe certain whirling movements in sacred Oriental dances. It is used frequently in the Old Testament, usually when describing dances by women.

Mahori. The Polynesian language considered as a whole.

mahr. A dowry among the Kababish, also called mal.

maiming. Punishment through cutting off part of the body. There was often a connection between the part cut off and the organ involved in the crime for which punishment is made. Thus, in Anglo-Saxon times, a thief might be punished by having his hand cut off.

Maine, Sir Henry J. S. (1822-1888). An English historian and lawyer who made substantial contributions to the study of ethnological jurisprudence and who was one of the founders of comparative law. He was the first person to use the historical method in the study of legal questions. His *Ancient Law* (1861) emphasized the early power of the patriarchal family, and his *Village Communities in the East and West* (1871) is a classic study. He pioneered in the philosophical study of institutions. His tracing of the development of societies from those with group relations and tradition determining duties and rights to those in which contract and le-

gal power were important has become a classic; he epitomized the process in his phrase "from status to contract." He defined the concepts of blood tie and territorial bond, later used by Morgan, and also influenced Durkheim, Maxim Kovalevsky, and Herbert Spencer. See SHIFT, MAINEAN.

maize. The tallest cereal, growing as much as 15 feet high. Its grains are produced on the cob, in rows. Among the different kinds of maize are pod, pop, flint, dent, flour, sweet, and waxy. It was probably first domesticated by Paraguayan Indians and intensively cultivated in Peru. It is also widely distributed and used in southeast Asia, since it grows best in warm countries. It used to be the major foodstuff of a good deal of the Americas and is also a valuable stock feed. Maize is called corn in the New World. It is not a good bread-maker.

majuscule. The use of capital letters only .

mak. See CLOTH, MUMMY.

Makalian. The first so-called wet period recognized in geological strata in Kenya. It was more moist than the present climate of Africa, but less wet than in the pluvial periods.

makara. A fishlike monster found on carvings in India.

Makers, Basket. The predecessors of today's Pueblo peoples. The Basket Maker and Pueblo cultures are continuous in character as well as in time. The term Anasazi (q.v.) indicates this joint development, which centered in the New Mexico-Arizona upland. The Anasazi sequence begins with Basket Maker II; Basket Maker I is left for the yet undiscovered culture believed to have developed earlier. The period of Basket Maker II is ca. 300 A.D.-500 A.D. The heart of the culture was in the area of the San Juan River. The culture was agricultural and preceramic, with coiled and twined baskets and bags. The atlatl (q.v.), not the bow (q.v.), was in use. Basket Maker III dates ca. 500-700 A.D. There are pit dwellings, domesticated turkeys, varieties of maize, pottery, baskets, fiber bags, and sandles.

mal. The pidgin name for loincloth (q.v.) in Melanesia. See MAHR.

malafu or **malebu.** A palm wine in Africa.

malanggan or **malagan.** Elaborately carved mortuary slabs, found in New Ireland. At a person's death, the slabs are made by someone from the opposite moiety (q.v.) and paid for by someone in his own moiety. The term also refers to the ceremonies for the dead.

malar. The zygomatic bone, which constitutes much of the outer and lower borders of the eye's bony orbit.

Malay. The Indonesian language element in the Austronesian linguistic stock; the Mongoloid post-Indonesian migration to Indonesia.

Malay, Deutero-. A hypothetical Mongoloid subdivision which left Southeast Asia for Malaysia after the migration of the proto-Malay Mongoloid subdivision.

Malayo-Polynesian. A language family found largely in island Oceania, except New Guinea and Australia. Affixation is important morphologically. The roots usually consist of two syllables. It has Indonesian, Melanesian, Micronesian, and Polynesian subfamilies.

Malay, Proto-. A hypothetical Mongoloid subdivision from Southeast Asia which migrated to the East Indies and the Philippines. It has a fairly broad nose and short stature.

Malaysian. A Mongoloid subrace with broad head, slight body hair, medium prognathism, brown skin, small stature, and straight head hair.

malga. An aboriginal implement with a sharp point. The New Caledonia type had a handle at right angles to the point, while some Australian types were practically a straight stick with a sharp point. The term war pick is sometimes used.

malim. A name given to a holy or learned man among the Arabs.

malo. See MARO.

maloca. A large multi-family thatched house, a common form of residence among the Indians of Tropical South America.

malocclusion. Malposition of the teeth so that there is interference with their normal opposition, as in mastication.

malting. Dissolving in water the ground grist of sprouted grain.

Mamaia. A form of nativism (q.v.) in Polynesia. Its prophet identified himself with Jesus Christ ca. 1827, and it lasted only until ca. 1833. It developed among professing Christians. Although ridiculed when it began, the Mamaia movement al-

most swept the islands. It was a reaction to missionary influences and
tried to combine Christianity with
some older native doctrines.

mammalia. A class of organisms
characterized by suckling of the
young, lung breathing, body hair,
and a four-chambered heart. Most
are placental.

mammals, placental. All extant
mammals, other than the marsupials
and the egg-laying. A placental
mammal carries the fetus within the
female's body and nourishes it
through a temporary organ called
the placenta.

man. The subject matter of anthropology is generally defined as
a hominid (q.v.), namely Homo
sapiens (q.v.), who makes tools, but
it also may include some types
which are now extinct, like Homo
neanderthalensis and Pithecanthropus. The word man is popularly
used in a much more narrow manner than taxonomy would indicate,
and its emotional connotations make
it difficult to use in an objective
manner. The major characteristics
that distinguish man from monkeys,
apes, and lemurs are the following:
the nose's prominent bridge and
well-developed tip, a median furrow in the upper lip, possession of
the chin, the convex lumbar curve
in the spine, the fact that the great
toe is nonopposable and is in line
with the other toes, the double arch
of the foot, relative hairlessness and
lack of tactile hairs, large brain
(2½-3 times the size of the gorilla's), slight projection of the canine teeth and the noninterlocking
of the upper and lower canine teeth,

outrolling of the lips and visibility
of the mucous membrane as a continuous red line, long life span, bipedal locomotion, narrower upright
trunk, head poised on spine, feet
bearing the body's weight, erect
posture, symbolic expression, edu-
cability, and advanced culture. See
MAN, EVOLUTION OF.

man, Afalon. A North African
fossil type, similar to Cro-Magnon
man in many ways.

man, ape-. The popular name for
the ancestors of man who possessed
apelike characteristics. They are
primates who walked erect, but
their ability to use fire or speech is
doubtful.

man, cave. A hypothetical early
man who lived in caves. Since caves
are damp and rheumatism was
prevalent in early days, as shown by
fossil remains, it is not unlikely
that on the baiss of this and other
evidence, some Neanderthal and
Upper Paleolithic men lived in
depths of the caves, although they
may sometimes have inhabited cave
mouths when they were not
draughty.

man, dawn. A hypothetical independent line of men which sprang
from an Oligocene stock, which also
presumably gave rise to the anthropoid apes.

man, evolution of. As seen by
students like Clark, the process of
evolution by which man developed
involves the growth from tree shrew
to Eocene lemuroids and tarsioids,
through progressive tarsioids with
some simian features and Oligocene
gibbons and Miocene generalized
apes. Subsequent development is to

the South African Australopithecinae and Pithecanthropus, leading
to the Pleistocene Mousterian man
of Neanderthal traits in one line,
while another line led to Acheulian
man, from which in turn arose
Homo sapiens. The growth of the
brain was great in the primates, and
the presence of primitive and generalized anatomical qualities endowed primates with a bodily plasticity that facilitated their evolution.

One theory holds that all men
began as a kind of ape in the Tertiary. This type broke up into a
number of lines. Homo sapiens is
an old form and Homo neanderthalensis (q.v.) is not necessarily
an ancestor. Another theory maintains that Homo sapiens is young
and is a stage of other species, not
a species in itself. The different fossil men evolved toward Homo sapiens until they resembled each
other. Thus, Rhodesian man became
the Negro, Peking man the Mongoloid, the Neanderthals the Europeans, and Solo man the Australians. Weidenreich has suggested that
prehominids like Peking man or
Java man produced Rhodesian, Solo,
and Neanderthal man, who became
Homo sapiens. Today Homo sapiens is one species. The other species of man exhibit greater differences among themselves than do the
extant races of man. See HOMO
SAPIENS; MAN.

man, fall of. The Mesopotamian
myth, later adapted by the Israelites,
which tells of the temptation and
disobedience of the first man and
woman, and their subsequent expulsion from the garden of Eden.
The story as set forth in the Bible
tries to interpret three facets of the
human lot: universal death, toil for
man and sorrow for the woman, and
woman's subjection to man. Its implication is that human beings have
learned the ability to discern by an
act of transgression, but it does not
necessarily include the doctrine of
original sin as developed by Christian theologians.

man, feral. A person raised in
complete isolation from other humans, usually by animals. Some students of the subject have said that
in recent times there are no genu-
inely authenticated cases of feral
men.

Man, Galley Hill. A fossil, probably one of the Middle Pleistocene
era, found in 1888 in England, and
perhaps an ancestor of the Mediterranean stock. The fossil, almost
complete, was of a modern European man about five feet three
inches tall. The large brows, thick
skull, and small mastoid processes
are primitive features.

Man, Heidelberg. See HOMO
HEIDELBERGENSIS.

man, marginal. An individual associated with two culture patterns
without really feeling a member of
either. A marginal man, thus, is not
a fully participating member of a
social group.

man, medicine. The popular early
name for an American Indian who
treats the sick or has special powers.
More specific terms are used by contemporary scholars. Medicine men
also exist in other primitive societies. Some practice magic or are

shamans (q.v.) acting as intermediaries between the world of spirits and the members of the society. The medicine man is often associated with the use of sweat baths, herbs, and simple surgery. His status and role change from one tribe to another, ranging from magician to doctor and priest. The training of medicine men was usually elaborate. Often they were selected from a special family.

man, Neoanthropic. A modern man, usually Homo sapiens.

Man, Peking. See SINANTHROPUS PEKINENSIS.

man, primitive. Prehistoric, or ancient men, or men of the Eolithic, Paleolithic, Neolithic, and Bronze Ages. Also, contemporary societies that are not civilized.

mana. A nonindividualized supernatural force, independent of specific supernatural persons. It is widely believed to be responsible for the effect of magic (q.v.) and for unusual qualities and to have power for good and evil. Codrington first found it in Melanesia, although Polynesia probably had the most refined concept; there mana was indestructible and was transmitted through the chiefs. The Algonkian *manitou,* the Sioux *wakan,* the *hasina* of Madagascar, the *baraka* of Morocco, and the *manngur* of the Queensland Kabi are related concepts. Codrington defined mana as ". . . a force altogether distinct from physical power which acts in all kinds of ways for good and evil and which it is of the greatest advantage to possess and control . . . shows itself in physical force or in any kind of power or excellence which a man possesses."

manak. A device to bring a seal from the water in which it floats to the hunter who killed it. It consists of a pear-shaped wooden ball several inches in diameter, with three sharp steel hooks and a ring with thong attached. The hunter throws the manak at the seal and pulls in the rope.

mancala. In Africa, a game played by moving pieces (shells or pebbles) from one cavity to another on a board, in accordance with set rules. Holes in the ground may be used instead of a board.

mandible. The lower jaw. The bone composing the mandible is well condensed and well calcified. This has led to the extreme resistance that mandibles oppose to the process of inorganic breakdown, so that there are many fossil mandibles as compared with other bones. The mandible's degree of prognathism (q.v.) is a valuable clue to the fossil's place in the evolutionary hierarchy. Through the late teens, the mandible and the lower face show a much greater degree of growth than the upper part of the face and head.

mandioca. See MANIOC.

mandrake. A poisonous Mediterranean plant often mentioned in folklore. It has strong sleep-inducing qualities and has been used as an aphrodisiac and to induce fertility. The root is forked and often vaguely resembles a human body, which has led to the mandrake's being given human attributes and being used in magic.

manes. The spirits of the deceased, or underworld gods.

mangabey. A species of African Cercopithecidae, which are slender and arboreal, with long tails and white spots on the eyebrows.

mangke. An age grade (q.v.) society of southern New Hebrides.

mango. A large east Asiatic fruit tree, the fruit of which has an aromatic and juicy pulp. One of the oldest cultivated tropical fruits, it is very important to the economy of Southeast Asia.

manguare. A slit log signal drum of the Tropical Forest area.

manic-depression. A psychosis characterized by mood swings from elation to melancholia.

Manicheism. A doctrine from Persia, established by Mani, a Magian who had been converted to Christianity and who tried to combine various religio-philosophical concepts. Manicheism incorporated the concept of good and evil from Zoroastrianism and of illumination among men from Buddha and Zoroaster; the symbolism of suffering and crucifixion from the life of Jesus; and the moral and ethical codes of Hinduism.

manilla. An ornamented copper semicircle, used as a medium of exchange in West Africa, notable in Benin.

manioc or mandioca. A sweet plant grown by the Indians of South and Central America. It produces yields for several years after it is first planted. Special treatment is required to purify manioc of the poison it contains and to render it edible. An important manioc derivative is tapioca.

manism. Worshipping the spirits of the dead. It occurs almost everywhere in the world and is usually based on the ancestors' helping the living and on placating the jealousy the dead have for the living. The term is also used for the worship of ghosts and for Herbert Spencer's theory that ancestor and ghost worship gave rise to religion.

manitou. The mysterious and unknown powers of the universe and of life, especially as exemplified in the holiness inherent in certain objects; a spiritual being which controls these powers. The word is Algonkian in origin. See MANA.

mano. A cylindrically shaped grindstone slightly tapered at both ends. It was held in the hand (whence its name handstone) and used as the upper stone in milling. See METATE, SIMPLE.

manor. An English territorial unit containing a village community in serfdom and belonging to a king, lord, or the church. It consisted of the lord's demesne and the land in villenage occupied by tenants.

mantic. Referring to magical activities that result from the intercession of an alien power. The mantic is intermediate between religion and magic.

Mantis. An insect-god who personifies the forces of good to the southern Bushmen of South Africa.

mantra. A sacred Vedic prayer often used by Brahmans as a spell.

manufactory. A place where artifacts are made.

manumission. Setting a slave free. It may be effected gradually or at once. The slave may be freed or become a serf, and he may retain an obligation to his former master, which may be handed down to the ex-slave's children.

manus. A husband's authority over his wife, usually in the sense of paternal authority.

manyatta. A Wondorobo hut.

Maori carving. See CARVING, MAORI.

map, mantle. A simplified schematic geological map of an area.

map, sky. The reflection of arctic terrain in clouds. Water appears black, snow white, and ice and land are variously mottled depending on their appearance.

mapping, village. A technique of field work in which the relationships of every person in a community are recorded, along with the nature of each relationship and where it is manifested.

marabout. A Mohammedan saint or hermit or his tomb.

maraca. A West Indian gourd rattle.

marae. In Polynesia, a ceremonial place, especially a low-walled stone temple, which also served for burials.

marawot. A lodge of the Ingiet secret society.

marble, breccia. Any marble composed of angular fragments.

Märchen. Fictional folk stories, much like fairy tales or folktales.

Marching Rule. See RULE, MARCHING.

margaritomancy. The art of divining the events of the future by observation of the position of pearls when thrown on a flat surface.

marginal area. See AREA, MARGINAL.

marginality, internal. Referring to a group of people with a low level of culture—usually of a hunting, fishing, and gathering type—who are surrounded by peoples of higher culture, as the Pygmies in Africa, the Mura in Brazil, and the Nilgiri Hill tribes in India.

Mariette, Auguste F. (1821-1881). A French archaeologist, the first director of the Egyptian Service of Antiquities. He conducted over 30 excavations and systematized the various archaeological diggings in Egypt. He established the first Near Eastern National Museum at Boulak. Mariette helped prevent the export of many Egyptian treasures in Egypt and was responsible to a considerable extent for the development of a conscience about removing archaeological materials from the country of origin.

marigold. A scented garden herb, with multi-colored flowers. It was the sacred flower of the Aztecs.

marimba. A simple kind of xylophone found in South Africa and Central America. The form mahambi is also found.

marinba. A pointed wallaby bone used for tooth avulsion among the Wongapitcha.

Mariology. The study of the life and teachings of the Virgin Mary.

mark, crop, or mark, soil. A crop site that shows signs of an archaeological find underneath. Aerial photography is especially useful in finding crop marks. Corn growing over an ancient filled-in ditch may look greener, through the depth of loose soil. Sparse corn may indicate a hidden wall or road underneath, so that the roots get little moisture from the shallow soil over the masonry.

mark, diacritical. See DIACRITICAL. A written symbol placed over, below, or across a letter, used most often to show how the sound should be pronounced in the given word.

mark, property. A mark on an object to indicate that it belongs to a given individual or group.

mark, quantity. A phonetic term used to describe the symbol placed over a vowel or diphthong to show that it is long or short. The macron (q.v.) indicates a long sound, the breve (q.v.) a short sound.

mark, soil. See MARK, CROP.

marker. A linguistic unit that shows the grammatical class to which a particular word belongs. It may indicate plurality, tense, etc. An example of a zero marker in the plural is the word "deer," which does not change from singular to plural but whose plurality may be marked by a plural verb form or a numerical adjective. Another example of a marker is the *s* added to nouns in English to indicate a plural. See ELEMENT, ZERO.

marks, recognition. Marks or deformations intended to identify a person or his social group. Cicatrization (q.v.), tattooing, and other means may be used for this purpose.

marl. A clay with a good deal of calcium carbonate.

marmoset. A small South and Central American monkey of the family *Hapalidae,* characterized by a long, nonprehensile tail and claws instead of nails. It is one of the most primitive of the platyrrhine monkeys.

maro or **malo.** A tapa breechcloth worn by Polynesian men.

marouvane. An Egyptian stringed instrument. The earliest forms were made of bamboo tubes with strips of bark cut between two joints and raised from the surface by small bits of wood placed at top and bottom of each string. A resonator made of palm leaf is frequently found, with the point of the leaf fastened to one end of the tube and the stem to the other.

marriage. The established institution for starting a family. Both monogamous and polygamous marriage is found. There is often an exchange of economic goods in a marriage, and involved is a legal, physical, and moral union between a man and woman, continuing through the raising of their children. Marriage regulates relations between the sexes and helps establish the child's relation to the community. It is usually associated with a ceremony, magical, religious, social, or civil, which formalizes the group's approval. In marriage, the children produced by the women are usually accepted as the legitimate offspring of the married couple. See FAMILY.

marriage, adoptive. Marriage by a man's adoption into his wife's family, so that he is a son in her family. Thus, a patrilineal family may get a son, so that his children belong to his wife's family.

marriage, affinal. A marriage with a relative of a spouse.

marriage, avuncular. Marriage of a man with his sister's daughter. Since forms of marriage are regularly described from the point of view of a male Ego, this type of marriage should more properly be referred to as cross-niece marriage. Avuncular marriage is sometimes defined as incestuous in modern countries.

marriage, child. The marriage of a child under about 15 years old. Usually the girl is the younger marriage partner. Child marriage was found among the Melanesians, Australians, and Hindus. In India great numbers of girls under 15 have married up to the fairly recent past, although governments have tried to stop the practice. Among nonliterate groups, marriage is usually permitted after puberty.

marriage, common law. A marriage that has not been solemnized but is founded on the consent of both parties and their openly living together as man and wife. The term common law marriage is most exactly used with reference to such unions occurring in a place that otherwise prescribes certain marital formalities, e.g., the State of Texas.

marriage, cross-cousin. Marriage between cousins related through the siblings of unlike sex, e.g., between the child of a woman and the child of her brother.

marriage, extended affinal. Marriage with an affinal relative of a generation other than one's own.

marriage, fictive. A sham marriage, conducted in the same way as a regular marriage, e.g., among the Kwakiutl.

marriage, group. A group of females married to a group of males. Caesar, for example, says that in the interior of Britain, fathers could have marital relations with their son's wives, so that parent and sons formed a group of this type. Although this concept often appeared in the writings of some early theorists, it was probably never a cultural norm, and the supposed descriptions were probably based on the erroneous impressions of untrained observers.

marriage, half. Among the Yurok, marriage without full payment of the bride price.

marriage, interfamilial exchange. Marriage between a brother and sister and another sister-brother combination. It is common in Australia and Melanesia.

marriage, patrilocal. A marriage in which the wife lives with her husband's tribe. It is associated with the patronymic system.

marriage, preferential. Marriage between two people of specific status, whether it is enjoined or preferred.

marriage, primary. A person's first marriage.

marriage, secondary. A secondary marriage contracted after a first marriage. The levirate (q.v.) is the most common type, and the sororate (q.v.) is also found.

marriage, symmetrical cross-cousin. A marriage in which either type of cross cousin (q.v.) is acceptable or sought after as a mate,

345

while marriage to the other cross-cousin might not be permitted.

marriage, term. A marriage contracted for a specified terminable period. It is found in Ethiopia, Tibet, and parts of the Near East. Traders in North Africa sometimes engage in a term marriage for specific periods.

marriage, tree. A symbolic ceremony that unites a tree to a person in marriage, often as part of a wedding, occasionally in order to permit one marriage before that of an older brother or sister. Tree marriage is especially common in India.

marriage-beena. A man's being required to leave his home and live with his wife's family; the marriage is usually matripotestal. It is found in India, although it is atypical.

marriage by capture. Getting a wife by abduction, whether genuine, ritual, or pretended.

marriage by exchange. Marriage which involves two men's exchanging daughters or sisters, so that each man obtains a wife for himself or for a brother or son.

marriwirri. An Australian wooden sword.

maschalismos. A murderer's cutting off the limbs and sense organs of the person murdered and tying them near the arm pits, so that the corpse's ghost is immobile and cannot achieve vengeance.

mask. A cover for the human face or head, whether worn for ritual, disguise, as symbol of authority or prestige, or to effect cures. Many masks are artistically executed and have inspired much modern art. They have been made of practically every material. There may be great distortion of the actual features or appearance of the model for the mask, or the mask may represent an animal or some nonhuman forces or beings. Masks may be representational or symbolical, starkly simple or highly ornamented. Masks were employed by American Indians, Africans, Chinese, and many other groups. The death mask was widely used by the Egyptians and Romans.

Mason, Otis T. (1838-1908). An American anthropologist, who contributed to the study of early technology. He wrote on the origins of inventions, the role of women in early culture, and early American basketry.

masonry, Cyclopean. Very large irregularly hewn chunks of stone used in ancient architecture for the construction of heavy walls and battlements.

masonry, Greek. A technique of wall construction in which every other stone is the full thickness of the wall.

masquerade. A public or private celebration in which the participants conceal their identities by wearing a mask or the like.

Massasoit. An Algonkian Indian who taught the Pilgrims how to plant corn.

Massenerhebung effect. See EFFECT, MASSENERHEBUNG.

masseter. The muscles which control the closing of the mouth. The origin is attached to the lower edges of the cheek bones, with the insertion attached to the outside of the ascending ramus of the lower jaw.

massif. A large mountain mass; a part of the earth's crust bounded by faults and displaced as a unit.

mastaba. A bench usually found at the entrance of Arab doorways. The term was applied by Arabs to Egyptian tombs of the Old Kingdom period so that it came to mean a low massive quadrangular building with inclined walls and no opening except the door. The ancient mastaba has a flat top and is made of brick or stone. It consisted of a chapel, passage, and sarcophagus chamber.

mastoid. A process of the temporal bone which is behind the ear, found in many mammals. It is conical and well-developed in adults.

matai. In Polynesia, the head of a household.

Matambala. A secret society (q.v.) of Florida Island, in the Solomons.

matapi. A squeezer used to press the poisonous juices from the cassava.

maté. An aromatic and mildly stimulant drink of South America, especially found in Paraguay.

materials, survival of. The material of which an object is made is the major determinant of how long it will survive. Inorganic materials are less likely to decay than organic. Stone masonry lasts well, although its surface tooling may be destroyed fairly easily. Kiln-fired bricks are fairly lasting, while bricks fired in the sun are likely to disintegrate rapidly. Flint and stone survive the best, although they may show surface changes. Gold is very enduring, while silver tarnishes considerably. Iron has little survival power, and lead and bronze seem to last fairly well. Early open-kiln fired pottery loses its surface easily. Of organic substances, horn, antler and ivory have the greatest resistance power, while vegetable remains are virtually without such power. Climate is a major factor in preservation, with the warmest climate the most oppressive. Very dry or very cold climates provide the best preservative conditions.

matha. A stick used by the ancient Brahmins to obtain sacred fire by friction. This may be the root of the name of the Prometheus who went to Olympus to get fire, especially as the prefix *pra* adds the concept of robbing by force.

mathala. See MRIDANG.

mating. Persons of the opposite sex pairing off through the agency of the sex drive.

mating, assortative. The mating of those individuals who have similar genetic traits, as short with short.

mating, preferential. Rules approving the marriage of individuals who have a specific kinship relationship.

mating, random. A situation in which any individual has an equal chance of mating with any other individual of the opposite sex within a given population.

matres lectionis. A consonant (q.v.) which also has a vowel value, especially in Hebrew. The Hebrew alphabet is completely consonantal, but four letters (aleph, he, waw, yod) have become long vowels. The terms vocalic consonant or vowel letter are also used.

matriarchate. An early society, suggested by some writers, in which women constituted the major authority. There is no group which was ever strictly matriarchal, although there are many which allot special prerogatives to women. Thus, only women own homes in Hopi and Khasi culture, and Iroquois women nominate the chiefs, but these are exceptional cases and do not represent a matriarchate. The theory of the matriarchate as a predecessor of the patriarchal system is tied to the theory of the family's originating from promiscuity. This theory has it that the earliest family relations were between mother and child, since the father was not known. Thus the mother was the important member of the family, with descent traced through her, and larger groupings fell under the control of the matriarch.

matriarchy, free. A matrilineal (q.v.) community without local exogamy (q.v.).

matrilineal. Referring to the transmission of authority, inheritance, or descent primarily through females. The Swiss Bachofen (q.v.) was the first to emphasize this, in *Das Mutterrecht* (1861), although he mainly used material from the classical civilizations, especially Lycian society. The Scotsman J. F. McLennan (q.v.) wrote on the significance of matrilineal descent, independently of Bachofen, although later. Matrilineal descent is sometimes called uterine descent.

matriliny. A unilateral female-dominated culture, which may have such features as matrilocal (q.v.) marriage and matrilineal (q.v.) descent.

matrilocal. Having reference to a married couple's residing with the wife's family or kin group. The term uxorilocal is also used.

matripotestal. Referring to the manifestation of authority by the mother or the maternal grandmother.

matting. A method of fabricating articles that is a link between weaving and basketry. A diagonally worked mat is started at a corner and plaited as a basket is. A horizontally worked mat may have a warp with parallel components, with the weft inserted as the work advances. A mat made by hanging on a horizontal bar or stretched on a frame is made by a process like weaving, with the threading done by hand rather than shuttle.

mattock. A kind of pickax with broad ends. It is used to loosen soil and for grubbing and digging. The term zappetta is also found.

Mau Mau. The Kikuyu terrorist society of East Africa.

Maudsley, Sir Alfred P. (1850-1931). A British archaeologist who spent 15 years (1881-1894) among the Maya ruins and wrote what were probably the first scientific reports of Central American archaeology.

Mauer. See HOMO HEIDELBERGENSIS.

Maui. The great mythical Polynesian culture hero, who is credited with fishing up islands from the bottom of the sea, harnessing the sun to slow its pace, and introducing fire to the earth.

maul. A heavy hammer, used to drive piles, wedges, and similar heavy work, as among the American Indians of the northwest. It has blunted or rounded edges.

maupuk. The Eskimo technique of hunting seals by waiting for them at their breathing holes.

Mausoleum. The tomb of Mausolus, king of Caria in Asia Minor, which was built by his widow at Halicarnassus ca. 350 B.C. It was beautifully decorated with many sculptures and was considered one of the Seven Wonders of the World.

mausoleum. A structure specifically designed to house bodies above ground, as differentiated from structures designed for underground burial or receptacles for holding ashes.

maxillae. The upper jaw, consisting of two bilateral bones. It composes the bony support of the middle portion of the face, forming part of the eye orbits, nasal fossae, most of the palate, and part of the cheekbones. Incomplete fusion of the maxillae leads to cleft palate and hairlip.

maxpe. Among the Crow Indians, a vision given by supernatural entities. A maxpe made a person powerful and lucky, if it were true. If not, the visionary might die.

maxtlatl. An Aztec loin cloth.

Maya. The advanced Neolithic civilization of Yucatan and related areas. The ancient language was geographically placed in the part of Central America now encompassed by Guatemala, Honduras, and south-ern Mexico. Its many dialects, along with Huastec, comprise the Mayan family of American Indian languages.

Mayan art. See ART, MAYAN.

Mazateca. The Aztec frog and snake cult.

Mazda, Ahura. See AHURA MAZDA.

mbakia. A clam shell armband of the Solomons.

mbisimo. A soul among the Azande.

Mbori. The Azande supreme being.

Mdoki. A Congo evil spirit.

mead. A fermented mixture of honey and water, which was a sacrificial drink of the Teutonic peoples and the regular beverage of the Teutonic gods. Odin's goat provided unending supplies of mead for the gods.

meae. The Marquesan stone terraces used for ceremonies.

meal, sacramental. A ritual meal, found in many religions, which symbolized identity with a deity or effected absorption of the god into the body of the partaker. The Hebrew Passover feast, which took place in the spring, was itself merely commemorative of the deliverance of the Hebrews from bondage in Egypt. However, the early Christians adopted it by treating the paschal lamb (a burnt offering) as a symbol of the crucified Jesus and erecting the sacramental meal (or mass) into the central ritual. The Eucharist or sacramental food, is ingested by the worshipper together with wine. Modern Christian faiths variously interpret the Eucharist as either an actual or a symbolic participation in the body and blood of Christ.

mean, arithmetic. A measure of central tendency that gives an average by adding the values of a series and dividing by the number of items contained in the series.

meander. The Greek key pattern, or fret, which originated ca. 1000-700 B.C. and became a common theme in Greek art, including early pottery.

measurement, derived or **measurement, indirect.** See PROJECTIVE.

meatus, auditory. The channel that opens into the ear.

mecapal. A Mayan tumpline (q.v.).

mechanism, isolating. A factor or combination of factors, such as sociological, geographical, or physiological, which tends to isolate a population. Darwin in his study of some Galápagos Island species showed how they became differentiated from the parental stocks because the islands were detached from the mainland.

mechanistic. See THEORY, MECHANISTIC.

medial. Toward or referring to the center of the body.

medial accent. See ACCENT, MEDIAL.

median. A measure of central tendency which is that value in a frequency distribution that constitutes the middle item.

Medical Papyrus, Edwin Smith. A record of medical treatment compiled by an Egyptian doctor, probably between 3000 and 2500 B.C., and purchased by Edwin Smith. It is probably the first detailed medical treatise and the first to make the distinction between medicine and surgery. It discussed the brain and localization of some brain functions, the pulse, adhesive tape, and surgical stitching to close wounds.

medicine. The techniques used to cure disease or alleviate pain. Early medicine employed magical and nonmagical techniques, drawing upon herbology, astrology, and other branches of learning. Surgery has been known for thousands of years. Some medical techniques were in the knowledge of all the members of a society, while others were restricted to special persons.

medicine, clown. Among many Indian groups, the belief that the clown can cure.

medicine man. See MAN, MEDICINE.

medicine society. See SOCIETY, MEDICINE.

mediopalatal. Referring to a sound produced at the center of the hard palate, e.g., *r*.

Mediterranean. A southern Caucasoid subdivision, originally found around the shores of the Mediterranean. This subrace is characterized by dark eyes and hair, little prognathism, slender body build, dolichocephalism, considerable body hair, narrow nose, and wavy hair. It is found in such Upper Paleolithic deposits as Galley Hill and Combe Capelle. Current representatives are probably most widespread in Ireland, Scotland, and Wales.

Mediterranean, Classic. A Mediterranean subgroup including many Berbers, Italians, Spaniards, Arabs, and Egyptians. The hook-nosed type is particularly common in the Near East among Arabs and Jews, while the straight-nosed type is found in the Mediterranean basin and in parts of eastern, central, and northwest Europe.

Mediterranean, Crude. A Mediterranean subgroup which includes many Sicilians and Southern Italians and is characterized by short, square face, less prominent chin, and dolichocephalism.

mega-. A prefix meaning "large," e.g., *megalith* "large stone."

megacene or **megaseme.** Older terms for a hypsiconch orbital index (q.v.).

megalith. A large stone structure. The Megalithic was a western European culture of the Neolithic and Copper Age, distinguished by the presence of monuments made of large stones. These stones were used for funeral or other, often ceremonial, purposes. Little was done to dress the stones. See CROMLECH; DOLMEN; MENHIR; GRAVE, PASSAGE.

megalosplanchnic. See MACRO-SPLANCHNIC.

Meganthropus palaeo javanicus. A very large early form of man, identified by two mandibles found in 1939 and 1941 by G. H. R. von Koenigswald in central Java. It is often called the Ancient Java Ape Man.

megaron. A building with a long hall and central hearth and a pillared porch on the short side. The megaron is found in some early Aegean communities, ca. 2000 B.C.

megascopic. Referring to an object large enough to be seen with the naked eye, as opposed to microscopic.

megaseme. See MEGACENE.

megatherm. A plant that requires much moisture and constant high temperature.

Meigs, James Aitken (1829-1879). An American physician who made contributions to the study of craniology.

Meinhof's law. See LAW, MEINHOF'S.

meiosis. See DIVISION, REDUCTION.

meke. A Fijian dance including both sexes.

Melanesia. The islands of New Guinea, New Britain, New Ireland, the Admiralties, the Solomons, New Hebrides, New Caledonia, Fiji, and the Santa Cruz islands, in Oceania (q.v.). There is a wide variety of racial elements in Melanesia.

Melanesian. A Negroid subrace, characterized by narrow head, considerable prognathism, dark brown skin, medium size, woolly hair, slight body hair, and a broad nose.

melanin. The pigment that is largely responsible for the color of the eyes and hair and for skin complexion. It is contained in the lower layers of the epidermis. The melanin ranges from yellow to black. The amount of melanin is more important in visual effect than its color. The amount is largely a hereditary constant.

Melian amphora. See AMPHORA, MELIAN.

melanism. Dark pigmentation.

Melanochroi. Caucasoids who have dark hair and a pale complexion.

Melanochroid. In some classifications, including Huxley's, a racial

351

subdivision which includes Adriatic, Littoral, Ibero-insular, and Western European branches. It is characterized by wavy hair.

melanochrous. Having a dark complexion, often used to describe groups south of the Alps.

melanoderm. Referring to a dark skin; Von Eickstedt's term for Negroid.

melanophore. A skin cell containing diffusable black pigment.

melioration. The evolution in meaning undergone by certain words by which a complimentary or decent meaning is substituted for the original pejorative or obscene sense.

melon. The melon has a very long history and in its distribution indicates the existence of agricultural communication between India and Africa. It probably originated as a wild plant in Southern Asia.

membrane, sympathetic. A small slender membrane placed across a hole in many musical instruments. It absorbs the vibrations and gives them a reedlike quality. Flutes in Europe and China and drums and xylophones may be equipped with sympathetic membranes.

membranophone. A musical instrument in which the sound is produced by a membrane stretched over an instrument, e.g., in drums.

memento mori. An amulet or charm carved in the shape of a skull, and sometimes studded with precious stones, carried or worn as a reminder of the inevitability of death.

menarche. The initial menstruation (q.v.), often associated with special observances. The transition denotes a girl's becoming a woman.

Menat. In ancient Egypt, a magic amulet worn by gods, goddesses, kings, priests, and high ranking officials. It was made of stone, porcelain, or lapis lazuli. Representations of a goddess and a serpent were inscribed upon the surfaces. The Menat was supposed to insure fertility and was buried with the wearer in order that his sex instincts might be renewed in the outer world.

Mendelian. Referring to the theory of inheritance developed by Gregor Mendel (1822-1884), a Czech monk. Mendel conducted experiments with peas to determine why certain traits appeared in successive generations and others appeared to skip a generation. He determined that all the traits of the organism were paired, e.g., the seed was green or yellow, the plant tall or dwarf. The specific trait developed in the organism depended upon the genetic contributions of the parents (see GENE). If the parents contributed heterozygous (unlike) genes governing a particular trait pair, then the trait that would always appear was called dominant, e.g., green seed, tall plant. A recessive trait could appear only if both parents contributed the same gene, that is, the trait was necessarily homozygous. Since two plants manifesting the dominant trait might be heterozygous, a random assortment of their chromosomes paired in reproduction would result in 50 per cent heterozygous (which would show the dominant trait), 25 per cent homozygous dominant, and 25 per cent homozygous recessive.

Although Mendel promulgated his views in 1866, they were forgotten until rediscovered at the beginning of the 20th century. The year 1900 saw the Englishman Bateson, the Dutch De Vries, the German Correns, and the Austrian Tschermak each reporting results like Mendel's, which all four had reached independently.

Menehune. A people of small stature reputed to have been the aboriginal settlers of Polynesia.

menerik. A condition in which the patient lapses into unconsciousness and trances. Shamans (q.v.) in Liberia are usually selected from individuals having this condition.

menhir. A megalith (q.v.) consisting of a single large pillar. The term is also used for one or more columnar stone blocks, from 3 to 20 or more feet high. A menhir is also called a monolith, pierre fitte, a long stone, or a standing stone.

mennui. See CLOTH, MUMMY.

menstruation. The periodic discharge in women of an unfertilized ovum and its ancillary tissues, along with blood. It may occur during three or four decades, the entire span of life within which a woman can conceive. The menses last a few days to a week and occur on the average of once monthly. In many cultures, special behavior is appropriate during the menstrual period, sometimes for men as well as women. A woman may be covert or overt about her menstruation, depending on whether her society regards the process as dangerous. A menstruating woman may be prohibited from enjoying religious observance, or from sexual intercourse. She may also be forbidden contact with economic activities or even be isolated, as among many American Indian groups. The complex of ideas relating to the menses is carried over to the menstrual blood in many cultures.

menstruation, male. The practice of cutting the urethra in men in order to induce a flow of blood, as in certain groups in New Guinea.

mental. Having reference to the chin, e.g., the mental eminence.

mentality, prelogical. The distinctive and special kind of thinking which was assumed by some anthropologists to be unique to primitives. Lévy-Bruhl suggested that primitives think emotionally and not logically about socially created ideas based on mystical identification. See PARTICIPATION, MYSTIC.

merbok. A system of ceremonial exchange in Northern Australia. Some of the many articles traded in this system go hundreds of miles. The exchange is conducted among specific kin partners. Having a merbok partner is a sign of friendship.

mere. A flat-bladed Maori club with sharp edges made of stone, whalebone, or wood. It was used in warfare as a thrusting weapon.

merging. Designating relatives, whether collateral or lineal, by the same kinship term, e.g., *aunt, cousin.*

merging, forked or merging, bifurcate. Distinguishing between relations descended through the the female and those descended

through the male, along with classifying relatives who are geneologic-
ally unlike into like relationship
categories.

merissa. A grain beer of Africa.

meristic. Varying with respect to
number; divided into segments.

merliadda. Among the Kukata,
ceremonial fire walking by adoles-
cent boys.

mermaid. A female who lives in
the sea and has some supernatural
qualities. A *merman* is the masculine equivalent.

Meroitics. A group of exquisite
Egyptian funereal vases, dating
from the Twenty-Sixth Dynasty.
They were painted with a simple
well-executed design.

merry tale. See TALE, MERRY.

mesa. An isolated level-bedded
rock hill.

mesa-. A prefix meaning "intermediate."

Mesa Verde. A famous archaeological site in southwestern Colorado. It is an area 15 miles long and
8 miles wide containing many cliff
dwellings. The finest examples of
the Anasazi (q.v.) houses are found
in the cliffs of the canyon of this
mesa. The Cliff Palace with 200
round and rectangular rooms of
stone and adobe occupies a cave
high up in a cliff wall. The chambers of this tremendous structure
are lined with timber floors and
roofs.

mesati-. A prefix meaning "intermediate."

mesatiskelic. Referring to a stem-
leg length index (q.v.), between 85
and 89.9.

mescal. or **mescaline.** See PEYOTE.

mescalero. A tribal dance of the
Apaches, performed only by the
chiefs and leaders in the puberty
ceremonies of Apache girls. The
motions are forceful and dramatic,
stressing straight line and angularity
of movement.

mesenchyme. A kind of wandering mesoderm which is formed
from true mesoderm. It is active in
forming blood, muscle, and connective tissue.

mesene. Referring to an upper
facial index (q.v.) of between 50
and 54.9.

mesial or **mesio-.** The surface of
a tooth closest to the center of the
dental arch.

Mesoamerica. The area of high
culture of Mexico and the Maya.
On the north is a hunting and gathering culture; the southern boundary, running through Central America, divides it from a culture basically oriented toward South America.
It is a culture area with time depth,
which existed as far back as the
beginning of classic time. All Meso-
american culture has certain characteristics in common: it was agricultural at the time of the conquest,
used lime mortar, and had a calendar system of 260 days, a specific
pantheon of gods, the concept of
zero, and special ball courts. The
concept of Mesoamerica was developed by Paul Kirchhoff in 1943.

mesocephalic. Referring to a head
of medium breadth, having a
cephalic index (q.v.) of between 76
and 81 on the living head and between 75 and 80 on the dry skull.

mesochouranic. Referring to a maxillo-alveolar index (q.v.) of between 110 and 114.9.

mesocnemic. Referring to a platycnemic index (q.v.) of between 63 and 69.9.

mesoconch. Referring to an orbital index (q.v.) of between 76 and 84.9.

mesocranic. Referring to a cranial index (q.v.) between 75 and 79.9.

mesoderm. The middle germ layer in the human embryo. It forms the muscles, blood-forming organs, and connective tissue.

mesodiacritic. Referring to the condition in which between 30 and 80 per cent of the members of a race or subrace are recognizable as such.

mesognathous. Having an intermediate facial profile, with a facial profile angle of between 80 and 85 degrees.

Mesolithic. The Azilian, Tardenoisian, Maglemosian, Campignian and Capsian periods, from ca. 20,-000 to 7,500 years before the historic era. The culture is an extension of Paleolithic. Modern weather replaced the glacial, making a change in culture necessary. As a result of the new development, European Mesolithic culture looks meager; and though such inventions as pottery and the bow appeared, their full import was felt only after the Mesolithic. The sparse food supply is linked with the population's scattering out. Shellfish, waterfowl, and hares were typical of the humbler food used. Implements grew smaller. The European Mesolithic cultures are divisible into those, like the Azilian (q.v.) and Tardenoisian (q.v.), which had no ax and used no timber, and those middle and late Mesolithic cultures, like the Maglemosian (q.v.), Campignian (q.v.), and Asturian (q.v.), in which the ax was used. Dogs are found with the Azilian and Tardenoisian. Pottery stems from the Campignian period of the European Mesolithic. The name Mesolithic was first used by Torell in 1874, at a meeting in Stockholm, although it got wide currency only after 1921.

mesological. Referring to the kind of semilogical reasoning characteristic of the 19th-century evolutionary anthropological thinkers, who assumed that the sequential development of institutions could be described systematically from a given starting point.

mesomorphy. 1 In Sheldon's typology of body builds (see TYPES, CONSTITUTIONAL), a type characterized by the predominance of bone, muscle, and connective tissue, over nervous tissues and digestive viscera. Its associated somatotonia is athletic and assertive in behavior. 2 In the classification of R. Bennett Bean, a mesomorph is a medium form of man, e.g., Homo neanderthalensis.

mesophyte. An organism that lives under moderate conditions of moisture.

mesoprosopic. Referring to a medium faced person, one in whom the facial index is 84 to 88, or 85 to 90 on a skull.

mesorrhine. Having a nose of medium breadth, with a nasal index of between 47 and 51 measured on the skull, and between 70 and 85, measured on the living head.

mesostaphyline. Having a palatal index (q.v.) between 80 and 84.9.

mesotherm. A plant that requires a moderate supply of heat and moisture.

Mesozoic. Referring to the geological era characterized by the development of reptiles. It includes the Triassic, Jurassic, and Cretaceous life periods. The Mesozoic lasted from perhaps 195 to 70 million years ago.

mesquite. A leguminous tree or shrub found in the western United States, Mexico, and South America. Its wood is hard, and the pod has considerable grape sugar. It is a valuable source of food for Indians of the Southwest.

messenger. Messengers are often inviolable in early societies and may be outstanding or older and respected persons. Some nonliterate peoples have used women both as messengers and envoys. In early times, messengers were used to call others to tribal meetings, religious activities, or hunting and fishing expeditions. They may be given gifts and presents when they arrive.

messianism. A religious movement the central theme of which is the expected coming of a leader who is to deliver his followers from oppression or other hardship.

mestizo. An individual of mixed blood, notably the product of a mating between an American Indian and a European, or of a European and a Negro or Malay. In South America, there are 16,000,000 mes-

tizos, which is twice the number of Indians. In the New World, there are about 39 million. In Paraguay 97 per cent of the population is mestizo, and in Venezuela 70 to 90 per cent. Mexico and Central America have from 12 to 13 million mestizos. Mestizo has become a catchall term for South American groups which have non-Indian culture traits. In the New World, the term, in addition to its culture meaning, usually implies a person who is largely American Indian from the point of view of racial characteristics, with a number of Mediterranean features and some Negro traits.

mesuranic. Referring to a maxilloalveolar index (q.v.) of between 110 and 114.9.

metabolism, purine. The organism's breaking down purine, a complex crystalline substance that gives rise to uric acid through oxidation.

metacarpal. A bone in the hand, between the wrist and fingers.

metacone. The disto-buccal cusp of the upper first and second molar.

metaconid. The mesio-lingual cusp of the first and second lower molar and the second lower premolar.

metal. An element that is lustrous, opaque, and fusible and that conducts heat and electricity. It has been suggested that early man could not tell one metal from another and that the concept of metal did not exist. In many cultures, the name for one specific metal seems to be used also to mean many different metals, e.g., the Sumerian word *anna* was used for lead, tin, and meteoritic iron. Metals like gold or

356

copper that are yellow were not easily distinguishable from metals like tin or lead that are silvery. Gold and copper were, however, probably the most easily recognizable metals by early man and often the designation for either was sometimes used to refer to all metallic objects. Rickard has suggested that to early man, the logical developmental sequence is stone, copper, and metal, until the several metals could be distinguished. The metal supply in the ancient world was never very large. Metal implements were substituted only slowly for stone tools. Thus, in Egypt, even after bronze was known, it was used for special work, like swords, while copper was the metal for most weapons and rough objects like arrowheads were made of flint.

metal, coinage. A metal generally used for coins, e.g., copper, silver, and gold.

metalanguage. Any language which is used for the purpose of describing the symbols of another language. The concept of metalanguage is essentially a refinement of logical positivism.

metallography. A method used in archaeology, for determining of what a given metal object has been made. The surface of the metal is polished and etched by acid, after which its crystalline composition is studied. This method may enable the investigator to tell how the given specimen was made.

metallophone. A metal gong.

metallurgy. The use of such techniques as the application of heat in preparing metals for use.

metamorphosis. The belief widely held among early men that some persons, deities, and animals could change themselves to other shapes. The change of shape is usually accomplished by magic.

metany. A bowing of specified depth, for religious purposes. It may range from slightly dipping the head to touching the forehead to the floor.

metaplasm. A deviation or change from the conventional linguistic form.

metatarsal. A bone in the foot, between the ankle and toe bones.

metate, cylindro-concave. A rectangular stone block, used with a heavy rolling-pinlike mano (q.v.).

metate, simple. A semiporous stone used as the nether stone in milling. A smaller stone is used on top (see MANO). The simple metate was probably the first machine to which natural power was applied.

metathesis. A sudden sound change in pronunciation which could not have been reached by a series of variations. There are few such authentic cases. The term is also used to describe two phonemes (q.v.) being interchanged inside a word.

metempsychosis. The transmigration (q.v.) of souls, an idea widely held at one time. Although Herodotus in Book II of his history reported that the ancient Egyptians believed that the soul of a man after death entered an animal and migrated into other creatures on the new earth for many years, when it came back to a human body, no evidence to support any Egyptian belief in metempsychosis has been discovered. Around the sixth century B.C., the doctrine spread widely and entered Greek thinking as a metaphysical doctrine through Pythagoras, while Gautama Buddha in India turned it into a kind of moral metaphor. In Buddhism, since animals are below man, the soul's migrating through animals was seen as a punishment for evildoers, seekers after pleasure, and others animalistically inclined.

method, Bertillon. The method developed in 1883 by the French criminologist Alphonse Bertillon for identifying persons anthropometrically, originally used to identify criminals. His work as head of the French Service of Judicial Identity from 1889 on marked probably the first systematic application of scientific method to police procedure. Bertillon measured head length and breadth and the length of the middle finger, left foot, and forearm from the elbow to the end of the middle finger. Finger prints, which Bertillon did not have confidence in, have supplanted this method in identifying criminals. See DERMATOGLYPHICS.

method, crown. A method of making glass by blowing a hollow glass sphere and then rotating it till it became flat. The Romans used the crown method.

method, culture historical. See CULTURE HISTORICAL and KULTURKREISTHEORIE.

method, flint and pyrites. A method of making fire in which iron pyrites are struck on a flint surface to make a spark. Fire results from these sparks being caught in dry tinder.

method, gene frequency. A method for determining the degree to which particular genes are present in a group, if the manner of inheritance of the trait carried by those genes is known. The method hinges on the simple concept that $p + q + r = 100\%$. See P; Q; R.

method, genealogical. That technique of anthropology which involves collecting and compiling pedigrees into tables of genealogy, in order to determine kinship systems and the nature of the institutions. The technique was developed by W. H. R. Rivers while on the Torres Straits Expedition around the turn of the century. The informant gives the name of persons in a given biological relationship to himself, as well as what they call him and he calls them, so that the kinship terminology can be determined.

method, hand and thigh. The simplest method of spinning, as in cordage.

method, paddle and anvil. A primitive pottery-making technique.

method, spindle and spindle-whorl. See SPINDLE AND SPINDLE-WHORL METHOD.

Methodenstreit. A famous 19th-century dispute about the methodology to be used in the study of society and in social science. One viewpoint, represented by Gustav Schmoller, held that the historical approach was best, while another, represented by Carl Menger, upheld the analytic method.

metonymy. Using a word for another word it suggests, e.g., we read *Homer,* instead of *Homer's poems.*
metope. The decorative panel between triglyphs in a Doric frieze on ancient Greek architecture. It was in use during the fifth century B.C. and usually bore sculptures. The examples on the Parthenon were richly colored, with skillfully executed figures. Most of the myths represented were the studies of Heracles and Theseus and the battles of gods against giants, Greeks against Amazons, or Lapiths against centaurs.
metopian. The midpoint of a line that connects the two frontal eminences.
metriocranic. Referring to a cranial breadth-height index (q.v.) between 92 and 97.9.
metriometopic. Referring to a transverse fronto-parietal index (q.v.) between 66 and 68.9.
metronymic. Referring to the derivation of a name from the mother or maternal relative; such a name itself. See SYSTEM, METRONYMIC.
mevelavites. Whirling dervishes. A sect named after its founder Mevelava, who is supposed to have whirled unceasingly for four days and nights until he collapsed in a trance and made many prophecies.
mia-mia. An Australian aboriginal bough shelter or hut. The term is derived from the designation of a Victorian tribe.
micro-. A prefix meaning small.
microcephaly. A form of idiocy in which the brain stops growing at an early age, or the cranial capacity is subnormal. The head is

cone shaped (oxycephalia) and the chin and forehead show a marked recession. The brain may weigh as little as 170 grams, as compared with a normal weight of 1,375 for males and 1,240 for females.
microclimate. The climatic environment of a small local area like the north-facing slope of a hill.
Microdiacritic. The condition in which less than 30 per cent of the members of a race or subrace are recognizable as such.
microdont. Referring to small teeth. A supernumerary tooth is often microdont.
microevolution. The evolution of slight differences based on small mutations.
microlith. A very fine small pressure-flaked flint from the Neolithic, Epipaleolithic, and Magdalenian eras.
micromutation. A mutation of slight phenotypic effect which is very frequent and causes a good deal of individual variation.
micron. A measurement equal to .001 millimeter; the symbol is *u.*
Micronesia. In Oceania, the Caroline, Gilbert, and Marshall Islands and Guam and Truk. The population of Micronesia is diminishing fairly rapidly and seems to be largely Polynesian with some Indonesian characteristics.
micropaleontology. The study of microfossils to aid in dating archaeological remains or deposits.
microsplanchnic. In Viola's body build typology, referring to the thin extreme.
microtherm. A plant that requires a minimum of heat and moisture

and is thus able to stand cold winters and short summers.

Mictlantecuhtli. The principal god of death among the Aztecs. He was associated with the direction of north and wore a mask made of human skulls.

midden, kitchen. A pile of shells and refuse where a primitive shore-dwelling people, a major portion of whose food consisted of shellfish, used to live. Kitchen middens date from the Mesolithic or later periods and were found mainly in Denmark. The dog was probably the only domesticated animal of this period. Midden comes from the Danish mödden, which means muck heap. A characteristic tool is the chopper.

mid-vowel. See VOWEL, MID-.

midwife. A woman who assists women in childbirth.

migration. A large movement of a people seeking a permanent change of residence. Natural catastrophes, societal changes, and economic necessity have been responsible for most migrations. Glaciation, floods, and volcanic eruptions were important in some early migrations. Huntington has emphasized progressive desiccation as a cause of migration, e.g., in inner Asia. Lack of food is another common reason. War caused much migration, as in the case of the Indian tribes forced to go west to escape the power of the League of the Iroquois. Topography may have a considerable influence on the direction of migration, e.g., the southern Chinese Shan moved along the Menam and Mekong into modern Thailand.

The question of whether there was an ancient migration to the Americas, and how and when it took place, continues a much-debated topic. It has been said that the migrations to the New World represent the greatest migration in human history in both numbers and time. Three million Spaniards settled in Latin America in the century and a half following 1492. Fifty-five million other Europeans migrated to the New World between 1820 and 1935. Fifteen million Negroes were brought to the New World as slaves. Almost one hundred million people came to the New World over the last five centuries, and enormously increased the original New World population of eight to ten million.

Oceania has had important migrations. Africa has also had migrations, as in the case of the Hamitic people who moved into the Nile valley and then west, north of the Sahara. The early historical period saw many nomadic migrations, notably from Central Asia, as well as such movement on the part of maritime people. Intermarriage with the population in the area has made it difficult to trace the effects of migrations, and the major migrations of early man are not known with any certainty. The German term Völkerwanderung is sometimes used for migrations.

migration, dune. The movement of dunes over a long period of time. Dune migration is used to date archaeological deposits.

migration, great American plant. The introduction of the plants of the New World to the European and Pacific areas, primarily by the Spaniards, so that plants like manioc and maize spread to Africa, Europe, and the Pacific, along with their associated insects and parasites.

mika. The Australian name for subincision (q.v.).

miko. An Indian chief, especially among the Creeks.

military society. See SOCIETY, MILITARY.

milk and honey. A metaphorical phrase, used in more than one ancient culture, meaning prosperity and abundance. Since milk and honey were delicious foods, they gradually became symbols of plenty, happiness, and well-being and eventually of the material richness of the golden age to come.

milking. Obtaining milk from domesticated animals. Milking is a fairly recent development in animal husbandry and probably was invented in southwest Asia and then spread. The goat was perhaps the first animal milked. Once milking was introduced, it was possible to have a regular supply of the major necessary proteins. In addition to goats, cattle, sheep, mares, and reindeer have been milked.

mill, prayer. A device consisting of paper on which appropriate prayers have been written. By turning a handle and revolving the paper, it is as if the prayer were spoken. In Tibet the prayer mill is very widely used. See WHEEL, PRAYER.

mill, rotary. A mill consisting of a cone-shaped lower stone supporting an upper stone which was a hollow cone. Grain was thrown into a hopper, trickled down a slope between the two revolving stones, and came out as meal. The rotary mill is found for the first time in the fifth century B.C. in the Mediterranean world. It has been suggested that it may have been invented by the Greeks.

millet. An annual small-seeded grass used for forage and grain. The millets represent a staple in many Asiatic and African areas.

millimeter. A measure equivalent to .001 meter.

milling. The process of grinding grain between two stones.

milpa. The Mayan term for the slash-and-burn (q.v.) technique.

Mimbres. See ART, MIMBRES.

miming. Imitating or representing events by gesture or other nonverbal mimicry. Miming may imitate animals, battle activities, or sacrifices, and may range from realistic copying to stylization and symbolism.

miming, animal. Imitating or impersonating animals to get help from their spirits for the society or community. Animal miming is believed to lengthen animal life and help obtain game.

mimorate. See ULTIMOGENITURE.

mina. An early Asiatic measuring unit, worth one sixtieth of a talent. It was worth 50 to 60 shekels in Babylonia and 100 drachmae in Greece.

minagnghinim. An ancient Hebrew musical instrument made in the form of a table with a handle over which were strung hollow brass or wood balls on a chain. In moving, the balls collided with the table and emitted clear sounds that carried great distances.

mind, concentration of the. A Winnebago rite used before hunting bears. It consisted in a symbolical enticement of the bear through gifts of food.

mind, social. A term suggested (1912) by the French sociologist Emile Durkheim for a collective religious consciousness that he felt, on the basis of his analysis of Australian aboriginal culture, was the origin of the religious experience. Later work has served to bring this concept of the social mind into question.

Mindel. The second glacial period in Europe, probably extending from 450,000 to 500,000 years ago.

mineralized. Referring to the condition of a bone all the organic material of which has been replaced by stone, with the general shape of the bone surviving.

Ming. The Ming dynasty in China, 1368-1644 A.D., was famed for its porcelain of underglaze copper red, polychromes, colored and monochrome glazes, and underglaze blue decoration.

Mingo. The Six Nations of the Iroquois; also an independent Iroquois tribe.

mining, placer. A method of mining for gold by shoveling gravel into a sluice with obstructions. When water sweeps the sand along, the gold is collected in the obstructions. Fat may be used to cover the sluices in placer mining.

mining, vein or **mining, reef.** A method for extracting gold from quartz rocks.

miniscule. Referring to the lower case letters, or to a style of writing that was fairly rapid and partly cursive. Miniscule became widespread in the ninth century A.D. and was the most widely used script for the manual copying of books.

minority, linguistic. Any group, generally a racial minority, whose ordinary language differs from the language used by the majority of the inhabitants of the country.

Miocene. A Cenozoic period, in which apes were in the process of development, and ancestral gibbons appeared. It is usually dated from 35 to 15 million years ago.

Miolithic. The Upper Paleolithic.

mir. The village assembly of old Russia.

miracle. An event that cannot be explained by the rules of natural forces and thus may be regarded as a sign of supernatural intervention, whether divine or diabolical. Almost every religion has important epochs when the god intervened.

Miru. A soul-devouring ogress in the Cook Islands.

miscegenation. Race mixture through marriage. There is no biological evidence of any resultant deterioration; in fact, hybrid vigor (q.v.) may occur.

mistletoe. An evergreen plant with white berries, widely used in connection with various popular beliefs as a cure for disease, a device to increase fertility, and an aphrodisiac. Aeneas' Golden Bough, which enabled him to visit the underworld safely, was mistletoe. It was a sacred plant among the Druids, who appear to have viewed it, because of its association with the oak, as that tree's genitalia. Its use at Christmas may stem from druidic practices. Some people, even today, will not cut mistletoe.

mistral. A cold north wind in southern France.

mita. The labor required of taxpayers in the Inca empire. One man was drafted from each administrative unit of 10 able-bodied men until the requisite labor force was obtained for a specified imperial task, e.g., construction of roads and public buildings, defense, or mining. The term mita applies as well to the system of enforced labor imposed on the Indians by the Spaniards after the conquest of Peru.

Mithraism. The worship of the Persian god Mithras, the god of light and devotee of truth.

mitimaes. The system of transplanting whole villages in the Inca empire and replacing them by pacified populations.

Mitla. A Mexican archaeological site that dates from the third Monte Alban period and existed up to the time of the Conquest. The buildings of this Mixtec site are of adobe with stone facing.

mitosis. Cell division in which the chromosomes (q.v.) split longitudinally and are distributed equally to the daughter cells.

mitote. An Aztec dance, probably originally associated with fertility rituals.

mixed terminology. See TERMINOLOGY, MIXED.

mixoploidy. The condition in which contiguous cells, cell masses, or tissues have different chromosome (q.v.) numbers.

mixovariation. An intermediate form.

Mixtec. A group of Mexican people who speak the Mixtec language. In the 11th century A.D., there flourished among the Mixtecs a religious art that seems to have migrated and replaced previously established religious arts in Middle America. The art style is also known as Mexteca-Puebla, because it was originated in that area and was carried by Aztecan Nahuas in addition to Mixtec-speaking peoples.

mixture, race. The production of offspring by two individuals each of whom is from one of the three great divisions of mankind—Caucasoid, Negroid, and Mongoloid. About one sixth of the population of the New World, or some 39,000,000, consists of mixed populations (see MESTIZO). South Africa has about 1,000,000 hybrids and Southeast Asia about 4,000,000. Eurasians number about a quarter of a million, largely Dutch-Indonesian. India has about 140,000 Eurasians. Oceania has some 100,000 persons showing race mixture. Shapiro has estimated that 2.5 per cent of the population of the world is mixed in race. No reliable evidence on the biologically dangerous effects of race mixture exists (see MISCEGENATION), and it has been maintained by some geneticists that race mixture might have positive biological effects by creating a greater range of types. There was considerable race mixture among early men, judging from the many intervening types found. One of the first authoritative proponents of race mixture was Jehovah, who afflicted Moses' sister Miriam with a plague when she objected to Moses marrying an Ethiopian (Numbers 12:2-15).

MN. A blood group system with three divisions: M, MN, and N. The blood grouping of a population can be expressed in terms of two genes that are allelomorphic (q.v.). There is not so much variation within a population as with other systems. Most Asians and American aborigines are high M. Australia and the Pacific islands are high in N. There seem to be subgroups within the MN system. See GROUP, BLOOD; RH.

Mobilian. A lingua franca (q.v.) of the Indians of the southeastern United States which was based on a corruption of Choctaw.

mobilier. See ART, MOBILIER.

moccasin. A soft leather shoe with no heel. The sole is brought up and over the toes and the sides of the foot, where a U-shaped piece is joined by a raised seam. The moccasin is found in almost all cold countries, although the term derives from an Algonkian word.

mode. The most representative of a series of values; the most frequently occurring score in a series.

modes, prayer. The musical structure on which services of Jewish holidays were built. It is constructed of five musical modes, each of which in turn is based on a certain scale. The cantor, while he may modulate from one mode to an-

other, always returns to the original mode.

modesty hypothesis. See HYPOTHESIS, MODESTY.

modification, phonetic. A modification in the primary phonemes (q.v.) of a linguistic form.

modifier. A gene (q.v.) that helps the dominance of another gene.

modulation. The use of secondary phonemes (q.v.).

Mogollon. An early culture, about which little is known, which existed in southwestern New Mexico. The people appear to have lived in pit dwellings, their art was completely unconnected with the surrounding cultures, and their red and brown pottery was made by the paddle and anvil method (q.v.). Certain shell gorgets are similar to objects from the Far East, although such an origin is not easily acceptable because of the great distance.

mogya. "Blood" among the Ashanti, inherited from the mother.

moi. An island monarch in Hawaii.

moiety. A primary social division in which the tribe is made up of two groups. Each moiety often includes one or more interrelated clans, sibs, or phratries, and moiety exogamy is common. The two groups may be of different size or function. The members of a moiety need not be related. A moiety may be formed for games or ceremonies.

moiety, compound. A moiety with phratries and/or sibs (qq.v.).

moiety, simple. A moiety that consists of a large sib (q.v.).

moko. 1 Staining the skin by making scratches with a small chisel and rubbing in pigment. The term is from the Maori for tattoo patterns. 2 A brass gong of the Alorese.

molars. The three teeth on top and bottom and on either side which are behind the premolars. They are grinding teeth, used to crush and chew food. The crowns have four or five cusps.

mold. A form, usually metal or stone, with one surface shaped or carved as the obverse of the desired cast. A mold will be lined or filled with a substance (metal, clay) that hardens on the application of heat or cooling. On solidifying, the cast is taken out and has the reverse design of the mold. See CASTING. Molds were originally open on one side so that the metal could be flattened. They developed into the double mold, in which two halves of the object were separately cast and then put together. The solid mold was made by constructing a model of the object in wood or wax, coating it with clay, and baking in a fire. The wood or wax was burned and left a cavity of the desired shape. Copper which was cast in a closed mold would blister until tin and similar agents were added. Molding techniques improved with the development of metals.

mold, post. The shape and discoloration of the earth which indicate that a post existed in an archaeological site. The post, usually of wood, will have rotted away, but its position can be deduced from the mold stains.

mold, valve. A mold used for casting bronze in the Middle and Late Bronze Age in Europe. Each half

of the negative outline of the object to be cast was carved into a smooth stone. When the two stone pieces were opposed, the resultant hollow was the negative of the cast.

moldavite. See STONE, BOTTLE.

mon. 1 A plank canoe of the northern Solomons. 2 A badge, usually circular, of a Japanese family, especially an old family. It bears conventionalized representations of natural objects.

monadnock. See MOUNTAIN, RESIDUAL.

monandry. The marriage of one man to one wife. The term is used even where the marriage need not be permanent and the man may have had several wives.

monaulos. An ancient Roman musical instrument. It has a reed attached to one end of a cylindrical tube with a large bore and four finger holes.

money. A measure of value and a medium for the purchase of goods and services. Its units are usually portable, durable, homogeneous, and divisible, and, in advanced culture, fungible. A wide variety of objects has been used for money, including cattle, shells, stones, teeth, seeds, iron bars, knives, salt, metals, cocoa beans, and ivory.

money, blood. Settlement made for a killing.

money, brick tea. A medium of exchange consisting of loaves of tea leaves, found in parts of China.

money, dog tooth. A medium of exchange consisting of a dog's four fangs placed on three parallel strings. Dog tooth money is found

365

in New Guinea, the Solomons, and the Bismarck Archipelago.

money, feather. A medium of exchange consisting of rolls of feathers, often the feathers of hummingbirds and pigeons. This money is used in Polynesia.

money, moon. An early Chinese medium of exchange, usually made of bronze and often in half-moon shape, with excellent ornamentation. Moon money is sometimes called sounding coin.

money, paper. A kind of money invented by the Chinese in the ninth century A.D., originally consisting of sheets of paper, of different values and sizes, made from the bark of the mulberry.

money, pig. Shell disks, clay with beads, dog teeth, and pig tails strung together and used as money on New Ireland.

money, ring. Early money in the shape of rings, sometimes strung on bracelets, found in the early Bronze Age.

money, token. A medium of exchange which has either limited temporary value or else only a symbolic value, e.g., chips in a card game.

Mongol, Afghan. Nearly extinct language in the Mongol branch of the Altaic subfamily of the Ural-Altaic family.

Mongol, American. A Mongoloid subgroup found among some American Indian groups, e.g., the Pueblo.

Mongol, Arctic. A Mongoloid subgroup found in northeast Asia and the Arctic. Its members are characterized by broad faces, narrow cheekbones, skin color ranging from yellow to brown, and short stature.

Mongol, Classic. A Mongoloid subgroup found in Central Asia, Northern China, and Mongolia. It is characterized by a broad face, square jaws, yellow skin, and brachycephaly.

Mongol, Indonesian. A widely distributed Mongoloid subgroup which may have some Ainu and Mediterranean features. It is characterized by a broad face, dark yellow-brown to red-brown skin, and broad to medium noses.

Mongolism. A kind of mental deficiency featured by upward sloping and slitlike eyes, large, transversely fissured tongue, sparse dry hair, and small round skull.

Mongoloid. In physical anthropology, a racial group centering around the Pacific Ocean. Some of its characteristics include sparse body hair, straight head hair of coarse texture ranging in color from brown to brown-black, skin color ranging from saffron to yellow brown, height ranging from medium short to medium tall, medium broad to very broad face, brown eyes, and nose with a low to medium bridge. This group includes the Malayan, southern and northern Chinese, Mongolian, Siberian, Eskimo, and American Indian subraces. The eye has a total internal epicanthic fold (q.v.). B type usually predominates in the blood composition. Classic and Arctic Mongoloids are the major subdivisions. The **Mongoloid languages** are spoken by approximately 3 million persons. They belong to the Altaic subfamily of the Ural-Altaic family. Its three subbranches are Kalmuk, Buryat, and an Eastern subbranch including Dhalkha, Tangut, and Shara, and perhaps Yakut. The Mongol branch also includes the almost obsolete Afghan Mongol.

monkey, capuchin. A small South American monkey, especially *Cebus capucinus,* whose head hair resembles a cowl, hence its name. It is the familiar organ grinder's monkey.

monkey, cynomorphic. A monkey with a long snout, like a baboon.

monkey, proboscis. A monkey with a long protruding nose, probably the only such primate species. The proboscis monkey belongs to the Semnopithecinae subfamily.

Mon-Khmer. A South Asian linguistic stock, which includes the Annamite language.

monochord. 1 An early device for exhibiting the mathematical relations among musical sounds. It has a string stretched over a sounding board, with a movable bridge as a graduated scale. The string is divisible into measurable vibrating parts. 2 A musical bow (q.v.).

monochorial. Referring to the concept that a pair of twins has only one chorion.

monoculture. An agriculture that concentrates on the cultivation of a single crop, excluding all others. Certain American Indian tribes, e.g., restricted their agriculture to tobacco or maize.

monogamy. The marriage of one man to one woman. This form of marriage is probably the most widespread and seems to be suited to raising children and solidifying family life. Monogamy is mandatory in only a few societies, although one mate at a time, for most peoples, is the indicated kind of marriage. The average Mohammedan, even, practices monogamy, in spite of permissive polygamy.

monogenesis. The early view that all of mankind is descended from one pair of progenitors. Such early anthropologists as Linnaeus, Buffon, Blumenbach, and Prichard were monogenists.

monogenesis of speech. See SPEECH, MONOGENESIS OF.

monogenic. Referring to the theory that one or several genes (q.v.) control each organ. This theory has largely been replaced by the polygenic (q.v.) theory.

monoglacialism. The doctrine which holds that there was only one glacial period in the northern ice field. See POLYGLACIALISM.

monoglot. A person who uses only one language.

Monokoutouba. A contact vernacular (q.v.) spoken in French Equatorial Africa. It combines certain dialects spoken by the natives who worked in building the railroad from Brazzaville to the seacoast.

monolatry. The worship of one god, even though other gods may be recognized to exist. The ancient Hebrews seem to have been monalatrous, since they apparently regarded Yahweh as being their god, while other peoples had other gods.

monolith. See MENHIR.

monophasic. Satisfying a need in one continuous period, during the 24 hours of the day, e.g., an adult's sleeping for eight consecutive hours a day. See POLYPHASIC.

monophone. One sound; also, the written symbol that stands for such a sound.

monophthong. A minimum unit of sound which is articulated with one emission of breath. The term is sometimes used to describe two vowel symbols which together signify one vowel sound.

monophthongization. The process through which a diphthong (q.v.) becomes a single sound.

monophyletic. Referring to a single race or parent form. **Monophyletism** is the belief that all the races of man developed from one original race or group. See POLY-PHYLETIC.

monotheism. Belief in a single deity. This view holds that the cosmos is a unity, with one God who created and ordered all. Around 440 B.C., in the exile, this concept was introduced in Israel by Second Isaiah, and it became established in the post-exilic period. Some scholars hold that Pharaoh Ikhnaton (1375-1358 B.C.) was monotheistic, and some have said that Moses was a monotheist. Most scholars, however, believe that Ikhnaton and Moses were in the stage of henotheism (q.v.) or monolatry (q.v.), with each championing one god but not denying the existence of others.

monotreme. The most primitive of the mammals, e.g., the platypus.

monotypic. Referring to a species of which all the members are fairly alike.

monoxylon. See DUGOUT.

monster. A combination of bird and animal in one creature. There were occasionally some human qualities included, as well. The centaur and griffin are monsters.

Montelius, Oscar (1843-1921). A Swedish archaeologist who made important contributions to the study of the Bronze Age in Europe. He gave numerical designations, from 1 through 5, and absolute dates to the techno-typological periods he reported within the Bronze Age. Montelius was an enthusiastic adherent of the theory that European culture stems from the East (see EX ORIENTE LUX).

mood, cohortative or **mood, hortatory.** A syntactical form in certain languages used when expressing an exhortation, encouragement, or suggestion. It is usually applied to the imperative of subjunctive moods.

moorlog. Peat from the surface of an early swamp. It is used in dating archaeological remains.

mopuka. Small bars of iron used for exchange in the Congo.

mora. A term in phonetics used to describe the components of a phoneme (q.v.) which may receive different tonal inflections, e.g., in classical Greek.

moraine. The deposits of boulders and other detritus carried down on a glacier's surface and dropped when the ice melts.

moraine, ground. A moraine laid bare by the retreating glacier tongue (q.v.).

mordant. A substance that combines with a dyestuff to fix a color in leather or textiles. It may also be used to corrode fibers and prepare them for further work.

Mordvin. The language of one million inhabitants of Asiatic Russia. It belongs to the Finno-Ugric subfamily of the Ural-Altaic family of languages. Certain linguists classify it further within a Lapponic group.

mores. Behavior patterns that are accepted, traditional, and usually change slowly. A mos is generally believed to be conducive to the society's welfare. The breach is punished more severely and formally than the breach of folkways (q.v.).

Morgan, Lewis Henry (1818-1881). A lawyer of Rochester, New York, whose interest in the American Indians led him to become a pioneer ethnographer and social evolutionist. His studies of the Iroquois and other Indian tribes led him to compile kinship data on over 200 separate societies, published in *Systems of Consanguinity and Affinity of the Human Family* (1871). This, the first treatise on kinship, established its study as a branch of comparative sociology. Morgan proposed the terms *classificatory* (see SYSTEM, CLASSIFICATORY) and *descriptive* (q.v.) to designate the two fundamental types of kinship nomenclature. His *Ancient Society* (1877) was a synthesis of the social history of aboriginal Oceania, the American Indians, and ancient Greece and Rome. Morgan divided all history into three stages of development— savagery, barbarism, and civilization —correlated with economic and social achievements.

morisca. A kind of battle mime found in parts of Europe and Central America.

Morning Star ceremony. See CEREMONY, MORNING STAR.

morpheme. A basic discrete sound unit with definite function and meaning. A morpheme is the smallest structure unit that has lexical or grammatic meaning. Thus, in English, the sound represented by the plural *s* at the end of a word is a morpheme signifying "two or more."

morpheme, bound. See FORM, BOUND.

morpheme, free. See FORM, FREE.

morphology. The branch of grammar that deals with the analysis of words into their parts, the morphemes (q.v.).

morphophonemics. The study of the phonemic form of morphemes (q.v.) and their variations in different grammatical contexts.

morra. An Italian game in which two players guess the number of fingers extended on the hands of both. It was played so violently in Rome that it was prohibited by law several times.

Mortillet, Gabriel de (1821-1898). A French scholar, who suggested the name *Anthropopithecus* for the Tertiary predecessor of man. De Mortillet held important academic and museum posts and was responsible for the introduction of an archaeological nomenclature for different cultural periods, instead of the paleontological nomenclature of Lartet. Thus, he called the Hippopotamus Age the Chellean period, after a site at Chelles, and the Mammoth Age became the Mousterian period, after the site at Le Moustier. The Robenhausian and Aurignacian were other periods he distinguished. In 1872, he proposed classifying the Paleolithic into Lower and Upper periods.

mortise *or* **mortice.** A hole cut in stone or wood for the reception of a tenon (q.v.) or other part.

mortmain. Church-held property. The name derives from the early legal conception of ecclesiastics as being civilly dead.

morula. A mass of cells in the fertilized ovum resulting from the multiplication of the segmentation nucleus, which is the product of the male and female pronuclei.

mos. See MORES.

mosaic, feather. A mosaic design of brightly colored feathers widely found in Mexico.

mosaic, stone. A surface decoration constructed with tesserae or small fragments of stone set into mastic. There are many fine examples in Mayan art.

mosque. A Mohammedan place of worship. The architecture is characterized by a group of dome-shaped buildings surrounded by several balconied minarets and enclosing a courtyard.

moss, copper. Copper in the form of fine intertwined threads.

Mother, Great. See GODDESS, MOTHER.

mother-kin. See KIN, MOTHER-.

motif. An underlying theme around which a work of art is polarized.

motif, diving. The theme of certain myths in which a deity commands various animals to dive into the deep in order to supply some earth from which the deity can create the world.

motif, filling. Ornamentation or decoration used to fill the spaces between figures on Greek pottery. The forms, including spirals, rosettes, and circles, appeared on the pottery of the eighth to sixth centuries, B.C.

motif, glutton. An art motif, of swallowing and ejecting a figure. It is found in ancient Chinese art and in the New World, notably among the Maya and on the Northwest Coast of North America. Carl Hentze has shown the relationship of this theme to lunar cycles, dark and night against light and regeneration, and other themes of opposition.

motif, sickle. A Greek decorative pattern, made up of a long row of crescent-shaped curves, used on pottery.

motif, split animal. A graphic art form, particularly on the Northwest Coast of North America, in which animals appear to be cut sagitally and spread so that their body appears in duplicate, back-to-back or end-to-end.

mot-phrase. A sentence word, used by children, in which the meaning is implicit in the context of the environment.

mould. See MOLD.

mound. A heap of earth. Three general classes are the conical mound for burial, the effigy mound, made in the likeness of some bird or animal, and the platform mound, which served as a foundation for temples or houses. See MOUND, SYMBOLIC.

Mound, Cahokia. A large archaeological mound containing 85 lesser mounds, in the midwest United States. It is a truncated pyramid on a rectangular terrace, which measures about 700 by 1,000 feet and 100 feet high and is the kind of mound generally used as the base of a ceremonial structure. It is called the Monk's Mound after a Trappist monastery built at its base in 1809.

mound, funeral. A mound, consisting of one or more chambers, which covers a corpse. The size is usually in proportion to the rank of the deceased. The body is often in a wooden or stone sarcophagus. Elaboration of funeral mounds is typical of certain parts of the New World.

Mound, Monk's. See MOUND, CAHOKIA.

mound, symbolic. A mound in the shape of a man, animal, pipe, or other object, found in parts of the New World. Such mounds were often very large. The Alligator Mound, in the Mississippi Valley, was 250 feet long; it was made of stones and a stiff fine clay. The Great Serpent Mound near the Ohio River is 1,000 feet long; it represents a serpent with an open mouth swallowing an egg 100 feet in diameter.

mound builders. See BUILDERS, MOUND.

mountain, block. A mountain in which the slope of each side is of different steepness, e.g., the Sierra Nevada.

mountain, folded. A mountain that derives its form from a wavelike folding of the earth's crust, e.g., the Jura.

mountain, residual. Part of a mountain which resists wearing away by water because it is especially hard. The term monadnock is also used.

mounting, loom. That part of the weaving process in which the warp is arranged in a parallel series.

mourner, hired. A person hired to help observe mourning. Hired mourners have been used in many parts of the world for thousands of years.

mourning. Expressions of grief for the dead may be conventionalized, stylized, and extended or individualized and brief. Fasting, as among some North Americans, or heavy eating may be practiced. Cutting off the hair, abstention from sexual intercourse, and many other prohibitions may be enforced, and special cleansing ceremonies for the survivors may be necessary. The mourners are usually in a specific kin relationship to the dead person.

Mousterian. See AGE, MIDDLE PALEOLITHIC.

movements, eustatic. Changes of sea level on a world-wide basis.

movements, forced. The concept of tropistic behavior of organisms expounded (1890) by Jacques Loeb. He suggested that behavior could be explained mechanistically, with the stimulus regarded as causing chemical changes in protoplasm and forcing the movements.

moxa. An ornamental scar resulting from applying a caustic to the skin.

mridang. The earliest drum found in India. It is made of a wooden shell which is larger at one end than the other. Both open ends are

371

covered with tightly stretched parchment. The performer plays the drum with the finger and the wrist. The mridang is also called the mathala.

Mu. A hypothetical sunken Pacific island where civilization allegedly began. There is no evidence to support this concept, which has often been ascribed to Plato, although Plato described the civilization of Atlantis in the Atlantic.

mud, gel. A humic colloidal material found as a fresh-water deposit. Gel mud often comes from peat bogs.

mud, nekron. Organic material in a lake, largely derived from plankton and similar organisms.

muet. An African stringed musical instrument of the French Congo which is played by being plucked. The muet is made of a palm stalk to which one or more resonators are attached. The strings are stretched over a notched bridge and fastened with loops.

mugwort. A tonic perennial herb, tall and grayish, related to wormwood. It is usually symbolic of femininity and is prescribed to help cure women's diseases and in many other medicinal and folk uses.

mukluk. An Eskimo moccasin in which sole and side are of one piece. It is water- and snow-resistant.

mukuru. The first ancestor of patrilineal line among the Herero; also, a lately deceased chief.

mulatto. A person with one Caucasoid and one Negroid parent. It has been estimated by Rosenblatt that there are 8,113,180 mulattoes in the New World. It is difficult to designate all persons in this category in the United States because of the social difficulties that lead many mulattoes to "pass" as Whites to census takers and in their social relations, and the frequent categorization of mulattoes as Negroes. In Brazil the calculation is impossible because of the official avoidance of racial distinctions.

mulberry, paper. A tapa-like bark from which paper is made.

mule, spinning. A power-driven device for spinning.

mullen. A woolly herb used for skin disorders and chest troubles.

Müller, Max (1823-1900). An Anglo-German philologist and orientalist, who developed the "Aryan" (q.v.) concept and wrote voluminously on problems of the Indo-European languages and the Indian classics of philosophy.

muller. A smooth rounded stone used as a pigment grinder in conjunction with a grinding slab of the same material upon which the pigments were placed in a paste. Instead of stone, it may be made of metal or glass. Grains, ore, and drugs were also ground by a muller.

multiple origin. See ORIGIN, CONCEPT OF MULTIPLE.

Mumbo Jumbo. A secret society (q.v.) of West Africa which punishes unfaithful wives.

mummification. The Egyptian technique for preserving the bodies of the dead. The Egyptian term is setekh. The body was thoroughly dried and the viscera were removed through an incision in the side. The body cavity was cleaned with palm wine and filled with cassia and myrrh. A bent instrument was used to remove the brain through the nostrils. After the incision was sewed, the body was put in a natron bath for 70 days, or treated with solid natron; it was then washed and wrapped in many gummed bandages and a canvas shroud. In a cheaper method, cedar pitch was injected into the abdomen before the natron bath. The purpose of mummification was to preserve the body so that the soul could return and revivify it. The first evidence of Egyptian mummification dates from the Fourth Dynasty. Mummification on a lesser scale has been found in other cultures.

mummification, chance. Mummification that occurs fortuitously because of favorable climate as in the Andean highlands among the Peruvian Indians.

mummy. A body which has been subject to mummification. The word probably derives from the Persian *mummia* or "bitumen," and was used because preserved bodies were black and appeared to have been soaked in bitumen, although there is almost no sign of bitumen ever having been used.

Munda. A language family spoken by several million in central India. It is an Austro-Asiatic language and is usually divided into Chota-Nagpur, or Southern Munda, and Himalayan, or Northern Munda.

Mungi. A secret society (q.v.) of the Basa of the Cameroons.

muniments. Writings or evidences through which a person can defend title to an estate or maintain a claim to various rights or privileges. The muniments include papers and title deeds.

mura. A Japanese village administrative unit.

murder, funeral. The practice of killing someone at a funeral, as in the Egyptian practice of slaughtering a slave in order to bury him with the master. This was done so that the master would be assured of servants in the outer world. See SLAVE, TOMB.

murmur. A position between voicing and breathing, so that the voice sound is not pure and is mixed with the friction of the breath going through the glottis (q.v.).

murra. A material reported in ancient sources as having been used for making rich vases. It is not known whether it was Chinese jade, porcelain, iridescent glass, or another substance.

museum. A systematic collection of scientific, archaeological, or artistic objects. Probably the first European archaeological collection was that of the Danish Olo Worm (1588-1654). The first museum in the United States was opened in Charleston in 1773. The world currently has some 7,000 listed museums, of which some 1,500 are in the United States. The United States' first anthropological museum was the William Clark Indian Museum opened at St. Louis in 1818.

music, Greek. A style of musical composition which had a single melodic line and a mournful scale, especially suited to tragic expression. There were neither chords nor harmony.

music, mundane. The inaudible harmony of the heavenly bodies. The ancients believed that the movements of the planets produced the seven notes of the scale. Pythagoras and Plato wrote a great deal on this "music of the spheres."

music, primitive. Music which does not have formally delineated scales, theories, or centrally accepted standards, and is usually played with instruments of a simple type. Ceremonies often use vocal music. The musician as a professional person in early society is not very common because music is so widespread. Melody as such is a fairly late development in the growth of music. Primitive music may be quite complex.

music, religious. The tonal accompaniment of religious rites, probably beginning with early man's magical incantations that hinge on the effect of instrumental and vocal tone in manipulating unseen powers. Early religious music was thus largely utilitarian, and this phase blended into the early historic religions with their more formalized music.

musicology. The formal study of music and music history.

musimo. The ancestral spirits in Nyasaland.

muskeg. A surface which is permanently waterlogged, often covering quantities of peat.

Muskogean. A language family of North America. It is found in the southeast part of the United States, largely to the east of the Mississippi.

mustache lifter. See LIFTER, MUSTACHE.

mutagen. The capacity of a gene locus to mutate, or a gene locus with a higher capacity to mutate than other genes.

mutant. An organism which is the carrier of a mutation. **A mutation** is a spontaneous change in the genes of some individuals, thus bringing about new hereditary effects. De Vries suggested that evolution arises through mutations, instead of slight cumulative changes, as supposed by the older evolutionists. A mutation rate of one per 100,000 organisms has often been suggested as an average.

mutation, chromosome. A mutation that stems from the genes in a chromosome undergoing rearrangement.

mutation, gene. A mutation that results from the gene's changing physically or chemically.

mutation, initial. The alteration of the first consonant of a word. It has been observed in many languages and is of first importance in the Celtic languages, where the first consonants alter according to the last sound of the preceding word or the place the word occupies in the sentence. This initial mutation takes place in the form of aspiration (q.v.), lenition (q.v.), or nasalization (q.v.).

mutation, somatic. A mutation in a soma cell, thus one which cannot be inherited.

mutation, vowel. The alteration of a vowel because there is another vowel or sometimes even a consonant in the next syllable. See UMLAUT.

mutilation. The practice of surgically or physically changing the appearance of parts of the body as a symbol of penance, rank, family, skill, etc., or for beautification. The sexual organs are traditional objects of mutilations, e.g., circumcision, often symbolizing the passage to maturity. Mutilation may enable one to control natural forces or be used as punishment, as of a felon until recent times.

myall. An Australian aboriginal who lives away from a white settlement. The term is derived from the Botany Bay tribe's word for stranger.

Mylitta, temple of. In Babylonia, the temple where every woman had to yield herself to a stranger once in her life. Mylitta is probably a variant of Aphrodite and Ishtar, and thus represents fertility. Each Babylonian woman was required to wait inside the temple for the first stranger—believed to be a god in disguise—who would give her a coin in the goddess' name. Herodotus said that some ugly women waited several years for a man to appear.

myomancy. A method of divination (q.v.) in which the movements of rats and mice are observed.

mysteries, Dionysian. A ritualistic cult of the ancient Greeks founded in Phrygia and spread by migratory devotees. Its adherents originally indulged in highly orgiastic rites, including drinking sacred wine, eating the raw flesh of a sacrificial animal and drinking its blood, and venting themselves in ecstatic frenzies supposed to have

been inspired by the presence of the god within them. At times the celebrants were reputed to have torn a living person to pieces and devoured gobbets of still hot flesh. In time the mysteries became refined and attenuated and centered about a genteel phallicism.

mysteries, Eleusinian. The most ancient of all Greek mysteries, held near Eleusia, outside Athens, and first performed as early as the 19th century B.C. They were built around worship of the mother goddess Demeter and her daughter Persephone, who was taken into the underworld by Hades and later given back to Demeter by Zeus, the king of the gods, for eight months every year. The motivating force of the rites, therefore, seems to have been the need for divine assistance in assuring the fertility and productivity of the soil, since Demeter was symbolic of the earth and Persephone of the seed. Later rituals were believed to have the power to insure happiness in the world after death.

mysteries, Orphic. An ancient Greek mystery cult, believed to be an outgrowth of the Dionysian mysteries. They did not have the orgiastic elements of the early Dionysian rites, however. These mysteries had a speculative and sober character and were concerned with the soul's immortality and reincarnation. The Orphists tried to influence what happened after death by practicing austerity.

mysteries, Phrygian. Rites centering in the Mediterranean area, dealing with Cybele, the mother goddess who lamented Attis' death until he came back to life in the spring.

mystery. A ceremony that can be attended only by members of a special social group and that involves secrets vital to the group or the preservation of its means of existence. Initiation ceremonies through which a person enters a class, age grade (q.v.), or new status, as well as special repetitions of ceremonies for specific seasons, are found in mysteries.

mystery cult. See CULT, MYSTERY; RELIGION, MYSTERY.

myth. A story that recounts purportedly historical events to explain how traditions, major doctrines, religions, and similar nuclear concepts arose. The major protagonists in a myth are deities. Myths probably were attempts on the part of early man to explain natural phenomena. The sun, the universe, the sky and the life after death are prolific sources of myth. An example of a functional myth is the American Indian notion that a fish buried in a hill of corn gave its spirit to the growing grain. By this myth, In-dians could facilitate the process of growth although they did not understand it.

myth, emergence. A myth held by some southern United States Indian tribes, as well as by the Great Lakes Huron-Iroquois, dealing with the emergence of the first human beings from a cave or an underworld hole and subsequent events.

myth, iconic. A myth that arose through the misinterpretation of a monument.

mythology. An organized group of myths with a common tradition and origin; also, the study of myth (q.v.). The scientific study of myths dates from the 18th century. After De Brosses and Schelling, myth was interpreted philologically by Max Müller, anthropologically by Tylor, Lang, and Frazer, and psychologically by Jung and Freud, among others. Mythologies have been found in almost all religions. They were important early teachers.

myxedema. Hypothyroidism that does not exist from birth. It is associated with muscle weakness, tremors, dullness, slow reaction time, and lethargy.

N

na vilavilairevu. Fiji "fire walking."

nacom. An elected military head of a Maya city-state.

Nadené. An American Indian linguistic subdivision, perhaps related to Sinitic. It includes the Athapaskan, Haida, and Tlingit subfamilies.

nagana. A disease which the tsetse fly transmits to cattle.

nagara. A kettle drum of India beaten with two curved sticks and used only in the temple.

naggareh. An ancient Arabian and Syrian small double drum of brass with a parchment stretched over the head. It is beaten with wooden drumsticks.

nagual. In Central America, a personal totem or an individual guardian spirit. The identity of the nagual is determined through fixed rules and consultation of an elaborate calendar. The person and his nagual—usually an animal that becomes the person's spirit soon after birth—have the identical soul. The nagual is usually half spirit and half real, and the individual is believed to suffer injury or death along with his nagual. The concept of the nagual was erected into a cult opposed to the religion and government of the conquerors in Mexico and Central America.

naif. Referring to a gem that is shiny even before being polished.

naka. A Maori war dance.

nakokus. Ancient Egyptian cymbals. They consisted of two brass plates suspended on strings and struck against each other. Their chief use was marking the rhythm for a religious procession.

Nakuran. The second so-called wet period recognized in the geological strata of Kenya.

name. In early thinking, a name was not only a designation but often an entity in itself, necessary to obtain power over the person or object named. In many early groups, the real name was secret, so that an enemy might not use it. Even in some religions, the gods tried to mask their names; thus Yahweh's real name might be uttered only once a year by the high priest in the Holy of Holies. Naming a person after another or after a deity was thought to transmit some of the original's characteristics.

name change. See CHANGE, NAME.

"Nancy." One of the many West Indian and African stories dealing with the mystical spider (anansi); among the Creoles, any myth, fairy tale, or legend.

Nanga. A secret society (q.v.) of Fiji to which women are admitted. Nanga also designates the stone enclosures within which the rites are held.

nangarri. An Arunta medicine man (q.v.).

nanism. The arrest of growth. It may be caused by inadequate development or by defective pituitary and thyroid glands. Nanism is often used for a kind of dwarfism in which the head is proportionately large for the age and the rest of the body stunted.

naos. A small wooden or stone Egyptian shrine in which the spirit of a deity was supposed to be present at all times.

Napiwa. An anthropomorphic (q.v.) white god among the Blackfoot.

nardoo. A plant whose seeds are ground and made into a cake by the Australian aborigines.

narrowing. The process by which a word that formerly represented a general class refers only to special cases of that class. It is often found when a word is taken over by one language from another. Thus, the French *cérise* ("cherry") in English is applied to the color only, not the fruit.

narwhal. A large arctic cetacean with a long pointed tusk protruding from the upper jaw. Narwhal tusks cast up on shore were believed in Medieval times to be the horn of the mythical unicorn.

nasal. In phonetics, referring to a sound made with the uvula in a lowered position so that the air escapes through the nasal cavity, which acts as a resonator, e.g., *m* in English.

nasal, palatal. A nasal in which the contact between the highest part of the palate and the tongue effects closure, e.g., *ni* in *onion*.

nasalization. The process of making a speech sound with the velum (q.v.) incompletely raised, so that some breath escapes from the nose and the sound has a peculiar resonance.

Nasamonian. The rite whereby the bride submitted to every male guest at her wedding before submitting to the bridegroom.

nasion. The midpoint of the nasofrontal suture (q.v.).

nassa. A Melanesian currency based on a small sea snail with a humped shell. The shells are collected with considerable ceremony. The hump is removed and the shell is cleaned and bleached, after which it is ready to be strung on liana tendrils. It is extremely valuable and tremendously important in the islanders' daily lives. The strings of money are wrapped in leaves and tied with rotang cord.

natality. The measure of the birth rate of a population.

nation. A group of persons who have a common language and geographical area. There is usually a clearly defined central authority which has ultimate legal, military, and administrative power. They may or may not have uniform culture and racial origin.

Nation, Tobacco. A name given to the Huron Indians.

nativism. A movement that proclaims the return to power of the natives of a colonized area and the resurgence of native culture, along with the decline of the colonizers, e.g., the cargo cult (q.v.), the ghost dance (q.v.) cult.

nativistic. See THEORY, NATIVISTIC.

natron. A neutral carbonate of sodium procured from the natron lakes of Egypt. It was obtained by evaporating the lake water or washing the earth in which it appeared. Natron was used in mummification (q.v.).

Natufian. An assemblage (q.v.) from the upper layers of some Palestinian caves, probably dating ca. 10,000 B.C. There was some bone-working and flint sickles and evidence that much of the food was hunted or collected. Childe thinks it possible that the agricultural revolution occurred during this culture.

nau. The transitional stage before adulthood among the Hottentots.

naualla. Vertical body marks in Australia.

naus. A rectangular stone structure with an apse at one end.

nave. The hub on a wheel.

navicella. A small boat; a Hallstatt fibula (q.v.).

naviform. A boat-shaped representation, found in early art.

Ndembo. A bisexual initiation society of the Congo.

Ndengei. The supreme deity in Fiji.

ndomi. Wooden shoulder shields of Kenya.

Neanderthaloid. Referring to the most widely distributed and most numerous of paleoanthropic men, of which some 100 skeletons, in whole or part, have been found. See HOMO NEANDERTHALENSIS.

neanthropic. Referring to the type of man that has persisted into recent times. The form neoanthropic is also used.

Nearctica. The New World half of Holarctica.

near-human. During the early to middle Pleistocene, the term sometimes used to describe the population of the Old World.

necromancy. Foretelling the future, or influencing others, usually by communication with the ghosts of the deceased. The term has been extended to mean almost any kind of magic. The underlying theory of necromancy is that the ghosts of the dead are omniscient, and if they reveal what they know to a mortal, he will have great powers. Necromancy has been widely found in most early societies and has lasted up to fairly recently. The Homeric Greeks, and probably the early Hebrews, practiced it.

necropolis. A cemetery, usually large or old.

necrosis. The death of a piece of tissue, through burning, interference with the blood supply, or a similar cause.

needle. A Magdalenian bone implement, probably first made by grinding a small bone fragment with a rough hard material. The eyes of these needles were probably

379

made with flint awls (q.v.). Needles vary greatly in size.

needle, Cleopatra's. Either of two obelisks built during the reign of Thothmes III (1501-1447 B.C.) in ancient Egypt. They were originally set up in the great temple of Heliopolis and later removed to Alexandria by the Romans in 14 B.C. At present, one is on the Thames embankment in Great Britain and the other in Central Park in New York City. Voluminously inscribed, they were called sun fingers by the Egyptian priests because they served as a gigantic sun-dial pointer and the time could be determined by the length of their shadows on the ground. They are not connected with Cleopatra in any way.

neeskotting. An American Indian term for catching fish in shallow water at night with a lantern and a long hooked pole.

nefer. An exquisitely designed Egyptian necklace or pendant worn by both the living and the dead, usually made of beads inscribed with representations of gods. The art of gem-cutting was at its height during the Twelfth and Thirteenth dynasties. The individual beads of gold, porcelain, silver, lapis lazuli, or emerald were supposed to have magical powers and to protect the wearer.

Negrillo. The African pygmy, who is shorter than all other pygmies (4 feet 6 inches on the average). The Negrillo is generally found in the Congo forests. Mesocephaly and an average cranial capacity of 1,300 cc. are other characteristics.

Negrito. The pygmies (q.v.) of the Philippines, who average about four feet eight inches in height. They are prognathous, with broad flat noses, and range from reddish to dark brown in color. In some classifications, Negrito is used for pygmies of Southeast Asia, while in others it designates all pygmies with a hunting and gathering economy. Some writers consider Negritos the most primitive humans. It has been contended by some writers that the Negrito type is found in the Congo region, the Malay peninsula, and New Guinea. Early India, in this view, was inhabited by Negritos, who have survived in pure form in the Andaman Islands, believed to be the only area of the world where the entire indigenous population is Negrito.

Negro, Forest or Negro, African. A Negroid subrace with broad nose, thick lips, sparse body hair, substantial prognathism, and dolichocephalic skull. The Forest Negroes are found in the western, central, and southern parts of Africa.

Negro, Nilotic. A Negroid subrace found in the Eastern Sudan and upper Nile areas. The individuals are tall, with fairly thin lips and broad, short faces.

Negro, Oceanic. A Negroid subrace found in the New Guinea area. The members display variable skin color and frizzly hair. There are two subtypes, the Melanesian and Papuan.

Negroid. One of the major racial groups of mankind. Some of its characteristics are slight body hair, small ears, black head hair which may range from a light curl to woolly or frizzly, brown to brown-black eyes, nose likely to have a low bridge, brown to brown-black skin, height from very short to tall, narrow to medium broad face, and everted lips. This race includes Forest, Nilotic, and Oceanic Negroes.

Negus. A chief in North Africa; a ruler of Ethiopia.

neoanthropic. See NEANTHROPIC.

Neoasiatic. A central-eastern Asiatic Mongoloid subdivision, with an extreme development of the internal epicanthic fold (q.v.).

neolinguists. Linguists, including Bertoni and Bonfante, associated with the idea of linguistic development emerging from complex chronological and geographical factors that are difficult to summarize in phonetic laws.

Neolithic Age. See AGE, NEOLITHIC.

neolithicum. The age of newer, or polished, tools of stone.

neonatal. Referring to newly born infants.

neopallium. G. Elliott Smith's name for the new part of the cerebral covering concerned with consciousness and the higher associative brain functions. This area is 3.4-6 times larger in man than in gorillas and chimpanzees.

neophyte. One recently initiated into a mystery cult.

neoplasm. New tissue growth that does not have a physiological function, e.g., a tumor.

neotechnic. The name given by some scholars to the period of recent technological advances, notably the rise of atomic energy.

neoteny. Stagnation in the growth of an organism, so that the adult is like an ancestral embryonic form. Bolk, a Dutch anatomist, has ascribed this condition to man, saying that he is like the fetus of an ape in many ways. In this view, man is a neotene ape, while the chimpanzee and gorilla have gone beyond man through specializing as acrobats. See PEDOGENESIS.

nephelomancy. A method of divination (q.v.) by observation of the clouds.

nephrite. A jade stone used for ornamentation and implements among the Thompson River Indians, the Eskimo, some groups of northern South America, and others.

net, carrying. A woven or braided net for carrying hand luggage.

net, cast. A fishing net with a weight at its edges to sink and trap fish.

net, dip. A fish net fixed to a circular frame and equipped with a handle.

net, gill. A net used in fishing for salmon off the mouth of a river, notably the Columbia River. A gill net has a wide mesh that catches the salmon behind the gills when it puts its head through the net.

net, hand. A manually operated fishing net.

net, trawl. A fishing net shaped like a bag and weighted to sink to the bottom. It remains open to permit fish to enter as it is towed (trawled) along.

Neter. The deity in Egyptian lore.

netting. A primitive kind of plaiting consisting of a single element plaited in an open mesh. The oldest surviving specimen, from Antrea in Finland, was part of a fishing net. Most of the recovered early specimens of netting are knotted.

netting, knotless. A kind of crocheted netting used to make bags in Oceania, Australia, and parts of the Western Hemisphere.

neuron. A nerve cell, the structural element of the nervous system. The dendrites are the receiving end, the cell body contains the nucleus, the axon transmits the nervous impulse, and the collaterals are side branches from the axon. Bipolar nerve cells have the axon and dendrite on opposite sides of the cell body, and multipolar cells have dendrites branching off at different angles.

neurosis. A mental illness that causes pain but does not prevent functioning. Common are anxiety, a gap between the individual's potential and actual achievement, and difficulties in object relations and interpersonal situations.

neutral territory. See TERRITORY, NEUTRAL.

new fire ceremony. See CEREMONY, NEW FIRE.

Nez Percés. A French term for some American Indian groups that they believed pierced the nose in order to insert dentalium (q.v.). These groups were found largely in Washington, Idaho, and Oregon.

Ngandong. The site in Java where Homo soloensis (q.v.) was found.

nganga. Witch doctors in the Congo and West Africa.

Ngbe. See EGBO.

ngiemah. See KOUNDYEH.

ngoma. A cask-shaped African kettle drum. The parchment head is struck with the fingers. It is named after a Kafir dance.

ngonge. An African wooden bell with two or more clappers hung inside on a cord. The ngonge keeps track of African dogs (which do not bark), hangs on the backs of mourners during a funeral, or is worn by women as an ornament.

nicchia. A niche, especially in a rock tomb.

night. The time of the day when the sun does not shine, often regarded symbolically as death or unpleasantness. See LIGHT AND DARKNESS.

Nigritian. An African culture believed by some Africanists to be a relic of a hypothetical Negroid original culture. It is also called Old Sudanese, because the area from the upper Nile to the sources of the Niger seems to have had the Nigritian as its homogeneous culture at one time. This culture has both Egyptian and Indian elements.

nikki. Stick tobacco in the Northern Territory of Australia.

nilam. A rice field in southern India.

Nili-an-can. An anthropomorphic white god among the Arapaho.

Nilote. Tall, very dark inhabitants of Ethiopia and the Sudan, who speak the Hamitic languages.

Nilotenstellung. A postural position fairly widely distributed throughout the world, consisting of a one-legged resting stance. It seems to be confined to males.

Nilotic. Referring to an early theory which postulates that the Nilotes represent an African culture resulting from a blending of Hamites and Forest Negroes, with a Nilotic southern migration taking place around the 17th century. Nilotic culture is believed by some scholars to be an eastern offshoot of the Nigritian (q.v.) which has been strongly influenced from Hamitic-Ethiopian quarters.

Nilsson, Sven (1787-1883). A Swedish zoologist, who wrote *Primitive Inhabitants of Scandinavia* (1838-1866). He suggested that waves of invaders had made changes in the early Scandinavian cultures and that human beings are ". . . constantly undergoing a gradual and progressive development." He listed the principles to be followed in the study of the development of culture. The four human stages he analyzed were savagery, herding and nomadism, agriculture, and civilization, and preceded related classifications by Tylor and Morgan.

nimbus. A representation of the halo of divine light and glory which usually appears surrounding the head of Christ, the Virgin Mary, or the saints. It is different from the aureole, which surrounds the whole body. The nimbus first appeared in Christian art during the fifth century, but earlier representations in India and Egypt and among the Greeks and Romans show that it was not Christian in origin.

nipper. A device to hold an object tightly while it is being worked.

nirvana. In Buddhist doctrine, the ultimate state of nonbeing after which all souls yearn. Nirvana is not attained until many transmigrations of the soul have permitted it to attain perfection.

nitrification. Conversion to nitrous and nitric acids of nitrogen or ammonia, usually through the action of bacteria in the soil.

nivation. Freezing followed by thawing.

nixtamal. Wet ground hominy in Mexico.

niyoga. In India, the selection by a childless man of a substitute male to beget a son and heir on his wife.

nkasa. A poison used in the Congo poison ordeals.

nkele. Arable land in Fiji.

Nkumba. A secret society (q.v.) of the Congo.

noa. In Polynesian religion, the state of being free from taboo (q.v.). Thus, noa also designates an object that is free from the supernatural.

nobility. A social class with a high hereditary status, prestige, and power.

nock. The notch in an arrow to fit into the bowstring. It may be cut in the shaft butt or in some harder material in the butt.

node. A small clay spot placed on a pottery vessel as decoration. It is common on vessels of the North American Indians, especially in the Mississippi area.

nodule, tooth. A measure of tooth size computed by multiplying the length and breadth and dividing the result by two. Using this criterion, the smallest molars are those of the Bush Negro and the largest are those of the Australian aborigines.

383

noeme. The meaning of a glosseme (q.v.).

nomad, pastoral. A person who lives completely from his flock and does not domicile himself to plant.

nomadism. Regular seasonal or cyclical movements of a group to obtain sustenance. According to the food supply, it may assume different forms, depending on topography and climate. There are nomads who hunt and nomads who collect food, as well as pastoral and even agricultural nomads. Nomads are usually found in small kin bands.

nomadism, primitive. Regular changes of locale, usually from one recognized site to another. These changes are correlated with variation in the procurement of food.

nome. The important divisions of the kingdom of ancient Egypt. There were 42 nomes, each protected by one divinity and each with both a religious and civil capital. The office of governor (nomarch) was hereditary.

nomina sacra. The sacred names, particularly the great names of the Biblical figures. The early scribes used abbreviations for many of these names, using the first and last letters, with a line above them, so that Jesus might be written $\overline{\text{IC}}$. See NAME.

nomothetic. A study the purpose of which is to arrive at general propositions that are uniform for the data to which they pertain. Windelband, who introduced the term (1904), used it for those sciences that emphasize general laws, as opposed to the idiographic (q.v.).

nonliterate. A people without a written language. The term does not carry with it the implication of fixation at the prehistoric level, or commitment to a sequential concept of cultural progress, as do primitive and preliterate (qq.v.).

nonsecretor. A person whose internal secretions, urine, and saliva do not make it possible to analyze his blood group factors.

nonsyllabic. See SYLLABIC.

nontaster. A person unable to taste PTC (q.v.) when placed on the tongue.

nook, bench. The part of a bench that is sunken into the wall as in a kiva (q.v.).

Nordic. A supposed northern Caucasoid (q.v.) group, about the existence of which there is some question. Also, a white subrace that can be regarded as a depigmented variant of Mediterranean stock. Straight nose, light hair, blue or gray eyes, and robust body build are representative traits. A cephalic index (q.v.) of less than 80 is typical. This group is concentrated in Scandinavia, especially Sweden and the uplands of Norway.

Nordic fold. See FOLD, NORDIC.

norfe. An Egyptian stringed instrument made in a pear shape with a long fretted fingerboard. The frets were of camel gut and the strings were plucked with the fingers.

norimono. A Japanese palanquin.

normosplanchnic. In Viola's system of body build types, referring to the normal constitution.

Northwest, Pacific. A culture area comprising the tidewater communities from Yakutat in southern

Alaska to northwest coastal California.

nose, Iranian Plateau. A fairly convex nose with flaring and recurved alae and a depressed, thick tip. It may be high and prominent.

Notation, Analphabetic. A phonetic alphabet developed by Jespersen. A group of symbols composed of Arabic numerals and Greek letters, with Latin letters as exponents, represents each phoneme (q.v.). The numeral represents the degree of opening and the Greek letter the organ of articulation.

notch. A trimmed indentation on one or both sides of a blade. Notches may alternate down each side or be opposite each other. They are characteristic of middle Aurignacian industries and may be found on the side of a coup-de-poing (q.v.) near its point.

Notenschrift. A kind of pottery design somewhat like musical notation. The pottery of the latter part of the Danubian I period showed this design.

Notes and Queries on Anthropology. A detailed annotated check list prepared so that systematic information about nonliterate societies can be obtained even by those without formal anthropological training. It was originally issued in 1874 for persons living in "uncivilized lands," by the British Association for the Advancement of Science, which reissued it in 1892, 1899, 1912, and 1929. In 1951, it was reissued by the Royal Anthropological Institute. It reports field work thoroughly and is unusually strong in social anthropology and material culture, but gives little insight into the dynamics of a culture, inasmuch as it emphasizes observation rather than interpretation.

notochord. In lower vertebrates, a rod of cells that represents the origination of the backbone.

novaculite. A tough siliceous rock with a fine grain used in whetstones. It probably is of sedimentary origin.

Novial. An artificial language invented by Jespersen in 1928.

n'toro. One's spirit in Ashanti. It is inherited patrilineally.

nu. See CLOTH, MUMMY.

nubility. The degree of marriageability of a woman.

nuchal. Having reference to the neck.

nudity. Not wearing clothes. It is used symbolically to bring about, or stop, rain, or to drive away demons.

nuggar. A cargo boat used on the Nile.

nulla-nulla. An Australian club.

number, magic. A number symbolic of the mysteries of creation and divine secrets and regarded as possessing magic powers.

number, pattern. A number that occurs often in different contexts and is preferred in a given culture.

number, ritual. A number with a unique meaning for various American Indian groups. Important social activities and ceremonies are tied in with ritual numbers, of which 3 and 4 are the most widely found. Numbers 5, 6, 10, and 12 are sometimes used, while 7 is rare. One tribe can have several such numbers.

number, sacred. A number with a special status and sanctity. These numbers were selected for different reasons: 12 for the months, 5 for the digits of one hand or foot, 20 for the fingers and toes. Multiples of these numbers may also be specially regarded, as may be the multiple of such prime numbers as 3 and 5. Number 1 may represent unity, 4 the cardinal points, 3 the past, present, and future. The original reason for a number selection is seldom recalled.

nunatak. A driftless area in a region with considerable glaciation, often a mountain or tableland; or, a peak of rock that can be seen through ice.

nupturient. A marriage partner.

nuraghe. A Late Bronze Age structure, resembling a fort, found in Sardinia. The nuraghi are conical, with a truncated summit, about 30 to 60 feet high and 35 to 100 feet wide at the base. They are built of rough blocks without mortar. There is a low tunnellike entrance and one or more rooms. The nuraghi were probably the castles of martial leaders. The term *nuragic* refers to the Bronze Age in Sardinia.

nurtanja. An object similar in function to a churinga (q.v.), found in northern Australia. It consists of spears tied with human hair, with colored feathers for a cover. It was carried like a banner, worn by dancers, or used as a headdress.

nut. A hard-shelled dry fruit or seed with a distinct separable rind or shell and interior meat kernel.

nyeka. A whistle charm used in the Congo.

nymph. In Greek mythology, an attractive young woman closely associated with some natural forces. They had some extra human qualities, and were favorites of the gods as well as guardians of mountains, springs, or groves. Most of the nymphs were notorious for their orgiastic conduct with satyrs.

Nzambi. A Congo sky god.

O

oak. A widely worshipped tree, often associated with lightning, death, fire, and many gods.

oakum. A loose fiber resulting from untwisting worn ropes of hemp. Oakum is often used to calk ships' seams.

oath. A promise or affirmation, usually calling on a divine authority to punish the oath taker in case of perjury. Many early peoples believed that words and verbal formulae had a special existence of their own and an oath was felt to be a kind of self-curse with almost magical potency. The oath may be taken in connection with an object associated with what might befall the person if he perjures himself, e.g., the Kandhs touch the skin of a lizard, and call down its scaliness on themselves if they are lying. Other rituals involve grasping weapons and pointing toward the sky.

oath, drinking the. An ordeal (q.v.) in which there is drinking, e.g., the Masai drink blood if accused of a crime and request the god to kill them if guilty.

obeah. A medicine man, especially in vodun, in the West Indies and parts of Africa.

obelisk. An upright tapering pillar, usually monolithic, found in Egypt. An obelisk's height (at times over 100 feet) was usually 9 to 10 times the diameter. Obelisks were split from the quarry by making holes and inserting and then wetting tight wooden wedges, so that the wood's expansion acted more smoothly than a dynamite blast. Obelisks were removed on sledges to the river, ferried across, and then resledged to the erection site. They were dragged up an inclined plane with the butt leading and dropped on the prepared base. They were always erected in pairs. They were often square, with fairly convex faces. The best were of granite, from the Aswan quarries. Some, topped with gilt copper or bronze, were often found in front of either side of a temple's main entrance. The pyramidion (the pyramidal form at the top) often had representations of offerings, and hieroglyphics describing a pharaoh's achievements were often inscribed on the shaft.

Obelisks have been believed to be phallic symbols, especially in view of the Egyptian religion's having so many phallic elements. It has been suggested that rough phalluslike stone pillars found in the Hamitic and Semitic culture grew into the Egyptian obelisk. The obelisk has also been called a ray of light, a god's finger, a unicorn's horn, a place marking, and a memorial for a king. Some obelisks have sun god symbols on top. See NEEDLE, CLEOPATRA'S.

Obelisk, Luxor. One of the famed obelisks built for Rameses II at Thebes. It now stands in the Place de la Concorde in Paris, where it was transported from Egypt by King Louis Philippe. It is made of pink syene granite. Seventy-six feet tall and mounted atop a 16½ foot plinth, it soars majestically. All four sides of the shaft are voluminously covered with inscriptions recounting the reigns of Rameses II and III.

Obelisk, Parisian. See OBELISK, LUXOR.

obesity. Overweight due to the body's having a disproportionately large fat content.

object, intrusive. 1 An object found at an archaeological level other than that from which it originally derives. 2 An object that is believed to enter the body of a victim and sicken or kill him. Sorcerers often claim to treat disease by extracting intrusive objects.

object, magic. An object which is an agent of magic, e.g., Aladdin's lamp.

object, sacred. Sacred objects include both cult and ritual objects. The image of a spirit may be sacred as its temporary home. Objects used for ritual or in a cult may be sacred, along with objects used in ceremonies or installation of officials.

oboe. A wood wind with a double reed. It consists of a tube with devices for opening and closing the holes. The oboe was used for sad, pastoral, or phallic themes.

observer, participant. A person who in the study of a society engages to some extent in its activities as a means of gaining a better understanding and heightening rapport with the people he is studying.

obsidian. A natural glass resulting from the quick cooling of lava. Obsidian implements usually have a glossy black surface. Obsidian has a perfect conchoidal fracture and by some early men was regarded as better than flint for implements. It was so highly valued, especially for making blades, that it was used as a Neolithic barter item, e.g., ca. 3500 B.C., a Lake Van village quarried obsidian for export. It is found, among other places, in the Admiralty Islands, Mexico, Kenya, Melos in the Aegean, Lake Van in Armenia, and Kaisarieh in Turkey.

occhio. A hole in an implement.

occipital. Referring to the occiput or the occipital bone. The occipital bone is a single bone found on the posterior-superior-inferior part of the skull. Part of the bone can usually be felt on the back of the head as the occipital prominence.

occlusion. The way the mandibular teeth and maxillary teeth meet during the functional excursions of the lower jaw. The maxillae are stationary. Normal occlusion manifests itself in mastication, proper speech

388

and swallowing, maintaining the health of the surrounding and supporting structure, and cosmetic appearance.

occlusive. See STOP.

occupance. Living in an area, along with the resultant landscape changes.

Oceania. The Pacific island area which includes Indonesia, Micronesia, Melanesia, Australia, and Polynesia and was probably populated by groups from the mainland of Asia.

ocher or **ochre.** An oxide of iron mixed with earth and clay, varying in color from yellow to chocolate. The ochers occur naturally and were often used in Upper Paleolithic times in art. Red ocher appears in ceremonial burials. These colors are permanent and are still used.

ochingufu. A crude African drum made of an open box. It is played by striking the sides with two beaters.

ochlocracy. A government in which the final authority rests with the people themselves.

ochre. See OCHER.

octoroon. A person with seven-eighths white blood and one-eighth Negro blood.

oculus. An "eye" on the bow of vessels in classical times and of junks and sampans. It is supposed to enable the vessel to see its path across the sea. The custom began when the prow was the sanctuary of a patron deity.

odontology. The science of the growth and structure of the teeth.

odors, classification of. The taxonomy of olfactory sensations. Lin-naeus (1752) listed seven classes: aromatic, ambrosiac, nauseous, fragrant, hircine, foul, and alliaceous. In 1895, Zwaardemaker added empyreumatic and ethereal to Linnaeus' classes. Henning, in 1915, listed six classes: ethereal, spicy, putrid, burned, resinous, and fragrant.

oenochoe. A Greek ceramic wine jug. It has a delicately curved handle and a trefoil-formed mouth, and is unsurpassed in its beauty of line. The early Rhodian jugs were decorated with brown slip with birds and animals, while the slim Athenian oenochoe has a simple decorative panel on the side. Apulian ware of the fourth century B.C. shows a thin, tapering body, a tall stem, and a high-curved handle.

offering, burnt. An animal sacrifice the flesh of which was wholly consumed by fire upon the altar. A burnt offering is differentiated from offerings of cereal or liquor or animal offerings where only the blood and fat were put upon the altar while the flesh was eaten by the priests and worshippers.

offering, primitial. The custom of throwing away a choice morsel of food or the day's first catch as an offering to a deity.

offering, sin. A sacrifice used to relieve the worshipper of the penalty for sinning.

offering, votive. An offering made to fulfill a vow or to offer thanksgiving for a favor.

officialese. The overcomplicated, periphrastic, and polysyllabic language used in a bureaucratic government.

officina. A flint workshop.

Ogam or **Ogham.** A script used by the Celts and found on monuments in Scotland, Ireland, and Wales. It had a 20-letter alphabet, which was a kind of code substitute for the Latin alphabet. The individual characters are also known as Ogams. Some manuscripts in this form still exist. The Ogams may be related to runes (q.v.).

ogdoad. In Egypt, a cycle of eight goddesses and gods.

Ogham. See OGAM.

ogre. A stupid fairy tale monster who often eats humans. There are many different kinds of ogres.

ogre, cliff. A monster, found in Greek and American Indian tales, who threw persons over a cliff as food for her offspring.

Oikoumene. A hypothetical central area covering parts of Europe, Africa, and Asia, within which there was a fairly common culture. The boundaries of this area are Java, Japan, England, and Morocco. The term means "the inhabited" in Greek, and was used by the Greeks to refer to the total habitable world as they knew it.

oils, seven holy. Magical oils given to the mummy (q.v.) in the funeral chamber to accompany it on the journey into the outer world. Their powers were protective. The oils were named *nam, heknu, sefth, seth-heb, ha-ash, tuaut,* and *tet-ent-thehenu.* They were presented to the kings in marble flasks and to those of lesser rank on the alabaster anointing tablet, which had a few drops of each oil in the seven hollows provided.

okeyame. The Ashanti talking chief (q.v.).

okolehao. A Polynesian intoxicant made from the ti plant.

olag. A girls' dormitory among the Bontoc Igorot. Girls live in an olag from the age of two until they marry. The olag is small and made of mud and stone, with a grass roof.

Oldoway. An early Paleolithic pebble-tool industry represented in Lower Pleistocene beds at Oldoway (Olduvai) Gorge, Tanganyika. The tools, which are formed by removing a few flakes from one end of the pebbles, resemble Abbevillian (q.v.) tools and are thought to be among the earliest artifacts made by man.

oligarchy. Government by a small group.

Oligocene. The Tertiary period which gave rise to the early apes in Egypt and to the ancestors of Old World monkeys. It lasted from about 45 to 35 million years ago.

oliphant. An ivory horn, made from an elephant's tusk, used by knights ca. tenth century, when it was introduced from Byzantium.

olive. A small evergreen tree about 25 to 40 feet high. It has leathery leaves and a shiny purplish black fruit. The olive probably originated in Palestine. It was known in Egypt in the 17th century B.C.

olivella. A shell used by American Indians for beads and ornaments.

olla. An earthen jar of Mexico and Spain used as a water cooler. The water that penetrates to the outer surface of the jug evaporates, thus cooling the contents.

Olorgesailie. An East African series of camp sites discovered by Leakey in 1942. There are many Acheulian (q.v.) implements and fossils of various extinct mammals, which were probably hunted, as evidenced by bones split to get at the marrow. No signs of fire have been found. If these Acheulian artifacts are confirmed by human fossils, this would indicate that large groups of men were living in this area some 200,000 years ago.

olpe. A small vessel with an even rim, no spout, and a fairly wide neck used for pouring or dipping.

omen. A supernaturally inspired clue to the future. Omens may be deliberately sought out, like the Romans watching the flight of birds, or chance observations. They may happen anytime and under any circumstances. They are very common among North American Indians. Some Indian omens are indigenous and others are borrowed from European beliefs.

omen, birth. An unusual event that takes place during childbirth and may have special significance.

omen, chance. An omen, like a meteor or comet, that is fairly or entirely unexpected. They may be regarded as especially powerful. Thus, a meteor is likely to presage bad luck.

omerti. One of the earliest stringed instruments of the ancient Hindus. It is played with a bow.

Ometecutli. A supreme being of the Aztecs.

omnivore. An organism that eats both meat and vegetables.

onager. A catapult (q.v.) with a slinglike action that hurled stones from a wooden bucket or bag.

oneiromancy or **oniromancy.** Predicting the future from dreams.

onomasiology. The study of the connotations of names.

onomatology. The study of the genesis of names and their meanings.

onomatopoeic theory. See BOW-WOW.

ontogeny. The growth and development of the individual organism. In 1884, the German biologist Ernst H. Haeckel developed the theory that ontogeny recapitulates phylogeny or that the individual goes through all the stages through which the race passed in the evolutionary process. See PHYLOGENY.

ontogeny, human. The study of the physical changes in the course of the life history of the organism; it is also called growth study.

onychomancy. Divination (q.v.) with finger nails.

onyx. A multicolored quartz, often used to cure or increase love.

coid. Referring to a skull that is egg-shaped when viewed from above.

opal. A delicately colored silica stone. It has been used to improve vision and as a sign of hope or sorrow.

operation, mika. See MIKA.

operationism. A term suggested (1928) by the physicist Percy W. Bridgman for the application of empirical standards that are consistent, definite, repeatable, capable of leading to concepts of greater validity, and linked to objective reality. Operational definitions do not apply to absolute properties or values that transcend the limits of a given experiment.

ophyron. The point in the center of the forehead where the temporal lines approach each other most closely.

opisthion. The midpoint on the rearmost margin of the occipital foramen.

opisthocranion. The midplane point on the head which is the most backward projection and furthest from the glabella.

opium. A narcotic made from the opium poppy, first used by the Sumerians ca. 4000 B.C. and by the early Assyrian civilization. It is usually attached to the bowl of a pipe, heated, and the fumes inhaled, although it may also be taken in a tincture. Its effects vary with the source and the user, but it often interferes with the sense of time. Its use is especially common in the Far East. Opium was a major therapeutic agent of medicine for over 2,000 years, through the 19th century.

oppidum. A provincial town, especially a fortified hilltop town in central Europe during the Iron Age. Such towns were often fairly large and were found especially in the temperate zones.

opposability. The ability to oppose the thumb to the fingers and to bring the finger tips into contact with the ball of the thumb. It is a characteristic distinguishing man from the other primates.

opposition, bilateral. A pair of phonemes having an identical archiphoneme (q.v.) in conjunction with diametrically opposite variations of one pertinent characteristic, which is known as the mark of opposition.

Opsimiolithic. A term applied to a culture that preserves the Mesolithic economy (hunting, fishing and collecting) in Neolithic times and exhibits some traits, such as polished axes or pottery, normally associated with Neolithic cultures.

oracle. A person specially able to obtain guidance from supernatural agencies. The oracle is sometimes attached to a specific cult and sometimes consulted by a cult official only in connection with major matters. An expert who has no association with a cult may consult the oracle.

orangutan. An anthropoid ape, found in Borneo and Sumatra. The average weight is 165 pounds, and the nose and face are very flat. Orangutans are arboreal and often have cheek pads. The brain case is short and round.

orant. A representation of a supplicant female in ancient art. It is usually identifiable by the position of the arm with the palm outward and by the smaller size when compared with any god represented in the same scene.

orbit. A skull cavity that contains an eye.

orbit, bony. The eye socket, which in primates is encircled by a bone ring and is almost completely shut off behind with a bony wall. Higher primates have forward bony orbits, so that the eyes look forward, each sweeping the same field from a different angle and giving rise to stereoscopic vision (q.v.).

orbitale. The lowest point, in the orbit's margin.

orda. One of the three paramount Kazak social divisions; a grouping of tribes. The word is the ancestor of the English *horde.*

ordeal. A technique of trial in which the accused submits to a dangerous or difficult task, like holding red hot stones in his hand, in the belief that he will not be harmed if innocent. It is assumed that supernatural powers help settle the dispute or test the accusation. An ordeal may be imposed upon an animal instead of a human.

ordeal, ant. A test of courage in the boys' puberty rites of some Indian tribes of Amazonia. The initiate allows himself to be stung by large black poisonous ants without evincing pain.

order, composite. An order of architecture based on the Greek Corinthian but varied by the Romans by the addition of large Ionian volutes to the capital of the column.

order, pecking. The tendency of organisms to organize in terms of a dominance - submission hierarchy, originally named from the tendency of hens to form such hierarchies in pecking one another.

order, syntactic. The order of words in a sentence, which serves to point out the grammatical functions of the words, particularly in those languages lacking an inflectional system as such.

order of architecture. See ARCHITECTURE, ORDER OF.

Ordovician. A life period of the Paleozoic era, characterized by the development of vertebrate fishes. It lasted from perhaps 420 to 350 million years ago.

orenda. Among the Iroquois, the concept of supernatural and impersonal power inhering in certain objects. It is probably closely related to the Algonkian manitou (q.v.) and the Sioux wakonda (q.v.).

organization, dual. Dividing the community into two major classes, which are usually exogamic. See MOIETY.

organization, gentile. Lewis H. Morgan's name for the clan system among the Iroquois.

orgy. A ceremonial celebration distinguished by indulgence of the appetites, especially sexual, and dropping of restraints.

orientation. Placing an object in a grave in line with a cardinal direction.

orientation, family of. A nuclear family (q.v.) in which Ego is the child. He will also usually establish a family of procreation (q.v.).

origin, concept of multiple. The hypothesis that every people contains within itself the possibility of being the origin of the essentials of civilization. The evolutionary thinkers of the 19th century emphasized this view.

ornament. Devices and methods used to adorn the body. Ornament has been found among almost all peoples. It may consist of objects worn on or attached to the body, using paints, scarification (q.v.), and similar techniques, or changing the body's appearance permanently by mutilation (q.v.). Ornament may be related to sex, magic, or social display. Ornaments often represent

393

very widespread means of exchange, with gold, e.g., being used for ornamental purposes before it had value as money.

ornithomancy. Predicting the future and reading messages from birds' flight.

orogeny. The process of making mountains, especially through the folding of the earth's crust.

orongo. A Polynesian genealogist.

ortho-. A prefix meaning normal or straight, e.g., an orthognathous jaw does not project.

orthocolic. Having a medium length colon, from 160 to 175 cm. long.

orthocranic. Referring to a cranial length-height index (q.v.) between 70 and 74.9.

orthoepy. The science and art of correct pronunciation.

orthogenesis. A variation that follows a given line, in a number of generations, so that a new type not due to natural selection or external factors evolves. The term also designates a momentum and exaggeration that cannot be explained by natural selection with which some features develop and the theory that the development of societies follows in the same direction in all cultures. Recent students have generally tended to regard orthogenesis as an unsound idea that oversimplifies the evolutionary process.

orthogenesis, cultural. The comparative overdevelopment of one part of a culture.

orthognathism. Straightness, e.g., of the face.

orthognathous. Having a perpendicular face—a profile angle of 85 degrees or higher—and a comparatively receding jaw. Most modern populations are orthognathous.

orthograde. Referring to an erect posture, usually bipedal.

orthography. The rules of spelling.

orthorachic. Referring to a vertical lumbar index (q.v.) between 98 and 100.9.

oryctology. The study of fossils or whatever is dug from the earth, with the exception of archaeological material. A classification of oryctology in the late 19th century distinguished paleontology, geology, petrology, and minerology.

os centrale. A wrist bone which occurs in all lower primates, the gibbon, and the orangutan, but ordinarily not in man, the gorilla, or the chimpanzee. It is present as a cartilaginous nodule in the fetal human, but usually fuses later with the navicular bone.

oscillation, Alleröd. A period in which the climate was more pleasant than that preceding or following. Milthers, using varve (q.v.) criteria, estimated it was ca. 10,000 to 9000 B.C. in Scandinavia.

ossicle, auditory. Three small bones of the inner ear which convey sound to the vestibule.

ossuary. A place of deposit for the bones of the dead. The term is often used to describe the burial in one place of the skeletons of several different persons.

osteology. The field of study dealing with an organism's bone structure.

osteometry. The study and measurement of the skeleton and its components.

osteonia. A tumor made of bony tissue.

ostracoderm. An extinct armored fish with a three-part brain and other characteristics that have led it to be called the earliest vertebrate of which there is any record.

ostracon. In Egypt, a potsherd or a limestone fragment.

otiose. Referring to a deity who is not interested in the affairs of men or in the world he has created and who leaves them alone after the creation.

otobasion inferius. The bottom point at which the head and ear are attached.

oued or **wadi.** An intermittent river resulting from seasonal precipitation in the desert.

out, breeding. See BREEDING OUT.

outbreeding. Marriage and childbearing outside the group, or between two individuals from different groups.

out-group. The persons outside the in-group (q.v.); a group regarded by an in-group as an "others" group. There is an implication of the different and the separate.

outlawing or **outlawry.** The withdrawal by a society of rights and protection from one of its members. Early societies regarded outlawing as a very profound punishment. Sometimes the offender was excised from ancestral protection, his horse and goods destroyed, and himself forcibly driven out. Were he killed, a price could not be asked nor could a feud avenge him. In Greece, the outlaw was regarded as a wolf.

outline, boulder. A design or representation of human, animal, or other figures, made of small boulders on the ground. Boulder outlines are found in the western United States. especially in South Dakota.

outrigger. A pole bracing a canoe in order to cut down on the possibility of its capsizing.

outwash. Deposits formed through water and ice action, or of fluvioglacial origin. The term rubble is also used.

ovate. An Acheulian (q.v.) hand ax chipped in an ovoid shape.

oven, earth. In Oceania, a pit lined with stones in which a fire is kindled. After the fire burns out, wet leaves are placed on the rocks to serve as a resting place for the food, which is covered by additional leaves. The food cooks by steaming. The process is like the American clambake. The earth oven is sometimes called the Samoan pit oven.

oven, pot. See KILN.

oven, Samoan pit. See OVEN, EARTH.

over, crossing. See CROSSING OVER.

overdifferentiation. Additional forms of a paradigm (q.v.), e.g., *to be able, can, could.*

overlooking. Using an evil eye (q.v.) to effect magic. The person with the evil eye may unwittingly effect trouble, although he usually acts deliberately.

ownership. The total rights possessed over things. They involve socially recognized and enforceable command over an object, especially its use, transfer, and destruction. These rights can be partial or complete, shared or exclusive. They are socially limited and conferred.

ownership, use. See USUFRUCT.

oxybaphon. A wide-mouthed Greek vase, which looks like the crater (q.v.) and has some of the same uses. It is usually decorated with battle scenes.

oxytone. A word in which the emphasis falls on the final syllable.

P

p. The symbol for the frequency of the genes for blood group A, in a given group. See *q; r.*

pack, ice. Ice that is in continual motion but is usually fairly large and solid.

pack-a-mogan. See POGAMOGAN.

packing. A method of transportation in which a domestic animal carries a burden on its back.

paddle, crutch. A paddle with the top end carved so as to form a transverse piece for a grip.

paddle and anvil method. See METHOD, PADDLE AND ANVIL.

padiglione. An unroofed approach to a rock tomb.

pae-. For words beginning *pae-,* see under spelling PE.

pagan. A nature religion that does not belong to any of the great religions and is usually found among groups little subject to acculturation (q.v.).

pagne. In west Africa, a standard unit of exchange consisting of lengths of cloth.

paho. 1 A walnutlike fruit of Hawaii. 2 A stick with feathers attached used as a prayer stick in the religious rites and snake dance

(q.v.) of the Hopi. The stick indicates the god to whom prayers are offered.

paint cup. See CUP, PAINT.

painting, dry or **painting, sand.** Making designs on the earth or floor with colored sands. Earths of different colors are used for the various ceremonial observances. Dry painting is found among various Southwest Indians. The Navaho are especially noted for their paintings, which may be 10 feet wide. The Navaho complete the paintings, and destroy them, in a day. The origin of dry painting is not known. The size varies from 3 to 20 feet in diameter, with the ground sand base about one-third of an inch deep and batten-smoothed. Five colors are used: red, white, yellow, black, and gray-blue. The artist trickles the colored sand onto the base and he works outward from the central part. The number of artists varies from one to 12, depending on size. Among the subjects are lightning and gods. The sand is thrown away after some ceremonies. Some white men who have seen the rite have made reproductions from memory.

painting, negative. A method of painting a design on pottery by covering part of the vessel with wax and then applying the appropriate colors. When the wax melts as the pot is being fired, the covered area remains the natural color of the vessel, thus providing a background for the design.

painting, zone. A pottery design in which paint is applied to zones blocked out by incised designs. The design is fired into the object.

Palace, Cliff. See MESA VERDE.

palae-. For words beginning *palae-,* see under spelling PALEO.

palafitta. A lake dwelling, or the piles of a terramara (q.v.).

palanquin. A device for carrying a person, usually a box with wooden shutters, carried on the shoulders of men through projecting poles at either end. It is found in China and India.

palatal. In phonetics, referring to a consonant produced with the tongue held in an arched position near, or in contact with, the hard palate, e.g., *j̑, ç.*

palatal, alveolo-. See ALVEOLO-PALATAL.

palatalization. Assimilation (q.v.) in which a consonant followed by a palatal semivowel is shifted from its original position, e.g., the *s* in *sugar.* Palatalization is especially frequent in some Slavic languages, and usually refers to velars and dentals being assimilated to a following palatal sound.

palate, soft. The rear of the roof of the mouth. It is also called the velum.

palatograph. A method for observing movements of the articulators (q.v.). A powder placed on the roof of the mouth rubs off as it is touched by the tongue. The articulatory movements are derived from a study of disturbance of the powder.

palaver. In Africa, a conference or parley, often used to describe a council of elders.

pale-. For words beginning *pale-,* see spelling PALEO-.

palenque. A stockade in Middle America.

paleoanthropic. A hypothetical type of early man that no longer exists. The term is often used for an intermediate human group, e.g., Homo neanderthalensis.

paleoanthropology. The study of the early types of man.

Paleoarctica. The Old World part of Holarctica (q.v.).

Paleo-Asiatic. See HYPERBOREAN.

paleobotany. The study of prehistoric flora.

Paleocene. The beginning of the Tertiary epoch, in which lemurs appeared.

paleoclimatology. The study of prehistoric climate.

paleoecology. The study of past biota (q.v.) from the point of view of ecological ideas.

paleography. The systematic investigation of ancient writing from the standpoint of how it was produced, the types of symbols, and the deciphering and interpretation of all types of manuscripts.

paleolith. A Pleistocene stone implement.

Paleolithic Age. See AGE, LOWER PALEOLITHIC; AGE, MIDDLE PALEOLITHIC; AGE, PALEOLITHIC; AGE, UPPER PALEOLITHIC.

paleolithicum. The age of older, or chipped, stone implements.

paleomagnetism. See MAGNETISM, REMANENT.

paleontology, human. The study of the development of man, particularly the early development, through the investigation of skeletal remains.

paleontology, linguistic. The technique, probably originated by Benfey in 1868, of studying root words in order to discover a people's original culture. Benfey used this technique to show the dispersal of the original language presumably spoken by our first ancestors from Asia to Europe. Thus, from the fact that the word for *snow* differs markedly among the Indo-European languages and is entirely absent from some, it has been concluded that the homeland of those who spoke the hypothetical primitive Indo-European language was warm.

paleopathology. The study of pathologies in early men or animals. The original studies in the field, in the late 19th century, were of animals. Recently, attempts have been made to link pathologies to the society in which they appeared.

Paleosimia. A probable ancestor of the orangutan, dating from the middle Miocene period.

paleotechnic. In the development of the techniques of western civilization, referring to the period in which mineral resources became prominent and coal power and iron were widely used. It flourished around 1750. The factory system, finance capital, and competition developed.

Paleozoic. An early major geological period in the development of the world, often called the Secondary period, or the Age of Reptiles. Land plants, amphibians, and reptiles appeared in its later epochs. Almost all the invertebrates, except the insects, culminated in the Paleozoic. It lasted from perhaps 520 to 195 million years ago. For its subdivisions see CAMBRIAN. CARBONIFEROUS, DEVONIAN, ORDOVICIAN, SILURIAN, PERMIAN, PRIMARY.

palimpsest. A parchment that has been reused by blotting over the original material and writing another message over it.

Pallaike Cave. CAVE, PALLAIKE.

palmette. A painted or carved ornament resembling a palm leaf.

palolo. A sea-worm, *Palolo viridis,* which inhabits the coral reefs around Samoa. In late October each year it rises in great numbers to the surface to spawn and is caught by the natives, who eat it as a delicacy.

palpation. Examining, especially the internal organs, by touch or prodding.

palstave. A celt (q.v.) with a stop ridge between the flanges to engage the ends of the shaft prongs.

palstave, Bohemian. See CELT, CONSTRICTED.

palynology. See ANALYSIS, POLLEN.

pan. To wash gravel, earth, or crushed rock in a pan by agitation with water so as to obtain the particles of greatest specific gravity it contains, as in panning for gold.

pan, warming. A prehistoric pottery article, probably used to warm ovens and perhaps beds, often found with ashes enclosed, as in some Vinca remains.

pan bomba. A crudely constructed European musical instrument made of an earthenware jar covered at one end with parchment. One or more thin rods are passed through this membrane to produce sound.

panchayat. A village council in India, usually consisting of five persons.

Pandanus. A tropical tree the leaves and branches of which are used in thatching huts.

pandemic. Referring to that which occurs widely in a number of natural areas.

pandiacritic. Referring to the condition in which every member of a race or breed is recognizable as such.

panecumenical. Referring to an organism found in all kinds of environments.

pan-Egyptian. See HELIOLITHIC.

pangat. Political leaders among the Kalinga.

panmixia or panmixy. Sexual promiscuity.

pannikin. A tin cup used for drinking, especially in Australia.

panopticon. A form of prison architecture, devised by Jeremy Bentham, in which corridors radiate out from a central watch tower. Bentham called it panopticon be-cause the guards could keep all the prisoners under surveillance simultaneously from one point.

panpipe. A type of aerophone (q.v.) consisting of a number of end-stopped hollow pipes, often reeds, fastened together side by side. It is among the most primitive wind instruments.

pantun. A short improvised Malay poem. The pantun relies heavily upon an elaborate system of rhymes, assonances, and alliterations to reinforce its typically epigrammatic or punning content.

paopao. A dugout canoe in Fiji.

papaya. The fruit of a small soft stemmed tree found in tropical America. It is a widely used tropical breakfast fruit, and was probably domesticated in the Amazon basin. Its dried sap is an important medicinal aid. An extract of the fruit contains an enzyme that makes meat tender.

paper. Paper was originally developed in China (105 A.D. is the traditional date) and was made in Spain by 1144. The end of the 14th century saw paper available throughout Europe, which learned how to make it from the Moors.

paper, squeeze. The unsized paper used to take impressions of inscriptions in archaeological research. The stone must be cleaned and soaked. The sheet, which should be tough when wet, is soaked in a basin of water, rolled into a ball between the hands to break the grain, and then shaken out and applied to the stone so that there is enough slack to go into all the hollows. In order to force it into the hollows, it is beaten gently with a spoke brush. When it is dry and hard, the cast can be pulled off.

Papuan. A New Guinea linguistic stock, non-Melanesian or non-Austronesian. It consists of 132 languages and is spoken in New Guinea, New Britain, Halmahera, and the Tolo, Ran, Tidore, and Ternate islands.

papyrus. A writing material used in ancient times. It came from Cyperus papyrus, a plant that grows in marshy places, notably in Egypt. The outer rind of the stem was removed and the pith was sliced into thin layers that were laid side by side and then pressed together and dried. The extant specimens range from dark cream to dark brown. An average papyrus sheet is from 9 to 11 inches high and 6 to 9 inches wide. Usually papyri (the plural form) are made out of several pieces of payrus from 6 to 17 inches wide attached together so as to form long sheets that were rolled from left to right. The roll was tied with papyrus string and sealed with a clay lump. In writing on papyrus, a reed pen was used. There were two kinds of ink: one, of gum and lampblack dissolved in water, dried black; and the other, of green vitriol, and nutgalls dissolved in water, dried rusty brown.

The writing on papyri was usually in columns about two to three inches wide separated by narrow margins. Generally it was confined to the side on which the fibers ran horizontally. Both hieroglyphic and hieratic writing are found. Some papyri are illustrated.

The earliest papyri date from the Fifth Dynasty in Egypt. Its use spread to other countries, including Palestine, Rome, Greece, and Mesopotamia. It was the principal writing material of the early Christian era, and instances of its use occur as late as the eighth century A.D. With a history, thus, of some 4,000 years, it has been used longer as a writing material made of plant fibers than any other substance.

The earliest papyri found in Europe were presented to the library of Basel in the late 16th century. Later, there were systematic efforts to locate papyri in the Fayum.

paracone. The mesio-buccal cusp of the upper first and upper second molars.

paradigm. In linguistics, a list of the variations of form of a word, used to illustrate certain rules of grammar. Thus, all the forms of a typical verb may be listed to demonstrate the construction of a conjugation. By extension, the term paradigm means a theoretical model to explain a type of social behavior.

paradigm, defective. A paradigm in which some inflections are missing.

paragoge. The addition of a sound to the end of a word for euphony or to facilitate pronunciation without effecting any semantic change.

paranchah. A mesh bag of black horsehair, used by Moslem women in Uzbekistan to cover the head and shoulders. As recently as 1930, Uzbek women who discarded their

401

paranchahs were burned alive by mobs led by outraged mullahs.

parang. A long Malay knife.

parallelism. The development of similar culture traits in areas that are not in contact. Parallelism also denotes the belief that all human societies have developed in approximately the same way.

páramo. Alpine vegetation in the mountainous areas of the Andes and the northernmost part of South America.

paranoia. A psychosis involving delusions of persecution and grandeur.

Paranthropus. A Pleistocene man-like ape fossil of Africa.

Parapithecus. A small monkeylike lower Oligocene animal, perhaps the earliest ancestral anthropoid ape. The lower jaw and teeth of the only known specimen were found in a dry lake bed in Egypt.

parasang. A Persian measure of length. According to Xenophon and Herodotus, it was probably about four miles long.

parasol. An umbrella used as a sun shade or in ceremonies. In the indigenous high cultures of America and Asia, the parasol signified the chief's rank, and might be carried by him or a bearer as a symbol of his authority. The feather parasol denoted rank among the Inca.

parataxis. A sequence of predictions in which the subordinate uses no special attributive forms; e.g., *You will arrive home, I hope,* involves no explicit indication that *you will* is subordinate to *I hope.*

parchesi. A game, originally from India, usually with four players. Each player has four cone-shaped markers of distinctive color. The aim of the game is to move the markers along the arms of the cross-shaped board on which the game is played to the center. The number of moves is determined by tossing dice. Many modern games are based on parchesi.

parching. Preparing food by rolling hot stones around a basket container. The food is parched without burning the basket. Parching also denotes any method of roasting food by applying indirect heat.

parchment. A writing material made of sheep hide. The hide is soaked in limewater, the hair and flesh are scraped off, and the skin is stretched and dried on and then rubbed with chalk or pumice stone. A famous parchment of excellent quality was made at Pergamum, ca. second century B.C. According to Pliny, Ptolemy was afraid that the library at Pergamum might become better than the one at Alexandria, so he forbade the export of papyrus from Egypt, thus driving Pergamum to invent parchment. The fourth century A.D. saw the rise of parchment and the decline of papyrus. In 332 A.D., Constantine had Eusebius prepare 50 Bibles on parchment.

pardon. Remission of the legal consequences of a crime as an act of grace. A pardon may be absolute or conditioned. Early man had some form of pardon on occasion. Thus, Hammurabi's son, Samsu-iluna, issued a pardon to a slave. King David issued pardons and Athens permitted pardons by the assembled populace. The head of a sovereign state, e.g., the Roman emperor, the President of the United States, may pardon criminals.

parentés à plaisanterie. See RELATIONSHIP, JOKING.

parenthesis. A kind of parataxis (q.v.) in which one form interrupts another, e.g., *I fed the dog—I mean Rover—this evening.*

parenthesis, close. A parenthesis in which there is no pause pitch between the components.

parfleche. A flat rawhide envelope used to store food by some Indian groups. A parfleche was about a yard long.

parash. A member of a despised class or caste. In its more specific use, it indicates an outcaste in India.

parica. A wild plant of South America from which snuff is made.

parka. An outer garment made of tailored skins worn by the Eskimo and Athabascan.

paronym. A word that derives from a basic word as a particular word; also a word like another in form but different in meaning.

parthenogenesis. Reproduction without the male's fertilizing the egg. Parthenogenesis has been induced by inserting a needle in frog eggs.

participation, mystic. Lévy-Bruhl's term for a special kind of link in nonliterate cultures between the perceiver and the object perceived. The individual sees trees or animals, e.g., through an emotional haze that gives them a human quality. This concept stimulated studies of nonliterate thinking, but is not used today by most anthropologists.

particularizing system. See SYSTEM, PARTICULARIZING; TERMINOLOGY, PARTICULARIZING.

partitive culture. See CULTURE, PARTITIVE.

parts of speech. See SPEECH, PARTS OF.

pasigraphy. A method of writing that uses symbols with universally understood meanings.

pasimology. The art of communicating by the use of sign language.

passage, rites of. See RITES DE PASSAGE.

passage grave. A long narrow burial chamber.

past, reconstruction of the. The establishment of the development of human life on earth. Astronomical and geological data, correlations with animal finds, biological data, and the study of implements have contributed to this study.

paste. The prepared material from which pottery is manufactured, consisting of clay, water, and usually some kind of temper mixed to form a smooth mass.

pastoralism. An economy that derives the bulk of the food supply from domesticated animals. Pastoralists usually do not eat plant products, except those obtained by trading or gathering. They often travel or migrate to get good pastures, and there is sometimes conflict betwen pastoralists and farmers. The animals may provide milk, meat, transport, hides, and hair. Pastoralism is essentially an African, European, and Asiatic mode of life, with the Navajo among the few pastoral people in the New World.

pastoralist. A person who depends on animal husbandry rather than plants for food.

pâte sur pâte. A pottery technique involving a dark ground with layers of colored and white slip (q.v.). The technique is especially associated with the Sèvres porcelain works.

paterfamilias. See FAMILY, PATRIARCHAL.

path, wild-animal. The theory, associated with Dressler, that the first human roads were based on the paths trod by the regular passage of wild animals, like herds of horses or bisons, or of animals going to a drinking pool.

patina. The skin of chemically weathered flint. It may vary from a fraction of a millimeter to several millimeters in thickness. The original color of the patina is white, but since it is porous, it may absorb color from minerals in the ground, e.g., reddish-yellow from oxide of iron, black from manganese. The color may penetrate the surface of the flint as far as one-eighth of an inch. The presence of patina helps in determining the genuineness of a flint and whether it has been reworked. The term patina also denotes the incrustation of surface texture acquired by bronze or other art objects through the action of time. This crust, resulting from oxidation, is used to help date objects on a comparative basis when they come from the same area. The heavier the patination the older is the object presumed to be.

patina, air. A surface deposit on metals caused by corrosion taking place in the air, e.g., the light green surface that forms on bronze.

patina, basket-work. A patina on the surface of a flint resulting from the action of ice and weather. In basket-work patina, the flint's surface is covered with irregularly crossing white lines.

patina, blue. An apparently blue surface on a naturally black flint resulting from the black showing through the white patina.

patina, toad-belly. An ochreous patina.

patination. See PATINA.

Patjitan. A chopper (q.v.) culture of Java, from the second interglacial period. It probably dates from before Homo soloensis and after Pithecanthropus erectus.

patolli. See PATTOLI.

patriarchate. A culture in which the male enjoys superior status. It is usually characterized by descent, inheritance, and succession reckoned through the male, patrilocal residence, and the subordination of women and children.

patriarchy, free. A patriarchal community without local exogamy.

patrilineal. Determining the transmission of name, property, or authority through males. Patrilineal descent is also called agnatic descent.

patriliny. A unilateral male-centered society. It can include such features as patrilineal descent and patrilocal marriage.

patrilocal. Referring to the practice of a married couple's living in the husband's community or of a wife's settling in the home of her husband. The term virilocal is also found.

patripotestal. Referring to the exercise of authority by the paternal grandfather or father.

patronymy. The derivation of the family or personal name from the father or other patrilineal relatives.

pattern, culture. The organization of the culture complexes and traits composing a given culture; the over-all direction and quality of a culture; a distinctive theme around which a culture polarizes itself. The term was introduced by Franz Boas in his description of area and tribal culture and was popularized by Ruth Benedict in her *Patterns of Culture* (1934).

pattern, grapevine. A Greek decorative motif of vine leaves and bunches of grapes arranged on a winding or straight stem. The leaves are usually placed at regular intervals, while the bunches of grapes are at irregular intervals.

pattern, net. A recurrent pattern of crossing lines. The net pattern was used on Greek pottery and in Roman mosaics.

pattern, plus. The four-cusp pattern of molars in Homo sapiens.

pattern, systemic. A hypothetical combination of organically associated cultural elements that is likely to persist as a unit, e.g., monotheism.

pattern, universal. An outline, suggested by Wissler, of nine schematic rubrics under which all the facets of a culture may be subsumed. These headings are: war, government, property, society, religion, knowledge, art, material traits, and speech.

pattoli or **patolli.** The Aztec version of parchesi (q.v.).

patu. A Maori term for a kind of short clublike weapon of wood, stone, or bone. It was originally long and adzelike and used to thrust and stab. Specialization led to the development of the *mere* or spatulate blade and knobbed handle, the *kotiate* or violin-shaped type, and the *waha-ika* or half violin-shaped type. The major development of the patu is on New Zealand, although there are related forms in Melanesia. The Pacific Northwest coast area in North America developed clubs said by some students to be similar to the patu.

pawang. A Malay expert in magic. The pawang has a wide variety of functions, offers advice on almost every projected activity and on the weather, and maintains contact with extranatural forces.

payak. The soul among the Chaco Indians.

paygun. The innate powers of the Hindu gods.

payment, marriage. See PRICE, BRIDE.

peace, king's. The act of a king in prohibiting private vengeance in his own household. The king's peace may in time extend to his whole kingdom. The degree to which it is effective marks the extent of centralized governmental power.

peace, market. See PLACE, MARKET.

peace, pipe of. See CALUMET.

peace chief

peace chief. See CHIEF, PEACE.

peach. A low tree, with velvety-skinned round fruit and a pitted, compressed, or furrowed stone. It is known to have been grown in China and Kashmir in the third century B.C.

peag. A term for shells used as money on the eastern coast of the United States. The term was used interchangeably with wampum (q.v.), although peag actually has no meaning by itself.

peanut. A creeping or bushy annual with a fruit that ripens underground. It probably was found in the New World before Columbus. The peanut supplies about one-sixth of the world's vegetable oils.

pearl, Cleopatra's. The pearl that Cleopatra was supposed to have dissolved in wine and drunk to the health of her lover Mark Anthony. Scientific evidence, however, proves beyond question that the pearl is insoluble in wine and that any possible solvent would have been most injurious to the health of Cleopatra.

Pearson, Karl (1857-1936). An English Scientist, who was the founder of biometrics. He pioneered in the application of quantitative methods to human qualities.

peat. The residuum from the decomposition of mosses that form on fallen and decaying tree trunks. The tannin and gallic acid contained in peat give it antiseptic qualities which help to preserve perishable materials embedded in it. This preservative quality makes peat bogs a valuable source of archaeological finds.

pedalfer. Soil formed under such humid conditions that its calcium has been leached out.

pedocal. Referring to soil formed in such a dry climate that the calcium is not leached out.

pedigree theory. See THEORY, FAMILY TREE.

pedocephalic or **paedocephalic.** The intermediate type of cephalic index (q.v.), between 78 and 82.

pedogenesis or **paedogenesis.** Von Baer's term (1828) for mature germ cells developing in a larval body. See NEOTENY.

pedology. The study of soil formation, growth, and weathering to determine the associated climate and time and thus help date archaeological remains.

pedomorphic. Referring to infantile morphological traits.

pedomorphism. The change from rugged to gracile in some of the traits used to describe fossil forms.

pedomorphosis. The appearance of the ancestor's early features in the descendant's adult stage. It is also called macroevolution.

Pedregal. A sheet of lava which covers an extensive area south of Mexico City and buried a number of formative sites, including Copilco and Cuicuilco (qq.v.).

pejoration. An evolutionary change in the meaning of a word by which the connotation becomes lowered; e.g., *knave* originally meant *boy* and now means *evildoer*. Pejoration is also the practice of adding a deprecatory suffix to a word.

pelagic. Referring to exclusively marine habitats.

406

pelele. A woman's lip plug in East Africa.

pelike. An ancient Greek vase similar to the Caeretan hydria (q.v.).

pelota. See BALSA.

pelota de hule. A complex ball game played in Mesoamerica, the West Indies, and parts of South America. A rubber ball was generally used, although a wicker ball was also found.

peltate. Shield-shaped.

pemmican. A preserved food consisting of dried pulverized buffalo meat mixed in fat. It is used by some American Indian tribes. **Berry pemmican** has dried chokeberries or other berries added.

penannular. Referring to an object that is almost in the shape of a ring.

penates. Roman household divinities, usually of the storeroom. Every hearth had a place for the penates. They were usually identified with Castor and Pollux. A fire was kept going for the penates and first fruits (q.v.) were given to them. Their worship was associated with that of Vesta and the lares (q.v.).

pendulum. A device to control the regularity of the verge rod of a clock. The pendulum became widespread in the late 18th century.

peneplain. An old mountain that is almost worn down to a plain.

penghula. A Sakai headman (q.v.).

pennyroyal. An herb used to treat varied ailments including headache, coughs, impaired vision, and colds.

pentadactyly. Having five fingers and five toes on each extremity.

pentadodechedron. A polyhedron formed by 12 pentagons.

pentagonoid. Referring to a skull which has a pentagonal shape when viewed from above.

peonage. Mandatory servitude because of indebtedness.

people, buzzard. A group that cleaned the bones of corpses among various Indian groups of the Southeast United States.

people, culture. A people possessing civilization and learning, presumably in contrast to primitives.

people, little. Gnomes, dwarfs, and the many kindred diminutive imaginary beings found in the folklore of nearly every country. The little people may be mischievous or helpful to humans. They are quite unpredictable and often represent future dangers.

pepper. A sharp condiment from an East Indian plant. It also has medicinal uses. It is among the best known and most widely used spices.

peppercorn. See HAIR, PEPPERCORN.

perçoir. See BORER.

percussion. Working flint (q.v.) by using a hammer stone to remove chips from a core (q.v.).

percussion, bulb of. A lump or mass at the end of a flake disengaged from a flint by a hammer blow. The bulb of percussion is directly under the point of impact of the blow. Its presence is an indication that a flint has been worked, particularly if the reverse impressions of similar bulbs appear where supplementary flakes have been dislodged. In any event, even the existence of such a bulb is not regarded as proof of human working unless the object shows evidence of

407

design and of conformity to a known type of implement. The **conchoid of percussion** is a shell-shaped concavity on a flint from which a flake or chip has been struck. The **cone of percussion** is the roughly conical projection of the bulb of percussion. It is surrounded by a swelling. The cone's magnitude depends on the force of the blow. The **negative bulb of concussion** is the hollow corresponding to the bulb of percussion.

percuteur. A hammer stone.

perennial. A plant that lives throughout the year and from year to year. All trees and shrubs are perennial.

periapt. An amulet or charm worn to fight disease or evil.

perihelion. The period in which the earth is comparatively near the sun, e.g., January.

perikymata. The small transverse ridges on the exposed surface of enamel on a permanent tooth.

Period, Glacial. In the Pleistocene era, the variable advance of a series of ice sheets over a good deal of the earth. Times of glacial advance alternated with periods of warmth. See GLACIATION.

period, reindeer. The last stage of the Lower Paleolithic era during which reindeer became more abundant and the climate became dry.

periodontal. Referring to being situated near a tooth.

periods, archaeological. The general breakdown of various periods based on skeletons, inscriptions, and artifacts found by excavation and otherwise. The groupings of the periods form sequential patterns.

periods, ethnical. A framework established by Lewis Henry Morgan in his *Ancient Society* (1871) to place any given society in the sequence: savagery, barbarism, civilization. The criteria are technological. All societies, in this viewpoint, must go through the earlier before entering the later stages, although some do not progress past the first or second.

periostitis. Inflammation of the periosteum.

peristalith. A circle of stones, often surrounding a mound or dolmen (q.v.).

permafrost. Ground which is frozen permanently because of the extreme cold attained.

Permian. A life period of the Paleozoic era in which early land reptiles first appeared. It lasted from perhaps 220 to 195 million years ago.

perpetuative. Referring to a native attempt to keep the old patterns against a new culture.

personality. See STRUCTURE, BASIC PERSONALITY.

personality, modal. The most representative core personality in an area. A stratified culture is likely to have several such modes.

personality, public. Those aspects of personality which reflect such acquired features as role and status.

personality, status. The elements of a personality associated with the specific status points of the social structure.

perspective tordue. Contorted perspective, as found in Upper Paleolithic art, e.g., horns and hooves of an animal face the observer while the torso is shown full-length.

Peschel's law. See LAW, PESCHEL'S.

pestle. An implement used to pulverize materials in a mortar.

pestle, bell. A grinding implement usually made of stone and resembling a bell. The grinding end is broad and rounded and the handle is somewhat long and pointed.

Petit Negre. A creolized French, spoken as a contact vernacular (q.v.) in French West Africa.

Petrie, W. M. Flinders (1853-1942). An English archaeologist, who systematized excavation methods in Egypt. He preserved as much material as possible from a dig, described it exhaustively, kept careful records of all work, and published his results promptly. Petrie was the first to show how unpainted pottery could be used as a clue to dating, and he invented the method of sequence dating (q.v.). Comparative archaeology profited from his cross-dating of Greek and Egyptian materials and from his emphasis on artifact analysis.

petrifaction. In mythology, transformation of a person into stone. It is often a punishment, although the Gorgon Medusa petrified persons because she looked so frightening.

petrified city. See CITY, PETRIFIED.

petroglyph. A picture incised on a rock. In archaeology, the term is often used to describe any drawing, inscription, or incision on a rock by early man.

petrograph. A picture painted on a rock.

peyote. A small cactus, or the liquid drug made from it; it is also called mescaline or mescal. Peyote has been used to minimize fatigue and hunger, as a medicine, an amulet or an intoxicant, and to induce visions. The peyote cult originated among some southern Indian tribes, and it spread to northern tribes, including the Crow and the Sioux. The drug's medical properties and effect on the imagination—likened to schizoid states by some students —lead many Indians to regard it as the vegetal incarnation of a deity, and a system of myths grew up about it. In the 19th century, a North American Indian religious cult developed around the worship of the rounded top of the peyote plant, although some Central American groups had eaten peyote ritually before Columbus. The contemporary peyote ritual involves smoking the plant, purification, and other ceremonials lasting all night to the accompaniment of songs. The cult in its emphasis on prayer and contemplation has certain aspects suggestive of pietistic Christianity. Mexico has a mescal rite which is older and is centered around a tribal dance.

peytrel. The breastplate of a horse.

Pfahlbauten. See DWELLING, LAKE.

pH. The hydrogen ion concentration of an individual. It indicates acidosis (less than 7), alkalosis (higher than 7), or a neutral condition (7).

phaeomelanin. Red and yellow pigmentation.

Phaistos disk. See DISK, PHAISTOS.

phallephoric. Referring to the use of phallic symbols in religious rites.

phallicism. Worship of the generative principle in nature, as symbolized by the phallus. Many early religions incorporated phallic features.

phallism. Religious observance and veneration of the sex organs, usually accompanied with magic. Such sophisticated peoples as the Greeks and Indians used phallism. It was often associated with a kind of sympathetic magic (q.v.) with the sexual activity representing the activity of rain and sun. A phallic symbol may be used as a charm against sterility, e.g., the Hindu lingam (q.v.).

Pharaoh. The title accorded all the monarchs of Egypt, erroneously assumed by many to be the name of the king. Pharaoh comes from the Egyptian *per-aah*, "great house" or "royalty."

pharyngal. Referring to a consonant that is articulated at the pharynx, e.g., the *q* in the Arabic pronunciation of *Iraq*.

pharynx. The chamber that lies between the back wall of the throat and the throat itself.

phememe. The minimal meaningless language unit.

phenotype. The actual form of the genetic type; the totality of the organism's functions and structure; an organism in which both dominant and recessive paired genes for a trait are present, so that somatic appearance does not show the recessive trait.

philology. The study of texts for linguistic analysis and cultural interpretation.

philter. See MAGIC, LOVE.

phonation. The opening and closing of the vocal cords from pressure from contraction of the muscles of expiration, giving rise to the puffs of air that constitute the voice.

phonatory. Referring to producing or causing vocal sounds.

phoneme. A complex of acoustical elements serving to distinguish a sound of a language. A phoneme, thus, comprises those elements that identify the sound regardless of any variation (see ALLOPHONE) it may undergo because of its position. Two acoustically similar sound complexes from different languages need not belong to the same phoneme. Thus, in English the sound typically represented by the letter *b* may resemble a Chinese sound commonly transliterated *p*. The distinguishing characteristic of the English sound is that it is a voiced bilabial plosive, while the Chinese is distinguished as being an unaspirated bilabial plosive. The English sound may be aspirated or unaspirated but must be voiced, while the Chinese may be voiced or voiceless but must be unaspirated. While any allophone of a phoneme will be recognized as constituting an instance of that phoneme, selection of the wrong allophone largely accounts for "foreign accent." A phonetic alphabet is constructed for a language by assigning a symbol to each of the phonemes. English has 45 phonemes.

phoneme, assimilated. The particular sound unit that undergoes

410

assimilation (q.v.) by another sound unit. An **assimilatory phoneme** is a sound unit that causes an assimilation.

phoneme, compound. A sound unity composed of smaller segments that are themselves phonemes. The compound, e.g., a diphthong (q.v.) has distributional characteristics typical of simple phonemes.

phoneme, intermediate. A phoneme that includes two sounds distinguishable as separate by some speakers of the language, e.g., *b* in *Athabaskan* (or *Athapaskan*), which includes the English *b* and *p* phonemes.

phoneme, primary. A simple phoneme.

phoneme, secondary. See FEATURE, SUPRASEGMENTAL.

phonemics. The study of the phonemes (q.v.) of a language, including the comparison of phonemic systems.

phonemics, synchronic. The study of the phonetic elements of the speech of a particular age or of a language at a specific date.

phoneticization. The representation of spoken sounds phonetically.

phonetics. The systematic study, description, classification, and analysis of the production and transmission of language sounds. It includes the application of physiology and physics.

phonetics, acoustic. The study of the physical qualities of speech sounds.

phonetics, articulatory. See PHONETICS, MOTOR.

phonetics, descriptive. The systematic observation of phonemic units and combinations the occurrence of which can be fixed in time.

phonetics, diachronic. The study of the evolution of phonetic laws.

phonetics, genemmic. The study of speech sounds after they have been produced.

phonetics, genetic. The study of the process of speech sound production.

phonetics, historical. The study and classification of the laws of phonetics and their operation in the evolution of linguistics. See PHONOLOGY.

phonetics, instrumental. Those features of phonetics that can be studied by physical instruments, like the sound spectrograph (q.v.).

phonetics, motor or **phonetics, articulatory.** The study of the articulatory and physiological elements of speech sounds.

phonetics, physical. The study of the sound waves resulting from speech.

phonetics, physiological. The study of the speaker's sound production and of the body movements that produce sounds. Physiological phonetics is part of laboratory or experimental phonetics.

phonetism. Symbols representing speech sounds.

phonogram. A symbol representing a phonetic form. Also, a graph of patterns produced by spoken phonemes (q.v.) obtained by the use of laboratory equipment.

phonology. The study and classification of phonemes (q.v.) on a functional basis. It studies the changes in phonemes from the point of view of a language's develop-

411

ment. The phoneme is treated as a unit without regard to its acoustic nature. The term phonology is sometimes used to describe historical phonetics (q.v.).

phorbeia. A leather bandage worn around the head of players of the aulos (q.v.) so that they would not overinflate their cheeks.

phorminx. An ancient Greek musical instrument similar to the lyre (q.v.).

phosphate determination. See DETERMINATION, PHOSPHATE.

photogrammetry. The measurement of humans by photographic methods. The term was first used in 1859 by a balloonist who mapped and measured a ground area by aerial photographs. Stereoscopic photogrammetry permits obtaining the surface and body area of a person as well as his dimensions.

photoperiod. The length of the daylight, used to describe plants which flower in days in which the period of daylight varies.

photosynthesis. The process by which green plants use the sun's energy to develop complex organic molecules out of the operation of the pigment-catalyst chlorophyll on water and carbon dioxide. Photosynthesis also enables plants to release the free oxygen which is essential for breathing in the higher animals.

phragmite. Peat (q.v.) formed from the reed and other shallow-water plants.

phrase. The minimum utterance characterized by an intonational contour (q.v.).

phrase, center of the. A word or words in an endocentric (q.v.) phrase which is of the same form class as the phrase.

phratry. A generally exogamous unilinear subdivision of a tribe, itself often divided into sibs (q.v.). A phratry is usually a union of two clans. It may be matrilineal or patrilineal. Kinship is an important element, along with a belief in an ultimate common ancestor. The phratry stems from an expansion of the clan (q.v.). Morgan used the term for clans with common goals.

phthiriophagy. The eating of lice.

phunga. A trumpetlike musical instrument of ancient India. It has a cup mouthpiece and is made of a long tube of thin metal that flares out into a small bell at the end.

phylactery. A small box which contains quotations from the scriptures. Jews bind it on the left arm and forehead in their daily prayer in order to remind themselves to keep the law.

phylad. A small phylogenetic stock, generally used to describe a few species that are linearly related.

phylogeny. The developmental or class history of an organism, usually referring to its evolutionary development. See ONTOGENY.

phylum. One of the 12 major divisions of animals. Man belongs to the phylum Chordata, which includes organisms with an internal skeleton and a segmented backbone or, in rare instances, only a spinal cord. The vertebrates are distinguished by a three-part brain, good muscular control, a heart, and a closed blood system.

physiometry. The measurement of the physiological functioning of the body.

physiomorphic. Referring to a design that represents phenomena of the physical world.

phytocoenosis. The totality of plants in a particular area, generally used to describe a number of smaller communities that are fairly homogeneous with regard to flora, life form, and surroundings.

piacular. Criminal, often in the sense of requiring expiation (q.v.).

piano, African. A musical instrument consisting of strips of metal of differing lengths so suspended above a resonator that each one emits a different note as the thumb presses and releases the end.

piblokto. Arctic hysteria characterized by extreme suggestibility, with some sexual delusions. It is usually found in adult women. Piblokto is especially prevalent among the Eskimo of western Greenland. It is likely to begin with the subject singing until consciousness is lost. Some victims remove their clothing, run from their home, throw objects about, imitate bird calls, and develop bloodshot eyes, head congestion, and foaming at the mouth. Attempts to calm them down are usually resisted.

pic. A flint implement that was the prototype of the pick.

pick. 1 A Campignian tool consisting of a flint bar with a blunt point at each end. It is usually 8 to 15 centimeters long. The pick is analogous to the ax (q.v.), except that it is used for piercing. 2 In weaving, an individual weft element.

pick, war. See MALGA.

picking. The process of putting weft lines between divided warp threads in weaving.

pickling. A technique for preserving food by wet-salting or soaking in brine.

picotah. A pivoted water bucket in southern India.

pictogram. A written symbol representing an object of which it is a complete or simplified conventionalized picture.

pictograph. A cartoonlike character of the type which usually precedes the hieroglyphic (q.v.) in the development of written communication. It is intended for communication rather than as art.

pictograph, gravel. A representation of an object, animal, or person made by removing surface stones from the natural pavement of a desert, so that the unweathered bedrock stones are visible. Exposure leads to the pavement developing a dark patina. Gravel pictographs are found in the Colorado Basin. They probably had a ceremonial significance and date from an early culture which has been called the Malpais Industry by Malcolm J. Rogers.

pictography. See WRITING, PICTURE.

Picts' houses. See HOUSES, PICTS'.

picture, rock. A representation on rock, often found in primitive art. A rock picture may be of groups, single persons, animals, or action.

pidgin. A language, usually for trade, formed by contact between English or another European language and an exotic language, e.g., Chinese.

413

piece, battle. A work of art representing a battle.

piece, trade. An object not characteristic of the people who inhabited the archaeological site at which it was found and which is often presumed to have been acquired through trade.

piedmont. Near or at the base of a mountain.

pier. An architectural structure which exists independently of and gives support to beams or arches. It may be of brick, masonry, or concrete. A pier is also any concentration of stone used to reinforce a wall where a heavy load is exerted.

pierre fitte. See MENHIR.

pig. A sexually immature swine, regarded by some groups, e.g., the Egyptians, as unclean or inedible, while other groups regarded it as sacred.

pigment, mummy. A dull brown coloring matter derived from the bones and remains of Egyptian mummies. It is composed primarily of the asphaltum that had been used in embalming the mummies.

piki. A thin corn bread found in Southwest America.

pilgrimage. A visit to a special place often for religious purposes. Pilgrimages may be made to graves or to places sacred to various deities or to implement a vow. The Crusades, which were a kind of pilgrimage, resulted from the need to protect pilgrims after infidels took over the Holy Land.

Pillar, Delhi. An iron pillar 23 feet 8 inches high, about one foot and one-third inches in diameter, and weighing six tons. It dates from A.D. 300 and is at Delhi. It was built to keep the Rajah's wish to have his kingdom last forever. The Delhi Pillar is perhaps the most famous of the Indian iron objects made by welding together a number of blooms (q.v.).

pillar, Pompey's. A Corinthian column 98 feet 9 inches high and 29 feet 8 inches in circumference which stands at Alexandria, Egypt. It was erected in honor of the emperor Diocletian, whose statue was once mounted on top. The pillar has no connection with Pompey.

pilosity. The degree of bodily hairiness.

pilou-pilou. The feast for the dead in New Caledonia.

Piltdown. See EOANTHROPUS DAWSONI.

pilum. A heavy javelin used by the Roman foot soldier.

Pima-Papago. A general term used to describe the art of the southwest Indians of the United States. It includes the techniques of several crafts.

pin, Aunjetitz. A Bohemian pin with an inverted conical head surmounted by a cast loop or ear.

pin, disk. An Early Bronze Age pin with the head in the shape of a circle and a small tang opposite the shaft as a loop.

pin, East German eyelet. A pin with a lateral spur on the neck, perforated by a hole parallel to the shaft. It is found in Late Bronze Age urn fields.

pin, eyelet. A pin with the thread passed through a hole in the pin shaft near the head.

pin, knot-headed. A pin in which the top is bent over and twisted around the shaft. It was used in predynastic Egypt and early Sumer and diffused up the Danube Valley.

pin, looped head. A pin in which the head is a loop through which thread can be passed.

pin, racket. A pin with a widened flat head. It existed in Sumer before 3000 B.C.

pin, roll head. A loop head pin in which the head is hammered out flat before being bent over.

pin, sunflower. A Bronze Age pin, found in Scandinavia and Great Britain, with a round head with concentric circular decoration. It has no eyelet or loop.

pin, wheel. A Middle Bronze Age variant of the disk pin in which the disk becomes an openwork wheel, with an ear for the original folded loop.

pineapple. A biennial plant with large fruits. It is one of the largest, best flavored, and most wholesome fruits. It probably originated in South America, where it was known long before Columbus.

Pink Castle. See CASTLE, PINK.

pinole. An alcoholic drink of North Mexico.

piñon. A pine nut of the Southwest with large edible seeds. The Indians used to observe where squirrels made their winter deposits of these nuts and then would rob the nests.

pintadera. A small Neolithic seal of stone or clay used to make ornamental designs on the body and face. It has been found in Crete, Liguria, Mexico, the Canary Islands, and elsewhere.

pipe, elbow. A pipe used by the eastern Woodlands Indians. The stem and bowl are at right angles in the shape of a bent elbow.

pipe, flue. See FLUTE.

pipe, monitor. A flat narrow-rimmed pipe used by the Ohio Mound Builder Indians for ceremonies.

pipe, Pan. See PIPES, PAN.

pipe, peace. See CALUMET.

pipe, portrait. A pipe with the head carved as a representation of animals or men. Portrait pipes were often made of soft stone or clay and were found on New World altars. They differ in form and size and in whether or not there is a tube connected with the bowl.

pipe, tomahawk. An iron hatchet combined with a tobacco pipe, common among American Indians in colonial days.

pipe, war. See CALUMET.

pipes, lip-reed. A wind instrument other than the flute, e.g., the trumpet.

pipes, Pan. A pipe made of several flutes tied together, the ancestor of our organ. Two or more tubes of different lengths can be combined and may be graduated or grouped to produce a given melody or note sequence. As the name indicates, Pan pipes are associated with woodland and pastoral mythology. They are a very common instrument. The terms syrinx and compound syrinx are also used.

pipestone, Indian. See CATLINITE.

pir. A highly decorated tomb found in India. It consists of a square burial chamber with domed roof.

piragua. A dugout (q.v.) propelled by a wooden board or plank. It is found on the upper Xingú.

piranha. Any of a number of species of carnivorous fish of the subfamily *Sarrasalmoninae*, which are found in the rivers of tropical America. The jaws of some species that bear sawlike teeth are used as cutting tools by Indians. These fish are known as caribe in Venezuela, palometa in Paraguay, and piranha in Brazil, and are also sometimes called pirai, piraya, or piriraya. The piranha is voracious and will attack mammals, including man, especially when aroused by blood from an open wound.

piraungara. See PIRRAURU.

pirogue. A small boat, made of a hollowed out tree trunk, found in the Atlantic and the South Pacific areas. It is usually paddle-driven, although some larger pirogues have sails and outriggers.

pirrauru or **piraungara.** In some Australian groups, a relative of the opposite sex, belonging to the marriage class from which a spouse can be taken, with whom sexual relations are permissible outside of marriage. This relationship was described by Howitt.

pisciform. Referring to an object designed in the shape of a fish.

pistol, tinder. A gunlock, used in England, specially adapted so that it can throw sparks into tinder.

piston, fire. A device for using the heat generated by suddenly compressing air to light fire. It operates by the movement of a plunger piston in a hollow cylinder.

pit, cache. A hole in the ground in which food or other objects are stored, often for preservation.

pit, stamped. A pit with a wooden top that is stamped on during fertility rites to make a resonant sound.

pit dwelling. See DWELLING, PIT.

pitch. The frequency of the fundamental tone of the voice. In some languages, like Chinese or Swedish, a difference in pitch can distinguish between otherwise identical words. See INTONATION.

pitch, absolute. The ability to locate a given pitch on the scale, with no other indication as a guide. Absolute pitch is probably acquired through practice.

pitch, exclamatory. A special distribution of pitch to indicate a very strong verbal response.

pitch, final. A special variation of pitch at the end of a sentence.

pitch, pause. A rise in pitch before a pause in a sentence.

pitch accent. See ACCENT, PITCH.

pitchi. In Australia, wooden troughs for carrying babies.

pitchuri. An Australian tobacco-like plant that is chewed.

pitfall. See TRAP, PIT.

pith. The spongy loose conjunctive tissue in the center of the stem in the vascular cylinder of dicotyledons.

Pithecanthropus erectus. A hominid discovered in 1891-92 by Eugene Dubois in Java. It was regarded by Dubois as a "missing link" between apes and men, with a primitive cranium but able to walk upright. A mandible, six femora, three skull parts, and other fragments have been found. It probably dates from the first or second interglacial periods, when Java was connected with the Asiatic mainland. The skull cap had some ape-like characteristics, while the thigh bone belonged to an erect person. The brain case capacity was around 900 cc., as compared with the largest apes (500 cc.) and contemporary man 1,350 cc.). A skull from Modjokerto in Central Java, perhaps from a two-year-old child, had a cranial capacity of around 700 cc., compared with around 1,000 cc. for a contemporary two-year-old. The infant skull had prominent brow ridges and a retreating forehead. Pithecanthropus had a skull with a sharply pointed back. The brain case is wider than high and is widest at the base. The nose is flat and broad. The jaw is quite strong and prognathous, with no real chin. The teeth are big and show some simian qualities. Pithecanthropus was about five feet tall and had strong neck muscles and beetling brows. He was probably a hunter and probably used fire. Some estimates place Pithecanthropus as about 450,000 years old, and it has been suggested that he made his own tools. Many scholars believe there is sufficient evidence to show that Sinanthropus pekinensis (q.v.) is a species of the Pithecanthropus genus.

The Pithecanthropus part of the name derives from Ernst Haeckel, who in his *General Morphology of Organisms* (1866) suggested that modern man and Neanderthal man were both descended from Dryo-

pithecus, a Tertiary tree-dwelling ape, and that there was an intermediate ancestor, yet to be found, called Pithecanthropus, or ape-man. Dubois added the specific erectus to his Java find because the thigh bone indicated that the creature could walk upright.

Pithecanthropus pekinensis. See SINANTHROPUS PEKINENSIS.

Pithecanthropus robustus. A hominid form discovered by von Koenigswald in Java in 1938. So far, a skull cap and upper jaw have been reported.

Pithecanthropus - sinanthropus. Hominids of the Early to Middle Pleistocene periods.

pithecoid. Referring to the higher apes.

pithos. An earthenware casklike container found in the early Greek world, probably beginning in the Minoan period. It was often ornamented and was frequently without a base, since such containers might be set in the earth for storage.

pitting. The earliest kind of underground mining, in which ore bodies are explored by dropping shafts at intervals. Each shaft was abandoned after the ore was extracted from the bottom.

Pitt-Rivers, Augustus (Lane Fox) (1827-1900). An English museum authority and archaeologist. He applied the evolutionary doctrine of complex organisms slowly developing from simple forms to the study of the human arts and technology. He originally developed his ideas while tracing the development of the English service rifle, which led him to think that similar principles were relevant to the study of the technologies of mankind.

pituri. An Australian drug that comes from dried plant leaves and is chewed.

place, high. Applied to Hebrew places of worship, the term is a translation of the Hebrew *bamah,* which means both "elevation" and "sanctuary." The Hebrew custom of placing sanctuaries at high points on hills or in the mountains may be responsible for the idea that the divinity is found there. In some cases, however, these *bamot* were in valleys and open air shrines. There the word *bamah* seems to apply to the raised construction of the shrine itself and this is possibly the origin of the word.

place, holy. A place regarded as sacred because of religious associations. The chief holy place in Judaism is the place where the Temple of Jerusalem once stood and where a part of the wall, known as the "wailing wall," still stands. It is one of the most popular places for Jewish pilgrims who there mourn the tragedies of the Diaspora.

place, market. A place where trade is conducted. There are instances of a market place being a place of asylum (q.v.). Some societies use salt deposits as market places. Market places often provide an area where warfare is absent. Thus, the Sumatran Battas cease hostilities at market time and bring a green bough in their weapons as a sign of peace. In the North American Chien Prairie market areas, even tribes that were enemies stopped fighting. Some-

times the roads to the market enjoy the market peace. Breaking the market peace was considered more serious than breaking the common law in Greece, Norway, and Denmark.

place, sacred. A place in the natural world that is sacred. It may be believed to be the home of a spirit or associated with a cult. Hills or bodies of water are often so regarded. Such places may be visited only under special circumstances.

placenta. A discoid vascular organ that connects the fetus and the mother by the umiblical cord. It is in the wall of the uterus and its processes are bathed in the mother's blood stream. Nutrition through the placenta is found in higher mammals. The placenta is expelled after birth, and thus is known as the afterbirth. Many societies have elaborate rituals surrounding the disposal of the afterbirth (q.v.).

placer. Gravel left by running water, often examined as a source of gold.

Plains. A culture area from the Rockies to the Eastern Woodlands and south to Mexico. Originally this was a big-game culture, the Folsom-Yuman. Marginal peoples from the Southeast introduced agriculture. Hunters sought game and engaged in agriculture in the summer or else lived with the Pueblos. The river valley groups lived in earth lodges (q.v.) and did some hunting in spring and fall. Almost every Plains Indian had a horse (q.v.) by the mid-18th century, thus permitting thorough exploitation of the buffalo. Many new groups came to the area, and the Plains nomadic bands became well organized, with much warfare. The questing vision (q.v.) and the sun dance (q.v.) were common.

plaiting. Weaving in which the two elements are manually placed over and under each other. It is primarily used for basket-making and mat-making.

plan de frappe. See PLATFORM, STRIKING.

plane. A flint tool with a flat base and a humped back.

plane, eye-ear. The plane made by the right and left tragion and the left orbitale in the same horizontal plane.

plane, Frankfurt. See LINE, FRANKFURT.

plane, midsagittal. The plane from anterior to posterior, dividing the skull into right and left halves. It is usually located by following the sagittal suture (q.v.). On the body, it is the vertical plane that divides the body in right and left halves.

planera. The ulmaceous tree genus.

planetesimal. Referring to the solar materials that are believed to have formed the planets.

planimeter. A device for measuring the area of a plane figure by running a tracer over the boundary. It is used in making certain measurements in physical anthropology.

planoccipitaly. A deformation of the back of the head, often associated with flattening the back of the head by the use of a cradle board as among the Pueblo Indians.

plantain. A bananalike plant cultivated in the tropics. Its large angu-

lar fruit is widely used as a food, especially in tropical America.

plantigrade. Referring to walking on the whole sole of the foot so that the heel touches the ground, as man does.

plasma, continuity of the germ. August Weisman's theory that the germ plasma is not produced by the body cells, even though it gives rise to them. He held that germ plasma is transmitted from one generation to the next, but that changes in the body (the soma) during life cannot be transmitted by heredity.

plasma, germ. The special kind of protoplasm found in germ cells, which produce the gametes.

plaster theory. See THEORY, PLASTER.

plasticity. Changing the shape of the body as the environment changes. Boas' study (1912) showing how the children of immigrants to the United States were physically tending to change in the direction of the American norm was the first large scale proof of plasticity.

plate, notched. A stone plate which is disk- or rectangular-shaped, found in Ohio and some of the southern states. Notched plates are made of sandstone and other gritty materials and were probably used to grind pigments. They may have had some religious functions.

plate, tympanic. A bony wall delimiting the lower margin of the ear hole. It is of a particular type and at a particular angle in Homo sapiens.

Plateau, Iranian. See IRANIAN PLATEAU.

419

platform, faceted striking. A striking platform prepared by removing a few facets at right angles to the direction of the main blow.

platform, hut. A shelf which was made level on sloping ground in order to accommodate buildings. It was used to attain a horizontal floor.

Platform, Stone. A mound at the Tres Zapotes (Vera Cruz) excavations, so named because of the trenchlike subterranean arrangement of stone. Several well executed ceramic figurines and a highly polished black stone head have been excavated from the mound in perfect condition. It is not thought to be a burial mound and is therefore different from the other mounds in the group.

platform, striking. A small flat surface on a lump of flint on which it is possible to strike the kind of blow needed to fashion an implement. The term plan de frappe is sometimes used.

platinum. A heavy, gray-white noncorroding metal. It is ductile and malleable. Most platinum comes from Colombia and the Urals. Platinum has been discovered only as a compound and is never found in a pure state. It is usually associated with other metals, such as iridium, palladium, osmium, ruthenium, rhodium, and gold.

platycephaly. A condition of considerable flattening of the cranial vault.

platycnemia. A flattening of the tibia found in some human groups. It was originally believed to be a racial characteristic found in groups like the Australoids, but it is now believed to be a result of muscular action.

platycnemic. Referring to a platycnemic index (q.v.) between 55 and 62.9.

platyhieric. Referring to a length-breadth sacral index (q.v.) of more than 106.

platymeric. Referring to a platymeric index (q.v.) between 75 and 84.9.

platyrrhine. Referring to a nose the breadth of which is more than 51 per cent of its length on a skull. The measurement is made by reckoning the relation between the breadth of the nasal aperture at the widest point and its length in the distance from the juncture of the middle point of the nasal bones and the frontal bone above to the inferior border of the nasal aperture. The term also indicates a nose, the breadth of which is 84 per cent of its length, measured on living subjects. Then the breadth is the distance between the two widest points of the fleshy wings, and the length is the distance from the nasion to the juncture of the septum with the upper lip.

Platyrrhini. New World monkeys, a division of the Pithecoid suborder. They have widely spaced nostrils and are found in the tropical areas of South and Central America. There are two families, the Hepalidae and the Cebidae (qq.v.).

plaustrum. A solid-wheeled Roman farm cart.

play. Bodily activity engaged in for its own sake. It is primarily found among warm-blooded vertebrates. In general, the nearer toward

420

man in the evolutionary scale, the more likely will a species engage in play. See THEORY, PLAY.

playa. A salt lake in a bolson. It is either shallow with fluctuating shores or a flat plain on which flood waters may create a lake.

pleiotropy. Individual genetic factors that have a multiple effect.

Pleistocene. The last million years of geological history, known as the age of glaciers, from which the earliest skeletal remains of man date. Except for the skull, man was probably well developed early in this period. Man probably was then about as large as he is now. A forest thinning which left gaps between groves might have led some of the prehuman arboreal apes to get used to the ground, even if only to move from one grove to another. Different foods might have made ground life interesting, until the trees came to be used less and less. It has been estimated that the Pleistocene lasted from 200,000 to 2,000,000 years. At present 500,000 to 1,000,000 years is regarded as the most probable duration.

pleochroic. Referring to the quality of exhibiting different colors when viewed from different angles. This is accomplished by light refraction, as in cut gems.

plesiadapids. A Paleocene and Eocene primate family with several genera.

Plesianthropus. An African man-like ape fossil from the Pleistocene period.

plethysmograph. A device for determining the blood volume in a part of the body. A finger, for ex-

ample, is immersed in water, with an air-tight collar. As the blood volume changes, the water level changes correspondingly.

pleurodont. A kind of teeth attachment to the jaw or skeletal support in which the base and one side of the tooth are attached on a ledge on the jaw's inner margin.

plication. Fissuration.

plied. Referring to a yarn in which more than one yarn is intertwined.

Pliocene. The last Tertiary epoch, in which prehuman levels were reached and apes of modern type appeared. It lasted for some 15 million years, from about 15 million years before the Pleistocene period.

plosive. A sound produced by the retention of air in the nasal and oral air passages, with the subsequent opening of the closure producing an "explosion," e.g., the *b* and *k* of *buck*. See STOP.

plow. An agricultural implement that applies the mechanical principle of the hoe and digging stick. It dates from 3000 B.C. and probably was first used in Egypt and Mesopotamia. A very early form was made of wood, shaped like two forked branches. The plow was first used without a wheel, and the contemporary Batak of Sumatra still use such a plow. The plow was not modernized until the 18th century, when iron and steel replaced wood, and two or more plows were combined. The plow cuts furrows in the soil and turns it up, thus greatly increasing crop yields. Both the spade and the hoe have been regarded as the plow's prototype. The plow usually has wheels, coulter, share, and mold-board.

plow, fire. A device used to make fire by rapidly pushing a stick forward and backward in a board to create friction and wood dust. This technique is largely found in some Pacific islands. It probably began in the East Indies and spread rapidly. The Samoan use of the fire plow is typical of the Polynesians. The Samoans held the rubbing stick at a low angle, raised to 45° for the final frictions. The term stick and groove is sometimes used for the fire plow.

plow, foot. An evolved type of digging stick found among the Peruvian Indians. It has a footrest and a hand hold to facilitate driving the point into the sod.

plow agriculture. See AGRICULTURE, PLOW.

plowshare. A stone implement that is flat on one side and curved on the other. Its major use was probably as a hoe.

plug, float. A plug used by the Eskimo to seal the inflated animal bladders that they use in harpooning animals and hunting whale.

plug, wound. A plug of bone or ivory inserted in an animal's wound so that it does not lose blood and floats.

plumbate. A leadlike pottery, especially in Central America. **Plumbeous** and **plumbiferous** refer to any ceramics containing lead or a lead compound.

plummet or **plumb.** A heavy object or substance, like lead, used to make soundings, check verticality of walls, and for similar purposes. It is usually attached to a line. The plummet was used as a weight for spinning and as a sinker. The term plumb bob is sometimes found.

plutonic. Referring to rocks formed by the action of fire, the oldest rocks. They are not stratified and contain no organic remains.

pluvial. Referring to rain, usually indicating heavy rain. The pluvials, or periods of excessive rain, were the equatorial equivalent of the European Ice Ages.

ply, single. A yarn with fibers twisted in one direction.

pneumatolytic. Referring to being formed by hot vapors and used to refer to ores and minerals the origin of which is conditioned by mineralizers given off by the cooling of molten rock material.

po. In the Maori cosmogony, the second stage of the universe, following kore, during which darkness was all-pervasive but out of which matter and life developed.

poata. A clam shell arm band of the Solomons.

podzol. Acid soil resulting from heavy rainfall and inadequate surface evaporation.

pogamogan or **pack-a-mogan.** A club made of reindeer horn from which all except the first branch has been removed. It was used for the chase and for war by the Canadian Indians.

poi. A common food in Hawaii consisting of taro root pounded into a paste and then left to ferment.

poikilothermic. Referring to cold-blooded organisms.

poinçon. A punch, usually made from a pointed bone.

point. An implement which probably served as the tip of darts, lances, and other devices used in hunting.

point, alveolar. The center of the alveolar margin of the upper jaw midway between the central incisor teeth.

point, auricular. The point at the top of the orifice of the ear.

point, bone lance. A thin piece of bone with one end pointed and the other varying in shape and size.

point, Châtelperron. A Lower Aurignacian small knife blade. The blunting along its back was skillfully accomplished by removing neat small flakes. It was somewhat like the Audi (q.v.), which it followed. See BLADE, BACKED.

point, Clovis. A fairly large dart point, probably made from a large chip, and with a channel going up the sides. Clovis points date ca. 10,000 B.C. in America.

point, corner-removed. A point with the corners of the base removed, usually to enable the stem to fit the haft.

point, Curie. See MAGNETISM, REMANENT.

point, Darwin's. A point of cartilage found on the inner margin of the helix, usually only on narrow long ears. This projection—also called Darwin's tubercle—has sometimes been interpreted as an atavistic sign of a flap-eared ancestor of man.

point, double-shouldered. A point with two shoulders at the base and a stalk between. It is also called the Font-Robert point, after a cave in France where examples have been found.

point, Emireh. A triangular point with a base that has been thinned through retouching on both surfaces.

point, Folsom. A thin leaf-shaped blade. It is made by pressure flaking of the edges and the removal of a longitudinal flake near the center of each side. It is named after its place of original discovery, in 1926, in northwest New Mexico. The typical Folsom point is made with great skill, with almost parallel sides. A number of rough artifacts, including side scrapers, gravers, snub-nosed scrapers, and choppers, were found at the site. The stone industry used flakes developed into fine blades. The Folsom culture is between 10,000 to 25,000 years old and was probably glacial, terminal Pleistocene of the Würm-Wisconsin period.

point, Font-Robert. See POINT, DOUBLE-SHOULDERED.

point, Font-Yves. A narrow small blade with pointed tip that shows nibbling retouch on an edge.

point, forked-base bone-lance. A point in which there is a definite V-shaped notch in the butt end. Such implements date from the Magdalenian era.

point, Gravette. A small blade with a square or pointed tip. It has a blunted back which is almost parallel to the sharp edge.

point, ignition. The temperature at which a substance ignites. Charcoal is ignitible at 580° and pine requires 800°. Some vegetable material is ignitible almost immediately.

point, laurel leaf. A fairly thin point of oval, tanged, or triangular shape. There is a delicate chipping over the entire surface. It is associated with the Solutrean period.

point, Mousterian. A pointed almond-shaped tool made of a flake. It is likely to show a faceted butt and step flaking. The upper surface is made of several primary flake scars. The trimming on both sides of the tool displays such extensive secondary working that little of the primary working remains apparent in the narrow tool.

point, plain-lance. A lance point made of a pointed bone which may or may not have bevels at its upper end for purposes of attachment.

point, shouldered. A point with a narrow pointed blade and secondary trimming at the butt end that makes a half notch and leads to a shoulder. It is found in late Solutrean times.

point, side-notched. A point with each side notched, usually for hafting and lashings.

point, split-base. A pricker (q.v.), 11 to 12 centimeters long, with a point at one end and a broad butt at the other. The butt often has a slit parallel to the long axis. The split-base point may have been an early bodkin (q.v.).

point, split-base bone-lance. A slender point in which the butt end is split a short distance up, probably for hafting. It dates from middle Aurignacian times.

point, willow leaf. A point like the laurel leaf point (q.v.), except that it has only one trimmed face.

point, Yuman. An unfluted slender long point, named for a New Mexico site. There is parallel flaking across the blade. It marks a hunting Plains culture.

pointe, audi. See AUDI.

pointe, châtelperron. See POINT, CHÂTELPERRON.

pointe à cran. A triangular laurel leaf point (q.v.) in which there is a tang in line with a side of the triangle, so that the opposite basal angle forms an elementary barb. The tang is made by chipping a hollow at the base of one edge.

pointe à soie. A tang on a Gravette point (q.v.) made by chipping a hollow at the base on both edges.

pointe de lance. A Solutrean spear point that may have either a concave, stemmed, or straight base.

pointing, bone. A form of magic, practiced in the Northern Territory of Australia, in which the victim becomes violently ill and sometimes dies as a result of a human or kangaroo bone being pointed in his direction. The victim, who may be miles away, believes that a lethal medium is pouring into his body, goes into a swoon, and remains in his wurley (q.v.), usually refusing to eat. He dies unless the Nangarri, or medicine man, administers a counter-charm. The close kin of the victim withdraw support from him, and help prepare him for his death and the ritual mourning that follows death, thus providing social sanction for what is happening. As the sorcerer points the bone, he usually sings malignly.

poison. A substance that causes deadly or noxious effects in an organism, especially if its potency is manifested in small amounts. Poisons have been used by many groups on the tips of arrow heads or on points to hasten death. Widely used poisons are Strophanthus hispidus (Africa), powdered red ants (African pygmies), a poisonous leaf beetle (South Africa), aconite (Malaya), and curare (South America. The Ebers papyrus, ca. 1500 B.C., mentions mineral and vegetable poison, so that it may be presumed that the Egyptians used poisons widely. One of the Vedas, ca. 900 B.C., indicates that the Hindus knew a good deal about poisons and their effects. Greek mythology mentions poison, and Nicander of Colophon (204-135 B.C.) wrote the first study of poison. See TEST, POISON.

poisoning, fish. The use of any of a large number of narcotic plants to kill or immobilize fresh-water fish.

poitrel. Armoring to protect a warhorse's breast.

pokey. An exceptionally long false sleeve found in medieval costumes, often trailing on the ground for some distance. Pokeys were usually well decorated.

polarity. A designation of a kin relationship that gives each member of the polarity a separate kinship term, e.g., father-son.

pole, carrying. A pole which is balanced on one shoulder and from either end of which a burden may be carried. It is found in China and Polynesia.

pole, punt. A pole used to propel rafts or other craft over a shallow body of water.

pole, square. In British measurement, 30.25 square yards.

pole, totem. A carved, and often painted, pole found in the North Pacific Coast area. Totem poles were used as house posts or grave posts and were placed along box graves. The animals represented were commemorative, heraldic, or legendary, and were not totemic in the usual sense. These poles were often made of cedar and ranged from 3 to 70 feet high.

poler, raft. A shaft used to propel a raft.

polisher. A chisel- or wedge-shaped device made of antler, used for dressing skins; a piece of rib or other flat bone with a slightly bevelled end and showing some traces of polishing. It is usually associated with the Lower Aurignacian era.

polissoir. A grooved stone used to finish needles, arrow heads, and similar implements.

poll. The butt end of an ax.

pollen analysis. See ANALYSIS, POLLEN.

poltergeist. See SPIRIT, HOUSEHOLD.

polyandry. Marriage in which a woman can have more than one husband at the same time. Polyandry is more than sharing or lending a wife. Many instances of supposed polyandry turn out not to be an institution of society but a local adjustment to special situations. Cooper has suggested that this kind of polyandry is most likely to be

425

found in marginal societies. The Todas practiced female infanticide (q.v.), which is a not unexpected counterpart of polyandry, since about equal numbers of both sexes are born. The wife usually remains in one abode in polyandry.

polyandry, adelphic. See POLYANDRY, FRATERNAL.

polyandry, attenuated. See LEVIRATE, ANTICIPATORY.

polyandry, fraternal. Several brothers marrying one woman. Usually the oldest marries the woman, while the other brothers have certain claims upon her. The purpose of this arrangement is to prevent the familial estate from dissolving. The term adelphic polyandry is also used.

polychrome. Referring to being of more than one color (i.e., monochrome), as in pottery.

polychronism. A species originating independently on more than one occasion.

polydactylism. Possessing more than the normal number of toes or fingers.

polydemonism. A religion involving the worship of several gods, as in Rome.

polygamy. Marriage in which a member of either sex has more than one spouse. If a community is called polygamous, it cannot be assumed that polygamy is the rule, but merely that it is permitted under certain circumstances. There are three kinds of polygamy: polygyny, polyandry, and group marriage.

polygenesis. The doctrine that an entity may have a multiple origin; the hypothesis that the different

groups of prehistoric men evolved from different Pliocene ape species; the hypothesis that similar cultural objects arose independently of each other, through different areas, having similar cultural milieus.

polygenic. Referring to the theory that the action of a gene is interwoven with the action of other genes.

polyglacialism. The doctrine that there were several glacial periods in the northern ice field.

polygyny. Marriage in which a man may have more than one wife at the same time. Some religions, like Islam (which allows four), are specific about the permissible number of wives. Polygyny is usually associated with the presence of more nubile women than men in a society. This surplus may stem from the loss of men through warfare and other hazardous occupations. Polygynous societies keep the plural wives in a fairly equal status that discourages jealousy. Polygynous wives may each have their own abode.

polygyny, sororal. Marriage in which one man marries several sisters; also, a man's marrying his wife's younger sister.

polymorphism. The occurrence of different forms in one species.

Polynesia. A triangular group of islands in Oceania east of the international date line and taking up half the Pacific area. It includes Hawaii, Samoa, Tonga, Easter, and the Marquesas, Society, Cook, and Tuamotu islands. (New Zealand, and Elice and Fiji in some classifications).

Polynesians are generally tall, with a mixture of Caucasoid, Mongoloid, and Negroid characteristics. They have some prognathism, moderate body hair, wavy hair, and are tall. Their skin color is light brown. The Polynesians used to be the world's leading seamen, maintaining considerable contact between islands, so that their culture has some homogeneity. They probably came from the west, possibly Indonesia, at about the start of the Christian era. Genealogies are very carefully kept. Arts, games, and social ceremonies are well-developed.

Polynesian. An Austronesion subfamily of the Malayo-Polynesian family of languages, which is spoken in Samoa, New Zealand, Tahiti, Hawaii, Easter Island, and the Cook, Society, Mangareva, Chatham and Marquesa Islands. There are 20 languages within the family, the chief among which are Maori, Hawaiian, Samoan, and Tahitian.

polyphasic. Referring to satisfying a need at periods throughout all 24 hours of the day; e.g., the infant's sleeping around the clock. See MONOPHASIC.

polyphone. A symbol or combination of symbols that stands for different sounds in different words or contexts. **Polyphony** consists in the use of such symbols.

polyphyletic. Referring to or derived from more than one original race or type. **Polyphyletism** is the belief that man developed from a variety of separate groups which evolved independently. See MONOPHYLETIC.

polyploidy. The condition in which an organism has more than one complete set of chromosomes. See DIPLOID; HAPLOID.

polystylodontism. Replacement of teeth as they are lost, typically found in lower vertebrates like sharks and dogfishes.

polytheism. Believing in and worshipping several gods.

polytypic. A group of species potentially or actually interbreeding in isolation from similar groups; a species with many variations in different environments.

pomander. A device used for medicinal purposes in the Middle Ages and early Renaissance. It consisted of a series of compartments, each of which had different perfumes and aromatic gums, or else of a vinegar-soaked sponge. It was often worn as a necklace or carried in a box.

pomegranate. A round berrylike fruit, two to four inches in diameter, that grows on a low tree or bush. It probably originated in Persia and by the Christian period had spread to Europe from China. It has been widely used as a vermifuge. Pomegranates were grown in the Hanging Gardens of Babylon.

pommel. The knob at the hilt of a sabre or sword or the front end of a saddle; a device for raising the grain or softening leathers by filing or rubbing.

Pompey's pillar. See PILLAR, POMPEY'S.

poncho. A loose garment or cloak worn by South American Indians. It is like a blanket with a slit in the middle for the head.

pongid. A species belonging to the **Pongidae**, an anthropoid family including the chimpanzee, gorilla, and orangutan. Available evidence seems to indicate that the Hominidae (q.v.) and the Pongidae may stem from a common ancestral stock. The most important single factor which led to the Hominidae's evolutionary segregation from the Pongidae was the development of erect bipedal locomotion and the attendant changes in the limbs and pelvis. The Pongidae kept the pelvic skeleton of the lower primates (q.v.) and their hind limbs became better developed for prehensile functions.

poniard. A slender dagger with a square or triangular blade.

pooh-pooh. See INTERJECTIONAL.

pool, drinking. The theory that roads resulted from following the paths made by animals going to their drinking pool. See PATH, WILD-ANIMAL.

poppy, opium. A rigid spiny-leaved annual with large flowers. Its use as a pain-reliever is known all over the world. It probably originated in Asia Minor and has been much used since Stone Age days. It is widely grown in India, China, and the Near East. The ripening seed heads are pricked and the milky sap dried to obtain the drug. The effects of opium are varied, but disturbance of the sense of time, stimulation of mental faculties, and a feeling of relaxation are common.

population, amphimictic. A population which has freely crossing fertile descendants.

population, inbreeding. A group of persons among whom mating takes place.

porcelain. A glazed earthenware developed by the Chinese ca. 700 A.D. A mixture of kaolin (a feldspar clay) and petuntse (decomposed granite), it is hard and waterproof. It was developed when the Chinese sought a substitute for the early nephrite dishes and plates. Recent excavations indicate that the early T'ang dynasty, 618-906 A.D., first showed a kind of semiporcelain ware, including the pale green type called celadon. In the Sung dynasty, 960-1279 A.D., Chinese pottery became known outside China. Sung porcelains are rare. The Ming dynasty, 1368-1644 A.D., saw the peak of ceramic development in China. As many as five colors on a piece were fired over a glaze. The imperial Chingtehchen porcelain factory was founded ca. 1560 A.D. It became famous for its white porcelain, used for religious and mourning ceremonials, and until recently considered by many the world's finest. The K'ang Hsi dynasty, 1661-1722, witnessed the development of a highly decorative porcelain. Old Nankin, a blue and white porcelain, was exported to Europe. Europe itself had little pottery manufacture between the decline of the Roman Empire and the 12th century. Italian majolica and the sgraffito (q.v.) process developed into Venetian, Florentine, and Capo di Monte porcelain. France developed its own porcelain, notably at Sèvres and Limoges. Dutch Delft ware dates from 1650. Between 1709 and

1745, Meissen, in Germany, was the site of a famous porcelain factory. Josiah Wedgwood in England became Europe's most renowned potter in the 18th century.

porcelain, Egyptian. Green ceramic ware shaped like a mummy or made to represent various Egyptian deities. The objects were composed of sand mixed with small amounts of pottery clay and fired. The product was glasslike in texture and was the color of the copper oxide applied to the surface. Many examples have been found in Egyptian tombs.

porcelain, true white. Earthenware in which the glaze evenly penetrates the whole vessel and is not a mere coating. True white porcelain was developed by the Chinese in the seventh century A.D.

porion. The topmost midpoint on the margin of the external auditory meatus.

Poro. See PORRO.

poros. Any stone other than marble, particularly in Greece.

Porro or **Poro.** A secret fraternity for men in Liberia and Sierra Leone.

portage. Carrying a canoe, or other vessel, and its contents on the shoulders of travellers over parts of the mainland where there is not enough water to float.

porte chaise. A closed litter (q.v.) widely used in fashionable circles in Europe in the 17th century.

portolan. A chart, designed for the use of mariners, that indicates harbors.

pose, kingly. A formal posture in which the right foot is raised to the seat level and the right arm rests on the right knee; often seen in East Indian art.

position, absolute. In a unit of expression no longer than a sentence, the position a word, phrase, or variant linguistic form occupies with reference to the phonetic system. The term is generally used to denote the first phoneme or the first word in a sentence which is said to be in absolute position.

position, anterior. A speech articulation in which the tongue touches the forward part of the palate. It is also called the palatal position.

position, cerebral. A speech articulation in which the tongue is in contact with a point high up in the palate. The tongue must be retroflexed in such articulations, whence the term inverted position.

position, contracted. A conventional method of putting the body in the grave, widely found in ancient burials. The body lies curled up on one side as if sleeping. The lower limbs are sometimes markedly flexed, with the knees drawn to the chin to make an angle of 90° or less with the spinal column. The body was probably swathed with ligatures, perhaps to keep the spirit from emerging and terrifying the living.

position, included. A linguistic form that is part of another larger form.

position, inverted. See POSITION, CEREBRAL.

position, palatal. See POSITION, ANTERIOR.

position, posterior. A speech articulation made by the back of the tongue touching the rear of the palate. It is also called the velar position.

position, standard erect. The position in which the subject stands during the taking of somatic measurements. The arms hang loosely extended and the palms are turned inward. The heels are in contact at an angle of about 45°. The head is in the Frankfurt line (q.v.).

position, standard sitting. The subject's sitting position during the taking of somatic measurements. He sits erect, knees at right angle, thighs parallel, hands on thighs, and upper arms along the side. The head is in the Frankfurt line (q.v.).

position, uvular. See ARTICULATION, UVULAR.

position, velar. See POSITION, POSTERIOR.

possession. An extranatural force that enters a worshipper of a deity, so that temporarily he is the deity. It is an ultimate religious experience, like that of the Siberian shaman or of the Christian saints, e.g., St. Teresa.

possibilisme. The doctrine, promulgated by Febvre and Vidal de la Blach, that geographic conditions make possible but do not determine the culture of a region. This theory holds that nonmaterial culture is as important as geography.

post and lintel. An early method of construction based on the principle of a horizontal beam or lintel supported at both ends by posts or vertical beams.

postaurale. The rearmost point on the helix of the ear.

postdental. Referring to an articulation in which the tongue is against the back of the upper teeth.

postulant. One who makes a request or demand, especially a person making a request of a deity through prayer.

pot, making a. The processes involved in making a pot include using clay to line or coat a mold, hand-modeling a lump of clay with simple implements, building up the pot by a method like coiling (q.v.), and using a potter's wheel (q.v.). The pot may be covered with a slip (q.v.) or polished and decorated.

pot, pepper. A dish commonly found among the Indians of Tropical South America consisting of vegetables, including peppers, meat or fish, and cassareep (q.v.). The pepper pot cooks indefinitely, and the ingredients are frequently replenished so that a meal may be had from it at any time.

pot, rommel. A drum made by stretching a skin over the mouth of a pot.

pota. Among the Bontoc Igorot, a woman who is the common mate of several men rather than the wife of one man.

Potala. The magnificent winter palace of the Tibetan Dalai Lama, containing over 1,000 rooms. It is over 900 feet high and constructed in tremendously large square sections of different colored stone on foundations hewn out of solid rock. The roof is sparkling gold and is the base for the tombs of the previous Dalai Lamas. The construction was begun in 1641. The five mile "sacred walk" around the palace is mandatory for every resident of Lhasa at least once a year. The walk is clockwise, keeping the building to the right in order to accord it the proper respect.

potato, sweet. A twining trailing perennial vine with roots with swollen tubers containing sugar and starch. It is an old American crop. Its wide use is due to the Polynesians' adopting it and taking it as far as New Zealand in the pre-Columbian era and the Spanish introduction of it to the Philippines in the post-Columbian era.

potiche. A ceramic vessel with a round shape and a short neck.

potion. See MAGIC, LOVE.

potlatch. Among the Indians of the Pacific Northwest, a ceremonial giving away or destroying of property to enhance status. The Kwakiutl used potlatch to validate and reinforce inherited position. Potlatching is a series of public distributions of property and has an important place in the social structure and economy. A potlatch might occur on taking a title or name. It may have to be returned in the future with interest. Persons of high status engaged in contests to see who could give or destroy the most. See KILLER, SLAVE.

potsherd. See SHARD.

pottery. Implements made of fired clay fashioned on a wheel or by hand. Pottery is a crucial factor in archaeological research, because of its abundance, variety, rapidity of change in style, and relative permanence, at least in shards. Once the clay is selected, stones are usually picked out and the clay is

kneaded into a fairly uniform consistency. If the clay is over-rich, organic matter like fine chaff or powdered animal dung may be added to cut down the stickiness, help water escape while drying, minimize shrinkage and the accompanying cracking, and improve the temper. The pottery is shaped, and a slip (q.v.) may be applied. It must be dried and polished when almost dry. A smooth hard object is used for polishing. Baking removes the chemically-combined water.

The color of pottery hinges on the type of clay, added ingredients, and the kind of firing. Brown is usually the same as the clay color. Black pottery probably began in trying to cover the smoke stains caused by a smoky fire. Red is usually caused by red oxide of iron or by using red ocher. Once water has been driven out of the clay by firing, a permanent chemico-physical change to a stonelike quality occurs. After being baked, the clay cannot be dissolved by water.

Earthenware is soft and fusible in a porcelain furnace, and includes unglazed, lustered, glazed, and enameled ware. Stoneware is hard and infusible because of the silica in the clay.

The first fired pottery dates ca. 6500 B.C. and is linked with early horticulture and agriculture. By that time the Sumerians in the Euphrates valley had made pots and other objects of sun-baked clay. Egyptian pottery from 4500-2457 B.C. consisted of bottles and bowls, with well-developed glazing techniques and ovens. Greek pottery advanced from the Neolithic finds at Cnossus and from Egyptian types carried by Phoenician merchants. The Athenian vase was the major piece of Greek pottery. Plant and animal figures are found in early vases from 2500-600 B.C. and legendary subjects are on the black figured vases of 600-500 B.C. The red-figured vases of 480-450 B.C. are commonly regarded as representing the peak. The Romans made Arretine vases which were smaller versions of earlier Greek pieces. Etruscan pottery (q.v.), made from 700 to 100 B.C. in Tuscany on the west coast of Italy, was varied in kind. Chinese pottery has been called the world's best. Predynastic pottery, ca. 3000 B.C., found in Honan, largely consists of utilitarian articles. The Han dynasty's pottery, 206 B.C.-220 A.D., was fairly simple, with some unglazed and simple decorations, although the first glaze was used at this time. See PORCELAIN; THEORY, PLASTER.

pottery, Assyrian. The pottery shards excavated from ancient Assyrian ruins are divided into four classes: tiles and bricks used in architecture, brilliantly decorated with enamel; "barrels," or cylinders and prisms, expressly designed for inscriptions; flat tablets or tiles for inscriptions, usually grouped together into libraries or sets classified by subject; vessels for various uses sparsely decorated and generally of plain unglazed clay.

Pottery, Black. Referring to a culture in China following the Painted Pottery (q.v.). It is char-

acterized by fine wheel-turned all-black pottery. Towns with wide walls were characteristic. The Chinese name for the culture is Ch'eng-tzu-yai or Lung-shan.

pottery, Celtic. The shards excavated in northern Europe, dating from the period before the Roman conquest of Gaul and Britain. They were found mostly in burial places and sometimes among ruins and appear to be pre-Roman in type. Among the vessels excavated were large cinerary urns and utensils. The color was gray or black and they were soft and fragile.

pottery, collar flask. A kind of pottery, found in northern Europe, shaped like a chemical flask.

pottery, comb. A kind of pottery, found in northern Europe, shaped like a semi-circular comb. **Combing** is a pottery decorating process in which slip of another color is splashed on the surface and a flexible toothed instrument like a coarse comb is dragged over the slip.

pottery, corded. See SCHNURKER-AMIK.

pottery, cordoned. Pottery decorated by strips of clay applied in relief.

pottery, Corean. See POTTERY, KOREAN.

pottery, crusted. Pottery on which paint has been applied after firing.

pottery, Cypriote. Named for the island of Cyprus, coarse baked clay vessels, geometrically decorated and similar in many respects to ceramics produced on the Greek mainland and in Asia. It is archaeologically and artistically significant in showing the connecting links between

Greek art and the art of other countries, e.g., it displays many examples of the Egyptian lotus motif in varying stages of change toward the Greek.

pottery, decoration of. Decorating pottery, either through burnishing, polishing, smoking, varnishing, making an impress, adding surface ornament to the clay before firing, adding foreign materials, adding a mineral glaze, or painting.

pottery, Etruscan. Etruscan ceramics are divided into four rough classes: cinerary urns somewhat like canopic vases, the covers of which were modelled in the shape of human heads; unglazed earthenware of a black color with a design impressed upon it in bas-relief; painted vases generally copied from (or perhaps arising from the same tradition as) the Greek; brilliantly varnished black vases with reliefs, also known as Etrusco-Campanian ware.

pottery, incrusted. Pottery decorated by incised lines filled with colored or white paste.

pottery, killed. A specimen of pottery, usually found archaeologically in graves, which has been intentionally broken to release its spirit or for some similar supernatural reason.

pottery, Korean or **pottery, Corean.** A type of pottery made in Korea, characterized by its medium hardness, cloudy white surface, and decorated with coarse paintings of black, dark red, and dark brown geometrical and conventional patterns.

pottery, Mexican. Pottery made by Mexicans before the Spanish conquest. Most examples were skillfully executed grotesque idols and images. Extant specimens were found in tombs and the ruins of temples.

Pottery, Painted. In China, a culture phase beginning in Neolithic times and running to ca. 600 B.C. In this period, some millet and some animals were raised. The dwellings were pits with a roof entrance.

pottery, particolored. Pottery fired by part being reddened by oxidization of iron oxides in contact with a free air access, while part is made black by these oxides being reduced.

pottery, rusticated. Pottery decorated by roughening the surface, which usually has a thick slip, by pinching, brushing, etc.

pottery, tulip. In western Europe, a kind of pottery like the Badarian (q.v.).

potto. A reddish-gray West African lemur of the genus *Periodicticus*. It is arboreal, nocturnal, and slow-moving.

Powell, John W. (1834-1902). American anthropologist who was first head of the Bureau of American Ethnology, founded in 1879, the first government department in any country to be devoted to the study of the aborigines. He also directed the official Geological and Geophysical Survey.

power, speech. The comparative rate of expenditure of speech energy.

powwow. A council or get-together among American Indians. It largely connotes a social rather than an official meeting.

pozzolana. A volcanic cement found at Pozzuoli near Naples. It was probably used in stucco reliefs and modeled figures.

praetorianism. The practice of a minority group's seizing a society and functioning through the nominal officials.

prairie. A midlatitude grassland with rich subsoil.

Prakrit. The literary languages of non-Sanskrit vernaculars of ancient India. The Prakrits were the basis for the Apabhramsa vernaculars on which the modern Indic vernaculars are based.

pramantha. A lighting stick among the Brahmins. It consisted of a hemp cord twisted with cow's hair, which was rotated sideways around the stick. This stick was turned in a little hollow formed at the point of intersection of two pieces of wood placed one above the other in the form of a cross. The extremities of the cross were bent at right angles and were fixed by four bronze nails. See SWASTIKA.

prau. A Malayan term for a boat.

Praxiteles curve. See CURVE, PRAXITELES.

prayer. A verbal request of a supernatural being, often made simultaneously with a sacrifice (q.v.). A prayer tries to obtain the intervention of the forces of the universe in men's affairs. It may be highly stylized or casual. The length of prayers varies considerably. Prayer can be interpreted as a religious self-expression, which, in higher religions, may include the expression of moral ideals. Prayer has developed from early man's superstition to the highest attempt to reach the deity. The posture and ritual of prayer are often prescribed.

preadaptation. Having characteristics that make it possible for a change in adaptation to occur and that are the basis of the new adaptation.

preanimism. The theory that the belief that many, or all, objects are alive, or have immanent energy, is the original element in religions, rather than animism; also R. R. Marett's name for the feeling of fear, awe, and wonder caused by the supernatural.

preaspiration. Preceding a sound by an unvoiced breath.

pre-boreal. See BOREAL, PRE-.

pre-Cambrian. See CAMBRIAN, PRE-.

pre-Chellean. Referring to artifacts from the early Pleistocene period, found in western Europe and made from flint.

predental. A phonetic term used to describe any consonant produced with the front part of the tongue near or touching the upper teeth, e.g., the *t*'s in *title*.

predicate. The verbal form associated with the subject of a sentence.

predication. A sentence that can be divided into subject and predicate.

pre-Dravidian. A hypothetical southern Asian population, also called Veddoid (q.v.).

Predynastic. Referring to the fourth millennium B.C. and earlier in Egypt.

prefixation. The process of affixation (q.v.) in which the affix appears before the underlying form, e.g., *pre* in *prehistory*.

prehistory. The study of the life and activities of mankind up to the beginning of recorded history, ca. 3000 B.C. Archaeological evidence is largely used by the prehistorian. Relics, implements, monuments, dwellings, fossils, and all remains of the culture are studied. The prehistorian is concerned with developing a period's chronology. The term was first used in Daniel Wilson's *Archaeology and Prehistoric Annals of Scotland* (1851).

prehominid. Weidenreich's name for such primitive men as the Java, Peking, and Eyassi types.

preliterate. An early term to describe a group with no written language, "natives" or nonliterate (q.v.) persons or cultures. It is not used widely today because it carries an implication of a linear evolution in a preordained sequence, with the preliterates being in a state of arrested development, and failing to attain literacy.

preman. A human being of the fossil era.

premolars. The bicuspid teeth. They are behind the canines and before the molars.

pre-Pueblo. See MAKERS, BASKET.

present, ethnographic. The practice of discussing ethnographic matters in a manner which presents the activities of a people in the present tense, as if they were still going on. It conveys a feeling of stasis and has sometimes meant disregarding

the history and dynamics of a culture.

preservation, self-. See SELF-PRESERVATION.

preservation, state of. The degree to which objects are in a state of comparative preservation when found by the anthropologist or archaeologist, who must consider such factors as the chemical changes which have taken place, and the extent of mechanical rolling (q.v.).

presle. See TALUS.

press, tipiti tube. A device woven of diagonal fibers, used to press juice from the mandioca pulp. It extracts the juice when it is pulled at both ends.

pressure, impulsive. Producing long blades of flint by sticking the core in the ground and gripping it with the feet. The flaker places one end of a wooden staff against his chest and the other end, with a spike attached, against the core. By moving his chest forward, the body's leverage is used to split a flake.

pressure technique. See TECHNIQUE, PRESSURE.

price, bride. Valuables given to the father, or appropriate relatives of the bride, by the groom or his representatives. These valuables usually serve to recompense the family for the loss of the woman's services and confirm the status of the marriage in the society. They also guarantee that the husband will take good care of the new wife, since if she returns home if badly treated, the husband loses the amount paid for her. The valuables may consist of objects used in daily life, livestock, ceremonial objects, currency, food, or service.

Prichard, James Cowles (1786-1848). An English ethnologist who emphasized the physical unity of men. He suggested that Whites had been developed from dark-skinned groups, and established the existence of the Celts as a people. He discussed the comparative influence of hair, color, height, and his *Researches into the Physical History of Man* (1826) contained a remarkable anticipation of modern viewpoints about evolution. The five volumes of his *Researches* and his *Natural History of Man* (1843) constituted a synthesis of data on the races of mankind which had a great influence on the development of anthropology in England.

prick spur. A spur with a single point.

pricker. A Lower Aurignacian rounded or flat slip of bone, pointed at one end.

priest. In more advanced cultures, a specialist in magic and religion. He is the intermediary between gods and men. The priest at first was probably merely the person organizing worship for his social group. The priests may have grown out of the witch doctor, shrine guardian, medicine man, or shaman. Priests may carry on other activities, or may specialize in one god of a polytheistic religion. The priesthood became exalted and often turned into a self-perpetuating inheritance, or special caste. Although good health may be required of a priest, sometimes an abnormal physical condition is seen as an example of special qualities, e.g., among the Ojibway Indians, where some deformed persons were made priests. Some taboos (q.v.), notably celibacy, are often found where there is a priesthood.

priest-temple-idol cult. See CULT, PRIEST-TEMPLE-IDOL.

Primary. A geological era, often called the period of ancient life.

primate. The order that includes man, the great apes, monkeys, tarsiers, and lemurs. It probably evolved, in the Eocene period, from the Insectivores. Typical primate traits include digit mobility, opposable thumb or big toe, a fairly large cerebrum and many-folded cortex, prehensile or near-prehensile feet and/or hands, a clavicle, nails rather than claws, menstruation and two mammae. Other than baboons and man, most primates live in trees. The primates advanced the ability to twist the radius on the ulna, so that the hands could be rotated without moving upper arm or elbow.

The Lemuroidea, Tarsioidea, and Anthropoidea are the three primate suborders. Simpson has suggested that the primates be divided into the suborders of prosimii (tarsiers, lemurs, tree shrews) and anthropoidea (monkeys, anthropoid apes, man).

primatology. The study of the primates, usually the non-human primates. Tyson, in 1699, started the study by describing a chimpanzee's anatomy. Such studies offer comparative norms that help explain human development.

primigenius. Referring to the early types of man which had heavy supraorbital ridges and low-vaulted skulls, e.g., Sinanthropus, Pithecanthropus, and Neanderthal man.

primitive. This term was formerly used to describe a "native" or nonliterate (q.v.) population. It is not so used today because it implies that nonliterate peoples are retarded and resist social change along the lines of western civilization, that they have not undergone any cultural evolution of their own, and that their way of life is like that of our prehistoric ancestors. This view is implied in the expression "our living ancestors." Primitive has been used also to describe prehuman men, early examples of Homo sapiens, and primate characteristics.

primitivism. The glorification of an earlier stage of human development. Almost every period has had a memory of a vigorous and happy past. A lost Paradise is mentioned in the Bible, and the Iliad praises the warriors of old, who could single-handed lift a stone too heavy for even two degenerate men of the poet's epoch. Aristotle harks back to early Attic simplicity and more recent writers like Rousseau and Nietzsche have called for a return to the presumably better ways of early man. The growth of anthropology has often heightened this interest in the ways of life of nonliterate man. Although anthropologists have repeatedly called attention to the many difficulties of life of noncivilized groups, their cautions have seldom dimmed the enthusiasm of primitivists. See SAVAGE, NOBLE.

primogeniture. The favored inheritance right of the oldest heir or son.

primordium. A region of the body in which there is localized growth or an embryonic area.

principle, site-name. The principle of designating archaeological materials by the site in which they were found.

print, block. A block of wood on which a transparent sheet with writing is placed. The background of the block is cut away and the characters are inked so that paper can be placed on it to take an impression. The block print was first used ca. 700 A.D., in China.

print, finger. See DERMATOGLYPHICS.

printing. A process for reproducing standardized writing by applying inked types or blocks to paper. It was invented in China, perhaps as early as 1041. Turkestan saw the invention of wooden type ca. 1300, and Korea had metal type ca. 1390. Gutenberg and Schaeffer developed the European printing press ca. 1440.

prism, Weld-Blundell's. An eight-column list of Babylonian dynasties, giving the name and length of reign of all the monarchs up to the end of the 19th century B.C., from which it probably dates.

privates, talking. Among some North American groups, the genitals of a man that advise him. This motif occurs frequently in Great Basin and Plains Indian stories.

privative. Referring to suffixes, prefixes and other grammatical elements that show absence or lack, e.g., *un* in *unloved*.

privilege. Discriminatory advantage usually based on exploitation. Sex, age, skill, birth, race, status, position, and wealth may be bases of privilege. The term privilege is often pejorative.

proa. An outrigger canoe with a large triangular sail. It is found in Indonesia.

process. A specific protrusion on the skeleton.

process, styloid. A process that juts out from the temporal bone's base.

process, supra-condyloid. A small process that may occur on the inner surface of the humerus in man. It is a reversionary trait found in lower mammals.

proclitic. A form that functions like a word (q.v.) in all respects except that, lacking a stress of its own, it "leans" on the following word, e.g., English *the*.

Proconsul africanus. An ape that flourished on an island of Lake Victoria, in Kenya, during the Miocene era, some 30 million years ago. It was reported in early 1955 that its hand bones were being studied to see if they were thin, monkeylike, and adaptable, in which case Proconsul might be at the beginning of the road of evolution which led to man. Proconsul probably lived in a considerable range of habitats. Leakey has found evidence, at Songhor and Lake Victoria in Kenya, of a substantial number of fossil apes. The different Proconsul forms vary in size from gorilla to chimpanzee, and there is reason to believe that they were able to walk on their hind legs. Teeth and jaw structure were probably more human than that of living anthropoid apes.

procreation, family of. A nuclear family (q.v.) in which Ego is the parent. He also belongs to a family of orientation (q.v.).

prodomestic. Referring to animals that were not domesticable at a given time but which are known to have become domesticated later.

profile, pollen. A summary of the changes in the percentage of pollen grains of different species, taken from a consecutive sample series.

profile, soil. The geological method of dating archaeological sites by studying the composition of the soil. Such a profile enables the investigator to infer the environmental circumstances under which the soil was formed.

prognathism. The extent to which the jaw protrudes. Man is the least prognathic mammal. Prognathism is measured by using the Frankfurt line to measure the angle between the nasion and the alveolar point.

prognathism, alveolar. Projection of the region of the teeth.

prognathous. Referring to a facial profile angle of less than 80 degrees, with a sloping face and comparatively projecting jaw. Early forms of man were more prognathous than recent populations.

projection, axonometric. A drawing in which objects are shown in three dimensions. It is executed by setting up all horizontal lines to scale and projecting scaled vertical lines from it. Any diagonals and curves on the vertical plane are distorted.

projection, isometric. A drawing in which an object is shown in three dimensions with the lines drawn at an equal angle to the horizontal and verticals projected from it to scale. All the diagonals and curves are distorted.

projective. Referring to a dimension in anthropometry obtained by measuring perpendiculars between a fixed plane and measuring points. Although these measurements are shorter than those from direct measurement, they can be obtained very easily. Such measurements as thigh length are best obtained by projection, because of the difficulty of measuring them directly. Projective measurements are sometimes also called derived measurements, indirect measurements, or subtractive measurements. For the use of the term in psychology, see TECHNIQUE, PROJECTIVE.

projectivism. Viewing the next world in terms of schemes of imagery of this world.

proliferation. Growth through cell splitting.

promiscuity. Indiscriminate sexual intercourse, with particular reference to a hypothetical early human society in which promiscuity was the rule.

pronasale. The tip of the nose.

pronation. A forearm position in which the palm is turned down and the two bones are more or less crossed.

pronograde. See QUADRUPEDAL.

property. Things over which persons have a totality of rights. Early man may not appear to have had much material property but may have been concerned about immaterial things which may secure the material. Property can be held by a person, a kinship group, or a society. Ideas on property cannot be separated from the social fabric in which they are found. Different rules may hold for different kinds of property.

property, communal. Community-owned property.

property, incorporeal or **property, intangible.** The elements of a culture, like dances or songs, which may be privately owned in primitive economies.

property, joint. Property owned by a group within the community.

property, real. Property which consists of land or what is built on land. Ideas about real property vary depending on whether the society is agricultural, hunting, etc., and on the degree of mobility of the possessor. Lowie has suggested that the Navaho usage might be a primitive agricultural norm: the first person to use a tract or his heir had rights over it, although it could be appropriated by anyone if the first owner did not use it. The crop was the property of the household.

Herders regard land as important for its value as pasturage, so that the incidence of food and water for their animals has a good deal to do with their ideas of property. Nonagriculturists and nonherders usually are in local groups that do not permit others to take advantage of natural resources without permission. Hunters or their families do not normally have a pre-empting right to land.

prophet. A person with an outstanding personality who is the founder of a cult or a cult official. A prophet speaks for someone else, often a deity, and may prophesy.

propitiation. The process of conciliating, or evoking favorable emotions, in others, or in officials or religious figures.

Propliopithecus. A small gibbonoid ape, dating from Lower Oligocene times. A lower jaw was found in Egypt. It may have been related to a common ancestor of man and apes.

propulseur. See THROWER, SPEAR.

propulsor, javelin. A bone or horn bone with a hook at the end in which the butt of a javelin shaft rests. By turning the shaft through a quarter circle and releasing the javelin, the shaft goes forward with additional force because of the added leverage. The javelin propulsor may have been the first machine invented.

proselytism. Converting others to a religion or other strongly-held belief system.

prosimian. A lemur or tarsier, often seen as a kind of halfway stage between monkeys and mammals that are not primates.

prosthion. The gum's lowest point, between the maxillary central incisors.

prostitution, hospitality. See LENDING, WIFE.

prostitution, temple. See HARLOTRY, SACRED.

protection hypothesis. See HYPOTHESIS, PROTECTION.

proterogenesis. A concept developed in 1950 by Schindewolf, closely related to fetalization and neoteny (qq.v.).

Protoanthropic. In some terminologies, referring to the earliest types of human beings, e.g., Java and Peking man.

protocone. The mesio-lingual cusp of the upper first and second molar and the lingual cusp of the upper premolar.

protoconid. The mesio-buccal cusp of the lower first and second molar and the buccal cusp of the lower premolar.

protoculture. An anticipatory or fragmentary culture, as among some anthropoids.

protocyte. A hypothetical ultramicroscopic primal organism, which presumably began as the result of a number of amino acids formed from the atmosphere when the condensations of water vapor were continuous and the evaporation of small isolated bodies of water concentrated the amino acids and synthesized them into complexes. One of these complexes had the promise of life.

protohistory. Early history.

Proto-Malay. See MALAY, PROTO-.

Protoneolithic. In some classifications, the Lower, or early, Neolithic era, consisting of the Campignian and Ertebole cultures.

provenience. The place where something is produced or found; the location of a fossil or find.

proverb. An abbreviated traditional instructional statement. It may deal with weather, health, morals, the law, or other areas of living. Proverbs often make use of rhyme, alliteration, and word play to reinforce their meaning. It is well known that the advice given in one proverb is often controverted by that in another equally well known, e.g., "Look before you leap," seems to conflict with "He who hesitates is lost."

pry hole. See HOLE, PRY.

psaltery. An early zitherlike stringed instrument, with a sound-board and differently tuned strings played by plucking.

pschent. The sovereign crown of Egypt, which combines the red crown of Lower Egypt and the tall white miter of Upper Egypt. The great king Menes united these two kingdoms, thereby founding the greatness of the Egyptian monarchy.

psychology, race. The study of likenesses and differences among different races with respect to interests, intelligence, reaction time, aptitudes, sense acuity, etc. Woodworth made the first experimental study in 1904, while the Torres Straits Expedition (q.v.) conducted the first systematic psychological examination of nonliterates.

psychosis. Mental illness that causes a person grave difficulties in functioning and adapting effectively. Paranoia, manic-depression, and schizophrenia are the major psychoses in our culture.

Psychozoic. The Quaternary rock system or development period, often called the "age of mind," beginning about one million years ago and including the Pleistocene and Holo-cene life periods, in which men first appeared.

psykter. A wine-cooling vase of Greece. It has a conoid body with a short cylindrical neck and a somewhat tall foot. It was alternately inserted in the crater and stood on the table. Occasionally a tripod supported it. The fifth century B.C. artist Euthymides made an excellent psykter in red-figured pottery.

PTC. Phenyl-thio-carbamide, a white powder used to determine whether one is a taster or non-taster (qq.v.).

pterion. The meeting place of the frontal, parietal, temporal, and sphenoid bones, on the side of the cranial vault.

pteroma. The walkway or space situated between the main walls of a temple and the surrounding row of columns (peristyle).

puant. See STINKARD.

puberty. The period in which the organism first attains reproductive power.

puberty school. See SCHOOL, PUBERTY.

pueblo. An adobe or stone dwelling, with several terraces, found among the Indians of New Mexico and Arizona (called **Pueblo Indians**). It is entered by ladder through a trap door in the roof. Some pueblos, of the period 1000-1300 A.D., had several hundred rooms and were several stories high. Pueblos are usually flat-roofed. The term is also used for a whole village of such buildings, as well as the culture of a linguistic group living in southern Puebla.

Pueblo, pre-. See MAKERS, BAS-KET.

puito. A South Congo friction drum.

pulka or **pulk.** A Lapp reindeer-drawn sleigh used to transport humans.

pulp. In a tooth, the area consisting of nerves and blood vessels.

pulque. A fermented drink found in Mexico, made from the agave flower's shaft. It probably existed prior to the Conquest.

pulsatile. Referring to the quality of percussion instruments.

pulverization. The process of reducing food to flours, either by pounding or milling.

pump, fire. A method of making fire found in Borneo and India. A piece of tinder is compressed by moving a piston up and down in a cylinder of wood until sparks emerge.

Puna. The cold, bleak elevated tableland which covers parts of southeastern Peru and northwestern Bolivia. Also, a cold wind which blows there.

punalua. Intermarriage of a number of sisters with one another's husbands and the intermarrying of a number of brothers with one another's wives. It is a hypothetical kind of marriage involving sexual communism (q.v.).

punctate. To decorate pottery by pressing into the unfired clay a fingernail or small, often sharp, instrument. Also, a ware which is so decorated.

punishment, legal. The manner of punishment that a society decrees for violation of its laws. Rules of punishment differ widely in different societies. Lowie has pointed out that imprisonment does not occur often in early societies, because of the scarcity of means for enforcing it as well as because of its probable disagreement with early ideology.

punta. A roughly worked sharp pointed flint implement.

Purah. A secret society (q.v.) of west Africa that exercises political control.

puraka. In Polynesia, the variety of taro that grows only under water.

Puranas. Eighteen books of religious poems that comprise the essential scriptures of Hindu popular religion. They represent the bases of sectarian teaching, each of the books being used by one or more sects. They contain much of the history and myths of gods and heroes.

purchase, bride or **purchase, wife.** See PRICE, BRIDE.

purification. The process of cleansing oneself. It may involve a ceremony of cleansing, washing, sacrifice, or similar symbolic techniques. Bloodshed, birth, and death may be occasions for purification. Such cleansing was common before engaging in certain activities or rites. Purification may be necessary to restore a state of holiness to an object. Although water is the most common agent used in purifying objects or persons, fire, cutting the hair, changing garments, abstinence from food, sexual activity, or the usual pursuits of life, confinement, and painting the body are also found.

purity, gametic. The splitting of each pair of the parent's genes or chromosomes prior to fertilization. The process is also called segregation.

purlin. A roof's horizontal support.

push plane. A nosed flint scraper, probably from the Aurignacian era.

pusu. A Congo palm bast cloth.

Putnam, Frederic W. (1839-1915). An American anthropologist, who was curator of the Peabody Museum for 40 years.

putta ildurra. An Arunta stone dagger.

pygmy. A member of a racial group characterized by being markedly below the average height of other racial groups. Pygmies average four feet eight inches in stature. The Bushmen in South Africa, five groups in the Congo Basin, the Andamanese in India, the Semang in the Malay Peninsula, the Aeta in the Philippines, and the Tapiro and Aiome dwarfs in New Guinea are among the major pygmy groups. In general, they are characterized by dark pigmentation and woolly hair.

It has been maintained that pygmies' facial features and color resemble groups of normal stature who lived or live in the same area, e.g., the Tapiro in New Guinea are smaller versions of their Papuan neighbors. An inference drawn from this is that pygmies are not a stock but that they have developed as mutations in different places and at different times. However, Taylor has shown that the brachycephalic Negrito pygmies of the Congo Forest do not have much in common with the nearby dolichocephalic Negroes. Moreover, Luzon

has Negritos with no Negroes nearby.

Pygmy stature seems related to the genes which cause woolly hair, and there are no pygmies where there is an absence of woolly hair. The African chimpanzee has a pygmy form. Another theory about the pygmies' development is that they constitute relics of an early racial group, with the pygmy culture presumably being one of the earliest cultures of mankind and best preserved among the central African pygmies. In large parts of Africa, in this view, the aboriginal population consists of pygmies who had been partly ousted and partly assimilated by the Bantu. Other Africanists point out the agreements between pygmy and Nigritian culture and that pygmy culture seems to have a dearth of material elements. **Pygmy, Negrito** or **Pygmy, Black.** A Negroid subrace found in some marginal tropical areas. The adult type is a dolichocephalic and fairly hirsute, while the infantile type is brachycephalic and has little body hair.

pyknic. In Kretschmer's system of constitutional types (q.v.), the short and fat extreme, presumably highly susceptible to manic-depression. This type is rounded and has heavy body cavities. Its cyclothymia manifests itself in a personality which is happy but sometimes moody. Extroversion and realism are other characteristics.

pylon. The great gateway which forms a temple's façade, as in Egypt. It had great blocks of masonry surrounding a large entrance.

Pylon temple. See TEMPLE, PYLON.

pyramid. A large structure, often on a square ground plan, with four triangular faces meeting in a point. There are over 70 ruined pyramids on the Egyptian plateau. They were probably built between the 1st and 12th Dynasties as tombs for royal mummies. The best pyramids were made of limestone, although mud brick was also used. The Egyptian pyramids are oriented in the direction of the cardinal points. The Great Pyramid was of blocks 4 by 6 by 20 feet which were well smoothed and finished with great precision. Flat-topped or truncated pyramids are also found in Central and South America.

pyre, funeral. A pile of wood on which a body was placed for destruction by fire. Most pyres were not completely successful, since the body was only partially consumed. The overtones of pagan sacrifice in the use of the pyre may have stimulated the Christian opposition to cremation. A resinous wood, like pine, was generally used, along with grass or twigs. Pitch, gums, and oil were later added to pyres to increase their effectiveness.

pyriform. A pear-shaped design, often found in early pottery; the anterior opening of the skull's nasal cavities.

pyrite. A mineral used in striking a fire, e.g., flint.

pyrolizing. Using fire for decorating and ornamenting materials like horn, leather, bone, and bamboo.

pyromancy. Divination (q.v.) by the observation of fire.

Q

q. The symbol for the frequency of the genes for blood group B in a given group. See P; R.

qanon. An ancient Turkish musical instrument.

Qat. A secret society (q.v.) of the New Hebrides.

qeres. A general term including all the equipment used in the Egyptian mummification process. Also specifically used to refer to the portion of the process which includes wrapping the corpse in bandages.

quadriga. A sculpture of a chariot drawn by four horses, frequently seen atop a monument.

quadritubercular. Referring to having four tubercules or cusps, as the human molars.

quadrumanous. Referring to being "four-handed," that is, capable of using both hind and fore limbs for grasping. The term is applied especially to some of the lemurs, the New World monkeys, and the orangutan, which sometimes hang downward by their feet. **Quadrumana** was once the name for the order Primates, except for man, who was in the order Bimana ("two-handed").

quadrupedal. Referring to walking or springing on all fours. The term pronograde is also used.

quahog. A clam, *Venus mercenaria,* from whose shell wampum or shell money was made by the Indians of the northeastern United States. The meat of this clam was—and still is—eaten.

quandong. A small Australian tree, *Fusanus acuminatus,* which yields a drupaceous fruit eaten by the aborigines.

quant. A pole with a flange at its end used to propel boats.

quantity. The duration of a sound, particularly if that is a distinctive feature distinguishing between phonemes (q.v.).

quantity, criterion of. A judgment of the degree of contact or the likelihood of common origin based on the number of similar cultural objects or practices in two different cultures. Leo Frobenius developed this concept as a result of his study of Melanesia and West Africa. The many elements in common indicated to him that these areas were connected.

quantity mark. See MARK, QUANTITY.

445

quartpot. A tin vessel used for heating liquids in parts of Australia. It has two wire handles on one side.

quartz. A mineral, crystallized silicon oxide, found in many parts of the world. The color varies. It was used for tools, ornaments, and magic. North American Indians used quartz long before Columbus. In parts of Australia, it figures in rain-making ceremonials.

quartzite. A hard silicified sandstone that varies in color from white to red and may be coarse- or fine-grained.

Quaternary. The geological period in which the present mammalian genera arose. Its climate was alternatingly warm and cold. It is generally dated in the last million years.

Quatrefages de Breau, Jean Louis Armand (1810-1892). A French anthropologist who engaged in a lengthy debate with Virchow (q.v.), maintaining that the Prussions were not Europeans but Huns. He emphasized that anthropology must include the study of man's habits and instincts as well as his biology. He wrote (1887) one of the earliest studies of the pygmies.

qubba. A highly decorated tomb of India with a square burial chamber and a dome-shaped roof. It was sometimes ornamented with pictures of scenes from the life of the deceased.

quebracho. An extremely hard type of iron wood. The bark is used to tan leather in northern Argentina, although it is poorly suited to this purpose.

quebrada. A canyon, especially in Peru.

Quechua. A family of South American Indian languages having as its chief dialects Ayacucho, Bolivian, Chinchaya, Tucumano (or Argentine), Cuzqueno, Huancaya, Lamano, and Quiteno. Quechua is spoken by an estimated 4 million Indians in central South America. It was the language of the ancient Inca civilization.

quena. An end-blown flute played by the Incas and still played today in the Andes area.

quern. An early mill used to grind grain. It consists of circular stones, with the upper stone turned by hand.

quern, rotary. A hand mill. The nether stone is circular and the upper, disk-shaped, rotates.

quern, saddle. An early quern, consisting of an elongated lower stone with a concave upper surface and an upper stone, shaped like a bolster, which was pushed back and forth on the lower. It was the only method of grinding corn used in the ancient world.

quest, vision. See VISION, QUESTING.

Quetelet, Adolphe Lambert Jacques (1796-1874). A French scientist, the first to write (1846) on the application of statistics to anthropological problems. In a series of publications from 1835 to 1871, he showed how anthropological qualities could be plotted in terms of a normal probability curve.

quffa. A circular coracle (q.v.) common in Iraq, used to transport both persons and goods through calm water. It is a large reinforced lidless basket made like coiled basketry. It has been in use for over 3,000 years.

quid, betel nut. A mixture of lime with the nut of the betel (q.v.). The lime removes some of the burning sensation from the betel and stains the saliva red. Chewing the quid is a widely distributed custom in the Pacific, but not beyond Melanesia. It is not found in Polynesia, where kava (q.v.) serves much the same purpose.

quilate. The purity of gold or precious stones; the carat.

quillon. An arm of the cross guard of a sword.

quillwork. Embroidery of the American Indian made with porcupine quills and bird feathers. The hardness of the materials made it necessary to use angular designs.

quinary. Referring to a counting system based on 5's and springing from the use of the digits of a hand as a major unit.

quinary-vigesimal. Referring to a system based mainly on 20's and secondarily on 5's.

quinoa. An annual herb, four to six feet high, with very nutritious seeds. It was an important pre-Columbian crop in the New World, used for flour and porridge, is still the staple of millions of South Americans. The Incas regarded it as sacred. Quinoa is probably a native of Peru.

quipu or **khipu.** A device used by the Peruvians as an arithmetical and mnemonic aid. It had a main cord from which smaller cords of different color hung at various distances. Each color had a definite meaning. Numbers were expressed by tying knots in the smaller cords. Numerical values were indicated by the location of the knots.

quitclaim. An instrument, ordinarily a deed, releasing to the purchaser whatever right the grantor may have in given property. A quitclaim is used ordinarily when the grantor is uncertain of the extent of his right because of a cloud on the title or possible contingencies.

quiver. A container for holding arrows, darts, and similar weapons.

quotient, intelligence. A person's mental age divided by his chronological age and multiplied by 100 to give his intelligence as compared with others of the same age in the general population. The mental age is supposedly indicated by given scores on an intelligence test. If a person 10 years of age indicates a mental age of 10, the intelligence quotient would be 100, average or normal. A person chronologically 10 years old with a mental age of 12 would have an I.Q. of 120, while such a person with a mental age of 8 would have an I.Q. of 80.

R

r. The symbol for the frequency of the genes for blood group O in a given group. See P; Q.

Ra. In Egyptian mythology, the creator of the world and of men.

rabbet. A longitudinal groove in a piece of timber to receive for fitting a plank or other object.

rabies. A disease which can have permanent effects on the central nervous system. It attacks animals and can be passed on to humans through a bite from a rabid dog. There has been much folk discussion of rabies and its cures.

race. A major division of mankind, with distinctive, hereditarily transmissable physical characteristics, e.g., the Negroid, Mongoloid, and Caucasoid races. It may also be defined as a breeding group with gene organization differing from that of other intraspecies groups. Thus, the morphological and metrical features which members of a race have in common derive from their common descent. Each race has a tremendous range of internal variability. Such identifying criteria as skin color, hair and eye color, prognathism, cephalic index, nasal index, skull capacity, hair texture, and the degree of hirsuteness and lip eversion are generally used. There is no completely pure race, and the criteria for a given race may not be manifested by all the members although any one member will probably manifest most. Current criteria for determining whether characteristics are racial include: hereditary transmission, comparative unalterability, lack of variability from external causes, and comparative independence of age and sex.

Blumenbach first divided mankind into races: Ethiopian, American, Malayan, Caucasian, and Mongolian. In Von Eickstedt's classification, there are now usually said to be three main races, 29 subraces, three intermediate and three special races. Coon, Garn, and Birdsell distinguish 30 races.

race, composite. A race that is a stable blend of two or more primary races and represents combinations of features from the different racial stocks involved. There are often geographic areas in which the blend has been stabilized.

race, genetic theory of. The classification of races on the basis of gene structure rather than morphology. At the present time, not enough is known about genes to make such a theory workable.

race, great. One of the major divisions of human beings.

race, kicking. A foot race of the Southwest Indians in which the participants run to the goal while kicking a stick.

race, secondary. A race which results from two primary races mingling.

race differences. See DIFFERENCES, RACE.

racial likeness. See LIKENESS, COEFFICIENT OF RACIAL.

raciation. Differentiation into racial groups.

raciology. The study of the races of mankind.

racism. The doctrine that the race, or physical type, generates culture. Count Arthur de Gobineau and Houston Stewart Chamberlain helped spread racist ideas in the 19th century. In its extreme form, racism preaches the inherent superiority of certain races and stirs up prejudice and hatred for races said to be inferior. While racist doctrines are still a stock in trade of demogogues, serious anthropologists no longer subscribe to them.

rack, skull. A large rack, often found in the central plaza of Aztec towns, on which the skulls of sacrificial victims were displayed.

racloir. A stout, thick flake used as a side scraper in Mousterian times.

radial. Referring to the thumb.

radiation. The exchange of heat between environment and body because of radiative interchanges with surrounding surfaces. It is stated in terms of calories per person or per square meter of body surface.

radiation, adaptive. The division of a successful animal group into several adaptive types that take advantage of the varied ecology and opportunities available. In such groups, the major structural changes may be in the comparative size of parts of the body. Adaptive radiation is especially well shown in reptiles. Mammals are a development in reptile radiation, and the mammals themselves radiated and replaced the reptiles to a considerable extent, as the dominant vertebrate class.

radiation, nonadaptive. The appearance of several related and morphologically divergent forms evolving without evident ecological diversification.

radiation, solar. See HYPOTHESIS, SOLAR RADIATION.

radical. The portion of a derived word that phonetically and semantically carries the basic meaning; one of the 214 primary characters used for classifying characters in the most widely adopted system of Chinese lexicography.

radioactive dating. See DATING, RADIOACTIVE.

radiocarbon dating. See DATING, RADIOCARBON.

radish. A very ancient cultivated plant, used for oil and food in Egypt.

radius. The outer bone of the forearm, articulating with the humerus and the wrist bones.

raft. See FLOAT.

raft, chatty. A raft kept afloat by jars or pots. It was used in parts of Europe in the classical civilizations and is currently used in India on rivers without rocks or rapids and with mud, loam, or sand banks. The chatty raft is also called the gharnao.

railway, contractor's or **railway, Decauville.** A small railroad with narrow-gauge track sections that can be moved from site to site and cars that may be pushed manually. It is used in archaeological research to remove earth. The French engineer Paul Decauville was the inventor.

rain, female. Among some North American Indian groups, a mild gentle rain. They term a driving rain a **male rain.**

rainbow. A circular arc showing the colors of the spectrum seen opposite the sun when its rays are refracted and reflected in drops of rain. Two or more rainbows may occur at once. Much folklore deals with the rainbow, which may be a bridge between earth and heaven (Norse mythology), a serpent (American Indians), or a sign of God's covenant never to subject the world a second time to universal inundation (Hebrews).

rake. An implement which stirs and spreads earth and gathers some products, like hay. It has prongs set at approximately 90 degrees to the handle.

ram, battering. A large beam, with an iron head (occasionally resembling or intentionally fashioned like a ram's head). It was used to knock down walls of a be-

sieged fortress. It might be swung from a tripod, be moved on wheels, or cradled in the arms of soldiers. It was developed by the Babylonians.

ramage. The branches or boughs of a tree; a group of relatives who trace their descent unilinearly from a common ancestor. It is also an internally stratified social organization, as in east central Polynesia.

Ramapithecus. A Pliocene genus of India, which may have been a generalized human predecessor.

Ramayana. An immensely popular epic poem of India. It includes the story of the prince Rama, his wife Sita, and the monkey-god Hanuman. Several authors probably contributed to it.

ramganny. In some Hindu temples, a dancing girl whose function is to excite desire.

ramus. The part of the jaw that extends upwards and articulates with the skull.

Rangi. The heaven or sky-space deity in New Zealand mythology, the husband of Earth Mother.

rapier. A sword with a straight two-edged narrow pointed blade. It is mainly used for thrusting and is probably an Aegean invention.

rappel. A musical instrument that looks like an ordinary hand drum. It was used by the ancient Egyptian or Hebrew people.

rasp, musical. A musical instrument with at least one surface or edge with either grooves or serrations. A stick is drawn across these grooves or serrations and produces a harsh sound. Several of these in-

struments, tuned differentially, can play a melody when used together.
Rassenkreis. A group of closely related subgroups within a species distributed according to a geographical replacement pattern.
rat fender. See FENDER, RAT.
Rata. A legendary navigator who is credited with having explored the islands of eastern Polynesia.
rath. A wall of earth, sometimes fortified, surrounding an old Irish dwelling; by extension, the dwelling of an Irish leader.
rattan. The stem of any of several slender, flexible palms of the genus *Calamus,* which is used in Southeast Asia as a lashing and to make baskets and furniture.
rattle. A musical instrument consisting of an object which encloses or is in contact with smaller objects and is shaken to produce sounds. Rattles may be shaken by hand or worn on the clothing and are sometimes used in rituals.
rattle, gourd. A rattle made by placing some small objects in a gourd. It is shaken by the player who carries it.
Ratzel, Friedrich (1844-1904). A German zoologist and geographer who helped develop the concept of the culture area (q.v.). Ratzel emphasized the importance of borrowings and migrations in the spread of culture. He was one of the founders of the anthropogeography movement.
rau. The name for moiety (q.v.) on Guadalcanal.
ravanastron. An ancient Hindu stringed instrument. It has a sound box that looks like a pipe bowl and

a long neck with two pegs from which two gut strings are strung. The strings pass over a bridge which raises them from the belly. They are played with a bamboo bow strung with hair. Some Chinese and Buddhists still play the ravanastron.
rawhide. An animal skin that has been fleshed and turned hard.
Rawlinson, Sir Henry W. (1810-1895). An English archaeologist who worked on cuneiform writings. Between 1835 and 1851, he completed the first translation of a cuneiform inscription that was carved on an almost inaccessible rock in the Persian Zagros mountains.
rebec. A three-stringed ancestor of the violin. It had a pear-shaped body and no finger board. It was made from a hollowed out piece of wood and had a carved figure at the end of the peg box. It was held by the performer under the chin or against the chest and bowed. It originated in ancient Europe.
rebus. A puzzle in which a picture stands not only for the object it represents but also for anything with a similar name, e.g., a drawing of a heart in an English rebus would represent all of the meanings of "heart" and also "hart." The early Greeks used the rebus, which was perhaps associated with the cryptic responses of the Delphic oracle.
recapitulation. The theory that the major stages in the history of the race are reenacted in the individual's growth. See ONTOGENY.
recessive. A gene carrying a trait the appearance of which is blocked

when it is paired with a dominant gene. A recessive gene will be evident only if two recessives are paired. It is abbreviated *a*.

reciprocity. 1 Returning objects or favors to others, since a person does not expect a gift or free service from one not his kin. 2 This term has also been used for the criteria of the linguistic means by which the two members of a social group refer to each other, usually a pair of relatives, of different generations, who use the same term reciprocally. 3 Malinowski's conception that social relations develop through a collection of reciprocated duties and privileges.

recoil, anchor. A device on a clock, introduced ca. 1680, to replace the verge escape. It alternately connected and disconnected with the clock's control wheel.

rection. The process through which a word's form differs in accordance with its relationship to other words in the sentence, e.g., in Latin.

reduplication. A kind of affixation (q.v.) in which there is repetition of the whole word or a part of it, e.g. *goody-goody*. It is often used to expand or diminish the concept of number or size. There are some Indo-European languages in which reduplicating the initial consonant or syllable of the verb root is a kind of tense formation. In some languages, like Malay, noun plurals are formed by reduplication.

reed. A device used to "beat up" a pick of the weft. It looks like a frame heddle (q.v.) which has no eyes.

reed, double. A valve musical instrument in which there is a thin opening with elastic walls that vibrate when the performer blows on them so that vibrations are set up. Stops are used to develop different notes.

reed-batten. A comb used in weaving so that each comb tooth goes between each pair of adjacent threads of the warp.

reference, cross-. See CROSS-REFERENCE.

reference, term of. A term used to refer to a relative when talking with a third person about him.

refuge, city of. In the period between individual vengeance and state control of criminals, a city to which a person might flee if he had unintentionally wronged another. There he could find sanctuary. Churches and other places of worship also provided sanctuary. Anyone who breached the sanctity of such a place by taking vengeance there committed sacrilege.

refuge area. See AREA, REFUGE.

refugium. An area that did not change so radically as the larger region of which it is a part. The term is generally used to delineate climatic change. A refugium is usually a center for relic species and postglacial dispersal.

refuse, cultural. The residuum or debris from man's cultural activities.

refuse, kitchen. Deposits consisting of the bones of animals eaten by early man. These bones are usually broken and are sometimes split longitudinally, showing that the marrow was extracted.

regalia. The symbols of the king, or, by extension, of any office or authority.

regelation. In glacial ice, the process by which parts of the ice melt at certain points under pressure and the film of water slips to a position at which there is less pressure and there refreezes. This gives the ice a pseudo-plastic motion.

regolith. The loose material, such as broken rock and soils, that overlays the earth's solid rock.

regression, filial. The principle enunciated by Sir Francis Galton (q.v.) in 1869 that the offspring of abnormal parents have a tendency to approach the normal.

reincarnation. The belief in many religions, e.g., the Pythagorean, that the soul returns in consecutive bodies. The soul may improve in its various reincarnations. An idiosyncrasy may be presumed to reflect the reincarnation of a dead ancestor. Appropriate ceremonies may be used to try to determine whose spirit has been revived.

Reindeer Age. See MAGDALENIAN.

reject. A worked stone that was apparently intended to be a tool but was discarded, usually unfinished, without being used.

relatedness. The integration of activities within a culture or cultural unit.

relationship, avoidance. A relationship characterized by avoidance between a woman and her daughter-in-law or a man and his son-in-law. Among the Dakota, e.g., the husband is not permitted to use his father-in-law's name during the first year in which he lives in the latter's home.

relationship, joking. Playing tricks and teasing among members of the same tribe. The conduct is usually directed toward specific members, generally relatives, of the opposite sex and may have originated between potential marital partners. Thus, a man may make teasing remarks to his sister-in-law. In a joking relationship, an individual may not only be permitted but also required to make fun of the other, who is not permitted to take offense. The joking may be verbal, physical, and obscene. The two individuals involved may mutually tease each other, or one may tease the other with the recipient responding mildly or not at all. Relationships of this sort are found chiefly in North America but also in Oceania and Asia. Joking is sometimes associated with avoidance relationships (q.v.), and often involves what Radcliffe-Brown calls a privileged disrespect. The French term parentés à plaisanterie is sometimes used.

relationship, privileged. A kinship relationship within which sexual access is allowed before, and sometimes after, marriage. Siblings-in-law are often in a privileged relationship.

relatives, affinal. Relatives, at whatever level, between whom there is a marriage tie.

relatives, consanguineal. Relatives who have common blood or ancestral ties.

relatives, cross. Relatives or offspring of siblings of the opposite sex.

relatives, genetic. Relatives in a biological relationship.

relatives, parallel. Relatives or offspring of siblings of the same sex.

relatives, primary. Relatives in the same nuclear family (q.v.) as a given individual, such as his parents.

relativism, cultural. The principle that experience is interpreted by each person in terms of his own background, frame of reference, and social norms, and that these factors will influence perception and evaluations, so that there is no single scale of values applicable to all societies.

release, Mediterranean. Drawing a bow by placing three fingers across the string and holding the arrow lightly between the first and second finger. The thumb is not used.

release, Oriental or **release, Mongolian.** Drawing a bow by placing the thumb across the string. The first finger is across the thumbnail.

release, primitive or **release, primary.** Drawing a bow by holding the arrow between the first finger and thumb. There is no digital contact with the string.

release, secondary. Drawing a bow by holding the arrow between the second joint of the first finger and the thumb. The tip of the first finger and of any other finger may rest on the string.

release, tertiary. A form of arrow release in which the ends of the forefinger and middle finger hold the nock and the first three fingers hold the string.

relict. An organism that survives after its group has largely become extinct or that occupies a smaller area than the earlier members of its group. Simpson has distinguished relicts as numerical, geographic, phylogenetic, and taxonomic. A relict is also a form that is a reflection of former environments.

relief-bas. See BAS-RELIEF.

Relief, Imgig. A copper representation of the lion-headed eagle of Ningirsu, a god, holding two stags by their tails. It was made in the early Sumerian dynastic period, ca. 3100 B.C. It was over the door of a shrine at Al'Ubaid.

religion. A system of beliefs and practices, found in every culture, that formalizes the conception of the relation between man and his environment. It helps explain difficult and seemingly inexplicable events. Religion embodies the idea of a supernatural power and of personified supernatural forces. Ceremonies, rituals, and observances are used to communicate with the supernatural, with certain persons believed to have greater access. Religion organizes a group's members in a condition of solidarity and gives a broad base to social interaction, being a symbolic statement of the social order. Religion suggests a system of authority, which enables one to know what is right. It permits imagination to express itself.

religion, comparative. The comparative study of religions, largely originating in the 19th century. It applies the scientific method and the social science armamentarium to discover the history and significance of religion.

religion, mystery. A religion in which the person rather than his community is most important. Participants join it on their own initiative and go through a specific, usually hidden, initiation (q.v.). In Greece, Eleusis, near Athens, was the scene of one such religion that attracted considerable fame. Its secrets were so well guarded that even today they have not been completely discovered. A heightened sense of closeness to the deity presumably resulted from the initiation, along with fairly solid arrangements for the success of the soul.

The cult of Dionysus was not attached to any one locality in Greece but was observed in different parts of the country. It was orgiastic. The Orphic mysteries, also practiced in Greece, were much like the Dionysiac. They began ca. seventh century B.C. The Phrygian mysteries celebrated the mother-goddess Cybele and Attis, her associate, whose death she mourned. Attis was resurrected, thus symbolically reassuring the worshippers of their return from the grave.

Mithra was the hero of a Persian mystery religion, which became very popular in the third century A.D. Astarte, in Syria, was a mother-goddess very much like Cybele. The death of Osiris and his recovery by Isis featured the Egyptian mysteries.

The mysteries have been called variations of the early nature cults where the mother symoblized the earth and her slain and resurrected associate symbolized the waning of the year and its return in spring. The secrecy may have stemmed from the desire to keep strangers out of the ceremonies, so that they could not acquire this symbolic knowledge. The fundamental purpose was to insure the crop. As agriculture advanced, this interest in crops changed to a more abstract concern for the soul and eternal life. See CULT, MYSTERY.

religion, sociology of. The application of sociological concepts and thinking to the study of man's religious behavior. It studies the genesis and development of different religions in different cultures, relates a culture's deities to its daily life and social and environmental conditions, and correlates specific religions and their settings, e.g., a fiercely competitive culture may have competitive gods.

religion, techniques of. The different behaviors and devices included in religions. They include magic (q.v.), or compelling the supernatural to act; reverence; cajoling; scolding; hospitality; prayer (q.v.); divination (q.v.); sacrifice (q.v.); taboos (q.v.); fetishes (q.v.); and amulets (q.v.).

religion, theories of. Numerous theories have been advanced to explain the origin and nature of religion. Spencer felt that religion's fundamental datum was the current generation's respect for the older generation, thus making it a kind of ancestor worship. Tylor said that visions and dreams gave rise to man's developing the concept of his soul as apart from his body, extending it to the whole material universe so that he reached the concept of a belief in spirits, or animism, which is the least common denominator in religion. Durkheim believed that religion arose from the crowd excitement in group ritual, such as totemism, and stressed the difference between things with power—sacred—and those without power—profane. Hauer saw religion as deriving from the mystic experience peculiar to some persons in a community being transmitted with such authority that it becomes more important than any other experience. Lowie treats religion as a cultural phenomenon. Frazer said that religion is a kind of individual, emotional, supplication to spiritual beings. Marett emphasized that animatism (q.v.) is personification of inanimate powers.

reliquary. A religious relic used for worship of any person considered immortal and sacred by a cult.

remains, vestigial. Organs that are degenerate and functionless analogues of structures that were entire and functional in an ancestral form. An example is the human vermiform appendix, which in some lower animals is an organ for storage of surplus food.

remedy, apotropaic. A remedy to avert evil. Spittle, which has some enzyme properties and can bring about fermentation, and blood, are among the earliest such remedies.

rendzina. Soil of limestone source, common in Italy. Such soils are usually dark.

rennet. An ingredient, used in cheese-making, that curdles milk without souring. It comes from the stomach lining of a suckling animal.

Rensch's rule. See RULE, RENSCH'S DESERT; RULE, RENSCH'S HAIR.

repartimiento. A Spanish form of land division found in South America.

repetition, incremental. A ballad technique in which each stanza repeats the preceding stanza, with another element of the story added.

reposición. In Central America, a child's being given the name of one who has qualities which the parents would like to see in the child. The person whose name is taken is told that the child's relation to him is that of reposición.

repoussé. A metal formed in relief and decorated by being worked mostly from the reverse side.

reredos. A carved or ornamented screen that stands behind an altar.

residence. The rule establishing where a married couple will locate its household, either matrilocal or patrilocal, or a combination of the two.

residence, ambilocal. A custom whereby a newly married couple is permitted to choose freely to reside with or near the parents of either the bride or groom. It is also called bilocal residence. See RESIDENCE, UNILOCAL.

residence, matrilocal. The practice of a married couple establishing its household near or with the parents of the wife for either a short or long time. Matrilocal residence is found usually in horticultural societies.

residence, patrilocal. The practice of a married couple establishing its household near or with the parents of the husband for either a short or a long time.

residence, unilocal. A customary post-marital residence in or near the home of the bride or of the groom. The choice is not free as in ambilocal residence (q.v.) but is culturally prescribed. Unilocal residence can be patrilocal, matrilocal, or avunculocal.

residue. An unusual language form that cannot be explained by a phonetic law and is assumed to be a vestige of some rule that has fallen generally into desuetude. An example is the plural *children,* which is a residue of a Middle English plural represented once by such forms as *shoon* for the plural of shoe.

resistivity survey. See SURVEY, RESISTIVITY.

resonance. The effect caused on sound quality by the vibration of the vocal cords in pronouncing voiced consonants. It sometimes also involves adjusting the opening and size of the oral and nasal cavities to result in nasal resonance.

resonator. 1 The sound box or body, particularly in stringed musical instruments. 2 An organ that produces resonance in speech sounds, namely the pharynx, nose, lungs, and mouth. They modulate and amplify the various pitches produced by the vocal cord's vibration.

resorting. A disturbance of the soil that upsets the original stratification. Resorting may complicate the archaeologist's task in dating finds.

responsibility, collective. The principle widely operative in primi-

tive society that holds fellow tribesmen, usually kinsmen, responsible for an individual's crime.

rest, neck. A piece of furniture, often of carved wood, used as a pillow, especially in the Pacific area.

retainer. An individual on the staff of a household or chief who has a status higher than that of servant or slave.

retaliation. A type of private vengeance in which the punishment of the offender is like the injury he inflicted. It is the lex talionis, expressed in the typical formulation, "An eye for an eye, a tooth for a tooth." See RETRIBUTION.

retouche. See FLAKING, SECONDARY.

retouching. The process, common in the Mousterian period, in which small bits of flint are removed from the area near the edge of the tool, so that its cutting edge is improved by making it like a miniature saw.

retribution. A punishment like the injury the offender inflicted. Based on what Aristotle called "corrective justice," it is designed to restore the balance of the social universe, which was upset by the crime. See RETALIATION.

retting. Detaching the fibers of a plant, like flax, from the woody cores through bacteriological decomposition.

Retzius, Anders Adolf (1796-1860). A Swedish anatomist who concentrated attention on the quantitative study of the skull, rather than the skin color, as a race criterion. He developed the cephalic index (q.v.) in 1840.

457

revenant. A person or animal who returns from the dead, often as a ghost. The person may be seen as a symbol, like fire. Revenants may come back to earth to execute various missions for themselves, or to communicate with the living. They have many human qualities and are often feared.

revenge, blood. The tradition whereby one is bound to kill any murderer of his kin. Early tribes enforced a crude justice in this manner by taking a life for a life.

revolution, food - producing. Childe's term for the change from food-collecting to systematic crop-growing, animal-raising, living in houses, and the other concomitants of planned food-raising. The food-producing revolution probably began in the Near East ca. 8000-6000 B.C., in China ca. 3000 B.C., and in the New World ca. 1000 B.C.

Rh. A blood factor of which there are several types. Persons with this factor are Rh+ (or positive); those without it are Rh— (or negative). In some cases, the offspring of an Rh+ male and an Rh— female may not live. There appears to be racial variation in the presence of Rh+ and Rh— factors. The name derives from the rhesus monkey, which provided the first evidence for the factor. The Rh factor is expected to be of great value to the study of racial compositions. There are about 50 groups that are theoretically distinguishable. Some 15 gene complexes can be distinguished, and 7 seem to occur quite frequently. The fairly few non-European groups studied exhibit great variability. Rh— seems to be associated with populations which originate in Africa, Western Asia, and Europe. A child whose Rh factor is incompatible with his mother's may develop anemia and jaundice.

Rhodes, Colossus of. A memorial statue 105 feet high, one of the seven wonders of the world, built in honor of the saving of Rhodes from Demetrius Poliorcetes. The Colossus of Rhodes was supposed to have been constructed by the sculptor Chares of Lindus from the abandoned weapons of Demetrius over a period of 12 years.

Rhodesian. See HOMO RHODESIENSIS.

rhombas. A bull roarer (q.v.) in ancient Greece.

rhyparography. Sordid, foul, or mean representations.

rhythmograph. An apparatus that records the sounds of drums, rattles, or other devices used to mark time. The sounds are translated into lines on a rotating smoked surface.

rhyton. A horn-shaped Greek cup that ran to a point in which there was a hole for drinking. Later examples were made in the shape of an animal or human head and were open at the top.

ricasso. The blunting of part of a rapier's edges, just below the butt, as a thumb and forefinger rest.

rice. A large annual grass that grows from two to four feet high. It produces an inflorescence which terminates in a grain. There are some 3,000 varieties. Rice probably provides more of the diet of man than any other crop. It needs much water and warm weather for its growth, like that found in the East Asia monsoon region. It is relatively deficient in proteins and fats. Rice is eaten by over half the world's population, with the Orient producing 95 per cent of the supply. Rice originated in Southeast Asia, and records of its cultivation in China go back 4,000 years. In fact, the same word represents both rice culture and agriculture in classical China. Rice is the standard food of South China, where the regular greeting is the question whether the other person had his rice that day.

In wet-rice cultivation, rice seeds are planted in flooded fields. It is found primarily in southeast Asia and the contiguous islands, although it has spread to other parts of the world. Wet-rice areas need substantial irrigation or river valleys that are regularly flooded. The sometimes complicated methods of channeling water used in mountainous wet-rice areas may lead to a substantial class and social superstructure, as has been pointed out in Madagascar, in Ifugaoland, north Luzon, Philippines, and South China. In dry-rice planting, the rice seeds are sown in the area to be developed. Considerable ritual often surrounds rice. Gautama placed rice in the second of the 10 classes into which he divided mankind.

Rich, Claudius James (1787-1820). A British Resident in Baghdad, one of the founders of field archaeology. He visited and described the sites of many of the ancient Mesopotamian cities and collected antiquities and manuscripts.

ricksha or **jinrikisha.** A vehicle with a hood and two wheels, usually drawn by man. It was invented by an American missionary in Yokohama and was introduced to China in 1847 by a Frenchman.

riddle. An educational question or statement, often cryptically phrased. Some riddles are thousands of years old. Riddles may be asked on ceremonial occasions to influence important events, since correctly answering a riddle may help a social group solve a problem.

ridge, alveolar. The area directly to the rear of the upper teeth.

ridge, brow. A large bony ridge across the forehead and above the eyes, at about the level of the eyebrows. The brow ridges have both an internal and external aspect. They constitute a distinguishing mark of Homo sapiens. The term supraciliary ridge is also used.

ridge, pressure. A long piece of pressure ice (q.v.).

ridge, supraciliary. See RIDGE, BROW.

ridge, supraorbital. The bony prominences over the sockets of the eye. They are often more prominent in males than in females and are today most noticeable among the Australoids. They are usually associated with Protoanthropic and Paleoanthropic fossils.

rigging, running. On a sailboat, rigging largely used to control the sails and the spars that can be moved.

rigging, standing. On a sailboat, permanently fixed rigging. It provides support for the spars and consists of stays and shrouds. The shrouds usually are attached to the mast to keep it from falling sideways.

right, father. A kind of societal organization with succession and inheritance reckoned through patriliny, patrilocal residence, and largely paternal authority. All these elements are not necessarily present in a father-right society, although they are usually associated.

right, junior. See ULTIMOGENITURE.

right, mother. A form of societal organization in which descent and inheritance are reckoned in a matrilineal manner, residence is matrilocal, and authority is maternal or avuncular. All these elements are not necessarily present in mother-right, although most of them are associated in such a society.

right, nephew. A special relationship between mother's brother and sister's son, particularly the nephew's succession to, or inheriting from, his uncle.

rimshard. A piece of pottery from the rim of the pot.

ring, climbing. Either of two types of rings used to climb trees. One type encircles the trunk of the tree and the waist of the climber. The other type encircles the ankles of the climber and keeps his feet together while ascending the tree.

ring, complacent. An annual growth ring on a tree which is approximately as thick as other rings on the tree. See RING, SENSITIVE.

ring, gimmal. Two rings that could either be locked together or worn separately. They were used as betrothal gifts in the Middle Ages.

ring, kula. Among the Melanesians of the Trobriand Islands, the stylized economic exchanges described by Malinowski which involve a spell connected with an aromatic mint plant and intertribal exchanging of shell necklaces and arm bands. These exchanges are formalized and without haggling. The necklaces are usually long and of red shell and the bracelets of white shell. They have mainly prestige value, with the more trading done by a person the more honorific his social position.

ring, sensitive. An annual growth ring on a tree in which the width varies. See RING, COMPLACENT.

riot. A short-lived group disorder, usually violent. Riots usually indicate social unrest.

Ripley, William Z. (1867-1941). An American anthropologist whose book *The Races of Europe* (1900) was for long a standard reference. He used many different criteria in distinguishing the three groups of Teutons, Mediterraneans, and Alpines.

ripostiglio. A hoard (q.v.) of bronzes or other valuable objects.

risings, heliacal. The time of the year at which some bright stars are seen rising before the sun. See SETTINGS, HELIACAL.

Riss. The third glacial period in Europe, probably extending from 250,000 to 125,000 years ago.

rite or **ritual.** A set or series of acts, usually involving religion or magic, with the sequence established by tradition. Rites are not likely to be so persistent as a cult. They often stem from the daily life of a people, e.g., Toda rites center on dairy matters and the temple is the dairy, with the dairymen priests.

rite, birth. A ritual performed on the birth of a child to purify mother and child and to insure the strength and good fortune of the child and protect him from evil spirits.

rite, fertility. Ritual observance to assure the fruitfulness of sources of food and of the human race. Such rites often involve sexual license.

rite, increase. A ceremony performed, especially in aboriginal Australia, to increase the supply of wild plant and animal species, particularly those relied upon for subsistence.

rite, initiation. See INITIATION.

rite, marriage. The socially approved activities attendant on a marriage, including promulgation of the marriage and appropriate festive observances.

rite, medicine. A medical activity dependent for success on contact with supernatural forces. Such rites may involve plants and herbs, exorcism, dancing, and singing.

rite, puberty. A ceremony attendant on a person's attaining puberty. A puberty rite may involve dances; fasting, isolation, and prohibitions, e.g., the prohibition among North American Indians against a menarchal girl's using her fingers to scratch her head. Boys were symbolically initiated into adulthood among North American Indians and were sent on a questing vision (q.v.).

rite, purification. See PURIFICATION.

rite, social. Behavior in accordance with custom or religion.

rite, transition. See RITES DE PASSAGE.

rites de passage. Van Gennep gave this name, in 1909, to the ceremonials surrounding the arrival of key periods, such as birth, puberty, marriage, and death. He suggested a tripartite classification: rites which separate a person from previous associations, rites which prepare for a marginal period, and rites of aggregation which incorporate him in his new existence. Rites of passage develop an emotional state which facilitates bridging the gap between old and new.

ritual. See RITE.

ritualism. Using or observing a rite.

roach. A head ornament, widely used by American Indians, consisting of a crest running along the middle of the head from front to back. It may consist of deer tails or similar materials. The tuft of hair in the center of the head is also called a roach.

road, ceremonial. A road in cities like Thebes or Babylon or in temple enclosures used to carry carts and persons to a place of worship or a special site. Such roads usually had well-drained surfaces and even gutters.

roads, classification of. Forbes has suggested that there were four major types of roads: the highway for traffic or trade; roads for transporting special materials for a short distance, like the stone blocks moved by the Egyptians from the Nile; strategic roads, like the Roman

461

Limes roads; and religious processional roads. Many of the Greek roads of the last type incorporated the right of asylum (q.v.); some marked the path followed by the god in establishing his temple.

The river valley civilizations preferred water transport to roads, and there are few cases of road building between 3000 B.C. to 600 B.C., when those civilizations flourished. In ca. 300 B.C., the Romans began reorganizing the old Italian track system and building roads. The Romans learned from the Persians, Egyptians, Greeks, and Etruscans. When an area was conquered they built roads so that it could be reached by trade and soldiers. As private property spread, roads became more necessary in order to delimit plots. Gravel and earth roads developed into paved roads, with the Appian Way to Campania the first (312 B.C.). The Roman Empire had 180,000 miles of paved roads, including 53,000 miles of major highways. The Roman state post averaged along these roads five to six miles an hour, which remained a standard for some 1,500 years.

The Inca Empire (1438-1532) had better roads than any people before them, with the probable exception of the Romans. Inca roads were narrow because they were made for runners, and were usable in all kinds of terrain and weather. Post houses along the route had couriers who took messages from other runners. These wayside stations (see TAMPU) were 4 to 8 miles apart.

There was a road through the mountains which was 2700 miles long and a 2400 mile road along the coast. Connecting and lateral roads brought the mileage to 10,-000. The roads were paved where the earth was damp. Stone walls bordered the roads, which were from 6 to 45 feet wide. Elaborate staircases, tunnels, culverts, drains, and masonry and bridges were part of the road system. The roads were constructed and repaired by the inhabitants of the districts in which they ran. The Bridge of San Luis Rey was a suspension bridge hung from rope cables, and was replaced every other year.

road, log *or* **road, corduroy.** A road made by covering the earth with a layer of boughs. It probably was the first kind of artificial road in Europe, and there are some extant specimens in Federnsee, Switzerland, ca. 1800 B.C. The log road reached its chief development in the area stretching from the Ukraine to Holland, where it was used to cover the many swamps, bogs, and other obstacles to communication. Many such roads from ca. 1500 B.C. have been found.

roads, theories of. See PATH, WILD ANIMAL; POOL, DRINKING.

roarer, bull. An implement usually consisting of a thin elongated blade of wood with a string at one end, used as a toy and in ceremonials to produce a whirring sound. A stick may be attached to the other end of the string. The blade is whirled rapidly so that it presents the flat surface and the sharp edge to the air successively. The bull roarer is often a means of advising the uninitiated to keep their distance. It is sometimes called a buzzer, hummer, or spinning valve.

roasting. Preparing food by keeping it over a fire or surrounding it with hot ashes, embers, sand, or similar materials.

robbery, soil. Early farming methods that lead to the depletion of a soil.

robe. An untailored garment wrapped around the body. It is usually made of a piece of skin.

robe, buffalo. A winter garment made of buffalo hide and used by the Plains Indians. It is often painted and decorated with porcupine quills and similar objects. The robe is usually worn·with the decorated side out, but during rain the fur side is out. It is also used as a spread on tipi floors.

Robenhausian. Referring to the Swiss lake-dwelling phase of the Upper Neolithic period.

rock, acid. Rock rich in silica.

rock, Aeolian. A type of rock composed of wind-drifted materials, used in architectural construction. The drift-sand rock of Bermuda is an example.

rock, Archaean. Rock forming the solid crust or first covering of the earth's surface after it cooled.

rock, crystalline. Volcanic rock that has changed because of pressure and heat.

rock, igneous. Crystalline rock which was once molten and then solidified.

rock, metamorphic. Rock which was igneous or sedimentary and was altered through heat or pressure.

rock, sedimentary. Rock stemming from the erosion of earlier rocks.

rod, Aaron's. A wand supposed to contain the sacred fire used in the Mosaic initiation ceremony. It is a staff with a serpent twined around it, similar to Hermes' caduceus.

rod, lease or **rod, laze.** A device to keep the threads of the warp from entanglement. It is usually placed under and over alternate threads. The lease rod is especially useful if the loom is portable or the work is stopped and recommenced before completion.

roebuck. A male roe deer, very graceful and nimble. It is found in forest country.

role. In Ralph Linton's usage, the dynamic aspect of a status (q.v.). It is the putting of the rights and duties of the status into effect.

rolled. In phonetics, referring to a consonant produced by tapping the tongue against the teeth or the uvula against the back of the tongue.

rolling, mechanical. The weathering or rolling of an artifact from water action, usually being hurled on a beach or rolled in a stream. Mechanical rolling rounds the edges of materials like flint or stone and often destroys fragile materials like bones. The study of the effects of rolling is used as a check rather than as a direct source of information.

Romance. An Indo-European language group including Italian, Catalan, Spanish, French, Rumanian, and Portugese.

rondelle. A round object, especially a disk of bone cut from the cranium.

Rongo. The Polynesian god of agriculture, also in some islands regarded as the god of oratory and eloquence, in others the god of peace, in still others the god of war. Cook (q.v.) was mistaken for the god Rongo. Other forms of the name are Lono, Ro'o, and 'Ono.

rood. A measure equal to 40 square poles (q.v.).

roof, hip. A roof with the end formed by a sloping face enclosed by hips, i.e., external angles formed by the meeting of two sloping roof surfaces.

root. 1 In linguistics, that element of a word left after all flectional endings and formatives have been taken off. The root is usually present in all members of a group of words relating to the same idea, and is thus the ultimate semantic vehicle of a given concept in a language. 2 The portion of a tooth implanted in the socket and within the gingiva.

root, insane. A mandrake or mandragora, which is highly sought for its aphrodisiac and medicinal qualities. It has been used to induce fertility, effect invisibility, find treasure, and arouse love.

Rorschach. A psychological test developed by a Swiss psychoanalyst, Hermann Rorschach, in which the subject describes what he sees in a series of 10 standardized ink blots. On the basis of the subject's report, it is possible to determine his personality structure. The responses are evaluated in terms of sequence and specific formal characters. This test has been used by investigators in various societies to gain information on personality characteristics.

rose, wind. A device to indicate wind direction. The directions were indicated by names instead of degrees.

rosette. A design made by one line connecting a star's extremities, or a collection of intersecting coiled lines.

rostrocarinate. A hypothetical eagle beak core form which has been called the predecessor of the true coup-de-poing (q.v.). It has been considered to be characteristic of the late Pliocene period. The core is a flint nodule with lower and upper flat surfaces and a pointed working end. The terms beak and keel and eagle beak are sometimes used.

round, holy. See CIRCUMAMBULATION.

roving. A loose collection of fibers in one strand. It does not have much twist.

rowlock. A device used as an oar fulcrum in rowing.

royal, blood. The belief that those of kingly ancestry have a unique and special type of blood. In order to keep this hypothetically unique blood pure, persons of the blood royal do not marry outsiders.

rubber, grain. A stone used to grind corn.

rubble. See OUTWASH.

rug, prayer. A Mohammedan floor covering. Each rug has a representation of a mosque or other public temple showing the prayer niche that indicates the direction of Mecca.

rug, primitive felted. Before carding, spinning, and weaving were discovered, the animal skins used for mats and rugs. It is thought that this practice developed into the Asian technique of working hair or fur into a matted texture.

ruga. A Fulani beehive hut.

ruin. In lapidary art, a stone with a cut face exhibiting markings that resemble ruined buildings.

ruk-ruk. The Bougainville version of duk-duk (q.v.).

rule, Allen's. In physiology, the tendency of warm-blooded animals in a cold climate to have the heat-radiating body surfaces reduced through diminishing the extremities and appendages.

rule, Bergmann's. The generalization that in a given wide-ranging warm-blooded animal species, the subgroups in colder climates attain greater size than those in warmer climates. This rule was formulated by Carl Bergmann, a 19th-century German biologist. Recent work by Marshall T. Newman on the physical attributes of Indians south and north of the Equator suggests the applicability of this rule to man, the widest ranging mammal. Newman found aborigines in the tropics were likely to be smaller than those in cooler areas to the south and north.

rule, Gloger's. A statement of the relation between pigmentation and climate. Warm and humid climates tend to be positively associated with much pigmentation. The higher the humidity and temperature, the more eumelanin, while high temperatures and low humidity are associated with phaeomelanin. Cold climates are associated with little pigmentation. These relations hold for lower mammals as well as man.

Rule, Marching. A movement of some natives in the Solomon Is-

lands protectorate toward self government. It was distinguished by extreme efficiency of organization.

rule, Rensch's desert. The generalization that fat stored on the bodies of desert animals will tend to be in lumps.

rule, Rensch's hair. The generalization that animals in colder areas are likely to have hair longer than that of animals in warmer areas.

runes. Angular characters forming an alphabet used by Germanic tribes after the third century A.D. They were believed to have some magical properties and were mainly in memorial, divinatory, and message inscriptions cut on stone, wood, and metal. There are also runic calendars. The runic script has been called the Teutons' national writing. Most scholars suggest the Latin alphabet as the basis of the runes, although there is some evidence that they come from a North Etruscan alphabet. The replacement of runes by the Latin alphabet probably is related to the development of the Catholic Church.

ruuruu. In the Society Islands, protective armor made of wood and covering the upper part of the body. It was padded with thick folds of cloth bound on with rope.

rye. A widely used grain which originated as a weed in grain fields in Asia Minor after the Iron Age. Its kernel matured more easily than those of barley or wheat, so that it was more widely used than they were on the northern edge of the wheat belt and in mountain areas. It is usually grown in dry cool climates or where the soil is poor.

S

sabertooth. An animal often erroneously cited as an example of maladaptation in evolution. It is contended that its canine tooth became so long that it could not bite and was starved into extinction. Actually, sabertooths are found some 40 million years ago and did not become extinct until about 30,000 years ago. During this period the relative size of the canine tooth did not increase and the variations in size were fairly constant.

sac, amniotic. A membranous sac that encloses the embryo in fluid. It is characteristic of all mammals, including man. It is also called the amnionic sac or the amnion.

sacerdotal. Relating to priestly activities.

sacerdotalism. A religion that has a priesthood as its central force. The term is sometimes derogatorily used to describe a philosophy that permits the clergy and ceremonial activities to take precedence over the deeper moral values contained in the religion.

Sachem. The head or peace chief of a tribe or group of New England Indians; by extensior, the head of any group of Indians in northeastern North America.

sacra. Sacred objects.

sacra privata. The ceremonials of family worship in ancient Rome. The father was priest and the children acolytes in observances for the Lares (spirits of ancestors), the Penates (blessers of the family store), and Vesta (goddess of the hearth).

sacra publica. Ceremonials in ancient Rome held on Liberalia (March 16), to mark the Roman youth's assuming the toga virilis, or manhood. After a ceremony at the family altar and in the public forum, the boy was taken to the Capitol and sacrifices were made to the Roman national gods.

sacrament. A rite that gives a natural function a supernatural authority through sanction or positive blessing. A sacramental rite involves a change in the person present at the ritual or in the person for whom the rite is conducted. A sacrament is sometimes defined as the outward sign of a spiritual state of grace. In the majority of nonliterate societies, marriage is not a sacrament. The

466

Catholic sacraments are baptism, confirmation, the eucharist, penance, marriage, holy orders, and extreme unction. Some Christian rites are not unlike nonliterate rites. Baptism is analogous to an infant's being received by its group through lustration. Confirmation is analogous to initiation (q.v.) ceremonies. Penance is not unlike the public confession of groups like the Manus. Extreme unction has no immediate analogue but may be related to some rites in which a dead person is helped into an appropriate condition after death, rather than being given a spiritual easing out of life. In early societies, the rites de passage (q.v.) are the most significant sacramental rituals. They involve a permanent change in the person, while a sacramental rite like communion marks a temporary change.

sacrifice. The giving, sometimes including the destruction, of a symbolic offering for religious or sacred purposes. It may consist of food or drink tendered to the object of the sacrifice. Among the explanatory theories is that the sacrifice is a gift to the god for present or future favors. The substitutionary theory has it that sacrifice is a means of atoning for sin, with the sacrificed animal's death symbolizing the death of the sacrificer. The sacramental theory sees sacrifice as a means of the sacrificer's attaining a kind of sanctity through the device of the sacrifice. The communion theory suggests that sacrifice is a kind of symbolic eating of the god.

Sacrifice is a major part of early religion and is also found in ad-vanced religions like Shintoism, Brahmanism, Taoism, Buddhism, and others. Food and drink, flowers, incense, and whole burnt animals are widely found offerings and such times as the solstices, the fall, and the new moon are commonly celebrated by sacrifice. Sacrifice is present in almost all ritual observances. The death of the victim may be accomplished in many ways, and the body is usually disposed of in a manner similar to the disposition of the dead in the culture.

sacrifice, arrow. The sacrifice of a flaming arrow by shooting it at the sun. It is found in the southern part of the United States and in Mexico.

sacrifice, building. In ancient times, slaying a person and placing the corpse as a sacrifice in the wall or at the foundation of a new building. This gave the building a protective spirit. The sacrifice was often an especially purchased child. The term foundation sacrifice is also used.

sacrifice, child. A public function involving the ritual killing of a child. The sacrifice usually was not arranged by the parents. Often the victim was the first born, who was destroyed so that additional progeny might be granted.

sacrifice, foundation. See SACRIFICE, BUILDING.

sacrifice, human. Human sacrifice is usually found in comparatively advanced cultures, e.g., the Peruvians. Generally the benefit of the whole community is intended, including such ends as saving crops, stopping epidemics, removing barrenness, and obtaining victory or good weather. A sacrifice may also be a scapegoat (q.v.), a messenger to the gods, or a guarantor of safe passage.

sacrifice, White Dog. The immolation by the Iroquois of a white dog at the New Year. This ceremony was in response to a dream of the god Teharonhiawagon, who personifies life.

sacrum. The fused part of the vertebral column, to which the pelvic girdle and ilia are attached.

sacs, laryngeal. Air sacs, occurring in most anthropoid apes, that communicate with the larynx' ventricles. They can be inflated.

sadhu. A Hindu holy person or religious teacher. He has a bowl for begging, a staff, rosary, water pot, and brush. He usually wears a light colored robe and often coats his body with ashes. He sleeps outdoors and is buried in a sitting position when he dies, since he is believed to be in a trance.

saga. A historical or legendary story dealing with the early Norse kings. Included are stories of the first settlement of Iceland 930-1030 A.D., sagas of the legendary past, and translations of foreign romances into Scandinavian languages and saga form. Some Norse sagas were orally transmitted before they were recorded.

sagaic. See ASSEGAI.

sagamore. A leader among the Algonkians and other New England Indian groups.

Sagen. In German folklore, tales that deal with historical events.

sagger. A container used to protect fragile pottery during the firing process.

sagittal. Referring to the median antero-posterior plane of the body or a plane parallel thereto.

sago. A dry mealy material or granulated paste that comes from the pith of various palms, like the sago palm, especially in Indonesia.

saguaro. A giant columnar cactus found in Arizona, Mexico, and Central America. Some Indian groups, like the Pima, used it to make a syrup and an intoxicating beverage.

sagum. A hooded cloak of the La Tène period.

saiga. An antelope that resembles a sheep. It is found in steppe country.

sail. The foot of a sail is the lower margin, the luff the anterior margin, the leech the posterior margin, the throat the anterior top corner, the peak the posterior top corner, the tack the anterior bottom corner, and the clew the posterior bottom corner.

sail, lateen. A triangular sail that is extended by a long yard slung to the mast, which is likely to be low. It is found on the Mediterranean and among Arab seamen.

sailing, great circle. Navigation that follows circles with centers at the earth's center, rather than what would appear to be the shortest course on a map.

St. Elmo's fire. See FIRE, ST. ELMO'S.

saka. The Hindu year.

sakti. Among Hindus, supernatural power that averts the evil eye

468

or the female component or energy in the gods. In art, it is a triangle that points downward, perhaps symbolizing the male and female forces in a state of harmony (see YIN; YANG). Often, especially in Tibetan art, the unity of the male and female elements is represented by a carnal embrace of the god and his sakti.

salenodont. A flat low unpointed cusp, found on omnivores and herbivores.

salt. Sodium chloride, used to preserve and season food. It is obtained from rock salt, or from certain plant ashes, by boiling salt spring water or brine, or by letting sea water evaporate in flat pans. Early men who lived on fish or meat did not need extra salt for their diet. As vegetables became used for food and there was a move from the sea, salt was more necessary. As a preservative, salt acquired a symbolic meaning of permanence and purity that led to its being used in religious offerings and to affirm important social arrangements.

saltation. In evolution, a new taxonomic group originating in a single step. There has not been any wide acceptance of this evolution by leaps since its promulgation by Schindewolf.

salting. A technique of preserving food by coating it liberally with salt.

salutation, weeping. In South America, greeting those who are coming back from a journey with overt signs of grief. It may represent feelings of commiseration, or the one arriving may be asked to mourn for members of the group who have died.

sambaqui. A prehistoric kitchen midden found on the Brazilian coast.

samisen. A lutelike Japanese musical instrument to accompany songs and dances. It has three strings played with a bone pick.

Samoa. Fourteen volcanic islands in the South Seas inhabited by Polynesians.

Samoyed. A language or dialect group spoken by some 10,000 persons in Asiatic Russia and made up of Yenisei-Samoyed, Ostyak Samoyed, and Sayan (or Southern Samoyed). It is a member of the Finno-Ugric subfamily of the Ural-Altaic family. The Samoyeds call the language *Nenets;* the Russian meaning of Samoyed is "cannibal."

sampan. An open skiff found in the Far East. It is shallow, wedge-shaped, and with a broad beam in the after end. The rail of the gunwale continues beyond the stern as a curved projection facing upward. The sampan is usually sculled with two long handled oars.

samurai. The Japanese lower nobility or military officials.

sanction. A society's reaction to behavior, either approval (positive sanction) or disapproval (negative sanction). Negative sanctions are generally more definitely outlined than positive.

sanction, legal or **sanction, organized.** A penalty involving force that may be imposed for the violation of a particular norm.

sanctuary. A place that provides a haven for an accused person, especially against an avenger. It is usually a sacred building or a consecrated grove. The fear of profaning a sacred spot kept pursuers from violating a sanctuary. See REFUGE, CITY OF; ASYLUM.

sandal. A primitive kind of footgear consisting of leather covering the sole of the foot and held in place by thongs crossing the foot.

sandalwood. A compact and closely grained heartwood of an Indo-Malayan parasitic tree (*Santalum album*). Its wood is fragrant.

sandhi. Phonetic modification and modulation of a word when it is included with other forms. A sandhi-form is the form found when a word is included with others. See FORM, ABSOLUTE.

sandhi, compulsory. A sandhi the usage of which is mandatory, e.g., using *an* for *a* before a word beginning with a vowel.

sandhi, optional. A sandhi which is not mandatory because there is an unaltered variant of the form, usually with a more formal implication, e.g., *can't* for *cannot*.

Sandia. Referring to a pre-Folsom culture. It includes some rough side scrapers, end scrapers, cutting tools, and projectile points which are thicker, larger, and heavier than the Folsom point (q.v.) and less finely chipped. Sandia implements are shouldered but not channeled.

sandr. Sheets of glacifluvial sand and gravel.

sandstone. A stone of quartz sand from the disintegration of older rocks cemented by clay, oxide of iron or silica, and calcium carbonate.

It has been widely used for building.

sannup. A male member of an American Indian community who is married to a squaw.

sansa. A musical instrument consisting of several flexible tongues one end of which is attached to a resonant object or board. The tongues are attached to a bridge, so that their free ends vibrate easily when they are plucked. Notes can be produced by varying the length of the tongues.

Santa Marta urn. See URN, SANTA MARTA.

sapphire. A gem widely used for good luck, health, and to cure disease.

sarcophagus. The outer stone casing in which the mummy (q.v.), with its wooden coffins, was kept. Sarcophagi were made of the hardest and best stone available and exhibited excellent workmanship. The shape and decorations varied.

sari. A silk or cotton outer garment worn by Hindu women. It consists of a rectangular fabric wrapped around the person, usually as the chief garment.

sarnai. A raft consisting of a pole or bedstead spread over two or more inflated animal skins. It is found in parts of India.

sarong. A garment for both sexes, consisting of a long cloth strip, the ends of which are sewn together. It is worn like a petticoat, tucked around the waist. It is especially common in the Malay Archipelago and in parts of India.

satem. Those languages of the Indo-European family in which the gutteral (*k*) sound of the proto-Indo-European classification has evolved into the sibilant (*s*) found in Balto-Slavic, Albanian, Armenian, and Indo-Iranian.

sati. See SUTTEE.

satrap. A provincial governor of ancient Persia.

saturation, zone of. The portion of the earth's surface that is saturated with water.

saturnalia. A period of considerable license. It may occur at times of crisis, or regularly as part of an emotionally important activity, like the harvest-home. The Ashanti *Apo* ceremony was an example of license in which, once a year, people speak out on whatever has been bothering them. In ancient Rome, the saturnalia (named for the creator of the universe and the deposed ruler over the vanished Golden Age) featured extreme sexual license and a reversal of the roles of master and servant or slave.

satyr. A spirit of male sexuality in Greek legend. The hindquarters were typically those of a goat and the ears were pointed. See NYMPH.

savage, noble. The concept, developed by Rousseau and 18th- and 19th-century romantics, that primitive man, being in a state of nature and unaffected by the corruptions of civilization, in his conduct demonstrates the virtue and honor inherent in man. Among the writers who have presented the noble savage with greatest art are James Fenimore Cooper and René de Chateaubriand.

savagery. A state of society characterized by a hypothetical cultural stage in which there are no crops or language. Modern anthropologists try to avoid this term, because of its vagueness and pejorative connotations. V. Gordon Childe has used it to describe the earliest human organization, in which gathering and hunting predominated. Gustav Klemm, in the mid-19th century, suggested that human beings have developed through the three stages of savagery, tameness, and freedom. In 1795, Condorcet had shown the development of primitives from savagery to animal husbandry, agriculture, the alphabet, and enlightenment.

savanna. In low latitudes, a wide zone with both grasslands and forests. The tree growth is usually scattered.

savin. A plant widely used by European witches and called the Devil's herb. It was an agent to bring on abortions and sterility.

saw. A denticulated flake. It is sometimes called a scie.

saw, fire. A device for fire-making in Malaysia. A split bamboo is sawed, with the dust dropping and being ignited by the heat occasioned by the friction. It is concentrated in the East Indies, but is also found in Australia and the Asiatic mainland. It is related to the fire plow (q.v.).

saw, flint. A piece of flint, usually about two or three inches long, fixed in the groove of a wooden blade. Many such tools were found among the ruins of the Swiss lake dwellings.

sawak. Wet land rice fields.

Sbaïkian. A Middle Paleolithic industry discovered near Sbaïkia in North Africa and comprising a variety of chipped stone implements intermediate in type between Acheulian and Solutrean blades.

sbieco. A cutting edge formed by two planes with an inclination different from the implement's plane of symmetry .

scale, weight beam. A scale used in somatometry, usually expressed in grams.

scalping. Among some North American Indians, cutting off part of the scalp, with hair, of an enemy. The victim did not necessarily die.

scapegoat. A creature that symbolically carries the sins of a society. The term was derived from the Hebrew practice on the Day of Atonement of having the high priest transfer to a goat selected at random the transgressions of the Jews during the past year, after which the goat was taken away or killed. During the Thargelia Festival, the Athenians beat and then dismissed two human scapegoats. The term scapegoat has come to be applied to the process of blaming a group's or individual's difficulties on another, as Hitler did with the Jews. Some Pacific Islanders use plants for scapegoating and discard them in running water.

scaphocephaly. A condition in which there is a keel-like projection from the front to the back of the skull.

scaphoid. Being in the shape of a boat.

scapulomancy. Predicting the future by the study of the bones of animals, often by interpreting the cracks developing in a shoulder blade (scapula) which has been heated in a fire.

scar, bulbar. A small flake facet on the bulb of percussion (q.v.), often produced naturally when the main flake flint is detached.

scar, flake. A rippled hollow on the parent lump of flint, which shows a negative bulb of percussion (q.v.).

scarab. In Egypt, an amulet (q.v.) in the shape of a beetle. Scarabs were made in almost all kinds of material known at the time. They were associated with the god Khepera, who moved the sun across the sky as the beetle rolled its ball. The sacred beetle was worshipped as a symbol of fertility and resurrection. A scarab was put in a corpse's body to replace the heart, and later it was placed in the mummy bandages. The different positions represented different meanings. Most high-ranking individuals used scarabs as a seal.

scaraboid. An oblong stone that is flat on one side and convex on the other. It derives its name from similarity in shape to the scarab beetle.

scarification. Cutting the skin for beautification, bloodletting, ritual, or self-torture.

scarnimento. The practice of cutting the flesh from a corpse before burial.

Schaber. See SCRAPER, SIDE.

Scheffer, John (1621-1679). 17th-century Swedish scholar, at the University of Uppsala. He wrote the first adequate ethnological discussion, *A History of Lappland* (1674).

schizophrenia. A psychosis characterized by a withdrawn personality that has lost contact with reality.

Schliemann, Heinrich (1822-1890). A German business man who retired when 46 to devote himself to the study of Greek archaeology. His excavations at Mycenae were followed with avid interest. In his excavations at Hissarlik, he aimed to prove that the Homeric account of the city of Troy was accurate. Although he incorrectly identified the second of seven superimposed cities at Hissarlik as Homeric Troy, he established the historical truth of Homer and, moreover, discovered the Eastern Mediterranean civilizations of the pre-Hellenic period. His work dramatized the potentials and methods of modern prehistoric archaeology. The romantic nature of his quest and his results served to humanize both archaeology and the ancient civilizations. He was the first to excavate a tell (q.v.) and to apply stratigraphic principles to excavating a mound.

Schnurkeramik. Cord-imprinted pottery of the Neolithic era in Europe. Twisted cords are pressed into the paste before it is fired. The terms corded pottery and string ceramics are also used.

school, bush. A puberty school in the Congo.

school, puberty. A school where young persons are trained in the puberty rites or in the nature of their post-pubertal status. The school is conducted usually before the puberty ceremony itself, as in Australia and Africa.

schotterfelder. Outwash (q.v.) deposits resulting from glacial action.

schumgha. A musical instrument of Africa consisting of a single back bow string. The string is attached to a bow shaft held horizontally between the hollow of the performer's thumb and his teeth. The sound is produced by blowing on the back of the bow. The schumgha is thought by some to be the most primitive of African instruments.

Schurtz, Heinrich (1863-1903). A German student of Ratzel who summarized the associational activities other than blood-ties which previous writings had ignored. Although he underestimated the associational activities of women, he emphasized the influence of men's organizations.

scie. See SAW.

science, hierarchy of. The orderly classification of the sciences in terms of the comparative complexity of their data, the degree of methodological precision, their interdependence, and the precision of their predictions. Physics is usually regarded as the highest science and the physical sciences generally are higher in this putative hierarchy than the social sciences. Anthropology is usually regarded in this hierarchy as one of the social sciences, although physical anthropology in particular is increasingly using the methods of the physical sciences.

science, mantic. Divination (q.v.) through the use of portents and signs.

473

scoop, ice. An Eskimo artifact used to remove chips from a hole chopped in the ice. It is usually a ladle made of baleen.

scopelism. Throwing charmed stones into a neighbor's field. It is sometimes intended to warn persons thinking about cultivating the field that they may die through the arts of those who threw the stones. The term scopelism sometimes is used to describe casting stones on the grave of one who died a dishonorable or violent death.

scraper. 1 An implement of flint used to scrape leather and remove fat from the under side of a skin and to smooth wood. It is retouched usually on one face only. The term scraper is sometimes used for flint implements that cannot otherwise be classified. 2 A notched musical instrument which is scraped. It may possess magical properties and express fertility symbolism.

scraper, beaked. A fairly rare form of scraper, a curved flint flake with a point like a beak. Either the convex or the concave side of the beak may be used for scraping. This implement began appearing in the Mousterian period and lasted until the Campignian. The beaked scraper is also called the grattoir à bec.

scraper, carinate. A Middle Aurignacian thick scraper that looks like an inverted boat. It has a flat base and a raised back. The scraping edge is at the end. There are characteristic long channelled flaked trimmings.

scraper, concave. A rough stone flake on the side of which there is a curved notch. It was used mainly for finishing wooden and bone weapons.

scraper, convex. A rough stone flake with a convex working edge, mainly used for scraping animal skins.

scraper, core. A scraper that resembles a small cone, with a working edge made by the intersection of a flat plane surface with several irregular flutings. The core scraper is sometimes called a tea cosy.

scraper, disk. A circular disk shaped like the ordinary side scraper (q.v.) and with a scraping edge at one side and an untouched edge at the other side for grasping. This implement is unusual in that the secondary chipping forming the edge is on the smooth or inner side of the flake.

scraper, double. A side scraper both edges of which are trimmed.

scraper, end. A scraper with the working end at the ends of blades or flakes. There is sometimes much fluting (q.v.). One short side was sharpened and used for scraping. The end scraper is sometimes called the kratzer.

scraper, hide. See FLESHER, HIDE.

scraper, keel-shaped nose. A large heavy flat-bottomed core with one well-worked nose. It is often large enough to be grasped by hand and may have been used like a push plane.

scraper, keeled. A scraper with narrow regular flutings that rise fan-wise to a point on the keel of the core or flake. It is very attractive. It dates from the Middle Aurignacian era.

scraper, keeled round. A small rounded scraper, umbrella-shaped, with chips removed to a peak in its center. It has sharp outer edges and was probably used for general scraping.

scraper, Levallois. A tool made by striking a flake from the nodule with one blow so that the face of the inner side is smooth and shows the bulb of percussion (q.v.). The edges of the outer side are trimmed by chipping, probably so that the flake could be used to scrape the inner surfaces of hides. The Levallois scraper is especially associated with the Mousterian period in Northern France.

scraper, Mousterian side. A scraper made by trimming the edge of a large flake into a somewhat convex form by step flaking (q.v.). Its sharp convex edge made it highly suitable for scraping skins.

scraper, nose. A scraper on which there is a small nose-shaped protuebrance that forms the scraping edge.

scraper, notched. A scraper with a fairly semicircular notch in its edge. It is touched with secondary chipping all around. It appeared in the Middle Mousterian period and is adapted for the scraping of round surfaces. The notched scraper is also called the **lame à encoche.**

scraper, round. A small circular flake that is sharpened practically all around its circumference. It is also called the thumb scraper.

scraper, side. A flake-tool with a sharp cutting edge formed by the intersection of the main flake surface with some small flake scars. Its working edge is usually convex, and the tool may be trapezoidal, rectangular, or triangular. It was probably mainly used to scrape the interior of hides in the preparation of garments. The side scraper appears chiefly in the Middle Mousterian period. The side scraper is also called the Schaber.

scraper, thumb. See SCRAPER, ROUND.

scratcher, head. A bone, wood, or shell object used to scratch the head without disturbing the coiffure.

scree. A pile of debris at a cliff base. The term talus is also used.

screen, fire. In Southwest American archaeology, a structure of undetermined function. Some archaeologists have suggested that the fire screen was used to block air from blowing on the fire, while the ventilator conducted air into the chamber. It has also been suggested that the ventilator afforded ingress and egress to the spirits and the fire screen was actually an altar.

screw, water. A device, developed by Archimedes, for raising water from a stream by action of a wooden cylinder, with power coming from men on a treadmill.

script, round. The contemporary Burmese writing, which consists largely of soft curves and circles or parts of circles. This unusual shape is largely due to the Burmese writing material being palm leaves on which the stylus traces.

Scripture, Diamond. A Buddhist document which is the first (A.D. 868) whole book to be found. It was printed in China and found in Tunhuang, Kansu province.

scrying. Divination (q.v.) by examining crystals or water.

sculpture, footprint. The representation of human or animal footprints in rock by North American Indians. There may be several footprints together. The purpose of these representations is obscure.

scutiform. Referring to a shield-shaped object, found in early art.

scythe. An implement used to mow by hand. It comprises a long curved blade attached to a bent handle. Scythes are classified according to whether they have long or short handles.

seal. A device that makes an impression in a soft material. It consists of a surface in which a name or inscription is cut. Seals are either flat or cylindrical, permitting a stamped or rolled impression. They are found in Mesopotamia ca. 3000 B.C. and were used in Egypt, Greece, and Rome. After the decline of the Roman Empire, they were not used very widely until late in the eighth century. In the 11th century Edward the Confessor was responsible for the pendant seal, which was attached to the document with a strip of parchment; this was the beginning of the great seal.

seal, cylinder. A fairly small stone cylinder that is rolled across a soft surface to leave an impression. The cylinder is carved in intaglio so that the image produced is in relief. Seal cylinders of distinctive design were used before writing was invented, originally to mark personal property; a package was sealed with clay and the cylinder rolled over it. After the growth of writing, such seal impressions were used to legalize documents on clay tablets. Cylinder seals first appeared in the fourth millennium B.C. in Uruk, and represent Mesopotamia's most important contribution to art. They were used for 3,000 years. Crude pictographs (q.v.) followed the introduction of the Uruk seal.

The Egyptians adapted the seal around 3100 B.C. and used a longer and slender shape with more decorative motifs and a more decorative type of writing, with hieroglyphics replacing cuneiform. Around 2300 B.C., the stamp seal appeared simultaneously in Egypt and western Asia. The stamp seal in Egypt gave rise to the button seal and the scarab seal. The use of seals in Egypt began declining around the time of the beginning of the New Kingdom, ca. 1500 B.C.

seal, Solomon's. See DAVID, STAR OF.

seasonal ceremony. See CEREMONY, SEASONAL.

Sebilian. Referring to the Aurignacian (q.v.) culture in Egypt.

seccotine. A cement used in archaeological work in dry climates to repair objects temporarily.

Secondary. A period or rock system, known as the age of reptiles (see MESOZOIC). Also, material formed after some other material, especially ores or minerals which result from the effect of atmospheric agencies or downward moving water on ores or minerals of an early generation.

section. A bilinear kin group and marriage-regulating division of some Australian societies; formerly called a class.

section, golden. A proportion such that a given line is bissected to make the shorter part in the same relation to the longer part as the longer part is to the whole. This concept of harmonious proportion has been found repeatedly in the history of cultures. Its best known exposition is in the writings of various Greek philosophers.

sections, law of three. A basic tenet in Chinese landscape painting, calling for ground, trees, and mountains as the three levels of composition.

sedan chair. See CHAIR, SEDAN.

sedentes. Individuals who remain in one place, often used for nonmigrants as compared to migrants.

seed. An annual plant with edible seeds, the plants most widely used for food, e.g., the cereals, legumes, and oil-seed plants.

segregation. See PURITY, GAMETIC.

seine. A large net used to catch a school of fish. It has floats on the upper edge and sinkers on its lower edges. It is thrown into the water to cover a large area and is then pulled to land.

seismology. The scientific study of earthquakes.

sekhem. The holy place in an Egyptian temple.

selection. The process of competition between a mutated and a nonmutated organism of a species.

selection, artificial. Permitting or restraining the reproduction of individual specimens so as to bring out certain traits and eliminate others. Artificial selection essentially is selective breeding.

selection, counter. Social forces of selection that operate in such a way as to give the biologically inferior an edge. War, with the toll it takes of the vigorous and healthy, has sometimes been regarded as making a counter selection of the weak and ill, who are exempt from military service.

selection, natural. The tendency of an adaptively valuable variation in an organism to become widespread because the individuals endowed with it have a better chance of surviving to reproductive maturity and passing the trait on to their offspring. In 1842, Darwin wrote that favorable variations facilitate survival while unfavorable may lead to extermination. Wallace developed a similar theory in 1858, when he and Darwin gave a joint paper. Darwin's *Origin of Species* (1859) developed the theory in detail. See EVOLUTION, BIOLOGICAL.

selection, sexual. The tendency of traits that make an individual attractive as a mate to become more widespread. It has been observed that certain traits that attract females, e.g., gaudy feathers in male birds, are deterrents to the survival of the species.

selection, social. The control of marriage and breeding by the application of artificial social barriers, so that mating takes place between persons who meet these social standards instead of at random. All human reproduction manifests social selection to some degree.

selenite. An ancient substitute for glass. It is crystallized gypsum which can be split into very thin sheets.

self-help. The process of avenging a wrong without any judicial assistance. Self-help is legally permissible in cases where it may be accomplished without violence or disorder. Thus, a landowner may demolish an encroaching wall, provided he does not use explosives or other dangerous means.

self-preservation. The attempt on the part of human beings to keep alive in the face of change. It is assumed that animals are motivated by such a drive, and some evidence exists to show that early man had a concept of something other than the body which was to be preserved.

selva. In the Amazon, a rain forest.

semantics. The systematic study of the meanings of words.

sememe. The meaning of a morpheme. Each sememe is presumed to have a specific unit of meaning.

semi-Mongoloid. A hypothetical Caucasoid-Mongoloid hybrid.

Semite. The name Semite—taken from Shem (or Sem), the son of Noah—was used for the first time in 1781 by A. L. Schlözer. The Arabian peninsula was probably the homeland of the Semites. They probably left Arabia in waves: ca. 3000 B.C. (Amorites), 2500 B.C. (Akkadians), 2000 B.C. (Canaanite-Phoenicians), 1500 B.C. (Arameans and Hebrews), and 500 B.C. (Nabataeans). Although the languages of these groups are related closely, their anthropological characteristics and religions vary considerably.

The monotheistic salvation religions—Judaism, Christianity, Islam—developed from the religion of the early Semites. It has been claimed that the first Semitic religion was monotheism (Renan), totemism (Robertson Smith), ancestor worship (Spencer), or polydemonism (Wellhausen). The early Semites were probably polydemonistic, regarding ritual objects and natural sites as the home of a separate spirit, usually called an *il,* although some were given personal names and were worshipped regularly. Some of these gods were attached to a domicile and others moved with the tribes. *El* became the proper name of a given god. At first there was no regular priesthood; the polytheism of the civilized Semitic kingdoms followed, and then the monotheistic religions. The nomadic Semites had a feeling of tribal solidarity, largely based on blood ties.

Semitic. A language group, part of the Semito-Hamitic family. Its two branches, East Semitic and West Semitic, are in turn divided into the extinct Akkadian language and Northern West Semitic and Southern West Semitic. The word roots of these languages are characterized by the inclusion of three consonants. Syntactically, they are characterized by a two-gender system. Current languages are Arabic, Ethiopian, Hebrew, and Maltese. Extinct languages include Phoenician, Moabite, Babylonian, Assyrian, and Canaanite.

Semitic-Hamitic. A family of languages with Cushite, Berber, Egyptian, and Semitic branches.

Semitism, anti-. See ANTI-SEMITISM.

semivowel. See VOWEL, SEMI-.

semn. Butter made of goat's milk, found in the Middle East.

sepo. In the Congo, a wooden charm thought to bring strength, courage and good luck.

septum. The cartilaginous dividing wall between the halves of the nose.

sending. An object or person, usually associated with some worker of magic, dispatched to cause difficulty for a victim. The impoliteness of pointing derives from its early use as a kind of sending.

senilicide. Killing of the aged. It is also called geronticide.

sennit. A braided cordage made of spun yarn or rope yarn, of which three or more threads are plaited. It is usually flat but may be round or square. In Oceania, sennit usually refers to a widely used coconut fiber braid. The spelling sinnet is also found.

sentence. In a language, the largest unit which has an internal grammatical organization and is characterized by an over-all or terminal intonational contour.

sentence, minor. A sentence not conforming to one of the language's favorite forms.

seppuku. See HARA KIRI.

sept. A group of persons associated through descent, usually measured through both the male and female lineage (q.v.) It is usually a local group which is part of a larger social group. In early Ireland, a tribal division with its own territory and village community.

Septuagint. The Alexandrian Greek into which the Egyptian Jews translated their Old Testament.

Sequoya. A half-breed Cherokee who invented a writing system for Cherokee.

Serdab. An Arabic word meaning a hidden chamber.

serf. One living on land and hereditarily obligated to perform certain duties to the person holding title. The serf generally farms but may have some other trade. Serfdom usually involves a kind of half-free status along with peasant tenure. It occurs when there is a weak central government, little trade, and usually, animal power. The serf is mostly found in conjunction with feudalism and in economies of fairly low grade, where there is more concern about the supply of labor than of land. The serf is in a condition of servitude related to custom, while one in slavery (q.v.) is dependent on his owner's whim.

Sergi, Giuseppe (1841-1936). An Italian anthropologist who viewed anthropology as the study of man, including the social elements of man's life, with sociology and psychology subbranches. He held that craniometry would prove anything one wanted and that physical indices might mask many individual differences. Sergi emphasized the importance of drawings and photographs in the study of physical differences. He published a detailed study of the Mediterranean race, including their physical and cultural characteristics and started the first Italian anthropological society and journal.

seriation. Arranging artifacts in some sequence, especially arranging pottery artifacts in a chronological series. Seriation is used to study the development of a quantitative picture of the chronological sequence of artifact development by placing samples of cultural materials in sequence of the rise and fall of specific types.

seriation, typological. The study of the chronological development of a type of artifact or art form. It has been used most widely to trace the evolution of specific artifact categories. This kind of seriation was originally used, mainly in the Old World, for descriptive purposes, so that artifacts could be placed in classes which were roughly alike. In the 1920s, archaeologists working in the American Southwest began to establish types in order to determine chronology. This concept of types enabled them to deal with the changes that took place during a given period so that the stream of cultural evolution could be followed. This work was originally done on middens, and the analysis of their fragments helped make clear the development and evolution of key artifacts, such as water bottles.

series. In phonology, horizontally listing a row of phonemes (q.v.) with the criterion of their relevant feature, e.g., voiceless series *(p, t, k)*, voiced series *(b, d, g)*.

series, typological. See SERIATION, TYPOLOGICAL.

Serpent Mound. A structure in Adams County, Ohio, of the early mound builders, more than 1,000 feet long. It is shaped like a snake with a large mound 39 by 110 feet at the head. Most researchers agree that it was built for burial or ceremonial reasons.

service, bride or **service, suitor.** Winning a wife by working for the parents of the bride, usually before the marriage takes place. This service is often in place of paying a bride price (q.v.).

service, marriage by. Marriage in which the groom moves in with the wife's family and works for them, e.g., among the Winnebago and Chuckchee.

service, suitor. See SERVICE, BRIDE.

set, age or **class, age.** A formally established group of persons of about the same age. The members may advance through age grades which have special ceremonies or military, ritual, or status activities at each level.

setekh. The mummification (q.v.) process in ancient Egypt.

seten hetep ta. The beginning of the formula found on Egyptian tombs, and a sort of prayer for benefits for the dead.

settings, heliacal. The times of the year at which some bright stars are last seen setting after sunset. See RISINGS, HELIACAL.

seven-color ware. See WARE, SEVEN-COLOR.

Sewall Wright effect. See DRIFT, GENETIC.

sex, heterogametic. That sex in which one pair of chromosomes is of unlike form.

sexagesimal. Referring to a system for counting in which 60 is a basic unit, e.g., the Babylonian.

sex-influenced. A characteristic, the expression of which hinges on sex, e.g., baldness.

sex-limited. A factor expressed in one sex but not the other. Its expression hinges on whether or not certain hormonal elements are present.

sex-linked. A trait present in the sex chromosomes.

sgraffito. In some early art, blackening a rock surface and then scratching around the outlines of the object drawn to achieve a relief effect. It is also a ceramic technique in which the design is made by scratching through an overglaze to reveal the different under-color. It was common in the Mediterranean area and also in Peru, where it was a parallelism (q.v.).

sha t'ai. The Chinese term for stoneware (q.v.).

shadoof. A pole on an upright post, or on a horizontal beam supported by two brick or mud columns, with a weight at one end serving to balance a bucket. It was used to dip water from the Nile.

shaft. 1 The section of a column between the capital and the base. 2 A vertical passage or excavation.

shaft, burial. A very deep grave. In Peru and Colombia, some burial shafts are 80 feet deep.

Shaker. A combination of Christian and Indian religions, originating with the Skokomish Indians of Washington in the late 19th century. Also, a Quaker group which displays strong emotionalism and some physical convulsions, whence the name.

shakti. See SAKTI.

shale. A fissile rock resulting from the combination of mud, silt, or clay. It has a finely stratified structure and is made up of minerals which have largely been unaltered since their original deposition.

shaman. Originally a Siberian medicine man; by extension, a medicine man in any primitive society. A shaman has supernatural power which stems from its original source, to which he has access. He has not only the power to cure but sometimes also the power to harm. Some societies had contests among the shamans.

Among the Siberian Chukchee, a shaman was a man who lived as a woman, taking the passive role in sodomy. The shamans and their "husbands" sometimes both had female mistresses. See HOMOSEXUAL.

shamanism. Religious practices based on the theory that a spirit outside the individual takes possession of him and that he thereafter operates only when motivated by the spirit. These practices were prevalent among the American Indians and in Siberia.

Shang. In China, a culture period extending ca. 1600 to ca. 1100 B.C. Writing, fairly advanced bronze artifacts, domestication of animals, and great underground tombs appeared. This culture in many ways

481

was similar to the earlier Near East bronze civilizations.

shape, beaker. A cylindrical form flaring at both ends or at one end. It is frequently used as a general style for flower vases and is often found in old pewter.

shape, shovel. See INCISOR, SHOVEL-SHAPE.

shapeshifter. Something or someone that can change in appearance. The shapeshifters may be forces for good or for evil. They may change appearance under specific conditions or permanently. Humans may assume the appearance of animals and vice versa, and gods may become mortals. Ghosts may also change their appearance. **Shapeshifting** is a transformation (q.v.) that occurs either voluntarily or without help from outside sources.

shaping. The process of giving a shape to pottery, by coiling, placing sections together, or patting.

shard or **potshard.** A pottery fragment that may give valuable archaeological clues. Often, even though few or no entire examples of pots will be extant at a site, some shards may be found since they are nearly indestructible. The spellings **sherd** and **potsherd** are also found.

Shari'a. The law of Islam, which includes Allah's rules for human conduct.

shears. An instrument that cuts by opposing two edges of metal.

sheath, penis. A protective covering for the male organ used among some peoples who otherwise wear no clothes. It may vary from a small cone which merely caps the penis, as among some Ge groups of east- ern Brazil, to a long, hollow gourd covering the entire member, as among some Pygmies of Dutch New Guinea.

shed. The open space between lifted and nonlifted warps through which the weft passes.

shedding. In weaving, creating a shed, or an opening, among several warp threads. See HEDDLE.

shedding of the skin. See SKIN, CASTING OF THE.

sheer. On a boat, the longitudinal curve of the gunwale.

sheets. On a sailboat, ropes that keep the sails at the appropriate angle with the wind when they are tied to the boom or the clew of the sail.

sheikh esh-sheshad. A war sheikh, who leads his people in battle.

shekel. A lump of silver of a given weight, used by the Babylonians as money.

shelf, continental. An underwater land platform that extends almost horizontally from the shore of each continent and ends in a fairly steep slope. It may vary from a few miles to 1,000 miles wide.

shelf, simian. A bony shelf between the two sides of the lower jaw in modern large apes. It developed along with an enlargement of the incisors. The simian shelf is not present in man.

shelter, rock. An early habitation of some early men, consisting of shelter from the weather provided by rocks, often under overhanging cliffs. Some such shelters are inhabited today in parts of Spain and France.

sherd. See SHARD.

shield. A defensive device to protect the body, usually carried on the arm or held in the hand. There are many different shapes. It was derived from the parrying stick.

shield, parrying. A shield for diverting the weapons of an opponent.

shieling. In Scotland, a group of huts where people lived during their stay at the summer pastures.

shift, language. The change from the everyday language of a bilingual person to other language that he uses less frequently.

shift, Mainean. The movement from status to contract in the development of early law, postulated by Sir Henry Maine (q.v.). It is noticed especially clearly in the period after the growth of cities, as the kinship tie becomes less important. In nonliterate societies, this shift is from regulation of the social norms by the individual and his kin group to the representatives of the larger social group.

shift, semantic. A transfer of meaning, so that a word acquires additional meaning.

shift, sound. An alteration in a phoneme (q.v.) which is seen as regularly recurrent in the evolution of a language, e.g., the change from *p* to *f* in the Germanic word for *father* (compare Latin *pater*).

shifts, Germanic sound. The first and second Germanic sound shifts. The first took place before Christ and separated the Proto-Germanic languages from the remainder of the Indo-European family of languages. The second occurred over the period between the first century B.C. and the eighth century A.D. These two sound shifts divided the Germanic languages into a High German and a Low German dialect group.

shimbi. In the Congo, a fairy or genii.

shinny. A widely distributed women's game among the American Indians. The participants propel a ball toward the opponents' goal with a canelike stick; they are not permitted to touch the ball with their hands.

ship, death. A coffin shaped like a boat or a stone-lined boat-shaped grave, suggesting a belief in a voyage to another world after death. Death ships have been found in southern England and other parts of the world.

ship, magic. A ship that is exceptionally large or has other special qualities.

ship, plank. A ship made of a minimum of three planks, one on each side and one on the bottom.

shipapulima. See SIPAPU.

shiwanna. Among the Cochiti, a masked dancer .

shoes, dead. Shoes given the dead so that they may use them in their trip to the nether regions. This old custom has survived almost to the present. The German term Totenschuh is also used.

shoes, Kurdaitja. Feather "sandals" worn by Australian scouts to disguise their tracks.

shofar. A kind of musical instrument, used by the Hebrews, made of a ram's horn which is put under great heat and straightened. It has a cup mouthpiece, and the few tones that can be produced are achieved only if the performer is highly skillful. It was used as a wind instrument, for religious ceremonies, and to rally the people.

shogun. A Japanese feudal military ruler.

shortening. The process by which an originally long vowel becomes abbreviated. It may occur with vowels before heavy combinations of consonants or when a syllable loses its stress.

shorthand. A script made for rapid writing and not based on the conventional alphabet. The first consistent system was developed by Timothy Bright in 1588.

Shoshonean. A subdivision of the Uto-Aztekan linguistic stock, in the western United States.

shott. On English farms during the Middle Ages, a strip of land parallel to or at right angles with other strips within an acre-strip.

shovel. A scooplike tool with a long handle, used to throw earth. It has been suggested that the first shovels came from the shoulder blades of oxen. This theory is supported by the fact that scapula, the Latin for shovel, means shoulder blade.

show, bride. The bride's being exhibited, either to increase the bride price (q.v.) or to get a dowry.

shrew, tree. In some classifications, the lowliest primates, in others, a family of the Insectivora. They are widely found in southwest Asia. They look like squirrels. Some are arboreal and some are bush animals. The part of the brain concerned with vision is well developed.

shrine. A place where sacred objects are kept and offerings made. The shrine is sacred for, and dedicated to, a spirit who may be immanent in it. Temples, trees, animals, pots, cenotaphs, and other objects have been used as shrines. Some shrines are empty. Kitchen, garden, or household shrines exist for special purposes.

shrine, wayside. A heap of rocks to which passersby add, as in the Southwest and in Mexico.

shtetl. The small-town, pre-World War II Jewish community of Eastern Europe, and its culture.

shuttle. On a two-bar loom, a capsule containing a bobbin on which the weft thread is wound.

siamang. An anthropoid found in Sumatra. It weighs about 25 to 30 pounds.

siapo. Tapa (q.v.) cloth in Samoa.

sib. A pseudo-kinship or unilateral extended lineage group in a community. It may be quite large, e.g., among the Bantu of East Africa. It has a name and often has ceremonial equipage. Such functions as a religion (totemism), marriage, and inheritance are discharged by the sib. Members have a common descent in a maternal or paternal lineage, although they may not be able to follow the specific genealogical ties among themselves. The sib was the general term for both clan and gens (qq.v.).

sibilant. A sound made by the breath's being passed along the furrowed tongue and directed against the edge of the upper front teeth, e.g., *so*. The term **gingival spirant** is used when the tongue is in contact with the alveolar ridge of the upper gum, as in English. A sibilant may also be called a **hiss.**

sibilant, abnormal. A sibilant made by drawing the tongue slightly out of its furrowed position, or slightly back, so that the breath eddies around slightly, rather than pushing against, the teeth and gums, e.g., *sh* in shin. An abnormal sibilant is also called a **hush.**

siblings. Children born of the same parents.

siblings, half. Children with one parent in common.

sibonga. A patrilineal clan among the Swazi.

sica. A short, thick curved knife with a handle used for fighting at close quarters in ancient times.

sickle. An agricultural implement consisting of a curved metal blade and handle fitted onto a tang. The blade used to be notched or toothed and the inside is sharpened. The sickle is really a hooked knife. Bronze sickles are found in the second epoch of the Bronze Age.

sickle, jaw-bone. A sickle made by placing serrated flint blades in the dental cavity of a domestic animal.

sickle motif. See MOTIF, SICKLE.

sicklemia. The tendency of the erythrocytes of some persons to show a sicklelike shape when in an oxygen-deficient medium. Sicklemia is fairly widespread and seems to be especially present in Negroid groups. It is a dominant characteristic.

Sicun. Among the Dakota, the essence of a deity, present at the birth of each human being.

sigmoid. Referring to being shaped like the Greek letter sigma, e.g., the sigmoid notch of the mandible.

sign, door. An object near or on a door in order to insure good luck and protect from evil. Such objects have been widely used for a long time.

sign, shift. A symbol used in phonetic writing to indicate any variations in the usual pronunciation of a vowel, e.g., a subscript under *o* denotes the open *o* sound in Italian.

signals. The methods used to communicate at a distance, including gesturing, waving objects, running in circles or at different paces, throwing dust in the air, and shouting. Smoke, mirrors, sparks, fire, marks on trees or hide, and music are pressed into use.

signals, attention. Signals, like fires, meant to attract attention to a visit, the return of a group, or the approach of an enemy party.

signary. See SYLLABARY.

signatures, doctrine of. A doctrine that plants were designed by God for the use of men, with the appearance showing the use. Thus, the walnut might treat brain disease because its appearance resembled the brain's convolutions.

signes obscures. Mystical symbols found on the walls of early caves in France and Spain, often with representations of animals. The nature of these symbols is unknown but it is believed that they are outline drawings of animal traps, dating from 20,000 to 10,000 years ago.

The term may be translated as "strange markings."

significs. The scientific investigation or analysis of significance or meaning.

Sikyatki. An old Hopi village after which Sikyatki pottery is named. It was located on the first Mesa and was a center of the ceramic industry during the Pueblo IV period.

silence, tower of. In the Zoroastrian religion, a place where corpses are exposed to birds of prey. After the birds have laid bare the bones, they are placed in the dakhamah (q.v.) to become dust.

silk. The strong fiber made by some insect larvae, especially the silkworm. Some Koreans learned the mechanics of raising silkworms, ca. 200 B.C., and it was introduced in Byzantium by Justinian in the sixth century A.D. There is no primitive group that has been able to make silk.

silt. Loose sediment with component particles less than one-sixteenth of a millimeter in diameter. This sediment is often suspended in a body of water.

Silurian. A life period in the Paleozoic era, characterized by the development of dogfish with cartilagenous skeletons. It lasted from perhaps 350 to 320 million years ago.

silver. A metallic, whitish element. It is highly malleable, sonorous, and ductile and has great thermal and electrical conductivity. Silver is found in both metallic and nonmetallic states. Native silver is not in great quantities and is usually crystalline. The commonest silver ores are silver sulphide and silver chloride. A good deal of silver is also found in zinc, lead, or copper ores. Silver is usually alloyed with copper to make it harder. Early objects made of silver are comparatively rare in Europe, except in those countries that border on the Mediterranean. Silver was used by 3000-2500 B.C., period of the lowest layers at Hissarlik, where pins, earrings, and wire were found. The second layer, 2500-2000 B.C., had a considerable collection of silver objects, such as jugs and ornaments.

simi. A long knife used by the Wandorobo.

Simian. A superfamily of Catarrhini consisting of monkeys having apelike characteristics.

Simiidae. The family within the primate order including manlike apes.

similarity, law of. Frazer's name for the process, important in magic, by which similar things are presumed to be the same.

Simo. A secret society (q.v.) in French Guinea.

simoon. A hot dry wind of the Middle East generated by the great heat of the deserts and sandy plains. It has a suffocating effect on travelers.

simulacra. Pictures and figurines found in ancient Egyptian tombs representing slaves, subjects, animals, or other beings who were supposed to accompany their master into the other world in order to minister to his needs and make him comfortable. They were excellently rendered, and some examples show the subjects occupied in their normal labors, such as reaping and plowing. Before the development of simulacra, animals and men were killed to be buried with their masters.

sin. Incurring the displeasure of the gods or of God because of an attitude that expresses itself in divinely disapproved actions. The displeasure may be incurred in different ways. Violating the sacred, offending the dignity of the divine, and not paying heed to the principles of humanity are among the causes of sin. In the early development of man, offenses against ritual and ceremonials loom as being very important, and sin changes to morality as standards develop.

sin eater. See EATER, SIN.

Sinanthropus pekinensis. A type of fossil man, also called Pithecanthropus pekinensis, discovered by W. C. Pei, Davidson Black, and Franz Weidenreich in the 1920s and 1930s near Peking. Several brain cases, facial bones, and other bones and teeth of about 40 persons have established the existence of this early Far Eastern man, who probably flourished some 450,000 years ago. He was about five feet tall. The bones are heavy but quite human. The skull is more advanced than Java man's. The brain capacity averaged 1,100-1,200 cc. There is no real chin. The features are definitely human. The teeth are transitional. The very few Sinanthropus bones found in their natural relation to each other and some chewed limb bones suggest cannibalism. Sinanthropus is probably

early Middle Pleistocene, from the second glacial or early second interglacial. He used fire, judging from some blackened earth, and made simple Lower Paleolithic chipping tools and scrapers from sandstone, quartz, and chert. His tools indicate that he was probably right-handed, which is important in evolution, since hand dominance seems essential in order to do two things simultaneously. The Peking Man bones disappeared in World War II, and it was charged, without proof, that they were removed to the United States.

sin-eater. A person who is paid and fed to take over the sins of the recently deceased, as in Wales.

sing-song theory. See THEORY, SING-SONG.

sinistrality. Using and favoring the left hand over the right.

Sinitic or **Sino-Tibetan.** A linguistic stock that includes Tai, Chinese, and Tibeto-Burman, also called Tibeto-Chinese and Sino-Tibetan. It is the second largest family in number of speakers. The major word form is the monosyllable, which is not inflected but which indicates its syntactical role in the sentence positionally. Pitch is very important in these languages.

sinker, net. An object attached to a net to help it sink below the surface of the water. Ordinary stones or carved objects are among the net sinkers, which are distributed fairly widely throughout the world.

sinnet. See SENNIT.

sinognathism. An S-shaped facial profile resulting from a concave face

487

and a short round brain case, as in the orangutan.

sinus. A space within a bone which is lined with epithelium.

sinus, frontal. An air chamber in the lower forehead which is lined with mucous membrane.

Siouan. A North American Indian linguistic stock, found in the western and mid-western part of the United States, mainly to the west of the Mississippi. It is also spoken by some groups in North and South Carolina and Virginia. The members of this stock are Assiniboin, Biloxi, Crow, Dakota, Iowas, Kansas, Katawba, Mandan, Missouri, Ogalala, Omaha, Osage, Oto, Ponka, Teton, Wahpeton, Winnebago, and Yankton.

sipapu. The name given by the Southwest American Indians to a pit in the floor of a ceremonial chamber. Although its origin is not fully known, the Indians seem to have believed that their ancestors came up into the world through this pit. Some tribes also believe that good deeds of the gods come through the opening. The word is sometimes spelled cibobe.

siri. A Malayan term for betel (q.v.) nut quid.

sirocco. An oppressive hot dry wind that blows over the Mediterranean from North Africa to Sicily and Italy.

sistrum. A rattle (q.v.) used in dancing, found in Egyptian fertility rites, in Aztec and other New World cultures, and elsewhere. It consists of a frame 8 to 18 inches long, with thin rods that shake strung in it. It was originally asso-ciated in Egypt with the goddess Hathor, whose head was usually the handle. The sistrum was carried to Rome, where it could be found even in the 11th century.

site, crop. An archaeological site characterized by crop differential growth and often discovered by aerial photography. It usually results from excessive or insufficient moisture in different parts of the site.

site, houte. A circular desert clearing, probably used as a temporary shelter in some parts of the American desert country, especially the lower Colorado River basin. Stones were often piled up to give low rims to the clearings.

site, shadow. An archaeological site with an irregular surface revealed by the shadow cast in the light of the setting or rising sun, especially as seen by aerial photography, although it is also visible to an observer on the ground.

site, soil. An archaeological site, often discovered by aerial photography, with a discolored or disturbed surface, usually found on once cultivated land not being used to bear a crop. Soil sites are especially visible in winter and the early part of spring.

site, type. An archaeological site considered to be typical of an archaeological unit, such as a focus, aspect, culture, etc., and often the source of the name of that unit, e.g., La Tène. The term type station is also used.

Sitting Bull (1834-1890). A Sioux warrior and tribal leader who conducted many raids and was an effective organizer. His "medicine-making" enabled him to predict that the battle at the Little Big Horn in 1876 would be Custer's Last Stand and enhanced his prestige.

situala. A bronze bucket-shaped vessel with a bail, from the Bronze Age; also, a Graeco-Egyptian bucket-shaped vase with two small handles near the top.

Sivapithecus indicus. An erect, omniverous, ground-dwelling ape of the Upper Miocene era found in India, and a possible source from which man derives.

skerries. Small rocky islands.

skeuomorph. A design representing a vessel or an implement; also, an object in the likeness of an earlier object, but made of a new material.

Skhul. See CARMEL, MOUNT.

ski. A slender long strip of wood, one of a pair, with the foot held in the center, used to enable the wearer to glide over snow speedily. It was developed in the northern parts of Asia and Europe and is often used with ski poles. Telemark, in Norway, originated the use of the ski for sport rather than hunting.

skiagraphy. The study, or depicting, of shadows; also, the study of vertical sections, or geometrical profiles of the interior, of buildings.

skin, casting of the. The widely found legend about men shedding their skins, following the example of animals or gods. It is used to explain the origin and cause of death.

Skraeling. The name given the natives by the Norsemen who came to the Americas almost 500 years

before Columbus. They probably saw the Algonkian Indians or Eskimo.

skull. The skeleton of the brain case, lower jaw, and face.

skull, clayed. A skull covered with clay and painted, used as a ceremonial object in the Pacific, e.g., in the Sepik river area of New Guinea.

skull, Cohuna. A skull excavated archaeologically in Australia. Its physical characteristics are those of a primitive Australoid type. The skull was once thought to be geologically ancient but is now interpreted as representing primitive characteristics of the modern aboriginal Australian type.

skull rack. See RACK, SKULL.

slab, grinding. A stone for the hand grinding of pigment, usually about 12 inches across. Grinding stones were ordinarily made of granite or porphyry. The paint was worked with a muller or smaller stone that fit into the palm. Tools of this type had been used in prehistoric times for grinding grain and were probably adapted for paint.

slash-and-burn. A technique for improving the quality of a soil and destroying weeds by burning branches on the ground and letting their ashes sink into the soil.

slave, tomb. A slave slaughtered in Egypt to be buried with his master. Some chiefs before 3050 B.C. had hundreds of slaves around them in their tombs so that they would be accompanied into the outer world by a number sufficient to minister to their needs. Later kings replaced the practice of tomb killing with simulacra (q.v.), i.e., artistic representations of the slaves. See MURDER, FUNERAL.

slavery. One person's legally owning and controlling another and denying him freedom of action or movement. Slavery may have originated because it was more rewarding to use captives as forced workers than to kill them. Men slaves could work the fields and women could perform a variety of indoor tasks. Slaves were often handicraft workers and even members of learned groups. The slave was protected by Hebrew law and had many special rights in other systems. Slavery seemed an irremovable part of the social fabric for a long time. Slavery is often confused with the subjugation of children, wives, members of a state, or tribes or classes. Early custom forbade members of a tribe from enslaving other members. Once extra-tribal slavery is established, it sometimes includes members of the kinship group, usually as a punishment.

Hobhouse has pointed out that slavery is not known by people in early stages of cultural development, like the lower hunting tribes. Slaves can only be effectively used if techniques have developed to a point at which a worker can make a surplus beyond what he needs; thus they are usually restricted to an advanced agricultural society.

Slavic. An Indo-European linguistic subdivision. It consists of Czech, Slovak, Polish, Russian, Bulgarian, Slovene, and Serbo-Croatian.

Slavonic, East. The Little Russian, Great Russian, and White Russian languages.

Slavonic, South. The Slovene, Serbo-Croatian, and Bulgarian languages.

Slavonic, West. The Polish, Czech, and Slovak languages.

sled. A traction transportation device with two runners.

sled, summer. A sled pulled by animals on dry ground. It is often used in Scandinavia for timber transport.

sledge. A flat-bottomed vehicle for hauling heavy objects over ice and snow. It dates from Neolithic times. The original form may have been a flat piece of wood or several boards put together.

sleeve, hafting. A solid haft for a stone ax consisting frequently of a perforated antler into which the ax blade is inserted. It is found especially in the European Neolithic.

sling. An early weapon consisting of a narrow thong, a plaited cord of bark fiber wider in the middle than at the ends, or a stick with a hole. A stone was inserted in the middle of the thong or cord or in the hole, and the weapon was pulled toward the user, so that the stone was propelled by centrifugal force toward its target when the pressure toward the user was suddenly stopped.

sling, dart. See STICK, THROWING.

slip. A thin surface coat of very fine untempered clay applied to pottery to make it harder and easier to polish. The slip is clay finer than that used in the body. It renders the pot less permeable to liquids and makes a good ground for painting.

It may also change the color of the pot to a more desired hue.

slug. A tool with a convex upper surface, with its under surface used as the blade. It has a glassy or waxy appearance because of its fine ripple marks.

slugi. A greyhound-like dog found in the Sahara.

smelting. Melting or fusing ore, usually involving separating or reducing metals. One of the major landmarks in human history was the initial smelting of metal from stone, ca. 4000 B.C. The Age of Metals originated with this discovery; before, metals had been hammer-shaped. Smelting perhaps began with a campfire in which stones with copper content enclosed a hearth, and the fire's charcoal changed the mineral to metal. In a copper area, this might have occurred with sufficient frequency to enable early man to see a link between the concept of heat and fusibility. Early remnants of copper smelting seem to come from a hole one foot in diameter. A charcoal fire was started, a layer of ore placed over it, then sufficient layers of fuel and ore so that a cake about 8 to 10 inches in diameter and about 1½ inches thick emerged. The slag was taken out and the metal removed when it was solid and easily breakable, so that it could be made into tools after being shattered into small pieces. The introduction of the mold (q.v.) simplified this stage.

Early smelting of copper probably resulted in a spongy metal mass which was not completely fused. The extra pieces of cinder and ore were removed by hammering.

Smelting involves heat which causes a chemical reduction as a result of the relations between fuel, ore, and flux. A new product results through combining with the metals in the ore. Smelting is distinguished from melting, which is a purely physical change of a metal to a liquid. The smith can change a metal's shape through melting.

smith or **smithy.** A metal worker. The major early types are those who smelted, the blacksmiths who fashioned metal objects, and metal workers who originated or repaired objects. V. Gordon Childe has called the smith the first expert, who had practically a full-time job. The smith's coming was termed a social revolution by Forbes. The early smith is usually held in awe, although he may be despised. Early smiths were probably in closed groups like castes. The group's religion usually determines the smith's ritual. His tools and his metals are also believed to be powerful.

Smith, George (1840-1876). A British archaeologist who found a part of the Chaldean tablet giving an account of the Deluge while sorting some clay tablets from Ninevah in the British Museum. He led an expedition to find the rest of the tablet and located it in Kuyunjik in 1873, on the fifth day of his digging. His books *Assyrian Discoveries* and *Chaldean Account of Genesis* were famous.

Smith, William Robertson (1846-1894). An English Near Eastern scholar and encyclopedist, who wrote books on family structure in Arabia and on Semitic religion. He showed that the religion of the Semites is based on totemism. Sigmund Freud was considerably influenced by Smith's views.

smoking. A technique for drying and preserving food by the use of fire.

smudge. A small heater in which herbs or dry wood are burned to smoke away insects. Its use is near universal.

snake, house. A snake in a house, regarded as a sign of good luck, and hence well treated, being fed with milk.

snake, snow. A winter game played by the American Indians of the northern Plains and elsewhere. A stick was skidded along the snow to see who could send it farthest or come closest to a target. The stick was often carved like a snake.

snakeroot. A plant, the roots of which are used to cure or relieve the effects of snake bite.

snare. See TRAP, SNARE.

snook. See COCKSNOOK.

snow snake. See SNAKE, SNOW.

snowhouse. Among the Eskimo, a dwelling made of snow. It is the only type of dwelling in which scaffolding is not required to construct a dome. The blocks of snow originally stick together by the force of gravity, because each course is parallel to the ground and overhangs the preceding course only a little. Soon the courses are welded together by water that is applied and quickly turns to ice. Access to the snowhouse is gained by crawling through a long bent tunnel of snow that cuts off the wind. The interior of an occupied snowhouse is so warm that skins must be stretched to catch the dripping water. The dome snowhouse was probably invented by the Eskimo but was not their only type of dwelling. The Eskimo group in northern Siberia, e.g., do not use a snowhouse and are not familiar with it. At present, there are probably less than 10,000 Eskimos who inhabit domed snowhouses regularly. The Eskimo term ini is sometimes used, and the form igloo (q.v.) is also found.

snowshoe. A device that is attached to the feet to prevent the wearer from sinking into soft snow. The snowshoe originated in Asia, but the North American continent has become identified with it. Many snowshoes have moccasins (q.v.) in the center, held in place by leather lacings. The shoe is a network of loosely woven thongs held in a more or less ovoid frame.

snowshoe, frame. A wooden frame that surrounds a filling made of pliable strands, or other materials which function as a footrest. It is usually found in North America.

snowshoe, plank. A slender plank ski in the middle of which the wearer's foot is attached. It is found mainly in the Old World.

Soan. A chopper (q.v.) culture of the Punjab in India, from the second interglacial period.

social structure. See STRUCTURE, SOCIAL.

socialization. The way in which a society integrates its members and the process by which individuals learn to adapt to their society.

society. A group of persons that lives as an entity and has its own culture; an organized aggregate of persons following a given way of life, persisting in time, and with a group consciousness. Linton has referred to a group of persons as a society when they have worked and lived together for a long enough period to become organized and to regard themselves as a social unit with clear limits.

society, caste. A group which has the same culture, with rigid hierarchical status groupings, each of which has a different role in the culture.

society, graded. A society which has a series of degrees or grades through which the members go. War societies, like those of North Dakota, were graded, and Central America and Mexico have many such societies.

society, Klallam. A secret society (q.v.) of the Northwest Coast.

society, leopard. A West African secret society whose members used an iron claw to kill human victims, so that it would look as if they had been clawed by leopards.

society, medicine. A secret initiation lodge of medicine men found among the Crow and Ojibwa Indians.

society, military. A society, the members of which are military men, e.g., among the Plains Indians.

society, secret. A special quasi-legislative group within a tribe, which may mete out justice as it sees fit; an association with secret membership and activities. A secret society may be concerned with war, religion, witchcraft, and similar pursuits. Members may join through inheritance, payment, social status, or as a gesture of civic responsibility. The societies are usually esoteric and formally organized. Membership is commonly limited to those of one sex, with male societies more numerous than female. There are likely to be several grades for initiates; it has been speculated that these are extensions of age sets (q.v.). A secret society probably has a lodge for its ceremonies; this is thought to be a development of the early men's house (q.v.). The society may have as one of its major functions initiation (q.v.) to manhood. The activities, designed to confuse outsiders, include signals to warn them away (see ROARER, BULL).

society, soldier. See SOCIETY, MILITARY.

sodality. An association based on voluntary or involuntary membership. Sodalities are often religious societies limited to a single objective, e.g., the veneration of a saint's relics.

soffit. The under surface of an arch.

sofki. A thin sour corn drink made by some American Indians of the Gulf area. Corn, water, and lye are the ingredients. The three kinds of sofki are plain, sour, and white.

soga. A sharpened bamboo spike used as a weapon in the Philippines.

soil, colluvial. Soil that collects at the foot of slopes.

493

soil, ectodynamorphic. A soil, the major features of which are attributable to external conditions like climate.

soil, endodynamorphic. A soil, the major features of which are attributable to its parent material. The soils of coastal areas are usually endodynamorphic.

soil, residual. Soil that has not been moved from its place of origin.

soil analysis. See ANALYSIS, SOIL.

soil mark. See MARK, CROP.

sojourn. The period between death and the ghost's departure for the spirit world.

solar radiation. See HYPOTHESIS, SOLAR RADIATION.

sok. A Kazak phratry (q.v.).

soldier society. See SOCIETY, MILITARY.

solifluction. In a periglacial zone (q.v.), the process by which material reaccumulates on frozen subsoil and is carried away by the water-logged and thawed upper surface of the soil.

solmization. A collection of syllables used to represent the tones of a musical scale.

Solo. See HOMO SOLOENSIS.

solstice. The sun's greatest north or south declination, when it appears to pause before it returns on its course. The dates are approximately June 21 and December 22. The solstices are the longest and shortest days of the year. The June solstice is the summer solstice in the northern hemisphere, with the December solstice the winter solstice; the opposite names apply in the southern hemisphere.

Solutrean. The Old World Upper Paleolithic period that succeeded the Aurignacian (q.v.) culture, ca. 70,000 years ago, around the time of the second maximum of the last glaciation. The name derives from the site uncovered at Le Solutre. It was fairly brief and was marked by a growth in making flint implements by pressure flaking and possibly by the needle. Stylized symbolic representations are found in its art. The bone industry did not continue to develop. Shouldered points and laurel and willow leaf points were widespread. The flint implements made were small and sliverlike, with an all-over ripple retouch. Horse hunting was found. The Solutrean peoples remained in the plains. They probably did not go beyond the Pyrenees, except at the eastern end.

soma. A leafless shrub that grows in India. It yields a rather acidulous milky juice that is used at religious ceremonies as a symbol of renewed life.

somatogenic. Referring to characteristics that are acquired and not hereditarily transmitted.

somatology. See ANTHROPOLOGY, PHYSICAL.

somatometry. Measurement of both the cadaver and the living body.

somatonia. In Sheldon's scheme of constitutional types (q.v.), an active and assertive personality, the counterpart of mesomorphy (q.v.).

somatotype. A classification of body builds by types. See TYPES, CONSTITUTIONAL.

494

sonant. A phoneme (q.v.) requiring synchronized vibration of the vocal cords. It can occur in syllabic (q.v.) as well as nonsyllabic positions.

song, cumulative. A song in which each refrain includes a recapitulation of all the elements mentioned in earlier parts of the song, e.g., *Old Macdonald Had a Farm.*

song, folk. A song with traditional subject matter, music, or words.

song, medicine. A song or a spell that functions at ceremonies among the American Indians.

song, mourning. A song to lament a recent or imminent death. Mourning songs may be simple or highly complex. They usually praise the dead person and express the sorrow of the survivors. There may be self-mutilation or other signs of distress.

song, swallow. A song of Greek children to signalize the return of the swallows and spring. The custom is several thousand years old.

sonograph, steno-. See STENO-SONOGRAPH.

sonority. The comparative force with which sounds strike the ear, e.g., a vowel is usually more sonorous than a consonant.

sonority, crest of. A phoneme (q.v.) which is more sonorous than the phoneme which it precedes or follows.

sonorous. Referring to sonority (q.v.).

soothsaying. Activities employed to gain insight into the future or into matters ordinarily beyond human perception. In Greece and

Rome, the soothsayer was almost a public official. Natural events, movements of the body, the changing position of the planets, drawing lots, and many other techniques are employed. Many contemporary superstitions are variants of soothsaying. See DIVINATION.

sorghum. A variety of grasses, both African and Asiatic, of different degrees of wildness. Sorghum has been used as forage, fuel, grain and syrup, and has a long history. It is possible that agricultural contacts between Africa and India may have given rise to sorghum.

sorcery. A kind of witchcraft (q.v.) especially linked with causing and curing disease. It is often used as a general designation for the acts of either a male or female sorcerer.

sororate. A man's marrying his wife's sister, on either a mandatory or permissive basis, after the wife's death.

sorting criteria. See CRITERIA, SORTING.

sortition or **sortilege.** Using a fortuitous choice to answer a question. It may be the oldest kind of divination (q.v.). Lots or dice are typical examples of sortition.

Sosom. The bull roarer (q.v.) god of the Kaya-Kaya in New Guinea.

Sothic. See CYCLE, SOTHIC.

soul. The essence or animating substance of individual life, especially human. North American Indians believe in the human soul, or souls, almost without exception, and some believe that animals have souls as well. Souls may be multiple and may be in the body, in shadow, or in reflections. An early notion saw the soul as a kind of human shadow that caused life, possessed an independent personal volition and consciousness, and could affect man's existence and appear in his fantasies. Factors making for acceptance of the idea of the soul include dreams and visions, the contrast between living and dead bodies, and the power of will.

soul, external. The belief that the soul may live apart from the body, or that a soul lives outside the body of the animal, plant, or object with which it is connected.

soul, ghost. Tylor's term for the totality of the parts of the general soul. Everyone has life, which leads to consciousness and is extinguished at death, as well as an image which appears in dreams. These can disconnect themselves from the body. Inasmuch as they both belong to the body, they belong to each other, and are part of the general or ghost soul.

soul-animal. An animal that exists simultaneously with and is the double of a person. The activities and lives of both animal and human coexist and are coordinate. See VISION, QUESTING.

soul catching. See CATCHING, SOUL.

soul substance. See SUBSTANCE, SOUL.

sound, bridge. A phonetic unit, commonly a vowel, which is put between the prefix and root of a word or between the root and suffix to make the pronunciation less difficult and more euphonious.

sound, double. A sound within which one stress syllable ends and the next begins, e.g., *nn* in *anno*.

sound, earthquake. A sound caused by an earthquake which can be heard by humans.

sound, friction. A sound between voicing and breathing, made by the vocal cords being separated and the glottis opened, e.g., *h* as in *hunt*.

sound, glottal. A sound primarily articulated by the vocal cords, e.g., the glottal stop *h*.

sound, musical. A sound such as the nasal, lateral, and vowel.

sound, noise. A sound such as the trill, spirant, and stop.

sound change, substratum theory of. A theory of sound change that postulates that a group taking over a new language will speak it with the mother tongue phonetics, thus incorrectly from the point of view of native speakers. An example is that of persons of German descent who dentalize English consonants that are normally produced on the alveolar ridge of the upper gum.

sounding box. See BOX, SOUNDING.

souterrain. An underground stone passage, probably from the Iron Age or later. It used to be interpreted as a place of refuge but is now considered as an early form of stone room. Animal, bird, and fish bones have been found in souterrains, in addition to carbonized grain and ash. The term fogous is sometimes used for souterrain.

Southern Death cult. See CULT, SOUTHERN DEATH.

spacer. A bead perforated with a number of holes, which are designed to maintain the proper distance among the several strings of a necklace.

spall. To break around or break into smaller pieces; a piece broken off in making a core tool; a fragment or chip.

span. Measured from the rear with both arms outstretched, the distance between the tips of the two middle fingers. It is often used to mean a distance of about six feet. The word span also means the distance separating the little finger and thumb with the fingers outstretched.

spanner, head. An instrument for measuring the height of the head.

spar. A support for sails.

spatula, lime. In chewing betel (q.v.) nut quid, a long spoon used to take the lime out of the container in which it is usually kept.

spear. A long pointed weapon, for throwing or thrusting, used in war and in hunting and fishing. It may be composite or solid. A composite spear usually consists of head, foreshaft, shaft, butt, counterpoise, and sheath. The head may consist of a point (plain or barbed), shank, and socket. The foreshaft connects the socket and main shaft. The butt is attached to the end of the shaft, unless it is replaced by a counterpoise. The sheath protects the point.

spear, bird. A spear used by the Eskimo with a spear thrower (q.v.).

spear, king. An ornate spear of the Solomons.

spear, throwing. A missile, either a javelin, harpoon, dart, or arrow.

spearhead. The point of a spear. It may be made of a variety of materials, such as obsidian and iron.

spear thrower. See THROWER, SPEAR.

specialization. An organism's developing strongly in one direction. It usually evolves in a straight-line fashion until an extreme form is achieved. Specialization leaves little opportunity to evolve to a higher plane. See ANIMAL, GENERALIZED.

speciation. The process of the formation of species.

species. A taxonomic group that probably cannot produce fertile offspring except with its own members. Zoologists do not completely agree on the meaning of the term. Several species make a genus. Within a species there are subspecies or varieties.

species, evolutionary unity of. The theory that evolution is responsible for every kind of organism. See CREATION, SPECIAL.

spectacle. A device to assist vision, usually consisting of two lenses in a frame, resting on the nose and held in place by hooks over the ears. Spectacles were used in Europe by the 15th century.

spectrograph, sound. A machine, used in phonetics, which makes a permanent record of the sound frequencies in every instant of a sample of speech lasting for 2.4 seconds.

spectrographic analysis. See ANALYSIS, SPECTROGRAPHIC.

spectrum, pollen. A statement of the percentage of pollen grains of different species taken from a single sample.

speech, inverted. A statement which is the opposite of what the speaker really means.

speech, monogenesis of. The supposition that all languages had a single origin.

speech, parts of. The parts or designations into which the words of a particular language can be separated, according to syntactical functions, forms, modes of inflection, or other criteria.

speech, visible. A phonetic alphabet (q.v.) which consists of simplified and schematized representations of the vocal organs as they appear when ready to utter each phoneme (q.v.). It was most widely used by Henry Sweet (1845-1912). Visible speech is expensive to print and difficult to write.

speech apparatus. See APPARATUS, SPEECH.

speech area. See AREA, SPEECH.

speleology. The science of cave exploration. It is a branch of archaeology and geology.

spell. A series of recited or sung words believed capable of effecting a desired magical end. The effect of the spell is mandatory and if it is properly presented, the expected result naturally follows. An archaic terminology may be used in spells so that they become fairly unintelligible or abracadabra. Spells often place great reliance on the effect of a name.

spelling, heterographic. A method of spelling wherein the identical letter or group of letters is pronounced differently in different words. English spelling is heterographic.

spelling, homographic. A method of spelling wherein the identical letter or group of letters is pronounced the same in all words. No conventional spelling is wholly homographic, although that of certain languages with recently reformed spelling, e.g., Spanish, comes close. Homographic spelling is found in a phonetic alphabet (q.v.).

spelt. A kind of wheat with a husk that must be partly dried before it is threshed from the grain. Spelt has helped archaeologists in the identification of sites, because it is found in the form of carbonized grain. This ancient cultivated wheat is still grown in parts of central Europe.

sphenoid. Having a wedge shape.

spheres, music of the. See MUSIC, MUNDANE.

spherocytosis. A condition in which the erythrocytes (red blood corpuscles) are unusually thick.

Sphinx. One of the oldest monuments in Egypt that still stands. It represents a lion with the head of a man. It probably dates from the IVth dynasty. It is made of solid rock and is some 150 feet long and 70 feet high. In Egyptian archaeology, a sphinx is any large carved figure, usually with an animal body and an animal or human head. The androsphinx has a human head, the criosphinx a goat's head, and the hieracosphinx a hawk's head. The Greek sphinx was in the form of a winged lion with a woman's head and breasts. It was believed to have posed a riddle to all passersby and to have killed everyone unable to solve it.

sphragistics. The study of the seals on coins and medals, including old metal and stone signets. The wax and lead impressions of heraldic seals that appeared after the 12th century sometimes yielded more accurate information to genealogists than did the emblazoned arms.

spikenard. An ointment made from a spikenard plant, which also yields a famous ancient perfume. It has had special meaning in India as well as among the Hebrews. It is traditionally identified as the major ingredient in Mary Magdalene's ointment.

spinach. An annual which produces many basal leaves and may be the most widely used herbage vegetable for greens. It probably originated in Persia, and was brought in medieval times via Spain to Europe.

spindle. A rounded rod which tapers at both ends, with yarn twisted on one end. Its origin is closely tied in with the beginnings of agriculture. The spindle is perhaps the tool most widely used for spinning in cultures where the wheel is unknown. It usually has a weight to keep the stick whirling. Wood is the most widely used material for spindles.

spindle, drop. A simple spindle consisting of a rod with a whorl placed near the lower end. The drop spindle is allowed to whirl while suspended in the air or resting on the ground instead of being twisted continuously on the thigh or other surface.

spindle and spindle-whorl method. A fairly simple method of spinning, using a wooden spindle and a circular weight.

spinnaker. A large triangular sail on a light long pole, found on the side opposite the mainsail. It is used in running before the wind.

spinning. Making yarn out of fiber through lengthening and twisting it.

spirant. A sound made when the speech organs are so arranged that there is a very narrow passage for the outgoing breath, so that friction is produced, e.g., f or z.

spirant, bilabial. A spirant in which the two lips narrow the sound, e.g., phi or beta in Greek.

spirant, dental. A spirant in which the upper teeth are touched by the blade of the tongue, e.g., th in *thin*.

spirant, gingival. See SIBILANT.

spirant, glottal. A spirant in which the breath passing through the slightly opened glottis produces friction, e.g., h as in *hot*.

spirant, groove. A sound produced by an elongated front-to-back channel in the tongue, e.g., $ſ$ in Sanskrit. It is between a hissing and a hushing sound.

spirant, labiodental. A spirant made by forcing the breath stream between the lower lip and the upper teeth, e.g., f.

spirant, palatal. A spirant, found in German, in which there is contact between the highest part of the palate and the middle of the tongue, e.g., ch in *ich*.

spirant, rounded labial. A sound made by puckering the lips, e.g., w in *witch*.

499

spirant, slit. A sound articulated with a comparatively flat opening between the tongue and roof of the mouth, e.g., the *rs* in the Swedish word *fors.*

spirant, unrounded labial. A rubbing sound made by the breath's coming from the lips when they are in slight contact. as in the Japanese *b* (usually transliterated *f*) coming before *u;* e.g., *Hujiyama* or *Fujiyama.*

spirit. An immaterial nondivine being of fairly independent existence. It may be associated with a particular natural feature. There may be many different kinds of spirits, even in one culture. Spirits cannot be perceived directly by the senses. The wind, the sun, a disease, may be regarded as having a spirit or being one. Spirits may be linked with fairies, gnomes, and similar figures. The concept of a soul (q.v.) that can be separated from the body is the model for the nonhuman spirit. The spirit helped the growth of advanced religion by facilitating dualistic conceptions of the material and the immaterial. Usually there are more spirits on the earth than human beings. Many spirits in nonliterate religions worked for man or against him, and their force could be seen in almost any unusual happening. The notion in some religions that each person enjoys the protection of a guardian angel and faces the snares set by a tempting demon may derive from the belief in spirits. Spirits are sometimes confused with ghosts (q.v.) who loiter around their homes.

spirit, corn. A spirit which typifies the living power of growing grain. Its existence is coterminous with that of the grain.

spirit, familiar. A personal protective spirit, often identified in a dream or vision, or an evil spirit which is controlled by a sorcerer. Among the American Indians of the Plains, the protective spirit is usually termed a tutelary guardian (see VISION, QUESTING). The form, usually that of a cat, assumed by a demon that served a witch was known as a familiar spirit or familiar. See SPIRIT, GUARDIAN.

Spirit, Great. A single all-powerful deity often assumed to be the god of the American Indians. This assumption is erroneous, as in fact they had many deities.

spirit, guardian. A personal protective spirit, often obtained from a visitation or dream. Possession of such a spirit had to remain secret, or it might be lost. The knowledge acquired from a spirit might not be used till a person reached middle age. It was possible to have more than one guardian spirit. The shaman (q.v.) might use a guardian spirit's advice. The guardian spirit was sought throughout life. See VISION, QUESTING.

spirit, household. A supernatural person found in or near dwellings in Europe. They may be tricky or helpful, as well as unpleasant. The mischievous poltergeist may be a household spirit. Fairies often frequent barns and kitchens to milk the cows dry and sour the butter.

spirit, water. A god among the southern Bushmen of South Africa.

He is an evil spirit who withholds rain.

spirochete. A spiral-shaped bacteria. The organism responsible for syphilis is a spirochete (*Treponema pallidum*).

spitting. Ejecting saliva through the mouth is often of considerable symbolic significance. As it is a sign of good luck to spit on something, spitting may be a means of counteracting bad luck.

spitzharfe. An ancient two-sided musical instrument, a double psaltery so constructed that duets could be played on it. One set of strings is bass and one treble. It is played by plucking.

split animal motif. See MOTIF, SPLIT ANIMAL.

split-line technique. See TECHNIQUE, SPLIT-LINE.

spokesman. See CHIEF, TALKING.

spokeshave. A concave scraper (q.v.) with a notch, usually used to scrape shafts.

Spondylus. A shell used for ornaments in Neolithic Europe.

sponsalia. The ceremony attendant on plighting a troth.

sport. An organism that shows a mutation or the mutation itself. Geneticists try to avoid using this word because of its connotation that the mutant is causeless or inexplicable rather than dictated by the gene structure. The term sport also suggests a throwback or atavism, which geneticists feel should not be associated with the concept of mutation.

sports. Activities, now largely recreational, which were at one time man's preparation for keeping alive.

Contests between animals and men were once to obtain food source and not a diversion. Activities like the chase were largely war preparations.

spot, Mongolian. A bluish-gray spot in the lumbar area, which usually disappears some time after birth. It is most common in East Asia.

spot, vulnerable. The folktale theme that a special person is only vulnerable in one spot, e.g., Achilles in the heel.

spout, bridge. A type of double spout on jars, the two vertical elements of which are connected by a horizontal strip. It is especially characteristic of southern Peruvian ceramics. The **stirrup spout** comprises two arched tubes which meet in a single cylindrical spout. This type was characteristic of much of the pottery of northern Peru.

Sprachgefühl. A native's feeling toward his language, based on an intuitive grasp of its structure.

spring, balance. A small weighted regulatory bar on a watch, held to the center of a coiled spring. It replaced the pendulum.

Springtanz. See ESPRINGALE.

sprit. On a sailboat, a spar which runs from tack to peak of a sail. It keeps the sail expanded.

spunk. Wood that takes fire readily.

squama. A shell-shaped bone, e.g., the temporal bone.

squamous. Covered by or largely composed of scales.

square-field plot system. See SYSTEM, SQUARE-FIELD PLOT.

squaw. A woman of an American Indian tribe.

squaw, lazy. A kind of simple oversewn coil (q.v.) in which a long stitch passes over two coils simultaneously. The sewing goes in front of, up, and then over the new coil, around which it winds. Then it goes behind and under the previous coil, then right up over the new coil.

squeeze, dry. In archaeological research, a method of taking a graphic impression of an inscription on paper. It is used with fragile or colored stones, where squeeze paper (q.v.) is unsuitable. A thin sheet of paper is held over the stone against every edge of the cutting, so that there will be a corresponding bend in the surface. The bends are then drawn with pencil on a drawing board and checked against the stone. The drawing is started at the bottom right hand side of the paper, to keep the impression from being pressed out by the hand.

squeezer, cassava. See MATAPI.

sraddha. A Hindu ceremony which expresses respect for a family's ancestors or gives a spirit an intermediate body. It involves offerings of different foods to various ancestors.

stab-and-drag. Pottery decorated by continuous lines made by repeatedly jabbing a point into the clay, drawing it back, and stabbing it in again.

stadia. A series of variations in climate, often the four major glaciations (q.v.), which led gradually to modern conditions. The Bühl, Gschnitz, and Daun stadia are usually distinguished. They date roughly from 22,000 to 9,000 years ago.

staff, cross or **staff, Jacob's.** A device used by early astronomers to measure latitude and the angle between stars. Later it was used by sailors to measure altitudes while at sea and to gauge the sun's height.

stages, economic. The three stages in the economic development of man. In the 19th century they were said to be fishing and hunting, pastoralism, and agriculture.

staining, alizarin. Using red alizarin to measure bone growth. It stains growing calcifying tissues red; bone which was produced before or after the dye was used remains white. It helps to determine the developmental stage at which particular bony tissue is laid down.

stalactite. A deposit of carbonate of lime found hanging from cave roofs. It is kept in solution by water trickling through the roof. The occurrence of stalactites is erratic, depending on minute fissures in the limestone and the subsequent percolation of water carrying carbonate of lime in solution. They may grow fairly rapidly under favorable conditions. Their presence is often used to set a maximum date for paintings or engravings which they may cover.

stalagmite. A limey, compact, hard material that may be formed in a damp period from limestone on the walls of rock shelters (q.v.) being redeposited on the floor. A stalagmite may be kept in solution by water trickling through the roof of the cave.

stamnos. An ancient Greek ceramic vase with a very high shoulder, a short neck, and two handles.

stamping, rocker. A pottery design made by a convex stamp being impressed in the wet clay and rocked back and forth.

stand, fruit. A pot, usually a shallow bowl, mounted on a high stand, as in the Alisar pottery of Neolithic times.

stane, Cat. A battle memorial of ancient Scotland. The word comes from the Celtic *cath,* "battle."

star, morning. The planet Venus, which rises just before sunrise, of importance as a religious object, notably among North American Indians.

state. A political or governmental grouping, ranging in complexity from the autonomous village to the nation. It usually arises through several tribes voluntarily joining or through strong groups subjugating weak. War is probably the major means of producing a state. There are more conquest states than confederacies. Conquest states usually enjoy settled life and technological achievement that permit a population to produce a surplus. The state includes all the persons living in an area who recognize or are subject to the force which can be applied by those exercising control. Max Weber defined the state as the human association that successfully claimed the monopoly of legitimate physical force in a given sphere. The early study of social organization was the study of the state.

station. An early site with artifacts that typify a culture.

station, open. An exposed site for a settlement, usually near a body of water. Open stations are helpful in dating some developments in material culture, since the inhabitants merely threw aside tools or food remnants, which can be correlated with the geologist's sequence.

station, trading. A place where trade was conducted on a semipermanent basis. Some trading stations became cities eventually, e.g., Byblos in Syria, which developed into a city to meet Egypt's need to import timber from Lebanon. This development occurred particularly in the Near East, ca. fourth millenium B.C.

station, type. See SITE, TYPE.

statoreception. An organism's ability to adjust to equilibrium and gravity.

stature. See HEIGHT, STANDING.

status. Comparative prestige rank in a community. It is a collection of both rights and duties. Ascribed status—the more common type—is that which individuals get without reference to their individual capacities by inheritance. Achieved status is that established by special qualities, through individual effort. See ROLE.

status group, endogamous. A bilateral kinship group within which the individual must marry, e.g., a caste (q.v.) in India.

stave, perforated bone. See BATON-DE-COMMANDEMENT.

steamer. A cooking vessel for steaming food. It is double, with the bottom of the upper portion perforated and placed over the lower vessel, which contains hot water. Rice especially lends itself to cooking by steaming.

steatite. A soapstone used to make stone bowls and pottery by the Indians of the eastern United States.

steatopygia or steatopygy. Unusually fatty buttocks, as in Hottentot and Bushmen women.

stecca. A small piece of wood or a stick.

Steinheim. A fossil skull from Steinheim, Germany, reported in 1933. It is from the second or third interglacial era, and may be 150,000 years old. The prominent brow ridges and strong upper jaw are primitive features, while the back part of the skull and the muscular ridges of the occipital bones are like modern man. This skull had a brain capacity of about 1,000 cc. and seems to be between that of Pithecanthropus and Homo sapiens, with many characteristics of the latter. The forehead is beginning to fill out and the skull has a generally rounded contour.

Steinmetz, Sebald Rudolph (1862-1940). A German ethnologist who studied the development of the concept of punishment and traced the idea of the psychology of vengeance. He examined the connection between vengeance and religion.

stele or stela. A small carved stone slab usually without capital or base. It is used as a monument, milestone, to indicate a site, or as a gravestone. The first sculptured stele is Sumerian; it dates ca. 2550 B.C. and shows the king leading his army. Buddhist and Mayan steles often have religious scenes. Many Athenian steles of the fifth and fourth century B.C., used as tombstones, are very beautiful. A typical scene is an episode from the life of the dead person. Demetrios of Phaleron's decree against ostentation caused a decline in this type of sculpture, although it continued elsewhere.

Stele B. A stone pillar among the Maya ruins at Copan on which was carved a figure which has been interpreted variously as a mastodon, an elephant, and a mosquito.

stenomeric. Referring to a platymeric index (q.v.) of more than 100.

stenometopic. Referring to a transverse fronto-parietal index (q.v.) of less than 65.9.

steno-sonograph. An instrument developed by Dreyfus-Graff, which he claimed could transcribe spoken sounds into written symbols.

Stephens, John Lloyd (1805-1852). An American archaeologist who made two visits to the sites of the Maya civilization between 1839 and 1842. He went with the English artist Frederick Catherwood, who illustrated Stephens' books and wrote a popular volume about the Maya cities.

steppe. Grassland with a cover of rapidly growing short grass. Steppes are very cold in winter and hot in summer and often have windstorms.

sternum. The breastbone, forming the ventral midline of the thoracic cage. It is made up of three parts. The first seven ribs of the human body articulate on the sternum.

stibium. A cosmetic used in Egypt to paint around the eyes and to treat some eye diseases.

stichband. A pottery design found in the Danubian I period. It consisted of a kind of arrow design with lines criss-crossing the shaft of the arrow.

stick, broiling. A stick placed on the ashes of the fireplace as a broiling spit, e.g., among the Ainu.

stick, counting. A stick with notches cut in it used for counting.

stick, digging or **stock, digging.** A wooden branch with a pointed end, sometimes forked and fire-hardened. Probably man's oldest wooden tool, it was used to dig out roots. From it the spear may have developed.

stick, diplomats'. A bundle sent to the United States government by American Indians. It often contained a hollowed corn ear filled with tobacco, representing the pipe of peace, and was accompanied by an appropriate message about peace.

stick, joss. A thin cylinder or stick of wood powder and paste, burned for incense or to measure time at night. The odor has ceremonial significance and keeps away insects. Joss sticks are found in the Far East, especially China.

stick, kicked. A game of some Southwest Indian groups in which two small sticks are kicked along a ceremonial course. It is especially associated with the Zuni.

stick, message. A notched stick used to identify the messenger and to act as a mnemonic device for him. A typical stick may be four to eight inches long, with notches, curves, and lines. The receiver could read the markings. It was very common among the early Australians, on the Malayan Archipelago, and among the Bushmen of Africa and the North American Indians. Handing over the message stick may be accompanied by a ceremony, with the messenger representing the chief.

stick, notched. A stick with notches in it, used by some North American Indians as reminders or as tally systems. The meaning of each notch may vary with the purpose of the stick.

stick, parrying. A stick used for parrying, instead of a shield.

stick, prayer. A stick with feathers attached, which is painted and has special religious meanings, as among the Pueblos. Prayer is made over the sticks, after which they can be hidden or presented on an altar.

stick, rabbit. A boomeranglike flat curved stick used as a hunting weapon by the Indians of the Basin Plateau area in Nevada and Southern California. One of its surfaces was grooved. It was usually made of oak and was not self-retrieving.

stick, sounding. A stick suspended from a tree used to beat rhythm.

stick, scratching. A stick, often in the shape of a fork or a hand, used by many primitive peoples to scratch the skin, especially during certain ritual occasions when scratching with the bare hand is considered dangerous.

stick, swizzle. A stick, usually of wood, which is twirled between the palms, so as to provide a swirling motion to beat and soften various materials. In Central America, the swizzle stick is used to beat up chocolate and make a foaming drink.

stick, throwing. A part of a tree or shrub used as a weapon that was thrown or hurled at a target. Its shape varied considerably. The throwing stick is sometimes called the dart sling.

sticks, bundles of. Sticks tied together in a bundle, used as mnemonic devices by some North American Indians. The marks and appearance of the sticks can serve as summaries of ideas or documents.

sticks, termite. Two sticks of different kinds of wood, taken to a termite mound by the Azande, who pose a question to the termites. They are told to give one of two alternative answers by eating one stick or the other.

stigma. 1 A brand made on a person with a red hot iron, used to identify criminals or slaves. 2 A spot on the skin that bleeds during some mental states. The Roman Catholic Church says that in certain cases these stigmata have been impressed upon the body miraculously as a reminder of the wounds suffered by the crucified Christ. The Church recognizes, however, that some cases of stigmatization are hysterical.

stigmata. Physical abnormalities believed to be associated with abnormal behavior. Lombroso (q.v.) in 1876 expounded the theory that criminals can be identified by the stigmata of atavisms (q.v.). In 1905, the psychiatrist Rosanoff suggested the following as signs of arrested development: microcephaly, macrocephaly, scaphocephaly, and extreme brachycephaly and dolichocephaly. The theory of stigmata has largely been disproved, although some types of mental defect occasioned by glandular malfunctioning, e.g., cretinism, are marked by distinctive physical signs.

Stillbay. A Middle Stone Age industry of South Africa. Also, a type of leaf-shaped stone lance head characteristic of this industry and reminiscent of Solutrean leaf points.

stinkard. A man of the common people, as distinguished from a sun (an honored man or the chief) among the Natchez and Creek Indians. The term puant (French "stinker") is also used. See SUN, GREAT.

stock. 1 A term often used to designate a collection of racial groups. Objections have been made to the use of this term because it implies an earlier parent group. 2 A linguistic family containing several closely related languages. 3 A large biological division, usually roughly equated with RACE.

stock, digging. See STICK, DIGGING.

stock, linguistic. A group of interrelated languages that are not related to other such groups.

stodge. Steamed and mashed fruit.

Stolpe, Hjalmar (1841-1905). A Swedish ethnologist, once director of the ethnography department of the Stockholm Museum. He wrote on early art and showed the importance of religion in the development of art and ornamentation. Stolpe studied the social nexus of a work of art and its possible polygenesis.

stomion. With the lips closed, the midpoint of the oral fissure.

stone, apex. The uppermost stone in a gable end.

stone, Armenian. The ancient name for azurite, called after the place where it was found.

stone, baking. A flat stone found in Southern California, usually with a perforation at one end, about a foot long and one inch thick. It was used as a boiling stone, a dipper, and for baking bread by the Indians of the area.

stone, banner. An axlike implement of polished stone, often with two winglike projections and axial perforations. It was made in prehistoric North America. Its use has not been established.

stone, bird. A weight for a spearthrower shaped like a generalized bird, found among some American Indians of the Hopewell period and earlier. It is lashed on to the shaft of the spearthrower. It had a pair of projecting knobs to represent eyes and was usually made of banded slate, suggesting feathers. It was symmetrical and polished. Other uses have been suggested for the bird stone. See STONE, BUTTERFLY.

stone, birth. The belief that a special stone is sacred to each month and that it has a special virtue for people born in that month. Josephus and St. Jerome are largely responsible for this belief, although the practice of wearing such stones did not originate until the 18th century, in Poland.

stone, boat. A polished stone, usually in the shape of a canoe, made of slate and steatite. It is found in Canada and the United States among several Indian groups and is especially common in almost all the states east of the Mississippi. It may have been used as a charm or talisman. Perforated specimens suggest ornaments hung around the neck.

stone, bottle. The mineral chrysolite or any mineral that will melt and combine with glass without first being prepared in any way. Bottle stone is also a unique type of glass found in the form of clear, green pebbles in the Moldau Valley, Old Bohemia, whence the name Moldavite. Moldavite is thought to be prehistoric slag or glass.

stone, butterfly. A weight for a spear thrower lashed to its shaft, characteristic of the Mound Builders in the United States. Its name derives from the shape like a butterfly with outstretched wings. See STONE, BIRD.

stone, collar. A yoke made of stone and found in central Vera Cruz, Teotihuacan and southern Olenec. Most of the collar stones are found in Totonac sites like Tajin. They were probably used as belts. Most of the specimens are in the shape of open horseshoes but some are closed. They average 50 pounds in weight and often are decorated with tiger or snake motifs.

stone, Ethiopian. An Egyptian embalmer's tool used for incising the side of the corpse to remove the vital organs. This was preparatory to mummification (q.v.).

stone, figure. A natural piece of flint which resembles some object, e.g., an animal, if held in a particular way. These pieces are sometimes erroneously attributed to human workmanship, which was believed to have been applied in order to enhance a fancied resemblance.

stone, grease. A smooth stone used to hold grains and fats.

stone, grinding. A stone used to wear down a surface or to shape a softer material. Grinding stones are difficult to detect archaeologically.

stone, hook. A heavy hook-shaped object, made of soapstone or a similar soft rock, often shaped like a Z and from one to five inches long. Its function is not established with any certainty. It is characteristic of the California area.

stone, Khenem. An Egyptian amulet (q.v.) which was placed on the dead body during the burial ceremony prior to the reading of inscriptions from the Book of the Dead just before the coffin was closed.

stone, long. See MENHIR.

stone, milling. See QUERN.

stone, nardoo. A slab metate among the Australians.

stone, notched. A stone with notches, used to polish and sharpen various implements. The edge of the tool to be polished was applied to the grooves, and a backward-forward motion produced friction to bring about the desired graining and polish.

stone, nut. A boulder with depressions used by American Indians to crack nuts. Such stones are especially common in the Tennessee area.

stone, pecked. A stone which is abraded rather than chipped.

stone, polishing. A stone, usually in the shape of an oblong polyhedron, used to polish tools and implements. One surface is usually furrowed in grooves that show the wear of small instruments like the chisel or gouge.

stone, precious. A mineral sought because of rareness, strength, color, or other unusual or attractive features. It is probable that early man collected precious stones as ornaments or for medicinal or magic purposes.

stone, religious. Stones often are found in religious contexts, involved with magic, as charms and amulets, as sacred boundary or phallic symbols, as gods or gods' residences. Their shape sometimes helped make them objects of devotion. The Black Stone of Mecca is kissed by many Moslem pilgrims. The lingam (q.v.) in India is worshipped. Rocks with Gautama Buddha's footprint were sacred. Almost every religion has had its sacred stones. In the Old Testament, Jacob gave the name "God's house" to the stone on which he slept and anointed it.

Stone, Rosetta. A basalt stone, about three feet nine inches long, two feet four and one half inches wide, and eleven inches thick, on one side of which were three parallel columns, in Greek, demotic, and heiroglyphic writing. When deciphered by Champollion, it gave the meaning of the hieroglyphs. It was found near the Nile's Rosetta mouth in 1789 by a French officer named Boussard. When Alexandria fell, the British government captured the stone and in 1802 put it in the British Museum. There are 32 lines of demotic, 14 of hieroglyphs, and 54 of Greek. The subject is a decree of the priests of Memphis awarding divine honors to Ptolemy V, Epiphanes (c. 203-181 B.C.), because he conferred various benefits. The Greek text proved easy to read, and Silvestre de Sacy of France and J. D. Akerblad of Sweden studied the demotic text and identified its names. The inscription afforded the first clue to the deciphering of hieroglyphics.

stone, sacred. See ALTAR.

stone, sarsen. A silicious sandstone block from a valley between Swinden and Salisbury in England.

stone, sedimentary. One of the three architectural and sculptural categories of stone. Gypsum, limestone, slate, shale, and sandstone belong to this classification.

stone, sling. An intentionally shaped stone, usually cylindrical with pointed ends, used as a missile to be hurled with a sling, especially in Polynesia and Peru.

stone, standing. See MENHIR.

stone, three-cornered. A triangular carved stone of unknown use, frequently zoomorphic, found in Taino archaeological sites in Hispaniola and Puerto Rico.

stone, thunder. A polished stone, formerly believed to have fallen from the sky in a thunder storm.

Stone Age. See AGE, PALEOLITHIC.

stone count. See COUNT, STONE.

Stone Platform. See PLATFORM, STONE.

stone table. See DOLMEN.

Stonehenge. The group of upright and horizontal stones located on Salisbury Plain, England and thought to be the ruins of an ancient temple of the druids. The transportation of the "bluestones" from a quarry in the Prescelly Mountains of Wales, 150 miles away, probably by sledges, has been called one of the most remarkable feats of prehistoric initiative in Europe. Thousands of men were probably working on the job for many years. The first Stonehenge earthwork dates from ca. 1800 B.C. The second monument was begun ca. 1650 B.C. and consisted of two stone concentric circles oriented toward the midsummer sunrise, with a two-mile-long processional avenue. The third period of Stonehenge construction took place ca. 1500 B.C., and consisted of a circle of 30 uprights, capped by a ring of stone lintels which surrounded a horseshoe of trilithons, each consisting of two uprights and a lintel. The chieftans of the Wessex aristocracy, who are buried in large numbers near Stonehenge, were probably responsible for this building. The graves of these chiefs have artifacts indicating that the basis for their power was trade with central Europe and the Mediterranean, primarily in the products of Irish gold and bronze smiths.

stoneware. A kind of earthenware made of clay fired at such a high temperature that it fuses into a very hard substance that is resistant to liquids and scratching. Cologne is usually credited with being the site of the first stoneware, in the early 15th century, although it was made in France in the early 13th century. Stoneware is often glazed with salt, and the clay used may have flint particles suspended in it.

stool, cucking. A chair used to punish shrews and dishonest merchants. It is shaped like a toilet seat. Sometimes the victims were ducked in a pond. It was used in England by the 13th century.

stop. A complete stopping of the breath passage by raised velum and lips and tongue, or by the closed glottis, e.g., in *p, b, d.* Some linguists consider the nasals *m, n,* and *ng,* which are made by oral and not nasal closure, to be stops also. The breath gathered behind the closure emerges with a slight pop when the closure is suddenly opened. Stops probably exist in every language. A stop cannot be prolonged. A stop is sometimes described as an occlusive sound or as a stop-plosive.

stop, alveolar. See STOP, DENTAL.

stop, bilabial. See STOP, LABIAL.

stop, dental, stop gingival, or **stop, alveolar.** A stop made by the tip of the tongue effecting a closure against the ridge (the alveolar ridge) on the rear of the upper gum (whence also the name gingival) or against the back of the teeth (dental), e.g., *t.*

stop, glottal or **stop, laryngal.** A slight cough made by the vocal cords being abruptly forced apart after lung pressure compresses the air behind the glottis. Such stops

often occur in the Semitic languages, which treat them as consonants. The letter alpha in Greek and aleph in the Semitic languages represent the glottal stop. In English the glottal stop is generally deplored as a bad, albeit common, speech habit. It is recognized as correct in order to separate consecutive occurrences of the same consonant at the end of one word and the beginning of the next, e.g., *Hit Tom.*

stop, labial or **stop, bilabial.** A stop made by the two lips forming the closure, e.g., the *b* in but.

stop, laryngal. See STOP, GLOTTAL.

stop, sonant. A stop in which the vocal cords vibrate while it is being pronounced, e.g., the *d* in German.

stop, surd. A stop in which the vocal cords do not vibrate when it is pronounced, e.g., the *t* in Latin.

stop, velar. A stop made by the back of the tongue being pushed against the velum, e.g., the *tt* in guttural.

story, cumulative. A story in which plants and animals have human qualities. There is usually an extended accumulation of statements, which may be reversed in order to end the story properly.

story, edifying. A medieval story dealing with the lives of the saints or the Madonna.

story, origin. A folk story about how various natural phenomena began, particularly among North American Indians.

story, true. An American Indian description of certain stories or myths, as opposed to lies or jokes.

strabismus. The inward turning of the axes of the eyes, popularly called cross-eyes.

straightener, arrow. 1 A part of an antler with one or more oval or circular holes. It has been suggested that these objects may also have served as brooches, scepters, or devices to make pliable thongs or reins from reindeer hide. 2 A device for straightening bent arrows, by wetting the arrow, binding it tightly to the straightener, and then leaving it to dry and set. The modern Eskimo use such straighteners.

strain, culture. A condition of uneasiness resulting from the disequilibrium which is a product of acculturation (q.v.). It results from the conflict between wanting to accept and to reject a new culture. In India, thus, many copied the behavior of the British colonials at the same time that Ghandi was urging adherence to the peasantry's traditional customs. The Kikuyu in Kenya probably represent the best known example of recent culture strain, with acculturation causing a collapse of marriage traditions, mores, and old modes of exchange, while confusion was worsened by overpopulation and the fact that the colonials did not observe the precepts of the Christian religion taught by the missionaries.

strainer, kava. A bundle of fiber used to strain out the solid parts from the juice of the pepper root from which kava is made.

strake. On a boat, planking going fore and aft.

strake, bilge. A strake situated where the side and bottom merge.

strake, wash. The top strake, or a plank placed on the gunwale to keep spray out.

strake, yarboard. On a boat, the strake next to the keel on both sides.

stranger. A person who comes into face-to-face contact with a group for the first time. Strangers often occupy a special place in early society. A stranger sometimes may not settle in a group without the chief's permission, and may be excluded from religious rites, refused burial, and subjected to mendacity. The stranger may bring bad luck or disease or have a baleful supernatural influence.

On such data, some writers have suggested that in early society a stranger is an enemy. Westermarck and Briffault suppose that the stranger is a god in disguise, thus explaining sacred harlotry (q.v.), inasmuch as the man is often specifically described as a stranger. The idea that a god is entertained in honoring a stranger may have been quite widespread. The relation between a host and his stranger guest is often confirmed by a ritual or ceremony. See GUEST; HOSPITALITY.

strata cut. See CUT, STRATA.

stratification. The layers that can be seen in an archaeological site, as determined by the application of the geological law of superposition (q.v.).

stratigraphy. The picture of the changing culture content of an archaeological site, usually based on the content of its stratification.

stratum, contact. The topmost layer of an archaeological site.

511

Stratz den Haag, Carl (1858-1924). A German anthropologist who used a considerable number of characteristics to differentiate races, and integrated his races with geographic concepts. He suggested the possibility of human beings being divided into a progressive group and a static group.

stream, crown. A stream of hair which begins at the crown.

stream, glabellar. A stream of hair beginning at the root of the nose.

strength, dynamometric. A score obtained by averaging three squeezes of the dynamometer, a device for measuring muscular power.

stress. The comparative emphasis, intensity, or loudness given to speech sounds. The more stress a sound has, the higher the number of sound waves, the closer together the vocal chords are for voicing, and the more energetically the sound is produced. The term stress accent is preferred by some writers.

stress, fixed. When speaking of a word, the emphasis which is always placed on the same syllable, no matter what inflectional or other changes take place and regardless of grammatical function.

stress, syllabic. An increase in stress which makes a syllabic of a sonant. It may have the effect of a secondary phoneme.

stretcher, sound. A device that permits the playback of a speech sample at a rate differing from that at which it was uttered while retaining the original pitch.

striae. Tiny channels or grooves in flint, radiating out from the bulb of percussion (q.v.), toward which they converge. They can be used to help determine the location of the point of percussion on a flint artifact.

strike-a-light. An early technique for fire-making, in which flint was struck against a hard stone to produce sparks. Flint and pyrites probably represent the earliest kind of strike-a-light, although the decomposition of pyrites may make it difficult to trace this method accurately. Sparks from pyrites are dull and will ignite only quick tinder. Even true pyrite pieces, struck together, may give a spark. The use of flint is more precise and is less likely to break the flint. The flint method was used by the eastern and central Eskimo. Later strike-a-lights used steel rather than pyrites. One of the earliest steel strike-a-lights is found in the late Iron Age pile buildings of Ueberlinger See. The first literary mention of steel in fire-making is by Lucretius, 95-91 B.C. Steel for early strike-a-lights probably first came from India. This steel was made by the cementation process, in which iron was heated in a closed vessel along with animal matter like horn or skin. This formed a layer of steel on the iron by casehardening. Steel probably did not become widespread for fire-striking until the late Iron Age, because most of the steel was used for weapons. The subsequent use of flint and steel for fire-making was the result of trade.

strike-a-light, bamboo. A strike-a-light found in Malaysia, Cochin China, the Waigiou Islands, and

512

West Africa. It consists of a piece of broken china which is struck on the side of a piece of bamboo. Bamboo with a hispid siliceous coating appears to be most useful for this purpose.

striker. A circular tool with a fairly flat lateral surface, made of a hard stone like granite or quartz, used for a hammer, a weight, and other purposes.

string, bowed. A musical instrument the tones of which are produced by drawing a bow across strings.

string, loop. A string which goes over a digit.

string, sympathetic. A strong thin string which is under the major strings on an instrument. Sympathetic strings are either tuned together or in some relation with the major strings. When the major strings vibrate, the sympathetic strings pick up the vibration. Their vibrations have a rich quality and take some time to die away, so that they provide resonant background. They are found widely in India.

string figure. See FIGURE, STRING.

structural theory. See THEORY, FUNCTIONAL AND STRUCTURAL.

structure, basic personality. The nuclear personality which is common to all members of a culture, developing from certain basic patterns of child rearing and institutional interaction. The term has been used in several studies by Abram Kardiner and his associates.

structure, social. The ordered relation which the parts of a society have to each other, seen from a reasonably long-range point of view.

Anthropological viewpoints of social structure have ranged from seeing it as the web of all the interpersonal relations in a community to the relations among only the major groups. Social structure has also been defined as the ideals and expectations of a society.

studies, area. Studies of a given area's human and natural resources. Such studies are usually cooperative.

stuff, soul. Extra-natural power, or that part of it relating to particular persons or objects.

Stukeley, William (1687-1755). A British field archaeologist, a pioneer in the ". . . account of places and things from inspection, not completed from others' labors, or travels in one's study." He was greatly interested in Druid remains.

stupa. A mound of varying size, widely distributed in Asian countries. Stupes have been used for thousands of years. Large stupas are believed to contain relics of Buddha or of saints and are venerated. In India, they were used for the burial of early kings. The large stupas have platforms and a staff or dome on top. The proportions were carefully prescribed. Stupas have sometimes been classified according to whether they resemble the female breast or the phallus more closely.

stupefacient. A material that paralyzes or immobilizes. Many different stupefacients are used in fishing, especially in quiet waters.

Stupika. An immense sculpture carved directly out of a rock quarry. It is located in India at Ellura and is actually a gigantic stupa (q.v.).

513

It is one of the best-known tombs in Indian art .

style, horizon. A spatial continuum which is found throughout the wide distribution of a given art style. The concept was developed in Andean archaeology by Max Uhle in 1913.

subarea, culture. An element of a larger culture area, characterized by its relative completeness and the relatively advanced degree of development of a particular trait.

subaurale. With the head held in the Frankfurt line (q.v.), the low point on the inferior border of the ear lobule.

sub-boreal. See BOREAL, SUB-.

subbrachyskelic. Referring to a stem-leg length index (q.v.) between 80 and 84.9.

subincision. A ritual operation on a male initiate, consisting of a posterior opening of the urethra for about one inch. It is especially found in Australia, where it is always associated with circumcision (q.v.). A stone may be placed in the subincised penis in order to keep the urethra open. Subincision may be an attempt to imitate the female genitals, an interpretation favored by the fact that some groups further incise the penis on anniversaries after the operation to make it bleed. The drawing of penile blood is probably the most important part of the operation; this may be used to anoint or paint the initiate or as a symbol of his new status. Hogbin believes that subincision is a cleansing operation against disease. Pitt-Rivers has noted its use in Fiji as a therapeutic blood letting. Little credence is now given to the view that subincision prevents normal ejaculation of semen and demands a special copulatory posture to effect impregnation.

submacroskelic. Referring to a stem-leg length index (q.v.) between 90 and 94.9.

subnasale. The point at which there is a merger of the nasal septum and the upper cutaneous lip in the midsagittal plane (q.v.).

subordination. An exocentric (q.v.) language combination in which a clause or phrase is subordinate to a subordinating expression, e.g., *If Arbuthnot were sick; richer than Arbuthnot.*

subplatyhieric. Referring to a length-breadth sacral index (q.v.) between 100 and 105.9.

subrace, primary. A subgroup within a primary race. It results from intensification, localization and continued operation of the factors which produced the primary race. These factors, along with mutation, inbreeding, selection, and adaptational changes, work on more restricted groups than the race.

subsection. Half of an Australian section.

subspecies. A subdivision of a species which is genetically and taxonomically different from other subdivisions. The major human races are probably less distinct than subspecies, while the same is perhaps not true of the major dog breeds.

substance, soul. A substance, found in the lore of Indonesia and Melanesia, which is believed to permeate humans, plants, and animals, as well as the bodily exuviae, like nail pairings. The body will suffer if the soul substance is not returned. Animals and plants give up their soul substance by being eaten. Much magic is based on soul substance.

substitute. A language form which may replace another form in specific circumstances.

substitute, anaphoric. A substitute which implies that the word replaced has recently been used.

substitution. Using a word which has been superseded to describe a new device or subject.

substratum, linguistic. A set of features of an extinct language that survives in the language which replaced it. The term is sometimes applied to the extinct language as such. In English, part of the linguistic substratum is composed of the few surviving Anglo-Saxon plurals, like children, sheep, and mice.

substratum theory of sound change. See SOUND CHANGE, SUBSTRATUM THEORY OF.

subtractive. See PROJECTIVE.

succession. The procedures for the handing down of rank, privileges, or authority in a social group, through kinship or other means.

succubus. A female demon who disturbs humans at night. Succubi typically tempt men to carnality.

Sudanese. A group of languages spoken south of the Sahara. They include Yoruba, Hausa, and Nuba.

Sudanese-Guinean. A family of African languages which includes the individual languages of some 50 million persons. Linguists have classified from 171 to 435 languages. The principal languages within this family are Ewe, Efik,

Hausa, Mandingo, Mende, Masai, Nubian, Twi, and Yoruba.

sudatory. A sweat bath.

suffix. An affix which appears at the end of a word and subsequent to the underlying form, e.g., *ness* in *coolness*.

suicide. Taking one's own life. Early men as a group did not have a definite view on suicide. It is not practiced or even known in some groups, while in others the incidence is fairly high. Societies in which there is little emphasis on status and competition are less likely to have much suicide. Some Brahman and Buddhist thought implies that the body can be abandoned whenever its owner wishes. Islam regards suicide as reprehensible. The Old and New Testament do not specifically prohibit suicide although both Judaism and Christianity condemn it as flouting God's will and spurning the temple He provided for the soul. Under the old common law, the estate of a suicide escheated. At present in many jurisdictions it is criminal to attempt suicide.

suku. A New Guinea term for tobacco.

Sukwe. A graded society in the Banks and Torres Islands.

sukya. In Central America, a sorcerer who can cure disease.

sulcus. In anatomy, a groove.

sullung. In Kent, a hide (q.v.).

sumac. A plant used for dyeing, tanning, smoking, and perfume.

Sumerian. An ancient language, now extinct, which has no verifiable common origin with any known langauge. The geographical distribution was from Babylon to the Persian Gulf in Mesopotamia. It was spoken from 4000 B.C. till the third century B.C.

sumpitan. A Malay blowgun.

sun. See STINKARD.

Sun, Children of the. The belief in several parts of the world that ruling families have descended from the sun.

Sun, Great. The title of the Natchez chief, used to distinguish him from other members of the noble class, who were called suns. The French term was "Grand Soleil." See STINKARD.

Sung. Referring to the Sung dynasty in China, A.D. 960-1279, in which many porcelain manufacturing centers developed. Stoneware with overglaze enamels was first made at Tz'u Chou.

sun-language theory. The belief that awe of the sun generated man's first aweful or thoughtful sound, so that human speech is related to observing solar phenomena.

sunspot. A dark spot observed on the sun. Sunspots appear on an average of one in every 11.2-11.4 years, although they have appeared as close together as 5.6 years and as far apart as 11.9 years. Many cultures attribute special meaning to them.

sunwise. Referring to handing an object around or organizing processionals or movements in the same direction as the sun's apparent diurnal movement.

superaurale. The top point on the superior border of the helix.

supercision. Making a longitudinal incision in the foreskin. It is a variant of circumcision (q.v.).

superlative, absolute. A superlative used to show the high position of a quality without implying comparison, e.g., *supreme.*

superorganic. Referring to the concept of culture as an entity over and beyond the human beings who live under its sway. Originally used by Herbert Spencer to describe the high point in evolution, the term was given anthropological currency by A. L. Kroeber in 1917.

superposition. In the case of aggradating deposits, if there has not been any subsequent disturbance, lower geological levels are older than upper. The bottom layer is the oldest, the top the most recent, the level below the top is fresher than the one below it, etc. The *law of superposition* is a general statement of this rule.

superstition. A belief for which there is no real basis in either science or religion. Most superstitions are vestiges of decayed systems of belief.

superstratum. The language of a conquering or culturally and economically superior nation which has been superimposed on the language of the subjugated or dependent nation.

supination. A forearm position in which the ulna and radius are parallel and the palm is turned upward; also, a standing position in which the outer side of the foot bears the weight.

suppletion. The complete absence of phonetic relation between the members of a class, e.g., *go, went.*

supraorbital. Referring to being above the eye's orbit, e.g., the supraorbital ridges.

suprasegmental feature. See FEATURE, SUPRASEGMENTAL.

surd. A sound made without the synchronized vibration of the vocal cords, e.g., *t.*

surface, measure of. The terminology generally used to express the size of a surface, such as the area of an animal's hide, a day's plowing on the part of a given animal unit, or a land that can be sown with a particular seed unit.

survey, archaeological. A network of grids over an archaeological site. It is used for measuring profiles, mapping features, and excavation. An archaeological survey is also the exploration of an area to obtain samples from each culture phase contained. Samples from several sites are collected, often by means of a strata cut for purposes of establishing the chronology.

survey, resistivity. A method for determining the extent of human habitation of different parts of an archaeological site by sending an alternating electric current through the ground. It is possible to detect those areas which have been disturbed and thus are more likely to have human remains by the differential degree of resistance to the current of the disturbed as compared with comparatively undisturbed ground. The method was successfully used by De Terra in his study of Tepexpan sites in Mexico.

survival. A holdover from previous times still present in contemporary culture. Tylor called attention to the importance of survivals in *Primitive Culture* (1871). W. J. Thoms in 1846 emphasized how folklore was based on survivals. Laurence Gomme's *Folklore As An Historical Science* (1908) contained much information on survivals as folklore, and Otis Mason traced survivals in material culture in his studies of primitive women and invention (1895). The comparative anthropologists of the late 19th century studied survivals as clues to the development of early society. To some extent, modern ethnologists have tended to regard the survival of nonmaterial traits without change as unlikely and to insist upon the significance of the trait in the total cultural complex.

survival of the fittest. See FITTEST, SURVIVAL OF THE.

susu. A kinship group consisting of the brother and children of a woman, as well as the woman. The emphasis is matrilineal and unilateral. The term is Dobuan and means "mother's milk."

suttee or sati. Among the Hindus, cremating a woman on her husband's funeral pyre. It has been banned in India since 1829. It was voluntary on the part of the woman and regarded as a very honorable act. The word comes from *sate* "virtuous life." Suttee began in the fourth century B.C. and was given religious approval in the sixth century A.D. The widow's reward was complete cleansing of evil for her

517

family and her husband's family and sainthood for herself.

suture. A seam connecting the several bones that form the brain case. These sutures remain open while the brain is growing, and their obliteration commences when the growth stops. In man, this process of obliteration begins around age 18 but is not completed until late in life. At birth, the sutures are lines of dense membranes but turn to bone. There is a relation between the growth of the brain in a given area and the suture's complexity. Thus the lambdoidal suture will be the most complex if the rear part of the brain develops most rapidly, the usual condition in Negroes. In Caucasians, the coronal suture is often the most complex, and in Mongolians, the sagittal suture.

suture, coronal. A transverse suture running across the top of the head.

suture, metopic. A median suture in the cranium's frontal bone. It generally disappears in childhood.

suture, nasofrontal. The line of union of the frontal and the two nasal bones.

suture, sagittal. The middle suture that lies between the parietal bones.

Swanscombe. A skull of a woman, probably about 20 to 25 years old, with a brain capacity of 1,325 or 1,350 cc. The skull is that of a primitive sapiens although the bones are thick. It indicates that a fairly high and narrow brain case appeared before the middle of the Pleistocene. These fossil remains were found in England in 1936 by A. T. Marston. They consisted of a parietal and occipital bone, in a very good condition of preservation. An endocranial cast has indicated that the folding of the gray matter was about as complicated as modern man's. On the basis of these two bones, it would appear that Acheulian man did not differ greatly from modern man, thus making Homo sapiens older than was supposed.

swaraj. In the East Indian language, independence or self-rule.

swastika. The name given to the pramantha (q.v.) by the Brahmin priests. From the many swastika-like devices found by Schliemann in the ruins of Troy, he concluded that the Trojans were Aryans. The devotees of Vishnu make this sign on their forehead. Among American Indians, the swastika was used in the sun worship of the Kickapoos, the Pottawatomies, and other groups, who called it a symbol of good luck. The swastika represented the sun, with its hooks the solar movements, according to Max Müller. The good-luck swastika turns sunwise, to the right; the bad-luck turns to the left. The swastika is also called the fylfot.

sweep. In metal casting, a pattern used in making molds for symmetrical articles.

Swiderian. A culture found in Poland, with the tranchet ax a typical tool. Its remains, mostly kitchen middens, resemble the Campignian (q.v.) culture, which is found further south.

swinging, hook. A form of self-torture, often for religious reasons, by suspending the body by hooks inserted under the large muscles of the shoulder or back. Hook swinging was often part of the sun dance (q.v.) ritual of the Plains Indians.

sword. 1 In warfare, a weapon used for thrusting and slashing. The first sword was probably a tanged blade, with flanges bordering the flat tang and round shoulders. The center of balance is usually nearer the hilt than the point. Swords are either solid or composite, with each type further divisible into cutting swords, like the cutlass or broadsword, and thrusting swords, like the rapier. The sword consists of blade, guard, hilt, and sheath. The guard may be separate or attached. The hilt comprises the grip and the pommel, while the sheath protects the blade. 2 In weaving, a flat bar with a sharp edge, used to "beat up" a pick of the weft.

sword, antennae. An early Swiss sword in which the pommel is a heavy bronze ribbon bent into opposing spirals. Often the spirals are fashioned like tiny snakes.

sword, chastity. A sword placed between a couple sleeping together to insure that they remain chaste.

sword, Hallstatt. In the Early Iron Age of Central Europe, a bronze sword that lost the flanges around the hilt and developed a wide extension of the hilt that could accommodate a cone-shaped pommel.

sword, Ronzano or **sword, Mörigen.** A sword with a pommel shaped like an oval saucer.

syllabary. A table of written characters each of which represents a syllable. Japanese uses two syllabaries, both independently of or in association with Chinese characters. The term signary is also used.

syllabic. A phoneme which is a crest of sonority (q.v.), e.g., *e* in *red; l* in *apple*. A nonsyllabic is a phoneme which is not such a crest, e.g., *r* in *red*.

syllabic, non-. See SYLLABIC; ASYLLABIC.

syllabication. The analysis of speech into its component syllables. A syllable is a segment of speech including a crest of sonority (q.v.) and extending from one trough of sonority to another. It can also be described as a group of phonemes (q.v.) made up of a vowel or a continuant and a consonant or consonants which form a complete articulation and constitute a unit of word-formation. An open syllable ends in a vowel while a closed syllable ends in a consonant.

syllable, common. A syllable that may be sounded either long or short, with or without accent, according to its position in the word.

symbiosis. The living together in close association of two dissimilar organisms.

symbol, arbitrary. A symbol the form of which does not have a natural or necessary link with its meaning. The characters of the alphabet are arbitrary, while pictograms and ideograms at least tend to be representative.

symmetry, bilateral. The similarity and likeness between right and left sides of an organism or en-

519

tity. **Radial symmetry** is the symmetry on a circular plan of such organisms as the starfish or of snowflakes.

sympathy, law of. Frazer's hypothesis that most magic formulas hinge on association between two objects. Sympathy is the basis for imitative magic (q.v.) and contagious magic (q.v.), which function on the basis of like being drawn to like. The term **principle of sympathy** is sometimes found.

sympatric. Referring to groups that occur in contiguity or overlap geographically.

symphysis. Two bones joined by cartilage which may be replaced after childhood by a bony suture.

sympodial. Lester F. Ward's term for the meandering nature of evolution. The term, derived from botany, indicates a main stem giving off a branch which is a new axis of growth, with the original stem becoming reduced to a twig. Ward confirmed this theory by paleobotanical researches and extended it to the evolution of peoples and cultures. If evolution is sympodial, a given genus and species may not stem from the specialized forms of preceding epochs but from more primitive generalized forms.

synapsis, somatic. The fusion of body-cell chromosome pairs.

synchronic. Referring to the functional approach to the study of culture, as of a given time. See DIACHRONIC.

synchronism. The practice of representing two or more events that took place at different times in the same picture or work of art.

syncretism. 1 In religion, a merger of two analogous elements in two different cultures. Each of the elements retains its being, e.g. the identification of African deities and Catholic saints among some African cult devotees in Haiti. 2 In language, the use of a particular grammatical form to perform the functions of another form or other forms in addition to its own.

syncretic. Referring to an act which gears in with the actions of other group members in performing a social function.

syndactylia. The growing together of two or more fingers or toes or web fingers or toes. It is a Mendelian (q.v.) trait.

syndiasmian. An impermanent man-woman association in which the participants do not cohabit exclusively with each other.

syngenism. The feeling of union resulting from being brought up together.

synostosis. The growing together of bones, like the sutures on the skull.

syntax. The branch of grammar dealing with the combination of words into larger constructions up to the sentence.

syringe, fire. A fire-making device, used by the Malays and Siamese, consisting of a cylinder with a closely fitting piston that holds tinder. When driven down, the piston kindles the tinder.

syrinx or **syrinx, compound.** See PIPES, PAN.

systadial. Referring to the same stage in the sequence of evolution.

system, baksheesh, bakshish or bakhshish. The system of paying rewards to workers on archaeological excavations for the finds they make. Experience has shown that where this system is used, it adds 5 to 10 per cent to the regular wages. The term baksheesh means essentially a tip or gratuity.

system, classificatory. The name given by Lewis H. Morgan (q.v.) to kinship systems in which the remoteness of a blood relationship does not lessen its importance. Under a classificatory system, it is more important to express kin-solidarity than exact genealogical relationships. Thus "mother" may not indicate the parent alone but her sisters as well. This system may have arisen, he believed, because of the necessity to unite fighting men for common protection, as well as because the sustained thought necessary to devise a descriptive (q.v.) system was lacking. Recent research suggests that Morgan's distinction between classificatory and descriptive is too sweeping, and that these are terms which should not be applied to systems of terminology, since almost every known system of kinship uses classificatory terms widely. Morgan introduced this term to designate a pattern of nomenclature which classed to-

gether lineal with collateral (qq.v.) relatives.

system, eight-class. A characteristic of the kinship structure of some Australian tribes in which all the members are divided into eight classes. An individual is permitted to marry into only one of these classes, which must not be his natal class.

system, grid. A co-ordinate field of an archaeological site which is staked out by survey methods to control excavations and record information.

system, metronymic. Tracing kinship exclusively through the mother. In matrilocal societies, property rights also are transmitted through the female. The Pueblo Indians were an outstanding example of the application of this system.

system, particularizing. A kinship system where every term for a relationship applies only to one genealogical status.

system, square-field plot. Cultivation of crops on a group of squares and small fields about one half to two acres in area. It is found in many parts of Europe and first appeared in England ca. 1000 B.C.

system, three-field. A method of land cultivation which allows one or two out of three plots to lie fallow for a year.

T

taap. An Australian saw knife.

tabbalat. An ancient Arabian drum. It is made of a shallow wooden shell which is carried around the neck, and it is played with the hands. The instruments are often played in pairs and are then called tabbalat arrakeb.

tabl. An ancient Egyptian drum made by stretching a parchment head over an earthenware jar or a hollowed wood block. It is played by beating with the fingers and wrists.

table, ground-water. The top of the zone of saturation (q.v.).

table, libation. A shallow pottery bowl on a stand. Examples are found in some Vinca remains.

table, stone. See DOLMEN.

tablet, anointing. An alabaster slab with seven hollows for the seven holy oils. It was used in ancient Egypt in one of the final ceremonies at the tomb. The oils were intended for magical protection on the journey to the next world. See MUMMIFICATION.

tablet, duck. An object of wood, bone, or metal approximately shaped like a duck. Its function is debatable. The duck tablet is found in the Florida area.

tablet, votive. A vow marker; a religious stone marker commemorating fulfillment of, or devotion to, a sacred oath.

Tablets, Eugubine. Bronze tablets found in 1444 at Gubbio Eugubium, Italy, inscribed in Umbrian, Etruscan, and Latin. There are seven tablets, which are believed to have been written between 400 and 300 B.C.

tablier. A Hottentot apron.

taboo or **tabu.** A prohibition, which, if violated, leads to an automatic penalty inflicted by magic or religion. Captain James Cook discovered the Polynesian term on his third voyage around the world, in 1777. In the early study of religion, the term taboo was used to indicate the signs of caution established to guard against basically dangerous things, i.e., those possessing mana (q.v.). Once the approved pattern of behavior was violated, early man might feel apprehensive. Some things could best be dealt with by avoiding them, rather than coming in contact with a contagion that might automatically punish. Taboo was widely applied to blood and death, warriors returning from battle, and even some property.

In the specifically Polynesian usage, the word referred to the forbidden and sacred. Frazer explained taboos as the result of applying beliefs based on erroneous reasoning processes, with an accidental effect of maintaining society. Radcliffe-Brown has suggested that both positive and negative rites continue because they have a function in maintaining society and its values.

taboo, looking. The belief that something is lost if it is looked at.

taboo, name. The restriction against mentioning the name of certain persons, objects, or deities.

tabu. See TABOO.

Tabueriki. The chief god of the Gilbert Islands.

Tacitus (55-120 A.D.). A Roman historian, the first person, in his account of Germany, to write a study of a culture.

taclla. The Peruvian name for the foot plow (q.v.).

taclobo. See TRIDACNA.

tagmeme. The minimum formal meaningful unit of grammar (q.v.). It may contain several taxemes (q.v.).

taiaha. A long wooden sword-club used in warfare by the Maori. Formalized fencing with taiahas took place, and they were also symbols of chiefly authority.

t'ai chi. In Chinese art, the symbol of the Great Absolute. It consists of a wavy or double curved line bisecting a circle, one half of which is red (see YANG) and the other black

(see YIN). In representations of this symbol, there are usually eight trigrams, which are the basis of Chinese divination. Each trigram is made of a number of lines, with each pair representing two of the major contrasting phenomena resulting from the yang-yin interaction when matter was formed. The 12 zodiacal symbols are also often found.

taiga. A swampy coniferous forest region in Siberia, which begins where the tundra (q.v.) ends. The term is used for similar regions in other parts of the world.

tail, rat's. An argot term for straight hair.

tale, animal. A fairly short tale which is essentially etiological, in that it explains the cause of some feature of animal life. Thus, how the bear lost his tail was explained by a tale in which a fox induced a bear to dip his tail into water in the winter to catch some fish. When ice froze around the tail, the bear freed himself, leaving the tail behind. A widely repeated story is how the snake learned to shed his skin: since this ability was interpreted as a sign of the snake's immortality, it was said that the snake obtained it by tricking man out of his immortality. This may have been the beginning of the myth of the fall of man. Out of these attempts to explain natural facts, developed such important literary types as the beast epic and the fabliau (q.v.).

tale, chain. A folktale in which there is a schematic series of objects, events, or persons in specific relations to each other.

tale, endless or **circular.** A kind of folktale characterized by the repetition of a theme, incident, or turn of phrase to the point of tedium. The auditors cannot stay to hear the end, as in the story of the mountain which was moved a grain of sand at a time.

tale, etiological. See TALE, ANIMAL.

tale, formula. A tale in which the pattern is more important than the plot. It follows a traditional formula. An example is *The House That Jack Built.*

tale, merry. A fairly short narrative that relates an event that culminates humorously. A merry tale may be in verse or prose, and its subject matter comes from everyday life. Homer tells several such tales, and they were often used in the medieval exempla literature of the Roman Catholic Church to explain the truths of Christianity by allegory and parable. Boccacio and the French fabliaux draw on many merry tales.

Taleb. Among the Arabs, a holy or learned man.

talent. In Mesopotamian money, 60 minas (q.v.).

Talgai. An Australian skull fragment from the late Pleistocene era. It was found in 1884 but not described until 1918.

tali. The ceremonial first marriage of a Nayar girl.

talisman. An object which has the power of effecting unusual and wondrous happenings. Sometimes the special qualities of the talisman are absorbed by its owner, even in the absence of the object. A talisman may also guard against evil.

talking chief. See CHIEF, TALKING.

talonid. A cusp organization on the lower molar of Homo sapiens made up of hypoconid, entoconid, and hypoconulid formations. In the evolution to the talonid form, the tooth went through the trigonid stage, which was composed of the paraconid, protoconid, and metaconid formations, and developed a heel or shelf which was the beginning of the hypoconid, hypoconulid, and entoconid, which constitute the talonid form. The protocone occludes in the distal fossa of the talonid in the lower first molars.

talu. See INTICHIUMA.

talus. 1 The sloping heap of fragments of loose rock at the foot of a cliff or steep slope; a sheet of waste which covers a slope below a cliff. In Great Britain, **scree** is used instead of talus, and the term **presle** is also found. 2 The ankle bone, that transfers the body's weight from the tibia to the foot.

talus cone. A piece of broken rock found at the base of a cliff after being dislodged through the action of frost.

talyot. A stone building in the form of a truncated cone. It resembles a nuraghe (q.v.).

tamate. A term for spirit in Melanesia and also for a New Hebrides secret society (q.v.) centering around the spirits of the dead.

tamberan. A cult, found in many New Guinea tribes, involving bull roarers (q.v.) and masks (q.v.).

tambourine. A cylindrical rim with a membrane head. Bits of metal are usually hung on the rim. The instrument is struck by the hand or with a stick.

tambu. Shell money of New Britain. See NASSA.

tamburan. In New Guinea, a sacred house.

Tamenend. The Delaware chief from whose name Tammany is derived.

tamouanehan. The Aztec repository of unborn souls.

Tampanian. The chopper culture of Malaya.

tampu. A wayside station in the Inca road system. See ROADS, CLASSIFICATION OF; INCA.

Tane or Kane. The Polynesian god of beauty and the creator god.

T'ang. Referring to the glazed pottery and tomb figures of the T'ang dynasty in China, A.D. 618-906. Porcelain (q.v.) first appeared in this period.

tanga. A pubic covering worn by Indian women, especially in tropical South America and the West Indies. The most common form of tanga today is a beaded apron. Others consist of a small triangle of inner bark. Concave pieces of baked clay found archaeologically on Marajó Island have been interpreted as tangas.

tangena. In Madagascar, an ordeal (q.v.) involving swallowing three pieces of a fowl. Those who do not vomit up the skin after an emetic are innocent.

tangi. Among the Maori, a mourning ceremony.

tanning. The process of curing (q.v.) skins by using a vegetable substance containing tannic acid. Water-soaked oak or willow bark can effect tanning. Tanning is only found in fairly advanced cultures.

tao mata. In Polynesia, a mnemonic device consisting of a knotted cord used in reciting genealogies.

t'ao t'ieh. A basic motif in Chinese art, representing the generalized primitive concept of the forces of life. See LEI WEN.

tapa. A fabric made chiefly in the Pacific islands from the finely pounded pulp of the inner bark of the mulberry tree. The bark is dried in the sun and then decorated by painting with natural vegetable stains. Most tapa cloth is some hue of brown. Tapa cloth-making may have influenced the Chinese invention of paper, which originally consisted of mulberry bast stiffened with plant fibers. See CLOTH, BARK.

tapeino-. A prefix meaning flat or low.

tapeinocranic. Referring to a cranial breadth-height index (q.v.) of less than 91.9.

tapia. A material consisting of clay, sometimes mixed with lime, used to construct walls. It is usually poured into a frame and compacted by stamping. A tapia is also a wall so made. This type of construction was practiced in pre-Columbian Peru as well as in Spain and Colonial Latin America.

tapirage. The growing of brightly colored feathers, usually red, by birds whose natural feathers were less colorful. A dye, such as the blood of the frog *Rana tinctura,* is applied to the skin of the bird after its original plumage has been plucked in order to modify the color of the next growth. This technique is known only among the Indians of the Tropical Forest of South America.

Taputapuatea. A great Polynesian temple.

tarappam. A raft, often about 18 by 4 feet, made of a number of pieces of light straight wood, side by side, connected by bars of the same wood. It is found today in the Laccadine Islands.

taraud. A French term for awl.

Tarde, Gabriel de (1843-1904). A French sociologist who emphasized the power of imitation and the non-intellectual components of social behavior.

Tardenoisian. A transitional Epipaleolithic culture area in western Europe. It was most common on sandy soils. Its small flint implements had geometric form. Some regard it as contemporary with the Azilian period, while others believe that it came just after. The naming station is at Fère-en-Tardenois in France, but similar implements have been found elsewhere in western Europe, in North Africa, and in parts of Asia. Composite tools were made widely at this time. A very small micro-graver is the typical tool, and there were no axes.

tarn. A small lake covering an ice-gouged basin.

taro. An aroid grown in the tropics for its edible root stocks and as an ornamental plant. There are many different species of the genus, found in southeast Asia and Polynesia. It was probably first cultivated in upper Burma or Assam.

Tarots. A collection of playing cards, often 22, included in European decks of cards and containing legends and pictures. They are used to tell fortunes.

tarpan. A wild horse found northwest of the Black Sea. It may have been the major ancestor of the domestic horse.

tarriance. Delaying or awaiting.

tarsier. A primate of a type which was the predecessor of the Oligocene monkeys, found in Indonesia and southeast Asia. These small rat-sized animals have some vaguely human traits. The occipital lobes are fairly well developed and the big toes and thumbs are opposable. Posture is usually semierect. The tarsier leaps in a froglike manner.

tarsus. The bones in the posterior portion of the foot. In man, they include the ankle bone, the heel bone, and five small instep bones.

Tasmania. A mountainous fertile island 150 miles from the southeast coast of Australia. The Tasmanians become extinct fairly recently. Some scholars believed that they were Pleistocene (q.v.) relics, perhaps the most primitive humans, but they were largely killed off by white settlers before it was possible to prove or disprove this theory.

taster. A person who tastes PTC (q.v.) when placed on the tongue as bitter.

tattler. In American Indian lore, an animal closely associated with a man which takes him into its confidence and tattles to him about such matters as the infidelity of his wife. The animal dies, in many stories, as a result of these confidences.

tattoo. A colored pattern on the skin, made by placing pigment under the surface. Tattooing is especially practiced in Polynesia. The methods used are puncture, incision, and sewing.

tattoo, scar. A design on the skin, made without color, as in Tasmanian culture.

tattoo, thread. Tattooing in which thread is impregnated with soot or coloring materials and then drawn through the skin.

tau. Red feather money of the Santa Cruz Islands.

tauari. A type of thick bark cloth in the Tropical Forest area of South America. See TURIRI.

taupon. A Samoan girl who has acquired prestige in her village as a result of the sponsorship of a chief.

taura. A Polynesian priest.

taurobolium. A kind of blood baptism into the mysteries of the great Mother Goddess, e.g., Cybele, and into the Mithraic cult. A bull was sacrificed and its blood flowed through a grating onto the initiate. It symbolized capturing a strong animal's blood through contact, and thus being reborn into a new and purified life. Early Roman architecture used a platform above a pit, with many small apertures in the flooring. The worshipper, going in the pit, was baptized by the blood of the bull which had been sacrificed on the platform. A taurobolium is also a work of art with a represen-

tation of a bull sacrifice or killing as its major theme. Such taurobolia are especially common in the Near East. The typical representation is of a bull being slain by a swordsman while a dog bites at its throat and a crab attacks its testicles.

taurodontism. Large pulp cavities in the molar teeth, so that the pulp cavities are deep and extend to the roots, which fuse into a kind of stump, instead of being long and separate. It is characteristic of Neanderthal Man.

tauvia. A headman on Guadalcanal.

Tawhid. The oneness of Allah.

taxeme. An individual facet of grammatical arrangement, which is a minimal unit of formal grammar. See TAGMEME.

taxonomy. Scientific classification, particularly as applied in biology to organisms.

tchama. A papyrus roll on which the ancient Egyptians inscribed their most important documents, e.g., government reports, state proclamations, literary and religious compositions. The Book of the Dead, one of the best known tchamas, is 123 feet long, second only in length to the Harris Papyrus, which is 135 feet long and 16½ feet wide.

tchernozem. See CHERNOZEM.

tea. The leaves and shoots of the Chinese tea plant, which probably originated in tropical eastern Asia. It usually grows as a small bush. In the Orient, its leaf was chewed to counter fatigue before it was used to prepare a beverage.

technique, bipolar. Producing rock flakes with a bulb of percussion at each end as a result of rebounding from the anvil. This technique was used by Sinanthropus pekinensis.

technique, block-on-block. An early method of producing flakes by swinging the core against the edge of a larger stone. It produces thick flakes.

technique, burin. An Upper Paleolithic technique for removing a small facet along a side of the flake. The blow is delivered vertically with the flake also held vertically.

technique, damascene. See DAMASCENING.

technique, Levalloisian. See CORE, TORTOISE.

technique, lost wax. A process of bronze-casting in which a clay figure is covered with wax with a coat of clay on top. When the figure is heated, the wax melts and the bronze is poured in. After the alloy cools, the clay core and the outer mold are removed. This technique was used in Peru and West Africa and during the Renaissance.

technique, pressure. A flint-working technique that involves the use of a blunt tool to press off flint chips where needed.

technique, projective. A method for appraising personality by subjecting the person to a comparatively unstructured and ambiguous stimulus, like the Rorschach (q.v.) ink blots, incomplete sentences, pictures or cartoons (Thematic Apperception Test), and doll play. The purpose of the tests is to supply a means by which the individual can express himself on subjects on

which he would otherwise be inarticulate, either by choice or because he is not aware of his own unconscious psychodynamic mechanisms. This technique is being used increasingly in anthropological field work to develop insights into personality structure.

technique, split-line. Analyzing the patterns of stress in bone by partly decalcifying the bone, inserting an awl in the surface, and marking the ensuing lines of split in ink. These lines show the inner structure of the bone.

technique, tranchet. Using a transverse blow to produce an edge on flint celts.

technique, wood. Flaking flint and other rocks by striking them with hard wood or bone.

Tecpatl. The third year, in Aztec writing; also the word for flint knife.

tectiform. Referring to triangular designs of the Magdalenian period that resemble the frameworks of dwellings or tents. Such designs often have a vertical line from base to apex. They are found on the walls of caves in France and Italy, and may occur by themselves or cover the middle of the body of animal representations.

tecuhtin or **tecutli.** The Aztec noble class.

teepee. See TEPEE.

teeth, vaginal. A widely distributed myth about women with teeth in the vagina. In some forms of the myth on the Northwest Coast of North America, men use a stone pestle to remove the teeth. In certain South African tribes, soreness in the glans penis resulting from frequent intercourse in a short period is attributed to the vaginal teeth. The term **vagina dentata** is also found.

Teke. The first settlers of the Marquesas.

teke. A Congo fetish (q.v.).

teknonymy. The practice of designating a person as the parent of his named child rather than by his individual name. Thus, one is known as "A" until he has offspring "B"; thereafter he is called "Father of 'B.'"

Telanthropus capensis. Perhaps one of the most ancient true men so far known, reported in 1952 by J. T. Robinson of the Transvaal Museum, who found a well-preserved portion of the nose with part of the palate intact about 25 miles northwest of Johannesburg, South Africa. The region of bone below the nose has an angle of slope like that of a true man and the nose is human. The socket for the left canine tooth is intact and is too small for nonhuman tooth roots. The palate is deep.

teleconnection. The process of correlating annual layers over considerable distances, usually on the basis of varve (q.v.) analysis.

teleolith. A deliberately shaped stone artifact.

tell. A mound consisting of debris from villages built over each other on the same site. It is an ancient Babylonian word, still used in Arabic today, meaning "high." Tulul (plural form) are very common in the Middle East. They are shallow truncated cones. Often they are found on hilltops, because they were well located for defense and observation. Subsequent groups would take over the area once it was abandoned or destroyed. As many as 20 layers of habitation have been found on one tell. Some tulul had adobe buildings, which made them unusually high, sometimes attaining 70 feet.

Tellings, Great. Extremely long war and migration tales, among the Mohave Indians. It might take a day to recount one of these stories.

tellurism. The capacity of the earth or soil to produce disease.

telpuchcalli. An Aztec youth home maintained by each clan to train its children and give instruction in citizenship, warfare, arts and crafts, history, and religious observances. Children began going at the age of 15.

temazcalli. See TEMEZCAL.

tembe. A rectangular mud-wall house of East Africa.

tembetá. A long plug suspended from the lower lip and held in the mouth by an enlargement at the upper end. The tembetá was widely used by Tupí-Guaraní tribes in South America. See BOTOQUE.

temezcal or **temazcalli.** A vapor bath in Mexico, consisting of a rectangular stone structure with a low door and ventilating apertures. A rounded oven was at one end. It was dedicated to a divinity, who was credited with supernatural power.

temper. 1 The process whereby metals are given the desired degree of hardness and malleability by controlled heating and cooling. The term is also applied to the hardening of clay and glass. Mica, straw, sand, pulverized sherds, lime, and feldspar are used in pottery. 2 Copper alloyed with tin. It is used by pewterers in making receptacles such as tankards, beakers, and spout pots.

temperature, sensible. The effect of temperature on a person's senses.

temple. A place or building dedicated to a god's worship and usually including an altar (q.v.) and a central holy place. It is possible that the first temples were caves, as in India and Egypt. Originally simple, temples became substantial structures. Each area and religion modified its temple to meet local needs and conditions. Egyptian temples developed from a one-room wattle structure with a representation of the animal or god worshipped, to a large stone building of many rooms. Far Eastern temples differ in size and design. The Altar of Heaven in Peiping, which covers 737 acres, is probably the largest and best known Eastern temple. Almost every county in Korea and China has a Confucian temple, usually of three courts on a central axis. There are over 150,000 Shinto temples in Japan.

Greek temples probably were first constructed ca. ninth century B.C. They usually faced east and were on a platform. On different sides of the Aegean, Doric and Ionic temples developed at about the same time. The Doric temples had sturdy lines and conveyed a feeling of dignity, while the Ionic temples suggested grace and slen-

derness. The Acropolis, from fifth century Athens, had both Doric (the Parthenon) and Ionic (the Erechtheum) buildings, with the Propylaea, or gateway, showing signs of both styles. The Corinthian, a highly decorated variant of the Ionic, developed by the late fifth century. Roman temples emphasized the frontal view and favored the Corinthian order, with a more ornate style, the Composite (involving all three orders), becoming popular, as in the Roman arena called the Colosseum.

India has many temples, with some 1,500 in Benares alone. Most Hindu temples have a room or cell in which there is an image of the deity.

Mesopotamian temples were believed to be the home and workshop of the deity for whom they had been built. Native unbaked brick was the main building material. Vertical T-shaped indentations are often found. Many temples were built on a ziggurat (q.v.).

temple, Pylon. A colonnaded central hall or chamber. The columns are situated at unequal intervals. The architectural term for Pylon temple is hypostyle.

Tenochtitlan. An island city in the Valley of Mexico founded in 1325 by the Tenochca people. This city, the greatest example of Aztec civilization, was the religious center of the Tenochcas. Present-day Mexico City is built on the ruins of Tenochtitlan.

tenon. A projection on a stone or timber made to fit into a mortise (q.v.).

tent. A mobile kind of shelter used by nomadic peoples. It originated in the windbreak (q.v.). It usually consists of a framework, covered by felt, hide, or bark.

tent, conjuring. A kind of tent, usually barrel-shaped, inside which a conjurer kneels at work. It is found among the Ojibwa.

tent, Monger. A tent with a cylindrical frame topped by a cone.

tent, umbrella. A tent with usually four to eight bamboo ribs. It is a European invention widely used in cold countries. In very windy areas, double umbrella tents, one within the other, are often used.

teocalli. A Central American temple, usually on the summit of a truncated pyramidal mound, or the mound itself; also, the Aztec temple at Tenochtitlan.

teocentli or **teocintle.** A wild grass domesticated in Middle America. It gave rise to all the subsequent varieties of corn.

tepe. In Persian archaeology, the term for a tell (q.v.).

tepee, teepee, or **tipi.** A cone-shaped tent, usually of dressed skins, mounted on poles meeting near the top. The tepee is found in some North American Indian groups of the Plains culture area. These portable dwellings were usually disassembled and erected by the women as the Plains tribes went from place to place following the buffalo. A group of tepees often were placed in a large circle, perhaps around a central council tepee.

Tepexpan. A site in the Valley of Mexico where De Terra in 1946-47 found a skeleton of Homo sapiens along with flake tools and some elephant bones. The materials were scattered but in the same stratum. It is possible that the skeleton is 10,000 years old, thus making it one of the oldest authentic and geologically dated human finds in the Americas.

tephrochronology. A chronology used to date archaeological discoveries on the basis of volcanic ash layers. Thorarinsson in Iceland has applied tephrochronology.

tepidarium. An early Greek or Roman heated bath chamber.

tepochcalli. An Aztec men's house for commoners.

teponatzli or **teponastly.** A South American or Mexican tom tom (q.v.) drum, which is audible for large distances. It is often used with rubber-topped drumsticks.

term, classificatory. A kinship term that may designate several relatives, e.g., *aunt.* See MORGAN, L. H.

term, denotative. A kinship term used only to refer to relatives in one kinship category, delimited by sex, generation, and specific genealogical ties, e.g., *mother.*

term, derivative. A kinship term consisting of a simple kinship term and another lexicographical component, e.g., *stepson.*

term, descriptive. A kinship term that amalgamates two or more basic terms, in order to describe a given relation, e.g., the Swedish *farbror,* father's brother.

term, elementary. A kinship word that is not reducible into smaller lexicographical units of kinship meaning, e.g., *father.*

term, kinship. See preceding entries commencing TERM.

terminology, mixed. A system of describing kin in which both classificatory and particularizing terms are used, as in some compound terms in Chinese, in which the total expression designates the individual.

terminology, particularizing. A system of describing kin in which each individual is designated by a different term and no classificatory term (q.v.) is used, as in the Latin distinction between *avunculus,* mother's brother, and *patruus,* father's brother.

ternary. Made up of or involving three elements.

terp. In northern Holland, a mound heaped up in stages. The exact use of terps is not known, although it has been suggested that they may have been constructed to cope with the beginning of coastal subsidence, which was affecting the North Sea coast.

terra cotta. A natural ferruginous clay, which may be glazed, unglazed, or painted. The body of a terra cotta object is usually porous and soft but may be hand-fired. Colors vary from brick red to buff. The Greeks made small adornments, like pendants, of terra cotta. The Greek Tanagra figurines are excellent early examples. In Egypt, vases were made of terra cotta as early as the pre-dynastic period.

terrace. A level and narrow plain with a steep front bordering a body of water.

terrace, river. A terrace consisting of gravels, usually parallel with the river running through the valley. Such terraces are laid down by the river's action.

terramara. An oblong mound, from 12 to 15 inches high, consisting of debris of extended habitation. It is characteristic of the Middle Bronze Age in Upper Italy. A terramara is trapezoid and is surrounded by a moat some 15 to 25 yards wide supplied with water from a neighboring stream. There were a number of such settlements, some covering 50 acres. The terramaricoli cultivated beets, beans, barley, millet, flax, and the vine, domesticated horses, and were good traders. Their pottery and metallurgy were well developed.

terrine. An earthenware dish in which food is cooked and served, or such a dish or jar sold along with its food contents.

territoriality. Among vertebrates, the general behavior pattern concerned with defending an area and sustaining an environment conducive to survival and maintaining offspring. Its effects are seen in the degree of density of a population as well as its equilibrium. Every complex human society shows territoriality. The trait is strongly manifested among certain birds during reproductive periods.

territory, neutral. A territory set aside as neutral through mutual arrangement among several tribes.

Tertiary. The geological era corresponding to the Cenozoic (q.v.).

tessera. A tiny fragment of stone, glass, tile, marble, or other material used in making mosaics. Tesserae are set into a type of cement called mastic.

test. A difficult task or quest which the protagonist of a folktale must successfully undergo in order to prove himself.

test, chastity. A test, usually involving an ordeal (q.v.), to determine if a woman has been faithful.

test, fluorine. See FLUORAPARTITE.

test, poison. An ordeal using poison. It is widely distributed.

test, son-in-law. A task which a son-in-law is required to undertake by his wife's father. It may involve very difficult feats, including various quests or measures of prowess.

testudo. A screen over a group of Roman soldiers made by holding their shields over their heads to form a solid wall so as to protect themselves from missiles. This screen resembles a tortoise shell, from which the name is derived.

tetraphthong. A compound sound consisting of four vowel sounds.

Teutonic. An Indo-European language group which includes English, Dutch, German, and Scandinavian.

tewha-tewha. A stone club with a broad rounded flat blade used in warfare by the Maori and also carried as a symbol of chiefly authority.

texture, hair. See HAIR.

tezontle. A red lava building stone from the Valley of Mexico. It is porous and resembles pumice.

thalassemia. See ANEMIA, COOLEY'S.

thanatomania. One's belief that he has been doomed that leads to his death shortly thereafter. It is found, e.g., among the Australian aborigines studied by Roth.

Thangawalu. A giant Fijian god.

thaumaturgy. The technique of working wonders; see MAGIC.

thecodontism. A tooth attachment to the jaw or skeletal support, of the most efficient and highly developed type. Nerves and capillaries enter the pulp cavity by the open tips of the hollow roots. Homo sapiens is thecodont.

theocracy. The government of a state by religious officials.

theodolite. An instrument that measures horizontal, and often vertical, angles. It usually consists of a telescope mounted to swivel vertically and attached to a revolving table with a device for reading horizontal angles. It usually also has a horizontal compass and a graduated arc for altitudes. The theodolite is used in archaeological research.

theogony. The study of the origin and descent of the gods.

theolatry. Worship of a deity who is essentially invisible.

theology. The elaborated corpus of the religious ideas of a community.

theomachy. Opposition to the gods.

theomancy. Divination by oracles that are believed to be divinely inspired; also, the part of the Hebrew Cabala dealing with God's majesty and the sacred names that are the key to divination and magic (qq.v.).

theophagy. The practice of ingesting the god. It probably stemmed from the ancient habit of eating the sacred animal to secure blessing, grace, and identity with the deity. See MEAL, SACRAMENTAL.

theophany. The action of a god in manifesting himself to a human at a definite time and place. It is a sensory experience which is more intimate and personal than mere revelation. Descriptions of it in the Iliad and in Genesis are altogether physical. It becomes more spiritual in later times, as in the accounts of Moses at the burning bush or on Mt. Sinai, Elijah on Horeb, and Jesus at the Transfiguration.

theory, age and area. A hypothesis originated in 1928 by Bartoli that the periphery of a speech area changes more slowly than its center and therefore reflects older stages of development of the language.

theory, arboreal. The theory, associated with F. Wood Jones and G. Elliot Smith, that arboreal life helped the development of early primates into man. Life in trees, according to this theory, encourages the development of limb differentiation, thumb opposability, forelimb emancipation, and upright posture; the increased use of the forepaws replaces the smelling function of the snout to a degree and thus decreases its size. The theory also holds that the brain grows as a result of the greater development of the auditory and visual senses in arboreal life and of the hand. This theory has been attacked by many, notably Earnest Hooton.

theory, area production. The theory, associated with Vavilov, that a plant is likely to exist in the greatest number of varieties in the area where it originated. Vavilov has suggested that on the basis of varietal density there were seven major centers of plant production: Southwest Asia, India, the east or central Chinese river valleys, the Mediterranean basin, the east African mountainous area, Southern Mexico, and Peru and Bolivia. These centers are all in warm mountainous regions. This theory has not been completely accepted.

theory, culture epoch. A culture epoch is a major stage in human development. The phrase is frequently connected with the early but now outmoded belief that each person develops through the stages of culture through which all of humanity has passed. That view was related to the theory in embryology that the ontogeny recapitulates the phylogeny. Lewis H. Morgan is mainly responsible for reviving the 18th-century classification into savagery, barbarianism, and civilization, giving it subepochs and detailing the cultural features of each age. Most anthropologists today hold that cultural evolution is neither unilinear nor unitary.

theory, family tree. The theory of language development holding that languages arose through a parent language family splitting off into daughter languages that then developed independently, e.g., Germanic split off from Primitive Indo-European and then West Germanic split off from Germanic. It is also called the **pedigree theory** and the **tree-stem theory.**

theory, functional and structural. The hypothesis that all languages are orderly structures within which the individual elements make human speech possible by distinguishing the linguistic signs one from the other. Therefore, the instability in human speech is caused by the varying needs of society. These needs are manifest in functional changes of the elements, eventually resulting in modifications of the linguistic structure.

theory, gestural. Paget's theory that language arose through gestures. He believed that man made gestures miming the behavior about which he wanted to converse, and the organs of articulation joined in the mimicry by assuming expressive shapes. The sounds involuntarily produced while these organs were "gesturing" ultimately became transformed into speech.

theory, mechanistic. The hypothesis that the changeableness of human speech is caused primarily by man's physiological structure in general and his nervous system in particular.

theory, monogenesis. See SPEECH, MONOGENESIS OF.

theory, nativistic. The hypothesis originated by Max Müller, that an esoteric accord exists between sound and meaning and that human speech was caused by a primitive instinct in man that forced him to vocalize each outside impression.

theory, onomatopoeic. See BOW-WOW.

theory, pedigree. See THEORY, FAMILY TREE.

theory, plaster. The theory that the art of pottery was discovered by making women's bags or calabashes more watertight through covering them with a clay layer and baking. The theory arises from the fre-

quency of pieces of early pottery with the shape of women's bags or calabashes.

theory, play. The theory that fine art is produced independently of the struggle for existence and that the imagination is exercised for the sake of the sense of freedom (Schiller), or power (Groos), or for conscious self-deception (Lange).

theory, sing-song. Jespersen's designation of his theory that languages arose through vocal play during courting or from the inarticulate chants of primitive man.

theory, sound change or **theory, substratum.** See SOUND CHANGE, SUBSTRATUM THEORY OF.

theory, tree-stem. See THEORY, FAMILY TREE.

therblig. In motion study, a part cycle or cycle of work.

theriomorphic. Referring to beings, especially gods, who resemble animals.

thermocouple. A thermoelectric couple that measures differences in temperature.

thief, master. A folktale character who is an extremely ingenious thief. He accomplishes handily the task of performing an incredibly difficult series of thefts from his master. If he is sentenced to death, he generally uses his sharp wits to get off.

tholepin or **thole.** A pin in the gunwale of a boat that functions as fulcrum for an oar.

tholoi. Circular buildings on wide foundation walls made of river stones and built of pisé. Examples are in the excavations at Arpachiyah, ca. 4000 B.C. They ranged from one to many rooms. Their

535

exact use is not known, but they are believed to have had some religious significance.

Thomsen, Christian Jurgensen (1788-1865). The first curator of the Danish National Museum. He divided the collection into the three categories of Stone, Bronze, and Iron, based on the materials used to make implements. He believed that these periods were chronologically successive. The concept of the three ages is set forth in a museum guide book published in 1836.

Thomson, Arthur (1858-1935). An English anatomist, physical anthropologist, and artist who helped develop anthropological teaching at Oxford and made some classic studies of physical characteristics. He showed how the nasal index is related to climate.

thong, fire or **thong, sawing.** A fire-making device consisting of a rattan thong or flexible liana drawn over a grooved piece of wood. This method has been found in Europe, Africa, and Asia.

thread, sacred. In parts of India, a thread that figures prominently in ceremonies marking a person's entry into a certain status. As the symbol of membership in certain castes, it is worn after it has been received by the boy initiate.

three-field system. See SYSTEM, THREE-FIELD.

threshing. Beating out grain by trampling or flailing. In parts of Asia and Egypt, a hard dry flour was made in the open air. The crop was spread out and oxen were driven over it. See FLAIL.

thrill, religious. A unique reaction that some believe to be so peculiar to religion that religion is erected into a special area of human behavior.

thromboasthenia. A defect in the formation of the blood, especially the fibrin, thrombin, and blood platelets.

throwback. The appearance, some generations after an offspring is produced by a single act of miscegenation, of an individual who is an unhybridized example of the interloping race. The belief in throwbacks is probably a folk rationalization designed to discourage miscegenation by warning that the racial taint will eventually manifest itself to disgrace future innocent generations. Students of heredity doubt that throwbacks are as common as they are popularly believed to be.

thrower, flexible spear. A cord or flexible object attached to a javelin to increase its range and accuracy. It may be a loop permanently attached to the weapon or be detached by the force of the hurl so that it remains in the thrower's hand. The term **throwing cord** is sometimes used.

thrower, spear or **thrower, rigid spear.** A throwing stick, about two feet long, used to give more speed and leverage to a weapon by lengthening the arm of the user. The fingers hold one end of the spearthrower and the other is attached to the weapon's butt. The spear throw is used by the Eskimo and Australians. It probably developed in Upper Paleolithic times. It may sometimes have other uses, in fire-making or as a tool. The terms **throwing board** and **propulseur** are sometimes used.

throwing, bone. The custom of hurling gnawed bones during a feast so that they could be caught in mid-air and thrown back, with no one injured. It was particularly common in northern Europe.

Thunder. A person or natural force personifying thunder in a number of North American Indian groups. Sometimes Thunder is one of a pair of men, or one of twin boys, who live in the sky or in cliffs.

thunderbird. A conception of a bird as thunder, widely found in America and Asia. The bird is believed to be very large and to produce thunder by flapping its wings.

thunderbolt. The name given by many groups to a flint tool of some Stone Age groups. Such objects were often used as trinkets.

thyme. An herb widely used to bestow strength, love, health, and sound sleeping habits.

ti. Any of several species of small trees of the genus *Cordyline.* The fleshy roots are used as food in East Asia and Polynesia.

Tibetan. A group of languages which belongs to the Sino-Tibetan family and is part of the Tibeto-Himalayan branch of the Tibeto-Burmese subfamily. It comprises Balti, the classical language of Tibet, and several dialects. The term is also used as a name for the dialect spoken in the central part of Tibet.

Tibeto-Burmese. The four branches of this subfamily of the Sino-Tibetan family of languages are Tibeto-Himalayan, Arakan-Burmese, Lo-Lo-Bodo-Naga-Kachin, and the extinct Pyu language.

Tibeto-Chinese. A language family that is both agglutinative (q.v.) and isolating (q.v.). It has more languages, dialects, speakers, and a larger speech area (q.v.), than any other language family. It is spoken from Baltistan to Peiping and from South Burma to central Asia. It has two subfamilies: Tibeto-Burmese and Siamese-Chinese.

Tibeto-Himalayan. A language which belongs to the Sino-Tibetan family and is a branch of the Tibeto-Burmese subfamily. The languages within this branch are Tibetan and Himalayan.

tibia. The shinbone.

ticket, mummy. See LABEL, MUMMY.

tickling, fish. A form of fishing in which women wade out into the water, sneak up on fish, and tickle them to calm them so that they can be seized. It is found especially off the shores of Tierra del Fuego, and among the Yahgan.

tide, ebbing. It is universal folk belief that death is associated with the ebbing of the tide and birth with its rise.

tigare. An earthenware boat of East Bengal.

tiki or **ti'i.** A Polynesian term for a god, for the first man, and for small figurines.

tilde. A diacritical mark (˜) placed over certain letters to indicate the proper pronunciation. Its meaning varies from language to language, e.g., in Spanish *ñ* represents a simple palatal nasal, as in *niño* ("boy"); in Portuguese it represents a nasalized vowel, as in *são* ("saint"). ,

till, glacial. The unstratified deposit of a glacier, usually consisting of rock and earth.

tillage, brand. An early form of agriculture in which the land is fertilized by burning down the undergrowth.

time, cosmic. The period in which the earth solidified from a collection of burning gas.

tillage, hand. See HORTICULTURE.

time, cycles of. The concept of the world's being involved in a cyclical movement from decay to renewal. The rebirth of the seasons probably gave rise to this concept. See CATASTROPHISM.

time, geologic. All time after the earth's formation.

tin. A comparatively rare metal, which is alloyed with copper to make bronze (q.v.). The first recorded appearance was in a bronze alloy, most likely as an impurity in the copper, so it is probable that bronze was made for some time before tin was isolated. Its role would thus be analogous to that of zinc, which figured in brass (copper and zinc) before zinc was isolated. Tin is not found natively as a metal but usually as an oxide in veins (often in granite rocks) and also as pebbles or gravel. Tin was found in running streams and was panned like gold, in all probability, before it was mined.

tincture, Mollison's. A hardening mixture used in archaeological field work.

tinctura, Rana. See TAPIRAGE.

tinker. An itinerant smith, first appearing in the Iron Age. Gypsies are typical tinkers.

tipi. See TEPEE.

tipití. A tubular basketry container into which grated manioc is placed to remove the juice containing prussic acid and tapioca. This sleeve-like strainer is woven diagonally. When stretched lengthwise, the diameter of the tube decreases, thus compressing the contents and forcing out the juice.

tipoy. A cylindrical seamless cotton garment worn as a skirt or sack dress by Indian women of tropical South America. It is also a circular band of fabric worn diagonally over one shoulder to carry an infant.

tiputa. A poncho among the Peruvian Indians.

tiqa. A reed javelin thrown for sport in Melanesia and Polynesia.

titer. The comparative extent of agglutination (q.v.).

tithe. A religious levy consisting of one tenth of a person's income.

tjaele. A permanently frozen subsoil, as in Lappland.

tjulu. The stone knife used for circumcision by the Kukata.

tjurunga. See CHURINGA.

tlacatecuhtli. "Chief of Men," the supreme chief of the Aztecs, who concerned himself with external affairs, war, and alliances.

tlachtli. Aztec ball courts.

Tlazolteotl. The Aztec mother of the gods.

tmesis. Putting a word between the portions of a compound word or expression, e.g., in German, *Männer- und Frauenkleider.*

toa. A message stick (q.v.) used in aboriginal Australia.

tobacco. A genus of plants with broad leaves that may be dried and smoked. *Nicotina tabacum,* the most important cultivated species, is a true breeding hybrid from South America, where it probably developed in pre-Columbian days. In the 17th century, it was widely used as a panacea. It is a coarse and glandular-pubescent perennial. Tobacco was originally regarded as semisacred.

tobacco, Indian. *Nicotina rustica,* a plant cultivated for so long that it can hardly be found in the wild. It is small and hardy and has yellow flowers. It probably originated in South America.

tobe. Somali cotton clothing.

Tobias nights. In the Catholic church, postponing the consummation of a marriage for several nights. The term comes from the Apocryphal Tobias, whose wife was unable to conceive until late in life.

toboggan. A flat surfaced snow sled that is pulled by dogs or humans. It has a curved forward end and low hand rails.

Tochtli. The first year, in Aztec writing; also the word for rabbit.

toggle. A button or pin attachable at the center and tapering at both ends.

tohunga. In Polynesia, a skilled craftsman generally. In some islands the meaning is restricted to a house- or canoe-builder, a wood-carver, or a carpenter. The spelling tufunga is also found.

token, sex. An object that predicts the sex of a child or a visitor to come. Two objects, one associated with the male and one with the female, are manipulated; the one that falls is the clue to the sex.

Tokharian. The easternmost language of the Indo-European group, once spoken in Eastern Turkestan.

toki. A Maori war adze.

toldo. A skin tent in Patagonia.

toloache. See JIMSONWEED.

tom tom. A drum of Eastern origin. It is beaten with the hands.

tomahawk. An Indian weapon consisting of a pointed or spherical stone head attached to a wooden handle. Hide often covers the head.

tomb, beehive. A Cretan or Minoan tomb of beehive shape of which the masonry, carving, and vaulting are particularly fine. All other Mycenaean stonework is on a more primitive level.

tomb, corbelled. A tomb made of courses of stones that project beyond the courses below.

tomba a camera. A tomb shaped like a room. It may be hewn from rock or built of brick.

tomba a forno. A circular rock-cut tomb pointed at the top.

tomba a pozzo. A narrow, often circular, grave.

tombé. A large American Indian ritual drum found among the tribes of the southwestern United States.

Tonacatecutli. A supreme being of the Aztecs.

Tonatiuh. The Aztec sun god.

tone. See INTONATION.

tone, pure. A sound with only a single frequency component.

toneme. An accent or tonal emphasis that shows the difference between two words or forms that are otherwise alike.

tong-a-tong. A Tinguian bamboo musical instrument.

tongue, gift of. A spontaneous cry or statement arising out of religious experience. It may be strange and unintelligible and is often received as supernatural. The utterances are sometimes called speaking in tongues.

tongue, glacier. The part of a glacier below the snow line.

tool. A manually operated implement. Tools represent the best clues to the early history of man. The core or bifacial, the flake, and the chopper are three major types of early tools. It has been shown that baboons and chimpanzees use rocks and sticks as tools and even animals like the sea otter and a Galapagos finch use sticks and rocks to reach food. The traditional statement about man being a tool-using animal, it has been suggested, thus should be changed to designate man as the only mammal regularly dependent on tools in order to survive.

Different techniques were used in making tools. Direct percussion resulted in the coup-de-poing (q.v.), developed about 400,000 years ago. The striking operation was performed first on one side and then on the other. In indirect percussion (see ACHEULIAN), the tool material rested on a flint block, and finer results and straighter edges were achieved. Tools of this type were found in Spain, France, Italy, Africa, India, and Java, but not in

China. Thus, this development was south of the Himalayas.

In the next phase of tool development (see AGE, MIDDLE PALEOLITHIC) the use of flint became highly skilled and standardized. A pointed object was a standard tool. A side scraper (q.v.) with a blunt back and a sharpened edge was made. When man took off the top part of the flint and long flint slivers, the blade industry came in with Aurignacian (q.v.) culture and the bone industry began. Lance points were made of bone, often with a split base for hafting. A flint engraving tool, or burin (q.v.), was used to make bone tools. The Solutrean (q.v.) culture made tools by pressure. The Magdalenian (q.v.) period saw the resumption of the manufacture of burins. During the Middle Stone Age or Mesolithic era, flint and bone implements were made.

tool, beaked. A tool with a beak-shaped end.

tool, blade. A tool made of long parallel-sided flakes.

tool, chopping. See CHOPPER.

tool, composite. A tool with several elements, each one of which has special properties. Thus, a bone haft can have little pygmy flakes fixed into it so that it can be used both as a knife blade and a saw.

tool, core. A tool made by removing flakes from a lump of stone until it is in the desired shape.

tool, flake. An object made from a large flint flake.

tool, generalized. A tool that has more than one function.

tool, incising. A flake tool that is more pointed and has a straighter back than a knife.

tool, pebble. A tool resulting from a pebble being split.

tool, tertiary. An implement that requires the use of primary and secondary tools in its shaping and is not used to shape other tools, e.g., the dart thrower.

tooth. A bony substance which grows out of the jaws of vertebrate animals. Teeth usually consist of enamel, dentine, cementum, and a pulp chamber. A tooth is usually anatomically divided into crown, neck, and roots. It functions in mastication, speech, and swallowing. The human being develops a baby or deciduous set of 20 teeth followed by a permanent set of 32 teeth (see FORMULA, DENTAL).

Predecessors of Homo sapiens have larger, and generally more, teeth than that species. Homo sapiens usually has four or five rather than six cusps in the lower first molars. Large cuspy teeth are often found among comparatively thick-skulled groups. The reason for teeth getting smaller as civilization progresses is not known.

The tooth's wear facets indicate the kind of food habitually eaten and are useful in fossil identification. The degree of caries, which was less prevalent in early man than in modern man, is another clue to the diet.

In reconstructing a skull, the occlusion of the teeth is often important. The extent to which teeth can identify a fossil is illustrated by Davidson Black's ability, in 1927,

to infer the existence of a new Hominidae genus and species, Sinanthropus pekinensis, on the basis of a single lower molar tooth.

Carnivores have well developed canine teeth, which are used in tearing food. Herbivores have short rami on the mandible and chew straight up and down. Omnivores, like man, have teeth equally developed for tearing and chewing. Canine teeth function primarily to tear, incisors to cut, and molars and premolars to grind and chew.

tooth, canine. A fairly pointed tooth behind the incisors. Apes have long strong canine teeth, which they use to protect themselves. In men, the canines are not outstanding but they show signs of their ancestry in very substantial roots, which are not in proportion with either other teeth or their functions.

tooth, dragon. A pulverized fossil tooth, used by the Chinese for many years as a medicine. Von Koenigswald discovered several large teeth which provided clues to human evolution among dragon teeth in Chinese drug stores.

tooth, supernumerary. A tooth that is not part of man's normal dentition (32 teeth). It is usually a duplicate of a tooth found in the normal dentition and is usually not so well formed as the tooth of which it is a counterpart.

tooth avulsion. See AVULSION, TOOTH.

toph. A tambourinelike instrument of the early Hebrews.

Topinard, Paul (1830-1911). A French physician who attempted to relate evolutionary ideas to anthropology, notably in his writings on Oceania. He suggested a trifurcate racial division in Europe. Topinard divided anthropology into the general study of the human species and the study of the several races.

toponomasiology, toponomastics, toponomatology or **toponymy.** The systematic investigation and analysis of the names of places within a particular geographical area or peculiar to a language.

torch. A persistent flaming light. At one time, the torch was the only artificial light. Torches were used in ceremonies to symbolize light or destruction. It has been suggested that torches developed from fireflies kept in a perforated vessel, or candlefish attached to a split stick.

toreutics. The art of sculpturing by embossing or chasing, usually in metal.

tornak. Among some Eskimo groups, a shaman's guardian spirit. Some are in bears, some in stone, and some in humans. The tornak notifies its bearer of incipient danger.

torque. A twisted neck chain, worn by some early peoples, like the Britons, Germans, or Gauls. It may also be a twisted wire ornament or any kind of neck ring.

Torres Straits Expedition. See EXPEDITION, TORRES STRAITS.

torus. A rounded smooth protuberance; a convexly profiled large molding, usually the lowest in the base of a pilaster or column, just above the plinth; a thickening or a reinforcement on a bone.

torus, frontal. The supraorbital-ridge and the glabella, fused in anthropoids and in palaeonthropic fossils.

torus, mandibular. The degree of bony thickening on the inner sides of the mandible usually below the premolars.

torus, maxillary. A protuberance usually found at the intermaxillary suture.

torus, occipital. A bony swelling extending across the back of the head. It delimits the area of attachment of the ligaments and neck muscles. It is exaggerated in anthropoid apes and is found especially in fossil men with projecting jaws.

totem or **totemism.** A totem is an object toward which members of a kinship unit have a special mystical relationship, and with which the unit's name is associated. The object may be animal, plant, or mineral. Tylor denied the existence of the individual totem, attributing it to a mistake in 1797 by John Long, who identified the Ojibwa guardian spirit (manitou) with the totem animals of the tribe's clans. Tylor and others have shown that a totem may have different functions in different cultures.

In totemism, the totem animals cannot be killed or eaten except under very special circumstances. The totem will be treated both in life and death like a fellow tribesman. Many writers erroneously refer to totemism as a complex with specific content, although modern anthropologists avoid this usage. The totem's essence or religious power is often linked to the clan's emblem and is often a sacred object. Totems are sometimes taken out to be rubbed against the body, to transmit power. See FEAST; TOTEM.

Totenschuh. See SHOES, DEAD.

Totonac. A group of peoples speaking the Totonac language, who live in what is now Vera Cruz in Mexico. It is also a descriptive term applied to archaeological objects found in that area.

touchwood. Wood that serves as tinder.

tournette. A pivoted disk, perhaps first used in Old Kingdom times in Egypt to make pottery. It revolved readily while the piece of pottery was being shaped. It was used in Brittany up to fairly recently.

tovodun. The ancient Dahomean gods, whose name is the root of the word vodun.

tower, Picts. In Scotland, a stone tower with a very thick wall, a circular court inside, and a guard cell. A Picts tower may also be called a doon.

trabeated. Referring to nonarcuated architecture or to any type of architecture that incorporates post and lintel (q.v.) construction.

traction. A method of transportation in which a domestic animal pulls a burden.

trade, silent. See BARTER, DUMB.

trade, symbiotic. A type of trade in which an advanced society trades with one less advanced that has no real division of labor and develops a trading surplus only in response to the trade need. The relation between the Great Plains Indians and American traders was thus symbiotic.

Tradescant, John. (1608-1662). An English official who started the idea of the public museum, in the 17th century. His collection was the origin of the Ashmolean Museum in Oxford.

tragion. The notch just above the tragus of the ear.

trailing. A technique of making broad incised lines in pottery.

trait, complex. A collection of culture traits, forming a distinctive combination and distinguishing a part of a culture.

trait, culture. The simplest basic unit into which a culture can be analyzed. Such a unit is a specific entity within the culture. A combination of traits is a culture complex. A trait may be diffused independently and may join freely with other traits.

tranchet. A hatchet blade or flake chisel that is an outgrowth of the side scraper (q.v.). It was probably used for chopping and had a transversely sharpened cutting edge. It was usually quadrangular. The tranchet is sometimes called a coupoir. See TECHNIQUE, TRANCHET.

transad. A plant organism found on both sides of a barrier and that probably once extended across it.

transcription, broad. A representation of the outstanding phonetic characteristics of an utterance, usually very close to a phonemic transcription (q.v.).

transcription, critical. A version of an ancient or medieval document altered in an attempt to clarify the text or make it more comprehensible and logical by reconstructing a hypothetical original form.

transcription, diplomatic. An absolutely faithful and precise transcription of an ancient or medieval manuscript.

transcription, narrow. The reproduction of all the features of a speech utterance.

transcription, phonemic. The reproduction of the phonemes (q.v.) in a speech utterance, so that only the relevant features are reproduced.

transcription, phonetic. Speech represented by using the phonetic alphabet (q.v.).

transformation. A change from one shape to another, often through magic. Humans changing to animals or inanimate objects is a common motif in American folklore. Gods may change themselves, for various reasons, into human or animal shapes. Transformation may take place to reach a goal, avoid punishment, or win a contest. Folktale heroes may undergo several transformations in a comparatively short period of time.

transformer. A mythic person who transforms the world into its present condition and gives it the elements of culture. This person was especially found in North American mythology. He travels around, changing people and things into their present shape. See HERO, CULTURE.

transformism. A hypothetical mechanism by which early 19th-century theorists explained changes in species, mainly through the inheritance of acquired characteristics,

as first suggested by Lamarck in 1799.

transhumance. Seasonal movements of domestic animals from one area to another in which different climatic conditions prevail. This usually refers to mountainous regions, where such climatic differences in a fairly small area are common. Transhumance means also a kind of nomadism in which villages migrate annually with the herds to upland pastures during the summer months.

transition. The process by which the organs used in speech change from silence to the expression of a phoneme, from the expression of a phoneme to silence, or from expressing one phoneme to expressing the next.

transition, close. A transition used in uttering consecutive sounds, in which the second closure is formed before the first is opened. Close transition is usual in English.

transition, open. A transition in which the speech organs completely disengage themselves after one sound and then begin making the following sound. Open transition is common in French.

transliteration. The matching of the letters of one alphabet by the letters of another, e.g., Russian P is transliterated by Latin R.

translocation. The transfer of a gene from one chromosome to another not paired with nor homologous with it.

transmigration. The entrance of the soul of a deceased person into another body or series of bodies or a soul's rebirth at death in another body. It implies the ability to cross the boundaries of all forms of life, including plant, animal, human, demonic and divine. Some early societies had concepts of a man's multiple souls in animals, of the dead appearing as animals, or of ancestors appearing in new-born children. The concept of transmigration probably flourished mainly in higher cultures, perhaps as a way of tieing the idea of personal survival of death to moral responsibility, or as a kind of future life which may be more attractive than immortality. See METEMPSYCHOSIS.

transmutation. The process by which a word is used in an unchanged form in grammatical functions given to different parts of speech.

transvestite. One who wears the clothes and does the work traditional to the opposite sex. Transvestitism was found in a number of American Indian groups. It also appears in vegetation dances and in the Oriental theater.

trap. A device to catch animals, which operates usually in the absence of the hunter.

trap, basket. A simple conical fisherman's trap placed over fish in shallow water.

trap, cage. A simple conical fisherman's trap the door of which is lowered and closed by the fisherman when he sees the fish inside the trap.

trap, gravity. A trap that uses either the weight of the target animal or the power of a falling object that is released so as to hit the animal when the mechanism is sprung.

trap, pit. A gravity trap consisting of a deep hole dug in an animal's track. Its opening is camouflaged by leaves, branches, and other natural objects. The animal steps on the covering and falls into a hole which almost exactly contains it, leaving no room to scramble out. The term **pitfall** is also used.

trap, snare. A trap set up vertically to take advantage of the target animal's forward movement. The snare is so arranged that the prey's head enters the noose, which then tightens around the neck.

trap, spirit. A bait intriguingly planted so that spirits will see it and be attracted by it, rather than continue to follow their quarry.

trap, spring. A branch bent and held down by an object to which a noose is attached. When the animal caught in the noose tries to escape, the weight is dislodged and the branch snaps up.

trap, spring pole. A hunting trap consisting usually of a noose attached to a bent-over tree. The animal attracted to the bait sets off the trigger, and the force of the tree snapping back into its normal position closes the noose upon it and hoists it into the air.

trap, torsion. A trap based on the principle that a twisted string will tend to regain its original form. A leverage device attached to roots, sinews, or fibers can direct the force of the torsion. These traps are made for close action. The modern steel trap is an example. The Romans used this principle very successfully in the catapult (q.v.).

trap, wheel. A trap consisting of a number of pointed flexible sticks inserted from the outside into a fiber wreath. This trap is attached to a pole or tree and put in the path of the game, often over a small pit. When the prey steps on it, the flexible spikes are thrust into the tender fetlock, and the animal's efforts to free itself only drive the spikes deeper into the flesh. The wheel trap is found in West Africa and the Cameroons.

travertine. A crystalline calcium carbonate formed from spring waters; it is used for building.

travois. Two poles trailing from the rear of a single dray dog or horse to support some baggage. It is found in the Plains culture area.

treasury, Cnidian. An early Greek structure (550 B.C.) that used caryatids.

tree, birth. A tree planted when a child is born on the assumption that there is a relationship between the development of the tree and of the child. A birth tree is also called a tree of life.

tree, family. See THEORY, FAMILY TREE.

tree, sacred. A tree associated with a religious cult. Trees have been widely used in connection with worship from early times, e.g., the Canaanites worshipped on high hills on which there were trees planted for protection.

tree of life. See TREE, BIRTH.

tree-stem theory. See THEORY, FAMILY TREE.

trepang. A Malay name for bêche-de-mer (q.v.).

trepanning, trepanation, or trep- **hination.** A widespread early custom involving cutting a good-sized hole in the skull of a patient suffering from pains in the head in order to take out part of the skull vault and thus release the source of the pain. Trepanning was also used in healing fractures of the skull. **Posthumous trepanning** is that performed upon a corpse before burial.

triad. A grouping of threes, especially used of deities. Thus, there are three furies; earth, air and heaven; the Christian Trinity; Brahma, Vishnu, and Shiva; and Jupiter, Juno, Minerva.

triangulation. Measuring the body's surface area by marking geometric figures on the body and computing their areas from the linear dimensions.

Triassic. A life period of the Mesozoic era, characterized by the development of such small mammals as the marsupial and insectivorous types. It lasted from about 195 to 170 million years ago.

tribadism. The practice of sexual relations among women.

tribe. A social group, usually with a definite area, dialect, cultural homogeneity, and unifying social organization. It may include several subgroups, such as sibs or villages. A tribe ordinarily has a leader and may have a common ancestor, as well as a patron deity. The families or small communities making up the tribe are linked through economic, social, religious, family, or blood ties.

Tribes, Five Civilized. The Cherokee, Chickasaw (or Chickarow), Choctaw, Creek, and Seminole tribes, so called because of their advanced customs. The term was first used in 1876 in an Indian Office report.

tribula. A press of wood with many small sharp flints hafted into it. It was used up to fairly recently in various parts of the world.

tribute. Payment by subordinate groups to a dominant group in order to maintain certain rights and often to derive some services. This practice is tied in with the beginnings of political life. Settled agriculturalists have had to give tribute to more martial groups, including pastoralists (west Mongols), semi-nomads (Semito-Hamites), maritime groups (Vikings), and hunters (some American Indians). The payment of tribute was widely demanded in a number of the early Oriental civilizations, e.g., Hittite, Assyrian, Lydian, Median, and Persian. The Persians under Darius I had probably the most carefully planned early type of tribute, with 20 satrapies required to contribute definite scaled amounts. Tribute was found in the Homeric period as well as in later Greek communities. The Roman rulers made subordinate peoples pay a *stipendium,* and some later Roman emperors themselves paid tribute to powerful barbarian leaders, e.g., the Dacians in the first century A.D. The Mongolian Empire got tribute from Asia and Europe up to Germany.

Tribute is often also used to describe not only a long term financial budgeted commitment but also the contributions that a people pays to its conquerors. The imposition of reparations after a modern war may be likened to tribute.

trichion. The border of the scalp, where the hair begins; the center of the hair line on the forehead.

trickster. A character in world folklore who plays tricks on his adversaries or opponents. In North American Indian lore, he is usually the tribe's culture hero (q.v.) and is a combination of human and animal. Coyote is the best known North American Indian trickster. Often the trickster is on the side of the irrational and evil, but his victims are not pitied. He usually has an animal companion, which may be a foil for his cleverness or even cleverer than he. The trickster usually displays negative qualities, like stupidity and pretentiousness, or perhaps duplicity and other antisocial qualities, which may enable him to vanquish his opponents. Stories of the trickster are usually told to amuse an audience, which usually identifies with the trickster and thus symbolically asserts itself over the forces of the world and nature. The trickster may be killed, but it is understood that he can come back to life.

Tridacna. The giant clam of Oceania. The shell was used in Polynesia to manufacture adzes and other tools. It is also called the taclobo.

trident. A fish hook with three arms and at least three barbs.

trigram. See T'AI CHI.

trigraph, consonantal. A grouping of three consonant letters that produce a single consonant sound, e.g., the German *sch.*

547

trihedron. Three planes meeting in one point.

triliteralism. In the Semitic languages, the groupings of three consonants which provide many root words.

trilithon. A gateway monument with two upright megaliths that hold a third as a lintel.

trill. A type of articulation in which an articulator vibrates rapidly as an air current passes over it, e.g., r.

trill, apical or trill, tongue tip. The most common kind of trill, in which the tip of the tongue vibrates rapidly and briefly against the gums, e.g., the Italian rolling r.

trill, uvular. A trill characterized by the uvula's vibrating against the uplifted back of the tongue. It is found in the Parisian pronunciation of the French r.

trimmer. A float (q.v.) that drifts with the wind or current so as to tire the fish. It is not connected to the fisherman.

Trinil find. See FIND, TRINIL.

triphthong. A compound phoneme with three components, including vowels and sonants.

triploid. Characterized by having three sets of chromosomes.

tripsacum. An early wild grass, perhaps an ancestor of maize.

triradius. A tiny triangle made by lines that meet at the corners in fingerprints.

triskele. A symbol consisting of three human legs bent at the knee and joined at the thigh.

trituberculy. Cope's and Osborn's theory of molar teeth evolution. It holds that in developing from simple conical teeth, the molar crowns became tritubercular (three-cusped), with the triangle's base outward in the upper part of the jaw and inward in the lower part. Other than the Australasian egg-laying mammals, the modern mammals' ancestors had tritubercular teeth, which were efficient because they grasped, sheared, crushed, and chewed. The simple tritubercular molar gave rise to the complex molars of placental mammals.

trivet. A three-footed iron stand for raising vessels above fire. It appeared in the Iron Age and is a development of three-stone supports set in a fire.

trivu. In New Caledonia, a village.

troglodyte. A person or group dwelling in a cave.

troll. In Scandinavian folklore, a gifted craftsman. Trolls were first very large but were later regarded as being dwarfs who lived in caves or dark forests. They are believed to be strong and stupid and possibly very harmful.

Tronder. A hypothetical Paleolithic strain found among the Scandinavians and the British.

tropenkoller. A neurotic condition, probably the result of isolated living, often found in Caucasians and Chinese in Indonesia.

trophoblast. An outer mass of cells that covers the embryo in its early stages. It helps to interpenetrate the maternal tissue.

tropical costume. See COSTUME, TROPICAL.

trough, glacial. The flattened U carved by valley glaciers as they deepen the bottom and scrape spurs away.

trousers. Bifurcated nether garments that cover each leg individually. Trousers probably developed as a part of arctic costume (q.v.), and were probably brought to Europe by the northern invaders at the end of the Roman Empire, as well as from the East. The eastern peoples who have been in contact with northern groups seem to have been among the first to wear trousers. In some cultures women often wear trousers, e.g., Mohammedans, Chinese.

trumpet. A tube-shaped wind instrument played by blowing into one end or into a hole. The trumpet has been widely used in ceremonies and religious rites. Its loudness contributes to its importance among early men.

trumpet, seal. A device to help determine the approach of a seal. It is a tube placed against the ice and held to the hunter's ear.

truth, act of. An occurrence subsequent to and resulting from truth or falseness of a statement. Thus, if perjury is committed thunder will sound immediately, even in winter.

truth, bird of. A bird that speaks the truth and sometimes exposes criminals.

tsama. A melon eaten by Bushmen.

Tsimshian. A northwest British Columbia linguistic group.

Tsuma. An anthropomorphic white god among Arawak-speaking peoples.

tuahu. See AHU.

tualcha mara. Among the Arunta, a relationship arranged by the parents in which a girl becomes the mother-in-law of a boy by giving him the right to marry her future daughters.

tube, blow. A device used to propel a dart. It consists of a tube and mouthpiece through which the operator blows. The tube may have an inner tube or consist of two grooved halves. Sights are sometimes found.

tube, stamping. A musical instrument made of a bamboo tube closed at its lower end so as to produce sounds when it is stamped against the ground. It may also consist of an open tube which is struck against the ground.

tube, sucking. A tube of bone or reed. It may be used by shamans to ingest liquids for magical operations. Those who are not supposed to touch foods, like menstruating girls, drink through it. It is used by the Bushmen and Hottentot to suck water from the earth, especially in the desert. It is especially found in the American Southwest, in parts of Africa, and in Tierra del Fuego.

tubercle, Darwin's. See POINT, DARWIN'S.

tubercles, genial. Two bony spicules inside the anterior portion of the mandible. The genio-glossal muscles, involved in speech, are connected to the genial tubercles.

tuberculare. The tubercle on the upper portion of the helix.

Tubuan. A female counterpart of duk duk (q.v.).

tufanga. See TOHUNGA.

tui. A wooden drum of Melanesia.

tuiana. A king over several districts in Samoa.

tukula. A red vegetable coloring substance of the Congo.

tulafale. In Samoa, a talking chief (q.v.) who makes public pronouncements in the name of the actual chief.

tule. A bull rush or reed used to make boats and bridges in California and parts of Latin America.

tulul. See TELL.

tumbaga. An alloy of gold, silver, and copper. It is widely found in Central and South America, especially in Colombia and Chiriqui.

tumpline. A cord device over the forehead or chest used to support burdens carried on the back. The tumpline is the most widely used device of its kind.

tumulus. See BARROW.

tun. A Mayan year, consisting of 360 days.

tundra. The great treeless plains within the Arctic Circle, which are marshy in summer and frozen in winter. Their subsoil is permanently frozen. The surface soil supports lichens and mosses.

Tungus-Manchu. A Ural-Altaic linguistic subdivision. It is a branch of the Altaic subfamily and includes the Chapogir, Kile, Lamut, Mangum, Orochon and Orop dialects. It is spoken by approximately 70,000 inhabitants of the Yenisei River region of Siberia.

Tupaia. A member of the tree shrew family which is associated with the pre-Tertiary period and has nonprimate claws as well as some primate features. The Tupaia are largely arboreal.

Tupi. A language of the South American Indians. It belongs to the Tupi-Guarani family of languages and is used as a common language by Indians in Brazil.

Tupi-Guarani. A family made up of 68 languages of the South American Indians, 14 extinct. Tupi-Guarani is spoken in Paraguay, Brazil, and parts of Argentina.

tupik. An Eskimo skin tent.

tupilaq. In some Eskimo beliefs, a soul of a deceased person. It is avoided because it may bring on disease, and its touch means death.

turban. A male headdress, originated probably by the Arabs. It consists of a cap with a shawl wound around it.

turbat. Highly decorated, domed monumental tomb of India, most often ornamented with inscribed picture stories about the life of the deceased.

turbinated. Shaped like a top.

Turco-Tartar. In some classifications, a language family which includes Tartar, Kirghiz, and Turkish.

turiri. A type of thin bark cloth in the Tropical Forest area of South America. See TAUARI.

Turkic. Languages belonging to the Ural-Altaic family and which are within the Altaic subfamily, including the Eastern, Western, Central, and Southern groups. Some 40 million persons speak them.

Turkic, Eastern. A division of the Turkic branch of the Altaic subfamily of the Ural-Altaic family of languages, sometimes called Altaic.

Turkic, Southern. A subdivision of the Altaic subfamily of the Ural-Altaic language family.

Turkic, Western. A division of the Altaic subfamily of the Ural-Altaic language family.

turmeric. A gingerlike plant formerly used as a body paint in Micronesia and still used by orthodox Hindus to indicate caste. It is also used in India and the Malay Peninsula as a spice, a skin rejuvenant, and a symbol of femininity.

turn, sunwise. See CIRCUMAMBULATION.

turtle ceremony. See CEREMONY, TURTLE.

turtleback. A stone form which has been rejected by its maker. It has a faceted upper side and a smooth lower surface. It is found in North America.

tusca. The seasonally harvested plant food of the Chaco.

tutelary divinity. See DIVINITY, TUTELARY.

tutulus, spiked. A Middle Bronze Age ornament consisting of a metal disk with a small protuberance in the center surrounded by concentric ridges.

twilling. A technique for making basketry (q.v.). It involves going over two strands and then under two strands. Since each row is slightly offset, the appearance is of a group of staircases.

twine. A yarn plied with the twist going in opposite directions.

twining. A basketry (q.v.) technique in which there are parallel foundation strands. Between them two strands of material are woven in and out, so that each strand is given a half twist, making the weaving stronger. Since the wefts are twisted on each other in half turns

going from one warp to the next, each warp is encircled and usually does not show on the completed surface.

twining, diagonal. Twining in which the surface has diagonal rows through the wefts' passing over two or more warps at a time.

twining, three-strand. Twining made by braiding the wefts into each other by each weft element being passed under one and over the other remaining weft element, while carried behind a warp.

twins. Two offspring produced at a single birth. Some cultures are afraid of twins; others dote on them. In some cultures, e.g., early Aztec, one of the twins was killed.

twister, sinew. A cord twister consisting of a stick with a handle at one end. A doubled thread is attached to the stick, and as the stick is turned the threads are twisted together, thus strengthening them. The sinew twister is used on sinew, cord, and thread.

Tylor, Edward Burnett (1832-1917). An English anthropologist who used a cultural evolutionary approach. Tylor evolved the theory of animism (q.v.). He coined the terms "cross-cousin," "local exogamy," and "teknonymy." Tylor contributed substantially to the study of social organization but his greatest work was probably in early religion. His *Primitive Culture* (1871) established him as the leading English anthropologist of his generation.

type, culture. The total of qualitatively similar characteristics that distinguish a given culture.

type, morphological. A division of a subrace in which differentiation has been carried even further. Although it is possible to observe morphological types visually, they are difficult to sort metrically because of the blending of many subtle features.

type, substitution. The specified circumstances in which a substitute (q.v.) can be replaced.

type life cycle. See CYCLE, TYPE LIFE.

types, constitutional. Personality types that correspond to morphological characteristics, or the morphological analysis of body build into standard categories. Lombroso (q.v.) suggested a typology to account for habitual criminals. In 1921, the German psychiatrist Ernst Kretschmer postulated the existence of the asthenic, pyknic, athletic, and dysplastic (qq.v.) types, each with a corollary personality syndrome. In 1940, the American physician William Sheldon identified ectomorphy, mesomorphy, and endomorphy (qq.v.). Most scholars maintain skepticism about the usefulness of typologies.

types, sound. The categories into which the sounds of a language may be divided, i.e., vowels, consonants, and sonants.

typology. The classification of artifacts by families and groups, on the basis of their form and method of manufacture; also, the taxonomic and evolutionary phases of archaeological research.

typology, linguistic. A method by which languages are classified in the light of their structure, rather than from the standpoint of origin.

Tyson, Edward (1650-1708). The English founder of primatology, author of the first comparative anatomy of an ape.

tzitzimitl. Aztec ghosts.

tzolkin. The Mayan cycle, measured by permutation and consisting of 260 days.

U

udakea. An hourglass-shaped drum of India with both ends covered with parchment and the overhanging edges laced with strips of skin. It is played by beating with the fingers.

Ugaritic. Referring to the early (ca. 1500 B.C.) pre-Phoenician alphabet of the city of Ugarit, in Syria. It has 28 letters.

ugubu. Among the Zulu, a musical bow.

ugwala. See GOURA.

Uijatao. The Zapote priest-king.

ullyinga. A pointed wooden hook used in Australia to avulse teeth.

ulna. A bone of the forearm that articulates with the humerus and the wrist bones.

ulnar. Referring to the little finger.

ulo. In Eskimo culture, a semicircular woman's knife, shaped like a chopper with a handle.

ulotrichi. Referring to frizzly hair.

ultimogeniture. Leaving property to the youngest born member of a family. It is distributed fairly widely. Frazer and Vinogradoff have pointed out that the youngest born gets the property involved because he remains with the parents after his elders have left. The term junior right is also used.

ultrabrachycranic. Referring to a cranial index (q.v.) of more than 90.

ultradolichocranic. Referring to a cranial index (q.v.) of less than 64.9.

ulu. See ULO.

ulumaika. Discoidal stones used for bowling in Hawaii.

umbilical cord. See CORD, UMBILICAL.

Umgangssprache. The native tongue; idiomatic language; the everyday language of a people.

umiak. An open polar boat made of walrus hide stretched over a wooden framework (usually spruce). It can carry about 12 passengers. The average length of an umiak is some 30 feet, and it lasts about three years. It is especially useful for tracking upstream. Since it is flat-bottomed and tall, it rides very high and is thus hard to propel against or tack into the wind. Women often are the operators.

umlaut. A Teutonic root inflexion, in which a word's meaning is changed by changing a vowel, e.g., *man* and *men*.

umu. A Polynesian earth oven.

uncial. A handwriting style found in vellum codices, notably the New Testament codices of ca. 300-800 A.D. The name probably derives from the Latin word for one-twelfth, since each character covered about that portion of a line. A fairly tedious script to write, it was eventually replaced by miniscule (q.v.) writing.

uncle, cross. Mother's brother, so called because the relationship involves a brother and a sister rather than with two brothers. It is contrasted with father's brother, who is called **parallel uncle.**

unction. Anointing for medicinal or consecrational purposes, often with oil.

underworld. In many religions, a place below the surface of the earth where the souls of the deceased live on. There is a surface entrance to the underworld, and a special guide is needed to conduct the dead.

undine. A fairy that lives in a small body of water.

unicorn. A legendary animal formed like a white horse and with a horn two to three feet long growing from its head. It could be captured only by a virgin maid. Narwhal horns were deemed to come from unicorns.

unicum. An entity unique in its way.

unifacial. A flint or other implement that has been worked on only one side.

uniformitarianism. See FLUVIAL-ISM.

unilinear. Referring to succession, descent, or inheritance measured through either the father's or the mother's line alone. The term **unilateral** is also found.

unilocal. Referring to the practice of a married couple's living with or near the parents of one of the partners to the marriage only.

union, ritual . Sexual intercourse on special occasions, as part of a ceremonial.

unit-custom. The minimal unit of socially learned behavior in a culture system; also, a culture trait or culture element.

unity, psychic. The doctrine that the human race is one in mental life and the ability to abstract.

unity of species, evolutionary. See SPECIES, EVOLUTIONARY UNITY OF.

univallate. A ditch with a bank on one side.

universal. Referring to behavior characteristic of all the members of a society.

unvoicing. See DEVOICING.

Upanishads. The 13 basic texts of Hinduism, which contain speculations on the nature of the world and of man.

uraeus. The sacred asp appearing on the headdress of ancient Egyptian rulers.

Ural-Altaic. A family of languages. It comprises two subfamilies, the Finno-Ugric (the Uralic) and the Altaic (Turco-Tartar). Linguists are in disagreement whether these two subfamilies are actually related.

Uralic. A hypothetical language stock that may have given rise to Finno-Ugrian and Samoyed.

urn, cinerary. A large pottery vessel used to hold the remains of cremated persons.

urn, face. An urn modelled after the shape of a human face. The type was made during the Bronze Age and after.

urn, Santa Marta. A jar with an ovoid body and a cylindrical neck. It is usually decorated with a design representing a face, and is characteristic especially of archaeological sites in northwest Argentina.

urnfield. A type of cemetery, characteristic of central Europe during the Bronze Age, in which the cremated remains of the dead were buried in urns.

urstromtal. A dune field.

uru. Kazak kin units of various levels, including some unrelated persons.

urucú. A cultivated shrub of tropical America, *Bixa orellana,* bearing pods the seeds of which are widely used as red pigment by the Tropical Forest Indians of South America.

urupe. A round straining basket in the Tropical Forest area.

urus. A large extinct wild ox that used to roam the German forests.

uruya. A rope stretched across a river as a track for a basket. The uruya is found at river crossings in western South America. A similar device exists in the Himalaya region.

usage. The concurrence of members of a language community concerning speech.

ushabtin. Mummylike figurines left with the dead in Egypt.

usufruct. Use with ownership. This concept is particularly useful in discussions of land tenure in early agricultural and among contemporary nonliterate peoples, especially in situations in which a tribe or family "owns" land and while a given individual is free to use it. In many early societies, the land's fruits are more important than the question of ownership.

usury. Originally, the fee paid for the use of money, a practice followed since ancient times. It has often been resented because of the penalties for defection. Although usury once denoted no more than "interest," the attitude of the early Christian church that, since nothing was given away, a charge for lending money was theft, led to its perjorative current meaning of an illegal or unfair interest rate.

uten. A measure of value in Egypt. It consisted of a wire weighing 91 to 92 grams.

utensil. An object in or on which something can be used or prepared.

Uto-Aztekan. An Indian linguistic stock, found from Costa Rica to Southern Oregon.

uvala. A large trenchlike sinkhole, resulting from several caverns collapsing along the same line, or from the roof of an underground stream falling in.

uvula. The flexible small body at the back of the soft palate.

uvular. A sound made by the rear of the tongue articulating with the uvula, e.g., *q* in Arabic.

uxorilocal. See MATRILOCAL.

V

vagina dentata. See TEETH, VAGINAL.

vahine. In Polynesia, a woman.

valerian. An herb widely used as incense, a poultice, and a sedative.

valley, aggraded. A floor built up through river deposits.

valley, wind. A valley originally formed by the action of a stream that no longer exists. The term wind gap is also used.

valuta. The worth of a currency, especially in terms of other moneys.

valve, slit. A fairly uncommon wind instrument played by the performer blowing air through a thin slit cut into a stalk of grass or a reed.

valve, spinning. See ROARER, BULL.

vampire. A corpse that emerges from the grave to drink blood from living persons. Vampires have been reported in many lands, although the Slavic areas are the major centers of belief. The vampire works only at night. Its victims themselves become vampires.

vang. On a sailboat, a rope that keeps the sail at the proper angle with the wind when it is tied to the yard.

varat. Voluntary groups of families among the Chuckchee.

variation, family. A difference existing between families.

variation, fraternal. A difference existing within a family.

varnish, desert. The polished surface of a desert stone, developed by the effect of wind-blown sand on the surface oxidation. The degree of polish is a clue to the age of the stone.

varve. A regular annual clay level resulting from melting glaciers. It helps determine the comparative age of changes on the earth's surface. The first use of varve was by Baron Gerard de Greer in Sweden in 1878.

vasa. See VELE.

vase, Aegean. A small vase with delicate brown, white, and gray coloring patterned with white veining. Aegean vases were produced ca. 3400 B.C.-2100 B.C. (the early Minoan period) by the people of Crete for enjoyment and for export. After the appearance of the potter's wheel ca. 1800 B.C., they began to produce the famous kamares ware, metal vases with geometric and stylized patterns.

vase, black figured. A terra cotta pottery made in Greece during the sixth century B.C. Figures were painted in black glaze on the terra cotta background and details were added by scratching. This style was developed in Attica. See VASE, RED FIGURED.

vase, Canopic. A container for the organs removed from the body of the deceased before the mummification process. The vases were slightly different from the Canopic jars (q.v.) in that they were more ornate and had tops in the form of human or divine heads. They were ordinarily made of terra cotta, but many examples were of fine stone. Certain seventh- and eighth-century cremation vases found in Etruscan tombs are also called Canopic.

vase, red figured. A terra cotta pottery made by the Athenians toward the end of the sixth century B.C. The drawing was first incised on the vase and the background filled in with a black glaze, so that the figures look red on a black background. The technique permitted a greater freedom of style than that of the black figured vase (q.v.).

vasu. Giving a Fijian nephew unusual rights that can be exercised against the maternal uncle.

vavatoa. Kite fishing (q.v.) in the Solomons.

Vedas. The ancient scriptures of India, believed to be the revealed word of divinity. The four Vedas consist of the basic Rig-Veda, written before 800 B.C. by several authors, ten books of which contain hymns and prayers; the Sama-Veda or chant-Veda, 75 of its 1,225 stanzas coming from the Rig-Veda; the Yajur-Veda, a ritualistic collection of prose formulas; the Atharva-Veda, the last Veda, which has hymns, prayers, charms and incantations and represents a stage of religion earlier than the Rig-Veda although it was collected later. The Vedas date from the early Aryan migration to India, and contain elements of the later Indian caste society.

Veddas. Food-gathering Ceylonese, among the least hybridized Veddoids.

Veddoid. A hpyothetical population in Southern Asia, hybridized by Caucasoids, Pre-Dravidians, and Indo-Australians. It is characterized by some prognathism, brown skin, short stature, wavy hair, moderate body hair, and narrow head.

Vedic. The earliest stage of the Indic language group, in which the Vedas were written.

vein. Among the Riffs, part of a generation of brothers. It is analogous to a lineage (q.v.).

vela. A puberty initiation hut in the Congo.

velar. A phonetic term for a sound produced with the back part of the tongue raised toward the soft palate, e.g., *k* or *g*. The term **guttural** is also used.

vele. A form of black magic (q.v.) practiced on Guadalcanal, Savo and Russell Islands. The container that holds the magical implements is called a **vasa.**

vellus. Delicate short downy hairs, found on the scalp, forehead, and face.

557

velocity, air. The mean air movement, stated in centimeters per second or feet per minute. It is measured by a hot wire anemometer.

vellum. The best kind of parchment (q.v.), prepared from calfskin. Also, a term for the soft palate (q.v.).

velvet, black. An Australian slang term for an aboriginal woman.

vendetta. A blood feud.

vengeance, blood. Avenging the slaying of a kinsman either by killing the person responsible for the death or someone close to him.

ventifact. A stone that has been faceted by sandstorms.

ventilator. See SCREEN, FIRE.

Venus figure. See FIGURE, VENUS.

ver sacrum. A vow by which children born in a given spring are required to colonize another community when they grow up.

vernacular, contact. A vernacular language that arises from contact between indigenous peoples and Europeans.

vertebra. One of the bones making up the spinal column. In primates, the cervical vertebrae (usually seven) are those between the thorax and skull. The lumbar vertebrae are between the sacrum and thorax. They bear no ribs and have no lateral masses that participate in forming sacral foramina. The sacral vertebrae compose the sacrum; they possess intervertebral and sacral foramina, ringed by bone in adults. The thoracic vertebrae bear ribs. The number of such vertebrae varies among the primates. There are usually 12 in humans.

vertebrates. Members of the phylum Chordata. They include fish, amphibians, reptiles, birds, and mammals.

vertex. With the head held in the Frankfurt Plane (q.v.) or erect, the head's highest point, in the midsagittal plane. It is usually near the bregma (q.v.).

vervain. An herb used by witches or used to drive away witches, cure ulcers, arouse love, purify, and ease childbirth.

Vesalius, Andreas (1514-1564). A Belgian physician whose book on the construction of the human body (1542) represented a turning away from Galenic medicine and the beginning of modern anatomy. He showed that Galenic anatomy was really the anatomy of an ape rather than of man. Vesalius emphasized the need for direct observation. He noted some differences in the head shape of different races and attributed them to artificial deformation.

vessel, food. A pottery vessel that holds food for the dead, found in English and Irish graves. Some are elaborately ornamented.

vessel, hollow. A hull that stays afloat because of its shape.

vessel, mortuary. An urn used to hold the ashes of a corpse.

vessel, sacred. A utensil or a vessel used in religion and believed to be associated with the deity whose rites are celebrated. Such utensils may embody tradition, as in the employment of flint knives

558

for sacrificial purposes after iron or bronze came into use.

viable. Capable of maintaining its own life.

Vietnamese. See ANNAMESE-MUONG.

vigesimal. Referring to a number system based on 20 rather than 10, e.g., among the Ainu. Such systems probably arose from the use of hands and feet both to suggest a major unit.

vigesimal, quinary. See QUINARY-VIGESIMAL.

vigor, hybrid. The belief that hybrids from healthy parents are larger and stronger than typical representatives of either of the contributing populations.

village. A small group of houses in a rural district; probably the most ancient type of settled group. A village is a collection of separate homesteads treated as a unit and sufficiently localized so that the inhabitants can know each other. The village arose in Neolithic times and may have existed ca. 8000 B.C. in Egypt.

village community. See COMMUNITY, VILLAGE.

Villanova. Referring to the early Iron Age (q.v.) in Italy, from about 1000 B.C.

viniculture. The domestication of the grapevine and its variants. The vine was probably first systematically cultivated in Europe during the Bronze Age. Vineyards were established in the East Mediterranean by Homeric times.

violin. A lute-type of musical instrument played with a bow. The bow probably is an Asiatic invention.

violin, nail. A musical instrument consisting of several rods attached to a resonant body. One end is free. The rods are tuned and differ in length. The instrument is played by drawing a bow across the rods.

virama. A negative diacritical sign used in Sanskrit.

Virchow, Rudolf Ludwig (1821-1902). A very influential German pathologist and humanitarian. He conducted an anthropological survey of the Germans (1877) in order to answer the charges of Quatrefages (q.v.). He edited several anthropological journals and made contributions to craniometry. Virchow, with Bastian, was one of the founders of the Museum für Völkerkunde.

virgate. In medieval England, an area of about 30 acres.

virgin birth. See BIRTH, VIRGIN.

virilocal. See PATRILOCAL.

viscerotonia. Sheldon's hypothetical type that is inclined toward comfort and relaxation, sociability, and gluttony for food and people. See TYPES, CONSTITUTIONAL.

vise. A device with two jaws that can be closed to hold an object to be worked.

vision, career. A vision responsible for imposing a particular career, as among the Crow Indians, who assume that the vision determines one's success. Some persons were almost compelled to adopt careers like that of sorcerer in spite of themselves, because of the power of the vision.

vision, color. The ability to see colors. Some 5 per cent of male humans are color-blind.

vision, questing. Among some North American Indians, a feature of puberty rites consisting in sending a boy to the woods without food or any implements other than bow and arrow. Boys were often sent on these quests in winter with a minimum of clothing. They were required to stay away from home until they had heard from a supernatural force, and they were often sent out again if they did not make contact on the first attempt. Some boys never succeeded.

vision, stereoscopic. Two pictures of an object blending into one image when seen from slightly different angles. Stereoscopic vision makes perception possible in three dimensions over short distances. It is found in primates.

vitalism. See ANIMATISM.

vocable. A word in the lexicographic sense.

vocalism. The systematic investigation of the history or nature of the vowel system of a given language or dialect.

vocalization. The process by which a consonant becomes a vowel.

vodun. A Caribbean Negro religious system with elements taken from African cults and Catholicism. The word, first used in the United States by Haitian Negroes, who had been brought to Louisiana in the early 19th century, is probably Dahomean. Vodun is a complex polytheistic system. The form voodoo is also found.

voiced. A sound produced with the vibration of the vocal cords, e.g., *b* or *z*.

voiceless. A sound produced without the vocal cords vibrating, e.g., *t*. It requires more effort to make a voiceless than a voiced sound.

volador. A sportive-ceremonial spectacle of ancient Mexico, still performed today, in which men dressed as birds leap off a rotary platform atop a high pole with ropes tied to them. The men circled through the air and slowly, as the ropes unwound, approached the ground.

Volapük. The first artificially constructed language which was actually written, printed, and spoken. It was invented in 1880 by Johann Martin Schleyer.

Völkergedanken. In Bastian's terminology, ideas, presumably universal, as modified by social and environmental conditions.

Völkerwanderung. See MIGRATION.

volute. A scroll-shaped spiral ornament.

Von Schwann's law. See LAW, VON SCHWANN'S.

voodo. See VODUN.

votive tablet. See TABLET, VOTIVE.

voussoir. One of the wedgelike pieces composing a vault or an arch.

vow. The act of committing oneself to a supernatural being or to a course of action, often because favor is expected. A vow is a kind of oath (q.v.). The taker of a vow assumes some holy qualities, which may account for the many abstinences, such as not cutting the hair and fasting.

vowel. Phonetically, a sound made without blocking the outgoing column of air as by friction or closure. Phonemically, a vowel is a sound that functions as a syllabic (q.v.).

vowel, abnormal. A sound that falls between a front and a back vowel, e.g., the French *u*.

vowel, back. A vowel made by raising the back of the tongue in the direction of the velum, e.g., the *u* in *put*.

vowel, central. An intermediate vowel made by the mid-part of the tongue approaching the mid-part of the roof of the mouth, e.g., the *a* in *father*.

vowel, closed. A vowel produced with the mouth opened less than in the articulation of another vowel sound.

vowel, connecting. A vowel sound which is placed between the stem or root of a word and an inflectional ending, or in general between two elements of word formation, to make the pronunciation of the word easier and more euphonius. An example is the added vowel in the colloquial pronunciation *athaletic* for *athletic*.

vowel, dark, or **vowel, deep.** A vowel, the sound of which is produced in the back part of the oral cavity.

vowel, front. A vowel made by raising the center of the tongue in the direction of the highest part of the palate, e.g., the *i* in *inn*.

vowel, high. A vowel produced with the tongue turned upward toward the roof of the mouth.

vowel, low. A vowel produced with the tongue lowered.

vowel, mid-. A vowel articulated with the tongue arched toward the center of the palate.

vowel, mixed. A vowel midway between a front and back vowel.

vowel, murmur. A vowel that is whispered or barely audible.

vowel, palatal. A vowel produced in the front part of the mouth with the front part of the tongue arched toward the palate.

vowel, retroflex. A vowel produced with the apex of the tongue directed toward the upper teeth or curled up and back to the alveolar ridge or the hard palate, e.g., the *i* in *bird*. In phonetic transcription, such vowels are indicated by a dot under the letter.

vowel, semi-. A sound which is phonetically like a vowel but because of its position next to another vowel functions as a consonant, e.g., *w* in water.

vowel, whispered. A vowel produced by friction between the arytenoids (q.v.) rather than vibration of the vocal bands.

Vulgate. A Latin version of the Scriptures, principally the work of St. Jerome in the fourth century A.D. The name comes from that of a previous Latin translation of the Septuagint and was first used in its present meaning in the 13th century A.D. by Roger Bacon.

W

waddy. A club notched at one end to give a grip and often knobbed at the other end. It is about two feet long and was used by the Tasmanians.

wadi. See OUED.

Wadjak. See HOMO WADJAKENSIS.

wagon, great. A structure shaped like a tent and carried on two wheels. In north China, it is used for long trips.

Waitz, Theodor (1821-1864). A German anthropologist. Between 1859 and 1872 he wrote five volumes summarizing what was known about all the nonliterate cultures which had been studied at the time. He divided anthropology into man's anatomy and psychology and social life. Waitz expected anthropology to mediate between the study of man from the physical and historical points of view.

wakan. See WAKONDA.

wake. A meeting of family and friends after a death. The host family usually is as generously hospitable as possible. The wake began with a gathering of relatives and friends who prayed for the soul and consoled the family in the presence of the body.

wakonda, or wakan. Among the Sioux, extranatural, impersonal power. It is mysterious and is found in certain objects, e.g., stones or spiders.

Walam Olum. A Delaware Indian sacred pictographic document, published in 1836. It is an authentic rendition of ancient tribal customs. Its narrator was probably a chief who preferred his tribe's customs to Christianity.

wali. In Malay groups, a young woman's guardian, for certain legal purposes, like marriage. The wali handles her side of marriage contract negotiations.

waling. Twining (q.v.) which uses three wefts.

walking, fire. An Eastern ordeal in which the celebrant walks over heated stones and remains unharmed. It is perhaps the best known and most widely used ordeal.

wall, mani or **wall, prayer.** A low long wall of mud and stone, covered with flat rocks, on which Tibetan characters are carved. Devout Tibetans walk with the mani wall to their right to get benefit from it. Such walls are frequently more than a quarter of a mile long.

wall, retaining. A structure designed to hold back a mass of earth or water.

Wallace, Alfred Russel (1823-1913). An English naturalist, who, in 1858, completed a study of the development of organisms which independently came to substantially the same conclusions as Darwin, to whom the study had been sent. Wallace's paper, "On the Tendency of Varieties to Depart Indefinitely from the Original Type," was printed along with a paper by Darwin in the *Journal of the Linnean Society.*

wallam. A cargo boat of the Malabar coast.

wampum. Beads used as money and ornaments among the Indians of North America. They are made of the disks from purple and white quahog shells. They were 2 to 5 millimeters thick and 4 to 17 millimeters long and were hollow or tubular. The white wampum was the most widely used. Wampum was sometimes made into belts used both decoratively and as a medium of exchange. The better kinds of wampum were displayed on occasions of tribal importance and became associated with them.

wand. A rounded bone rod with a point at one end, sometimes grooved longitudinally and often decorated.

waninga. An object similar in function to a churinga (q.v.), found in central Australia. It consists of spears tied with human hair, with colored feathers for a cover.

wanningi. A cross-shaped stick used in Australia as a ceremonial emblem.

war. Organized violence to compel one group to yield to another's will. Among early men, war was often conducted as if it were a hunting expedition, with magico-religious rites. To terrify the enemy was often more important than fighting. Early wars were usually of short duration and relatively rare, and there was little mass conflict, except among some North American Indians. Some Germanic peoples had special theaters of war. The Australian aborigines protected women in a war. A number of early wars were preceded by some kind of negotiations and were concluded formally. Common worship sometimes prevented war. Disputes over hunting or fishing territories or over women often led to war, rather than political considerations.

Recent research suggests that on the lower planes of culture, war was largely restricted to small groups and was not a permanent institution. Indirect evidence, such as an analysis of artifacts to determine a period's occupations, points to an emphasis on peaceful pursuits. The Bronze Age seems to have seen the first major warlike tendencies. Current thinking on primitive war is opposed to Maine's "universal belligerency of primitive mankind" and points, instead, to war as essentially the product of an economic surplus and the attendant leisure.

war, tong. A conflict among competing Chinese fraternal or family groups.

ware, Apulian. A type of ancient Greek vase chiefly identified by its egg-shape, thick mouth, and the merging neck and shoulder.

ware, channelled. Pottery with the design drawn on the clay while damp with a round-ended instrument that left a grooved line instead of the sharp V cuts resulting from a pointed tool. The design was a series of concentric semi-circles, often in vertical bands.

ware, corrugated. A kind of coiled pottery found among the Indians of the Southwest United States, the ancestors of the Pueblo. The coils overlap to create a scalloped effect and a rough surface.

ware, fired. A pottery that has been baked in a kiln at high temperature in order to render it harder, to fix the colors, or to melt the glaze.

ware, five-color. A type of delicate Chinese porcelain colored with yellow, red, green, blue, and violet.

ware, jasper. Pottery, associated with Josiah Wedgwood, with a blue background and white relief designs.

ware, plumbate. A gray, quasi-vitreous pottery that had a wide circulation through trade in Mexico and Middle America in late pre-Aztec times.

ware, seven-color. Chinese porcelain, colored red, yellow, green, blue, violet, black, and aubergine.

warning, death. A portent of a person's death indicated by the appearance of a raven or some other black-feathered bird, or another sign, near his home.

warp. The parallel foundation threads through and over which the weft (q.v.) is passed at a 90° angle. The warp is usually kept extended artificially and remains fairly passive as the weft is interwoven. It may be linked to the operator at one end and to an object like a post at the other, or it may be stretched on a loom.

warpath. The trail followed by North American Indians in pursuing the enemy, and, by extension, the act of going to war. The term probably originated in the northeast Woodlands of the United States, among the Iroquois, who had a marked capacity for creating such figures of speech.

warrior, eagle. A cult, originally of Toltec origin, which spread widely, as far as Peru and the Great Lakes and Alaska. In the ceremonies, the men dressed like eagles and engaged in an eagle dance. The best known was perhaps that of the Pueblo. Similar cults devoted to the jaguar and coyote were common among American Indians.

washing. In ceramics, covering a piece with an infusible powder that keeps it from sticking to its supports while receiving a glaze. In metallurgy, washing is the material retained after being washed or panned.

washing, pan. See PAN.

wassail. Songs sung to indicate good luck wishes, usually on a festive occasion, and often to the accompaniment of drinking.

564

watap. The split root of spruce, pine, or tamarack tree used by the northern Algonkians to sew birch bark canoes and make baskets.

watermelon. A trailing tendrilled vine with pinnatified leaves. It is of great antiquity and probably originated in Africa. It is likely that the Moors took it to Spain and thence it went to Mexico. It is found in early Egyptian painting.

watershed. A land surface that supplies a watercourse. It includes all the areas that receive the precipitation which gets to the channels of the parts of the watercourse.

wattle. 1 A method by which cattle were marked for identification in which the dewlap was slit so as to form a characteristic loop, knob, or pendant, which was visible when the animal was seen in profile. The dewlap was sometimes cut into the shoulder or jaw. 2 The process of weaving or twisting twigs or other materials into a network; a frame of interwoven poles and twigs.

wattle-and-daub. A method of building whereby a wattle or frame of poles and interwoven twigs is daubed with mud or plaster.

wave hypothesis. See HYPOTHESIS, WAVE.

wawi. Black magic (q.v.) in the Gilbert Islands.

wax, lost. See TECHNIQUE, LOST WAX.

Way, Enemy. A ceremony by which the Navaho Indians cured victims of witchcraft.

way, ridge. An early road built along ridges which had hard dry subsoil and where an open view was a protection against attack, e.g., the

Harrow-way from Salisbury Plain to Canterbury, mentioned in Chaucer.

wayang. Javanese puppets.

wealth, bride. See PRICE, BRIDE.

weapons, parrying. A weapon used to turn away an opponent's blow. Parrying weapons include clubs, shields, and wood lashed to the forearm.

weathering, profile of. The subdivisions of a weathered zone in a vertical geological section.

weaving. A technique for making cloth from cordage. The materials used are softer and narrower than in basketry and are worked on a loom. Weaving involves interlacing two series of pliable elements at right angles to each other.

weaving, finger. Weaving with the fingers rather than a loom to create special effects. Southern Peru is particularly noted for the excellence of its finger weaving.

weaving, pile. Weaving a fabric with weft threads forming upstanding loops, which constitute a pile when they are cut.

weaving, suspended warp. Weaving in which the warp is suspended from a raised horizontal pole and the weaver moves the weft in and out with her fingers. This is a primitive weaving technique found in parts of the Mississippi Valley, Southeast and Northeast.

wedging. Removing coarse stones and rough material from clay and mixing the clay with water and kneading it till soft for pottery-making.

weft. In weaving, the relatively active series of elements that interlaces with the warp (q.v.). It may be several separate elements or a single continuous component. A shuttle or the hand may be used to guide it between the warp threads. The word **woof** is sometimes used for weft.

weft, shooting a. Pushing a shuttle through a group of warp (q.v.) threads. See HEDDLE.

wefting. In weaving, passing the transverse threads between the warp threads.

Wei. Referring to unglazed pottery, often decorated with pigment and tomb figures of the Wei dynasty in China, A.D. 368-557.

weight, brain. The weight of the brain, usually as compared with the weight of the rest of the body. The human brain is about 2 per cent the body weight, the greatest of any species, and even in absolute weight, is greater than that of most land animals except the elephant.

weight, loom. A weight used to keep thread on a warp extended properly.

weight, measure of. The measure of weight is often expressed in plant seeds, or man or wagon loads.

weir. A fence of wood or stakes placed in a body of water to catch fish. Fish pass along a funnel into a basket, from which they cannot escape. Weirs are found in the African Sudan, South America, and the West Coast of North America.

well, artesian. A well made by digging until water is reached and flows spontaneously, driven by internal pressure. The name comes from Artois, France, where such wells were dug several hundred

years ago. They are often very deep, though of small diameter.

were-. A prefix denoting a human being who is metamorphosed into a specific kind of animal, e.g., were-tiger.

were-were. In the Banks Islands, the rubbing of a stick on a flat stone to create a sound like that of the bullroarer.

werewolf. A person who can be, or has been, transformed into a wolf. Werewolves prefer human flesh, which they usually seek at night. This belief was known in the classical civilizations. Other countries have legends of equally fierce transformed humans.

werf. The name for a kraal in southwest Africa.

wergild. The payment made by the responsible party to compensate an injured person or the relatives of a slain person. This payment was reckoned by the injured person's status, and if it were not paid, private retaliation was available. The payment was divided among the dead person's relatives in accordance with their degree of kinship. In Anglo-Saxon, the term means "man money," i.e., compensation for taking a life.

werowance. The title of the chief among the Indians of Virginia and Maryland.

Westermarck, Edward (1862-1939). A Finnish sociologist who made a major study of the forms and history of human marriage (1891). He did not believe in the existence of primitive promiscuity and maintained that the family has always been the basic component of society. He documented man's being naturally monogamous.

whare wananga. In Polynesia, a house where craftsmen, or tohunga, learn their trade.

wheat. A hybrid grass, probably first developed in western Asia. The river valleys of the Tigris, Euphrates, and Nile first saw the extensive cultivation of wheat. The river basins' flooding made it easy to plant wheat. Wheat is often associated with European development and is grown best in a temperate, subarctic, or subtropical climate. It has long been a center of ritual, and magical practices are often found in connection with its growth. The species of wheat can be divided into three groups, with 42, 28, and 14 chromosomes respectively.

wheel. A rounded artifact permitting rotary motion. It uses the principle of a circular moving support and minimizes the size of the surface touching the ground, so that little friction is generated and a heavy object can be moved. The original wheels were of solid wood, joined to an axis that moved with the wheel. It was first used for transportation in the New Stone Age, in Mesopotamia and Egypt. The spoked wheel was known in 2700 B.C. Inasmuch as travel by cart was not common in antiquity, the wheel was largely used in war. The nomads from the northern steppes and the Hittites, ca. 1500 B.C., used a two-wheeled war chariot to great advantage. Early Mexicans used the wheel for toys. The wheel's shape suggests protection. The wheel is often linked with the sun.

wheel, Persian. A wheel with dippers along the rim, used to lade water from brooks and rivers.

wheel, potter's. A whirling turntable used to mold pottery, invented ca. 3000 B.C. in Egypt; it was used in Crete in the Bronze Age. It appeared in Germany and France, ca. 500 B.C., but was not known in the Americas. A lump of soft clay is placed in the center of a horizontal wheel. This wheel is rotated rapidly, and the clay, assisted by the potter's hand, assumes the desired cylindrical contours. The foot-powered wheel, which was widely distributed among the Chinese and Greeks, was the next step, and improvements continued until the wheel was motorized.

wheel, prayer. A wheel-shaped device, usually moved by hand, to facilitate praying. Sacred inscriptions are inside. The wheel symbolically moves with the sun. Prayer wheels may be small and portable or large and requiring the efforts of several persons to move them. Some were even moved by water or wind power. Buddhism has made the greatest use of the prayer wheel. The prayer wheel is usually moved sunwise, except in the Hindu rites of the dead.

wheel, spinning. A technique for spinning in which the thread is both twisted and wound on the rotating spindle.

wheel, water. A device operated by water current against a paddle wheel with a vertical or horizontal shaft. Vitruvius invented, ca. 20 B.C., a water wheel with vertical gears.

whey. The residue of curdling, mostly water.

whipping. Flogging for purposes of purification. It may be used to exorcise spirits, to install society officers, or as an initiation rite.

whisper. A sound between voicing and breathing, in which the vocal chords are in contact and the space between the arytenoids (q.v.) is open.

white. See CAUCASOID.

whorl. 1 A pattern found in dermatoglyphics (q.v.). It consists of concentric loops around a core. 2 The flywheel of a spindle (q.v.). Specimens going back to ca. 3500 B.C. have been found in Transcaspia and Crete.

whorl, spindle. A disk of pottery or some other material, used as a balance wheel on a spindle shaft.

wickerwork. Plaited basketry in which there is a rigid and thick warp and a flexible slender weft.

wickiup. A grass hut shaped like a beehive, e.g., among the Shoshone.

width, face. The greatest distance between points directly opposite on the cheekbones.

wife, big. The head wife in East Africa.

wife, chore. A wife who is a co-worker of her husband, e.g., among the Comanches of the Plains.

wigwam. A conical hut of the Indians of eastern North America, often covered by bark or mats. It has an arched-over roof.

wiitoka. A psychosis found among the Ojibwa and Cree of North Canada. The victim usually craves or feels that he will crave human flesh. If he yields to the craving, it is believed that he has become a cannibalistic ogre with an icy heart. Wiitoka is an Eskimo word for a person who has changed into a fearsome being after eating human flesh during a famine.

Wikhegan. Picture writing among the Abenaki.

Williston's law. See LAW, WILLISTON'S.

will-o'-the-wisp. Ignis fatuus, (q.v.) widely regarded as a manifestation of extranatural forces. It may be a sign of death or trouble in the future.

Wilson, Jack. A Paiute Indian prophet called Wovoka, who, while ill in 1888, was delirious and had a revelation that the Indians would soon be united with the dead and would recover their rightful inheritance and should practice various preparatory ceremonies. The ghost dance (q.v.) was strongly influenced by Wilson's revelations.

winch. A crank with a handle used to move a device.

Winckelmann, J. J. (1717-1768). A German archaeologist. He wrote the first systematic study of ancient art and is regarded as the founder of classical archaeology. In 1763 he published his *History of Ancient Art.*

windbreak or windscreen. A simple dwelling of branches or trees placed in the soil to make a semicircle or wall. Its framework is covered by leaves, brush, grass, and bark as protection against rain. Nomadic groups, such as the Negroes, Veddas, and Bushmen, use such dwellings.

Windigo. A mythical cannibal tribe believed by the Ottawa and Chippewa to live on an island in Hudson Bay. The Têtes de Boule of the upper St. Maurice River in Quebec regard the Windigo as a giant cannibalistic man. His name is often invoked to frighten children. See WIITOKA.

windlass. A machine for hauling or hoisting. The simple type has a horizontal barrel with a hoisting rope turned by a crank and handle. The early windlass, used to raise the anchor on ships, consisted of a horizontal barrel turned by handspikes inserted in holes near each end.

windmill. A mill operated by the force of the wind, often on oblique vanes attached to a horizontal shaft.

Windmill Hill. The southern culture of England during Neolithic times.

windscreen. See WINDBREAK.

wine, palm. A wine made from the palm tree, as in Indonesia.

wine, sugar cane. A mild distilled drink made from sugar cane and used in Central America. It is post-Conquest, inasmuch as the Spaniards brought sugar to the New World.

winter count. See COUNT, WINTER.

witch. A person, usually female, who has supernatural powers to do evil. Witches are reported from all parts of the world. They usually can look into the future, escape harm, transform themselves, and accomplish almost anything. The witch often has a magic rod and she has a concealed birthmark or other sign of her compact with the powers of darkness. There may be special ways of detecting a witch and frustrating her efforts.

witchcraft. Exercising control over another person through individual protective spirits, often to his disadvantage. Witchcraft originally meant the work of a female sorceress. Sometimes the person who exercises witchcraft is a public figure, while in other situations he may be disliked. In some societies, everyone practices witchcraft. Witchcraft may be believed to be a disease.

withe. A twig used to handle crucibles until metal tongs came into existence ca. 1500 B.C.

wife, King's. An "Amazon" (q.v.) among the Dahomey.

Wolff's law. See LAW, WOLFF'S.

Woman, Snake. The title of the Aztec male chief who directed the internal affairs of the state. Also, the goddess Cihuacoatl (q.v.).

wommera. See WOOMERA.

wood. A hard fibrous substance which largely makes up the stems and branches of trees and shrubs. There are few wooden artifacts of early man, except those found in peat bogs. The early Paleolithic era has yielded only two wooden implements, a yew spear at Clacton-on-Sea and one at Lehringen, Germany. The wide use of wood in early Paleolithic times is inferred from the considerable number of hollow scrapers, probably used to shape spears and other wood implements. Australian aborigines used wood widely, and boughs were probably used for windbreaks in the early history of man. In Neolithic days, the polished ax head permitted the wide use of wood, especially in dwellings. Some scholars have maintained that there was a "Wood Age," although there is little evidence for it. Wood and stone were probably used together, with stone used to cut wood and wood to haft stones. Petrified wood was used in Burma for tools.

wood, sliding. An early ski used in the Bronze Age.

wood technique. See TECHNIQUE, WOOD.

woodskin. A Guiana canoe made of a single piece of the tough bark of the purpleheart tree. It was 14 to 30 feet long, with great specific gravity.

woof. See WEFT.

woomera. A wooden Australian spear thrower, from two to three feet long with a hook at one end that fits into a notch at the end of the spear haft.

wootz. An early caked steel, found in India ca. 500 B.C.

word. A form intermediate between the morpheme (q.v.) and the phrase (q.v.). It is distinguished in many languages by its mobility in the sentence and a certain semantic independence, and in some languages by phonetic features such as stress (q.v.).

word, borrowed. A unit of speech that has been taken from one language and incorporated in another. The phrase also describes any word of foreign origin even though it has been somewhat changed.

word, cognate. A word that derives from the same root as another word in a different language, e.g., English *drink* and German *trinken*.

word, complex. A word resulting from a simple word and a bound form (q.v.) combined; e.g., *sophistication,* a combination of *sophisticate* and *ation*.

word, compound. A word made up completely from smaller words.

word, ghost. A word that came into being through the error, written, printed, or spoken, of a printer, author, or scribe.

word, head. The particular word that is modified by another word or words in a sentence, e.g., *man* in *the good man*.

word, native. A word that originates in a language and cannot be traced as a loan word from another language.

word, noa. A word the utterance of which is forbidden because of its profane connotation. See TABOO.

word, portmanteau. A word formed by putting the first part of one word and the second part of another together, e.g., *brunch* and *smog*. The expression originated in the explanation given of "The Jabberwocky" in *Alice in Wonderland*.

word, primary. A word that does not contain any free forms (q.v.).

word, prime. A word not made up of other words or linguistic elements.

word, sentence. A word that includes a sentence form characteristic of the language to which it belongs.

word, simple. A free form (q.v.) that cannot be broken up into smaller free forms.

word, telescope. A word that combines portions of two or more words.

Work of Works. The great encyclopedia compiled during the Ming Dynasty under the third emperor, Yung-lo. It required a large staff and two years to complete the 22,877 volumes.

workaday world. See WORLD, WORKADAY.

World, New. The archaeology of North and South America does not show a Paleolithic culture. Around the turn of the century, Hrdlicka and Holmes demonstrated that man's arrival in the New World was fairly recent. Although Old World cultural origins go back some 125,000 years, New World cultural origins are at most 30,000, and more probably, 12,000 years old. Agriculture may date back to ca. 8000 B.C. in the Old World and to ca. 3000 B.C. for Peru and Mexico, so that there is a possible lag of 5,000 years in the New World. Different crops and animals were domesticated. Maize was the basic grain in the New World, along with squash, beans, potatoes, manioc, tobacco, and rubber. Most of these were not known outside of the New World. Although the principle of the wheel (q.v.) was known, it was never used for practical purposes.

Some features are common to the Old and New World. Botanists have asserted that wild corn grows in Burma, and some scholars feel that South American cotton is a hybrid of New and Old World forms, although there is evidence that

these two kinds of cotton are different. The bottle gourd and coconuts are found in both the New and the Old World. See AMERICAS, THEORIES OF HABITATION OF.

world, spirit. The place where the souls of the deceased, or of ghosts, live.

world, workaday. Marett's term for the area of normal experience and reason, where there is an empirical correspondence between cause and effect, as opposed to the area of the mysterious and extraordinary.

Worsaae, Jens Jakob (1821-1885). A Danish archaeologist, who had several important academic, government, and museum appointments. His *Primeval Antiquities of Denmark* (1842) helped popularize the concept of the three ages of stone, bronze, and iron, especially after its translation into English (1849). He conducted stratigraphic research on Danish bogs, which confirmed the three-age hypothesis.

worship, ancestor. Religious worship of the spirits of dead relatives. In early times, it was widely found. Since it was believed that the immaterial part of man survives, this had to be placated lest it cause trouble. The family's father got special treatment because he had been so important while alive and it was easy to assume that he carried into the next world his concern for his family. The idea of the ancestor of the common father is an outgrowth of this approach.

Genuine ancestor worship is not often found in the history of religions. The Bantu, some Melanesian tribes, and some parts of Asia offer the best examples. Most evidence points to the transitory nature of ancestor worship.

working, secondary. Striking the surface and the sides of a flake tool (q.v.) to trim its edge and make it into the desired shape.

workshop. An archaeological site where there was considerable stone chipping and, therefore, a sizable accumulation of stone flakes, rejects, blanks, and artifacts.

world, ages of the. See CATASTROPHISM.

World, Book of the. See BOOK OF THE WORLD.

worship, animal. The veneration of animals, sometimes to the point of having prayers and temples for them. Among the best known divine animals was the Egyptian bull Apis. Deifying serpents still forms part of some African religions. In a later stage, the god may take human form but be associated with animals, like Zeus with the eagle. The term **zoolatry** is also used.

worship, devil. Devil worship is the cult of a religious group in Persia, the Yezidis. They consider themselves to be descended from Adam alone, as differentiated from the rest of mankind, who have sprung from Adam and Eve. There are about 20,000 believers living in Kurdistan and scattered near Aleppo, Diarbekr, and Bitlis. Their theological concepts are derived from Zoroastrian, Manichaean, Jewish, Nestorian, and Moslem ideals. Their sacred writings are *The Book of Revelation* and *The Black Book.* According to their teachings the supreme being is a passive transcendent god, who delegates the preservation of the world to seven angels, chief among which is the peacock angel or Malak Ta'us.

worship, fire. Fire was regarded as sacred by many early groups. Polytheistic religions deify fire in its many forms: lightning, inflammable gas, hearth fire. Some groups maintained a perpetual fire; sometimes these were put out and then rekindled. The use of fire for burnt offerings, divination, and ordeal is widespread.

worship, hero. Worship of men who have done much for their people or who possess divine qualities. Culture heroes (q.v.) who helped mankind and founders of a social group are widely worshiped. Dead kings, as in Egypt, and epic heroes, as in Scandinavia, may be worshiped. In Greece, heroes were widely regarded almost as deities.

worship, mother. The veneration of the mother, often found in religion. See GODDESS, MOTHER.

worship, nature. Worshiping all of nature. It is widely found in early 'religion, usually distributed in such a way that the aspects of nature that are worshipped and the nature of the worship are linked with economic and other necessities. Usually the features of nature worshipped seemed dangerous or uncertain.

worship, serpent. A form of religion that honors or deifies the serpent. Although it had many varied forms, it was quite widespread in the ancient world and may still be found among certain tribal groups. Its existence was especially noteworthy in early Indian Buddhism. The Romans honored the serpent as a healer and the Zulus kept them as household pets, believing them to be reincarnated ancestors.

worship, sun. Worship of the sun has been found in practically every country. The sun has been variously personified; as a great being, an ethical force, heaven's eye, etc. The sun may be presented as having a multiple personality and may also travel in a variety of ways: on horseback, by boat, chariot, or on foot. The sun god may have bad as well as good attributes. He may teach various subjects, or function as a fertility god. Clubs, battle axes, and arrows are among his weapons, and hawks, serpents, and bulls often function as his animals. Since the sun's rays are likely to hit the summit of topographic landmarks, sun worship may be connected with hill and mountain worship and with bodies of water.

Sun myths and symbols are not necessarily a sign of sun worship, since calendars, food, and weather prediction were linked to the sun. The worship of the sun probably reached its apex in Mexico, Egypt and Japan. In Mexico, it was linked to well developed mathematical and astronomical sciences. The Egyptian pyramids were probably tied to sun worship, judging from their orientation, and the sun god Ra persisted. The Mayans saw the sun god as a jaguar. The Plain Indians had a sun dance (q.v.) and the Arizonan Pueblo offered a ceremonial meal to the dawn. The Japanese royal family is said to spring from the sun goddess Amaterasu.

Wovoka. See WILSON, JACK.

wraith. A double of a living person, seen as in a vision. A wraith may indicate that death is near.

wrapping. A comparatively minor technique for making basketry. There is a fixed framework of parallel rods around which pliable strands are wrapped.

wreath. A floral ring, either hung or worn on the head, to symbolize various emotions.

wristlet. A band worn around the wrist to guard against a snapping bow string or a wound in combat.

writing. The use of conventionalized or standardized visual symbols to convey meaning. Writing first occurred in Egypt and Sumer ca. 4000 B.C. and developed independently in Mayan Yucatan. The usual stages in the history of writing are representation of objects (see PICTOGRAPH), followed by the representation of sound (see REBUS) and the use of symbols for sounds. The Egyptians had 24 consonants and added a picture after spelling a word. The wedge-shaped Sumerian writings (see CUNEIFORM) had little resemblance to material objects. The Chinese system combined the phonetic principle with arbitrary and pictographic symbols. The Phoenicians ca. 1000 B.C. developed an alphabet (q.v.) of consonants only.

writing, acrophonetic. A type of writing using symbols that began by expressing the abstract idea of an object without suggesting its name but came to stand for the first syllable or phoneme of the name of the object depicted.

writing, alphabetic. See ALPHABET.

writing, cursive. A quickly written script, simplified in form, for ordinary daily use. In it the characters are linked.

writing, defective. The Hebrew practice of writing consonants only, leaving the vowels to be supplied from memory or the syntactical context.

writing, ideographic. See IDEOGRAPH.

writing, linear. A writing system that uses symbols which are designs of lines or are not pictograms.

writing, logographic. See WRITING, WORD.

writing, Ogam. See OGAM.

writing, phonemic. Writing in which every phoneme (q.v.) is represented by a symbol.

writing, picture. The most elementary type of script, consisting of pictorial representations made on a fairly permanent material. A picture of a man, for example, would represent a man. Narrative can thus be presented by a picture sequence. Semantic but not phonetic representations can be conveyed. Picture writing is widely found. It was used by prehistoric men, as in Mesopotamia, Spain, and Crete, and is still used today in central Africa and Australia. Wood tables, animal skins, bones, and ivory are among the writing materials.

writing, plene. A Hebrew method of consonantal writing, in which vowel sounds are indicated by consonantal signs known as matres lectionis (q.v.). See WRITING, DEFECTIVE.

writing, syllabic. A system of writing in which each character stands for a syllable. See SYLLABARY.

writing, word or **writing, logographic.** Writing in which every word is represented by a separate symbol.

wrong, private. An offense that is usually punished by the victim or his kinsmen invoking the sanctions of the state. It differs from a crime (q.v.), or public wrong, where the state is directly interested.

wundu. The minor purification of Mohammedans, performed with water before each of the five daily prayers.

wurley. The bough shelter or hut of an aborigine in South Australia; hence, any aboriginal hut.

Würm. The fourth, and last, glacial period in Europe, probably extending from ca. 75,000 to 25,000 years ago. See GLACIATION.

wurt. In northeast Germany, a terp (q.v.).

X

X. The chromosome (q.v.) which determines that a given child will be female. Each egg has an X chromosome; if it pairs with the sperm's X chromosome, the child will be a female. See Y.

X ray. Referring to an art style found in northern Australia in which the inner parts of humans and of animals (e.g., spine or ribs) are represented along with the external form of the body.

Xanthochroi. A Caucasoid group, primarily consisting of fair-haired northern Europeans.

xanthoderm. Yellow skin color; Von Eickstedt's name for Mongoloid.

xeironomia. The language of gestures.

xeroderma pigmentosa. A congenital condition in which skin areas exposed to light are likely to become cancerous.

xerophyte. A plant that is adapted to dry conditions.

Xiuhcoatl. The "Fire Snake," one of the Plumed Serpent (Quetzalcoatl) cults of the Aztecs at Tenochtitlan.

xylography. Engraving on wood.

xylomancy. Divination (q.v.) through studying the shape and positions of twigs or other bits of wood on the ground.

xylophone. An early musical instrument played by striking sticks against pieces of wood of varying length. The pieces of wood are raised on two supports in more advanced types.

xylophone, compound. A xylophone in which the pieces of wood are tuned to different notes and arranged in a graduated series.

xylophone, hollow. A musical instrument consisting of a wooden gong hollowed to increase its resonance.

xylophone, single. A piece of hard wood shaped so that it gives off one note when it is struck.

Y

Y. The chromosome (q.v.) carried by the sperm cell, which determines that a given infant will be male. If the Y chromosome from the male pairs with an X chromosome in the egg, the child will be male. See X.

yang. In Chinese art and philosophy, the basic male component of life and the universe. It is usually portrayed as being red. Around the time of the Han Dynasty (206 B.C.-204 A.D.), it emerged as a circular diagram bisected by a wavy line, with both yang and yin (q.v.). Yang is linked with life, light, and heat. See T'AI CHI.

Yang Shao. A Chinese village culture, in which people lived in mud-walled pit homes. It developed ca. 2500 B.C. Wheat and millet were characteristic crops. See POTTERY, PAINTED.

yard. On a sailboat, a spar to which the head of the sail is attached in order to help maintain its expansion.

yarn. A longer textile fiber that can be used to make a fabric. A strand of yarn is usually composed of twisted fibers.

Yayoi. A full Neolithic culture based on rice agriculture in southwest Japan, dating ca. 250 B.C.

year, astral. See YEAR, SIDEREAL.

year, new. The cessation of one year and the beginning of the next, often marked by special observances to symbolize the change and its effect on man.

year, sidereal. The time in which the center of the sun makes the full circuit going eastward from the ecliptic meridian of a given star. The sidereal, or astral, year contains 365.242198 days.

yech. In Indian belief, a small animal that can take any shape and mislead travelers. It can become invisible through its white cap. If a human grabs a yech's cap and gets it under a millstone, the yech will work its great powers for him.

Yiddish. The language of the Ashkenazic Jews, formed through the fusion of dialectal German, medieval Romance, Hebrew-Aramaic, and Slavic components. It originated approximately in the tenth century in the Rhineland area and was spoken by about 11,000,000 people

576

in 1939. It is still the native or second language of millions of Ashkenazic Jews the world over, and has developed a rich literature of its own.

yin. In Chinese art and philosophy, the basic female component of life and the universe. It represents darkness, cold, and death. It is usually portrayed as being black. When represented, a wavy line divides a circle's diameter, with yin black and yang (q.v.) represented as red. See T'AI CHI.

yo-de-ho. Noiré's theory that language arose through sounds originally issued during physical exertion and that the first words stem from fixating natural sounds emitted in a group effort, e.g., *heave.*

yoke, coolie. A single piece of strong wood which is balanced on the neck and weighted by loads carried at each end. It is generally used to carry water containers or other objects of equal weight, so that each side balances the other. It probably was first used in Asia, although it was found widely in the western hemisphere.

Yomta. The priest-like head of a Pomo medicine society.

yoni. A Hindu religious symbol for the female generative power. It is widely worshipped in Tibet and India, usually together with the lin-gam (q.v.). It represents the earth and fertility. The yoni-lingam combination often symbolizes a merger of opposites in order to create. The yoni may have overtones of evil that can be warded off by the lingam. In addition to a pointed oval or a circle suggesting the vulva, the yoni is often shown as a cow, lotus (q.v.), woman, or sakti (q.v.).

young-dah-hte. See LATAH.

yourta. A spreading low tent used by central Asiatic nomads generally to cover pits in the ground. See YURT.

Yüan. The Yüan dynasty in China, A.D. 1280-1368. Decoration of porcelain in underglaze cobalt blue probably originated then.

yucca or **yuca.** A plant with long fibrous leaves, a member of the lily family. The sap of the roots makes suds in water.

Yuma. See IMPLEMENTS, YUMA.

yurt. Among the Kazak and several other Siberian nomadic groups, a tent of felt stretched over a light framework of wood. It has been called the best portable dwelling developed by man. The yurt is cylindrical with a dome top. There is a wattle wall about five feet high, and a wooden frame for the dome. Carpets cover the bare earth. The yurt can be disassembled in less than an hour. See YOURTA.

Z

zadruga. A community household found in the lowlands of the Pannonian plains of Yugoslavia. It is an agricultural community which communally owns land and other property. It consists of a group of unrelated families voluntarily associated. Men and women enjoy equal status. A male and a female manager direct the work of the zadruga.

zak. A water craft, found in India, consisting of a number of inflated goat skins fastened to a square wooden framework.

zappetta. See MATTOCK.

zariba. A cattle enclosure of West Africa.

zebu. Humped cattle, originally domesticated in India, kept by Africans.

zemi. An idol carved of stone or wood and worshipped by the Taino Indians of the Greater Antilles.

Zend. The earliest form of Indic. It was the sacred language of the Zoroastrians.

zero. A cipher; a number corresponding to naught; a constant less than any quantity; the number defined by the equation $x + 0 = x$. It was developed by the Hindus ca. 1,300 years ago, by the Maya ca.

third century B.C., and in Mesopotamia ca. fifth century B.C.

zeugma. A grammatical structure in which one word serves a double purpose, relating to one word specifically and to the other one in a supplementary sense.

ziggurat. A brick terraced tower, probably originally Sumerian. The ziggurat stood on its own platform. The Ur ziggurat was 70 feet high and 200 by 150 feet at the base.

zinc. A blue-white crystalline element. It is brittle when cold, malleable at 110-210° C, brittle at 260° C. It tarnishes slightly in moist air in usual temperatures. Zinc is seldom found in a metallic form. One of the few such instances is in basalt in the Melbourne area. Zinc is hard to smelt, which also contributed to the delay in its discovery. It can be extracted from its ore only by a very high temperature, along with powdered coal, and the end product must be condensed.

zither. A musical instrument consisting of a frame with strings that are either struck or plucked. They are primarily melody instruments, often used at religious ceremonies. The frame may be a flat board, a shallow body, or a box resonator. The strings are generally parallel with the resonator surface and are accurately tuned.

zoanthropy. The delusion that a person has been turned into an animal. Daniel 4 contains a description of Nebuchadnezzar's zoanthropic delusion.

zodiac. A division of the route of celestial bodies into 12 parts, each named after a star cluster. The zodiac probably originated in Babylonia. It probably arose from observation of the sun and moon traveling similar paths among the stars, as they made their circuit of the sky. The center of the zodiac and its constellations is the sun's annual path and is a belt about 16° broad. The connection with the sun's movements was made by observing heliacal risings (q.v.) and heliacal settings (q.v.).

zombie. In the vodun belief, a human whose soul has been stolen through evil magic. The magician can do as he likes with the body. Some believe that a zombie can be changed to an animal.

zone, life. An altitudinal and latitudinal belt characterized by specific flora and fauna.

zone, periglacial. An area in which tjaele (q.v.) prevailed in a given glacial phase.

zoolatry. See WORSHIP, ANIMAL.

zoomorph. An animal represented in decorative art.

zoophorus. The representation of men and animals in relief on a frieze.

zya. The Buriat designation for one's profile drawn so as to work magic against him. The picture is hidden near the home of the victim, who will die unless he counteracts the magic.

zygion. On the zygomatic arch, the most lateral point.

zygomatic arch. See ARCH, ZYGOMATIC.

www.ingramcontent.com/pod-product-compliance
Lightning Source LLC
Chambersburg PA
CBHW020559270326
41927CB00005B/101